Corwin & Peltason's
UNDERSTANDING THE
CONSTITUTION

THIRTEENTH EDITION

J. W. PELTASON
University of California

HARCOURT BRACE COLLEGE PUBLISHERS

Fort Worth Philadelphia San Diego New York Orlando Austin San Antonio
Toronto Montreal London Sydney Tokyo

Publisher: Ted Buchholz
Acquisitions Editor: David Tatom
Project Editor: Deanna Johnson
Production Manager: Erin Gregg
Senior Art Director: Don Fujimoto
Literary Permissions Editor: Julia C. Stewart

Cover photo © Tom Wachs

Address editorial correspondence to:
301 Commerce Street, Suite 3700
Fort Worth, TX 76102

Address orders to:
6277 Sea Harbor Drive
Orlando, FL 32887
1-800-782-4479 outside Florida
1-800-433-0001 inside Florida

ISBN: 0-15-500721-1
Library of Congress Catalog Card Number: 93–80865
Printed in the United States of America
3 4 5 6 7 8 9 0 1 2 067 9 8 7 6 5 4 3 2 1

PREFACE

This edition comes out at a time of significant change for the Supreme Court and the field of Constitutional law, with the election of a new president and the appointment of a new Justice to face the large number of five-to-four decisions that have issued from the Court in recent years. As always, the Constitution is a vital and evolving document, changing with American society as it has done for more than 200 years.

The Constitution has always held a special, even a unique, place in our history. Although during ratification struggles two centuries ago the Constitution was intensely attacked and its merits were searchingly examined, after its ratification Federalists and Anti-Federalists quickly began to vie with each other in proclaiming their loyalty to it. Throughout our history, despite intense differences, all (or at least almost all) Americans have insisted that they are the true defenders of the constitutional faith and have attacked their opponents as its enemies. Despite many significant political movements, only a few hard-core abolitionists have attacked the Constitution itself.

The Constitution of the United States is both symbol and instrument of government. It is today what it was in 1809, when James Madison referred to it as "the cement of the Union." Its role as the symbol of our unity is no less important than its role as the charter of our government. It is the tie that binds 250 million people who have no long common history and no long-established monarch to personify their nationhood. Unlike the Germans or the French or the Italians or the English or the Scots or most of the other peoples of the world, Americans share no centuries-long traditions of battles, heroes, kings, literature, poetry, or songs. We have existed as an independent nation only a few decades longer than we did as part of the British Empire. What we share—often almost the only thing we share—is a commitment to a constitutional system.

In 1787 "We the People" meant only white, male property owners. Today it means *all* the people. Perhaps "the people" do not always know what is in the Constitution; in fact, they often confuse it with the Declaration of Independence. Only a bare majority know that its purpose was to create a national government, and almost two-thirds cannot identify the Bill of Rights. Americans might not know in precise detail what is in the Constitution, but they revere it nonetheless. They do know, however, that the Constitution stands for the rule of law, for fairness and justice for all, for civil supremacy, and for restraints on those who govern. It is our shared long-term interest, an interest greater than any immediate political victory. Thus, it is not only fitting but probably essential that we have occasions to reassert our loyalty to and involvement with the Constitution, as we have done in recent years with the various celebrations marking the bicentennial of the signing and ratification of the Constitution and the Bill of Rights.

It is not enough, however, to celebrate the Constitution. We should also—or at least a considerable number of us should—cerebrate about it. We need to understand that, important as it is to see the forest, the forest is made up of trees, and unless someone tends them, there will be no forest to be seen. That is one of the purposes of this volume—to go beyond generalities and discover the major constitutional issues of our times.

The Constitution of the United States, the supreme law of the land, is by no means self-explanatory. In an attempt to make it understandable, this book sets forth the main features of the Constitution and the practical significance of its most important provisions as they are construed and applied today. Attention is given also to the immediate historical origins of the Constitution and to its basic principles. The central core of the Declaration of Independence and of the articles of the Constitution is discussed section by section, amplified, and interpreted in nontechnical terms. Because the constitutional system—the fundamental rules by which governmental power is organized and limited—also includes some basic practices and customs that have developed during the past 200 years, those elements of our government are also discussed. In addition, there is a brief essay pointing up the hallmarks of our constitutional system: federalism, separation of powers, and judicial review.

Although an attempt has been made to avoid excessive detail and over elaborate citations, this revision presents all relevant decisions of the Supreme Court though June 1993. The absence of extensive documentation and the attempt to simplify should not be seen as an expression of dogmatism. There is no such thing as a single "true" interpretation of the Constitution, and the reader should understand that others would find different meaning in the words of the Constitution and in the opinions of the judges who have interpreted it.

ACKNOWLEDGMENTS

On April 29, 1963, students of the Constitution of the United States suffered a major loss with the death of Professor Edward S. Corwin. I think it may be said without exaggeration that "the General," as he was affectionately known by his thousands of students, knew more about the Constitution of the United States than any person who ever lived. Those of us who had the privilege of studying under him know that Chief Justice Hughes was in error when he said that the Constitution is what the judges say it is. We know that the Constitution is what Edward Corwin said it is.

Professor Corwin combined his comprehensive knowledge of the Constitution with wisdom and powerful analytical skills so that his major works, many of which were written almost half a century ago, are as fresh and important today as when he wrote them. Although many of the views expressed and the words used are those of Professor Corwin, retained from earlier editions, the responsibility for this revision is mine. It is more than the usual cliche, however, for me to acknowledge that its merits are attributable to the teacher, its errors to his student.

I wish to thank Prentice-Hall, Inc., for permission to quote occasional sentences from previous publications.

In addition, I would like to thank the professionals at Harcourt Brace: Don Fujimoto, Erin Gregg, Mike Hinshaw, Deanna Johnson, and David Tatom.

I also wish to thank Patricia A. Pelfrey for her creative help and her good sense and good judgment in the preparation of this manuscript.

I am especially indebted to Professor Stephen L. Wasby of the State University of New York at Albany for his help on this and previous editions. He is an outstanding critic with an authoritative knowledge of our Constitution and the work of our courts. He patiently went through drafts of the manuscript, brought to my attention errors of fact and interpretation, and suggested many ways to make the presentation of materials more coherent and useful. Most of all, I appreciate his persistence and insistence in calling to my attention changes that were difficult to make but that, once made, greatly improved this book and its usefulness to students.

JWP
Oakland, California
January 1994

A NOTE ON CASE CITATIONS

The number of cases mentioned in the text has been kept to a minimum. It is more important for most people to know what the Supreme Court has said about what the Constitution means and to have some feeling for the issues involved than to know the names of the cases. Nevertheless, there are some cases of such significance that knowledge of them is part of a liberal education; still others are cited in footnotes for those who wish to inquire further.

Cases decided by the Supreme Court before 1875 are cited by the name of the court reporter. Thus, the citation *McCulloch* v *Maryland,* 4 Wheaton 315 (1819), means that this case can be located in volume 4 of *Wheaton's Reports of cases argued and adjudged in the Supreme Court of the United States,* on page 315, and that the case was decided in 1819. Cases after 1875 are cited by the volume number of *United States Reports,* a publication of the Government Printing Office that records the cases adjudged in the Supreme Court. Thus, the case *United States* v *Nixon,* cited 418 US 683 (1974), is found in volume 418 of *United States Reports,* beginning on page 683, and was decided in 1974.

For the special use of lawyers and scholars, commercial publishers make Supreme Court opinions available more quickly than does the United States Government Printing Office (GPO); now even the GPO's Preliminary Prints are not available until several years after a decision has been handed down. For this reason, cases decided in more recent years will be cited, for example, *Voinovich* v *Quilter,* 122 L Ed 2d 500 (1993), meaning that this case can be found on page 500 of volume 122 of *United States Supreme Court Reports, Lawyer's Edition,* second series, published by the Lawyers Co-operative Publishing Company, and that it was decided in 1993.

I call special attention to the comprehensive annotation of the Constitution published by the Library of Congress. A complete revision is scheduled every ten years, but a cumulative supplement to keep the volume current is available every two years. *The Constitution of the United States: Analysis and Interpretation* is available from the United States Government Printing Office in Washington, D.C. This monumental work builds on the first edition, published in 1952 under the editorship of Professor Corwin.

CONTENTS

CHAPTER SIX

THE CONSTITUTION OF THE UNITED STATES OF AMERICA 420

CHAPTER ONE

BACKGROUND OF THE CONSTITUTION

The Constitution can be understood best within the historical situations in which it was written and has been applied. By placing the Constitution in the context of history, we learn of the conditions and conflicts that produced it and continue to give it meaning. This book, therefore, begins with a brief consideration of the Declaration of Independence and the Articles of Confederation, the two most important documents affecting the background of the Constitution.

The Declaration of Independence is the first formal American state paper. It is not judicially enforceable, and it establishes no legal rights or duties. Nonetheless, the Declaration has had a decisive effect on the development of our governmental system. It sets forth the ideals and reflects the standards of the American creed. This creed, with its stress on the rights of people, equality under the law, limited government, and government by consent of the governed, infuses the structures and practices of the Constitution. The Declaration of Independence remains the American conscience, a constant challenge to those who would subvert our democratic processes or deny persons their inalienable rights.

THE DECLARATION OF INDEPENDENCE

In Congress, July 4, 1776 THE UNANIMOUS DECLARATION of the thirteen UNITED STATES OF AMERICA.

This was the first time that "the United States of America" was officially used. Previous practice had been to refer to the "United Colonies."

We celebrate our independence on the Fourth of July, the anniversary of the day it was proclaimed. The proclamation, however, had been approved by the Second Continental Congress two days before, when it adopted by a narrow vote Richard Henry Lee's resolution "to declare the United Colonies free and independent states." Thomas Jefferson, John Adams, Benjamin Franklin, Roger Sherman, and Robert R. Livingston were appointed to draft a declaration to accompany that resolution of independence, but it was Jefferson who did most of the work.

Jefferson had the task of rallying both American and world sentiment to the cause of independence. As he later wrote, "Neither aiming at originality of principles or sentiments, nor yet copied from any particular and previous writing, it was intended to be an expression of the American Mind."[1] Jefferson drew on precedents known to all educated Englishmen and Americans, especially on John Locke's often-quoted *Second Treatise of Civil Government*, written in 1689. That volume was thought to be an authoritative pronouncement of established principles. Locke's ideas provided ready arguments for the American cause, and their use for that purpose was especially embarrassing to an English government whose own revolution was based on them.

When in the Course of human events, it becomes necessary for one people to dissolve the political bands which have connected them with another,

One of the points at issue between the colonists and the English government was whether the Americans and the English were one people or two. Here the Americans asserted that they formed a separate entity, previously connected with the English people but not an integral part of them.

and to assume among the powers of the earth, the separate and equal station to which the Laws of Nature and of Nature's God entitle them,

Equality of sovereign nations was stated as a requirement of the law of nature; today it is part of what is called international law.

a decent respect to the opinions of mankind requires that they should declare the causes which impel them to the separation.

---

[1]Letter to Henry Lee, May 8, 1825, in P.L. Ford, ed. *The Writings of Thomas Jefferson*, Vol. 10 (New York: G. P. Putnam's Sons, 1892–1899), 343.

The favorable opinion of mankind was a military necessity. The demand for independence was slow in developing, and many Americans continued to hope for reconciliation with the mother country even as late as the summer of 1776. As long as the revolution remained a purely internal quarrel between England and her colonies, foreign governments were reluctant to give military assistance, and assistance was desperately needed if the Americans were to make successful their revolutionary acts. The French were especially anxious to support any move that would weaken English power, but they first wanted assurances that the Americans meant business. The Declaration of Independence notified the world that the Americans were serious, and it was both an appeal to the conscience of mankind and a call for military help.

The American Philosophy of Government

We hold these truths to be self-evident, that all men

Today we would speak of "people," rather than of men.

---

are created equal, that they are endowed by their Creator with certain unalienable Rights, that among these are Life, Liberty, and the pursuit of Happiness.

These ringing words introduced the American philosophy of self-government. About six weeks before, Virginia had adopted a constitution that contained the first American bill of rights. In it the same concepts that are found in the Declaration were stated as follows: "That all men are by nature equally free and independent, and have certain inherent rights, of which, when they enter into a state of society, they cannot by any compact deprive or divest their posterity; namely, the enjoyment of life and liberty, with the means of acquiring and possessing property, and pursuing and obtaining happiness and safety."

It did not necessarily follow that independence from England would lead to republican institutions in the United States. It is, therefore, highly significant that the Americans based their revolutionary acts on constitutional principles. The revolution was not justified so that one group of Americans could impose its will on other Americans free of English control, but so that Americans could govern themselves. The Declaration is not just a declaration of independence; it is also a defense of free government.

Many have scoffed at the assertion that all are created equal. They argue that such a statement flies in the face of the obvious facts that some have ability, talent, and virtue and others do not. The Declaration, however, does not assert that people are equal in all things. It proclaims that people are equally endowed with certain inalienable rights, among these being a right to their own lives, liberties, and pursuits of happiness. These are a person's birthrights; they are not secured by an act of governmental grace or received as a gift from others. As John Adams, a member of the drafting committee that wrote the Declaration, and a believer in equal rights but not in natural equality, wrote in 1814,

> That all men are born to equal rights is true. Every being has right to his own, as clear, as moral, as sacred, as any other being has. This is as indubitable as a moral government in the universe. But to teach that all men are born with equal powers and faculties, to equal influence in society, to equal property and advantages through life, is as gross a fraud, as glaring an imposition on the credulity of the people, as ever was practiced by the monks, by Druids, by Brahmins, by priests of the immortal Lama, or by the self-styled philosophers of the French Revolution.[2]

In 1776, people spoke of inalienable or natural rights; today, we speak of human rights, the rights that distinguish men and women from the other creatures that inhabit the earth. These truths that were self-evident to the people of 1776 underlie the culture and civilization of the free world.

How inalienable are inalienable rights? Such rights may be forfeited by wrongdoing. The government may call upon persons to sacrifice their lives and liberty in defense of the nation. But that some should be called to make the sacrifice and others favored arbitrarily, or that the innocent should be made the tools of others' happiness, is contrary to the concept of the equal right of each person to life and liberty.

How is the existence of slavery to be explained in a nation whose leaders proclaimed the doctrine of inalienable rights? The Declaration makes no distinction between black and white; in 1776 most Americans believed that slavery was an evil institution that sooner or later had to be abolished. In his original draft, Jefferson blamed the Crown for the establishment of slavery in the United States and condemned the king for waging "cruel war against human nature itself, violating its most sacred rights of life & liberty." This clause offended some of the delegates from slaveholding states. In the midst of their crisis, the Americans decided to fight one evil at a time, and Congress deleted that passage to secure united support against England. It was to be another eighty-seven years before the practices of the nation started to conform in this respect to the professions of the Declaration.

---

[2] Letter to John Taylor, 1814, quoted in Adrienne Koch, *The American Enlightenment* (New York: George Braziller, 1965), 222.

That to secure these rights, Governments are instituted among Men, deriving their just powers from the consent of the governed,

People create government for the purpose of securing their preexisting natural rights. That the rights come first, that government is created to protect these rights, and that government officials are subject to the natural law were not novel ideas in 1776. These ideas were based on the concepts of a state of nature, a natural law, natural rights, and the social compact. John Locke had written that, before the establishment of society, people had lived in a state of nature. Thomas Hobbes, an antidemocratic philosopher, had insisted that in the state of nature, where there was no government to make and enforce laws, people made war on each other and life was "solitary, poore, nasty, brutish and short." But Locke argued that even in a state of nature there was a natural law to govern conduct. This natural law, comprising universal, unvarying principles of right and wrong, was known to people through the use of reason. For example, if an Englishman were to meet a Frenchwoman on an uninhabited and ungoverned island, he would not be free to deprive her of her life, liberty, or property. Should he attempt to do so, he would violate the natural law and could rightly be punished.

Although the state of nature was not, according to Locke, a lawless condition, it was an inconvenient one. Each person had to protect his or her own rights, and there was no agreed-upon judge to settle disputes about the application of the natural law to particular controversies. Realizing this, people decided to make a compact with one another in which each would give to the community the right to create a government equipped to enforce the natural law. Thereby each agreed to abide by the decisions made by the majority and to comply with the laws enacted by the people's representatives, provided the laws did not encroach upon the people's fundamental rights. The power of government was thus limited.

Modern social scientists and historians agree with Aristotle that people are social animals and never lived in a presocial and pregovernmental state of nature. Government, instead of being a consciously created institution, has developed as naturally as the family. But rejecting the belief that government originated through a social compact does not invalidate the belief that men and women are primary and governments are secondary and that governments derive their coercive authority from the consent of the governed. The moral primacy of the individual remains. It is on the philosophical and ethical, rather than the historical, concept of priority of men and women over governments that Americans base their insistence that governments are to be evaluated by their improvement of the well-being and protection of the rights of individuals.

That whenever any Form of Government becomes destructive of these ends, it is the Right of the People to alter or to abolish it, and to institute new Government, laying its foundation on such principles and organizing its powers in such form, as to them shall seem most likely to effect their Safety and Happiness.

In other words, the people may abolish their government whenever it ceases to protect natural rights and becomes destructive of the ends for which it was established. In a free society, where the consent of the governed is regularly expressed through open debate and free elections, it is not likely that revolutionary action will be necessary to alter the foundations of government. The colonists tried first to use constitutional devices to adjust their grievances. Finally, they felt compelled to revolt and, in the eyes of English law, to become traitors.

The doctrine of revolution pronounced in the Declaration is not a legal doctrine; there is no constitutional right to engage in revolutionary conduct. Nor should the doctrine proclaimed by the Declaration be confused with that of those who advocate change by the use of violence. Jefferson did not defend the right of a fraction of the civic community to seize the government and use it to suppress the rights of others. The conservative nature of the revolutionary right asserted is underscored by the next sentence.

Prudence, indeed, will dictate that Governments long established should not be changed for light and transient causes;

Without denying that the people have the right to change government whenever a majority of them think it destructive of their rights, the writers of the Declaration counsel caution.

and accordingly all experience hath shown, that mankind are more disposed to suffer, while evils are sufferable, than to right themselves by abolishing the forms to which they are accustomed. But when a long train of abuses and usurpations, pursuing invariably the same Object evinces a design to reduce them under absolute Despotism, it is their right, it is their duty, to throw off such Government, and to provide new Guards for their future security. Such has been the patient sufferance of these Colonies; and such is now the necessity which constrains them to alter their former Systems of Government. The history of the present King of Great Britain is a history of repeated injuries and usurpations, all having in direct object the establishment of an absolute Tyranny over these States.

Charges Against the King

The Declaration makes no mention of Parliament. It directs its accusations at the king. The colonists were asserting the constitutional theory that their allegiances were to the Crown, not to Parliament, and that they were bound to England through the king. They were contending that Parliament had no authority over them and had no right to regulate their affairs. This colonial view of the nature of the British Empire eventually triumphed over the eighteenth-century English view that the English Parliament had authority to legislate for all the dominions. (To concentrate the attack on the king was also a good political tactic. Quite a few members of Parliament sympathized with the colonists, and there was no point in unnecessarily alienating them.)

The details of the specific charges leveled by the Declaration against the king are of less significance today than are the other parts of that document. As kings go, especially those ruling in the eighteenth century, George III was not all that bad. It is interesting to note, however, that when it came time to write the Constitution, steps were taken to guard against some of the abuses charged to the king, such steps as making sure a judge's salary and tenure of office did not depend on the will of the president, making the military dependent on and inferior to civil authorities, guaranteeing trial by jury in the jurisdiction in which a criminal offense was alleged to have taken place, and establishing fixed dates for the election of the members of the House of Representatives. The several charges against the king are listed here without additional comment.

To prove this, let Facts be submitted to a candid world

He has refused his Assent to Laws, the most wholesome and necessary for the public good.

He has forbidden his Governors to pass Laws of immediate and pressing importance, unless suspended in their operation till his Assent should be obtained; and when so suspended, he has utterly neglected to attend to them.

He has refused to pass other Laws for the accommodation of large districts of people, unless those people would relinquish the right of Representation in the Legislature, a right inestimable to them and formidable to tyrants only.

He has called together legislative bodies at places unusual, uncomfortable, and distant from the depository of their public Records, for the sole purpose of fatiguing them into compliance with his measures.

He has dissolved Representative Houses repeatedly, for opposing with manly firmness his invasions on the rights of the people.

He has refused for a long time, after such dissolutions, to cause others to be elected; whereby the Legislative powers, incapable of Annihilation, have returned to the People at large for their exercise; the State remaining in the meantime exposed to all the dangers of invasion from without, and convulsions within.

He has endeavoured to prevent the population of these States; for that purpose obstructing the Laws for Naturalization of Foreigners; refusing to pass others to encourage their migration hither, and raising the conditions of new Appropriations of Lands.

He has obstructed the Administration of Justice, by refusing his Assent to Laws for establishing Judiciary powers.

He has made Judges dependent on his Will alone, for the tenure of their offices, and the amount and payment of their salaries.

He has erected a multitude of New Offices, and sent hither swarms of Officers to harass our people, and eat out their substance.

He has kept among us, in times of peace, Standing Armies, without the Consent of our legislatures.

He has affected to render the Military independent of and superior to the Civil power.

He has combined with others to subject us to a jurisdiction foreign to our constitution, and unacknowledged by our laws; giving his Assent to their Acts of pretended Legislation:

For quartering large bodies of armed troops among us:

For protecting them, by a mock Trial, from punishment for any Murders which they should commit on the Inhabitants of these States:

For cutting off our Trade with all parts of the world:

For imposing Taxes on us without our Consent:

For depriving us in many cases, of the benefits of Trial by Jury:

For transporting us beyond Seas to be tried for pretended offences:

For abolishing the free System of English Laws in a neighbouring Province, establishing therein an Arbitrary government, and enlarging its Boundaries so as to render it at once an example and fit instrument for introducing the same absolute rule into these Colonies:

For taking away our Charters, abolishing our most valuable Laws, and altering fundamentally the Forms of our Governments:

For suspending our own Legislatures, and declaring themselves invested with power to legislate for us in all cases whatsoever.

He has abdicated Government here, by declaring us out of his Protection and waging War against us.

He has plundered our seas, ravaged our Coasts, burnt our towns, and destroyed the lives of our people.

He is at this time transporting large Armies of foreign Mercenaries to compleat the works of death, desolation and tyranny, already begun with circumstances of Cruelty & perfidy scarcely paralleled in the most barbarous ages, and totally unworthy the Head of a civilized nation.

He has constrained our fellow Citizens taken Captive on the high Seas to bear Arms against their Country, to become the executioners of their friends and Brethren, or to fall themselves by their Hands.

He has excited domestic insurrections amongst us, and has endeavoured to bring on the inhabitants of our frontiers, the merciless Indian Savages, whose known rule of warfare, is an undistinguished destruction of all ages, sexes and conditions.

In every stage of these Oppressions We have Petitioned for Redress in the most humble terms: Our repeated Petitions have been answered only by repeated injury. A Prince, whose character is thus marked by every act which may define a Tyrant, is unfit to be the ruler of a free people.

Nor have We been wanting in attentions to our Brittish brethren. We have warned them from time to time of attempts by their legislature to extend an unwarrantable jurisdiction over us. We have reminded them of the circumstances of our emigration and settlement here. We have appealed to their native justice and magnanimity, and we have conjured them by the ties of our common kindred to disavow these usurpations, which, would inevitably interrupt our connections and correspondence. They too have been deaf to the voice of justice and of consanguinity. We must, therefore, acquiesce in the necessity, which denounces our Separation, and hold them, as we hold the rest of mankind, Enemies in War, in Peace Friends.

Conclusion

We, THEREFORE, THE REPRESENTATIVES OF THE UNITED STATES OF AMERICA, in General Congress, Assembled, appealing to the Supreme Judge of the world for the rectitude of our intentions, do, in the Name, and by Authority of the good People of these Colonies, solemnly publish and declare, That these United Colonies are, and of Right ought to be FREE AND INDEPENDENT STATES; that they are Absolved from all Allegiance to the British Crown, and that all political connection between them and the State of Great Britain, is and ought to be totally dissolved; and that as Free and Independent States, they have full Power to levy War, conclude Peace, contract Alliances, establish Commerce, and to do all other Acts and Things which Independent States may of right do. And for the support of this Declaration, with a firm reliance on the protection of Divine Providence, we mutually pledge to each other our Lives, our Fortunes and our sacred Honor.

Did the Americans declare independence on behalf of the United States or on behalf of each of the thirteen sovereign states? The language is ambiguous. In later years the question became important as arguments arose about the nature of the federal system and, especially, about the source of the national government's authority in the field of external affairs.

The Supreme Court takes the view that in 1776 all powers in the field of foreign affairs passed from the English Crown to the United States and that the states never had power to make war and peace or to deal as sovereign nations with other governments. Other Americans have insisted that the separate colonies declared their independence and that all powers of the Crown passed to each state. Those states, it is argued, in turn created the central government, first by informal acquiescence and then more formally in the Articles of Confederation and the Constitution. Whatever the original intent, the first of these views was supported by the North's victory in the Civil War, the growth of national sentiment, and the sanction of the Supreme Court.

The men who signed the Declaration of Independence probably gave little thought to the matter; they had more immediate problems to solve. With full recognition of the gravity of their acts, they pledged their lives, their fortunes, and their sacred honor. John Hancock of Massachusetts, president of the Continental Congress, was the first to so pledge, with his famous, bold signature.

THE ARTICLES OF CONFEDERATION

Although the Second Continental Congress, which had assembled in May 1775, had no formal governmental authority, it raised an army, appointed a commander in chief, negotiated with foreign nations, coined money, and assumed all powers that, it claimed, belong to an independent and sovereign nation. However, it seemed desirable to legalize those practices and place Congress's operations on a more formal basis of authority. Accordingly, even before the Declaration had been proclaimed, Congress appointed a committee, headed by John Dickinson of Maryland, to draft articles of union. In 1777 Congress submitted the articles to the state legislatures, but not until March 1781 did all the states approve (Maryland, acting in behalf of the six states with no land claims, held out until the seven states with claims to western lands agreed to cede them to the Union) and our second national government begin to function.

The Articles of Confederation did not materially alter the structure or powers of the government that had been governing the United States—unofficially but effectively—since 1775. They established a league of friendship, a "perpetual Union" of states, resting expressly on state sovereignty. The state legislatures promised to treat each other's citizens without discrimination, to give full faith and credit to each other's legal acts and public proceedings, and to extradite fugitives wanted in another state.

The structure of the central government was quite simple. There was only a single-chamber Congress. There was no executive, although a congressional committee consisting of one delegate from each state managed affairs when Congress was not assembled. There was no judiciary, although Congress acted as a court to resolve disputes among the states.

Each state had one vote in the Congress, and each state legislature selected representatives to cast that vote, paid those representatives, and could recall them at any time. The only restrictions on a state's choice were that it could send no fewer than two nor more than seven members and that no person could be a delegate for more than three years in six or could serve at the same time as an officer of the United States.

The second article stated, "Each State retains its sovereignty, freedom and independence, and every power, jurisdiction and right, which is not by this confederation expressly delegated to the United States, in Congress assembled."

In short, Congress had only those powers that were expressly delegated.

Congress could determine peace and war, send and receive ambassadors, enter into treaties (except that it could not deprive states of the right to tax imports or prohibit exports), apportion prizes taken by United States forces, coin money, fix standards of weights and measures, regulate affairs with Indians not members of any state, establish a postal system, appoint United States military officers above the rank of colonel, and decide certain disputes that might arise among the states. Any action required the approval of at least nine states, and the articles themselves could not be amended without the approval of all thirteen states.

Congress did *not* have the power to collect taxes from individuals, to regulate commerce, or to prohibit the states from coining money. To secure funds, it determined how much each state should pay, but it was up to each state to collect taxes from its citizens and turn the money over to the national treasury. If a state refused to do so, there was little that Congress could do. Likewise, Congress could negotiate treaties with foreign nations, but it had no way of making states comply with the obligation thus assumed. Resembling an international organization composed of sovereign nations rather than a national government, Congress could not impose obligations directly on individuals or enforce its legislation through its own agencies. Enforcement of congressional commands would have required sanctions against the offending states, not against individuals.

TOWARD A MORE PERFECT UNION

In retrospect, it may appear that the Americans lacked vision when they failed to establish a more tightly knit union with a strong central government. Remember, however, that they had just fought a war against centralized authority and that, with communication and transportation so slow, they had good reason to believe that there could be no self-government except through local government.

The accomplishments of the government under the Articles of Confederation should not be overlooked. It successfully concluded the war; it negotiated the Treaty of Paris of 1783, which gave the United States de jure the status of a nation; it established an enduring system for the development of western lands; and it refined the practices of interstate cooperation, which gave Americans experience in handling national problems.

And there were plenty of those. The English refused to withdraw their troops from western lands until the states lived up to their treaty obligations to indemnify British subjects for property confiscated during the war, and Congress was powerless to make either the British or the states comply. The Spanish threatened to close the mouth of the Mississippi to American trade, so foreign commerce via the Gulf of Mexico languished. The Americans, having lost the privileges of membership in the British Empire, were unable to secure their own treaty advantages from other nations, which had no desire to make agreements with a nation that could not enforce its own compliance.

Once the Revolutionary War had ended, the pressures to cooperate were reduced, and each state started to go its own way. Some printed paper money that quickly became worthless, and some failed to contribute their share of funds to support the central government. Trade barriers were established by some states in an attempt to give their own merchants special privileges. The seaboard states levied taxes on goods going inland. Within states, conflicts between debtors and creditors were often bitter: defaulting debtors resented the harsh laws that caused them to lose their property and sometimes to go to jail; creditors resented laws that gave debtors more time to pay off debts or permitted them to pay with inflated paper currency.

Attempts were made to amend the articles to give Congress authority to collect taxes and to regulate interstate commerce. In 1781 Congress submitted an amendment to the state legislatures that would have given Congress power to collect taxes; a flaw in the articles was made apparent when the amendment failed because a single state, Rhode Island, refused to agree. Two years later New York vetoed a similar amendment. What could be done?

A relatively small group of important and articulate Americans had been agitating for a more vigorous national government, but general sentiment was against drastic changes. These nationalists had to move carefully. They needed an opportunity to present their proposals to the country. Interstate conferences to discuss navigation and commercial matters gave them such a chance. After successfully negotiating an agreement with Maryland, some nation-minded Virginians proposed that all the states send delegates to Annapolis in September 1786 to discuss the establishment of a uniform system of commerce for the entire nation. But only five states sent commissioners to the Annapolis Convention.

Although disappointed by this apparent lack of interest, Alexander Hamilton of New York and James Madison of Virginia persuaded the delegates who did come to try to salvage something. They adopted a report urging the states to send delegates to another convention to be held the following May in Philadelphia. The report further stated that such delegates should be authorized not only to discuss trade matters, but also to examine the defects of the existing system of government and "to devise such further provisions as shall appear to them necessary to render the constitution of the Federal Government adequate to the exigencies of the Union."

Even before Congress had authorized a convention, several of the state legislatures, following Virginia's lead, selected delegates. They chose distinguished men, thereby notifying the country that the approaching Philadelphia convention was to be taken seriously. Congress gave its consent, after carefully stipulating that the delegates should meet "for the sole and express purpose of revising the Articles of Confederation and reporting to Congress and the several legislatures such alterations and provisions therein as shall, when agreed to in Congress and confirmed by the states, render the federal constitution adequate to the exigencies of Government & the preservation of the Union." Ultimately, all the states except Rhode Island selected delegates.

THE CONSTITUTIONAL CONVENTION

Seventy-four persons were appointed delegates to the Philadelphia convention, of whom fifty-five attended, and thirty-nine took a leading part in deliberations. These delegates, for the most part, were anxious to create a government that would work. They were well equipped for the task. Seven had served as governors of their respective states, thirty-nine had served in Congress, and eight had previous experience in constitution making within their own states. Despite this wealth of experience, the convention was composed mainly of young men. The youngest was only twenty-six, six were under thirty-one, and only twelve were over fifty-four. They were men of consequence—merchants, manufacturers, planters, bankers, and lawyers. Small farmers and city mechanics were not represented, and the back-country rural areas were greatly underrepresented (but were fairly represented in several of the state ratifying conventions). There were no women, no African-Americans, no Native Americans, or any other minorities.

Conspicuous by their absence from the convention were Patrick Henry, Samuel Adams, John Adams, John Hancock, Tom Paine, and Thomas Jefferson—the fiery democratic leaders of the Revolution. Henry had been appointed but had refused to attend; he was not in favor of revising the Articles of Confederation. "I smelt a rat," he is reported to have remarked. Jefferson and John Adams were abroad, representing the United States in a diplomatic capacity; Paine had returned to England; Hancock and Samuel Adams had not been chosen as delegates.

Six men stand out as leaders of the convention: George Washington, James Madison, Edmund Randolph, Benjamin Franklin, James Wilson, and Gouverneur Morris—three from Virginia, three from Pennsylvania. Washington, first citizen of Virginia and of the United States, was unanimously selected to preside over the convention. He had been extremely reluctant to attend and had accepted only when persuaded that his prestige was needed to ensure that the convention would even be held and that it would be taken seriously. Although he seldom spoke, his influence was potent both in informal gatherings and in the convention sessions. The universal assumption that he would become the first president under the new government inspired confidence in it.

Madison, only thirty-six at the time, was one of the most learned and informed of the delegates. He had been a member both of the federal Congress and of the Virginia Assembly. Foreseeing the future significance of the convention, Madison always sat in the front of the room, where he could hear all that was said, and he kept a detailed record of the proceedings. Even today, *Madison's Notes*, although he edited them in the 1820s, almost forty years after the event, remain our major source of information concerning the convention.

Edmund Randolph, thirty-four, was governor of Virginia and a member of one of Virginia's first families. Although he declined to sign the Constitution, perhaps because he was unsure of its popularity, he later advocated its ratification.

Benjamin Franklin, at eighty-one, was the convention's oldest member. Second only to Washington in the esteem of his countrymen, Franklin had a firm faith in the people. Despite his great age, Franklin played an active role. At critical moments his sagacious and humorous remarks broke the tension and prevented bitterness.

Most of Franklin's speeches were read to the convention by his fellow Pennsylvania delegate James Wilson. This Scottish-born and Scottish-trained lawyer had signed the Declaration of Independence and subsequently had become a state representative in Congress. He was a strong supporter of Madison, and his work on the convention's Committee on Detail, although inconspicuous, was very important.

In sharp contrast to Franklin, Gouverneur Morris, the third Pennsylvania delegate, was strongly aristocratic in his sympathies. He was an eloquent and interesting speaker and addressed the convention more often than any other member. Because of his facility with the pen, he was chosen to write the final draft of the Constitution. Years later he began a letter, "The hand that writes this letter wrote the Constitution."

In addition to these six, other prominent delegates included George Mason, Charles Pinckney, Roger Sherman, Alexander Hamilton, and Luther Martin. Hamilton, representing New York, did not play as important a role as one might expect. His influence was nullified to a great extent by his associates from New York, who opposed the Constitution. Hamilton also lost influence through his advocacy of a strong and completely centralized national government. At the opposite extreme from Hamilton was Luther Martin from Maryland, who was an ardent—and fearfully boring—champion of the small states. As soon as it was apparent that his views were in the minority, Martin left the convention and traveled back to Maryland.

Convention Debates and Procedures

The Virginia delegates, anxious to establish a strong central government, took advantage of an eleven-day delay in the opening of the convention—a delay due to the failure of a sufficient number of delegates to appear at the designated opening time—to prepare a series of proposals. They prepared a plan that imparted to the forthcoming debates a general direction that the less nationalistically inclined delegates were never able to reverse. Eventually the *Virginia Plan,* with modifications, became the Constitution.

Immediately after Washington was chosen to preside and rules of procedures were adopted—of which the rule of secrecy was perhaps the most significant—Randolph introduced Virginia's fifteen resolutions. The Virginia Plan contained some startling proposals. The convention's mandate from Congress, and most of the delegates' instructions from their state legislatures, restricted them to the consideration of amendments to the Articles of Confederation. The Virginians, however, proposed a completely new instrument of government differing fundamentally from those articles. They proposed that a central government be established with power to pass laws and with authority to enforce those laws through its own executive and judicial branches. They proposed that Congress be a bicameral (two-house) legislature in which states would be represented on the basis of wealth or population and that it be given all powers vested in the existing Congress plus the authority "to legislate in all cases in which the separate states are incompetent, or in which the harmony of the United States may be interrupted by the exercise of individual legislation."

For the first two weeks, the convention discussed the Virginia Plan. Delegates from the less populous states were afraid that their interests would be overlooked by a national legislature dominated by representatives from the large states. They favored a less powerful national government with more independence of action by the states. They counterattacked on June 14, when William Paterson of New Jersey introduced nine resolutions—*The New Jersey Plan*—as an alternative to Virginia's scheme. Except for proposing that Congress be given the power to regulate commerce and levy taxes, the plan would not have significantly altered the Articles of Confederation. All states were to have the same weight in a single-chambered national Congress, a plural executive was to administer the law, and a single national Supreme Court was to supervise the interpretation of national laws by the state courts. Although some of its provisions were incorporated into the Constitution, the New Jersey Plan was ultimately rejected, and the delegates resumed discussion of the Virginia Plan.

As deliberations continued, there were threats of withdrawal as discontent grew among delegates from the small states, and eventually the convention became deadlocked over the crucial issue of representation in the upper house of the proposed Congress. Finally, a committee of eleven, one delegate from each state (remember, Rhode Island had refused to send delegates to the Constitutional Convention, and much of the time New York was unrepresented), was appointed to work out a compromise. Three days later, on July 5, the committee presented its report, known to history as the *Connecticut Compromise*. The nationalists conceded that each state would have equal representation in the upper house, but only on the condition that money bills originate in the lower chamber. Furthermore, three-fifths of the slave population was to be added to the free population both for determining representation in the lower house and for apportioning direct taxes among the states according to population. Delegates from the less populous states, thus mollified, were then ready to support the establishment of a strong central government.

There remained many differences to be reconciled: questions about suffrage, the structure and authority of federal courts, and the procedures for selecting the president. Yet, on many basic issues the delegates were in general agreement. All supported the idea of a republican form of government, and all agreed that the powers of the national government should be distributed among a legislative branch, an executive branch, and a judicial branch. Without extended debate, it was decided to impose limits on the power of the states to coin money or interfere with the rights of creditors. By the end of summer the delegates had a document to present to the nation.

The framers had not prepared a mere revision of the Articles of Confederation. Instead, ignoring instructions from their state legislatures, they called for an entirely different structure of government. Moreover, contrary to their instructions from Congress and the provisions of the Articles of Confederation, they called for direct submission of their work to a special convention within each state for ratification, rather than submission through Congress to state legislatures. They also asked that the new Constitution go into effect when approved by three-fourths of the states, without the unanimity required by the Articles of Confederation. In summary, the framers called upon the nation to engage in a second American revolution.

Final Day

On September 17, 1787, after four months of debate, the delegates took their seats. General Washington called the meeting to order, and the secretary began to read the final copy of the Constitution. When that was finished, Dr. Franklin rose. Too feeble to speak for himself, the good doctor turned to his fellow delegate James Wilson and asked him to read a speech that he had prepared for the occasion. The delegates stirred in their seats. "Mr. President," said Wilson, his strong voice giving emphasis to the wisdom of one of America's sages,

> I confess that there are several parts of this constitution that I do not at present approve, but I am not sure I shall never approve of them.... The older I grow, the more apt I am to doubt my own judgment, and to pay more respect to the judgment of others.... On the whole, Sir, I cannot help expressing a wish that every member of the Convention who may still have objections to it, would with me, on this occasion doubt a little of his own infallibility and to make manifest our unanimity, put his name to this instrument.

At the conclusion of his speech, Franklin shrewdly moved that the Constitution be signed by the members in the "following convenient form, viz., 'Done in Convention by the unanimous consent of the States present the 17th of Spr. & c...In Witness whereof we have hereunto subscribed our names.'" This ambiguous form had been drawn up by Gouverneur Morris in order to gain the support of those members who had qualms about giving their approval to the Constitution, but it was introduced by Franklin so that it might have a better chance of success.

The roll was called on Franklin's motion. The results: ten ayes, no nays, and one delegation divided. The motion was approved.

The delegates then moved forward to sign. Only three persons present at this historic meeting refused to place their names on the Constitution. Others who had opposed the general drift of the convention had already left Philadelphia. *Madison's Notes* tell us that Franklin, the last member to sign, looking towards the president's chair, at the back of which a rising sun happened to be painted, observed to a few members near him, that painters had found it difficult to distinguish, in their art, a rising from a setting sun. "I have," said he, "often and often in the course of the session, and the vicissitudes of my hopes and fears as to its issue, looked at that behind the president, without being able to tell whether it was rising or setting; but now, at length, I have the happiness to know that it is a rising, and not a setting sun."

Their work over, the delegates adjourned to the City Tavern to relax and celebrate a job well done.

Ratification Debate

Ratification of the Constitution was not without a bitter struggle within the states, especially in Virginia, Massachusetts, and New York. Both in the campaigns for the election of delegates to the ratifying conventions and in the conventions themselves, the Constitution was subjected to minute and searching debate.

By the end of June 1788, ten states had ratified—one more than was needed. But New York still had not acted, and because of its central geographic location, its approval was essential to the success of the new government. All during the previous winter and spring the debate had been intense. Hamilton, fearful of the outcome, had secured the assistance of James Madison and John Jay to write a series of articles to win over the people of New York. The influence of these articles, known as *The Federalist Papers,* on the outcome of the ratification struggle is sometimes exaggerated; but, without a doubt, they did help bring about the final favorable verdict. Written under pressure and for partisan purposes, they nevertheless quickly became the most important contemporary comment on the Constitution. Their penetrating discussion of the basic problems of government and their profound analysis of our constitutional system make them even today America's most outstanding contribution to the literature of political science.

CHAPTER TWO

BASIC FEATURES OF
THE CONSTITUTION

Underpinning the entire Constitution certain basic features establish the character of the American system of government: federalism, separation of powers, and judicial review.

FEDERALISM

A *federal government* is one in which a *constitution* divides governmental power between a central government and one or more subdivisional governments, giving each substantial functions. In contrast, a *unitary system* is one in which a constitution vests all governmental power in a central government. In a unitary system, the central government may delegate authority to local units, but what it gives, it has constitutional authority to take away. In a federal system, the constitution is the source of both central and subdivisional authority. Each unit has a core of power independent of the wishes of those who control the other level of government.

American federalism is only one variant of the many forms of federalism. Examples of other governments federal in form and practice are those of Switzerland, Australia, and Canada. In Canada a constitution reserves to the central government powers not given to the provinces. (Canadians are struggling over the very nature of their federal system. There are great pressures from French-speaking Quebec for greater autonomy.) In the United States we do it the other way around, reserving to the states powers not given to the national government.

Federal systems create tension over questions about where authority resides. In the United States we have resolved that tension by tilting toward the supremacy of the national government. Other federal systems, Switzerland, for example, tilt in the other direction.

The Constitutional Basis of American Federalism

1. The Constitution grants certain legislative, executive, and judicial powers to the national government.

2. It reserves to the states powers not granted to the national government.

3. It makes the national government supreme. The Constitution, all laws passed in pursuance thereof, and treaties of the United States are the supreme law of the land. American citizens, most of whom are also state citizens, owe their primary allegiance to the national government; officers of the state governments, of course, owe the same allegiance.

4. The Constitution denies some powers to both the national and the state governments, it denies some powers only to the national government, and still other powers are denied only to the state governments.

Conflicting Interpretations of American Federalism

Throughout our history, political conflicts have generated debates about the nature of nation–state relationships. Can slavery be outlawed in the territories? Does the national government have the power to regulate railroad rates or forbid racial discrimination? Does the national government have any responsibility to finance higher education? As issues and times have changed, so also have the details of the arguments. It is, however, a useful oversimplification to classify the views about the relations between the national government and the states into two broad schools: the states' rights position and the nationalist position.

The states' rights interpretation rests on the premise that the Constitution is a compact among the states. The states, it is argued, created the national government and gave it certain limited powers. A doubt whether a particular function has been given to the national government or reserved to the states should be resolved in favor of the principal parties to the constitutional contract, the states, and against their agent, the national government. Hence, the national government's powers should be construed narrowly and should not be expanded by interpretation. The clause giving Congress the power to legislate when "necessary and proper" to carry into execution the powers assigned to the national government (see page 97) confers authority to legislate only if it is absolutely necessary to effect one of the national government's express powers.

According to the states' rights interpretation, the existence of the national government does not in any way curtail the full use by the states of their reserved powers. However, the existence of the reserved powers of the states does restrict the scope of the national government's granted powers. For example, because the power to regulate agriculture is reserved to the states, the national government, contended states' righters, should not use its enumerated powers in such a way as to regulate agriculture. The states' rights orientation toward our federal system is based on the assumption that state governments are closer to the people and therefore more accurately reflect the people's wishes than does the national government. The national government has to be watched carefully to make sure that it does not deprive the people of their liberties.

Nationalists, on the other hand, reject the whole idea of the Constitution as a compact among the states and deny that the national government is an agent of the states. Rather, they argue, the Constitution is a supreme law issuing from "We the people of the United States." It was the people, not the state governments, who created the national government, and who gave it sufficient power to accomplish the great objectives listed in the Preamble. The national government is not a subordinate of the states. To avoid frustrating the people's intentions, the powers of the national government should be construed liberally. In addition, a liberal construction of the "necessary and proper" clause gives Congress the right to adopt any means convenient and useful to put into effect expressly delegated powers. The national government should not be denied authority to act unless its actions clearly conflict with express constitutional limits or have no constitutional basis.

Nationalists also deny that the reserved powers of the states limit the national government's use of its delegated authority. The national government, for example, may exercise its power to regulate commerce among the states, whether or not such regulation touches on matters otherwise subject to the reserved powers of the states. Furthermore, states may not use their reserved powers—the power to tax, for example—in a way that interferes with programs of the national government. The national government represents all of the people; each state, only a part of the people.

In 1819 the Supreme Court had the first of many occasions to choose between these two interpretations of our federal system, when the celebrated case of *McCulloch* v *Maryland* came before it.[1] Maryland had levied a tax against the Baltimore branch of the Bank of the United States. McCulloch, the cashier, refused to pay the tax, on the ground that a state could not tax an instrumentality of the national government. Maryland's attorneys argued that the national government did not have the power to incorporate a bank in the first place but if it did have that power, the states had the power to tax the bank.

Chief Justice John Marshall, speaking for the Supreme Court, gave his full support to the nationalist position. Although the power to incorporate a bank is not among the powers expressly delegated, he said, it is a necessary and proper— that is to say, convenient and useful—means of carrying into effect such delegated powers as caring for the property of the United States, regulating currency, and promoting interstate commerce. Marshall wrote, in one of the most celebrated judicial statements of all time, "Let the end be legitimate, let it be within the scope of the Constitution, and all means which are appropriate, which are plainly adapted to the end, which are not prohibited, but consist with the letter and spirit of the Constitution, are constitutional." Moreover, although the states have the power to tax, they may not tax instruments created by the national government, inasmuch as "the power to tax involves the power to destroy."

---

[1] *McCulloch* v *Maryland*, 4 Wheaton 316 (1819).

The nationalist interpretation has been supported, with varying emphases, by Abraham Lincoln, Theodore Roosevelt, and Franklin Roosevelt and, throughout most of our history, by the Supreme Court. However, notwithstanding *McCulloch* v *Maryland*, many have continued to champion the states' rights interpretation. Chief Justice Roger B. Taney (Marshall's immediate successor), for example, was an advocate of dual federalism, the position that the national and state governments are equal sovereigns, each with its own sphere of supremacy; John C. Calhoun believed in the doctrine of concurrent majorities, a view that effectively would give states a veto over the actions of the national government. A Supreme Court majority in the 1920s espoused dual federalism. Most recently, Presidents Ronald Reagan and George Bush championed the view that the national government's responsibilities should be narrowly construed.

Classification of National Powers

By Constitutional Source

1. *Enumerated powers* are those the Constitution expressly grants—for example, the power to raise and support armies and navies.

2. *Implied powers* are those that may be inferred from power expressly granted—for example, the power to operate an air force or the power to draft, from the express power to raise armies and navies.

3. *Resulting powers* are those that result when several enumerated powers are added together. For example, the authority to make paper money legal tender for the payment of debts results from adding together the enumerated powers to coin money, to regulate commerce among the several states, and to borrow money.

4. *Inherent powers* are those powers in the field of foreign affairs that, the Supreme Court has declared, do not depend on constitutional grants but grow out of the very existence of the national government. These powers—for example, to discover and occupy territory, to make treaties with other nations, to send and receive representatives—are powers the national government would have even if the Constitution were silent, because they are powers all nations have under international law.

By Relation to State Powers

1. *Exclusive powers* are those only the national government may exercise—for example, the power to conduct foreign relations or to establish uniform rules of naturalization. In some cases, the Constitution explicitly gives the national government exclusive power or expressly denies states the right to act; in others, the Supreme Court has found that the nature of the national power involved rules out state actions.

2. *Concurrent powers* are those the national government shares with the states—for example, the power to tax. Whenever action by the national government conflicts with state action, the former prevails.

3. *Expressly forbidden powers* are those the Constitution denies to the national government in relation to state governments. For example, the national government may not tax states' exports. (Remember, here we are describing the limitations on national powers in the context of nation–state relations. There are other limitations on national powers designed to protect civil liberties.)

4. *Implied limitations on national power* are limitations that grow out of the nature of the federal system—created by the Constitution—in which states are integral units. The national government may not use any of its powers—the power to tax, for example—in such a way as to destroy the states or make it impossible for them to govern. However, whatever implied limitations on national power flow from our federal system are limitations that are primarily enforceable through the political process and only secondarily through the courts (see pages 173–76).

Reserved Powers of the States

The reserved powers of the states may be classified according to the nature and subject of the power.

1. *To tax and to spend.* This power, like all powers reserved to the states, may not be used to place a burden on the national government, to frustrate its activities, or to conflict with national regulations.

2. *To regulate persons and property in order to promote the public welfare.* This power, known as the *police power,* must be exercised in a manner consistent with constitutional limitations, as must all state powers. The Supreme Court, an agency of the national government, makes the determination when a conflict is alleged between a state's exercise of its powers and a national constitutional limitation.

3. *To regulate intrastate (local) commerce* and those aspects of interstate commerce that in the opinion of Congress (or in the case of Congress's silence, in the judgment of the Supreme Court) are appropriate for state regulation.

4. *To take private property.* This power is known as the power of eminent domain. Under the Constitution (see page 304), the states, as well as the national government, may take property only for public purposes and must compensate the owners.

5. *To establish a republican form of state and local government.* Subject
only to the constitutional requirement that each state is to have a
republican form of government (see page 163), each state is free to
establish whatever kind of state and local governments it wishes.
Moreover, the people of each state, through their own state constitution, may impose limitations on state officials beyond those contained
in the national Constitution. They cannot, however, deprive state officials of the responsibilities the Constitution gives them. To illustrate,
the power to ratify or reject constitutional amendments is vested by
the Constitution in state legislatures or state conventions, and the
people of a state cannot take that power from the legislature or a
state convention and vest it in the electorate.

Federalism Today

Speaking precisely and technically, Congress has no general grant of authority to do whatever it thinks necessary and proper to promote the general welfare
or to preserve domestic tranquility. However, as a result of the emergence of a
national economy, the growth of national allegiance, and the existence in a
world with weapons that could destroy us in seconds, our constitutional system has evolved to the point where the national government has ample constitutional authority to deal with any national or international problem.

As recently as the Great Depression of the 1930s, scholars and Supreme
Court justices seriously debated whether Congress had the constitutional power
to regulate labor, business, education, housing, social security, and welfare.
Only decades ago there were constitutional questions about the authority of
Congress to legislate against racial discrimination. Despite an occasional "flash-
back" to prior, more restrictive interpretations, nowadays it is hard to think of
any subject that the Supreme Court might consider to be completely beyond
the scope of national regulation. In fact, it is accurate, even if technically incorrect, to make the generalization that Congress has the power to do whatever it
believes is necessary and proper to promote the general welfare.

Today the national government is involved with the hospitals in which we
are born, the families in which we grow up, the schools we attend, the places
we work, the ways we travel, the places we keep our money, and the conditions
under which we are buried. In fact, one is hard put to think of anything we do
that is not in some way affected by a rule, regulation, or program of the
national government.

The principles of federalism no longer impose constitutional restraints on
the powers of Congress, the president, or the federal courts—most especially
not on Congress. As Justice Rehnquist commented, not altogether with
approval, "It is illuminating for purposes of reflection, if not for argument, to
note that one of the greatest 'fictions' of our federal system is that the Congress

exercises only those powers delegated to it, while the remainder are reserved to the States or to the people."[2] (See the Tenth Amendment.) There are significant restraints today on the powers of the national government, but they stem primarily from constitutional provisions designed to protect the liberties of the people rather than from provisions designed to preserve the powers of the individual state governments.

SEPARATION OF POWERS AND CHECKS AND BALANCES

Separation of powers refers to the constitutional distribution of national powers among three departments, each of which is given constitutional and political independence from the other two branches. The personnel of each branch is chosen by different procedures and holds office for terms that are independent of those of the other branches. It is this constitutional and political independence of the three branches, not just the distribution of functions, that is the central feature of our system of separation of powers. Great Britain also has executive, legislative, and judicial branches, but the British government is not established according to the principle of separation of powers, inasmuch as the legislature chooses the prime minister and the cabinet and the executive depends on the legislature both for retention of office and for authority. In the United States, the president's power comes not from Congress but from the Constitution.

The framers of the Constitution feared concentration of powers in a single branch. To them, separation of powers and checks and balances were desirable to prevent official tyranny and, even more important, to prevent a single segment of the population, majority or minority, from gaining complete control of the government. It was hoped that making each branch accountable to different groups would cause a variety of interests to be reflected. Hence, compromises and a balancing of interests would result.

In addition to separate functions and considerable political and constitutional independence, each branch has weapons with which to check the others. The president has a qualified veto over laws enacted by Congress, and the courts interpret the laws, but the president and the Senate select the judges; the president is commander in chief of the armed forces, but Congress provides those forces; and so on. This doctrine of separation of powers is more accurately described as "separated institutions sharing powers."[3] Each department is given a voice in the business of the others, and each is made dependent on the cooperation of the others in order to accomplish its own business. It is through this blending of powers by politically independent branches that the doctrine of checks and balances is made effective.

The constitutional provision for separation of powers has been altered by the growth of national political parties and the increased legislative influence of the

---

[2] *Hodel* v *Virginia Surface Min. & Recl. Assn,* 452 US 264 (1981).
[3] Richard E. Neustadt, *Presidential Power* (New York: John Wiley & Sons, Inc., 1980), 26.

president. National parties, however, are such loosely organized political instruments that they are often ineffective devices for coordinating governmental action, even when the president and a majority of the Congress belong to the same party.

A more significant alteration of the original constitutional arrangements has been the president's expanding role as chief legislator. Today presidents are expected to have a legislative program of their own and to use their powers and prestige to secure its adoption by Congress. This growth of presidential leadership has brought the legislative and executive branches into a closer relationship than many of the Founding Fathers anticipated, and undoubtedly many of them would be surprised to discover that the president has been able to take over so many, and such important, legislative responsibilities.

Despite the growth of the presidential role, the traditional independence of Congress has remained intact, as the president is frequently compelled to deal with legislators who have political security greater than the president's.

There are a variety of corollaries flowing from the separation of powers principle. One is the doctrine of *nondelegation of legislative powers*—namely, what the Constitution gives to Congress, it may not give away. In reality, a blending of duties is often necessary to accomplish the business of government. The Supreme Court has recognized that it is impossible for Congress to make all policy decisions. In fact, the Supreme Court has been willing to tolerate so much delegation of policy making to executive agencies that many consider the doctrine against the delegation of legislative power to be obsolete. As Justice Thurgood Marshall wrote: "The notion that the Constitution narrowly confines the Congress to delegate authority to administrative agencies, which was briefly in vogue in the 1930s, has been virtually abandoned by the Court for all practical purposes, at least in the absence of delegation creating the danger of overbroad, unauthorized, and arbitrary application of criminal sanctions in the area of constitutionally protected freedoms."[4]

He is correct as far as actual declarations of unconstitutionality are concerned. Only in two cases in the 1930s was any legislation ever set aside for being an unconstitutional delegation of legislative power.[5] Legislation, however, occasionally continues to be challenged on the grounds of an unconstitutional delegation of legislative powers, and Justice Scalia has occasionally voiced an older view of the prohibition against delegation of legislative power. In 1974, in order to avoid any suggestion that Congress had given away its power to levy taxes, the Supreme Court narrowly construed an act of Congress that gave independent regulatory agencies the right to collect fees against those they regulate.[6] In 1986, although the Court sustained the practice in the particular instance considered, the justices warned Congress that it should not go too far in giving administrative agencies responsibility to deal with matters historically within the province of courts (see page 142).[7]

---

[4] *FPC v New England Power Co.,* 415 US 345 (1974).

[5] *Schechter Poultry Corp. v United States,* 295 US 495 (1935).

[6] *National Cable Television Assn. v United States,* 415 US 336 (1974).

[7] *Commodity Futures Trading Comm'n. v Schor,* 478 US 833 (1986).

Yet, when all is said and done, it is sufficient nowadays for Congress to set down a general policy and then to authorize administrative officials to make rules to carry out the general policy. "So long as Congress lays down by legislative act an intelligible principle to which the person or body authorized to [act] is directed to conform, such legislative action is not a forbidden delegation of legislative power."[8] By acting in this way, Congress maintains the form of constitutional propriety: it retains its "essential" legislative duties and merely delegates what the Court has labeled "quasi-legislative" power. Thus, the Supreme Court has sustained congressional delegation of authority to the Interstate Commerce Commission to establish "fair and reasonable" interstate railroad rates; to the Federal Trade Commission to make regulations to prevent "unfair methods of competition"; to the Federal Communications Commission to regulate radio and television in "the public interest, convenience, and necessity"; to the secretary of labor to promulgate nationwide standards governing health and safety in the workplace; to the United States Sentencing Commission to set binding and detailed guidelines for federal judges in setting sentences for federal offenses; and to the secretary of transportation to establish pipeline user fees.[9] The Court has also upheld the right of Congress to delegate to the attorney general responsibility to outlaw traffic in new drugs "when necessary to avoid an imminent hazard to the public safety."[10]

The doctrine of separation of powers has other corollaries. Among them is that Congress should not interfere with the president's appointive or removal powers or with the president's responsibilities to execute faithfully the laws of the United States. Until recent years, these rules were more likely to be discussed in political science classes than to be the basis of judicial decisions. In the last decade, however, the Court has struck down some major congressional legislation on the grounds that Congress has strayed into fields reserved to the executive: the Court set aside the congressional veto of the actions of administrative agencies (see pages 66–67).[11] It also declared unconstitutional a provision of the Federal Election Campaign Act of 1974 calling for the appointment of some of the commissioners of the Federal Election Commission by the House and the Senate because this interfered with presidential appointing powers (see page 128).[12] The Court also set aside a provision of the Gramm-Rudman-Hollings Budget Act because it had assigned an executive responsibility to the comptroller general, an officer removable by Congress.[13] The Court has also held that Congress violated the separation of powers principle by condition-

---

[8] *Touby* v *United States*, 114 L Ed 2d 219 (1991) quoting from *J.W. Hampton, Jr., & Co.* v *United States*, 276 US 394 (1928).

[9] See *Skinner* v *Mid-American Pipeline*, 490 US 212 (1989) and *Mistretta* v *United States*, 488 US 361 (1989) for the most recent visits to the doctrine of nondelegation of legislative powers.

[10] *Touby* v *United States*, 114 L Ed 2d 219 (1991).

[11] *INS* v *Chadha*, 462 US 919 (1983).

[12] *Buckley* v *Valeo*, 424 US 1 (1976).

[13] *Bowsher* v *Synar*, 478 US 714 (1986).

ing approval of an agreement between the District of Columbia and Virginia to create an agency to operate National and Dulles Airports on the establishment of a board made up of members of Congress with veto power over the actions of the agency. "If the [Board of Review's] power was executive, the Constitution did not permit an agent of Congress to exercise such power.... If such power was legislative, Congress was required to exercise it in conformity with the bicameralism and presentment requirements of the Constitution (Art I, Sec. 7)."[14]

Although the Supreme Court does not always side with the White House—it upheld Congress's right to create independent prosecutors to investigate allegations of executive wrongdoing—the Burger and Rehnquist Courts have used the doctrine of separation of powers to protect the executive from congressional interferences. Skeptics point out that the Republican-appointed justices' concern for protecting the constitutional independence of the executive power from congressional infringment may be related to the fact that between Johnson's departure in 1969 and Clinton's arrival in 1993, except for the four Carter years (1977–1981), Republicans controlled the White House while the Democrats have been in charge of Congress.

Yet the White House did not win all the battles. As noted, the Court sustained Congress's right to create a system of independent prosecutors who, once appointed, can be removed by the president only for cause and who are free to investigate and prosecute executive officials free from routine supervision by the attorney general.[15] And the Court upheld the right of Congress to keep Nixon, unlike every other president before or since, from taking custody of his presidential papers, by placing these papers under the control of the administrator of the General Services Administration. Nixon challenged the law for, among other things, violating the doctrine of separation of powers, and he argued that Congress had improperly delegated to a subordinate officer of the president the power to decide when and how to disclose presidential materials. Such a delegation, he contended, encroached on the president's powers over his own files and reversed the presumption of confidentiality of such materials. The Court, however, rejected Nixon's argument as resting on "an archaic view of separation of powers requiring three airtight departments of government." Chief Justice Burger, in dissent, responded, "If separation of powers principles can be so easily evaded, then the constitutional separation is a sham."[16] (The doctrine of executive privilege, another corollary of the separation of powers doctrine, is discussed on page 115.)

Separation of Powers and Judicial Independence

Both the mores of our politics and the design of the Constitution give federal judges a large measure of protection from the Congress, the White House,

---

[14] *Metropolitan Washington Airports Authority* v *Citizens for Abatement of Aircraft Noise*, 115 L Ed 2d 236 (1991).

[15] *Morrison* v *Olson*, 487 US 654 (1988).

[16] *Nixon* v *Administrator of General Services*, 433 US 425 (1977).

and the electorate. The framers took special precautions to isolate the judiciary from executive and legislative influence. They did not wish the judges to be subject to executive dominance because they remembered how English kings had used judges to punish enemies and to reward friends. They were also afraid that there might be times when Congress and the president might respond to political and social convulsions and act hastily and oppressively. The judges, it was hoped, with their independence and political security, would be more likely to withstand transitory gusts of popular passion and to take a more detached and long-range view. The relative independence of the judges from political influences takes on additional significance because they have the important power of judicial review.

JUDICIAL REVIEW AND JUDICIAL POWER

Judicial review is the authority of judges to interpret the Constitution and to refuse to enforce measures that, in their opinion, are in conflict with the Constitution; the ultimate authority is that of the justices of the Supreme Court. The study of the American Constitution is therefore in large measure a study of judicial decisions and opinions, although it is not limited to them because the president, members of Congress, and other officials, national and state and local, must also interpret the Constitution as they carry out their tasks. Members of Congress, presidents, governors, legislators, school boards, sheriffs, police officers, and all public officials have a duty to act constitutionally. Often they have to measure their actions against their own reading of the Constitution, most especially if there is no Supreme Court decision that is relevant. Judges are the authoritative, but not the only, interpreters of the Constitution.

The Constitution does not specifically grant the courts the power to interpret the Constitution, but it furnishes sufficient verbal basis for the power. The first assertion of that power against an act of Congress was made in 1803 in Chief Justice John Marshall's famous opinion in *Marbury v Madison*.[17]

The case arose out of the following situation. The Federalists had lost the election of 1800 but, before leaving office, they succeeded in creating several new judicial posts. Among these were forty-two positions of justice of the peace for the District of Columbia, to which the retiring Federalist president, John Adams, appointed forty-two Federalists. The Senate confirmed the appointments and the commissions were signed and sealed, but Adams's secretary of state, John Marshall, failed to deliver seventeen of them. When the new president, Thomas Jefferson, assumed office, he gave instructions not to deliver these commissions, including one for William Marbury.

Marbury decided to act. He found that Section 13 of the Judiciary Act of 1789 declared, "The Supreme Court shall have the power to issue writs of man-

---

[17] 1 Cranch 137 (1803).

damus, in cases warranted by the principles and usages of law, to persons holding office, under the authority of the United States." (A writ of mandamus is a court order directing an officer to perform a certain ministerial duty, that is, a nondiscretionary act required by law.) Without further ado, Marbury, through his attorneys, went before the Supreme Court and asked the justices to issue a writ of mandamus to Secretary of State Madison ordering him to deliver the commission.

The Court, speaking through Marshall, who was now chief justice, held that Section 13 of the Judiciary Act of 1789 was repugnant to Article III, Section 2, of the Constitution, inasmuch as the Constitution itself limited the Supreme Court's original jurisdiction to cases "affecting ambassadors, other public ministers and consuls, and those to which a state is party." Since Marbury fell in none of these categories, the Court declined to take jurisdiction of his case despite the fact that Congress in Section 13 gave such power to the Court.

Where did the Supreme Court derive the authority thus to contradict Congress? Marshall reasoned that the Constitution is law, that it is the duty of courts to interpret the law in order to decide cases in accordance with it, and that therefore the Supreme Court had the authority, and indeed was duty bound, to interpret the Constitution and of course to prefer it to any other law. He also pointed out that the Constitution enjoins the courts to enforce, as the supreme law of the land, only acts of Congress that are "in pursuance of the Constitution" (Article VI, Section 2). Therefore, the Court must first determine whether a law is in pursuance of the Constitution before it is entitled to enforce it as the "supreme law of the land."

Although the argument sounds plausible, Marshall's logic and the assumptions on which his contentions rest have been continually questioned over the years. To this day, a heated debate rages about whether the consequences of judicial review are favorable or unfavorable to the maintenance of our democratic system. Critics, including several presidents, have argued that the Constitution is supreme law because it emanates from the people. Therefore, the most politically accountable and responsive agencies, Congress and the president—who, like the justices, have also sworn to uphold the Constitution—have a better claim to interpret its meaning than does the least politically accountable agency, the Supreme Court. Also questioned is Marshall's assertion that the Constitution is a law of the same kind and character as ordinary law and that the judges therefore have a superior claim to interpret it. The Constitution, it is argued, is not ordinary law but political law. The Constitution is the prime political document of the nation.

Other facets of Marshall's argument are also attacked. He assumed that Article III and Section 13 were in conflict, but this is not obvious. A perfectly reasonable construction of Article III is that it does not restrict the Supreme Court's original jurisdiction to the types of cases listed. Or the Court could have construed Section 13 as authorizing the Supreme Court to issue writs of mandamus if it had jurisdiction. Moreover, in order to rule Section 13 unconstitutional, Marshall had to ignore several canons of constitutional interpretation; for example, he decided a constitutional issue that was not necessary in order to dispose of the case. Once the Court had concluded that it lacked jurisdiction, it need not have gone on to deal with other issues, such as whether Madison had improperly failed to give Marbury his commission.

Finally, critics of judicial review have not accepted the argument that it is a necessary check on Congress and the president. They argue that Congress and the president are checked by the voters, whereas the only regular check on the judges is their own self-restraint, which seems at times to be lacking.

Most of the criticism of judicial review is directed, it should be noted, against review of acts of Congress. That there must be a central review of state action by the Supreme Court is generally conceded. As Justice Holmes once put the matter, "I do not think the United States would come to an end if we lost our power to declare an Act of Congress void. I do think the Union would be imperiled if we could not make that declaration as to the laws of the several states."[18]

Marbury v *Madison* might have been interpreted in a more limited way, so that the Supreme Court had the right to determine the scope of its *own* powers under Article III, but that Congress and the president had the authority to interpret *their* own powers under Articles I and II, respectively. One scholar insists that is what Marshall intended and that a more expansive interpretation of *Marbury* v *Madison* is part of a myth designed to perpetuate judicial dominance.[19] However, Marshall's decision has not been interpreted in this way. On the contrary, building on Marshall's precedent over the decades, the Court has taken the commanding position as the authoritative interpreter of the Constitution.

Restrictions on Judicial Review

John Marshall's successful assertion in *Marbury* v *Madison* that constitutional questions are justiciable—that is, appropriate for judges to decide—has meant that the Supreme Court has played a central role in constitutional interpretation. It also has meant that litigation is often as important a means for policy making as is legislation.

As important as litigation is to our policy-making processes, judges do not have a roving commission to make policy or to interpret the Constitution whenever and however they wish. Courts operate within a prescribed setting and are subject to certain limitations. First, operating within an adversary legal system they can only decide real legal cases and controversies. Second, individuals are not free, by filing a lawsuit, to invoke judicial power whenever they have a grievance they want the judges to decide. They must have standing and must present judges with a justiciable—that is, non-political—question. The doctrines of *standing* and *justiciability* and other doctrines that have grown up around the limitations set on courts—*a real case and controversy,*

---

[18] *Oliver Wendell Holmes, Collected Legal Papers* (New York: Harcourt, Brace & World, 1920), 295–296.

[19] Robert Lowry Clinton, *Marbury* v *Madison and Judicial Review* (Lawrence: University of Kansas Press, 1989), 4–42.

mootness, ripeness—"relate in part, and in different though overlapping ways, to an idea, which is more than an intuition but less than a rigorous and explicit theory, about the constitutional and prudential limits to the powers of an unelected, unrepresentative judiciary in our kind of government."[20]

As a result of the doctrine of political questions, the standing-to-sue requirements, and the restriction of judges' decisions to real cases and controversies, there are some constitutional questions for which there are no judicial answers. The nature of the president's responsibility to formulate legislative programs; the constitutional authority of the president to send arms to other nations or factions, such as the Contras in Nicaragua, without congressional authorization (or even in the face of a prohibition); and the extent of the president's power to abrogate treaties are not the kinds of questions that can readily be raised in the form of a lawsuit. Even those questions that can more readily be formulated as lawsuits are often not brought before the courts for many years, if at all. For example, not until 1926 was there a judicial interpretation of the president's authority to remove executive officers,[21] or until 1969 of each congressional chamber's authority to determine the qualifications of its members,[22] or until 1974 of the prerogative of the president to withhold information,[23] or until 1981 of the question whether Congress had the authority to require a male-only registration for a possible military draft.[24] We still lack authoritative Supreme Court interpretations of the extent of the presidential pocket veto. (See pages 65.)

Three limits on judicial review flowing from the doctrine of separation of powers are of special importance: the standing-to-sue requirement, the political doctrine limitation, and the canons of judicial interpretation.

Standing to Sue

A person, an organization, a corporation, or a group of persons must have standing in order to invoke judicial power, that is, be able to show past injury or immediate, concrete threat to a legal right. A speculative or abstract interest is not sufficient; a mere wish to vindicate one's preferences will not do. Nor is it enough to show a general desire to prevent Congress from acting unconstitutionally or to keep the president from exceeding presidential authority. No matter how qualified an organization may be to evaluate a problem, such qualification does not give it standing to invoke judicial power.[25]

The question that determines standing is "whether the party seeking relief has alleged such a personal stake in the outcome of the controversy as to assure

---

[20] Judge Robert Bork as quoted by Justice Sandra Day O'Connor, writing for the Court in *Allen* v *Wright*, 468 US 737 (1984).

[21] *Myers* v *United States*, 272 US 52 (1926).

[22] *Powell* v *McCormack*, 395 US 486 (1969).

[23] *United States* v *Nixon*, 418 US 683 (1974).

[24] *Rostker* v *Goldberg*, 453 US 57 (1981).

[25] *Sierra Club* v *Morton*, 405 US 727 (1972).

that concrete adverseness which sharpens the presentation of issues upon which the Court so largely depends for illumination of difficult constitutional questions."[26] Justice Thomas summarized for the Court the teachings about standing of a long line of cases as follows: "A party seeking to invoke a federal court's jurisdiction must demonstrate three things: (1) 'injury in fact,' by which we mean an invasion of a legally protected interest that is '(a) concrete and particularized, and (b) actual or imminent, not conjectural or hypothetical'... (2) a causal relationship between the injury and the challenged conduct, by which we mean that the injury 'fairly can be traced to the challenged action of the defendant,' and has not resulted 'from the independent action of some third party not before the court'...(3) a likelihood that the injury will be redressed by a favorable decision, by which we mean that the 'prospect of obtaining relief from the injury as a result of a favorable ruling' is not 'too speculative'.... These elements are the 'irreducible minimum'...required by the Constitution."[27]

The Rehnquist Court has emphasized that "purely abstract claims of noneconomic injury do not provide the kind of particular, direct, and concrete injury that is necessary to confer standing to sue in the federal courts."[28] Moreover, persons seeking federal court jurisdiction have the "burden of showing standing by establishing...that they have suffered an injury in fact, i.e., a concrete and particularized, actual or imminent invasion of a legally protected interest."[29]

As Justice Scalia explained for the Court, even Congress cannot confer standing on persons whose only claim is a generally available grievance about government, unconnected with a concrete interest of his own. To permit Congress to convert such a general interest 'into an individual right' and allow all citizens to sue, regardless of whether they suffered any concrete injury, would permit Congress "to transfer from the President to the courts the Chief Executive's most important constitutional duty, to 'take Care that the Laws be faithfully executed.'"[30]

Yet despite these caveats the Supreme Court and Congress have broadened and "modernized the concept of standing," to permit a wider range of persons to resort to the courts than was the case in earlier decades. First, the Court has slightly lowered what was previously an absolute barrier to suits by persons whose only claim to standing is that they are taxpayers who believe a federal appropriation is unconstitutional (see page 72). In addition, "economic interests that at one time would not have conferred standing have been reexamined and found sufficient,"[31] and the Court has expanded the "zone of interests" that could serve as the basis for standing. Data-processing firms were permitted to challenge regulations that

---

[26] *Baker v Carr*, 369 US 186 (1962).

[27] *Fla. Gen. Contractors v Jacksonville*, 124 L Ed 2d 586 (1993).

[28] *ASARCO v Kadish*, 488 US 887 (1989).

[29] *Lujan v Defenders of Wildlife*, 119 L Ed 2d 351 (1992).

[30] *Lujan v Defenders of Wildlife*, 119 L Ed 2d 351 (1992).

[31] Justice Powell concurring in *United States v Richardson*, 418 US 166 (1974).

allowed banks to compete with them, and tenant farmers were allowed to challenge regulations of the secretary of agriculture affecting their economic status.[32]

Some noneconomic interests also have been recognized, such as concerns for protecting the environment. The mere fact that one belongs to an environmental organization does not confer standing to challenge actions affecting the environment,[33] but groups which claim that damage to the environment limits their members' enjoyment of nature were granted standing to challenge some regulations of the Interstate Commerce Commission.[34] However, simply being '"in the vicinity" of a threatened ecosystem or the fact that one might someday visit such a system does not give people standing to sue, and the mere fact that one belongs to an environmental organization, or might someday visit a threatened ecosystem, does not give one standing.[35] Clearly, in the 1990s the Supreme Court, although willing to allow federal judges to listen to some people claiming loss of their use of the environment, is a long way from the view of Justice Douglas, who would have given standing to trees and other inanimate objects "about to be despoiled, defaced, or invaded by roads and bulldozers."[36]

When black "testers," that is, people trying to find out if African-Americans seeking to rent a particular apartment were being treated differently from white applicants, were told that no apartment was available while a few hours later white testers were told that the same apartment was available, the black testers had standing, even though they did not intend to move. They had standing because they were being denied the statutorily created right to truthful housing information. Since the white testers were given truthful information they did not have standing as testers, but they did have standing as persons who had been injured by being denied "the right to the important social, professional, business and economic, political and aesthetic benefits of interracial associations that arise from living in integrated communities free from discriminatory housing practices."[37] The Court has also held that persons who might be disadvantaged by affirmative action programs that seek to provide more government business for women- and minority-owned firms, such as white male contractors, have standing to sue without having to show that they would in fact have gotten a contract but for the challenged ordinance. The possible denial of equal treatment that provides standing flows "from the imposition of the barrier, not the ultimate inability to obtain the benefit."[38]

---

[32] *Association of Data Processing Service Organizations, Inc. v Camp,* 397 US 150 (1970); *Barlow v Collins,* 397 US 159 (1970).

[33] *Sierra Club v Morton,* 405 US 727 (1972).

[34] *United States v SCRAP,* 412 US 669 (1973)

[35] *Lujan v National Wildlife Federation* 497 US 871 (1990); *Lujan v Defenders of Wildlife,* 119 L Ed 2d 351 (1992).

[36] Dissenting in *United States v SCRAP,* 412 US 669 (1973).

[37] *Havens Realty Corp. v Coleman,* 455 US 363 (1982).

[38] *Fla. Gen. Contractors v Jacksonville,* 124 L Ed. 2d 586 (1993)

One important exception to the basic rules of standing applies to challenges of laws or regulations that may violate the First Amendment. Under what is known as *the overbreadth doctrine,* the Court has permitted persons whose own conduct may be unprotected by the First Amendment to challenge broadly written laws affecting rights under the First Amendment, most especially those relating to freedom of expression. The overbreadth rule is predicated on the assumption that such a statute's very existence may cause others not before the court to refrain from constitutionally protected expression.[39]

Here are some examples of how the standing-to-sue doctrine has been applied in more recent years. Although developers seeking to build in a suburb would have standing to challenge a zoning ordinance, neither low-income minority persons nor taxpayers living in a central city were allowed to challenge zoning laws that they claimed made it difficult for them to move to a suburb.[40] A person who offered no resistance after being stopped by the Los Angeles police, but who was rendered unconscious by a "choke hold," was allowed to sue for damages for that particular incident. However, because it was only speculative that he might be stopped and subjected to the same practice again, he was denied standing to challenge the constitutionality of the practice and to seek an injunction ordering the police not to use such tactics again except in life-threatening situations.[41]

The Court took a similarly restricted view of the doctrine of standing in *Allen* v *Wright:* Some black parents whose children were attending public schools in districts undergoing desegregation alleged that the IRS, by improperly allowing some private schools which discriminated on the basis of race to retain their tax-exempt status, was making it more difficult to integrate the public schools and that this action of the IRS was thus depriving their children of their constitutional rights to attend integrated public schools.[42] The majority denied the parents standing, saying they could not show that removing the tax exemption would assist public school desegregation. Justice Brennan, dissenting along with Justices Stevens, Marshall, and Blackmun, wrote rather angrily, "Once again, the Court 'uses' standing to slam the courthouse door against plaintiffs who are entitled to full consideration of their claims on the merits."[43]

The Doctrine of Political Questions

The doctrine that the Court does not decide "political questions" is still alive. Since the Supreme Court decides which questions are justiciable and which are not, the political question limitation on the authority of the courts

---

[39] *Secretary of State of Maryland* v *J. H. Munson Co.,* 467 US 947 (1984).

[40] *Warth* v *Seldin,* 422 US 490 (1975).

[41] *Los Angeles* v *Lyons,* 461 US 95 (1983).

[42] *Allen* v *Wright,* 468 US 737 (1984).

[43] *Allen* v *Wright,* 468 US 737 (1984).

is a self-defined one. What is a "political question" is a term of judicial art different from our ordinary descriptions of that term. The doctrine of political questions "is designed to restrain the judiciary from inappropriate interference in the business of the other branches of government...."[44] Political questions, constitutionally speaking, are (1) those questions the Constitution clearly directs to the Congress or the president; (2) those that lack judicially discoverable standards for resolution (there seem to be fewer and fewer of these, as the courts regularly apply standards that lack precise meaning); (3) those that cannot be decided without an initial policy determination of a kind clearly appropriate for nonjudicial discretion; (4) those that would be impossible for a court to handle without expressing lack of respect due the Congress or the president (the mere fact that the courts might hold that what Congress or the president did was unconstitutional does not mean that they "lack respect" for the offending branch); (5) those that involve an "unusual need" for unquestioning adherence to a policy decision already made (most of the time, if not always, such an "unusual need" arises in the area of foreign affairs); or (6) those that could create embarrassment by leading to conflicting pronouncements by Congress, the president, and the courts (most such examples relate to foreign matters since conflicting pronouncements by Congress, the president, and the courts are routine).[45] Examples of *political questions* include the following: it is for the president to determine which foreign government is to be recognized by the United States; for Congress to determine if a sufficient number of states have ratified a constitutional amendment within a reasonable time to make the ratification effective; for Congress and the president to determine, in a case of conflicting claimants, which government of a state is the legitimate one; for Congress to determine whether states have the republican form of government required by the Constitution[46]; and for the House to decide how to impeach persons and for the Senate to determine how to try such impeachments.[47]

In 1962 the Supreme Court significantly contracted the scope of the doctrine of political questions. Until that time, it had refused to allow federal judges to get involved in the "political thicket," to use Justice Frankfurter's words of warning, of determining what kinds of legislative districting schemes are constitutional. State courts followed suit. Voters in urban areas who objected to arrangements that gave rural counties a disproportionate number of representatives had no judicial recourse. The only redress available was from the legislatures themselves. Since the legislatures were the product of the allegedly discriminatory district arrangements, and since the rural voters who benefited from the status quo had no desire to alter the existing pattern of representation, appeals by city voters for more equitable representation were ineffective.

[44] *United States* v *Munoz-Flores*, 495 US 385 (1990).

[45] *Baker* v *Carr*, 369 US 186 (1962); *Oneida* v *Oneida Indian Nation*, 470 US 226 (1985).

[46] *Luther* v *Bordon*, 7 Howard 1 (1849); *Colegrove* v *Green*, 328 US 549 (1946).

[47] *Nixon* v *United States et al.*, 122 L Ed 2d 1 (1993).

In *Baker* v *Carr,* the Supreme Court ruled that schemes for determining the boundaries of legislative districts and for apportioning representatives among these districts raised justiciable questions under the equal protection clause of the Fourteenth Amendment.[48] Since then, the Supreme Court has expanded its ruling to cover the drawing by state legislatures of congressional district boundaries,[49] unit-voting schemes for choosing state officers,[50] and the drawing of districts for local governmental legislative or policy-making units such as county commissions.[51] The Court has held that not only is it a justiciable issue to determine whether legislative districts are properly apportioned in terms of population, but so are questions about whether electoral schemes improperly dilute the strength of racial minorities.[52] Furthermore, the Court has concluded that even the issue of partisan gerrymandering, that is, whether a state has violated the Constitution by drawing the legislative district lines in such a partisan fashion as to deny candidates of a political party their constitutional rights, is justiciable.[53] It is hard to imagine a question more centrally located in the "political thicket."

Canons of Judicial Interpretation

In addition to the rules of standing and justiciability, throughout its history, the Supreme Court has developed certain rules of interpretation to guide itself and other federal judges. These rules, like those on standing and justiciability, act to restrain judicial action. Among the rules—sometimes ignored but generally followed—are these:

1. Do not decide a constitutional issue unless it is absolutely necessary in order to dispose of a case.

2. Whenever there is a choice, interpret a law in such a way as to render it constitutional.

3. If it is necessary to make a constitutional ruling, restrict it as narrowly as possible and do not anticipate or decide issues not immediately before the Court.[54]

4. Whenever state law is unclear and is susceptible of an interpretation that will preserve its constitutionality, abstain from deciding the case until state judges have ruled on the law.

Many critics contend that judges pay little attention to these canons, but they are part of the conventions and environment in which judges work.

---

[48] *Baker* v *Carr,* 369 US 186 (1962).

[49] *Wesberry* v *Sanders,* 376 US 1 (1964).

[50] *Gray* v *Sanders,* 372 US 1 (1963).

[51] *Avery* v *Midland County,* 390 US 474 (1968).

[52] *Gomillion* v *Lightfoot,* 364 US 339 (1960).

[53] Davis v Bandemer, 478 US 109 (1986).

[54] Justice Brandeis, concurring, in *Ashwander* v *TVA,* 297 US 288 (1936).

Courts in the Political Process

Courts are deliberately isolated from political battles and partisan conflicts. Yet in a free society judges cannot interpret the Constitution in a manner at significant variance from the desires of most of the people and have such interpretations be effective or sustained. Judges have neither the power of the sword nor the purse, and in order to make their decisions meaningful they have to have the support of most of the people most of the time. Whenever judges hand down rulings that arouse the hostility of significant numbers, it is not at all certain that the rulings will stick; most of the time they do not.

Judges, unlike members of Congress and even the president, are not immediately accountable to the electorate. But in time, as judges resign, retire, or die, the president, who is elected by a national majority, nominates and the Senate confirms new judges to fill vacancies. The views of the new judges will probably reflect the demands of contemporary majorities. At times, congressional majorities and the president, and the groups they represent, have been so strongly opposed to certain Supreme Court decisions that they have changed the laws to alter the structure, size, or jurisdiction of courts to secure decisions more consistent with their wishes. Time after time, new judges—sometimes even the old ones—have found it necessary to reinterpret the Constitution to adjust it to changing demands. Judges interpret the Constitution, but they, like all other public officials, are servants, not masters, of the electorate.

Failure to recognize that courts have limited ability to influence the course of events may lull us into a false sense of security about our rights. The Supreme Court cannot guarantee, for example, freedom of speech, or ensure the preservation of our constitutional system. Judges both lead and respond to the values of the nation. But only insofar as they reflect the views of most of the people can they guarantee free speech or preserve republican government. If most of the people are strongly opposed to freedom of speech, chances are that we shall not have it. If most desire it, chances are that the Supreme Court will hand down decisions protecting it. In short, the Constitution ultimately is not what the judges say it is, but what the people want it to be.[55]

---

[55] J. W. Peltason, *Federal Courts in the Political Process* (New York: Random House, 1955).

CHAPTER THREE

THE CONSTITUTION OF THE UNITED STATES

THE PREAMBLE

We the People of the United States, in Order to form a more perfect Union, establish Justice, insure domestic Tranquility, provide for the common defence, promote the general Welfare, and secure the Blessings of Liberty to ourselves and our Posterity, do ordain and establish this Constitution for the United States of America.

The Preamble is the prologue of the Constitution. It proclaims the source of the Constitution's authority and the great ends to be accomplished under the Constitution. It does not, however, by its own terms create any governmental powers or vest any rights in the people.[1]

The phrase "We the People of the United States" is ambiguous. It was not the people collectively who created the Constitution, but the people of each individual state. The states established the voting requirements for delegates to the ratifying conventions, and the states administered the election machinery. It was a vote of the ratifying conventions of nine states, irrespective of the total popular vote in all states, that was essential for ratification. Whatever the historical case, there has since developed a national community of the people of the United States.

From the Preamble we learn that the Constitution claims obedience not simply because it is intrinsically excellent or because its principles have merit, but because it is ordained and established by the people. "The government of the Union," said Chief Justice Marshall, "...is emphatically and truly, a government of the people. In form, and in substance, it emanates from them. Its

---

[1] *Jacobson v Massachusetts*, 197 US 11 (1905).

powers are granted by them, and are to be exercised directly on them, and for their benefit."[2] The people are the masters of the Constitution, not the reverse.

ARTICLE I: THE LEGISLATIVE ARTICLE

SECTION 1

All legislative Powers herein granted shall be vested in a Congress of the United States,

---

It is significant that, of the three branches of the national government, the legislative branch is mentioned first. The framers of the Constitution desired "a government of laws and not of men,"[3] and they expected Congress, except in time of war or emergency, to be the central and directing organ of the government.

With one very important exception, Congress has no legislative power except those "herein granted" by the Constitution. Powers not granted or powers that cannot reasonably be inferred from the granted powers are denied to Congress and reserved to the states (see the Tenth Amendment). By way of contrast, the British Parliament has complete legislative powers over all matters. Having said all this, the fact is that today Congress's legislative powers are so liberally construed that this contrast between the unlimited nature of Parliamentary powers and the delegated scope of congressional powers should not be given too much significance. Nowadays, so long as Congress's actions do not violate specific constitutional rights of individuals or interfere with constitutional powers delegated by the Constitution to the president or the federal courts, there is little that Congress wants to do that it lacks constitutional authority to do. Moreover, in addition to those legislative powers delegated to it by the Constitution, Congress has "inherent" powers in the field of international affairs to do whatever any other legislature of any nation may do under international law.[4]

SECTION 1

[continued] which shall consist of a Senate and House of Representatives.

By granting legislative powers to two distinct branches of Congress, the framers created a *bicameral legislature,* as contrasted with a *unicameral,* or

---

[2] *McCulloch* v *Maryland,* Wheaton 316 (1819).
[3] Constitution of Massachusetts, Article XXX.
[4] *United States* v *Curtiss-Wright Export Corp.,* 299 US 304 (1936).

single-chamber legislature. Of the framers, only Benjamin Franklin favored a single-chamber legislature. The others felt that two chambers are needed so that representation in one chamber might be based on population with equal representation of the states in the other. Also, the two chambers would serve as a check on each other and prevent the passage of ill-considered legislation. Bicameralism also conformed to the framers' general belief in balanced government, a government that would represent the interests of all parts of society. The House, it was thought, would reflect the attitudes of the popular or democratic elements, and the Senate would reflect the views of the aristocratic elements.

SECTION 2

1. The House of Representatives shall be composed of Members chosen every second Year

---

Some of the framers favored annual terms, believing that "where annual terms end, tyranny begins." Others, including Madison, favored a three-year term. The framers compromised on a two-year term. Throughout our history various people at various times have proposed that members of the House be given four-year terms with the terms coinciding with that of the president. The advantage, it is argued, is that we would reduce the probability that one party would win the presidential election while another dominated one or both branches of Congress. If Congress were dominated by the party of the president, the presidential election mandate could be readily implemented. Those who oppose such an amendment respond that the present midterm elections provide a desirable check on the popularity of the presidential party. They also contend that if the terms of House members coincided with a presidential election, congressional elections would become so submerged in presidential politics that representatives would be overly subject to presidential influences.

The House has several times proposed an amendment to extend the terms of its members to four years but with off-year elections; the Senate has refused to concur, a decision perhaps not unconnected with the fact that four-year terms for members of the House would make it easier for them to run for the Senate. Presidents are also not likely to be very enthusiastic about such an amendment because it probably would produce members of the House less dependent on presidential "coattails" for election and reelection.

In recent years almost all incumbents have been winning their reelection campaigns and since most are Democrats, the Republicans have been unable to win control of the House. Some Republicans have suggested that we should amend the Constitution to set a limit on the number of terms for which any one person might be eligible. This is reminiscent of the Twenty-second Amendment. It seems unlikely that a two-thirds vote will be mustered in the House to support such an amendment.

Within the states there is a strong movement to limit legislative terms. Half the states have adopted amendments to their own state constitutions restricting the number of terms that may be served by members of their state legislature. Fifteen, Colorado being the first, have attempted to impose limits on the terms for members of the United States Congress. It is doubtful if a state can add a qualification to serve in the Congress beyond the age, citizenship, and residency requirements imposed by the United States Constitution. Those who argue to the contrary contend that states using Article I, Section 4, which gives states the right to regulate initially the time, place, and manner of congressional elections (see page 55), may make ineligible for party nomination—even for Congress—persons who have already served a number of terms. They point out that such a person could always mount a write-in campaign and is thus not being prevented from running for office, but only from being the candidate of a political party. Advocates of this means of imposing term limits on members of Congress concede that Article I, Section 4 gives Congress authority to supersede such regulations, but they believe that pressures in favor of term limits are so strong that Congress would not do so. Members of Congress, they argue, would fear that their vote to set aside a state-imposed term limit could successfully be used against them at the next election.

SECTION 2

1. [continued] by the People of the several States,

In the Great Compromise, the framers agreed that, although senators were to be chosen by the state legislatures, representatives were to be elected by the people. In 1963 the Supreme Court, in *Wesberry v Sanders,* gave this tenet additional significance by holding that a state legislature is required to establish congressional districts consisting as nearly as practicable of an equal number of people. Said the Court, "One man's vote in congressional election is to be worth as much as another's."[5]

Since then, using this clause and the equal protection clause of the Fourteenth Amendment, the Court has laid down very stringent standards to ensure the application of what is now called "the one-person, one-vote principle": a state legislature, in drawing congressional districts, must justify any variance from precise mathematical equality by showing that it tried in good faith to come as close as possible to absolute mathematical equality. Even minor population deviations are not permissible unless a state can demonstrate that they are absolutely necessary to achieve some legitimate goal, such as making districts compact, respecting municipal boundaries, preserving the cores of prior districts, or avoiding contests between incumbent representatives.[6] So far no state has been able to justify to the Supreme Court's satisfaction any variance from mathematical equality for congressional districts, even for these legitimate goals. The Supreme Court set aside a New Jersey

---

[5] *Wesberry v Sanders,* 376 US 1 (1964).
[6] *Karcher v Daggett,* 462 US 725 (1983).

reapportionment plan in which the difference between the largest district and the smallest was only 0.6984 percent of the population of the average district.[7]

State legislators are subject to less stringent equal-population standards when apportioning their own chambers, as are city councils, county commissions, junior college districts, and other policy-making state and local government units. For such apportionment the standard is not this clause but the equal protection clause of the Fourteenth Amendment. The standard of the equal protection clause allows for the limited accommodation of other legitimate governmental objectives besides population equality—for example, the keeping together of neighborhoods, cities, and counties, although the leeway the Court allows for such matter is limited. In fact the Court has stated that as a general matter an apportionment plan with a maximum population deviation under 10 percent does not require justification. Even disparities of the larger amount can be justified "by the rational objective of preserving the integrity of political subdivision lines."[8]

SECTION 2

1. [continued] and the Electors in each State shall have the Qualifications requisite for Electors of the most numerous Branch of the State Legislature.

The word *electors* in this paragraph means voters. The clause applies to primary as well as general elections. In the original Constitution, members of the House of Representatives were the only officials of the national government to be chosen directly by the voters. In 1787 the qualifications for voting varied widely from state to state. At the Constitutional Convention, a majority of the delegates believed that suffrage should be limited to those who possessed some kind of property; as they could not agree on the amount or kind of property to require, they finally left it to the individual states to determine the qualifications of voters for representatives.

Although this clause gives states authority to determine qualifications for voting in congressional elections, including primaries, the right to vote in such elections is conferred by the Constitution. Accordingly, the national government may protect the voter in the exercise of this right against either private violence or state discrimination.[9]

The clause should be read in conjunction with Section 4 (see pages 55–56), which permits Congress to supersede state regulations for election of members of Congress and presidential electors.

As long as a state law does not disenfranchise in a national election anyone qualified to vote for the more numerous house of the state legislature, this

---

[7] Ibid.

[8] *Voinovich v Quilter*, 122 L Ed 2d 500 (1993), reaffirming *Brown v Thomson*, 462 US 835 (1983).

[9] *Ex parte Yarbrough*, 110 US 651 (1884).

clause and its companion in the Seventeenth Amendment do not require that the qualifications to vote in state elections be the same as those to vote in a national election. The question came up because the Republican Party of Connecticut, in conflict with state law, invited independent voters to vote in its primaries for United States representatives and senators and for statewide officers but not for state legislators. The Supreme Court, basing its decision on the constitutional rights of association (see page 238), said that Connecticut could not constitutionally restrict a political party's right to open its primaries in this way, and that the party's practice of allowing independent voters to participate in choosing its candidate for Congress but not its candidates for the most numerous branch of the Connecticut state legislature did not violate the Constitution.[10]

SECTION 2

2. No person shall be a Representative who shall not have attained to the Age of twenty five Years, and been seven Years a Citizen of the United States, and who shall not, when elected, be an Inhabitant of that State in which he shall be chosen.

In other words, persons who are twenty-five years old or older, who have been citizens of the United States for seven years, and who are citizens of the state they represent are constitutionally eligible for membership in the House of Representatives. The House of Representatives or Congress as a whole may not add to these constitutional qualifications, nor may any state legislature, although as noted some states are attempting to impose term limits.[11] Once someone is elected and seated, however, the House may expel him or her by a two-thirds vote, more than the simple majority required to refuse to seat someone.

Persons who lack the required age or duration of citizenship at the time of election may nevertheless be admitted to the House (or to the Senate) as soon as they become qualified.

Although the Constitution does not require members of Congress to reside in the districts they represent, voters normally refuse to elect a nonresident. By way of contrast, members of the British Parliament are often elected to represent districts other than those in which they live. Our insistence upon local residence reflects and supports the prevalent belief that representatives' primary obligations are to their own districts, rather than to the country as a whole.

---

[10] *Tashjian v Republican Party of Connecticut*, 479 US 208 (1986).

[11] *Powell v McCormack*, 395 US 486 (1969).

⌇

SECTION 2

3. Representatives [*and direct Taxes*[12]] shall be apportioned among the several States which may be included within this Union, according to their respective Numbers, which shall be determined by adding to the whole Number of free Persons, including those bound to Service for a Term of Years, and excluding Indians not taxed, three fifths of all other Persons.[13] The actual Enumeration shall be made within three Years after the first Meeting of the Congress of the United States, and within every subsequent Term of ten Years, in such Manner as they shall by Law direct. The Number of Representatives shall not exceed one for every thirty thousand, but each state shall have at Least one Representative; and until such enumeration shall be made, the State of New Hampshire shall be entitled to chuse three; Massachusetts eight; Rhode Island and Providence Plantations one; Connecticut five; New York six; New Jersey four; Pennsylvania eight; Delaware one; Maryland six; Virginia ten; North Carolina five; South Carolina five; and Georgia three.

Congress determines how representatives shall be apportioned among the states, subject only to the limitation that each state shall have at least one representative and that the number shall not exceed one for every thirty thousand population (see page 47). As a result of the 1990 census, beginning with the 1992 elections, New York lost three seats; Pennsylvania, Illinois, Michigan, and Ohio lost two representatives; Louisiana, Massachusetts, New Jersey, Kentucky, Iowa, Kansas, West Virginia, and Montana lost one seat. States gaining were California with seven more, Florida with four, Texas with three, and Arizona, Georgia, North Carolina, Virginia, and Washington, one each.

During the last two centuries Congress has chosen among four different methods for apportioning seats among the states. After seeking the advice of the National Academy of Sciences, for the last five censuses Congress has settled on what is called the "method of equal proportions." Following the 1990 census Montana challenged this method, which resulted in its losing a seat, alleging that this method provides too much variance among Montana's remaining one district and an "ideal district." The Supreme Court, acknowledging that the constitutionality of the particular method chosen raises justiciable and not political questions, concluded that in "none of these alternative measures ... do we find a substantive principle of commanding constitutional significance." As to Montana's allegation that Congress must apportion delegates in order to maximize equal representation, the fact is "the constitutional guarantee of a minimum of one Representative for each State inexorably compels a significant departure from the ideal." "The polestar of equal representation," wrote Justice Stevens for a unanimous court, "does not provide

---

[12] Bracketed section discussed on page 46.

[13] Replaced by the Fourteenth Amendment.

sufficient guidance to allow us to discern a single constitutionally permissible course." In short, Congress's decision to adopt this particular method, "although undoubtedly influenced by partisan considerations, makes as much sense as any other, and has stood the test of a half century of experience."[14]

Massachusetts was also unhappy with the way the 1990 census was conducted. It too lost a member. Its complaint was that the secretary of commerce had decided to count federal employees working overseas and allocate them to the state they had designated as their "home of record" even though overseas military personnel often designated a state with low taxes without having any intention of living there. The Court rejected Massachusetts' arguments, pointing out that the term "usual residence," the phrase used ever since the first census, always has had a broad connotation. For example, up until 1950, college students were counted as belonging to the state where their parents lived, not to the state where they attend school. The secretary's decision to allocate overseas military personnel to the state they designated on their records makes as much sense as any other definition and does not hamper the underlying constitutional goal of equal representation.[15]

After determining the number of representatives to which a state is entitled and ruling out the at-large system, Congress has left it up to the state legislatures to divide their respective states into congressional districts. After the 1990 census, whether a state gained, lost, or kept the same number of seats in the House of Representatives, each state except those that have only one member had to redraw its congressional districts to ensure compliance with the constitutional requirement that the districts represent as much as possible an equal number of people. The party in control of the state legislature, subject only to a loose judicial supervision to ensure that it does not permanently lock out the opposition party,[16] may carve up the state in such a way that the voters of the opposing party are concentrated in as few districts as possible or are so spread out that they can never win a district. This practice is known as *gerrymandering*.

The *Wesberry* requirement (see page 41) that congressional districts be composed, as nearly as practical, of an equal number of people and the subsequent *Bandemer* decision (see page 385) have made gerrymandering a little more difficult, but far from impossible. Federal courts have jurisdiction under this and under Section 2 of this Article and the federal Voting Rights Act (see page 36) to ensure that state legislatures comply with their constitutional responsibilities in the drawing of both congressional and state legislative district lines. However, "The Constitution leaves with the States primary responsibility for apportionment of their federal congressional and

---

[14] *Department of Commerce v Montana*, 118 L Ed 2d 87 (1992).

[15] *Franklin v Massachusetts*, 120 L Ed 2d 636 (1992).

[16] *Davis v Bandemer*, 478 US 109 (1986).

state legislative districts."[17] "We say once again," announced the Supreme Court, "what has been said on many occasions: reapportionment is primarily the duty and responsibility of the State through its legislature or other body, rather than of a federal court." "Absent evidence that these state branches will fail timely to perform that duty, a federal court must neither affirmatively obstruct state[18] reapportionment nor permit federal litigation to be used to impede it."[19]

SECTION 2
[continued]...*and direct* [20] *Taxes shall be apportioned among the several States...*

Direct taxes are not defined in the Constitution but are generally thought to be limited to taxes on property and a head tax, so much per person. The requirement that direct taxes be apportioned among the states according to population is of little significance today because of the Sixteenth Amendment. Other than income taxes, which the Supreme Court once ruled to be a direct tax,[21] Congress does not levy any such taxes. (See also Article I, Section 9.)

SECTION 2
3. [continued] *which may be included within this Union, according to their respective Numbers, which shall be determined by adding to the whole Number of free Persons, including those bound to Service for a Term of Years,* [emphasis added]

Note that the clause does not talk about citizens, but about "free people." All resident aliens, legal or undocumented, are counted by the Bureau of the Census and included in the apportionment. As the 1990 census approached, representatives and senators from Northeastern states facing the loss of a large number of representatives proposed legislation to instruct the Census Bureau not to count the estimated five million illegal aliens. Representatives from California, Florida, and Texas, where most such aliens live, successfully objected, arguing that to exclude any persons from the count would violate this clause.

---

[17] *Growe v Emison,* 122 L Ed 2d 388 (1993).

[18] *Chapman v Meier,* 420 US 1 (1975).

[19] *Growe v Emison,* 122 L Ed 2d 388 (1993).

[20] Modified by the Sixteenth Amendment.

[21] *Pollock v Farmers' Loan & Trust Co.,* 157 US 429 (1895). The Sixteenth Amendment made this decision of no consequence and it was expressly overruled in *South Carolina v Baker,* 485 US 505 (1988).

SECTION 2

3. [continued] and excluding Indians not taxed, *three fifths of all other Persons.*

The term "Indians not taxed" also has been rendered obsolete. States may not, generally speaking, collect income taxes from the income earned by Native Americans working on reservations, but all Native Americans today, in one way or another, pay taxes. They are citizens and voters. They are now counted in the census and are included in determining the number of representatives to which each state is entitled in the House of Representatives.

The term "other Persons" meant slaves. Because of the Thirteenth and Fourteenth Amendments, these emphasized words are obsolete.

SECTION 2

3. [continued] The actual Enumeration shall be made within three Years after the first Meeting of the Congress of the United States, and within every subsequent Term of ten Years, in such Manner as they shall by Law direct.

The Census has become a highly charged political event. Not only does it determine the number of representatives from each state, but it has a major consequence for the distribution of federal grant dollars. When the 1990 Census approached, questions arose, as we have noted, not only about whether or not to count undocumented aliens, how to count overseas military-related people and their families and how to assign them to specific states, but also about whether the Census Bureau should adjust the actual enumeration to take into account the fact that certain categories of persons—the homeless, the destitute, undocumented aliens, minorities—are not likely to be reliably included with the regular count with the same accuracy as middle-class homeowners. Democrats and big city officials urged the Census Bureau to make an "adjustment." Republicans and those from rural areas and middle-sized cities opposed making such adjustments. As we have seen, although noting that these questions are justiciable, the Court has nonetheless tended to defer to the expertise of the Department of Commerce.

SECTION 2

3. [continued] The Number of Representatives shall not exceed one for every thirty Thousand,

---

The restriction placed by this paragraph on the size of the House of Representatives is now meaningless. By the 1990 census our population, excluding the District of Columbia and Puerto Rico, was 249,022,783. The constitutional limit would allow 8,300 members (249,022,783 divided by

30,000). Obviously, a chamber that size would be of little value; for many decades Congress has by law limited the number of representatives to 435, approximately one representative for every 572,466 persons counted in 1990.

SECTION 2
    3. [continued] but each State shall have at Least one Representative;

After the 1990 census, three states—Alaska, Wyoming, and Vermont—had fewer than 572,466 inhabitants; each, however, was given its constitutional minimum. Delaware, North Dakota, South Dakota, and Montana, with populations above the national average for one representative, have only one representative as their numbers are not sufficient to win them an additional seat. Because of this requirement that each state have at least one representative, not even the House of Representatives can provide that every person in the United States has equally weighted voting power with every other person; one person in the least populous state has more voting power than one person in a more populous state.

SECTION 2
    3. [continued] and until such enumeration shall be made, the State of New Hampshire shall be entitled to chuse three, Massachusetts eight, Rhode-Island and Providence Plantations one, Connecticut five, New-York six, New Jersey four, Pennsylvania eight, Delaware one, Maryland six, Virginia ten, North Carolina five, South Carolina five, and Georgia three.

This was a temporary provision until a census could be taken to determine the basis of representation. It has no significance today.

SECTION 2
    4. When vacancies happen in the Representation from any State, the Executive Authority thereof shall issue Writs of Election to fill such Vacancies.

The chief significance of this clause is that vacancies in the House of Representatives are not filled by gubernatorial appointment, as are vacancies in the Senate. In many instances, when the next election is less than a year away, governors do not call special elections.

SECTION 2

5. The House of Representatives shall chuse their speaker and other Officers;

In principle, the speaker of the House is chosen by the House of Representatives; in fact, the speaker is chosen by the majority party or, more precisely, by a majority of the majority party. The duties and powers of the speaker and of the other officers are determined by the rules and practices of the House. Curiously enough, the Constitution does not specify that the speaker must be a member of the House. The framers simply assumed that the examples of the British House of Commons and of the state assemblies would be followed.

SECTION 2

5. [continued] [the House] shall have the sole Power of Impeachment.

It is a common error to think that the power to impeach means the power to remove a person from office; in fact, impeachment is only the first step toward removal. The power of impeachment is the power to accuse and to initiate formal charges. The House ordinarily exercises its authority in a two-step process: After an investigation and a report from its Judiciary Committee, the House first considers a resolution of impeachment; if the resolution carries, the House then votes on detailed articles of impeachment. (The House has established a special commission to study whether there should be changes in handling impeachment procedures for federal judges.)

The House has adopted impeachment resolutions against sixteen federal officers, one of whom then immediately resigned, so articles of impeachment have actually been prepared and voted on only fifteen times. Those involved included one senator, one president, and one Supreme Court justice; the rest have been judges in the lower federal courts.

The most celebrated impeachment deliberations of recent times were against President Nixon. Although the House Judiciary Committee recommended to the House that it impeach the president, he resigned before the issue was brought to the floor of the House. The House then dropped the matter. It need not have done so, since resignation does not necessarily prevent the House from acting, or the Senate from trying, a person impeached by the House, but in every such case resignation has terminated the matter.

SECTION 3

1. The Senate of the United States shall be composed of two Senators from each state, *chosen by the Legislature thereof for six Years*; and each Senator shall have one Vote [emphasis added].

The emphasized portion of this paragraph has been superseded by the Seventeenth Amendment. The framers adopted equal representation of all states in the Senate at the insistence of the smaller states, which made it their price for accepting the Constitution. As a result, the 453,588 inhabitants of Wyoming have the same number of representatives in the Senate as the 30 million inhabitants of California. On the one hand, the New England states, with 5.2 percent of the total population, have 12 percent of the Senate seats, and the mountain states, with only 5.4 percent of the total population, have 16 percent. On the other hand, the Middle Atlantic states, with 15 percent of the total population, have only 6 percent of the Senate seats; the East-North-Central states, with 17 percent of the total population, have only 10 percent. These figures account for the disproportionate influence that mining and agricultural interests—especially mining—have sometimes exerted on legislation in the Senate.

SECTION 3

2. Immediately after they shall be assembled in Consequence of the first Election, they shall be divided as equally as may be into three Classes. The Seats of the Senators of the first Class shall be vacated at the Expiration of the second Year, of the second Class at the Expiration of the fourth Year, and of the third Class at the Expiration of the sixth Year, so that one third may be chosen every second Year;

As a result of this original division of senators into three classes, the Senate is a continuous body. Only one-third of the senators' terms expire at the same time; hence, at least two-thirds of its members at any time have been members of the preceding Congress.

That the Senate is a continuing body, whereas the House is not, sometimes has constitutional significance. The Supreme Court, for example, has pointed out that, although a Senate subpoena issued five years earlier is still clearly valid, a subpoena issued by the House at the same time may not be valid, because "the House is not a continuing body" and the subpoena thus comes from a prior Congress.[22] That the Senate is a continuing body also has generally been interpreted to mean that its rules continue from Congress to Congress. Thus, its rule that an extraordinary majority is required to terminate debate cannot be set aside by a new Congress except in accord with the rules of the Senate in the previous Congress.

SECTION 3

2. [continued] and if Vacancies happen by Resignation, or otherwise, during the Recess of the Legislature of any State, the Executive thereof may make

---

[22] *Eastland v United States Servicemen's Fund*, 421 US 491 (1975).

temporary Appointments *until the next Meeting of the Legislature, which shall then fill such Vacancies* [emphasis added].

This clause was modified by the Seventeenth Amendment, which provides for the direct election of senators. When a senator leaves office before the end of a term, the state's governor can appoint a replacement to serve until either a special election or the next general election, when the remainder of the term is filled.

SECTION 3

3. No Person shall be a Senator who shall not have attained to the Age of thirty Years, and been nine Years a Citizen of the United States, and who shall not, when elected, be an Inhabitant of that State for which he shall be chosen.

You have to be a little older (but not necessarily wiser) and have lived in the United States a little longer to be eligible to serve as a senator than to be a member of the House of Representatives.

SECTION 3

4. The Vice President of the United States shall be President of the Senate, but shall have no Vote, unless they be equally divided.

The vice president has much less control over the Senate than the speaker has over the House. In fact, the vice president seldom presides over the Senate. He is more inclined to do so when the issue before the Senate is controversial and a close vote is expected. The first vice president, John Adams, exercised his casting vote at least twenty times, a record that continues to stand to this day.

SECTION 3

5. The Senate shall chuse their other Officers, and also a President *pro tempore*, in the Absence of the Vice President, or when he shall exercise the Office of President of the United States.

With the adoption of the Twenty-fifth Amendment, there is much less likelihood that we will be without a vice president, but even when we have one the vice president does not spend much time presiding over the Senate.

The president pro tempore of the Senate is chosen by the majority party. This officer is normally the member of the majority party with the longest continuous service in the Senate. Unlike the vice president, the president pro tempore can, being a senator, vote on any matter before the Senate.

SECTION 3

6. The Senate shall have the sole Power to try all Impeachments. When sitting for that Purpose, they shall be on Oath or Affirmation.

When the House of Representatives impeaches a federal officer, the officer is tried before the Senate subject only to three procedural requirements: the Senate shall be on oath or affirmation; the chief justice shall preside when the president is tried; and conviction shall be upon the concurrence of two-thirds of the members present. In the recent impeachment hearings of Judge Harry Claiborne (1986) and Judges Alcee L. Hastings and Walter L. Nixon, Jr. (1989), the actual recording of testimony and hearing of witnesses were done by the special twelve senators, not the full Senate, with the full Senate hearing oral argument once the panel made its recommendations. (Judges Claiborne, Hastings, and Nixon addressed the full Senate.) This was a controversial procedure since some argued that the full Senate had to hear all the evidence and hear all the witnesses, but the Supreme Court has decided the decision to delegate these matters to a committee is well within the discretion of the Senate.[23]

In hearing an impeachment, the Senate deliberates behind closed doors, reconvenes in open session, and each senator votes on each of the articles of impeachment.

The word "try" does not mean that the Senate must hold a trial in the sense of a full hearing by the full Senate or that it must follow the process of a criminal trial. Moreover, when the Constitution vests in the Senate, the "sole" power to try all impeachments, the Senate's decisions about how to do so and who shall be impeached are not subject to judicial review; that is, they are political questions, a "textually demonstrable constitutional commitment of the issue to a coordinate political department."[24] Justice Souter, while agreeing that most questions flowing from this clause are political questions not reviewable by any court, nonetheless would not categorically deny all possibilities of judicial review. He argued that there might be "unusual circumstances" justifying a more searching review of impeachment proceedings, for example, "say, upon a summary determination that an officer of the United States was simply 'a bad guy.'"[25]

SECTION 3

6. [continued] When the President of the United States is tried, the Chief Justice shall preside:

---

[23] *Nixon v United States*, 122 L Ed 2d 1(1993).

[24] Ibid.

[25] Ibid.

This provision disqualifies the vice president, who might be personally involved because he or she is in the line of presidential succession, from presiding over a trial of the president.

SECTION 3

6. [continued] And no Person shall be convicted without the Concurrence of two thirds of the Members Present.

Of those impeached by the House, the Senate has convicted seven, all judges of the lower federal courts. Others have resigned before Senate trial. The most celebrated Senate impeachment trials were those of Supreme Court Justice Samuel Chase in 1802 and President Andrew Johnson in 1868. In neither case did the Senate sustain the impeachment charges, although in Johnson's case, the vote to sustain the impeachment charge was only one vote shy.

SECTION 3

7. Judgment in Cases of Impeachment shall not extend further than to removal from Office, and disqualification to hold and enjoy any Office of honor, Trust or Profit under the United States:

Despite its ambiguous language, the Constitution has always been construed to make removal from office automatic upon conviction by a two-thirds vote of the Senate. Disqualification, however, is not mandatory. Of its seven convictions, the Senate voted for disqualification in only two. In those two cases, disqualification required a simple majority vote. In the most recent instance, in which the Senate voted guilty on the impeachment of Judges Harry Claiborne, Alcee L. Hastings, and Walter L. Nixon, Jr., it did not vote to disqualify them from any "Office of honor, Trust, or Profit under the United States," but their chances of being appointed to such an office seem negligible. However, after being removed from his judgeship, in 1992 Alcee Hastings was elected to Congress from Florida. A question was raised before a federal district judge that Hastings' conviction by the Senate disqualified him from serving in Congress, but the district judge held that the person raising the issue lacked standing to sue because he did not live in Hastings' district[26]

Prior to impeachment, Judges Claiborne and Nixon had been sentenced to prison terms, and at the time of their impeachment they were serving prison sentences. In fact, it was their failure to resign and to give up their salaries that accelerated demands for impeachment. Judge Hastings, on the other hand, had been acquitted in a criminal trial, which he argued unsuccessfully should

---

[26] Adam Clymer, "Impeached Judge Clears Hurdle to Seat in House," *The New York Times,* January 5, 1993, p. A 8.

bar impeachment. In each instance of these three recent impeachments, the House and Senate concluded that, although they could take the fact of conviction or acquittal into account and that the trial records could be introduced, the House and Senate were not bound by the findings of the courts and were free to determine whether the conduct in question should result in removal from office.

SECTION 3

7. [continued] but the Party convicted shall nevertheless be liable and subject to Indictment, Trial, Judgment and Punishment according to Law.

This provision clearly says that it is not double jeopardy to subject an officer of the United States both to trial before the Senate on impeachment charges and then to trial before the courts on criminal charges. Conviction of a crime, or even acquittal of a crime, may prompt impeachment procedures, but these are separate proceedings.

President Ford's pardon of President Nixon was predicated on the assumption that, after leaving the White House, a president may be tried criminally for actions undertaken while serving as president.

No one may sue the president, however, either in or out of office, for damages for any injury the president might have caused. This "absolute presidential immunity from damage liability extends to all acts within the outer perimeter of the President's official responsibility." The Court has suggested very strongly that presidential immunity stems from the Constitution itself. "We consider this immunity," wrote Justice Powell for the Court, "a functionally mandated incident of the President's unique office, rooted in the constitutional tradition of separation of powers and supported by our history."[27] Justice White, speaking for three dissenting justices, responded, "Attaching absolute immunity to the office of the President, rather than to particular activities that the President might perform, places the President above the law. It is a reversion to the old notion that the King can do no wrong." Cabinet members and presidential assistants have only a qualified or good-faith immunity from civil suits for damages.[28] (Judges have this same absolute immunity from civil suits for damages, but judges may be liable for payment of attorneys' fees to those who have secured injunctions to prevent the judges from depriving persons of their constitutional rights. By acts of Congress prosecutors have absolute immunity from liability for the initiation and pursuit of a criminal prosecution but not for actions such as giving legal advice to the police or making statements to the press.[29])

What of a related issue? May officers of the United States be brought to trial and imprisoned and thereby kept from performing their duties before

---

[27] *Nixon v Fitzgerald,* 457 US 731 (1982).

[28] *Stump v Sparkman,* 435 US 349 (1978); *Harlow v Fitzgerald,* 457 US 800 (1982).

[29] *Stump v Sparkman,* 435 US 349 (1978); *Pulliam v Allen,* 466 US 522 (1984); *Imbler v Pachtman* 424 US 409 (1976); *Buckley v Fitzimmons,* 125 L Ed 2d 209.

being removed from office through impeachment? In the case of judges, the answer is yes, as Judges Claiborne and Nixon can testify. In the case of the vice president, the answer also is probably "yes," but whether the vice president could be imprisoned raises more serious doubts. (Vice President Spiro T. Agnew resigned and pleaded no contest to certain criminal charges.) In the case of the president, the answer is probably "no." The difference is that, whereas the business of government is not seriously jeopardized if a judge is brought to trial and imprisoned or even if the vice president is forced to defend himself (or herself) in a criminal court, the entire business of government would be endangered if the president were prosecuted for a crime, let alone thrown into prison. Fortunately, only once has the issue involving a president been a serious one. The grand jury investigating the coverup of the Watergate scandals named President Nixon as an unindicted coconspirator. The grand jury did not indict him, largely in order to avoid the thorny question of whether or not he could be forced to trial while still serving as president.

SECTION 4
1. The Times, Places, and Manner of holding Elections for Senators and Representatives, shall be prescribed in each State by the Legislature thereof;

This clause, which is modified by the one below, confers on legislatures in each state, subject to congressional revision, "authority to provide a complete code for congressional elections, not only as to times and places, but in relation to notices, registration, supervision of voting, protection of voters, prevention of fraud and corrupt practices, counting of votes, duties of inspectors and canvassers, and making and publication of election returns; in short, to enact the numerous requirements as to procedure and safeguards which experience shows are necessary in order to enforce the fundamental rights involved."[30]

Because persons wishing to restrict congressional eligibility for reelection have little hope that Congress will propose an amendment to do so, they rather ingeniously point to this clause and argue that it gives states authority to restrict congressional terms. (See page 40.)[31]

SECTION 4
1. [continued] but the Congress may at any time by Law make or alter such Regulations, *except as to the Places of chusing Senators* [emphasis added].

---

[30] *Smiley v Holm*, 285 US 355 (1932).
[31] Stephen Glazier, "Each State Can Limit Re-Election to Congress," *The Wall Street Journal*, June 19, 1990.

The emphasized portion has been modified by the Seventeenth Amendment.

The paragraph covers primaries and preprimaries in which candidates for the Senate and the House are nominated, if such primaries effectively control the choice or are state-required.[32] Congressional power as to times, places, and manner consequently extends to such primaries.

Congress has established the first Tuesday after the first Monday in November in even-numbered years as the date for the election of representatives, except where other times are prescribed by state constitutions. All states hold these elections on the same day, and all states now elect senators on that same date.

Congress has placed a limit on contributions to congressional candidates and has adopted extensive regulations to prevent corrupt and fraudulent practices in connection with these elections. Congress exercises this authority to regulate campaign finances, however, subject to First Amendment limitations (see pages 222–223).[33]

This section authorizes Congress to set aside state age requirements for voting for Congress and for presidential electors, but not for state and local officials as it once tried to do.[34] Then the Twenty-sixth Amendment settled the issue so far as the eighteen-year old vote is concerned.

SECTION 4

2. The Congress shall assemble at least once in every Year, and such Meeting shall be on the first Monday in December, unless they shall by Law appoint a different Day [emphasis added].

The Twentieth Amendment has superseded this paragraph. Congress now convenes in January.

SECTION 5

1. Each House shall be the Judge of the Elections, Returns and Qualifications of its own Members,

Does this section authorize each chamber to add to the stipulated constitutional qualifications, or does it merely authorize each house to determine if a particular member has those qualifications? Until 1969 both the House and the Senate had adopted the former construction, and on occasion each chamber had denied duly elected persons their seats because they were morally or politically objectionable to a majority of the chamber. For example, in 1900, the

---

[32] *United States v Classic,* 313 US 299 (1941).

[33] *Buckley v Valeo,* 424 US 1 (1976).

[34] *Oregon v Mitchell,* 400 US 112 (1970).

House refused to admit Brigham H. Roberts from Utah because he was a polygamist. That and other precedents, which sprang in the first instance from the practice of the British Parliament and of the early state legislatures, were relied on by the House of Representatives in 1967 when it excluded Adam Clayton Powell, Jr., for alleged misconduct and for being held in contempt by a court for refusing to pay a judgment against him for slander. The speaker ruled that, since the question was whether Powell should be excluded rather than whether he should be expelled (see paragraph 2 of this section), only a majority was necessary, although in fact the vote on exclusion was passed by more than two-thirds.

Powell and thirteen voters from his district asked the District Court for the District of Columbia for a declaratory judgment that the House had acted unconstitutionally and for an order requiring House officers to pay Powell his salary. Both the district court and the court of appeals dismissed Powell's complaint, stating that the case raised a "political question" and that it would violate the doctrine of separation of powers if judges got involved.

By the time the case was before the Supreme Court, Powell had been reelected and admitted to Congress. Many observers felt that the Court would avoid handling such a politically ticklish issue by holding the question moot or that if it did accept the case, it would rule either that the issue was a political question or that the long historical practice of Congress had settled the construction in favor of allowing each chamber to add to constitutional qualifications. However, the Court ruled that Section 5 authorizes the House only to determine if its members meet the qualifications prescribed in the Constitution.[35] Since Powell met those qualifications, the House had no power to refuse to admit him to its membership.

Subject only to the limitation that it may not add to the qualifications stipulated by the Constitution, each chamber determines finally which person is entitled to be seated, for example, when there is a challenge to the validity of an election (as on grounds of vote fraud).[36] Each chamber may, if it wishes, defer a disputed matter until after a decision by the courts, or a state may recount votes in a senatorial or congressional race in the event of a challenge. But neither chamber is bound by a state's verification of the accuracy of returns or a court's decision in an election contest.

SECTION 5

1. [continued] and a Majority of each [house] shall constitute a Quorum to do business; but a smaller Number may adjourn from day to day, and may be authorized to compel the Attendance of absent Members, in such Manner, and under such Penalties as each House may provide.

2. Each House may determine the Rules of its Proceedings, punish its Members for disorderly Behaviour, and, with the Concurrence of two thirds, expel a Member.

---

[35] *Powell v McCormack*, 395 US 486 (1969).
[36] *Roudebush v Hartke*, 405 US 15 (1972).

Although it takes only a majority to prevent a member-elect from being seated, it takes two-thirds to expel a member once he or she has been admitted to membership. Since members of Congress are not subject to impeachment, expulsion by their respective chambers is the only way they may be unseated, except, of course, by defeat at the polls.

SECTION 5

3. Each House shall keep a Journal of its Proceedings, and from time to time publish the same, excepting such Parts as may in their Judgment require Secrecy; and the yeas and Nays of the Members of either House on any question shall, at the Desire of one fifth of those Present, be entered on the Journal.

This requirement is consistent with the belief that, in a republic, the proceedings of the legislature should be published, except in unusual circumstances.

The journals should not be confused with the *Congressional Record*. The journals are the official record of congressional acts, resolutions, and votes, whereas the *Record* purports to be a report of what is said in each house. In fact, because of the practice of freely allowing members to "revise and extend their remarks," as well as to print articles, speeches, poems, and so on by nonmembers, much appears in the *Congressional Record* that was never said on the floors of Congress.

By the parliamentary device of resolving itself into a Committee of the Whole, a quorum for which is 100, the House of Representatives avoids the constitutional necessity of a roll-call vote on the demand of one-fifth of those present.

SECTION 5

4. Neither House, during the Session of Congress, shall, without the Consent of the other, adjourn for more than three days, nor to any other place than that in which the two Houses shall be sitting.

Nowadays, although the two chambers take "recesses," they do not "adjourn," but remain in continuous session. They do this in part to avoid a presidential pocket veto (see page 64). Moreover, these days there is never any question about holding meetings of the entire House or Senate in any place except the Capitol in Washington, D.C.

SECTION 6

1. The Senators and Representatives shall receive a Compensation for their Services, to be ascertained by Law, and paid out of the Treasury of the United States [modified by the Twenty-seventh Amendment].

The salary for both senators and members of the House is $129,500.

Although elected by the people of the states, members of Congress must look to the national treasury for their compensation. During the struggle for ratification of the Constitution, many persons objected to this provision because it permits members of Congress to determine their own salaries. The First Congress proposed an amendment as part of the Bill of Rights which, finally ratified in 1992 as the Twenty-seventh Amendment, prohibits any change in the salary of members of Congress until an election for representatives has intervened.

In practice, members of Congress have been reluctant to increase their salaries for fear of public displeasure. When in 1816 Congress abandoned a $6 per diem stipend and voted itself a raise to $1,500 per year, the outcry was so great that nine members resigned and many others were defeated at the polls. At the next session Congress backed down and replaced it with an $8 a day stipend.

In recent decades, Congress has tried without success to decrease the political liability of members of Congress for increasing their own salaries by delegating responsibility for recommending salary increases to a commission that brings in periodic recommendations about the the salaries of cabinet officers, members of Congress, and federal judges. The commission's recommendations are submitted to the president, whose recommendations become effective unless both chambers disapprove within thirty days after receiving the president's recommendations.

Out of fear of giving challengers an issue at the next congressional election, Congress has set aside most proposed increases, not only for itself but for civil servants, cabinet officers, and federal judges. In 1989, however, it tried quietly to allow a substantial (51 percent) congressional (and executive and judicial) pay increase to go into effect. The political outcry, stimulated in part by radio talk show hosts, was so loud that Congress defeated this increase. Part of the outrage was because the Congress had tried to maneuver the increase so that the raise would become effective without voting on it.

At the end of 1989, after the political turmoil died down, a bipartisan agreement among House and Senate leaders was reached and, with the support of President Bush, the 1989 Act required the House and Senate to take recorded votes on all future congressional pay increases except for the annual cost-of-living increases. (Some have questioned whether the annual cost-of-living increases are consistent with the newly ratified Twenty-seventh Amendment.) The Act replaced the "quadrennial commission" with a Citizens Commission on Public Service Compensation, consisting of five persons to be chosen by lot from voter-registration lists—two by the president, two by congressional leaders, and one by the chief justice—which is to report every four years to the president, who is then to make recommendations to be effective after the next congressional election, but only if both the House and Senate adopt a resolution of approval by recorded vote within 60 days of submission.

SECTION 6

1. [continued] They shall in all Cases, except Treason, Felony and Breach of the Peace, be privileged from Arrest, during their Attendance at the Session of their respective Houses, and in going to and returning from the same;

The words "breach of the peace" are construed, not as a particularly defined crime, but as a term covering all criminal offenses. The exemption extends, therefore, only to arrest for civil offenses—failure to pay debts, for example, while engaged in congressional business. With the abolition of imprisonment for civil offenses, this clause lost its significance. As the Supreme Court has emphasized, by quoting approvingly from Jefferson, "legislators ought not to stand above the law they create but ought generally to be bound by it as are ordinary persons."[37]

SECTION 6

1. [continued] and for any Speech or Debate in either House, they shall not be questioned in any other Place.

The protections of the speech and debate clause extend not only to members, but also to those who are acting as their authorized agents. Still undecided is whether members of Congress can waive their rights under this clause, or even if the Congress could do so.[38]

State legislators obtain no protection from this provision.[39] They may have equivalent protection before their state courts under their respective state constitutions.

The speech and debate clause exempts members of Congress from arrest, prosecution, or suit for anything they say on the floor of Congress, in committee, or in committee reports. What they say with respect to these legislative matters cannot be introduced as evidence in any criminal prosecution, nor may there be a judicial inquiry into motives for making a speech related to the legislative process or into why a member has cast a particular vote.[40] The protection extends, however, only to a legislative act that has been performed. A promise to deliver a speech, to vote or solicit others to vote, or to introduce a bill at some future date is not "speech or debate," and matters relating to such conversations may be introduced in trials of members of Congress for bribery or conspiracy to commit bribery.[41]

---

[37] *Gravel v United States*, 408 US 606 (1980).

[38] *United States v Helstoski*, 442 US 477 (1979).

[39] *United States v Gillock*, 445 US 360 (1980).

[40] *United States v Johnson*, 383 US 169 (1966).

[41] *United States v Helstoski*, 442 US 477 (1979); *United States v Brewster*, 408 US 501 (1972).

The Court has narrowly construed "legislative functions" to exclude such ordinary activities of legislators as issuing news releases, making speeches outside Congress, performing errands for constituents, and keeping voters informed, and thus these nonlegislative functions are not protected by congressional immunity. Thus, although a senator and his assistants could not be compelled to respond to any questions about the senator's introduction in a Senate subcommittee of the famed but classified "Pentagon Papers," the senator had no such immunity from questioning about arrangements he had made for the subsequent publication of those papers by a private publisher or about the way the papers had come into his possession. Introducing materials in a committee is a legislative function; having the materials published by a private publisher is not.[42] Nor did the speech and debate clause protect former Senator William Proxmire of Wisconsin from the threat of standing trial for libel when his staff issued press releases and made telephone calls about his accusations that a scientist had wasted public funds on a project for which the senator granted his famous—or, some would say, infamous—"Golden Fleece Award."[43] (The senator settled the suit out of court.)

House members and their staffs were immune, decided the Supreme Court, from suit for publishing and distributing to other members of Congress a report that allegedly violated rights of privacy (the report told of the grades and disciplinary problems of named students). But no such immunity protected the superintendent of documents, who distributed the same report to the general public, even though he acted in response to a congressional request. Distribution of a committee report inside Congress is a legislative function; distribution of the same report outside Congress is not.[44]

The speech and debate clause protects a congressman only from being questioned in "any other Place" about speeches and debates, making it quite clear that the clause does not limit the power of each chamber to discipline its own members, for example, for defaming others under a cloak of congressional immunity. This is a power that the chambers understandably have been reluctant to exercise.

Although this clause extends only to members of Congress, the separation of powers principle, as we have noted, confers upon presidents absolute immunity for anything they say or do that has any remote connection with their official responsibilities. In fact, presidents have greater immunity from lawsuits for what they have said and done than do members of Congress. Judges, both federal and state, when acting in their judicial capacities, share this absolute immunity with the president.

SECTION 6

2. No Senator or Representative shall, during the Time for which he was elected, be appointed to any civil Office under the Authority of the United

[42] *Gravel* v *United States*, 408 US 606 (1972).
[43] *Hutchinson* v *Proxmire*, 443 US 111 (1979).
[44] *Doe* v *McMillian*, 412 US 306 (1973).

States, which shall have been created, or the Emoluments whereof shall have
been encreased during such time;

The ineligibility clause has resulted in little litigation. A taxpayer tried to
challenge Justice Hugo Black's appointment to the Supreme Court on the
grounds that as a senator he had voted for legislation improving the retirement
benefits of members of the federal judiciary. The Court ruled that the taxpayer
lacked standing to raise the issue.[45] Justice Black, who served for thirty-four
years, died eight days after retiring and never received any benefits of the
Retirement Act.

The issue was raised again after President Carter nominated Representative
Abner Mikva, a liberal Democrat from Illinois, to the Court of Appeals for the
District of Columbia. Some senators challenged Mikva's nomination as a violation of this clause because a judicial pay raise had gone into effect during his term,
though after he had resigned his House seat. Shortly after his nomination was
confirmed, Congress passed a law granting members of Congress standing to
contest such judicial appointments on eligibility grounds. Senator McClure, a
conservative Republican from Idaho, raised the challenge in a suit financed by the
National Rifle Association. A three-judge district court ruled, however, that,
despite the law, a senator lacked standing to challenge a nomination confirmed
by the entire Senate. The Supreme Court affirmed that ruling without comment.[46]

SECTION 6
2. [continued] and no person holding any Office under the United States,
shall be a Member of either House during his Continuance in Office.

The incompatibility clause, which stems from the doctrine of separation of
powers, contrasts sharply with the British system, in which most high executive ministers are also members of Parliament. It makes members ineligible to
serve in the executive branch while retaining membership in Congress. It does
not, however, prevent the appointment of members of Congress as temporary
representatives of the United States at international conferences. Senators and
members of Congress have sometimes served temporarily as members of the
United States delegation to the United Nations General Assembly.

Does the clause prevent members of Congress from serving in the military
reserve forces? Some reservists who opposed our involvement in Vietnam
thought so, and as taxpayers and citizens they sought a judicial order to require
the secretary of defense to strike congressional members from the reserve lists
and to declare that service by members of Congress in the reserves is prohibited
by the incompatibility clause. The Supreme Court dodged the issue by holding
that those who raised the question lacked standing to sue.[47]

---

[45] *Ex parte Levitt,* 302 US 633 (1937).
[46] *McClure v Regan,* 454 US 1025 (1981); these materials are taken from Stephen L. Wasby, *The Supreme Court in the Federal Judicial System,* 3d ed. (New York: Nelson-Hall, 1988), p.113.
[47] *Schlesinger v Reservists to Stop the War,* 418 US 206 (1974).

Although these days most states forbid members of Congress from holding appointed or elective state office, there is nothing in this clause, or the ineligibility clause, "to bar congressional service in state or State-created offices," as was the practice in the early days of the Republic, if a state wished to make it possible.[48]

SECTION 7

1. All Bills for raising Revenue shall originate in the House of Representatives; but the Senate may propose or concur with Amendments as on other Bills.

Although not constitutionally required, there has been a tradition, often breached, that appropriation bills, as well as those raising revenues, ought to originate in the House.

This provision, based on the assumption, which made more sense before the Seventeenth Amendment, that the House is more directly responsive to the will of the people than is the Senate, was inserted at the insistence of the more populous states, to relate taxation to representation. It has not, however, kept the Senate from originating revenue measures under the pretense of amending House bills, by striking out an entire measure except the title and the enacting clause. This paragraph, moreover, does not have the same significance that it had in 1787, when senators were chosen by state legislatures.

The House, by refusing to concur, has the opportunity to keep any revenue bill originating in the Senate from becoming a law, but in 1990 the Supreme Court, in one of the rare cases interpreting this clause, decided that the question of where a revenue bill originated is a justiciable issue within the scope of judicial enquiry, not a political question. At the same time the Court gave a very narrow definition to "revenue bill": "A statute that creates a particular governmental program and . . . raises revenue to support that program, as opposed to a statute that raises revenue to support government generally, is not a 'Bill for raising Revenue' within the meaning of the origination clause."[49] Thus, a statute creating a governmental program and providing specific sources for its financial support is not a revenue measure even if it raises revenue. In short, the clause does not apply to statutes that create fines or fees or funds earmarked for specific purposes, but only to those that raise general revenues.

SECTION 7

2. Every Bill which shall have passed the House of Representatives and the Senate, shall, before it becomes a Law, be presented to the President of

---

[48] Justice White concurring in *MWAA* v *Cann*, 115 L Ed 2d 236 (1991).
[49] *United States* v *Munoz-Flores*, 495 US 385 (1990).

the United States; if he approve he shall sign it, but if not he shall return it, with his Objections to that House in which it shall have originated, who shall enter the Objections at large on their Journal, and proceed to reconsider it. If after such Reconsideration two thirds of that House shall agree to pass the Bill, it shall be sent, together with the Objections, to the other House, by which it shall likewise be reconsidered, and if approved by two thirds of that House, it shall become a Law. But in all such Cases the Votes of both Houses shall be determined by yeas and Nays, and the Names of the Persons voting for and against the Bill shall be entered on the Journal of each House respectively. If any Bill shall not be returned by the President within ten Days (Sundays excepted) after it shall have been presented to him, the Same shall be a Law, in like Manner as if he had signed it, unless the Congress by their Adjournment prevent its Return, in which Case it shall not be a Law.

The framers expected Congress to be the dominant branch of the government, but they did not wish it to be in a position to arrogate to itself all powers. So they gave the president a qualified veto, both to prevent Congress from overstepping its boundaries and to enable the president to influence the actual course of legislation.

After a bill has been passed in *identical* form by both houses of Congress, it is presented to the president, who can do one of three things:

First, the president can sign the bill; it then becomes the law of the land.

Second, the president can veto it and return it to the house in which it originated, stating the reasons for disapproval. If the bill is then repassed by a two-thirds vote of *both* houses, which means two thirds of a quorum of the members thereof, it becomes law despite the president's veto. On the other hand, if the bill does not secure the approval of two thirds of members of each chamber, the veto is sustained, and the bill does not become law.

Third, the president can refuse to sign the bill but can retain possession of it. It then becomes law at the end of ten days (excluding Sundays) after its receipt "unless," as the Constitution says, "Congress by their Adjournment prevent its [the bill's] Return, in which Case it shall not be a Law." The bill is thus subject to what is called the *pocket veto.*

The pocket veto applies differently to the three different kinds of adjournments. It probably does not apply to the first, there is a dispute about the second, and it clearly applies to the third.

The first type, to which it probably does not apply, is the intrasession recesses that Congress frequently takes for short periods, for example, over Christmas and other holidays. In 1970 President Nixon tried to pocket veto a health bill during such an intrasession recess. Senator Edward Kennedy argued that the pocket veto could not be used for such adjournments and took the question to federal court. The lower federal courts agreed with him.[50] The Department of Justice decided not to take the matter to the Supreme Court.

Second, there are the intersession congressional adjournments. These days Congress does not end its first session until November or December, and then

---

[50] *Kennedy v Sampson,* 364 F. Supp. 1075 (DDC 1973); affd, (D.C. Cir. 1974) 511 F.2d 430 .

it starts the second session the following January. (In the early days of the Republic, Congress went home during the summer and did not start its second session until the following December.) There continues to be a debate between Congress and the president as to whether the pocket veto can be used between sessions. In 1976 President Ford, in response to another suit by Senator Kennedy, agreed that, as long as the House and Senate designated officers to receive veto messages during such between-session recesses, he would not use a pocket veto. President Reagan, however, abandoned that policy and pocket vetoed measures during intersession adjournments; one such measure tied aid for El Salvador to that nation's compliance with certain human rights conditions. Thirty-three House Democrats and the Senate filed a suit charging that such pocket vetoes are unconstitutional. A federal district judge sided with the president, and the Court of Appeals sided with the members of Congress, but the Supreme Court "punted." It held that, since the El Salvador aid statute had expired, there was no longer a live case or controversy.[51]

Despite these decisions of two courts of appeals, President Bush's Office of Legal Counsel in the Department of Justice insisted that "any adjournment of either house for longer than three days gives occasion for a pocket veto."[52] But he never forced a showdown on this issue and returned to the Ford and Carter practice of asserting the right to pocket veto intersessional bills while at the same time returning them to the chamber where they originated. After withholding approval of a bill—related to the rights of Chinese students living in the United States—sent to him in December 1989 after the expiration of the first session of the 101st Congress, President Bush issued a "memorandum of disapproval," the usual method of exercising a pocket veto, rather than a "veto message" normally used with return vetoes. President Bush nonetheless returned the bill with his memorandum of disapproval to the clerk of the house, the official designated by the House to receive presidential vetoes of bills that originated in that chamber. (The House failed to override the veto, but if it and the Senate had done so the bill presumably would have become law.)

The third type of adjournment, called adjournment *sine die*, comes at the end of the second session, when a particular Congress adjourns never to return again (although in one sense the Senate, as a continuing body, has never adjourned). Everyone agrees that the pocket veto applies to such adjournments.

Unlike many state governors, the president cannot approve parts of a bill and veto other parts; approval or disapproval must be given to the bill as a unit. Because the president does not have an *item* veto, Congress has been able to get measures past the president by using *riders*, provisions that are not germane to the main purpose of a bill. Riders are most effective when tacked on to appropriation bills, thus forcing the president to accept them in order to secure funds for the operations of the government.

Presidents Reagan and Bush urged Congress either to grant the president an item veto or to propose a constitutional amendment that would do so.

---

[51] *Burke v Barnes*, 479 US 361 (1987).

[52] William P. Barr, assistant attorney general in charge of the Office of Legal Counsel, quoted in Robert Pear, "Pocket Veto Dispute: President Calls a Truce," *The New York Times,* December 7, 1989, A22. *Congressional Quarterly,* "Bush Tests His Pocket-Veto Power" December 2, 1989, 3285.

Congress, so far, has shown little enthusiasm for this enhancement of presidential powers. President Bush never carried out his threat to assert a novel interpretation of the presentment clause (see below)—that it require each item in a bill be presented to him separately. In effect he argued that the Constitution already gives the President an item veto.

Not only has Congress been unwilling to give the president an item veto, but in the Budget and Impoundment Control Act of 1974, as a reaction to President Nixon's refusal to permit the spending of funds that Congress had appropriated, Congress imposed a "legislative veto" (see below) over presidential "deferrals" and "rescissions." However, in the aftermath of the Chadha case (see below), and in the face of major budget deficits in recent years, and in view of the fact that the Democratic Party now controls both houses of Congress and the White House, Congress is considering ways to make it easier for the president to make rescissions.

Section 7

3. Every Order, Resolution, or Vote to which the Concurrence of the Senate and House of Representatives may be necessary (except on a question of Adjournment) shall be presented to the President of the United States; and before the Same shall take Effect, shall be approved by him, or being disapproved by him, shall be repassed by two thirds of the Senate and House of Representatives, according to the Rules and Limitations prescribed in the Case of a Bill.

Despite the inclusive language of what has come to be known as the presentment clause, there are certain orders, resolutions, and votes, in addition to questions of adjournment, that require the concurrence of both houses but are not presented to the president for action. For example, when a constitutional amendment is proposed by a two-thirds vote in both houses of Congress, it is submitted immediately for ratification without being sent to the president. Congress does not exercise ordinary legislative powers when it proposes constitutional amendments. It operates under the powers given it in Article V. Article V is a self-contained, complete statement of methods for amending the Constitution, and it omits the president from the procedure.

A second exception used to be the legislative veto. Congress started to use the legislative veto in a small way in the 1930s and in a big way beginning in the 1970s, until the Supreme Court in *INS* v *Chadha* (1983) called the practice to a halt. In 1932 Congress started to condition some of its more general delegations of powers to the president, and to executive departments, on the approval by Congress, or by one house, of a particular exercise of that power. (Sometimes it even gave veto power to a legislative committee.) The resolutions of approval or disapproval were not submitted to the president.

The legislative veto came in many forms. In some laws, Congress stipulated that the exercise of presidential authority was to be effective unless disapproved by either or both chambers within a certain number of days. In others, Congress provided that what the president did would be effective only if approved by both houses of Congress within a certain time period. For example, under the 1973 War Powers Act, unless Congress adopts a concurrent resolution of approval within sixty days, troops sent into combat by the president are to be withdrawn. Under the Budget and Impoundment Control Act of 1974, if the president withholds funds temporarily, thus making a deferral, it must be reported to Congress, and the action is effective unless overturned by a resolution of either chamber. If the president wishes to impound funds permanently, an act called rescission, the *rescission* of the appropriation is ineffective unless both the House and the Senate approve it within forty-five days.

The congressional veto was criticized by presidents of both parties as an evasion of the presentment clause and the one-house veto was said to be a violation of Article I's bicameralism provision. Often when presented with legislation delegating powers to them and their agents, but subjecting such delegation to a legislative veto, presidents complained that the provisions were an unconstitutional invasion of presidential powers. Nonetheless, they had little choice but to sign the bills and accept the practice. Congress looked upon the legislative veto as an essential means of exercising oversight of the executive departments to ensure that they were carrying out the intent of Congress. Without the legislative veto, Congress could overturn the actions of the president and executive officials only by enacting overriding legislation, which would have to be presented to the president for approval or veto. Congress was not about to give up the practice.

The Supreme Court kept out of the battle for half a century. Then in a sweeping decision in *INS* v *Chadha* (1983),[53] the justices declared the legislative veto unconstitutional. The particular provision in question granted the attorney general authority to suspend the deportation of certain aliens, but all such suspensions had to be reported to Congress. Either chamber could veto the suspension of deportation by passing a resolution of disapproval in the current session or in the next. If Congress did nothing, the aliens' status became that of lawful residents.

The Court could have worded its opinion so that it applied only to this particular use of the legislative veto, or only to one-house vetoes, but the language of the Court was so broad that it sounded "the death knell for nearly 200 other statutory provisions,"[54] more laws than the Supreme Court has declared unconstitutional in our entire history.

Even though the legislative veto is no longer enforceable, the substantive provisions of most laws containing a legislative veto are likely to be sustained. The test is whether the veto was critical to Congress's decision to pass the law in the first place. Not unless the delegations of power "to the executive or to an independent agency have been so controversial or so broad that judges believe Congress would have been unwilling to make the delegation without a strong oversight mechanism" is the entire law to be considered unconstitutional. Moreover, "it is not only appropriate to evaluate the importance of the veto

---

[53] *INS* v *Chadha,* 462 US 919 (1983).
[54] Justice White dissenting in *INS* v *Chadha,* 462 US 919.

in the original legislative bargain, but also to consider the nature of the delegated authority that Congress made subject to a veto."[55]

Despite the sweep of its language and the predictions of disaster by the judicial dissenters and other supporters of the legislative veto, so far the *Chadha* decision seems to have had little consequence. Most federal executives are sensitive to the fact that year after year they must return to Congress for funds. Although they are no longer subject to a legislative veto, nonetheless they are unlikely to act contrary to the express wishes of Congress or its leaders. The *Chadha* decision left intact the constitutionality of "report and wait" provisions: Congress may specify in the original act that no final rule or regulation may be issued until so many legislative days—usually 30—after the proposed regulation has been submitted to specified committees of both chambers. "This interval gives Congress an opportunity to review the regulations and either to attempt to influence the agency's decision, or to enact legislation preventing the regulations from taking effect."[56]

Congressional Organization and Procedure: The Unwritten Constitution

The Constitution provides the barest outline of congressional organization and gives only a partial description of how Congress operates. Basic practices have developed over the past two hundred years. Of special importance are the role of political parties, the selection of committee leaders, and the rules governing debate.

Political Parties in Congress

The nature of the party system is as significant as a formal constitution in determining how a governmental institution operates. The constitutional structure of the English and French parliaments is much the same, yet the French multiparty system leads to a kind of legislature very different from that produced by the English two-party system.

If political parties are so important, why is our Constitution silent about their organization and operation? The Founding Fathers considered parties divisive and baleful influences. Although they knew that "factions," as they called parties, might develop, they hoped that the constitutional arrangements would curtail party influences and make it difficult for parties to operate. To a considerable extent they were successful. While parties have always played a significant role in the operation of Congress, they have not always been decisive factors in determining the outcome of legislative struggles, nor have they served as important agencies in coordinating the executive and legislative branches. They have, however, always played a role of some considerable significance in the operation of Congress.

---

[55] *Alaska Airlines, Inc. v Brock*, 480 US 678 (1987).
[56] Ibid.

Congressional candidates are nominated by parties; they run in elections as representatives of those parties, and the majority party in each house "organizes" that chamber. Prior to the opening of a Congress, each party in each chamber holds an organizing meeting.[57] (The Republicans call their meetings a conference, the term also used by Senate Democrats; House Democrats keep the older name, caucus.) At those meetings the parties choose their officers and nominate their candidates for the various congressional offices, the most important being (in the case of the representatives) the speaker of the House and (in the case of the senators) the majority leader, and the chairs and ranking minority members of committees and subcommittees. The party conferences also confirm the assignment of party members to the standing committees of the Congress (the formal appointments are made subsequently by the chamber), elect the floor leaders and their assistants (the assistants are known as whips), and select policy committees to mold strategy during the coming sessions.

Committees, Subcommittees, and Chairpersons

The standing committees and subcommittees process bills, hold investigations, and recommend legislative action. They are composed of members of both parties, each party being represented in a ratio approximately equal to its strength in the entire chamber.

The influential chairpersons of committees and subcommittees for decades were picked by strict seniority: the member of the majority party who had the longest continuous service on the committee became chairperson. (The senior ranking minority member is also a person of importance.) No matter how much he or she might have differed with party colleagues, no matter how much his or her ideas might have been out of tune with those of the president (even if both belonged to the same party), the senior member became chairperson. But, beginning in 1971, Democrats and Republicans in both the House and the Senate began to make changes in their procedures. The custom of seniority still prevails, but there is now merely a presumption that the senior member will be chosen as chairperson, no longer an automatic guarantee. The chairpersons of all committees and subcommittees now know that if they displease a majority of their fellow party members, they may be voted out of their posts.

Each party may also hold conferences during the course of the sessions, but only the recommendations of the organizing conferences receive the united support of party members. All Democratic House members, for example, support their party's candidate for speaker; all Republicans support their conference's candidate. Thus, the party with the most members selects the speaker and other House officers. The vice president, who presides over the Senate, may belong to the minority party in the Senate, but the president pro tempore who presides in his absence is always a member of the majority party in the Senate.

---

[57] We have a new Congress every two years. The Congress inaugurates its first session in January of an odd-numbered year. The second session meets the following January, and unless the party lineup in the chamber has changed because of deaths, resignations, or special elections, the organization does not change.

Rules and Debate

With so many members and so many issues, the time of the House is carefully controlled. The House Rules Committee, except for certain privileged matters, normally stipulates the amount of time and the conditions under which the House may debate legislation; the Rules Committee merely recommends, but its recommendations are almost always accepted by the House, making it a key player in the passage of legislation. Representatives may be ruled out of order if their remarks are not pertinent to the topic at hand, and their speech is subject to rigorously enforced time limits.

In the Senate debate is usually structured through negotiations among senatorial leaders. But lacking a unanimous consent agreement, Senate debate is practically unlimited. Once senators gain the privilege of the floor, they may talk on any subject for as long as they wish. This rule of unlimited debate and the right to talk about anything even if it has no connection to the subject at hand permits a few determined senators to tie up the business of the Senate by *filibustering*—talking to delay or to prevent the Senate from voting. Senators who strongly object to a measure seldom have to engage in a filibuster. By merely threatening to do so, they are normally able to deter the Senate leaders from attempting to bring the objectionable measure before the Senate for consideration.

Once a filibuster is begun, it is difficult to stop. It takes a vote of three-fifths of the senators duly chosen and sworn in—in most instances sixty senators—to apply cloture (or closure, as it is sometimes called), that is, to end debate. (It requires two-thirds of those present and voting to close debate on a motion to amend Senate rules.) Although the Senate in recent years has been more inclined than in the past to invoke cloture, the power to talk and talk and talk remains a significant weapon of Senate minorities.

Enumeration of Congressional Powers

Section 8 enumerates the legislative powers granted to Congress. In interpreting these powers, we should, as Chief Justice Marshall put it, never forget that it is a Constitution we are reading, a Constitution "intended to endure for ages to come," and consequently to be adapted to the various crises of human affairs.[58] Furthermore, each separately enumerated grant should be read as if the necessary-and-proper clause (see page 97) were part of it.

SECTION 8

1. The Congress shall have Power To lay and collect Taxes, Duties, Imposts and Excises, to pay the Debts and provide for the Common Defence and general Welfare of the United States;

---

[58] *McCulloch v Maryland*, 4 Wheaton 316 (1819).

This paragraph grants to Congress the important powers of the purse: the power to collect taxes, pay debts, and spend money for the common defense and general welfare.

The power to pay debts is not restricted to the payment of the legal obligations of the national government. On the contrary, Congress may pay off obligations that are merely moral or honorary, and when this power is tied to the power to spend for the general welfare, it results in the power of Congress to decide who shall receive dollars from the federal treasury.

A word of caution: the general welfare clause is tied to the power to tax and to spend; no general power is granted to Congress to legislate for the general welfare. But, as noted in the discussion of federalism, liberal construction of congressional powers and the demands of our times have removed any serious constitutional limits stemming from this clause.

James Madison argued that Congress could tax and spend only to carry out one of its other granted powers—that is, Congress could tax and spend to establish post offices and post roads (Section 8, paragraph 7), to regulate commerce with foreign nations (Section 8, paragraph 3), and so on. From the first, nevertheless, the power of Congress under this clause has been interpreted as being *in addition* to its other powers and, hence, exercisable in its own right without reference to them. (Justice O'Connor appears to be a modern-day convert to the Madisonian position. She argued in dissent that Congress's use of the spending power to regulate the drinking age for liquor was an unconstitutional attempt to regulate what had been given to the states.[59])

There are four constitutional limits on the congressional power to spend, but they are not very constraining. First, the expenditure must be for the general welfare, but "the level of deference to the congressional decision is such that the Court has more recently questioned whether 'general welfare' is a judicially enforceable restriction at all."[60] Second, if Congress restricts the way states spend federal monies, it must do so unambiguously.[61] Third, the restraints must be reasonably related to the purpose of the expenditure. But the Court is also deferential to congressional conclusions about what is related; for example, the right of a state to use federal funds otherwise available to it to build highways may be conditioned upon the state's agreeing not to allow persons under 21 to buy alcoholic drinks in the state.[62] Fourth, the Congress may not, via conditions on expenditures, violate other clauses of the Constitution; for example, it cannot use its taxing powers in such a way as to deprive people of their First Amendment freedoms. (Congress may refuse to subsidize First Amendment rights such as limiting the tax-exempt status of nonprofit groups that engage in lobbying.[63])

---

[59] Dissenting in *South Dakota* v *Dole*, 483 US 203 (1987).

[60] *South Dakota* v *Dole*, 483 US 203 (1987).

[61] *Pennhurst State School and Hospital* v *Halderman*, 451 US 1 (1981).

[62] *South Dakota* v *Dole*, 483 US 203 (1987).

[63] *Regan* v *Taxation with Representation*, 461 US 540 (1983).

Congress raises and spends billions of dollars every year to aid agriculture, education, and business; to alleviate conditions of unemployment; and to take care of the poor, the aged, and the disabled, although not one of these activities is specifically within its other delegated powers. About one out of every five dollars that state and local governments spend comes from the federal government. Some of the money comes with relatively few strings, as with block grants for such purposes as education or manpower training, in which the state and local units have considerable flexibility in using the dollars. Some federal dollars come through "categorical grants," in which there are rather specific conditions that state and local governments must follow if they wish to receive the federal funds, sometimes including the requirement that the state use its own resources to match the federal grant. By tying conditions to the funds it makes available, Congress has been able to regulate vast areas, such as how highways are built, how the National Guard is trained, even how universities and colleges post student grades and assign faculty members to do research.

It is difficult, almost impossible, to secure a judicial hearing on the constitutionality of a federal grant program.[64] In rare instances, a state may raise the issue: South Dakota was allowed to do so in connection with federal highway funds. Taxpayers lack standing to challenge federal expenditures merely because they dislike them or believe them to be unconstitutional. They must show that there is a logical link between their status as taxpayers and the challenged legislative enactment, and that there is a "nexus" between this status and a *specific prohibition* in the Constitution, such as the limitations on the taxing and spending power imposed by the establishment of religion clause of the First Amendment.[65] In fact, in our entire history, the Court has allowed only one taxpayer suit against a federal grant. That suit challenged, as a violation of the establishment clause—and thus of a specific constitutional prohibition—a federal grant of funds for instructional materials to schools, including religious schools.[66]

The same rules constraining taxpayer suits prevail for state taxpayers who seek *federal* court review of the actions of their respective state governments. However, although it has not been clearly decided, municipal taxpayers may be given more standing to challenge the action of a city where the taxpayer can show a "direct and immediate" interest in the application of municipal revenues.[67]

State courts have much less stringent rules and often allow state taxpayers to challenge the federal constitutionality of state actions. Such taxpayers who lose at the state court level may not carry the case to the Supreme Court. However, if taxpayers prevail before the state courts and a state action is declared to be contrary to the federal Constitution, the Supreme Court may review the judgment of the state court at the behest of a losing party who can show direct, specific, and concrete injury from that ruling.[68]

---

[64] *Massachusetts v Mellon*, 262 US 447 (1923); *Valley Forge Christian College v Americans United for Separation of Church & State*, 454 US 464 (1982).

[65] *United States v Richardson*, 418 US 166 (1974); *Valley Forge Christian College v Americans United for Separation of Church & State*, 454 US 464 (1982).

[66] *Flast v Cohen*, 392 US 83 (1968).

[67] *Asarco Inc. v Kadish*, 490 US 605 (1989).

[68] Ibid.

Not only can Congress spend for regulatory purposes, it can also tax for such purposes. For example, Congress has taxed out of existence the manufacturer of dangerous white phosphorus matches and the issuing of bank notes by state-chartered banks; the fact that the impact of the tax makes the activity uneconomic raises no constitutional problems. Of course, Congress may not use its authority to tax to deprive persons of specific rights secured by the Constitution. For example, Congress has attempted to regulate gamblers and gambling, the sale of narcotics, and traffic in dangerous weapons through some rather elaborate tax laws. To the extent that, to comply with such laws, gamblers, narcotics peddlers, and sellers of dangerous weapons are, in effect, required to produce evidence that they are engaging in illegal activities, the measures unconstitutionally violate the guarantees against compelling persons to testify against themselves. (See page 275.)[69]

The power to tax and to spend has become one of the two major sources of the so-called national police power, the power to regulate persons and property for the safety, health, and welfare of society. (The other is the power to regulate commerce among the states.) Congress has no general grant of police power, but it may and does use its delegated powers for police-power purposes.

Section 8

1. [continued] but all Duties, Imposts and Excises shall be uniform throughout the United States;

This geographical limitation prevents congressional favoritism toward a particular state or set of states, but the uniformity clause neither keeps Congress from levying taxes that fall unequally on the people in various states nor from defining a tax in geographic terms. Thus, a unanimous Court upheld the Crude Oil Windfall Profit Tax Act of 1980, which raised oil taxes except for wells located in a northerly section of Alaska. The exemption was not drawn on state political lines. Rather, it reflected a congressional judgment that unique climatic and geographic conditions make drilling wells in that region so much more costly than elsewhere that they justified exempting that oil from the windfall profit tax in order to encourage further exploration in that area.[70]

Section 8

[The Congress shall have Power]

2. To borrow money on the Credit of the United States;

---

[69] *Marchetti v United States,* 390 US 39 (1968); *Haynes v United States,* 390 US 85 (1968); *Leary v United States,* 395 US 6 (1969).
[70] *United States v Ptasynski,* 462 US 74 (1983).

Congress borrows money by authorizing the sale of government securities to banks, businesses, and private individuals. The most important forms of government securities are bonds, treasury certificates, and treasury notes.

It is interesting to contrast this provision with that of most state constitutions. Here Congress is given unlimited power to borrow money without any constraints as to amounts, purposes, or conditions. Most state constitutions limit how much the state legislature can raise and go into great detail as to purposes, conditions, repayments, and so on.

SECTION 8
[The Congress shall have Power]
   3. To regulate Commerce with foreign Nations,

Prior to 1937, Congress's power over foreign commerce was greater than its power over commerce among the states. Nowadays Congress's power over commerce among the states is so expansive that the distinction between the two kinds of commerce is of little significance.

Still, of some importance is the fact that this clause imposes somewhat greater constraints on state powers than does the interstate commerce clause. State taxation of foreign commerce is subject to closer scrutiny than taxation of interstate commerce. As the Court recently reaffirmed, "the constitutional prohibition against state taxation of foreign commerce is broader than the protection afforded to interstate commerce . . . in part because matters of concern to the entire Nation are implicated. . . . We think that a State's preference for domestic commerce over foreign commerce is inconsistent with the Commerce Clause even if the State's own economy is not a direct beneficiary of the discrimination."[71] In addition to the tests used to determine whether a state tax violates the "dormant interstate commerce clause" (see page 79), a state tax on foreign commerce is subject to two additional tests: it is unconstitutional first if it "creates a substantial risk of international multiple taxation, and second, if the tax "prevents the Federal Government from speaking with one voice when regulating commercial relations with foreign governments."[72] A state can tax a domestic airplane or railroad car engaged in interstate commerce if the airplane or railroad car is in the state for a certain number of days, if the tax is proportioned to the time in the state, if the tax rate does not discriminate against interstate commerce, and if the tax is related in some way to services provided by the state, but such a test will not justify a state *property tax* on a container used by a ship of a foreign nation when the ship is docked in a port in that state.[73] (A state sales tax on the sale of such a container is permissible; see the following.)

---

[71] *Kraft General Foods v Iowa Dept. of Rev.* , 120 L Ed 2d 59 (1992).
[72] *Japan Line, Ltd. v County of Los Angeles,* 441 US 434 (1979).
[73] Ibid.

The Supreme Court's bold language against state taxation of foreign commerce should not be taken too seriously. The Court usually takes its cue on these matters from the president and Congress. The Court, for example, sustained a Florida tax on fuel purchased in the state by foreign air carriers, whether the fuel was used to fly within or without the state and regardless of whether the airline engaged in any business in the state. Although federal authorities had not specifically authorized such action, by implications arising out of more than 70 agreements with other nations, the federal government had made it clear that it did not object to such state taxation.[74] On the other hand, the Court struck down an Iowa corporation tax that treated dividends received from a foreign subsidiary less favorably than those from domestic subsidiaries even though the Executive Branch filed a brief urging that the tax be sustained.[75] As noted, the Court has struck down a state property tax on containers used in international shipping, but it sustained a sales tax on those same kind of containers without reversing its earlier decision. In the latter instance the Court pointed to the fact that the Executive Department, although its action is "by no means dispositive," nonetheless had indicated that it did not think that the state sales tax infringed on the national government's ability to speak with one voice when regulating commercial relations with other nations. As to the dangers of multiple taxation, the Court appeared to be influenced by the fact that the Tennessee sales tax in question provided for giving credits against any tax properly paid in another jurisdiction on the same transaction.[76]

SECTION 8
[The Congress shall have Power To regulate Commerce with foreign Nations,]
   3. and among the several States,

The commerce clause is another important basis on which Congress has developed a national police power. It is also an excellent demonstration that the vague words and phrases of certain sections of the Constitution have enabled a document written in 1787 in the days of the oxcart to be adapted to the needs of modern global economy.

From the commerce clause, Congress also derives its full powers over the "navigable waters of the United States," including waters that may be made navigable by "reasonable improvements." Those waters are subject to national planning and control; the authority of Congress over them "is as broad as the needs of commerce," including flood protection, watershed development, and the recovery of the cost of improvements through utilization of power.[77]

---

[74] *Wardair Canada* v *Florida Dept. of Revenue*, 477 US 1 (1986).

[75] *Kraft General Foods* v *Iowa Dept. of Rev.*, 120 L Ed 2d 59 (1992).

[76] *Itel Containers International Corp.* v *Huddleston*, 122 L Ed 2d 421 (1993).

[77] *United States* v *Appalachian Electric Power Co.*, 311 US 377 (1940).

Commerce, in the sense of this clause, includes not only buying and selling (traffic), but all forms of commercial intercourse, of transportation, and of communication. Congress's power extends to commerce if it is carried on with foreign nations or "concerns more states than one." The power of Congress over such commerce is the power to govern it. In the words of Chief Justice Marshall in *Gibbons v Ogden,* that power "is complete in itself, may be exercised to its utmost extent, and acknowledges no limitations other than are prescribed in the Constitution."[78] More recently, Justice Brennan wrote, "It would be difficult to overstate the breadth and depth of the commerce power."[79]

Congress is not obliged, when regulating "commerce among the several states," to consider the effect of its measures on matters that generally have been regulated by the states. In fact, it need not pay much attention to the effect of its regulations of commerce upon the operations of the state governments themselves (see page 173). Indeed, it may regulate intrastate activities (those within a state) when they substantially affect interstate or foreign commerce.

Although Congress's measures are usually intended to benefit commerce, they are not required to do so. Congress may even prohibit or greatly restrict commerce in order to promote the national health, safety, and welfare, or for humanitarian purposes. From 1808, as soon as it was constitutionally able to do so, Congress proscribed the slave trade. Many years later it prohibited the transportation of lottery tickets between the states and, still later, the transportation of liquor into states having "dry laws." Congress has made it a federal crime to use the channels of interstate commerce for the shipment of stolen automobiles or impure foods, in the traffic of "white slavery," in the business of "loan sharks," or for travel to commit certain specified crimes.

These days neither Congress nor the Supreme Court even bothers very much to find a connection between the activity it proscribes and interstate commerce. For example, Congress has made it a federal crime to destroy any building affecting interstate commerce. In sustaining this law as applied to the attempted arson of a two-unit apartment, the Court merely pointed to the fact that the rental of real estate "unquestionably" affects interstate commerce and "the local rental of an apartment unit is merely an element of a much broader commercial market in real estate."[80] Under this rationale, it is hard to imagine any activity that could not be brought within the scope of federal power.

Occasionally a member of the Supreme Court raises some questions about congressional use of commerce clause powers, especially if there are also some Tenth Amendment concerns because of the impact on state governments. And Justice Rehnquist and Chief Justice Burger warned "it would be a mistake to conclude that Congress' power to regulate pursuant to the Commerce Clause is unlimited."[81] But the fact is "the task of a court in reviewing congressional

---

[78] *Gibbons v Ogden,* 9 Wheaton 1 (1924).

[79] *Pennsylvania v Union Gas Co.,* 488 US 810 (1989).

[80] *Russell v United States,* 471 US 858 (1985).

[81] Concurring in *Hodel v Virginia Surface Min. & Recl. Assn.,* 452 US 264 (1981).

commerce clause regulations is exceedingly narrow." A court may invalidate legislation enacted under the commerce clause only if it is clear that there is no rational basis for a congressional finding that the regulated activity affects interstate commerce, or that there is "no reasonable connection between the regulatory means selected and the asserted ends."[82] What happened is that the Court has turned over to Congress the interpretation of the scope of its powers under the commerce clause. (See the discussion of *Garcia* v *San Antonio,* on page 173.) As a result, congressional regulations, when based on the commerce clause, have been seldom challenged in recent years. When challenged, the Court, with a cohesion that is rare, has no difficulty in concluding that Congress may regulate such purely local transactions as fees charged by real estate brokers and lawyers, or mining, or the preservation of farmland.[83] Yet in *Gregory* v *Ashcroft,* the Court drew back somewhat from giving Congress carte blanche. In holding that states could retain mandatory retirement for judges at a certain age, the Court, while resolving the matter by interpreting the Age Discrimination in Employment Act to permit such state action, hinted that Congress would raise serious constitutional problems if it were to override the states' authority to determine when their own judges must retire.[84]

Congress has used the commerce clause to provide extensive regulations of the workplace. It has regulated how and why employees can be hired, promoted, and fired, it has closed the channels of interstate commerce to goods of enterprises engaged in commerce or in production for commerce that do not pay all employees minimum wages and overtime pay as prescribed by federal law.[85] Congress not only has banned the interstate transportation of goods so produced, but has also made it a federal offense to produce goods under such conditions when the goods are "intended" for sale in interstate commerce (Fair Labor Standards Act). To safeguard interstate commerce from interruption by strikes, Congress has regulated employer–employee relations in businesses and industries that "affect" such commerce (the Wagner and Taft-Hartley Acts, for example). Congress has also used the commerce clause to justify comprehensive federal regulations of mining, agriculture—in fact every aspect of our economic life.[86]

The commerce clause is also the constitutional peg for most federal civil rights legislation. The 1964 Civil Rights Act, for example, forbids discrimination because of race, religion, or national origin in places of public accommodation and because of race, religion, national origin, or sex in employment. "Congress's action in removing the disruptive effect which it found racial discrimination has on interstate travel is not invalidated because Congress was also legislating against what it considers to be moral wrongs."[87]

---

[82] *FERC* v *Mississippi,* 456 US 742 (1982).

[83] *McLain* v *Real Estate Board of New Orleans,* 444 US 232 (1980); *Goldfarb* v *Virginia State Board,* 421 US 733 (1975); *Hodel* v *Virginia Surface Min. & Recl. Assn.,* 452 US 264 (1981).

[84] *Gregory* v *Ashcroft,* 115 L Ed 2d 410 (1991).

[85] *United States* v *Darby,* 312 US 100 (1941).

[86] *Hodel* v *Virginia Surface Min. & Recl. Assn.,* 452 US 264 (1981).

[87] *Heart of Atlanta Motel* v *United States,* 379 US 241 (1964).

Since Congress's power over interstate commerce extends to the regulation of local incidents that might have a substantial and harmful effect on that commerce, Congress can extend and has extended its power to regulate places of public accommodation to "remote places." Congress has authority to cover such places because discrimination there restricts the flow of interstate commerce and because interstate commerce is being used to support the discrimination. Thus, the Supreme Court sustained the application of the Civil Rights Act to what Justice Black in dissent characterized as "this country people's recreation center, lying in what may be, so far as we know, a little 'sleepy hollow' between Arkansas hills, miles away from any interstate highway" because the park leased its paddle boats from an Oklahoma company, its jukebox was made outside of Arkansas, and it played records manufactured outside the state. Ingredients served in the snack bar were obtained from out-of-state sources, and as the Court majority, speaking through Justice Brennan, wrote, "it would be unrealistic to assume that none of the 100,000 patrons actually served by the Club each season was an interstate traveler." Justice Black contended that the commerce clause should not be stretched "so as to give the Federal Government complete control over every little remote country place of recreation in every nook and cranny of each precinct and county in every one of the 50 states."[88] But he dissented alone.

Does the Commerce Clause Confer Rights on Individuals?

In a decision that further shows how Congress uses its powers under the commerce clause to protect civil rights and potentially may become of great significance, the Supreme Court held that 42 USC 1983 (see page 389), a federal statute which gives persons the right to sue for damages if deprived of any rights, privileges, or immunities secured by the Constitution and laws, "gives persons a cause of action for violations of the commerce clause."[89] Justice Kennedy and the chief justice in dissent distinguished between "power-allocating" provisions such as the commerce clause and "rights-securing provisions" such as the Fourteenth Amendment, and contended that this Reconstruction statute had been passed to protect basic civil rights against oppressive state action, but the majority held that the commerce clause confers "a 'right' to engage in interstate trade free from restrictive state regulation." The immediate effect was to allow a trucking firm to sue Nebraska for attorney's fees the firm had incurrred in order to oppose a tax which was held to violate the commerce clause. If this decision is broadly construed, it could produce a substantial enlargement of the civil rights business of federal courts.

Preemption and the Commerce Clause

If a state law conflicts with a federal law or regulation, the federal regulation supersedes it. And much of modern-day commerce clause litigation con-

---

[88] *Daniel v Paul*, 395 US 298 (1969).
[89] *Dennis v Higgins*, 498 US 439 (1991).

cerns judicial attempts to decide whether the state action has been "pre-empted." Congress may, but often does not, explicitly define the extent to which its enactments preempt state law. More commonly Congress implicitly takes over a field. A congressional purpose to take over may be inferred "where the pervasiveness of the federal regulation precludes supplementation by the States, where the federal interest in the field is sufficiently dominant, or where the object sought to be obtained by the federal law and the character of obligations imposed by it ... reveal the same purposes. ... Finally, even where Congress has not entirely displaced state regulation ... state law is pre-empted when it actually conflicts with federal law."[90]

Congress's control over preemption is so powerful that not only does a congressional regulation supersede a conflicting state regulation, "but an act of Congress conferring power on states under the commerce clause also preempts judicial judgments. ... When Congress has struck the balance it deems appropriate, the courts are no longer needed to prevent states from burdening commerce, and it matters not that the courts would have invalidated the state tax or regulation under the Commerce Clause in the absence of congressional action."[91] Thus, if Congress ordains that the states may regulate an aspect of interstate commerce, as it has done, for example, with respect to insurance, any action taken by a state within the scope of the congressional authorization is rendered invulnerable to commerce clause challenge.[92] (The state action, however, may violate other provisions of the Constitution; for example, the equal protection clause.)

The Dormant Commerce Clause

The commerce clause is important, moreover, not only as a grant of power to Congress but also as a limit on the power of the states. In giving this power to the national government, the Constitution took it away from the states, at least in large part. Therefore, whenever a state, in professed exercise of its police or taxing power, passes a law materially affecting interstate or foreign commerce, the question necessarily arises whether the law is not really an unconstitutional regulation of foreign or interstate commerce. These are what have come to be known as the "dormant principles" of the commerce clause.

When Congress is silent and has neither preempted state power nor authorized it, then the courts—ultimately the Supreme Court—must determine whether a state regulation affecting commerce conflicts with the dormant commerce clause. In the exercise of this great power, the Court has handed down hundreds of decisions, some of which involved vast commercial interests. It has laid down scores of rules about which volumes have been written. There is not space to discuss all those rules in a little book like this, but in essence, the

---

[90] *Schneidewind* v *ANR Pipeline Co.*, 485 US 293 (1989).
[91] *Lewis* v *BT Investment Managers Inc.*, 477 US 27 (1980).
[92] *Northeast Bancorp* v *Board of Governors*, 472 US 159 (1985).

Court weighs the local interest against the general commercial interest and then gives the right-of-way to the interest it deems, all things considered, the more important one.

In analyzing whether state economic regulations violate the commerce clause, the Court has a two-tiered approach with gradations inside the first tier. First, when a state statute *directly discriminates* against state commerce or when its effect is to *favor in-state economic interests*, the law is likely, without much inspection, to be struck down.[93] Discriminating laws may be struck down either for a discriminatory *purpose* against out-of-state commerce or for a discriminatory *effect* on such commerce.[94] "Where simple economic protectionism" is found, "a virtual per se rule of invalidity has been erected."[95]

If the purpose is not protectionist but the law has a *discriminatory effect,* the law, although not per se unconstitutional, nonetheless is subject to strict scrutiny, and the burden falls on the state to demonstrate that (1) the statute serves a legitimate local purpose and (2) the purpose cannot be served as well by available nondiscriminatory means.[96]

State laws passed for nonprotectionist purposes that have an *indirect* adverse effect on interstate commerce are judged by the less demanding second-tier test. In such an instance, the Court performs a balancing test and examines whether the state's interest is legitimate and whether the burden on interstate commerce clearly exceeds the local benefits.

Justice Scalia is leading what is so far a one-person crusade that the commerce clause contains no "negative" component. He contends, "The historical record provides no grounds for reading the Commerce Clause to be other than what it says—an authorization for Congress to regulate commerce."[97] Because of this claim, he is willing to support application of the dormant clause only against a state law that facially discriminates against interstate or foreign commerce or against a state law that is indistinguishable from a law previously held unconstitutional by the Court. Justice Scalia in this, as in some other instances, reads the Constitution literally, but he is the only justice who does not support some application of the dormant commerce clause.

In hundreds of cases the Supreme Court, when Congress was silent, performed this balancing role with respect to state police-power laws (those passed to promote the public health, welfare, and safety). Here are a few examples: Arizona was not allowed to impose a fourteen-passenger-car or seventy-freight-car limit on interstate trains, nor could it require interstate trains to carry a "full crew" as defined by the state legislature.[98] Illinois could not require inter-

---

[93] *Brown-Forman Distillers v NY Liquor Auth.*, 476 US 573 (1986).

[94] *Western & Southern Co. v Board of Equalization of California*, 451 US 648 (1981).

[95] *Minnesota v Clover Leaf Creamery Co.*, 449 US 456 (1981).

[96] *Maine v Taylor*, 477 US 131 (1986); *Hughes v Oklahoma*, 441 US 322 (1979).

[97] *Tyler Pipe Industries, Inc. v Washington State Dept. of Revenue*, 483 US 232 (1987); also concurring in *Itel Containers International Corp. v Huddleston*, 122 L Ed 2d 421 (1993).

[98] *Southern Pacific Co. v Arizona*, 325 US 761 (1945); *Fireman v Chicago, Rock Island and Pacific RR Co.*, 393 US 129 (1968).

state trucks to be equipped with specific kinds of contoured mudguards.[99] Wisconsin and Iowa could not ban trucks longer than fifty-five feet, because such a ban placed a substantial burden on interstate commerce and the evidence did not support the states' contentions that such regulations made the highways safer.[100] Washington could not ban supertankers from Puget Sound.[101] New Jersey could not prohibit the importation of solid or liquid waste that originated or was collected outside the state, since the prohibition imposed on out-of-state commercial interests the full burden of conserving the state's remaining landfill space and was a freeze on the flow of commerce for protectionist reasons.

Here are a few "coulds": Arkansas could regulate the wholesale electric rates charged by rural power cooperatives to their member retail distributors.[102] Maine could prohibit the importation of bait fish because the state proved to the satisfaction of the judges that its purpose was to protect its own wild fish and that there was no other available means to do so.[103] (If procedures are developed that make sampling of fish and inspection for disease feasible, Maine may no longer be able to justify its import ban.)

In recent years the attempts by Congress and the states to deal with the issue of the disposal of waste, especially hazardous waste, has presented the Supreme Court with a variety of issues. Trash may have no value, but it is an article of commerce. The problem is that we keep generating waste but nobody wants to take care of it. Those states that have created hazardous waste disposal facilities are not particularly anxious to handle the waste from other states, especially from states that have failed to provide their own facilities. When Alabama imposed an additional fee on hazardous wastes generated outside of the state but disposed of inside it, the Supreme Court struck the fee down. "No State may attempt to isolate itself from a problem common to the several States by raising barriers to the free flow of interstate commerce," said the Court, unpersuaded that Alabama had met its burden of showing the unavailability of nondiscriminatory alternatives. The justices indicated that there were other ways to cope with the problem, including an additional fee on all hazardous waste, regardless of its source.[104] Nor would the Court allow Michigan to bar private landfill owners from accepting solid waste originating outside the county in which the landfill was located. The fact that such a law treated waste from other Michigan counties no differently from waste from other states did not save the law: Michigan could not isolate its counties from interstate commerce. The Court pointed out, however, "Of course, our conclusion would be different if the imported waste raised health or other concerns not presented by Michigan waste."[105]

---

[99] *Bibb v Navajo Freight Lines*, 359 US 520 (1959).

[100] *Kassel v Consolidated Freightways Corp.*, 450 US 662 (1981).

[101] *Ray v Atlantic Richfield Co.*, 435 US 151 (1978).

[102] *Ark. Elec. Coop. v Ark. Public Serv. Commission*, 461 US 375 (1983).

[103] *Maine v Taylor*, 461 US 375 (1986).

[104] *Chemical Waste Management v Hunt*, 119 L Ed 2d 121 (1992).

[105] *Fort Gratiot Sanitary Landfill v Mich. Dept. of Natural Resources*, 119 L Ed 2d 139 (1992).

When Congress enacted the Low-Level Radioactive Waste Policy Act, imposing on states obligations to dispose of wastes generated within their borders and creating monetary incentives and allowing states to increase costs of access to their waste disposal sites, the Court upheld these incentives, but it struck down other provisions forcing states to enact regulations because of conflict with the Tenth Amendment (see page 175).[106]

The Court distinguishes between the role of state and local governments as participants in the market and their role as regulators of commerce. When acting as participants in the market, they are not subject to the restraints of the commerce clause. Thus South Dakota could give preference to in-state buyers for the cement it produced, and Maryland could favor in-state processors in getting rid of abandoned automobiles.[107] Similarly, Oklahoma could require its own state-operated electricity utility to burn at least ten percent coal mined in Oklahoma but it could not make such a requirement for private utilities in the state, for such was a discrimination against interstate commerce.[108] However, what a state may do as a participant in the free market without violating the commerce clause, may violate the privileges and immunities clause—the one in Article IV, not the one in the Fourteenth Amendment—by limiting the ability of out-of-state residents or businesses to participate in that particular business (see pages 156–57).

As difficult as the issues are when it comes to deciding whether a state law enacted to promote the public well-being should be applied to interstate commerce, questions relating to the application of state taxes to interstate commerce are even more complicated. These questions also get combined with Fourteenth Amendment considerations: Under the due process clause of that Amendment, a state may not tax that which is not within its jurisdiction, over which it has no control, and on which it confers no benefits, that is, it lacks "minimum contacts" with the entity it wishes to tax. Under the equal protection clause of that amendment, the tax must be for a legitimate purpose and have a rational relation to that purpose. If the Court concludes that a state may not tax a particular activity because of Fourteenth Amendment considerations, even Congress cannot give a state the authority to do so. However, if the state is kept from taxing a particular activity because of interstate commerce clause considerations, Congress may, if it wishes, allow state taxation.

The Supreme Court recently reaffirmed a "bright-line" physical presence test prohibiting a state from collecting a use tax from mail-order firms that neither have outlets nor sales representatives in the state. Such a tax, said the Court, creates an unconstitutional burden on interstate commerce. At the same time, however, the Court reversed that part of the earlier decision holding that such a tax also violates the due process clause. By so doing it threw the question of whether states should be allowed to collect use taxes from mail-order firms back to Congress. The Court distinguished between the commerce

[106] New York v United States, 120 LEd 2d 120 (1992).

[107] Hughes v Alexandria Scrap Corp., 426 US 794 (1976); Reeves v Stake, 447 US 429 (1980).

[108] Wyoming v Oklahoma, 117 L Ed 2d 1 (1992) sustaining in part and reversing in part National Bellas Hess, Inc. v Department of Revenue of Illinois, 386 US 753 (1967).

and due process clauses by holding that a corporation selling goods in a state even without a physical presence nonetheless has the "minimum contacts" required by the due process clause to subject it to state taxes, yet without that physical presence the corporation lacks the "substantial nexus" required by the commerce clause, absent the consent of Congress, that allows a state to tax it. [109]

In reviewing state taxes the Court acts "as a defense against state taxes which, whether by design or inadvertence, either give rise to serious concerns of double taxation, or attempt to capture tax revenues that . . . belong of right to other jurisdictions."[110] In *Complete Auto Transit, Inc.* v *Brady,* the Court attempted to clarify the apparently conflicting precedents it has spawned. The Court adopted the following four-pronged test to measure the constitutionality of state taxes as they relate to interstate commerce: (1) Is the tax applied to an activity that has a substantial nexus with the taxing state? (2) Is it fairly apportioned? (3) Does it not discriminate against interstate commerce? (4) Is it fairly related to the services provided by the state? If the answer to all four questions is yes, the tax is constitutional.[111]

In 1987 the Court added to this test an "internal" and an "external" consistency test. Under the internal consistency test, a state tax must be of a kind that, if applied by every jurisdiction, would cause no impermissible interference with free trade. The external consistency test "asks whether the state has taxed only that portion of the revenues from the interstate activity which reasonably reflects the in-state component of the activity being taxed."[112] As a result, a "flat tax," a tax at a single rate upon trucks, for example, that imposed the same rate on out-of-state trucks as on in-state trucks, even though out-of-state trucks used a state's highways much less, was declared unconstitutional since the state could not show that administrative difficulties made collection of more finely calibrated user charges impracticable.[113] On the other side, a state excise tax on telephone calls charged to an address in that state are permissible even on calls from or to other states.[114]

There is certainly no field in which the Court's reviewing power has been more valuable than in its review of state regulations and taxation under the commerce clause. Although we have fifty state legislatures, we have one national economic and industrial system—one prosperity. Nor is there any field in which the Court has, on the whole, done better work in maintaining the national authority "in full scope without unnecessary loss of local efficiency."[115] In interpreting the due process clause of the Fourteenth

---

[109] *Quill Corp.* v *North Dakota,* 119 L Ed 2d 91 (1992) sustaining in part and reversing in part *National Bellas Hess, Inc.* v *Department of Revenue of Illinois,* 386 US 753 (1967).

[110] *Trinova Corp* v *Michigan Treas. Dept.,* 112 L Ed 2d 884 (1991).

[111] *Complete Auto Transit, Inc.* v *Brady,* 430 US 274 (1977); *Mobil Oil Corp.* v *Commissioner of Taxes,* 445 US 425 (1980); *Exxon Corp.* v *Wisconsin Dept. of Revenue,* 447 US 207 (1980).

[112] *Goldberg* v *Sweet,* 488 US 979, 1001 (1989).

[113] *American Trucking Associations* v *Scheiner,* 483 US 266 (1987).

[114] *Goldberg* v *Sweet,* 488 US 252 (1989).

[115] *The Minnesota Rate Cases,* 230 US 537 (1913).

Amendment, the Court has frequently been lured into questionable positions by that will-o'-the-wisp word liberty, but commerce clause cases are generally down-to-earth cases, well-seasoned with facts and figures.

SECTION 8
[The Congress shall have Power to regulate Commerce]
     3. and with the Indian Tribes;

Indian tribes are not states within the meaning of the commerce clause. "It is also well-established that the Interstate Commerce and Indian Commerce Clauses have very different applications. In particular, while the Interstate Commerce Clause is concerned with maintaining free trade among the States . . . the central function of the Indian Commerce Clause is to provide Congress with the power to legislate in the field of Indian affairs."[116]

This clause confers on Congress plenary and exclusive power to deal with the Indian tribes.[117] Since 1871, when Congress declared that henceforth there would be no more treaties negotiated with Indian tribes, this clause has been the primary source of federal authority over Indians. It also "singles Indians out as a proper subject for separate legislation."[118]

Treaties, however, remain a basis of many Supreme Court rulings. Current doctrine is that treaties and statutes are to be interpreted to benefit Native Americans, although "Congress has the power to abrogate Indians' treaty rights, though we [the Court] usually insist that Congress clearly express its intent to do so."[119]

Because of the power conferred on Congress by this clause and because of the special historical relationship between the national government and the Indian tribes, the Supreme Court sustained an act of Congress giving Indians belonging to federally recognized tribes a preference in employment by the Bureau of Indian Affairs. "The preference . . . is granted to Indians not as a discrete racial group, but, rather, as members of quasisovereign tribal entities whose lives and activities are governed by the BIA in a unique fashion. . . . The legal status of the BIA is truly sui generis. . . . As long as the special treatment can be tied rationally to the fulfillment of Congress's unique obligation toward the Indians, such legislative judgments will not be disturbed."[120]

The national government, acting through the Bureau of Indian Affairs in the Department of the Interior, counts 280 Indian tribes, pueblos, and groups within the continental United States. There are also slightly more than 200 Native Alaskan communities served by the Bureau. Of the approximately one and one-

---

[116] *Cotton Petroleum Corp.* v *New Mexico*, 490 US 163 (1989).

[117] *Montana* v *Blackfeet Tribe of Indians*, 471 US 759 (1985).

[118] *Morton* v *Mancari*, 417 US 535 (1974).

[119] *South Dakota* v *Bourland*, 124 L Ed 2d 606 (1993).

[120] Ibid.

half million people who designated themselves as Indians in the 1990 census, about 600,000 live on or near reservations (this number includes all Native Americans in Alaska and those in Oklahoma who live on or near the former reservations in that state). Nonreservation Indians—any Indian is free to move anywhere he or she wishes—are entitled to be treated like any other citizen.

To be eligible for most benefits provided by the Bureau of Indian Affairs, one must live on or near a reservation. All Native Americans are American citizens by act of Congress. Today, by act of the states in which the reservations are located, reservation Indians have the right to vote in state and local elections.

Subject to congressional alteration, the tribes have inherent powers to govern themselves. They are "domestic, dependent nations."[121] In governing themselves, the tribes are unconstrained by the Bill of Rights or the Fourteenth Amendment. Although, by the Indian Civil Rights Act of 1968, Congress imposed restraints on tribal governments similar to, but not identical with, those contained in the Bill of Rights and the Fourteenth Amendment, federal courts have only limited power to review tribal actions for conformity with this law. When a female member of the Santa Clara Pueblo and her daughter, for example, challenged as illegal and unconstitutional a tribal regulation denying membership to children of women who marry outside the tribe, but not to children of men who do so, the Supreme Court refused to permit federal courts to consider the claim.[122]

Congress has excluded tribal courts from criminal jurisdiction to try and punish persons other than members of their own tribe for offenses committed on reservations. Included in the exclusion are Indians from other tribes and non-Indians for offenses committed on reservations.[123] Only federal and tribal criminal laws apply on reservations, except where Congress has specified to the contrary, which it has done by delegating to the states the right to exercise jurisdiction over some crimes committed on reservations. Most states have elected to exercise that jurisdiction. In recent years, some Indian tribes have operated high-stakes bingo games on their reservations for the benefit of non-Indians, even though such games are against the laws of the states in which they are located. So far the Supreme Court has sided with the Indian tribes. The state laws forbidding gambling, the Court has concluded, are "regulatory" and not "prohibitory" and thus not within the grant of criminal jurisdiction given by Congress to the states.[124]

Over non-tribal members, Indian tribes have only the jurisdiction conferred on them by Congress, but with Congress's approval they may exclude non-members from reservations.[125] The Supreme Court is continuing to define the jurisdiction of tribal courts over civil matter disputes

---

[121] *Santa Clara Pueblo v Martinez*, 436 US 49 (1978).

[122] Ibid.

[123] *Duro v Reina*, 495 US 676 (1990).

[124] *California v Cabazon Band of Indians*, 480 US 202 (1987).

[125] *Montana v United States*, 450 US 544 (1981); *Oliphant v Suquamish Indian Tribe*, 435 US 1911 (1979); *Merrion v Jicarilla Apache Tribe*, 455 US 130 (1982).

between non-member Indians and non-Indians over issues arising on or related to reservations.[126]

The clause conferring authority on Congress to regulate commerce with Indian tribes also places limits on the power of the states to do so. State regulation of the commercial activities of Indian tribes is allowed only if the state overcomes two independent but related barriers: a state may not act if its authority has been preempted by federal law or if its actions interfere with a tribe's ability to exercise its sovereign functions.[127] For example, a state may not apply its general rules on hunting and fishing to either Indians or non-Indians on reservations, even if there is no specific federal preemption, since such state regulations are "incompatible with federal and tribal interests reflected in federal law and there is no state interest at stake sufficient to justify overriding tribal regulations."[128]

The extent of a state's powers to tax Indians, Indian tribes, and people doing business on Indian reservations is a complex subject. The principles are simple, the applications difficult. Indians living off reservations pay state and federal taxes like everybody else. Indians living on reservations and Indian tribes may be taxed by states "only when Congress has manifested clearly its consent to such taxation." Moreover, statutes are to be construed liberally in favor of the Indians, with "ambiguous provisions interpreted to their benefit."[129] Applying these principles, the Court upheld the right of a county to impose a property tax on property owned by Indians which had been acquired during an earlier period—from 1887 to 1934—when the law authorized the president to allot tribal lands to individual Indians, but not to allow a county to collect an exise tax on the sale of such land.[130]

The Indian commerce clause does not of its own force bar all state taxation of matters that *indirectly* affect the economic interests of the tribes. It prevents only undue discrimination against or burden on Indian commerce. Thus, in addition to taxes imposed by tribes, the state of Washington was allowed to collect a sales tax on sales of cigarettes to non-members of a tribe, including non-tribe Indians, in stores operated by the tribes on reservations, even though the effect was to eliminate the tribes' economic advantage from cigarette sales.[131] New Mexico was allowed to tax non-Indian companies that, under lease from the Apache Tribe, were producing oil and gas even though they were also subject to taxation by the tribe.[132] On the other hand, states may not levy taxes that fall on reservation Indians or affect tribal activities unless Congress, by express authority, has conferred such powers on them. A state may not, for example, collect taxes on income earned by Indians on reservations,

---

[126] National Farmers Union Ins. Co. v Crow Tribe, 471 US 845 (1985).

[127] Ramah Navajo Sch. Bd. v Bureau of Revenue, 458 US 833 (1982).

[128] Antoine v Washington, 420 US 194 (1975); Mescalero Apache Tribe v Jones, 411 US 145 (1973); New Mexico v Mescalero Apache Tribe, 462 US 324 (1983).

[129] Montana v Blackfeet Tribe of Indians, 471 US 759 (1985).

[130] County of Yakima v Confederated Tribes and Bands of the Yakima Indian Nation, 116 L Ed 2d 687 (1992).

[131] Washington v Confederated Tribes, 447 US 134 (1980).

[132] Cotton Petroleum Corp. v New Mexico, 490 US 163 (1989).

collect a fuel tax from a non-Indian firm that cuts trees on a reservation and transports them to a tribal sawmill, or collect a sales tax on tractors delivered to an Indian tribe.[133] New Mexico was told that federal law preempted its collecting a tax on the receipts that a non-Indian construction company received from a tribal school board for building a school on the reservation.[134] (New Mexico could collect the same tax from the contractor for work he did for the federal government.)

These limitations that flow from congressionally imposed limits on the power of states to tax Indian activities on reservations do not extend to off-reservation activity. New Mexico was allowed to collect a sales tax on a ski resort operated by the Mescalero Apache tribe off the reservation, although it could not tax the property the tribe owned and used in operating the resort.[135]

SECTION 8
[The Congress shall have Power]
4. To establish a uniform Rule of Naturalization,

Naturalization is the legal process by which a foreigner is admitted to citizenship. In view of the inherent power of any sovereign nation to determine its own membership, the naturalization clause must today be reckoned superfluous.

By virtue of this same inherent power, Congress has the right to determine which foreigners may enter the United States, for what purposes, and on what conditions. "Over no conceivable subject is the legislative power of Congress more complete than the admission of aliens."[136] This power extends even to granting the attorney general discretion to determine which, if any, aliens who advocate "the economic, international and governmental doctrine of world communism" should be admitted to the United States.[137]

Although aliens are in the United States at the sufferance of the national government and may be removed through administrative procedures, while they are here this grant of authority does not permit Congress to deprive aliens, any more than it may citizens, of freedom of worship, freedom of speech, fair trials for criminal prosecutions, or other fundamental rights protected by the Constitution. Furthermore, congressional power to regulate the admission of aliens includes authority to preempt conflicting state laws. For example, "Congress has broadly declared as federal policy that lawfully admitted resident aliens who become public charges for causes arising after their entry are not subject to deportation; and that as long as they are here they are entitled to the full and equal benefit of all state laws for the security of persons and property."[138]

---

[133] *McClanahan v Arizona*, 411 US 164 (1973); *White Mountain Apache Tribe v Bracker*, 448 US 136 (1980); *Central Machinery Co. v Arizona Tax Comm.*, 448 US 160 (1980).

[134] *United States v New Mexico*, 455 US 720 (1982).

[135] *Mescalero Apache Tribe v Jones*, 411 US 145 (1973).

[136] *Fong Yue Ting v United States*, 149 US 698 (1893); reaffirmed in *Kleindienst v Mandel*, 408 US 753 (1972).

[137] *Kleindienst v Mandel*, 408 US 753 (1972).

[138] *Graham v Richardson*, 403 US 356 (1971).

SECTION 8
[The Congress shall have Power to establish]
    4. and uniform Laws on the subject of Bankruptcies throughout the United States;

Bankruptcy laws enable debtors to obtain release from their obligations upon surrender of their property to their creditors. Thus are the "wholly broke made whole again." Congressional enactments take priority over conflicting state laws. Congress's power under this clause is wide, but not unlimited. It is subject to the Fifth Amendment's prohibition of taking private property without just compensation. For example, there is substantial doubt that Congress could, by bankruptcy legislation, retroactively destroy a creditor's ownership in property sold to a debtor.

When Congress (1973) designed a special law to deal with the bankruptcy of eight northwestern and midwestern railroads, the act was challenged for violating the uniformity requirement of the bankruptcy clause. The contention was that this highly complicated act applied only to some parts of the country and dealt with those subject to its provisions differently from bankrupt railroads in other parts of the nation. The Court responded that the uniformity requirement does not call for geographic uniformity. It requires only uniform treatment for all creditors and debtors covered by the law. Furthermore, during the time the act was in effect, the only bankrupt railroads were those covered by it.[139]

A decade later, however, the Supreme Court seemed to give the uniformity provision a somewhat different interpretation. When the Rock Island Railroad was in the midst of bankruptcy proceedings, Congress enacted a law ordering the trustees to provide up to $75,000,000 as a priority item to pay the unemployment benefits of workers who might not find jobs with the successor organization. The bankruptcy court refused to implement this act because it amounted to an unconstitutional taking of the railroad's property without just compensation. Congress then reenacted the law with the additional provision that if the railroad's property were taken to pay for the unemployment benefits to its workers, the railroad had a right to bring an action against the federal government for compensation. On review, the Supreme Court, ignoring the taking of property issue, held that because the act applied only to one railroad, it was not uniform and therefore exceeded the authority of Congress.[140]

SECTION 8
[The Congress shall have Power]
    5. To coin Money, regulate the Value thereof, and of foreign Coin, and fix the Standard of Weights and Measures;

---

[139] *Regional Rail Reorganization Act Cases*, 419 US 102 (1974).
[140] *Railroad Labor Executives' Association* v *Gibbons*, 445 US 457 (1982).

This power, in conjunction with the power to borrow money on the credit of the United States, gives Congress the authority to issue paper money and to make it legal tender for the payment of all debts.

SECTION 8
[The Congress shall have Power]
    6. To provide for the Punishment of counterfeiting the Securities and current Coin of the United States;

It would seem that Congress has this power, even without this clause, as a result of the necessary-and-proper clause.

Pursuant to this authority, Congress has enacted two statutes designed to make it more difficult to counterfeit money, by restricting photographic reproductions of currency. The first, enacted during the Civil War to combat the surge in counterfeiting caused by the great increase in government obligations, makes it a criminal offense for any person to print or in any manner publish a likeness of currency. The second, adopted in a 1958 law codifying Treasury practice, permits the printing or publishing of the likeness of any federal security or currency for certain purposes and for those purposes only, namely, "for philatelic, numismatic, educational, historical or newsworthy purposes." In addition, publication must be in articles, books, journals, newspapers, or albums; the illustrations must be in black and white; the reproduction must be undersized by at least three-fourths or oversized by at least one and one-half; and the negatives used in making the illustrations must be destroyed after their final use. The Supreme Court has set aside the requirement that the likeness of currency may be published only "for philatelic, numismatic, educational, historical or newsworthy purposes." The Court assumed that the requirement that an illustration of any federal security had to be in a publication such as a book or magazine was unconstitutional, but it left for another day the final determination of that question. (Time, Inc., was the party to the suit and since the publication requirement caused *Time* no problems, the Court ruled that Time, Inc., lacked standing to raise the issue.) The Court upheld the constitutionality of the size and color requirement. It said nothing about the requirement that the negatives be destroyed.[141]

SECTION 8
[The Congress shall have Power]
    7. To establish Post Offices and post Roads;

This clause, combined with the power to regulate interstate commerce and to spend for the general welfare, permits Congress to subsidize airlines, railroads, and shipping companies, and to grant money to the states for road

---

[141] *Regan v Time, Inc.,* 468 US 641 (1984).

building and maintenance. The fact is that, through its powers to tax and to spend for the general welfare, Congress could perform those same functions even in the absence of this grant. Today, this provision is superfluous, but of course, the Founding Fathers could not have anticipated the liberal interpretation of the necessary-and-proper clause (see page 97). When they put this clause into the Constitution, they resolved any doubts about the ability of the national government to establish a postal system.

SECTION 8
[The Congress shall have Power]
   8. To promote the Progress of Science and useful Arts, by securing for limited Times to Authors and Inventors exclusive Right to their respective Writings and Discoveries;

Because of this clause, Congress may grant exclusive rights to authors and inventors for limited times only. To authors it provides copyright protection and to inventors it provides patent protection. Copyright protection is afforded to "original works," including books, plays, musical works, pantomimes, sculptural works, motion pictures, and sound recordings. The owner of a copyright is given certain exclusive rights with respect to such works, including the right to reproduce the copyrighted work and to license its sale. The copyright law does not protect ideas or principles, but rather the particular manner in which they are expressed or described.

Works are protected from the moment of creation, whether published or unpublished, and do not need to be registered or identified with a copyright notice. Registration with the Register of Copyrights is, however, a prerequisite for bringing suit for infringement; registration must occur within five years of publication or copyright protection is lost. The protection extends through the life of the author plus fifty years. For anonymous works and works prepared by an employee at the request of an employer, the protection is for seventy-five years from the date of first publication or one hundred years from the year of creation, whichever expires first.

Facts are not copyrightable but an original compilation of them is, although it is only the compilation, not the facts themselves, that is copyrightable. "Originality is a constitutional requirement," the Court has said in rejecting a "sweat of the brow" doctrine which would have given a copyright to reward those who compiled the facts for their efforts. The originality standard is not very stringent, but even so the court refused to allow a telephone company to copyright its white-page directory. "There is nothing," said Justice O'Connor for the Court, "remotely creative about arranging names alphabetically in a white pages directory."[142]

Notwithstanding the exclusive right of copyright owners, there are certain circumstances under which it is permissible to reproduce or display copy-

---

[142] *Feist Ub. v Rural Tel. Serv.*, 113 L Ed 2d 358 (1991).

righted works without the permission of the copyright owner. Traditionally, the courts have considered copying for such purposes as criticism, comment, news reporting, teaching, scholarship, and research to be *fair use*. The standards of fair use described in the current statute include (1) the purpose and character of the use, including whether it is for commercial or educational purposes, (2) the nature of the copyrighted material (e.g., periodical, film, book, videotape), (3) the amount of the work used in relation to the whole, and (4) the effect of the use on the potential market for or value of the copyrighted work.

The Supreme Court has decided that manufacturers of videotape recorders do not infringe the rights of owners of copyrighted television programs. The evidence indicated that the largest use of videotapes was for "time-shifting purposes," to allow the viewer to see the material at a time different from that in which it was telecast, and thus there was little evidence that copyright owners suffered financial harm.[143] Congress could override this decision, but in view of the millions of people with videotape machines in their homes, such action seems unlikely.

Persons who invent or discover any new and useful art, machine, manufacture, or composition of matter, certain types of plants—including microorganisms[144]—and so on may secure a patent from the Patent Office, part of the Department of Commerce. A patent gives its holder the exclusive right to the invention or discovery for seventeen years and, like a copyright, may be sold, assigned, or willed. Litigation in the federal district courts growing out of conflicts relating to patents, if appealed, must go to a special court, the U.S. Court of Appeals for the Federal Circuit in Washington, D.C., and the Supreme Court has left resolution of almost all patent law issues there.

Although the patent power is governed by the same introductory and limiting phrase as the copyright power, the Supreme Court has insisted on more stringent standards for patent than for copyright protection. To secure a copyright, originality is sufficient. To secure a patent, it is necessary to establish that the materials are *useful, innovative, and beyond the state of the art*. Congress, in exercising the patent power, may not "enlarge the patent monopoly without regard to the innovation, advancement or social benefit gained thereby.... Innovation, advancement, and things which add to the sum of useful knowledge are inherent requisites ... in a patent system which by constitutional command must 'promote the Progress of ... useful Arts.' This is *the standard* expressed in the Constitution, and it may not be ignored."[145]

Congress's power to protect trademarks—words, letters, or symbols used in connection with merchandise to point out the ownership and origin of the product—stems not from this clause but from the commerce clause. For a trademark to be registered with the Patent Office, it need not be original, merely distinctive. Registration of a trademark grants the right to its exclusive use in interstate commerce for ten years with unlimited rights of renewal.

Obviously, no state can adopt any regulation that conflicts with federal patent or copyright laws, but again copyrights are treated differently from

---

[143] *Sony Corp.* v *Universal City Studios*, 464 US 417 (1984).

[144] *Diamond* v *Chakrabarty*, 447 US 303 (1980).

[145] *Graham* v *John Deere Co.*, 383 US 1 (1966).

patents. The Constitution does not by its own force exclude states from copy-right-type protection for records and tapes not covered by federal law.[146] As to patents, while the Constitution does not "deprive the States of the power to adopt rules for the promotion of intellectual creation,...states may not offer patent-like protection to intellectual creations which would otherwise remain unprotected as a matter of federal law or protect processes that are unpatented or even unpatentable."[147] States may, however, limit the use of unpatented designs and products in order to prevent consumer confusion and to enforce laws protecting trade secrets.[148]

SECTION 8
[The Congress shall have Power]
   9. To constitute Tribunals inferior to the supreme Court;

All federal courts except the Supreme Court rest exclusively on acts of Congress. Any court, except the Supreme Court, can be abolished by act of Congress. It is not clear whether Congress must provide for the judges of the courts it abolishes. In 1802, when Congress first exercised its power to abolish a federal court, no provision was made for the displaced judges. But the only other time Congress has exercised this power, when the Commerce Court was abolished in 1913, Congress redistributed Commerce Court judges among the circuit courts.

The power to establish courts along with the necessary-and-proper clause gives Congress authority to "enact laws regulating the conduct of those courts and the means by which their judgments are enforced."[149] Under the Rules Enabling Act, committees of the Judicial Conference of the United States, a conference consisting of federal appellate and district judges, propose rules of criminal, civil, and appellate procedures, evidence, and bankruptcy and then the Supreme Court promulgates them. These rules are effective after a speci-fied time period unless Congress sets them aside or amends them.

SECTION 8
[The Congress shall have Power]
   10. To define and punish Piracies and Felonies committed on the high Seas, and Offences against the Law of Nations;

Congress can make any crime under international law a crime under national law. In the past, this has not been important because international law has dealt chiefly with governments rather than individuals. Developments since

---

[146] *Goldstein v California*, 421 US 546 (1973).
[147] *Bonita Boats v Thunder Craft Boats*, 489 US 181 (1989).
[148] *Kewanee Oil Co. v Bicron Corp.*, 416 US 470 (1974).
[149] *Willy v Coastal Corp.*, 117 L Ed 2d 280 (1992).

the end of World War II, placing individuals under the obligations of international law, could give this paragraph unexpected importance.

In 1988 the Supreme Court declared unconstitutional a provision of a law Congress had enacted in part pursuant to its authority under this clause. Congress had banned both hostile picketing in the immediate vicinity of foreign embassies as well as the gatherings of large numbers of hostile people in front of them. The Court struck down the former as a violation of the First Amendment, but sustained the latter provision (see page 219).[150]

SECTION 8
[The Congress shall have Power]
     11. To declare War, grant Letters of Marque and Reprisal, and make rules concerning Captures on Land and Water;

The purpose of this clause was to transfer to Congress a power that in Great Britain belonged to the king, the executive branch. This purpose has not been realized. The president has been primarily responsible for our participation in all our wars, although the role of Congress has recently been enhanced (see page 123).

Letters of marque and reprisal formerly authorized private individuals to prey upon the shipping and property of enemy nations without being considered pirates. The Pact of Paris of 1856 bans this practice.

SECTION 8
[The Congress shall have Power]
     12. To raise and support Armies,

Under conditions of total war, this and the following clause, plus the inherent powers of the national government in the field of foreign relations, confer greater powers than all of the rest of the Constitution. These include the power to draft people and materials; to requisition property; to allocate and ration materials; to direct the production, marketing, and consumption of all products; and to do whatever is "necessary and proper" to further the successful prosecution of a war. In the words of Chief Justice Hughes, "The power to wage war is the power to wage war successfully."[151] One must have a wide-ranging imagination to comprehend the full scope of these powers.

Congress used its war powers in 1946 when it passed a law giving the federal government control of materials, plants, and information dealing with atomic energy, a statute that has been termed "the most remarkable exercise of governmental power" in the entire history of the country.

---

[150] *Boos v Barry,* 485 US 312 (1988).

[151] Charles Evans Hughes, "War Powers under the Constitution," Reports of the American Bar Association (September 5, 1917).

Inasmuch as the framers did not foresee the development of air power, the 1947 act of Congress creating the air force as an independent element of national military power rests on the general *inherent* power of the national government in the fields of foreign relations and national defense. Thus, Congress has the power to raise and support modern military forces of all kinds.

The power to raise and support armies, along with the companion clause "To provide and maintain a Navy" and the necessary-and-proper clause, gives Congress the power to register and conscript people. Does it permit Congress to draft men while not drafting women? When the question was presented to the Supreme Court (1981), the majority concluded that, since Congress had decided that women as a group are not eligible for combat, Congress could choose to order only men to register. The dissenting justices did not challenge the power of Congress to exclude women from combat positions but argued that their exclusion from registration contravened the "equal protection component of the Due Process Clause of the Fifth Amendment".[152]

SECTION 8

12. [continued] but no Appropriation of Money to that Use [the raising and supporting of armies] shall be for a longer Term than two Years;

This limitation is to ensure the dependence of the army on Congress and is a reflection of the framers' belief in civilian supremacy and their fear of standing armies.

SECTION 8

[The Congress shall have Power]
13. To provide and maintain a Navy;

The navy was not thought to be a threat to liberty, and no limitations were placed on appropriations for it.

Does the two-year appropriation limit apply to the Air Force? It is not clear that the question has ever been raised, let alone answered.

SECTION 8

[The Congress shall have Power]
14. To make rules for the Government and Regulation of the land and naval Forces;

The power here conferred is shared, especially under combat conditions, by the president in the capacity of commander in chief. Congress's power under

---

[152] *Rostker v Goldberg*, 453 US 57 (1981).

this section, like all its powers, is subject to specific constitutional limitations, such as the First Amendment protection for religious liberty and freedom of speech or limitation on how it is to appropriate funds. However, "judicial deference...is at its apogee when legislative action under the congressional authority to raise and support armies and make rules and regulations for their governance is challenged."[153]

Constitutional freedoms, such as the right to speak or to be secure from unreasonable searches and seizures and so on, apply to persons in the land and naval forces in a much more modified way than to those not subject to military jurisdiction. But the Supreme Court has narrowed the definition of persons subject to the rules for the regulation of the armed forces to include only those currently having military status (see page 270).

Congress may legislate for those in the armed forces with more flexibility than it is allowed to do for civilians. Thus, the Court has upheld against the charges of vagueness and overbreadth Article 133 of the Military Code, which punishes "conduct unbecoming an officer and a gentleman," and Article 134, which proscribes "all disorders and neglects to the prejudice of the good order and discipline in the armed forces."[154]

SECTION 8
[The Congress shall have Power]
15. To provide for calling forth the Militia to execute the Laws of the Union, suppress Insurrections and repel Invasions;

From an early date, the president has been authorized by Congress to employ not only the state militia but also the armed forces of the United States against "combinations of persons too powerful to be dealt with" by ordinary judicial processes. Presidents have used their authority under these statutes to dispatch troops to break up combinations of persons interfering or threatening to interfere with the execution of federal court orders. Presidents have even "federalized" a state's militia, now known as the National Guard, just to take it away from the command of a governor. When the president calls the National Guard into federal service, the president exercises the same control over it as over any unit of the armed forces of the United States including the authority to send the Guard personnel wherever thought necessary (see the following). In the exercise of these powers, the president may, in case of "necessity," declare martial law. Of this there are various degrees and kinds, the most extreme being that in which military courts temporarily take over the government of a region.

---

[153] *Goldman* v *Weinberger*, 475 US 503 (1986).
[154] *Parker* v *Levy*, 417 US 733 (1974); *Secretary of the Navy* v *Avrech*, 418 US 676 (1974).

SECTION 8
[The Congress shall have Power]

16. To provide for organizing, arming, and disciplining the Militia, and for governing such Part of them as may be employed in the Service of the United States, reserving to the States, respectively, the Appointment of the Officers, and the Authority of training the Militia according to the discipline prescribed by Congress;

Congress and the states cooperate in the maintenance and training of the National Guard. Normally, it operates under the direction of the states, subject to provisions made by Congress. When called into the service of the United States, the National Guard becomes a part of the United States military forces and is subject to government by Congress and the president. When the National Guard is not in federal service, Congress exercises a considerable degree of control through conditions attached to grants of money to the states for the National Guard.

Under present legislation every member of the National Guard of a state is also a member of the National Guard of the United States who, when ordered to active duty, is automatically relieved from duty in the National Guard of the state. Thus, "[Members of a state guard unit] ... must keep three hats in their closets—a civilian hat, a state militia hat, and an army hat—only one of which is worn at any particular time."[155]

After several governors objected to the president calling their respective state guards into training exercises in Honduras, Congress enacted the so-called "Montgomery Amendment." This amendment repealed a provision that had limited peacetime presidential authority to call a state guard into active duty for training purposes outside the United States, saying it could only be done with either the consent of a state governor or a presidential declaration of a national emergency. Some governors contended that the Montgomery Amendment violated the militia clauses. They argued that Congress may authorize the calling of the guard to federal service only for the three reasons listed in clause 15, that is, "to execute the Laws of the Union, suppress Insurrections, and repel Invasions." However, a unanimous Court sustained the constitutionality of the Montgomery Amendment, pointing out that the militia clauses must be interpreted in terms of "the supremacy of federal power in the area of military affairs." The Court also noted that Congress has provided that, in addition to the National Guard, for which Congress provides most of the funds, a state may provide and maintain from its own funds a defense force that is exempt from being drafted into the armed forces of the United States. "As long as that provision remains in effect, there is no basis for an argument that the federal statuary scheme deprives [states] of any constitutional entitlement to a separate militia of [their] own."[156]

---

[155] *Perpich v Department of Defense*, 496 US 334 (1990).
[156] Ibid.

SECTION 8
[The Congress shall have Power]

17. To exercise exclusive Legislation in all Cases whatsoever, over such District (not exceeding ten Miles square), as may, by Cession of particular States, and the Acceptance of Congress, become the Seat of the Government of the United States, and to exercise like Authority over all Places purchased by the Consent of the Legislature of the State in which the Same shall be for the Erection of Forts, Magazines, Arsenals, dock-Yards, and other needful Buildings;

After many years in which Congress exercised direct authority over the District of Columbia, with the district having only appointed officials, the District of Columbia Self-Government Act of 1973 finally brought a considerable measure of home rule to the district. The citizens of the district elect their own mayor, city council, and school board; the council has limited authority to legislate and to levy taxes, but Congress still retains ultimate legislative authority. A National Capital Service Area consisting of the principal federal buildings provides a federal enclave within the district.

This clause probably requires Congress, if it should ever vote to admit the District of Columbia as a state (see page 160), to retain exclusive jurisdiction over a small part of it as "the Seat of the Government of the United States."

SECTION 8
[The Congress shall have Power]

18. And To make all Laws which shall be necessary and proper for carrying into Execution the foregoing Powers, and all other Powers vested by this Constitution in the Government of the United States, or in any Department or Officer thereof.

This clause (variously known as the implied powers clause, the necessary-and-proper clause, the elastic clause, and the coefficient clause) does not grant Congress the power to make all laws that shall be necessary and proper, as is sometimes said. Rather it gives Congress the power to make laws necessary and proper in order to execute its enumerated powers or to execute powers vested by the Constitution in the president, the Senate, or the courts. However, because of the expansive interpretation given to the several enumerated powers and the generous interpretation of the necessary-and-proper clause, nowadays there is hardly any subject that Congress cannot deal with. Thus, to be precise and technically accurate in noting that this clause is not a general grant of power is to convey the wrong impression. This may be one of those rare instances when those who are technically wrong are more accurate than those who are precisely right, and a classic example of how a little learning can be a dangerous thing.

As we have noted, in the famous case of *McCulloch* v *Maryland,* Chief Justice Marshall construed the word necessary to mean "convenient" or "useful" and rejected the narrow interpretation "indispensable." As an example, the authority to establish a Federal Reserve banking system is not among the enumerated powers of Congress, but Congress can so act because establishing such a system is a necessary and proper (that is, convenient) way of executing its powers to lay and collect taxes, to borrow money on the credit of the United States, and to regulate interstate commerce.

"Inherited" Powers: The Power to Investigate

In addition to specifically vested powers, each house of Congress enjoys important powers by inheritance, as it were, from the English Parliament and the early state legislatures. One important inherited power is that of conducting investigations to gather information needed to legislate, to propose constitutional amendments, or to perform other constitutional functions.[157] As a necessary adjunct to its investigating power, each house may subpoena witnesses and punish those who refuse to produce documents or answer questions. Each chamber may itself determine a witness's guilt and have that witness held in custody for as long as the chamber is in session. The more common practice is to turn the recalcitrant witness over to the federal prosecutor for action under a federal law making it a crime to refuse to answer pertinent questions or produce pertinent testimony when ordered to do so by a congressional committee.

Are there constitutional limits to Congress's investigating authority? Or to be more precise, what are the limits of the authority of Congress to compel persons to furnish materials or to answer questions? The Supreme Court has warned Congress that the First Amendment sets boundaries on its investigatory authority.[158] But a majority of the justices has never been mustered to sustain an actual claim that testimony compelled by Congress, even about political beliefs and activities, has in fact abridged rights secured by the First Amendment.[159]

The doctrine of separation of powers also limits Congress's investigatory power. As the Supreme Court has stated it, "The power to investigate must not be confused with any of the powers of law enforcement; those powers are assigned under our Constitution to the Executive and Judiciary." Congress "has no power to expose for the sake of exposure."[160] It may compel answers only if the information sought is needed by Congress in the pursuit of its legitimate business. However, few limits have been placed on what constitutes such pursuit. For example, legislative investigations need not be justified by the development of proposals for new legislation; investigations to determine whether and how government programs are functioning are appropriate.

---

[157] *McGrain* v *Daugherty,* 272 US 135 (1927).

[158] *Watkins* v *United States,* 354 US 178 (1957).

[159] *Barenblatt* v *United States,* 360 US 109 (1959).

[160] *Watkins* v *United States,* 354 US 178 (1957); *Barenblatt* v *United States,* 360 US 109 (1959).

Since witnesses before congressional committees are not on trial in a formal sense, the committees are not required to give witnesses the same rights they would have in a court of law. Committees, however, must comply with whatever procedural rules they choose to adopt.[161] In addition, witnesses have a right, under the Fifth Amendment, to refuse to answer questions if the answers would expose them to the risk of criminal prosecution. (Congress, by granting limited immunity from prosecution, may impose legal obligations upon persons to testify; see page 279.)

By far the most important restraint on congressional investigations has been the Supreme Court's insistence on a strict construction of the federal law defining the offense of contempt of Congress. Contempt of Congress, as defined by the law, is the refusal to answer *pertinent* questions. Before the Supreme Court will permit a conviction, the following must be met: (1) the parent chamber must have clearly authorized the committee to make the particular investigation (in the case of investigations by committees of the House of Representatives, since neither the House nor its committees are continuing bodies, the authorization must occur during the term of Congress in which the investigation takes place); (2) the committee must have authorized the investigation; (3) the committee must have made clear to the witness the subject under investigation, the pertinence of the question to the subject, and the reason the committee insisted that it be answered; and (4) the grand jury indictment must have specified the subject under committee investigation and the pertinent questions the defendant is charged with refusing to answer.[162]

Limitations on Congressional Powers

Whereas Section 8 enumerates the legislative powers of the national government, Section 9 limits them. Section 9—and Section 10, which restricts the powers of the state governments—were originally looked on as a kind of bill of rights.

SECTION 9
  1. The Migration or Importation of such Persons as any of the States now existing shall think proper to admit, shall not be prohibited by the Congress prior to the Year one thousand eight hundred and eight, but a Tax or duty may be imposed on such Importation, not exceeding ten dollars for each person.

This rather delicate language refers to the slave trade. Its inclusion was the high price that the framers paid to bring the slave-trading states of South Carolina, Georgia, Louisiana, and Mississippi into the Union. In 1808, when it had authority to do so, Congress promptly banned the slave trade.

---

[161] *Yellin v United States*, 374 US 109 (1957).
[162] *Gojack v United States*, 384 US 702 (1966); *Russell v United States*, 369 US 749 (1962).

SECTION 9

2. The Privilege of the Writ of Habeas Corpus shall not be suspended, unless when in Cases of Rebellion or Invasion the public Safety may require it.

Congress has the authority to order the suspension of the privilege, although in situations in which the president can validly declare martial law, the president can also suspend the writ. The greater power includes the lesser.

State courts may not inquire why persons are held under the authority of the United States; federal courts, on the other hand, do have jurisdiction to determine if persons are being improperly held by federal or state authorities.

The writ of habeas corpus—known in the eighteenth century as the Great Writ—was primarily a remedy against executive detention. By this writ a judge could inquire of an arresting officer or jailer why a particular person was in custody. If no proper explanation could be given, the judge could order the prisoner's release. But once it was determined that a person was being held as the result of a sentence imposed by a court with proper jurisdiction, that ended the matter.

Congress has expanded the use of the writ to permit federal courts to review the actions of officials to determine not merely whether a person is being detained as the result of a judicial sentence, but also whether that sentence was obtained as the result of a constitutionally proper trial.[163]

Under the Warren Court, the habeas corpus business of federal district judges grew tremendously, causing considerable resentment among state judges. Partly in response to that criticism, the Supreme Court has drastically limited the scope of federal district judges' habeas corpus jurisdiction. First of all, prior to seeking a federal habeas corpus writ to review the actions of state courts, a person must first exhaust state remedies, including a petition for review by the Supreme Court. The Court has also decided in *Stone v Powell* that, when a person has had a hearing in a state court on the allegation that the evidence used against that person was extracted in violation of Fourth Amendment search and seizure rights, the matter should no longer be looked into by federal courts upon a habeas corpus petition.[164] It has refused, however, to extend this ruling beyond its original boundaries to cover other claims, for example, a state prisoner's claim that his conviction rested on statements obtained in violation of the *Miranda* ruling.[165] However, unless it fairly appears that a state court's decision rested primarily on federal law, federal judges should assume that the state court made its decision for independent and adequate state reasons and federal judges should not intervene by way of a habeas corpus review.[166]

---

[163] *Wainwright v Sykes*, 433 US 72 (1977).

[164] *Stone v Powell*, 428 US 465 (1976); *Cardwell v Taylor*, 461 US 571 (1983).

[165] *Withrow v Williams*, 123 L Ed 2d 407 (1993).

[166] *Coleman v Thompson*, 115 L Ed 2d 640 (1991).

Moreover, if defendants fail to raise constitutional claims in state proceedings, they are not to be given any relief by means of a writ of habeas corpus in federal court unless they "demonstrate cause and actual prejudice"; that is, they have a valid reason for not having raised the issue earlier and their case was hurt by the alleged constitutional error. The mere proof that state courts committed an error will not suffice. The only exception is where a petitioner can demonstrate that failure to consider the claims will result in a fundamental miscarriage of justice.[167] The Court has reemphasized, "it is not the province of a federal habeas court to reexamine state court determinations on state law questions. In conducting habeas review, a federal court is limited to deciding whether a conviction violated the Constitution, law or treaties of the United States."[168] If a federal habeas corpus petitioner challenges a state court conviction, the petitioner is not even entitled to an evidentiary hearing, that is, an opportunity to present evidence and call witnesses, on the claim that the state court's proceedings were deficient because material and important facts were not presented to it, unless the petitioner can show a cause for the failure to develop the facts and actual prejudice resulting from such a failure, or that a fundamental miscarriage of justice would result from the failure to hold a federal evidentiary hearing.[169] Furthermore, if a state court concludes that a petitioner failed to follow proper state procedures, the same rules apply. The Court has also recently said that habeas corpus is not to be used to determine a defendant's innocence. As far as a habeas corpus petition is concerned, innocence is irrelevant; defendants must claim that there was a specific constitutional violation.[170]

The Supreme Court has also adopted this more stringent standard when a petitioner files a second federal habeas corpus petition. In the face of government objection, the petitioner, before getting a hearing, must meet the "cause and prejudice standard." The petitioner must show that he or she failed to present the issue in the first habeas corpus petition because "of improper interference by officials, or because a factual or legal basis for a claim was not then available," or because the attorney provided constitutionally ineffective assistance of counsel. Moreover, even if proper cause is shown for failure to raise the issue in the first habeas corpus petition, the petitioner must show actual prejudice resulted from the errors, that is, a likelihood that it would have made any difference in the outcome of the case. Again, the only exception to this requirement for getting a second federal habeas corpus hearing is the "extraordinary" instances when a constitutional violation probably has caused the conviction of one innocent of the crime, that is, to avoid a "fundamental miscarriage of justice."[171]

Despite the importance of these cases in limiting the flow of habeas petitions in the federal courts, the major constraints are to be found in a series of

---

[167] Coleman v Thompson, 115 L Ed 2d 640 (1991); Engle v Isaac, 456 US 107 (1982); Wainwright v Sykes, 433 US 72 (1977).

[168] Estelle, Warden v McGuire, 116 L Ed 2d 385 (1991).

[169] Keeney v Tamayo-Reyes, 118 L Ed 2d 318 (1992).

[170] Herrera v Collins, 122 L Ed 2d 203 (1993).

[171] McCleskey v Zant, 113 L Ed 2d 517 (1991).

decisions relating to petitions from death-row prisoners. Recently, the Supreme Court, in announcing a "no new rule" rule,[172] said that henceforth habeas corpus will not be available in federal courts to state prisoners seeking to establish a "new rule" or to benefit from any new rules announced in decisions since the date their own conviction became final except under two narrow exceptions (see below).[173] This doctrine, said Justice Kennedy in a later case, "is but a recognition that the purpose of federal habeas corpus is to ensure that state convictions comply with the federal law in existence at the time the conviction became final, and not to provide a mechanism for the continuing reexamination of final judgments based upon later emerging legal doctrine."[174]

A "new rule" has been defined broadly to be any rule that "breaks new ground, imposes a new obligation on the state or the federal government," or was not "dictated by precedent existing at the time the defendant's conviction became final."[175] Thus, there is to be no habeas corpus relief from "reasonable, good-faith interpretations of existing precedents made by state courts even though they are shown to be contrary to later decisions."[176] In other words, there is to be no use of habeas corpus for any person whose conviction was upheld by the state courts under law and precedents prevailing at the time the petitioner's conviction became final, even if the law and precedents were "susceptible to debate among reasonable minds."[177] According to Justice Brennan, in dissent, these no-new-rule precedents will preclude federal habeas corpus review "for all but the most indefensible state-court rejections of constitutional challenge."[178]

The two exceptions that allow habeas corpus to be used to consider the application of a new rule to those whose state convictions were "final" are as follows. First, a rule may be applied retroactively if the rule places a class of private conduct beyond the power of the State to proscribe; that is, if the rule "decriminalize[s] a class of conduct," or prohibits a certain category of punishment, such as the death penalty, for a class of defendants because of their status or offense. Second, habeas corpus may apply retroactively "watershed rules of criminal procedure" "implicating the fundamental fairness and accuracy of the criminal proceeding," that is, when the rule enhances the accuracy of the fact-finding process in a major way.[179]

SECTION 9
3. No Bill of Attainder [shall be passed]

---

[172] *Teague v Lane*, 489 US 288 (1989).

[173] *Teague v Lane*, 489 US 288 (1989); *Penry v Lynaugh*, 492 US 302 (1989); *Butler v McKellar*, 494 US 407 (1990).

[174] *Teague v Lane*, 489 US 288 (1989); *Penry v Lynaugh*, 492 US 302 (1989); *Butler v McKellar*, 494 US 407 (1990).

[175] *Teague v Lane*, 489 US 288 (1989).

[176] *Butler v McKellar*, 494 US 407 (1990).

[177] Justice Brennan's dissent in *Butler v McKellar*, 494 US 407 (1990).

[178] *Butler v McKellar*, 494 US 407 (1990).

[179] *Teague v Lane*, 489 US 288 (1989); *Penry v Lynaugh*, 492 US 302 (1989); *Saffle v Parks*, 494 USS 484 (1990).

A bill of attainder is the infliction of punishment by the legislature. Congress, by general law, determines what conduct will be considered a crime, but it may not impose punishment—this must be done by a court of law.

At common law, a bill of attainder was a death sentence, but early in our history we departed from that restrictive definition. Imprisonment, banishment, confiscation of property, denial of jobs, and other kinds of punishment are now recognized as attainders forbidden by this clause.

In the last half-century, the Court has entertained four serious challenges under this clause, twice holding that Congress had violated it. The first time, a provision of an appropriations bill named three federal employees and declared that they should receive no compensation from the federal treasury, other than for military or jury services, unless reappointed to office by the president with the consent of the Senate.[180] The second challenge was to a provision that no member of the Communist Party should be allowed to serve as a trade union officer.[181] In both instances Congress was found to have passed a bill of attainder in that it had inflicted punishment—that is, loss of job—without trial on named individuals or on members of a specific political group.

The third serious challenge was by former President Nixon, who argued that the Presidential Recordings and Materials Preservation Act of 1974, which took control of his presidential papers away from him and vested it in the administrator of general services, was a bill of attainder. As Justice Stevens said: "The statute before the Court... singles out one, by name, for special treatment. Unlike all other former Presidents in our history [and subsequent ones], he is denied custody of his own presidential papers. The statute implicitly condemns him as an unreliable custodian of his papers. Legislation which subjects a named individual to this humiliating treatment must raise serious questions under the Bill of Attainder Clause." But seven members of the Court, including Stevens, ruled that this was not a bill of attainder. Nixon, they argued, was a legitimate "class of one"; Congress was motivated, not by a desire to punish, but rather by a desire to provide an appropriate process for disposing of presidential papers. Justice Stevens, concurring, stated that the decisive fact was that Nixon had made himself a class different from all other presidents by resigning under unique circumstances and accepting a pardon. But it was precisely because of those facts, the dissenters contended, that Congress had "punished" Nixon and passed a bill of attainder.[182]

The fourth modern bill-of-attainder challenge was presented by some male students who charged that Congress had imposed a bill of attainder in the Solomon Amendment, which required all men who wished to apply for federal student financial aid to indicate that they had complied with the registration requirements of the Military Selective Service Act. Although a federal district judge agreed with the students, the Supreme Court did not. Chief Justice Burger, speaking for the Court, pointed out that any student who

---

[180] *United States v Lovett,* 328 US 303 (1946).

[181] *United States v Brown,* 381 US 437 (1965).

[182] *Nixon v Administrator of General Services,* 433 US 425 (1977).

wished to apply for aid could become eligible for it at any time by registration. In addition to not singling out an identifiable group as is characteristic of a bill of attainder, the Solomon Amendment was also said not to impose punishment, because the sanction was a mere denial of a noncontractual governmental benefit. "It imposed no affirmative disability approaching the kinds of disabilities historically associated with punishment."[183]

SECTION 9
   3. [continued] or ex post facto Law shall be passed.

In a celebrated early decision, *Calder* v *Bull* (1798), the Supreme Court interpreted this clause to apply only to penal statutes that disadvantaged the persons affected by them and defined four categories: "1st. Every law that makes an action done before the passage of the law, and which was *innocent* when done, criminal; and punishes such action. Every law that *aggravates a crime*, or makes it *greater* than it was, when committed. Every law that *changes the punishment*, and inflicts a *greater punishment*, than the law annexed to the crime, when committed. Every law that alters the *legal* rules of *evidence*, and receives less, or different, testimony, than the law required at the time of the commission of the offense, in order to convict the offender."[184]

In 1990 the Supreme Court, explicitly overruling 1883 and 1898 precedents, limited the definition of ex post facto to the four categories outlined in the *Calder* case and removed from the definition procedural alterations in the laws that might work to the disadvantage of the accused.[185] Thus, "To fall within the ex post facto prohibition, two critical elements must be present: first, the law must be retrospective, that is, it must 'apply to events occurring before its enactment'; and second, it must disadvantage the offender affected by it.... No violation occurs if a change does not alter 'substantial personal rights,' but merely 'changes modes of procedure which do not affect matters of substance.'"[186] Yet the Court seems to have accepted changes in death-penalty sentencing procedures that negatively affected defendants—or so the dissenting justices have charged.

The prohibition does not prevent passage of retroactive penal laws that work to the benefit of an accused—a law decreasing punishment, for instance. [187]

Although the due process clause imposes some barriers to retroactive civil laws, the ex post facto clause imposes no limitations on retroactive civil, in contrast to criminal, laws, even those that work against individuals—say, an increase in income taxes applied to income previously earned as Congress did in the summer of 1993 when it raised income tax rates retroactively to January 1993.[188] "So

---

[183] *Selective Service System et al.* v *Minnesota Public Interest Research Group et al.*, 468 US 841 (1984).
[184] *Calder* v *Bull*, 3 Dallas 386 (1798).
[185] *Collins* v *Youngblood*, 497 US 37 (1990) overruling *Kring* v *Missouri*, 107 US 221 (1883) and *Thompson* v *Utah*, 170 US 343 (1898).
[186] *Miller* v *Florida*, 482 US 423 (1987).
[187] *Dobbert* v *Florida*, 432 US 282 (1977).
[188] *United States* v *Darusmont*, 449 US 292 (1981).

much importance did the Convention attach [to the ex post facto prohibition] that it is found twice in the Constitution"[189]—here as a limitation on the national government and in Section 10 as a limitation on the states.

SECTION 9

4. No Capitation, or other direct, Tax shall be laid, unless in Proportion to the Census or Enumeration herein before directed to be taken.

A capitation tax is a poll or head tax. The precise meaning of the term direct tax is today uncertain.

SECTION 9

5. No Tax or Duty shall be laid on Articles exported from any State.

Although Congress cannot tax articles exported from states, it can, under its power to regulate commerce with foreign nations, prohibit those exports.

SECTION 9

6. No Preference shall be given by any Regulation of Commerce or Revenue to the Ports of one State over those of another: nor shall Vessels bound to, or from, one State, be obliged to enter, clear, or pay Duties in another.

By giving Congress the power to regulate interstate and foreign commerce, the states were prevented from discriminating against the commerce of other states. This section prevents Congress, in regulating such commerce, from discriminating against the trade of a single state or of a group of states.

SECTION 9

7. No money shall be drawn from the Treasury, but in Consequence of Appropriations made by Law; and a regular Statement and Account of the Receipts and Expenditures of all public Money shall be published from time to time.

It is this clause, more than any other, that gives Congress control over the acts of the other branches of government—the president, the courts, the mili-

---

[189] *Kring v Missouri*, 107 US 221 (1883). For due process considerations with respect to retroactive civil laws, see *Pension Benefit Guaranty Corp. v R. A. Gray & Co.*, 467 US 717 (1984).

tary—since all depend on Congress for money to carry out their functions. "Money may be paid out only through an appropriation made by law, in other words, the payment of money from the Treasury must be authorized by a statute."[190] "However much money may be in the Treasury at any one time, not a dollar of it can be used in payment of any thing not ... previously sanctioned."[191] In fact, Congress normally passes a law authorizing an appropriation, but the authorizing legislation does not permit any actual expenditure until after Congress passes another law actually appropriating the funds. Authorizations are sometimes for a five-year period; appropriations are for the fiscal year. Congress frequently appropriates much less than it has authorized.

Congress, and not the courts, determines with what specificity executive agencies are to account for their expenditures. Taxpayer suits cannot be maintained to force Congress or a federal agency to comply with this clause. Thus, a taxpayer was denied the right to challenge before the courts the constitutionality of an act of Congress that permits the Central Intelligence Agency to account for its expenditures "solely on the certificate of the Director."[192]

In one of the rare cases involving the appropriations clause, the Supreme Court went out of its way to cite it as an additional reason why a person who lost his disability pension because he acted on false information given to him by a government official and by an official publication, nonetheless could not secure a judicial order for a payment for his losses. Wrote Justice Kennedy for the Court, "If agents of the Executive were able by their unauthorized oral or written statements to citizens, to obligate the Treasury for the payment of funds, the control over public funds that the Clause reposes in Congress in effect could be transferred to the Executive."[193]

SECTION 9
8. No Title of Nobility shall be granted by the United States:

Section 10 imposes the same limitation on the states. One wonders how our lives might have been enriched if the Constitution had not prohibited the national government and the states from granting titles of nobility: Babe Ruth might have become not just the Sultan of Swat but the Duke of Swat, and Lindbergh the Earl of Flight. Elvis Presley might have become the Prince of Memphis, and who knows who might have become the Archduke of Albany, the Baron of Berkeley, the Duke of Dupont Circle, or the Marquis of Irvine? But then again, titles might have been passed out by the national government and the

---

[190] *Office of Personnel Management* v *Richmond*, 496 US 387 (1990).

[191] Ibid., quoting *Reside* v *Walker*, 11 Howard 272 (1851).

[192] *United States* v *Richardson*, 418 US 166 (1974).

[193] *Office of Personnel Management* v *Richmond*, 496 US 387 (1990).

states, not in recognition of outstanding public service, but for purposes of patronage.

SECTION 9

8. [continued] And no Person holding any Office of Profit or Trust under them, shall, without the Consent of the Congress, accept of any present, Emolument, Office, or Title, of any kind whatever, from any King, Prince, or foreign State.

Acquainted with the history of previous republican governments, and aware of the ability of foreign sovereigns to bribe and corrupt republican officials, the framers took precautions to prevent any foreign state from securing undue influence within the executive agencies of the national government.

Limitations on States

SECTION 10

1. No State shall enter into any Treaty, Alliance, or Confederation;

When the government of the United States was formed, the individual states lost their international personalities, if, in fact, they ever possessed them. Constitutionally, the states can neither negotiate with foreign states nor have any direct relations with them. The national government possesses a monopoly over the foreign affairs of the United States. States may not exercise their reserved powers in such a way as to intrude on the national government's exclusive right to deal with international affairs. For example, states traditionally regulate the distribution of estates, but those regulations must give way if they impair the effective exercise of the nation's foreign policy by conflicting with agreements between the United States and other nations.[194]

SECTION 10

1. [continued] [No state shall] grant Letters of Marque and Reprisal;

This power was given to Congress in Section 8, paragraph 11 (see page 93), and this section makes clear that states are not to have any authority over such matters.

---

[194] *Zschernig v Miller*, 389 US 429 (1968).

SECTION 10

1. [continued] [No state shall] coin Money; emit Bills of Credit; make any Thing but gold and silver Coin a Tender in Payment of Debts;

This provision makes quite clear that the national government is in charge of our currency system. The practice of states issuing their own currencies made commercial life difficult under the Articles of Confederation. That there is but one currency system for the entire United States is a major factor binding the Union together.

SECTION 10

1. [continued] [No state shall] pass any Bill of Attainder, ex post facto Law,

These limitations imposed on the national government are herein also imposed on the states.

SECTION 10

1. [continued] or Law impairing the Obligation of Contracts,

After the Revolution, the thirteen states, operating under the weak and ineffective Articles of Confederation, passed through a difficult period of readjustment as a result of the economic and political dislocations of the war's aftermath. Many citizens were in debt; the farmers who had speculated freely in land while prices were rising were especially burdened. Property and debtor laws were extremely harsh. Defaulting debtors were thrown into jail and deprived of all their holdings. In many states, the legislatures, responsive to farmers' pressure, passed laws to alleviate the lot of debtors. Paper money was made legal tender for the payment of debts, bankruptcy laws were passed, and sometimes the courts were closed to creditors. These laws, in turn, aroused the creditor classes, who, feeling that their rights had been infringed, demanded action to put a stop to such "abuses" of power by the state legislatures. Creditors, in fact, were foremost among the groups that brought the Constitutional Convention about; the prevention of such interferences with private rights by state legislatures was one of the major purposes of the convention. As James Madison put the matter in a speech to his fellow delegates, intrusions in private rights by state legislatures "were evils which had, more perhaps than anything else, produced this Convention." This paragraph of the Constitution was the principal result of this concern.

When the framers spoke of "contracts" whose obligations could not be impaired by state law, they had in mind the ordinary contracts between individuals, especially contracts of debt. The meaning of the word, however, was early expanded by judicial interpretation to include contracts made by the states themselves, including franchises granted to corporations. As a result, the "obligation of contracts" clause became, prior to the Civil War, the most important defense of the rights of property in the Constitution. States were prevented from passing any law, whether in the interest of the public welfare or not, that might materially disturb rights secured by contract.[195] In the late 1830s, however, the Supreme Court began to restrict the application of the contracts clause. By the 1890s,[196] it had been established that all franchises should be narrowly construed in favor of the states and that all contracts implicitly recognized the general police power of the states to regulate property (including contract rights) for the public welfare.

By the 1930s it came to mean no more than that a state could impair the obligation of contracts provided it did so to promote the general welfare and not "in a spirit of oppression" and "without reasonable justification." Then, after more than forty years, in 1977 and—to show that it was not a fluke—again in 1978, the Court, in the words of the dissenters, "dusted off" the contract clause and declared a state law unconstitutional. In 1977 the Court declared that New Jersey had violated the contract clause when it set aside a provision of an earlier law enacted to protect bondholders. Justice Blackmun wrote for the Court, "Whether or not the protection of contract rights comports with current views of wise public policy, the Contract Clause remains a part of our written Constitution."[197] In the 1978 decision, Justice Stevens reiterated, "The Contract Clause remains part of the Constitution. It is not a dead letter." The Court declared unconstitutional the application of a Minnesota law that imposed additional pension obligations on employers beyond those they had previously undertaken by contract with their employees.[198]

Despite these two holdings, more recent decisions make it clear that the contract clause is not likely to become once again a major limitation on the power of the states to regulate property. A unanimous Court upheld the application of an Alabama law prohibiting oil producers from passing on to purchasers any increase in severance taxes, despite preexisting contracts stipulating that purchasers were to absorb such increases. The Court pointed out that the Alabama law, unlike those involved in the 1977 and 1978 decisions, did not "prescribe a rule limited to contractual obligations or remedies, but imposed a generally applicable rule of conduct designed to advance a broad societal interest." Alabama was attempting to shield consumers from the burdens of tax increases, and its prohibition applied to all oil and gas producers, regardless of whether they happened to be parties to contracts providing for tax increases to be passed on to purchasers.[199] The Court

---

[195] *Fletcher v Peck*, 6 Cranch 87 (1810); *Dartmouth College v Woodward*, 4 Wheaton 518 (1819); *Sturges v Crowinshield*, 4 Wheaton 122 (1819).

[196] *Charles River Bridge Co. v Warren Bridge*, 11 Peters 420 (1837); *Stone v Mississippi*, 101 US 814 (1880).

[197] *United States Trust Co. v New Jersey*, 431 US 1 (1977).

[198] *Allied Structural Steel Company v Spannaus*, 438 US 234 (1978).

[199] *Exxon Corp. v Eagerton*, 462 US 176 (1983).

also ruled that Kansas could regulate natural gas prices even if it slightly impaired the contractual rights of an energy company because the company was operating in a highly regulated industry, and the state's interest in protecting consumers is a significant and legitimate one.[200] The Court did not find it difficult to conclude that Pennsylvania could prohibit mine owners from holding surface owners to their contractual waiver of liability for surface damages.[201] In short, if states avoid singling out contracts, laws passed to promote the general welfare are not likely to run afoul of this clause even if they do incidentally impair the obligations of a contract.

SECTION 10

1. [continued] [No state shall] or grant any Title of Nobility.

Fifty states granting titles of nobility would have made for an exciting social page in our daily newspapers.

SECTION 10

2. No State shall, without the Consent of the Congress, lay any Imposts or Duties on Imports or Exports, except what may be absolutely necessary for executing its inspection Laws: and the net Produce of all Duties and Imposts, laid by any State on Imports or Exports, shall be for the Use of the Treasury of the United States; and all such Laws shall be subject to the Revision and Controul of the Congress.

Without the express consent of Congress, but subject to its revision, states may levy an inspection tax on imports and exports. (Congress itself may not tax exports.) Inspection laws are concerned with quantity and quality. Congress, not the courts, decides whether or not the inspection tax is more than "what may be absolutely necessary for executing [the state's] inspection laws."

The ban on duties and imposts on imports and exports used to be construed to forbid taxation of imports until removed from their original package and of exports after they had begun to move to a foreign country. The Court has now removed such rigid limitations on state taxation. Today the clause provides little if any additional limitation on the powers of states beyond that contained in the commerce clause.[202] The clause is designed to prevent (1) state exactions that interfere with the exclusive power of the federal government to regulate foreign commercial relations; (2) exactions by seaboard

---

[200] *Energy Reserves v Kansas Power & Light*, 459 US 400 (1983).

[201] *Keystone Coal Association v DeBenedictis*, 480 US 470 (1987).

[202] *Itel Containers International Corp. v Huddleston*, 122 L Ed 2d 421 (1993).

states, taxing goods that flow through their ports, that might disturb the harmony among the states; and (3) in the case of state duties on imports, state exactions that interfere with the exclusive power of the federal government to raise revenues from tariffs which was thought to be at the beginning of our history a major source of revenue for the federal government. Short of these limitations, a state may collect non-discriminatory taxes—for example, a general property tax applied to imported tires, even though in their original package,[203] or a tax on imported goods, such as tobacco, stored under bond in a customs warehouse and destined for domestic manufacture or sale,[204] or a tax on the gross income from stevedoring activities for loading and unloading cargo ships.[205]

SECTION 10

3. No State shall, without the Consent of Congress, lay any Duty of Tonnage, keep Troops, or Ships of War in time of Peace,

---

A duty of tonnage is a charge on a vessel, according to its cargo capacity, for entering or leaving a port or navigating public waters.

A state has the constitutional right, without the consent of Congress, to provide for and maintain a militia, although as we have noted, even this state power is subject to the supremacy and militia clauses (see page 96). A state may not keep a standing army or maintain its own navy without the consent of Congress.

SECTION 10

3. [continued] [No State shall, without the Consent of Congress] enter into any Agreement or Compact with another State,

---

"Read literally, the Compact Clause would require the states to obtain congressional approval before entering into any agreement themselves.... But it has never been so interpreted. Congressional assent is required only for agreements that enhance the political power of states in relation to the national government" or those that might offend the sovereignty of other states.[206] Thus, an agreement between New Hampshire and Maine "locating an ancient" boundary did not require congressional assent.[207] Nor was congressional approval required for the agreement among twenty-one states to establish an

---

[203] *Michelin Tire Corp.* v *Wages,* 423 US 276 (1976).

[204] *R. J. Reynolds Tobacco Co.* v *Durham,* 479 US 130 (1986).

[205] *Washington Revenue Department* v *Stevedoring Association,* 435 US 734 (1978).

[206] *Northeast Bancorp.* v *Board of Governors,* 472 US 159 (1985); *US Steel Corp.* v *Multistate Tax Commission,* 434 US 452 (1978); *New Hampshire* v *Maine,* 426 US 363 (1976); *Virginia* v *Tennessee,* 148 US 503 (1893).

[207] *New Hampshire* v *Maine,* 426 US 363 (1976).

administrative headquarters to audit multistate taxpayers and to facilitate the collection of state taxes from such taxpayers.[208]

When congressional consent is required Congress may give it in advance, as it has done many times; for example, when it authorizes states to make civil defense compacts to be effective sixty days after such agreements have been transmitted to Congress, unless Congress disapproves by concurrent resolution. Sometimes congressional consent is granted in more general terms, as when Congress gave approval for two or more states to enter into agreements for the cooperative enforcement of their respective criminal laws.

Congressional approval of an interstate compact makes such compact federal law subject to construction by federal rules rather than the rules of a state.[209] Disputes over the interpretation of such compacts are disputes between states and thus are subject to the original jurisdiction of the Supreme Court.[210]

Section 10
3. [continued] [No State shall, without the Consent of Congress, . . . enter into any Agreement or Compact] or with a foreign Power, or engage in War, unless actually invaded, or in such imminent Danger as will not admit of delay.

This clause reflects conditions in the eighteenth century, when it was possible that a state government might have to assume some responsibility for repelling a foreign invasion until the forces of the national government could be alerted and mobilized to do so.

The framers made it very clear, in every way possible, that the states have no right to negotiate with foreign countries. States have no power whatsoever to declare war—that power belongs to Congress alone. As to engaging in hostilities, any invasion of any state is an invasion of the United States.

ARTICLE II: THE EXECUTIVE ARTICLE

Section 1
1. The executive Power shall be vested in a President of the United States of America.

---

[208] *US Steel Corp.* v *Multistate Tax Commission,* 434 US 452 (1978); *Virginia* v *Tennessee,* 148 US 503 (1893).

[209] *Cuyler* v *Adams,* 449 US 433 (1981).

[210] *West Virginia ex rel Dyer* v *Sim* 1 US 22 (1951); *Nebraska* v *Iowa,* 406 US 117 (1972).

What is the significance of the fact that the words "herein granted," which appear in the legislative article, are omitted in the executive article? Does Section 1 confer the executive power on the president, or does it merely designate the title of the person who is given certain specified duties by the rest of the article? The more general view, and the one that conforms to presidential practices, is that this section gives the president a power that has never been defined or enumerated and, in fact, cannot be defined since its scope depends largely on circumstances. Although not so broad, this executive power is akin to the prerogative formerly claimed by the English Crown to act for the public good "without the prescription of the law" and "sometimes even against it."[1] The president can issue proclamations of neutrality, remove executive officials from office, make executive agreements with foreign nations, and take emergency action to preserve the nation, although such powers are not specifically granted to the president by the Constitution.

During the Korean War, President Truman ordered the secretary of commerce to take temporary possession of the steel mills to avoid a strike that would disrupt production of steel desperately needed to produce weapons of war. No law authorized this action. The Taft-Hartley Act, passed over his veto, gave the president the authority to seek an eighty-day court injunction against strikes that jeopardized the national safety, but the president refused to do so because the union had previously agreed to postpone the strike for a much longer period and because it would have been politically unwise for him to use it.

Where did the president secure his authority to order this seizure? From his inherent executive powers as well as his power as commander in chief, argued the attorneys for the president. The steel companies challenged this contention, and the Supreme Court agreed with them that the president had acted unconstitutionally.[2] Although Justice Black announced the opinion of the Court, only he clearly denied that the president had any general executive powers. Five other justices joined with him to reject the president's claim to act in this particular instance, but did so because Congress had indicated by the Taft-Hartley Act that the president should not seize property to avert strikes. In the absence of that legislation, a different question would have been presented. Moreover, it is possible that, if the justices had been convinced the emergency action was necessary, they would not have interfered, even in the face of the Taft-Hartley Act. When it is remembered that three justices agreed with the president and four carefully limited their concurrence to the particulars of the immediate case, the steel seizure decision does not appear to undermine the general position that the president has authority to act without prescription of law—and perhaps, in desperate situations, even against the law—to preserve the national safety. Such actions are subject, however, to the peril of subsequent judicial reversal, of impeachment, or of political defeat.

Presidential powers are interrelated with those of Congress. As Justice Rehnquist, quoting Justice Jackson from the steel seizure case, observed:

---

[1] John Locke in *Second Treatise of Civil Government*, ed. Charles L. Sherman (New York: D. Appleton-Century Co., 1937), 109.

[2] *Youngstown Sheet & Tube Co. v Sawyer*, 343 US 579 (1952).

When the President acts pursuant to an express or implied authorization from Congress, it is an exercise not only of presidential powers but also those delegated by Congress. "In such a case the executive action would be supported by the strongest of presumptions and the widest latitude of judicial interpretation, and the burden of persuasion would rest heavily upon any who might attack it.... When the President acts in the absence of congressional authorization he may enter a zone of twilight in which he and Congress may have concurrent authority, or in which its distribution is uncertain.... In such a case the... validity of the President's action, at least so far as separation of powers principles are concerned, hinges on a consideration of all the circumstances which might shed light on the views of the Legislative Branch toward such action, including congressional inertia, indifference, or quiescence." Finally, when the President acts in contravention of the will of Congress, "his power is at its lowest ebb," and the Court can sustain these actions "only by disabling the Congress from acting upon the subject."[3]

It should also be noted that in *United States* v *Curtiss-Wright Export Corp.*, Justice Sutherland, for a unanimous Court, staked out a special role for the president in the conduct of foreign affairs. He wrote: "[T]he President alone has the power to speak or listen as a representative of the nation." And quoting from the great John Marshall prior to his service on the Court, "The President is the sole organ of the nation in its external relations, and its sole representative with foreign nations."[4]

Since the steel seizure case, the Supreme Court has four times specifically acknowledged that the president has inherent executive authority, although in each instance it rejected the assertion that inherent presidential power applied in that particular case. In the first, a majority of the Court ruled that, because of the presumption against prior restraint of publications (see page 207), the executive authority of the president did not justify a court's acceding to the president's request to restrain a newspaper from publishing secret documents (the Pentagon Papers) that had fallen into its hands.[5] In the second case, a unanimous Court, one justice not participating, held that the executive authority of the president does not extend to authorizing electronic surveillance of conversations of persons suspected of engaging in domestic subversion.[6]

The third instance was the celebrated case of *United States* v *Nixon* (1974).[7] The Supreme Court rejected President Nixon's claim that he had an inherent power, growing out of the doctrine of separation of powers, to have an absolute say about what information he would withhold and what he would release to a court. There is no such absolute executive privilege. The responsibility to decide what information should be released and under what conditions

---

[3] Justice Rehnquist for the Court in *Dames & Moore v Regan*, 453 US 654 (1981), quoting Justice Jackson concurring in *Youngstown Sheet & Tube Co.* v *Sawyer*, 343 US 579 (1952).

[4] *United States* v *Curtiss-Wright Export Corp.*, 299 US 304 (1936).

[5] *New York Times Company* v *United States*, 403 US 713 (1971).

[6] *United States* v *United States District Court*, 407 US 297 (1972).

[7] *United States* v *Nixon*, 418 US 683 (1974).

is a judicial one, not an executive one. The president, like other persons, is subject to a subpoena of materials needed for criminal prosecutions. In this particular case, the Supreme Court, holding that the tapes in President Nixon's possession were needed for a criminal prosecution, thus sustained the order of the trial judge that the president release the materials to the court.

The Supreme Court also ruled, however, that the president does have a *limited executive privilege,* stemming both from the doctrine of separation of powers and from powers granted by Article II. *Executive privilege* is something that most presidents have long insisted vests in their office, but this was the first time the Supreme Court had acknowledged that it existed, albeit in a limited fashion. The president does have the right *to claim confidentiality of executive communications,* especially if claiming that their disclosure would reveal military or diplomatic secrets. Faced with such assertions, the courts are to show "utmost deference." And even outside those areas, the president's "singularly unique role" requires that great efforts be made to ensure that presidential communications be kept confidential. To that end, the trial judge was instructed to inspect the subpoenaed materials in camera (in secret) and to release only the information he thought related to the trial. Other material was to be returned to the president and "restored to its privileged status." In short, the president has the right to claim executive privilege for materials under his control, subject only to the limitation that if they are needed for a criminal trial and do not reveal military or diplomatic secrets, a trial judge may have limited access to them.

Left unanswered by the Supreme Court, since the issue was not before it, was the right of the president to withhold information from Congress. The principles of *United States* v *Nixon* would seem to suggest that under certain circumstances—for example, when the House of Representatives or one of its committees is carrying out its responsibilities under the impeachment clause— the doctrine of executive privilege would not justify the president's refusal to submit materials in response to a congressional subpoena. When President Nixon refused to release materials in connection with the House Judiciary Committee's investigation of activities that might warrant his impeachment, the House chose not to take the issue to the courts; rather, the president's failure to respond to the congressional subpoena became one of the grounds for the committee to recommend that he be impeached.

The fourth case relating to the inherent executive powers of the president grew out of negotiations with the Iranian government, conducted by President Carter and confirmed by President Reagan—negotiations that led to the release of American hostages. The president signed an executive agreement with Iran under which the United States agreed to terminate all legal proceedings in the United States by our nationals against the Iranian government and to transfer such claims to a specially created Iran-United States Claims Tribunal for binding arbitration. In addition, one billion dollars of the assets of Iran held by U.S. banks were transferred to English and Algerian banks to be held to cover the settlement of claims by American nationals. The rest of the Iranian assets held by American banks was returned to Iranian control. A unanimous Court upheld the president's power to act, even though it infringed on judicial power. The Court stressed the long-standing exercise by the president of the power to enter into executive agreements to settle claims, the long-standing acquiescence by Congress in the exercise of such presidential power, and, in this specific instance, the fact that Congress had taken no action to disapprove of what the president did. The Court cautiously decided, "While it is not concluded that the President has plenary power to settle claims, even against foreign governmental entities, nevertheless where, as here, the settlement of claims has been determined to be a necessary incident to the resolution of a major foreign policy dispute between this country and another, and Congress has acquiesced to the President's action, it cannot be said that the President lacks the power to settle such claims."[8]

SECTION 1
1. [continued] He shall hold his Office during the Term of four Years, and, together with the Vice President, chosen for the same term, be elected, as follows

---

See also the Twenty-second Amendment, which limits the president's tenure, and the Twenty-fifth Amendment, which provides for replacement of the vice president, whenever the office becomes empty.

SECTION 1
2. Each State shall appoint, in such Manner as the Legislature thereof may direct, a Number of Electors, equal to the whole Number of Senators and Representatives to which the State may be entitled in the Congress: but no Senator or Representative, or Person holding an Office of Trust or Profit under the United States, shall be appointed an Elector.

At various times, some state legislatures have directed the selection of presidential electors by the legislature itself, some by voters in districts, some by voters of the entire state, and some by a combination of these methods. At present—except for Maine, which elects two of its four electors by congressional districts—all electors in all states and in the District of Columbia are elected by voters on a statewide ticket.

In exercising this power, state legislatures are subject to all constitutional commands. In addition to the obviously applicable Fifteenth and Nineteenth Amendments, other clauses that particularly apply are the First Amendment and the equal protection clause of the Fourteenth, which, among other things,

---

[8] *Dames & Moore v Regan*, 453 US 654 (1981).

protect the rights of association as applied to minor parties. In addition to the clearly unconstitutional denial of the right to vote because of race or sex, a legislature cannot enforce a scheme that would give the voters in one part of a state more electoral votes than voters in another district. A state may not use procedures for nominating electors that make it too difficult for minor parties to get their presidential electoral candidates on the ballot,[9] that impose greater demands on city folks than on country people in order to get the candidates they favor on a ballot,[10] or that set too early a deadline for filing and make it too difficult for independent candidates to run for president.[11]

SECTION 1

3. [This entire paragraph has been superseded by the Twelfth Amendment.] The Electors shall meet in their respective States, and vote by Ballot for two Persons, of whom one at least shall not be an Inhabitant of the same State with themselves. And they shall make a List of all the Persons voted for, and of the Number of Votes for each; which List they shall sign and certify, and transmit sealed to the Seat of the Government of the United States, directed to the President of the Senate. The President of the Senate shall, in the Presence of the Senate and House of Representatives, open all the Certificates, and the Votes shall then be counted. The Person having the greatest Number of Votes shall be the President, if such Number be a Majority of the whole Number of Electors appointed; and if there be more than one who have such Majority, and have an equal Number of Votes, then the House of Representatives shall immediately chuse by Ballot one of them for President: and if no Person have a Majority, then from the five highest on the List the said House shall in like Manner chuse the President. But in chusing the President, the Votes shall be taken by States, the Representation from each State having one Vote; A quorum for this Purpose shall consist of a Member or Members from two thirds of the States, and a Majority of all the States shall be necessary to a Choice. In every Case, after the Choice of the President, the Person having the greatest Number of Votes of the Electors shall be the Vice President. But if there should remain two or more who have equal Votes, the Senate shall chuse from them by Ballot the Vice President.

The framers of the Constitution had difficulty in working out the procedures for selecting the president and the vice president. Selection by Congress was rejected because it would make the president dependent on Congress and would violate the doctrine of separation of powers. Election by the state legislatures was rejected because of lack of confidence in those bodies, which "had betrayed a strong propensity to a variety of pernicious measures."[12] Direct

---

[9] *Williams v Rhodes*, 393 US 23 (1968).

[10] *Moore v Ogilvie*, 394 US 814 (1969).

[11] *Anderson v Celebrezze*, 460 US 780 (1983).

[12] James Madison as quoted in *The Records of the Federal Convention of 1787*, ed. Max Farrand (New Haven: Yale University Press, 1937), vol. 2, 110.

popular election was rejected because the less populous states felt that the more populous states would always elect the president, and because most of the delegates thought that the expanse of the country rendered "it impossible that the people can have the requisite capacity to judge of the respective pretensions of the Candidates."[13] So, for lack of something better, the framers devised the system set forth in Section 1, paragraph 3, which they expected would work in somewhat the following fashion: the several state legislatures would prescribe procedures to select the most eminent persons in the states—electors—who would then cast their electoral ballots for the two persons they considered the best qualified to serve as president. When the votes of the electors of the various states were collected, the person with the most votes, provided those votes were a majority of those cast by the whole number of electors, was to be declared president; the person with the second-highest number of votes was to be vice president. It was expected that almost every elector would cast one vote for a candidate from his own state and that the votes would be so dispersed that often no person would have a majority. In that case, the House of Representatives, voting by states, would make the final selection from the five candidates receiving the most electoral votes.

But the framers reckoned this system without political parties. Parties, by presenting a single slate for president and vice president, completely changed the operation of the electoral system and thus made the original provision for it unworkable. The failure became apparent in the election of 1800, when Jefferson and Burr, the presidential and vice-presidential candidates of what we now call the Democratic Party, tied for first place in the electoral college. It was a major breakdown of the constitutional system, and the Twelfth Amendment was needed to repair the breach.

SECTION 1

4. The Congress may determine the Time of chusing the Electors, and the Day on which they shall give their Votes; which Day shall be the same throughout the United States.

Congress has designated the first Tuesday after the first Monday in November in presidential election years as the day for the selection of electors. The electors do not give their votes, however, until the first Monday after the second Wednesday in December. On that date the electors of each state assemble at such place as their state legislature directs (normally the state capitol), give their votes, and certify six lists, which are distributed as follows: one is sent by registered mail to the president of the Senate, two are delivered to the secretary of state of their state, two are sent by registered mail to the archivist of the United States, and one is delivered to the federal district judge of the district in which the electors have assembled. No chances are taken of

---

[13] George Mason, quoted ibid., vol. 2, 31.

losing these precious documents, which usually record a foregone conclusion. Then in January (see the Twentieth Amendment) the president of the Senate, in the presence of the Senate and the House of Representatives (see the Twelfth Amendment), opens the certificates and the electoral vote is counted; the winners are formally proclaimed elected.

Electors remain constitutionally free to cast their ballots for any person they wish. There have been maverick electors, who ignored the wishes of the voters who had chosen them, but in no case have they affected the outcome of an election. States may authorize political parties to require electors to pledge in advance that they will vote for the party candidate,[14] but what could be done to enforce such a pledge remains unsettled.

The states choose the electors, and the legislature of each state determines how electors will be selected, but Congress counts the votes. Most of the time the counting is routine, but in 1876 Congress found that Rutherford B. Hayes, the Republican candidate, had 165 uncontested electoral votes, Samuel J. Tilden, the Democrat, had 184 clear votes, one less than necessary, and there were disputes about which was the right slate of electors from Florida, South Carolina, and Louisiana and about one electoral vote in Oregon. How those disputes would be resolved would determine who would become president. The House was controlled by the Democrats, the Senate by the Republicans. The practice up to that time had been that the consent of both houses was required to validate the electoral count.

To break the deadlock, Congress, by an act approved by the president, created an electoral commission consisting of five house members chosen by the House, five senators chosen by the Senate, and five justices of the Supreme Court, four of whom were designated in the act, with the fifth to be chosen by those four. The electoral commission ended up with eight Republicans and seven Democrats, and by a vote of eight to seven the commission resolved the dispute in favor of Hayes.

As a result of that disputed election, Congress enacted a provision that if the vote of a state is not certified by the governor, it shall not be counted unless both houses of Congress concur.

SECTION 1

5. No Person except a natural born Citizen, or a Citizen of the United States, at the time of the Adoption of this Constitution, shall be eligible to the Office of President; neither shall any Person be eligible to that Office who shall not have attained to the Age of thirty five Years, and been fourteen Years a Resident within the United States.

This clause contains the only constitutional distinction between naturalized and natural-born citizens. Whether a person born abroad of American parents is a natural-born citizen within the meaning of this section has not yet been

---

[14] *Ray v Blair*, 343 US 214 (1952).

decided. There is a considerable body of opinion that such a person is "natural-born" even if perhaps not native-born. The issue is likely to be resolved only if a political party nominates a person born outside the United States to American citizens and he or she is elected. The answer will come from the electorate.

The Twelfth Amendment states explicitly that the same qualifications are required for eligibility for the vice presidency.

Before the election of President Hoover, there was some question whether the fourteen-year residence requirement meant any fourteen years or fourteen consecutive years immediately prior to election. Although a legal resident, Hoover had been abroad a good part of the fourteen years immediately preceding his nomination. His election settled any doubts; the interpretation of this requirement came from the most authentic source—the same source that created the Constitution—the people.

SECTION 1

6. In Case of the Removal of the President from Office, or of his Death, Resignation, or Inability to discharge the Powers and Duties of the said Office, the Same shall devolve on the Vice President, and the Congress may by Law provide for the Case of Removal, Death, Resignation or Inability, both of the President and Vice President, declaring what Officer shall then act as President, and such Officer shall act accordingly, until the Disability be removed, or a President shall be elected.

This clause is supplemented by the Twenty-fifth Amendment. The Twenty-fifth Amendment confirms the precedent established by John Tyler when he succeeded to the presidency on William Henry Harrison's death. He signed all state papers "John Tyler, President of the United States" and established that on the death or resignation of the president, the vice president becomes president, not merely acting president. In the event of the president's disability, the "powers and duties" of the presidency devolve on the vice president who serves only as acting president.

If there is no vice president (a contingency less likely to occur since the adoption of the Twenty-fifth Amendment), by act of Congress the first in the line of succession is the speaker of the House, followed by the president pro tempore of the Senate, the secretary of state, and the other cabinet officers in the order in which their departments were created. No one, however, may act as president without possessing the constitutional qualifications of a president. Cabinet members would serve only until either a speaker or a president pro tempore became qualified.

The Twenty-fifth Amendment provides procedures for judging whether the president is unable to discharge the duties of the office.

SECTION 1

7. The President shall, at stated Times, receive for his Services, a

Compensation, which shall neither be encreased nor diminished during the Period for which he shall have been elected,

To preserve the president's independence, Congress is prohibited from increasing or diminishing the president's salary during the period for which elected.

SECTION 1

7. [continued] and he shall not receive within that Period any other Emolument from the United States, or any of them.

This provision was inserted to prevent the president's own state from paying compensation and to ensure the president's independence from any state. The president is totally dependent on the federal government for salary, which is now $200,000 a year. It has not been increased for several decades. Also received are the use of the White House, free secretarial and executive assistance, and generous travel and official allowances.

SECTION 1

8. Before he enter on the Execution of his Office, he shall take the following Oath or Affirmation: "I do solemnly swear (or affirm) that I will faithfully execute the Office of President of the United States, and will to the best of my Ability, preserve, protect and defend the Constitution of the United States."

The chief justice of the United States normally administers this oath or affirmation, but any judicial officer may do so. Calvin Coolidge's father, a justice of the peace, administered the oath to his son.

SECTION 2

1. The President shall be Commander in Chief of the Army and Navy of the United States, and of the Militia of the several States, when called into the actual Service of the United States;

This is another provision to ensure civilian supremacy over the military. A civilian, the president, is commander in chief of our armed forces. (Although the air force is not mentioned in the Constitution, the president's status as commander in chief of that branch of the armed forces is not in question.) The president appoints all military officers with the consent of the Senate, governs hostile territories subjugated by our armed forces until their disposition is determined by Congress or by treaty, and, as commander in chief, makes the ultimate decisions on all matters of strategy.

The president's war powers are vastly more than purely military ones. During the Civil War, President Lincoln, as a war measure and without congressional authorization, in the Proclamation of Emancipation, declared that all slaves in areas in rebellion were free. Moreover, the president's powers as commander in chief are augmented by the executive powers and by such powers as Congress may delegate. Under conditions of total war, when the distinction between soldier and civilian may be blurred, the resulting "aggregate of powers" may be very great, although not unlimited. Outside the theater of war, the courts will review presidential acts.

During World War II, President Roosevelt authorized the army to create "defense zones" on the West Coast; under his order, supported by an act of Congress, 112,000 persons of Japanese ancestry (two-thirds of whom were citizens of the United States) were first compelled to obey a curfew and then forced out of their homes and put into relocation camps. The Supreme Court sustained the constitutionality of those measures not only on the general ground of military necessity, but also because it found no improper racial discrimination. The Supreme Court ruled, however, that the executive order did not justify the continued detention of such persons after their loyalty had been established nor could it have done so.[15] Nowadays, there is a consensus that there was no justification for the military orders and presidential measures and that they were, in fact, largely motivated by prejudice. Several decades later Congress appropriated funds for the partial reparation of those who were forced from their homes, and lower courts have reversed convictions of those charged with violating the curfew and resisting relocation.

The Court has not always gone along with the president. In *Ex parte Milligan* (1866), martial law had been declared in Indiana because of a threatened invasion. The Court set aside the declaration, ruling that martial law can never be applied to citizens in states where the courts are open and their processes unobstructed.[16] President Roosevelt's order establishing martial law in Hawaii after the attack on Pearl Harbor was held unconstitutional by the Court because it lacked such justification and was contrary to statute.[17] It should be noted that both of those cases were decided after the conclusion of hostilities.

Congress shares with the president authority over the armed forces: it supplies the money and makes regulations for their governance. Although Congress has the power to "declare war," the president, as commander in chief, may send the military forces where he wishes and give them orders that may lead to hostilities. The president may direct our foreign relations to that end. President Polk, by sending troops into disputed territory, deliberately precipitated the Mexican War. President Truman ordered American forces to resist communist aggression in Korea; President Johnson used military power to intervene in the Dominican Republic; Presidents Eisenhower, Kennedy, and Johnson ordered American forces into Vietnam, although before the major

---

[15] *Korematsu v United States*, 323 US 214 (1944); *Hirabayashi v United States*, 320 US 81 (1943); *Ex parte Endo*, 323 US 283 (1944).

[16] *Ex parte Milligan*, 4 Wallace 2 (1866).

[17] *Duncan v Kahanamoku*, 327 US 304 (1946).

escalation of our military effort in Vietnam, President Johnson secured from Congress a resolution to support his action. President Reagan sent troops to invade Grenada and told Congress about it afterwards. He also ordered troops into Beirut and the Persian Gulf. President Bush sent troops into Panama to remove General Manuel Noriega from office, and he sent more than 400,000 troops into the Middle East to expel Iraqi forces from Kuwait and to prevent them from invading Saudi Arabia and from taking possession of a good share of the world's oil. President Clinton sent troops as part of a UN force to help feed the people and secure the peace of Somalia.

An example of the president's power over the armed forces that had less serious consequences occurred when President Theodore Roosevelt sent the navy halfway around the world after Congress had threatened to withhold appropriations for a global tour. Congress was then presented with the choice of appropriating money to bring the fleet home or leaving it where it was.

Throughout our history, Congress has resisted, but with little success, the president's predominant role in controlling our military forces. Whenever it chooses to do so, Congress clearly has the constitutional authority to refuse to grant funds for military uses or to place conditions on the use of the funds it does grant. As a practical political fact, however, it has been difficult for Congress to resist the president or to limit the way in which the authority of the commander in chief of the armed forces is exercised. The Vietnam conflict, however, caused Congress, near the end of that war, to become increasingly assertive of its authority. In 1970 Congress stipulated that no funds should be used to send ground troops into Cambodia or Laos, an unprecedented restraint on presidential discretion to send armed forces wherever the president thinks necessary.

Then, in the War Powers Act of 1973, Congress stipulated that thenceforth, in every possible instance, before the president commits the armed forces of the United States into the locations where "imminent hostilities" are probable, Congress should be consulted and that forces should be committed only (1) pursuant to a declaration of war by Congress, (2) by specific statutory authorization, or (3) in a national emergency. After committing the armed forces under the third condition, the president is to report within forty-eight hours to Congress, and the troop commitment is to be terminated within sixty days "after imminent hostilities" unless Congress concurs with the presidential action. Another thirty days are allowed if the president certifies to Congress that unavoidable military necessity, involving the safety of United States forces, requires continued use of the troops. The president is to end any deployment of troops at any time if so directed by Congress by a concurrent resolution, which is not subject to a presidential veto.

There has been a constant debate between presidents and congressional leaders over the application of the War Powers Act. Presidents have not been willing to adhere strictly to the reporting requirements and it is not always obvious whether or not our forces are in situations where imminent involvement in hostilities is clearly probable. For example, when President Reagan sent forces into Lebanon, there was considerable debate between the president and Congress about whether the act should come into play. President Reagan insisted that the American military forces had not been committed to engage in hostile actions and that therefore the War Powers Act did not apply. Congress insisted that it did. Congress adopted a resolution, and the president signed it. The resolution superseded the War Powers Act and set a time limit for the involvement of our troops in Lebanon. When President Reagan ordered the bombing of Libya, he called a bipartisan group of congressional leaders to the White House, after he had given final approval for the raid and after the bombers had taken off. After the raid, Reagan filed a report but, like his predecessors, did so "'in accordance with desire that the Congress be informed on this matter, and consistent with the War Powers Resolution,' thereby again refusing to acknowledge that he was reporting under the War Powers Resolution."[18] President Bush did the same thing when he sent troops into Panama. In his letter to congressional leaders he refused to put any time limit on the operation and to avoid any appearance of complying with the Act, he informed Congress of his notification as being "consistent" with the act, but not "pursuant to it."[19] He followed the same practice in August of 1990 when he dispatched troops to Saudi Arabia and imposed a military blockade of Iraq after that country invaded Kuwait.[20] Subsequently he asked Congress for authority to use troops to expel Iraqi forces from Kuwait, and after two days of debate Congress granted such authority to him.

President Clinton has shown a greater inclination to consult with Congress prior to the deployment of the military forces, in part to be explained by the fact that he and the congressional leaders are from the same political party, in part because by the 1990s the Cold War permitted somewhat greater time for deliberations and consultation not only with the Congress but with the United Nations.

Perhaps more significant than these attempts by Congress to limit presidential discretion to deploy the armed forces are growing political restraints. As recent history in Korea and Vietnam illustrates, presidents and their parties run a serious risk of defeat in the next presidential election if the armed forces are used, with or without congressional approval, as an instrument of foreign policy and the result is a substantial number of American casualties over an extended period of time.

SECTION 2

1. [continued] he [the President] may require the Opinion, in writing, of the principal Officer in each of the executive Departments, upon any Subject relating to the Duties of their respective Offices,

---

[18] Michael Rubner, "Antiterrorism and the Withering of the 1973 War Powers Resolution," *Political Science Quarterly* 102, no. 2 (Summer 1987): 210.

[19] *Congressional Quarterly*, December 30, 1989, 3557.

[20] L. Gordon Crovitz, "War Power Resolution Hasn't Saved Saddam Hussein—Yet," *The Wall Street Journal* (August 29, 1990): A9.

Although there is no mention of the cabinet in the original Constitution, that body came into existence as early as 1793; from the beginning, the president's power over the heads of the major executive departments has extended beyond merely requiring written reports upon subjects relating to the duties of their respective offices. Cabinet members serve at the president's pleasure, and presidential control over their official acts is complete. The executive departments, however, and usually their duties, are created by law, and the money needed for their operation comes from Congress.

The cabinet has never been a prominent feature of American government, and its collective advice is seldom significant. With the adoption of the Twenty-fifth Amendment the cabinet, in deciding whether the president may be "disabled," has been given a constitutional role of importance.

SECTION 2

1. [continued] and he shall have Power to grant Reprieves and Pardons for Offenses against the United States, except in Cases of Impeachment.

A reprieve postpones punishment. There have not been many requests for reprieves since the federal death penalty was struck down by the Supreme Court because of the procedures by which it has been imposed. We can anticipate that there will be more in the future since federal law is being amended to impose the death penalty for more and more federal crimes. A full pardon restores persons to all civil rights and revises their legal status in all respects. In most instances, however, the president merely grants a limited pardon and restores some civil rights, a practice upheld by the Supreme Court.[21]

The president can pardon persons before they are formally charged or have been brought to trial, during the trial, or after conviction. (The president cannot pardon people before they commit an offense, for no one can be excused from obeying the law.) The power extends only to offenses against the United States, not to those against the laws of a state. The most celebrated presidential pardon was President Ford's pardon of former President Richard M. Nixon. Nixon had not been charged with any crime, but President Ford pardoned him for any crimes that he might have committed while president.

The president's power to pardon extends to persons held in criminal (but not civil) contempt of court by a federal judge. "The power flows from the Constitution alone ... and ... it cannot be modified, abridged, or diminished by the Congress."[22] The president may reduce or commute sentences and may impose conditions even though the conditions are not provided by statute. The president may not, however, set conditions that offend the Constitution or that make the sentence more, rather than less, severe.

---

[21] *Schick* v *Reed,* 419 US 256 (1974).
[22] Ibid.

President Carter used the power when he first came into office to grant "full, complete and unconditional pardon" to all persons, whether or not they had been formally convicted, who had violated the draft laws during the Vietnam era, except military deserters, employees of the selective service system, and persons who had violated the draft laws through force or violence. Americans who had left the United States to avoid the draft and had become citizens of another country were permitted to return freely and reapply for their citizenship. Congress reacted angrily to this use of the presidential pardon, by barring the use of certain supplemental appropriations for the administration of the amnesty program, but since expenses were minimal and other funds were available, the congressional protest was symbolic.

Most of the time presidential pardoning power is exercised routinely. Each year about 400 people petition the president for executive clemency, asking for a reduced prison term or a pardon. The requests are processed by a pardon attorney according to guidelines established by the president.

SECTION 2

2. He shall have Power, by and with the Advice and Consent of the Senate, to make Treaties, provided two thirds of the Senators present concur;

The Senate as a body has provided the president with very little formal advice beyond votes approving or disapproving of treaties. The president nevertheless seeks advice from senatorial leaders from time to time, especially members of the Senate Committee on Foreign Relations. In general, the president negotiates a treaty and then presents it to the Senate for approval. The final step in the making of a treaty is its ratification, which, precisely speaking, is the president's act.

There are several reasons for the two-thirds vote requirement. The southern states were afraid the northern states, which were in a majority, would negotiate treaties disadvantageous to them. They remembered that John Jay of New York, secretary of foreign affairs for the Confederation, had proposed a treaty with Spain conceding the right to close the mouth of the Mississippi at New Orleans in return for concessions to northern merchants. The two-thirds rule gives sectional groups the power to veto such treaties.

In addition to being international compacts, treaties are the "supreme law of the land," and their self-executing provisions are, therefore, enforced by courts, just as any other laws; this fact, too, is sometimes urged in favor of the two-thirds requirement.

Now that the United States is continuously involved in international negotiations, the process of treaty making has achieved considerable significance. At the same time, the two-thirds rule makes it possible for a few senators representing perhaps a minority of the electorate to block treaties desired by the majority, and many have suggested that ratification be by a simple majority of *both* houses of Congress. There are, however, some senators who think that the treaty-making procedures should be made more difficult. Adherents to this view have proposed that, in addition to the two-thirds requirement, the approval of both houses be required before a treaty shall operate as law. In point of fact, since the House of Representatives must approve any appropriations or any legislation necessary to carry out the terms of the treaty, it already enjoys considerable power in this area.

Securing a two-thirds vote of the Senate for treaty ratification has at various times imposed obstacles to the ratification, and it is not surprising that various ways have been devised to get around those obstacles. One is the joint resolution of Congress, an ordinary legislative procedure. Texas was annexed in this fashion after the Senate refused to do so by treaty. The North American Free Trade Agreement (NAFTA) was considered in this fashion. Another device is the *executive agreement,* of which there are two types. (1) Inasmuch as Congress and the president have cognate powers in the field of foreign affairs, it is constitutionally permissible for Congress to delegate to the president more legislative powers than would be allowable in domestic affairs, although these days the Supreme Court places few obstacles in the way of congressional delegation of larger amounts of discretion in domestic affairs (see pages 24–25). Thus, the president is often empowered by Congress to make executive agreements, for example, reciprocal tariff agreements. (2) As part of undefined executive powers, growing out of the authority to appoint and receive diplomatic officials, and as the nation's official spokesperson, the president has the power to negotiate with foreign nations agreements that do not require the consent of Congress. As long as the agreements are not countermanded by Congress, they, like treaties, become the "law of the land."

It was once thought that executive agreements differed from treaties in that they were concerned with affairs of less importance; in fact, executive agreements have sometimes dealt with highly important matters. For example, in September 1940 President Roosevelt handed over to Great Britain fifty naval vessels in exchange for certain leases of military bases. The Atlantic Charter in 1941, the Yalta Agreement of 1944, and the Potsdam Agreement of 1945 are other examples of executive agreements. In 1970 President Nixon signed an "Agreement of Friendship and Cooperation" with Spain that constitutes a significant security guarantee. And in most years there are about five times more executive agreements implemented than formal treaties ratified.

As part of its reassertion of congressional authority in the field of foreign affairs, Congress, in the Case Act of 1972, required the secretary of state to notify Congress within sixty days of any executive agreement. If the agreement has national security considerations, notification may be made on a classified basis, with only members of the House and Senate Foreign Affairs Committees being told of the agreement.

Since the adoption of the Case Act, there has been considerable conflict between the president and the Department of State on one side and congressional leaders on the other over the definition of an executive agreement. The president and the Department of State define executive agreements as those reached with another nation under the president's constitutional powers to conduct foreign relations or to act as commander in chief, or under authority granted to the president by Congress. Administration spokespersons maintain that a mere exchange of understandings between the president and the head of another nation is not covered by the Case Act, not even the European Declaration signed in Helsinki in 1975, in which the heads of many nations indicated their agreement not to interfere with the existing boundaries in Europe. Some members of Congress take issue with this narrow definition of an executive agreement and have pressed, so far unsuccessfully, for legislation that would require the president to submit executive agreements for congressional review and possible veto.

Once a treaty has been ratified or an executive agreement implemented, courts have authority to construe the agreement.[23] But who has the power to abrogate treaties? The Constitution is silent. After President Carter terminated a mutual defense treaty with Taiwan as part of the agreements leading to recognition of the People's Republic of China, several senators filed a suit asking a federal judge to set aside the presidential action. They charged that the president could not abrogate a defense treaty without the consent of the Senate or Congress. The Supreme Court dismissed the case: four justices balked on the grounds that the issues were political—a dispute between Congress and the president in which courts should not intervene; the fifth, Justice Powell, balked on the grounds that the issue was not ready for judicial disposition, since neither the Senate nor the House had chosen to confront the president on the matter. Only Justice Brennan went to the merits, and he was of the view that abrogation of the defense treaty with Taiwan was a necessary incident to executive recognition of the Beijing government and was part of the presidential power to recognize and withdraw recognition from foreign governments.[24]

Section 2

2. [continued] and he [the President] shall nominate, and by and with the Advice and Consent of the Senate, shall appoint Ambassadors, other public Ministers and Consuls, Judges of the supreme Court, and all other Officers of the United States, whose Appointments are not herein otherwise provided for, and which shall be established by Law: Officers who are appointed by the president with the advice and consent of the Senate (only a majority vote is required) are known as superior, or senatorial, officers. Officers who can, if Congress permits, be appointed by the president alone, by the courts, or by heads of departments, are known as inferior officers.

There have been several significant appointments clause cases in recent years. Congress violated the appointments clause and the principle of separation of powers when it provided in the 1974 amendments to the Federal Election

---

[23] *Japan Whaling Assn.* v *Amer. Cetacean Soc.*, 478 US 221 (1986).
[24] *Goldwater et al.* v *Carter, President of the United States*, 444 US 996 (1979).

Campaign Act of 1971 for the appointment of two members of the Federal Election Commission by the president, two by the Senate, and two by the House, with confirmation of all six members by both the House and the Senate. It would have been different if the commission had been merely an advisory body like the Civil Rights Commission, some of whose members are selected by the speaker, some by the president pro tempore of the Senate, and some by the president. But the only way "officers of the United States," who exercise significant authority to administer government programs and enforce the law, may be appointed is in the manner prescribed by the appointments clause.

The 1974 procedures for the selection of members of the Federal Election Commission also violated the Constitution by calling for the confirmation of the officers of the FEC by the House and the Senate. The Constitution permits confirmation only by the Senate, not by the Senate and the House.[25]

An appointments clause issue was also raised by the Independent Counsel Case. Congress created an office of independent prosecutor to handle cases of alleged illegal conduct on the part of highly placed executive officials. These independent prosecutors were appointed by a panel of federal judges on petition of the attorney general. The fact that special prosecutors were selected by a special Article III court created little concern to the Supreme Court, which cited a recently decided case upholding the power of federal judges to appoint private counsel to prosecute contempt of court charges.[26] More difficult were the constraints on presidential powers to remove special prosecutors (see page 135).

Another appointments clause issue was presented by a challenge to the practice of every president since Eisenhower of asking the American Bar Association's Committee on Federal Judiciary to review the qualifications of persons being considered for presidential nominations to the federal bench. A public interest group, vexed by what it considered to be this committee's tendency to give low ratings to conservatives, sought a declaratory judgment that the Committee was an official advisory committee within the meaning of the Federal Advisory Committee Act which requires such committees to follow certain rules, including deliberating in public. The Court concluded, however, that, although the language of the act would seem to be to the contrary, the ABA committee is not governed by the FACA, in part because if FACA were to be construed to apply to these presidential deliberations, it would present "formidable constitutional difficulties" with respect to whether FACA unduly infringed on the president's appointive powers and thus violated the doctrine of separation of powers. Said Justice Brennan for the Court, "We are loath to conclude that Congress intended to press ahead into dangerous constitutional thickets in the absence of firm evidence that it courted those perils." Justice Kennedy, with the concurrence of the Chief Justice and Justice O'Connor, took issue with the majority's use of legislative history to set aside the precise words

---

[25] *Buckley* v *Valeo*, 424 US 1 (1976).
[26] *Morrison* v *Olson*, 486 US 654 (1988); *Young* v *United States ex rel Vuitton*, 481 US 787 (1987).

of a statute and held that the application of FACA in this context would be a plain violation of the appointments clause of the Constitution. Justice Kennedy pointed out that the clause divides the appointment power into two separate spheres. "The President nominates, the Senate gives or withholds its advice and consent, but neither the Senate nor the Congress has any role in choosing the person to be nominated."[27]

The Senate has normally refused to give its consent to federal appointments when there is objection from a senator from the state in which the office is located, provided the senator is of the same party as the president. This practice, known as *senatorial courtesy*, permits a senator to veto presidential appointments and gives each senator extensive control over federal patronage in his or her state. Because of this custom, senators from the state in which the appointment is to be made are usually consulted by the president before the appointment is sent to the Senate for confirmation. So strong is senatorial deference to each other on these patronage matters that the Democratic controlled Senate would not allow President Bush to ignore the wishes of their Republican senatorial colleagues.

The "consent of the Senate" part of this clause is subject to increasing attention these days. Until recently, once the Senate was assured of a candidate's integrity, fairness, and legal competence, the rules of the game called for the Senate to give its consent to the presidential nominations of a federal judge, especially to the courts of appeals where "senatorial courtesy" is less operative and most especially to the Supreme Court where senatorial courtesy is not operative. Although concerns about integrity, fairness, and legal competence often mask concerns about substantive issues of constitutional orientation, the conventions required there be a rather subdued discussion about constitutional issues and only a veiled reference to expected judicial policy choices.

Nowadays, with a more sophisticated understanding that the federal judges, especially Supreme Court justices, are key players in resolving the great issues of our times and that they must make choices among competing political values, there is a more open concern about how the nominees feel about current constitutional issues—abortion, affirmative action, privacy, rights of persons accused of crime, and so on. Many believe that the contentious 1988 Senate hearings (see page 141) on President Reagan's nomination of Judge Bork to the Supreme Court and the Senate's eventual refusal to give its consent created a watershed marking a new Senate vigor in exercising its "consent" power, although the Democratic Senate was more inclined to oppose Republican George Bush's nominations, especially particularly late in his term than is likely to be the case with respect to President Clinton's nominations. In any case, it is still considered improper for judicial candidates to respond to senatorial probes as to how they will vote in specific cases. And convention still call for considerable senatorial deference to presidential choices, since, as we have noted, the president's power to nominate judges is the major link between

---

[27] *Public Citizen* v *Dept. of Justice*, 489 US 1006 (1989).

the electorate and federal courts. Nonetheless, the Senate takes its consent role very seriously, and there is a growing tendency to search out the constitutional values of the future judges and justices, especially when the Senate is controlled by a different party from the White House.

SECTION 2.

but the Congress may by Law vest the Appointment of such inferior Officers, as they think proper, in the President alone, in the Courts of Law, or in the Heads of Departments.

This clause prevents Congress from dispensing the power to appoint officers of the United States too freely. Any appointee exercising significant authority pursuant to the laws of the United States is an "Officer of the United States," who must be selected according to this clause. "Neither Congress nor the president can waive this structural protection for the principles of separation of powers." It does not apply, however, to employees. Congress may vest the appointment of these "lesser functionaries," that is, employees, wherever it so decides.

The Court has dealt with the issue of what is a court of law or head of a department in only one case. It recently concluded that the Tax Court, an Article I court (see page 92), is a "court of law" and thus its chief judge can be vested with the appointment of special trial judges who hear and prepare findings and written opinions which become binding upon approval by the Tax Court. Justices Scalia, O'Connor, Kennedy, and Souter in concurrence agreed that Congress could vest the appointment of special trial judges in the chief judge of the Tax Court but not because that court in their opinion is a court of law, but because the Tax Court is really an administative agency and the chief judge is the head of an executive department.[28]

SECTION 2

3. The President shall have Power to fill up all Vacancies that may happen during the Recess of the Senate, by granting Commissions which shall expire at the End of their next Session.

The word "happen" here has come to mean "happen to exist." The clause allows the president to fill temporarily any vacancies while the Senate is recessed, no matter how or when they occurred.

This clause provides an interesting example of the questions that remain, after two hundred years, about the meaning of what appears to be uncompli-

---

[28] *Freytag v Commissioner*, 115 L Ed 2d 764 (1991).

cated constitutional language. From 1789 to 1980 many federal judges were appointed by presidents under this clause. Although there were doubts about the wisdom of such appointments, there was no constitutional challenge to the practice. Then, in December of 1980, President Carter, after he had lost the election and while the Senate was in recess, made an interim appointment to the federal district court. The man thus appointed had previously been nominated for approval by the Senate, but the Senate had recessed without having confirmed him or sixteen other Carter nominees. His nomination was withdrawn by President Reagan almost immediately after he assumed office, but the judge continued to sit for 50 weeks. His actions as a judge were challenged, and a panel of the Court of Appeals for the Ninth Circuit held the appointment unconstitutional but the decision was reversed by the appellate court en banc (the entire court),[29] thus maintaining the president's power to make recess appointments of a judge.

President Bush in 1992 used his recess appointment power to reappoint the eleven members of the board of directors of the Legal Service Corporation, which has been a continuing source of conflict between those who want it to provide help to poor individuals and those who see it as a source to empower the poor as a class. The appointees were the same eleven members Bush had previously appointed under a recess appointment which expired because they had not been confirmed by the Senate. This action breached a 1984 agreement with Congress that the president would make such recess appointments only when Congress was out of session for 30 days or more.

The Clinton administration, however, has taken the side of the Bush administration in arguing that the president has the power to make a recess appointment even if the Senate recesses as briefly as half an hour, that is, whenever "the gavel fails to summon the regular session into being."[30] Democrats in the Senate have argued that "recess" means between breaks in congressional sessions, that is, an "intrasessional adjournment." The argument is presently before the federal courts.

SECTION 3
He shall from time to time give to the Congress Information of the State of the Union, and recommend to their Consideration such Measures as he shall judge necessary and expedient;

The opening address of the president at each session of Congress is known as the State of the Union message. George Washington and John Adams gave their addresses in person, but Jefferson sent his in writing. President Wilson revived the practice of personally delivering the speech.

---

[29] *United States* v *Woodley*, 751 F 2d 1009 (9th Cir 1985).

[30] Bill McAllister, "Strange Bedfellows: The Clinton White House Goes to Court to Defend a Bush Position on Recess Appointments," *The Washington Post National Weekly Edition*, July 26–August 2, 1993, p. 34.

At the beginning of each session, the president is now also required by law to send Congress a budget message and an economic report. From time to time the president sends messages, addresses Congress on specific subjects, and makes recommendations for legislation. In this manner the president is able to focus national attention on national problems. As an extension of this practice, the executive branch develops many legislative proposals, which are then formally introduced by members of Congress.

SECTION 3

[continued] he may, on extraordinary Occasions, convene both Houses, or either of them,

---

Whenever it is thought necessary, the president can call a special session of Congress. Once in session, Congress has full powers. In contrast, most state legislatures, when called into special session, are limited to discussion and action on the particular matters laid before them by the governor.

Nowadays, Congress is in session almost all of the time, and there is no need for special sessions. In the past, in addition to special sessions of Congress, the Senate was occasionally called into special session by itself to ratify treaties and appointments, which it does without the concurrence of the House.

SECTION 3

[continued] and in Case of Disagreement between them, with Respect to the Time of Adjournment, he may adjourn them to such Time as he shall think proper;

The president has never been called upon to exercise this duty.

SECTION 3

[continued] he shall receive Ambassadors and other public Ministers;

The president is the only officer who can speak officially for the United States to foreign governments. Foreign governments may speak to the United States only through the president, or the president's agent, usually the secretary of state. The president's power to receive ambassadors includes the power to recognize new states or governments.

The increasing importance of foreign relations during the last several decades accounts in no small part for the increasing power of the president in all fields. The nature of the problems of foreign policy requires that the initiative and general direction be in the president's hands.

SECTION 3
[continued] he shall take Care that the Laws be faithfully executed,

The president's duty to see that the laws are enforced is supported by his powers as commander in chief. As already pointed out, Congress very early authorized the president to use the armed forces when necessary to overcome combinations too powerful to be dealt with by judges, federal marshals, and the regular federal police forces.

The president is constitutionally obliged by this clause to enforce all the laws of the United States, whether or not the president approves of them, including all federal court decisions and all regulations of federal agencies, as they apply to all the people all the time. But there are so many laws and regulations that the president of course has great discretion in deciding which laws and regulations will take priority. The Reagan and Bush administrations, for example, were less vigorous than the Carter administration in enforcing laws and regulations relating to the civil rights of minorities and women, but gave more attention to laws and regulations relating to the rights of children and fetuses. The Clinton administration has returned to the pattern of the Carter administration.

Does this clause require the president to comply with all laws? This question was raised when Congress, by what has come to be known as the Boland Amendment, prohibited any agency of the United States involved in intelligence activities, directly or indirectly, from using any funds to support any groups operating in Nicaragua. When it was discovered that federal funds from the sale of arms to Iran had been diverted to help the Contras, a group working to overthrow the then-communist government of Nicaragua, President Reagan at first denied knowledge of such activities. Subsequently he argued that such a law was only advisory to him and the National Security Agency, since that agency was not engaged in intelligence. Moreover, the president argued that, because of his own constitutional status as commander in chief and as the chief spokesperson for the United States, the Boland Amendment could not constitutionally be applied to him or his direct agents in dealing with foreign affairs. His critics, including many members of Congress from both parties, contended that Congress intended the law to apply and that the president had a responsibility under this clause to see to it that he and those who reported to him complied with it.[31]

President Bush also pressed the claim that as president he was not required to implement laws he believed to be unconstitutional. He did not assert, however, although some in his administration did so, what is known as "nonacquiescence," that is, the argument that the executive does not have to follow the policies found in the judicial rulings of the lower courts with which the president disagrees, before the Supreme Court has ruled definitively on the matters in question.

---

[31] Stuart Taylor, Jr., "A New Stand over Contras," *The New York Times* (May 25, 1987): 1.

In addition to being a grant of power to the president, this clause limits congressional power. Under the separation of powers doctrine, the president, not the Congress, executes the laws. Thus, the Court declared unconstitutional a provision of the Gramm-Rudman-Hollings Act that gave the comptroller general, an officer removable by Congress, a responsibility under certain circumstances to put into effect budget reductions. "The Constitution does not," said the Court majority, "contemplate an active role for Congress in the supervision of officers charged with the execution of the laws it enacts. . . ." To permit an officer controlled by Congress to execute the laws would be, in essence, to permit a congressional veto. Congress could simply remove, or threaten to remove, an officer for executing the laws in any fashion found to be unsatisfactory to Congress.[32]

SECTION 3
[continued] and shall Commission all the Officers of the United States.

How this clause, the appointments clause, the faithfully-execute-the-law clause, and the undefined executive power clause all add up to protect or limit presidential *removal* powers has generated a considerable number of pages of judicial opinions. In *Myers* v *United States* (1926), the Court announced that, since presidents are charged with the duty of faithfully executing the laws, they therefore must have control over those through whom enforcement takes place and Congress could not restrict the presidential power to remove *executive* officers.[33] Then in *Humphrey's Executor* v *United States* (1935), the Court held that this unlimitable removal power, however, does not extend to officers who have quasi-legislative or quasi-judicial functions conferred upon them by act of Congress, such as members of the Federal Trade Commission, the Interstate Commerce Commission, or the Federal Communications Commission.[34] The president has no authority to remove those officers except as outlined by Congress.[35]

What makes an officer quasi-legislative or quasi-judicial, and what are the distinctions between executive and legislative powers, are not questions to which there are easy answers or "bright-line rules."[36] In *Morrison* v *Olson* (1986) the Court upheld a constraint upon the president's powers (in reality the attorney general's) to remove special prosecutors—only for good cause, physical disability, mental incapacity, or any other condition that substantially impairs the performance of such independent counsel's duties. "The Court

---

[32] *Bowsher* v *Synar*, 478 US 186 (1986).

[33] *Myers* v *United States*, 272 US 52 (1926).

[34] *Humphrey's Executor* v *United States*, 295 US 602 (1935).

[35] *Wiener* v *United States*, 357 US 349 (1958); *Myers* v *United States*, 272 US 52 (1926); *Humphrey's Executor* v *United States*, 295 US 602 (1935).

[36] *Wiener* v *United States*, 357 US 349 (1958).

announced that whether the Constitution permits Congress to impose a 'good cause' type of restriction on the president's power to remove an official cannot be made to turn on whether or not that official is classified as 'purely executive.'" The issue is not to define "rigid categories of those officials who may or may not be removed at will by the President, but to ensure that Congress does not interfere with the President's exercise of the 'executive power' and his constitutionally appointed duty to 'take care that the laws be faithfully executed. . . .'" "The real question," wrote the Court, "is whether the removal restrictions are of such a nature that they impede the President's ability to perform his constitutional duty."[37]

In summary, there are a few executive officers who must be removable at will by the president. For most federal officers, however, although Congress may not insert itself into the removal process, it may by law limit their removal for cause, provided it does not impede the president's ability to perform his constitutional duty.

SECTION 4

The President, Vice President and all civil Officers of the United States, shall be removed from Office on Impeachment for, and Conviction of, Treason, Bribery, or other High Crimes and Misdemeanors.

Members of the House and of the Senate are not civil officers of the United States subject to this clause.

The interpretation of the impeachment provisions is primarily the responsibility of the House and the Senate. Fortunately, only a few precedents are available to give us guidance as to their meaning. The first person to be impeached was Senator William Blount from Tennessee in 1797, but the Senate dismissed the proceedings against him after deciding that members of Congress are not civil officers of the United States subject to impeachment. The Senate did, however, expel Senator Blount.

What are impeachable offenses? Throughout our history there have been three constructions:

1. A *loose construction,* that incompetent or politically objectionable officers, especially if they be judicial officers, are liable to impeachment and removal from office. This view appears to have been the position of Thomas Jefferson. If it had been adopted by Congress, it could have made our governmental system similar to the British system, in which government officials may be turned out of office because of lack of confidence in them, without any suggestion of wrongdoing on their part.

---

[37] *Morrison v Olson,* 486 US 654 (1988).

2. A *strict constuction,* that the only impeachable offenses are those that break criminal laws. This position was the view of President Nixon and the lawyers who defended him. It appears to have been the view also of many of those who voted not to sustain the impeachment charges against Justice Chase and President Andrew Johnson. (There is a related but separable question of the converse of this view: does conviction of a criminal offense call for impeachment and removal from office? Although conduct that causes criminal conviction may lead to impeachment, impeachment and criminal proceedings are separate. Judge Harry Claiborne, after a jury trial, was convicted by a federal court of tax evasion. He refused to resign. The House then brought in four articles of impeachment, three stating that the Senate should remove Judge Claiborne from office upon an independent finding by the Senate that he had willfully filed false tax returns. The fourth article was based on the view that conviction by a federal court of a serious crime is by itself sufficient grounds for the Senate to act. The Senate, by two-thirds, voted guilty on the three impeachment articles based on independent findings. Although a majority of those present and voting voted guilty on the fourth article, the vote was less than two-thirds, so Judge Claiborne was not found guilty as charged in that particular article. Likewise, when Judge Walter Nixon was convicted of impeachment charges, the Senate failed to adopt a charge that he had called the judiciary into disrespect by having been convicted of perjury.)

3. The prevailing *moderate construction* that impeachable offenses need not be criminal in character but must reflect a serious dereliction of duty, a substantial violation of constitutional and legal responsibilities, or a sustained failure to meet one's obligations. This construction was the view of those on the House Judiciary Committee who voted to impeach President Nixon. It was also the view of those who voted to impeach and then convict Judge Robert W. Archbald (1912–1913) and Judge Halsted L. Ritter (1933–1936), each of whom was convicted on charges of misconduct in office and judicial improprieties, although in neither instance were the offenses criminal.

That a person may be impeached even if not found guilty of a crime is also clear from the impeachment and removal of Judge Alcee L. Hastings after he had been *acquitted* early in 1983 of the charge that he had accepted a bribe in return for lenience toward defendants in a case he was handling. Four years later, after investigation by the Judicial Council of the 11th circuit, the Judicial Conference of the United States recommended to the House that it begin an impeachment enquiry. The House brought in seventeen articles of impeachment, the Senate voted on eleven, and by a two-thirds vote found Hastings guilty of eight of them, including conspiracy to obtain a bribe.

May a person be impeached and removed from office for misconduct performed before assuming office? We have no precedents. Vice President Agnew's
resignation and pleading no contest to certain offenses, some of which took
place while he was governor of Maryland, made it unnecessary for Congress to
face that issue.

ARTICLE III: THE JUDICIAL ARTICLE

SECTION 1
The Judicial Power of the United States

The Constitution merely prescribes the boundaries of the judicial power
of the United States. Except for the original jurisdiction of the Supreme Court
(see page 150), no federal court has jurisdiction over any case unless Congress
exercises its power under this clause. Although until recently Congress gave
federal courts jurisdiction rather grudgingly, federal courts have generously
interpreted Congress's authority to confer jurisdiction on them: it extends to
giving federal courts the power to construe "every law that the Legislature may
constitutionally make."[1] For example, Congress, by reason of its authority over
foreign commerce and foreign relations, may even give federal courts jurisdiction to hear civil suits brought by a foreign plaintiff against a foreign state.[2]
    Judicial power, the only kind of power that Article III courts may exer-
cise, is the power to pronounce a judgment and carry it into effect between parties engaged in a real and substantial controversy over a legal question. Unlike
the International Court of Justice and some state courts, federal courts have
no authority to give advisory opinions. Nevertheless, they may render "declaratory judgments." Such judgments, binding on both parties, define their respective legal rights. They may be used to free one or both parties from uncertainty
regarding their rights, say, under an ambiguous contract. However, they are
most likely to be sought by persons who believe that government officials are
threatening action that, if taken, will deprive them of their constitutional and
legal rights.
    In 1990, the Supreme Court gave a sweeping definition of the judicial
power of federal courts. A federal district judge, after finding that the Kansas
City School Board and the state of Missouri had caused racial segregation,
had ordered taxes be raised to provide the funds to improve local schools so
that they would attract back to them non-minority students and thus help to
integrate the schools. The Court said that the judge could not order taxes to
be levied, but he could order the board to ignore state law limitations so that

---

[1] *Osborn v Bank of the United States,* 9 Wheaton 738 (1824).
[2] *Verlinden BV v Central Bank of Nigeria,* 461 US 480 (1983).

the board could raise taxes. Making a distinction between the power to levy taxes, which courts lack, and the power to order school boards to levy taxes, the justices held: "When it is necessary in order to compel a local government to fulfill the requirements the Constitution imposes on them, a court order directing a local government body to levy its own taxes is plainly a judicial act within the power of a federal court."[3] Justice Kennedy, speaking for the minority of four justices, responded, "The power of taxation is one that the federal judiciary does not possess." Quoting from James Madison in *Federalist No. 48*, he continued, "In our system 'the legislative department alone has access to the pockets of the people,' for it is the legislature that is accountable to them and represents their will."[4]

The subject of relatively little Court discussion over the years and related to the nature of judicial power is the question of whether, once the Supreme Court has declared a particular state or federal law unconstitutional and does so in a holding that announces a new principle of constitutional law, this ruling is to be applied retroactively or only prospectively. After some sputtering around the Court declared that, as far as criminal cases are concerned, "newly declared... rules must be applied retroactively to all criminal cases pending on direct review," and did so in part because "the nature of judicial review strips us of the quintessentially 'legislative' prerogative to make rules of law retroactive or prospective as we see fit."[5] As to civil retroactivity there has been even more judicial backing and forthing. Take, for example, the Supreme Court's 1984 decision in *Bacchus Imports, Ltd.* v *Dias,* in which it announced that Hawaii's excise tax on imported distilled spirits, twice the rate on home-grown spirits, was unconstitutional (see page 105).[6] Prior to that decision prevailing constitutional interpretation would have sustained that law. Should the *Bacchus* holding mean that Hawaii should pay back taxes collected from the company that sued and stop collection of the tax after the date of the Court's decision, or would Hawaii have to pay back all the unconstitutionally collected taxes? What about other states who had levied similiar taxes? Should they be required to give back taxes in the event of legal action against them by distilling companies? After all, the states had in good faith collected the taxes, which they had every reason to assume they had a constitutional right to do. On the other hand, as a result of the *Bacchus* holding it is clear that the tax is unconstitutional. In a subsequent case raising these very issues, a majority of the Court concluded that the new rule of law must be applied retroactively to all litigants but could not agree why.[7] Justice Scalia, taking one of the several positions of the majority, argued that the nature of judicial power compelled such a result: judges say what the law is; they find it and do not make it. Justice O'Connor, with whom the Chief Justice Rehnquist and Justice Kennedy joined, dissented, arguing that before the *Bacchus* decision

---

[3] *Missouri* v *Jenkins*, 495 US 33 (1990).

[4] Ibid.

[5] Justice Thomas for the Court in *Harper* v *Virginia Department of Taxation*, 125 L Ed 2d 74 (1993) quoting *Griffith* v *Kentucky*, 479 US 314 (1987).

[6] *Bacchus Imports Ltd.* v *Diaz*, 468 US 263 (1984).

[7] *James B. Beam Distilling Co.* v *Georgia*, 115 L Ed 2d 481 (1991).

states collecting the tax did not violate the Constitution, and retroactive application, even for Hawaii, permits liquor manufacturers to reap a windfall from the taxpayers. Then the same issues were presented again after the Court held that a state violates the constitutional doctrine of intergovernmental tax immunity when it taxes retirement benefits paid by the federal government but exempts from taxation retirement benefits paid by the state to its own employees.[8] It is clear that after that decision states may not collect such taxes from federal employees, but do all twenty-three states have to pay back the taxes they had already collected? Applying *Beam,* the Court said yes. "When this Court applies a rule of federal law to the parties before it, that rule is the controlling interpretation of federal law and must be given full retroactive effect in all cases still open on direct review and as to all events, regardless of whether such events predate or postdate our announcement of the rule."[9]

SECTION 1

[continued] [The Judicial Power of the United States] shall be vested in one supreme Court, and in such inferior Courts as the Congress may from time to time ordain and establish.

The Supreme Court is the only federal court required by the Constitution. The Founding Fathers were purposely vague about the nature of the federal court system because they were unable to agree on the need for inferior federal courts (the term refers to the jurisdiction of these courts, not their quality). Some thought that since the supremacy clause (see page 173) imposes on state courts a responsibility, whenever appropriate, to apply the Constitution and federal laws, there was less need for lower federal courts. But the First Congress created such courts, and they have always been part of our federal court system.

Under present legislation there are ninety-four district courts, including territorial courts. (There are some specialized trial courts, such as the U.S. Court of Federal Claims, the Court of International Trade, and a Foreign Intelligence Surveillance Court.)

At the appellate level there are twelve courts of appeals with general jurisdiction including the Court of Appeals for the District of Columbia, which hears many cases from the federal regulatory agencies. It is a division of this court that on request from the attorney general selected independent prosecutors (see page 129). The United States Court of Appeals for the Federal Circuit has specialized jurisdiction to hear appeals relating to patents, trademarks, and copyrights.

Federal magistrates appointed by federal district judges now are attached

---

[8] *Davis* v *Michigan Dept. of Treasury,* 489 US 803 (1989).
[9] *Harper* v *Virginia Dept. of Taxation,* 125 L Ed 2d 74 (1993).

to district courts. Magistrates appointed to full-time positions, with authority over a wide range of matters, have eight-year terms; those serving only part-time, in less populated areas, serve four-year terms. Among their duties are the disposition of initial motions, including the making of recommendations to the district judge as to whether or not evidence in a criminal case should be suppressed (see the Fourth Amendment). Magistrates also have jurisdiction to preside over civil trials with the consent of both parties, over nonjury trials for misdemeanors with the consent of the defendant, and over trials for petty offenses. Magistrates' authority to take these initial actions, subject to final approval by the district judge, has been upheld against claims that it violates the due process requirement that persons have their criminal cases heard from the beginning to end by judges appointed by the procedures and for the terms set forth in Article III.[10] On the other hand, the Court has refused to countenance magistrates being given authority to select felony juries.[11]

Bankruptcy judges, appointed by the courts of appeals for fourteen-year terms, dispose of matters arising under federal bankruptcy laws. Their decisions may be appealed to the district judge or to a special appellate panel of bankruptcy judges established by the judicial council of each federal court of appeals.

In addition to courts created under Article III to exercise the judicial power of the United States, Congress has created other courts under its Article I authority to do whatever is necessary and proper to carry into execution powers granted to the national government, including the Article IV power to provide for the governance of the territories. These so-called legislative, or Article I, courts are district courts in Guam, Northern Marianas, and the Virgin Islands, the Court of Military Appeals, the U.S. Court of Federal Claims, and the Tax Court. Magistrates and bankruptcy judges, referred to earlier, are also Article I judges.

Judges of Article I courts may be selected by other procedures and serve for terms other than those prescribed by the Constitution for judges of Article III courts, which exercise the judicial power of the United States. Article I courts could be given nonjudicial duties, which might be inappropriate to vest in an Article III court, although at the moment no such duties are assigned to any Article I court.

Sometimes it is difficult to know whether a court is an Article III court created to exercise the judicial power of the United States under Article III or an Article I court created to exercise the legislative power of Congress under Article I. In practice, Congress indicates whether it considers a court to be an Article I or an Article III court by specifying in the case of Article I judges that they are to serve for a fixed number of years or, in the case of Article III judges, that they are to serve "for good behavior," although there is nothing to prevent Congress from giving Article I judges lifetime tenure if it wishes to do so, and it has done so in the past.

---

[10] *United States* v *Raddatz*, 447 US 667 (1980).
[11] *Gomez* v *United States*, 488 US 838 (1989).

Although the "legislative courts" are created under Congress's Article I authority, the Supreme Court has held that these courts are "Courts of Law," as that term is used in the appointments clause (see page 131) and that, in the words of Justice Blackman, "these courts exercise the judicial power of the United States."[12] Four dissenting justices argued that Article III vests not "some of the judicial power of the United States," or even "most of the judicial power of the United States," but in unequivocal terms, all the judicial power of the United States to courts created by Congress in accord with Article III. To the dissenters, Article I courts may be involved in adjudication but they are not exercising the judicial power of the United States.

Distinguishing the conditions that make it appropriate for Congress to delegate adjudication to officers who do not enjoy the tenure and salary protections of Article III judges is "one of the most confusing and controversial areas of constitutional law."[13] There appears to be a running battle between Congress and the Supreme Court over these issues, especially as they relate to the creation of a system of bankruptcy courts. In 1982 the Supreme Court declared unconstitutional the system of bankruptcy courts established by the Bankruptcy Reform Act of 1978. That act created bankruptcy courts whose judges, like earlier bankruptcy judges, did not have lifetime tenure, could be removed for nonimpeachable offenses, and were not given constitutional guarantees that their salaries would not be reduced. These courts were given jurisdiction over all civil proceedings relating to bankruptcy matters. The Supreme Court declared the act unconstitutional because it authorized bankruptcy judges to resolve cases normally within the purview of general jurisdiction state trial courts or Article III federal courts. Justice Brennan, speaking for a plurality, stated that the Constitution allows legislative courts to be used in only three situations: (1) to establish territorial courts, (2) to establish courts-martial, and (3) to enforce public rights—matters that arise between the government and one of its citizens. He argued that only Article III courts could decide disputes between two individuals.[14]

Four years later (this time Justice Brennan was in the minority), the Court explained that the distinction between public rights and private rights is not controlling. Rather, it is merely an understanding that when public rights are involved, the danger of encroaching on judicial power is less than when private rights are relegated initially to administrative adjudication. Article III, said Justice O'Connor for the Court, serves two functions: (1) to protect the role of the independent judiciary and (2) to safeguard litigants' right to have their claims tried before judges who are free from potential domination by other branches of government. Litigants may waive their personal rights and consent to have their claims heard elsewhere, but they may not cure by consent the things that undermine the independence of the judiciary. The Court warned

---

[12] *Freytag v Commissioner*, 115 L Ed 2d 764 (1991).

[13] Justice White dissenting in *Northern Pipeline Construction Co. v Marathon Pipe Line Co.*, 458 US 50 (1982).

[14] *Northern Pipeline Construction Co. v Marathon Pipe Line Co.*, 458 US 50 (1982).

Congress not to take too much business from Article III judges. In this particular instance, however, the majority held that Congress could confer on the Commodity Futures Trading Commission jurisdiction to settle disputes between traders and their brokers, including state law counterclaims. Here Congress had created a limited scheme to provide an inexpensive and expeditious alternative forum for a class of questions of fact that are peculiarly suited to resolution by administrative agencies.[15]

A few years later, faced with an issue related to the Seventh Amendment civil jury trial requirements, a five-justice majority of the Court, although declaring a provision of the bankruptcy laws unconstitutional, further delimited the "private right" category by holding that the "Federal Government need not be a party for a cause to revolve around 'public rights.'" In other words there are some causes of action involving disputes between private persons which are "so closely integrated into a public regulatory scheme as to be a matter appropriate for agency resolution with limited involvement by the Article III judiciary."[16]

Within any state, there are two court systems, the state court system and the federal court system, neither of which is superior to the other. Over some matters both systems have jurisdiction, over others only the state courts have jurisdiction, and over still others only the federal courts have jurisdiction. For example, a dispute between two citizens of New York over the terms of a contract signed in New York would be within the exclusive jurisdiction of the New York state courts. A suit involving more than $50,000 between citizens of different states would be within the jurisdiction of the federal courts and the state courts in either the plaintiff's or defendant's state. A suit arising under the Sherman Antitrust Act would be within the exclusive jurisdiction of the federal courts.

The power of the federal courts over certain types of cases does not in itself exclude state courts from exercising *concurrent jurisdiction*. But Congress is free to make the federal jurisdiction exclusive and has done so in the following kinds of cases, among others: crimes against the United States, civil cases of admiralty and maritime jurisdiction, prize cases (cases arising out of the capture of enemy or abandoned property on the high seas), cases to which a state is party (except cases between a state and its citizens or a state and citizens of another state or foreign country), and cases involving foreign ambassadors and other public ministers.

SECTION 1

[continued] The Judges, both of the supreme and inferior Courts, shall hold their Offices during good Behavior,

---

[15] *Commodity Futures Trading Comm'n. v Schor*, 478 US 833 (1986). See also *Thomas v Union Carbide Agric. Products Co.*, 473 US 568 (1985), where the Court struggled inconclusively with these same issues.
[16] *Granfinanciera v Norberg*, 492 US 533 (1989).

The Constitution provides for the appointment of judges by the president with the consent of the Senate, but it is silent about the number and size of the courts and the qualification of the judges. Today there are nine members of the Supreme Court; at various times there have been six, seven, and ten. The number of judges serving on a district court or a court of appeals varies with the number and nature of the cases to be handled. Usually one judge hears a case in a district court, and three circuit judges hear cases in a court of appeals, although courts of appeal at times hold hearings en banc (with all their judges participating).

Although the Constitution here refers to members of both the Supreme Court and the inferior federal courts as judges, in Article I, Section 3, paragraph 6, it refers to the "Chief Justice." Since the Judiciary Act of 1789, members of the Supreme Court have always been referred to as "Justice" and, until November of 1980, more formally as "Mr. Justice." In November 1980, anticipating the arrival of the first woman justice, the title "Mr. Justice" was dropped. The Chief Justice is properly designated as the Chief Justice of the United States, not of the Supreme Court, but is known informally to fellow justices as "the chief."

The phrase "during good behavior," which means virtually for life, has been interpreted by some to mean that Congress has the constitutional power to create procedures to terminate judges for "bad behavior," even if the behavior in question falls short of impeachable offenses. Congress has refused to go that far, but in 1980, following the example of the states, did clarify the authority of the judicial council of each circuit. The judicial council, consisting of some circuit judges and some district judges from the circuit, is to investigate complaints against judges. If the judicial council finds that a complaint is justified, it may request the judge to retire, censure or reprimand the judge in question, order that no cases be assigned to the judge, or take "other appropriate actions" short of removal. Appeals from the decision of a council may be taken to the Judicial Conference. If the council thinks that impeachment may be warranted, it refers the matter, through the Judicial Conference (which consists of the chief justice, the chief judges of the twelve courts of appeals, and a number of district judges elected by their peers), to the House of Representatives, the procedure followed in the case of the three previously mentioned federal judges impeached in recent years.

Some argue that the good-behavior language means that impeachable offenses for federal judges differ from those for other officers, such as the president, who is elected for a fixed term. In other words, in addition to "Treason, Bribery, or other High Crimes and Misdemeanors," for which the president, the vice president, and other civil officers may be impeached, federal judges, it is argued, may be impeached for willful misconduct in office, failure to perform their duties, habitual intemperance, or other conduct that brings the judicial office into disrepute. As we have noted, the House has impeached and the Senate has convicted federal judges for misbehavior that fell short of treason, bribery, or other "crimes and misdemeanors."

SECTION 1

[continued] and shall, at stated Times, receive for their Services, a Compensation, which shall not be diminished during their Continuance in Office.

To ensure judicial independence, Congress is prohibited from decreasing judicial salaries during the term of any particular judge, but unlike the president's salary, judicial salaries may be increased. The compensation clause prohibits Congress from repealing salary increases for judges when the increases have already taken effect automatically pursuant to a previously enacted formula—a process Congress used from time to time to establish judicial salaries;[17] it now specifically enacts judges' salary increases.

SECTION 2

1. The judicial Power shall extend to all Cases, in Law and Equity,

This clause and those that immediately follow outline the scope of federal judicial power.

The distinction between cases in law and cases in equity is inherited from England. In law, the party bringing the case usually asks for damages; in equity, an injunction is usually requested. The common law compensates for injury already done, whereas equity prevents or stops the injury from occurring. Nowadays the same federal judges can hear both types of cases and can hear both types of matters in a single case.

May Congress take from federal courts large "hunks" of the judicial power of the United States? Could Congress go so far as to strip federal courts of jurisdiction to hear any cases at all? Except for the original jurisdiction of the Supreme Court perhaps it could do so, but see page 151. If it did so it would profoundly alter the nature of our constitutional system.

SECTION 2

1. [continued] [The judicial Power shall extend to all Cases, in Law and Equity,] arising under this Constitution, the Laws of the United States, and Treaties made, or which shall be made, under their Authority;

If a *federal question* is involved, a case that starts out in a state court may be taken to the Supreme Court from the highest state court to which an appeal

---

[17] *United States* v *Will*, 449 US 200 (1981).

can be made. For example, if X is tried and convicted of murder under state law in a state court and exhausts her state appeals, she may then ask the United States Supreme Court to pass on her contention that her trial was not a fair one under the due process clause of the Fourteenth Amendment.

The Supreme Court, acting under terms of its own interpretation of federal jurisdictional statutes, reviews state court decrees and judgments only when these actions are final. There are exceptions, however, of which perhaps the more important is when First Amendment questions are involved.[18] As we have noted (see page 100) under some circumstances, by writ of habeas corpus, persons may seek a review of the actions of state courts in lower federal courts.

Often a state court will dispose of a matter on both federal and state grounds. If a state court rests its judgment on grounds that are both "independent" of the merits of a federal claim and an "adequate" basis for the court's decision, this precludes federal court review. In *Michigan* v *Long* the Court adopted a "plain statement" requirement: a state court must make it clear that it has decided on adequate and independent state grounds if it wishes to preclude subsequent federal court review.[19] This "plain statement" requirement is of some significance now that some state courts are citing their own state constitutions as the basis for extending some constitutional rights beyond the scope of the protection of the federal Constitution. State judges who wish to do this and protect their decisions from U.S. Supreme Court review cannot be ambiguous about whether they so decide in order to comply with the interpretations of the United States Supreme Court under the national Constitution, or whether they are stating their own interpretation of their own state constitution. Since state judges can no longer hide behind a Supreme Court decision, they are exposed to greater political peril. They cannot blame the U.S. Supreme Court and persons who do not like their decision may vote against them in subsequent elections. When state judges do clearly provide greater protection for rights under their own state constitution than the Supreme Court has upheld under the federal Constitution, the Supreme Court has recognized their power to do so.[20] The national Constitution sets a floor for rights, not a ceiling.

The Supreme Court recently skirted an interesting issue involving the federal courts' "arising under" jurisdiction. Two postal employees, while delivering the mail, were involved in accidents and were charged by California with manslaughter and driving outside a lane. They sought to utilize a federal law authorizing the removal of cases from state to federal courts of cases brought against federal officials who were acting under the "color of law." The Department of Justice supported their request. The Supreme Court held, however, that the statute in question should be limited to authorizing removal of only those cases where defendants had "a plausible federal defense." The Court stated that if the statute were interpreted to permit the removal of cases such as these traffic cases, where the only issues are liability under state law, it would

---

[18] *Fort Wayne Books, Inc.* v *Indiana*, 489 US 809 (1989).

[19] *Michigan* v *Long*, 463 US 1032 (1983) and also *Harris* v *Reed*, 489 US 255 (1989).

[20] *Prune Yard Shopping Center* v *Robins*, 447 US 74 (1980).

"unnecessarily present grave constitutional problems."[21] Justices Brennan and Marshall concurred, emphasizing that the Court had left open the possibility that, where a federal officer is prosecuted because of local hostility, then removal should be granted, even in the absence of a federal defense. "The days of widespread resistance," Justice Brennan wrote, "by state and local governmental authorities to acts of Congress and to decisions of the Court in the areas of school desegregation and voting rights are not so distant that we should be oblivious to the possibility of harassment of federal agencies by local law-enforcement authorities."[22]

SECTION 2.
    1. [continued] to all Cases affecting Ambassadors, other public Ministers and Consuls;

Since the national government is responsible for relations between the United States and foreign governments, cases affecting foreign public ministers are within the judicial power of the United States. For the federal courts to assume jurisdiction, such officials must be materially affected by the case without necessarily being parties to it.

SECTION 2
    1. [continued] to all Cases of admiralty and maritime Jurisdiction;

This jurisdiction is concerned with ships and shipping. Under the English rule, it extended only to the high seas and those rivers in which the tide ebbed and flowed. Under the Constitution, however, such jurisdiction reaches all "navigable waters of the United States, whether or not subject to the ebb and flow of the tide" and "all causes of damage or injury, to person or property, caused by a vessel on navigable water, notwithstanding that such damage or injury be done or consummated on land."[23] A collision between two boats, whether small pleasure craft or large commercial ones, on the navigable waters of the United States, even in a very small river inside a state, is within the admiralty jurisdiction of the United States.[24] So was a tort action involving the extent of liability from a fire on a private boat in a marina on Lake Michigan where the only other boats were also private boats. Jurisdiction over maritime activity is appropriate when a potential hazard to maritime commerce arises out of an activity that bears a substantial relationship to traditional maritime

---

[21] *Mesa v California*, 489 US 1023 (1989).
[22] Ibid.
[23] *Gutierrez v Waterman SS Corp.*, 373 US 206 (1963).
[24] *Foremost Insurance Co. v Richardson*, 452 US 668 (1982).

activity, such as navigating boats or storing and maintaining them at a marina on navigable waters.[25]

This grant of jurisdiction to federal courts is exclusive. States may not extend their laws, such as workers' compensation, to areas covered by maritime law. The rough dividing line—which has taken many cases to establish—between state and maritime jurisdictions is the gangplank, with some confusion and legal difficulties over the jurisdiction of the seaward side of the pier.[26]

Airplanes on domestic flights are not ships for purposes of admiralty jurisdiction. Congress can, however, exercise its power to regulate foreign and interstate commerce to provide rules for airplane crashes and to bring them under federal jurisdiction, as it has done by providing for wrongful death and tort suits for airplane accidents on the high seas.

SECTION 2

1. [continued] to Controversies to which the United States shall be a Party;—to Controversies between two or more States; *between a State and Citizens of another State* [emphasis added];—between Citizens of different States;

The Eleventh Amendment modified the emphasized portion of the section.

Article III authorizes Congress to extend federal jurisdiction to any case involving conflicts between citizens of different states. Congress has legislated that diversity cases—those founded on conflicts between citizens of different states where diversity of citizenship is the only grounds for federal jurisdiction—involving amounts of less than $50,000 shall not be entertained by federal courts. To come within the diversity jurisdiction, there must be *complete* diversity between *all* parties to the suit. If the amount is above $50,000 and involves citizens of different states, the plaintiff may bring the suit in either federal or state courts. If the plaintiff brings the case to a state court, the defendant may remove it to a federal court. When a federal court takes a case because of diversity, it is to apply the same substantive law as would have been applied if the case were heard in the state court.[27]

Many people, including many if not most federal judges, argue that Congress should eliminate all federal court diversity jurisdiction. They contend that the reasons to fear that state judges or juries will favor their own citizens no longer persist, and that elimination of diversity jurisdiction would free federal courts to devote more time to federal issues. However, Congress so far has failed to abolish diversity jurisdiction, although it and the Supreme Court have restricted it in a variety of ways.[28] Not only did Congress increase the dol-

---

[25] *Sisson v Ruby*, 497 US 358 (1990).

[26] *Victory Carriers, Inc. v Law*, 404 US 249 (1972).

[27] *Erie RR Co. v Tompkins*, 304 US 64 (1933).

[28] USC 1332. Russell Chapin, "Federal or State Court: Should Diversity Jurisdiction Be Abolished?" *Intergovernmental Perspective*, vol. 15, no. 2 (Spring 1989): 29.

lar threshold to $50,000 from $10,000 but the Supreme Court has also insisted on complete diversity of all parties to a lawsuit and "firmly resisted extending to other entities," such as partnerships, "the treatment given to corporations of allowing them to be considered citizens only of the state where they are incorporated or in which they do their principal business."[29]

The Court has also reinforced a "domestic relations exception" to diversity jurisdiction in order not to extend this jurisdiction to cases involving the issuance of a divorce, alimony, or child custody decree. The exception stems from dicta in an 1859 Supreme Court decision.[30] In 1992 the Supreme Court presumed that, although Congress had not specifically confirmed this exception when in 1948 it extensively revised the diversity statute, by saying nothing to the contrary in the face of such "a long-standing and well-known" domestic exception construction, Congress in effect had adopted the exception.[31]

SECTION 2

1. [continued] between Citizens of the same State claiming Lands under Grants of different States, *and between a State, or the Citizens thereof, and foreign States, Citizens or Subjects* [emphasis added].

At the time of the adoption of the Constitution, many states had conflicting claims to western lands. Today this clause is unimportant. The emphasized portion of this clause has been modified by the Eleventh Amendment.

In summary, the judicial power of the United States extends to the following cases in law and equity.

1. Cases in which jurisdiction is based on the *nature of the dispute:*
   a. Cases arising under the Constitution, under a federal law, or under a federal treaty.
   b. Cases arising under admiralty and maritime jurisdiction.
   c. Cases involving title to land that is claimed under grants by two or more states.
2. Cases in which jurisdiction is based on the *parties to the dispute:*
   a. Cases in which the United States is a party.
   b. Cases in which a state is a party.
   c. Cases in which the parties are citizens of different states.
   d. Cases that affect foreign ambassadors, ministers, and consuls.

[29] *Carden v Arkoma Associates*, 494 US 185 (1990).
[30] *Barber v Barber*, 21 Howard 582 (1859).
[31] *Ankenbrandt v Richards*, 119 L Ed 2d 468 (1992).

SECTION 2

2. In all Cases affecting Ambassadors, other public Ministers and Consuls, and those in which a State shall be Party, the Supreme Court shall have original Jurisdiction.

"The original jurisdiction of the Supreme Court is conferred by the Constitution, is self-executing and needs no legislative implementation."[32] This original jurisdiction, however, is neither mandatory nor constitutionally exclusive. Except for suits between states, which Congress has reserved exclusively for the Supreme Court,[33] Congress can give and has given concurrent jurisdiction to other courts. The Supreme Court hears the relatively few cases brought by a state against the United States, but ordinarily refers other categories of cases to lower federal courts for a first hearing. As to suits brought by states against other states, "In order to constitute a proper 'controversy' under our original jurisdiction, it must appear that the complaining State has suffered a wrong through the action of the other State, furnishing ground for judicial redress, or is asserting a right against the other State which is susceptible of judicial enforcement according to the accepted principles of the common law or equity systems of jurisprudence."[34]

The Supreme Court is reluctant to take cases involving its original jurisdiction since it is "ill-equipped for the task of fact finding."[35] It takes into account "the seriousness and dignity of the claim," and the availability of another forum."[36] "The model case for invocation of this Court's original jurisdiction is a dispute between States of such seriousness that it would amount to *casus belli* if the States were fully sovereign."[37] When it hears a boundary dispute between states, the Court ordinarily appoints a special master to hear the evidence and make recommendations to the Court on which it then hears argument.

The Supreme Court's role in resolving disputes between states is limited to deciding a legal dispute. It will not allow itself to become an arbitrator between conflicting states about nonlegal matters.[38] For that purpose, states must resort to an interstate compact or seek a settlement from Congress.

The Supreme Court will not accept original jurisdiction if a "state is only nominally a party and in reality is standing in to vindicate grievances of individuals."[39] But like so many judicial generalizations, there is a contrary one.

---

[32] *California v Arizona*, 440 US 59 (1979).

[33] *Mississippi v Louisiana*, 121 L Ed 2d 466 (1992).

[34] *Wyoming v Oklahoma*, 117 L Ed 2d 1 (1992) quoting earlier cases of *Maryland v Louisiana*, 451 US 725 (1981) *and Massachussets v Missouri*, 308 US 1 (1939).

[35] Justice Rehnquist dissenting in *Maryland et al. v Louisiana*, 451 US 725 (1981).

[36] *Wyoming v Oklahoma*, 117 L Ed 2d 1 (1992).

[37] *Texas v New Mexico*, 462 US 554 (1983).

[38] *Vermont v New York*, 417 US 270 (1974).

[39] *Illinois v Michigan*, 409 US 36 (1972).

Although a state may not invoke the original jurisdiction of the Supreme Court to forward the claims of individual citizens, it may act as a representative of its citizens, as *parens patriae,* as the lawyers call it, when the injury alleged affects the general population of a state in a substantial way. Thus, the Supreme Court permitted Maryland and a number of other states to challenge a Louisiana tax on natural gas taken from the continental shelf and brought into the state for processing prior to being shipped out of state. The tax fell not on just a few of the states' citizens, but on a great many of them. In addition, the states, as purchasers of natural gas for governmental purposes, had a substantial interest in the matter.[40] Similarly, the Court accepted jurisdiction when Wyoming sought relief from an Oklahoma statute that required Oklahoma coal-fired electric generating plants producing power for sale in Oklahoma to burn a mixture of coal containing at least 10 percent Oklahoma-mined coal. This act reduced the amount of severance taxes that Wyoming could collect from Wyoming coal-mining companies. The Supreme Court agreed with Wyoming that Oklahoma's action violated the commerce clause.

SECTION 2

2. [continued] In all the other Cases before mentioned, the Supreme Court shall have appellate Jurisdiction, both as to Law and Fact, with such Exceptions, and under such Regulations as the Congress shall make.

Appellate jurisdiction is the power to hear and decide appeals of decisions of lower courts. In all cases, except those few within its original jurisdiction, the Supreme Court has only appellate jurisdiction. Unlike its original jurisdiction, the Supreme Court has only that appellate jurisdiction granted it by Congress. The completeness of congressional control of the Supreme Court's appellate jurisdiction is illustrated by the 1869 decision in *Ex parte McCardle.* In 1868 the Supreme Court announced that it would hear the appeal of a newspaper editor who had challenged the constitutionality of one of the Reconstruction Acts. After the Court had heard arguments on the merits of the case and was considering the decision, Congress, anticipating that the Court might declare the act unconstitutional, repealed the habeas corpus provision that had allowed the issue to be appealed to the Supreme Court. The Court thereupon held that it had no power to decide the case.[41]

Those members of Congress who from time to time have proposed to restrict the Supreme Court's appellate jurisdiction, as well as the original jurisdiction of the lower federal courts, on such subjects as abortion, busing, and school prayer point to *Ex parte McCardle* as evidence that Congress may do so. Some scholars, however, pointing out that *McCardle* had another route to the

---

[40] *Maryland et al. v Louisiana,* 451 US 725 (1981).

[41] *Ex parte McCardle,* 6 Wallace 318 (1868); *Ex parte McCardle,* 7 Wallace 506 (1869).

Supreme Court, argue that the *McCardle* case does not stand for the principle that Congress may cut off all appeals to the Court on constitutional matters.

Although Congress has some considerable, if not complete, power to restrict the Supreme Court's and other federal courts' jurisdiction, it cannot specify how a court should decide a particular case. The Supreme Court first made this clear in a post–Civil War case dealing with an attempt by Congress to order courts to treat the acceptance of a presidential pardon as proof of aid to the Confederacy but to ignore the pardon when determining loyalty to the United States; the Court struck down that limitation on its discretion.[42] In 1992, however, the Court upheld the action of Congress which had changed the law relating to protecting the habitat for the spotted owl in the Pacific Northwest and specified particular pending cases to which the new law was to apply. Congress, concluded the Supreme Court, had not dictated the way courts should decide these cases but had only changed the standards which courts were to apply in deciding them.[43]

Despite the great and increasing volume of federal litigation, the Supreme Court has been able to keep up with its work, more or less, because Congress has given it the authority to choose which cases it will review. Until 1989, when asked to do so by the proper party it was obligated to review certain types of cases, primarily those in which a federal statute was called into question or those in which a state action had been challenged on the grounds of violating a federal law or the federal Constitution. These cases were said to go to the Court *on appeal.*

Although there are still a few cases which Congress has mandated must be reviewed by the Supreme Court, primarily concerning voting rights, today the Court reviews almost all cases by granting *a writ of certiorari.* It grants that writ for those cases it considers to be of sufficient public importance to merit its attention. It does so under the rule of four: whenever four justices vote to grant a writ of certiorari the case is put on the Court's docket. The denial of a writ of certiorari has no value as precedent. All it means is that, for whatever reason, four or more justices could not agree that the Supreme Court should accept the case for review.

SECTION 2

3. The Trial of all Crimes, except in Cases of Impeachment, shall be by Jury; and such Trial shall be held in the State where the said Crimes shall have been committed; but when not committed within any State, the Trial shall be at such Place or Places as the Congress may by Law have directed.

---

[42] *United States* v *Klein*, 13 Wallace 128 (1972).
[43] *Robertson* v *Seattle Audubon Society*, 118 L Ed 2d 73 (1992).

This section guarantees the right to a trial by jury to persons accused of crimes by the national government. (See also the Sixth Amendment.) It also responds to one of the charges brought against George III in the Declaration of Independence, "For transporting us beyond Seas to be tried for pretended offenses," and requires that the trial be held in the state where the crime was committed. It is not always clear, however, where some crimes were committed. For example, federal statutes permit trial in any state from, through, and to which obscene materials are mailed. The statutes have been applied without effective constitutional challenge on this point.

SECTION 3

1. Treason against the United States, shall consist only in levying War against them, or in adhering to their Enemies, giving them Aid and Comfort.

Although treason is narrowly defined by the Constitution, this section does not prevent Congress from making it a federal crime to use force and violence against the government or to conspire to do so.

As to treason there are two separate grounds: (1) levying war against the United States and (2) giving aid and comfort to the enemy. Levying war is being part of a group of armed persons actually moving against the government. Giving aid and comfort means deliberately promoting the cause of a declared enemy of the United States. It may be possible for aliens to commit treason against the United States because while within the boundaries of the United States they owe our government temporary allegiance.

Since Congress never formally declared war against North Vietnam, it is doubtful that any person could have been convicted of treason for adhering to its cause and giving it aid and comfort, but there is no precise court holding on the matter. Those who take up arms against the United States as part of a hostile force, however, probably risk prosecution for treason even without a congressional declaration of war.

SECTION 3

1. [continued] No person shall be convicted of Treason unless on the Testimony of two Witnesses to the same overt Act, or on Confession in open Court.

No person may be convicted of treason on circumstantial evidence alone. The accused must make a confession in open court, or there must be two witnesses to an overt act that, either by itself or with other evidence, convinces the jury of the defendant's guilt.

SECTION 3

2. The Congress shall have Power to declare the Punishment of Treason, but no Attainder of Treason shall work Corruption of Blood, or Forfeiture except during the Life of the Person attainted.

In sixteenth- and seventeenth-century England, "attainders of treason" worked "corruption of blood," making it impossible for a traitor's family to inherit from him. Having been traitors themselves in rebelling against King George, the framers may have felt a certain tenderness for such unfortunates.

ARTICLE IV: STATES' RELATIONS

SECTION 1

Full Faith and Credit shall be given in each State to the public Acts, Records, and judicial Proceedings of every other State. And the Congress may by general Laws prescribe the Manner in which such Acts, Records and Proceedings shall be proved, and the Effect thereof.

Note that it is the acts of a state, not its laws, that get full faith and credit. Congress has supplemented the full-faith-and-credit clause by providing that "acts, records, and judicial proceedings or copies thereof, so authenticated, shall have the same full faith and credit in every court within the United States and its territories and possessions as they have by law or usage in the courts of such State, Territory, or Possession from which they are taken." The "every court" in this provision includes federal as well as state courts.

This clause applies especially to judicial decisions. Suppose that a Pennsylvania court awards X a $150,000 judgment against Y, also a Pennsylvanian; after moving to New York, Y refuses to pay. Thanks to the full-faith-and-credit clause, X does not have to prove her case all over again and secure a new judgment against Y in a New York court. The New York courts will give full faith and credit to the Pennsylvania judgment and will enforce the judgment even if it is not one that the New York courts would have granted originally.

Or suppose that X, a New Yorker, while driving his car in New Jersey, injures Y or his property and then returns to New York without doing anything about it. Following a certain procedure, Y may sue X in the New Jersey courts; if they decide in Y's favor, the New York courts must aid Y in collecting the judgment, whether X appeared in the case or not.

How much faith and credit must a state give to a divorce decree granted by another state? The material question raised is that of *domicile*. Each state has the power to regulate the marriages and divorces of its own residents. Clearly, a divorce granted by a state to two bona fide residents must be given full faith and credit by all the other states, although they might not themselves have granted the divorce for the grounds alleged. However, if one North Carolinian, for example, goes to Nevada and obtains a divorce after the brief time necessary under Nevada law, and then returns to North Carolina the Constitution does not require the North Carolina courts to recognize this divorce. The Supreme Court has ruled that under such circumstances the North Carolina courts could refuse to recognize the Nevada decree on the ground that Nevada courts lacked jurisdiction to grant the divorce because the plaintiff, in the eyes of North Carolina, had not acquired a bona fide domicile in Nevada.[1] If, however, both parties to the divorce make their appearance in the divorce-granting state and the issue of domicile is raised and decided, neither they nor their heirs can, in any other court, challenge the validity of the divorce on the ground that the state lacked jurisdiction. By a rule of American jurisprudence, *res judicata,* once a person has had a "day in court," that person may not raise the same issue again in a separate proceeding.[2]

According to the divisible divorce concept, although a state may have to recognize a divorce decree of another state when domicile has been acquired in that state, it may have greater discretion in deciding whether to recognize decisions about alimony, property, and custody of children. Some interesting legal problems stem from this concept. This is not the place to get involved in such highly technical matters, other than to note that situations have occurred in which the woman who had been the legal wife was not the legal widow.

The full-faith-and-credit clause is involved in the conflict-of-laws (choice of law) questions that arise so frequently in a federal system, particularly in suits by citizens of one state against those of another in federal courts under diversity of citizenship jurisdiction. Which laws should be applied to decide particular disputes? Take, for example, a case in which a widow sued an insurance company to recover for her husband's death. Ralph Hague had been killed in Wisconsin when the motorcycle on which he was a passenger was struck from behind by an automobile. Although the drivers of both vehicles were Wisconsin residents, as was Hague, and the accident took place in Wisconsin, his wife brought suit in a Minnesota court—she had moved to Minnesota after her husband's death.

Which law should the Minnesota courts apply, that of Wisconsin or that of Minnesota? It made a difference since the law of Minnesota allowed three times the damages allowed by the law of Wisconsin. The Minnesota courts chose to apply their own laws. The Supreme Court upheld Minnesota's action against a challenge that it violated both the full-faith-and-credit clause and the due process clause. (The tests under both clauses are in effect the same; but, as Justice Stevens in concurrence pointed out, the question was whether the full-faith-and-credit clause required Minnesota to apply Wisconsin laws or whether

---

[1] *Williams v North Carolina,* 325 US 226 (1945).
[2] *Johnson v Muelberger,* 340 US 581 (1951).

the due process clause prevented Minnesota from applying its own laws.) Since Hague had worked in Minnesota, the insurance company did business in Minnesota, and Hague's wife had become a citizen of Minnesota before instituting the litigation, the Supreme Court ruled that Minnesota had significant enough contact with the accident for it to apply its own laws if it chose.[3]

May a state be sued against its wishes in the courts of another state? The Court has ruled that it may. Nevada was being sued because of an accident in California that had involved a Nevada vehicle and a Nevada employee. The full-faith-and-credit clause does not require California courts to enforce a Nevada law requiring that such suits take place only in Nevada courts and limiting the amount of money that could be recovered.[4]

The trend in recent years has been to read the full-faith-and-credit clause as giving state courts more latitude in deciding whether to use laws of their own state, rather than those of a sister state, in dealing with issues brought before them. Nonetheless, the Court decided that Kansas had violated both the due process clause and the full-faith-and-credit clause when it applied its law to all claims in a class action suit brought in behalf of oil royalty owners. Most of the royalty owners lived outside Kansas, the defendant was a Delaware corporation whose principal place of business was Oklahoma, and almost all the oil leases were for land outside Kansas. Said the Court, "We conclude that application of Kansas law to every claim in this case is sufficiently arbitrary and unfair as to exceed constitutional limits."[5]

SECTION 2

1. The Citizens of each State shall be entitled to all Privileges and Immunities of Citizens in the several States.

This clause forbids discrimination against the citizens of another state by a state government or by municipalities, counties, or any other local unit of government.[6] "While the Privileges and Immunities clause cites the term 'Citizens,' for analytic purposes citizenship and residency are essentially interchangeable."[7] This clause was intended "to create a national economic union," but it also protects noneconomic interests as well.[8] It was "intended to 'fuse into one Nation a collection of independent, sovereign states.'"[9]

The privileges and immunities clause "does not preclude disparity of treatment in the many situations where there are perfectly valid independent reasons for it."[10]

---

[3] *Allstate Insurance Co.* v *Hague*, 449 US 302 (1981).
[4] *Nevada* v *Hall*, 400 US 410 (1979).
[5] *Phillips Petroleum Co.* v *Shutts*, 472 US 797 (1985).
[6] *United Building & Construction Trades Council* v *Mayor of Camden*, 465 US 208 (1984).
[7] *Supreme Court of Virginia* v *Friedman*, 487 US 59 (1988).
[8] *Supreme Court of New Hampshire* v *Piper*, 470 US 274 (1985).
[9] *Supreme Court of New Hampshire* v *Piper*, 470 US 274 (1985).
[10] *Hicklin* v *Orbeck*, 437 US 518 (1978).

Thus, a state may exclude nonstate citizens from voting in its elections or serving as elective officers. A state does not have to permit out-of-state citizens to attend its tax-supported institutions, such as schools, or to hunt its game or fish, for the same fees as charged its own citizens. On the other side of the constitutional divide, it may not ordinarily tax citizens of other states at discriminatory rates, deprive them of a means of livelihood, or deny them access to any part of the state.

The clause does not wipe out all differences between the citizens of a state and those of other states. "It is discrimination against out-of-state residents on matters of fundamental concern which triggers [this clause]."[11] If the discrimination affects fundamental rights, the state must show that: (1) there is a "substantial reason" for the difference in treatment and (2) the difference in treatment bears a close or substantial relation to that reason.[12]

States fell afoul of this clause when they tried to limit admission to the bar to their own residents.[13] The Virgin Islands did not get along any better in trying to restrict nonresident lawyers' admissions, although it argued that, because of its geographical isolation and unreliable telephone and airline service, it had a greater interest in limiting participation in its local bar to persons who resided on the islands.[14] South Carolina was told it could not require nonresident commercial shrimp boats to pay a substantially higher fee than its own residents paid.[15] Nor could Alaska attempt to alleviate its unemployment problem by requiring private employers in the oil and gas exploration and transportation business to give preference to Alaska residents.[16] (The Court has, however, sustained similar laws giving employment preference to citizens of a particular city.[17]) On the other hand, Montana was permitted to charge nonresident elk hunters a higher fee than its own residents. The higher fee did not interfere with out-of-state hunters' livelihoods, only their sport and amusement. "Whatever right or activities may be fundamental under the Privileges and Immunities Clause," wrote the Court, "we are persuaded, and hold, that elk hunting by nonresidents in Montana is not one of them."[18]

The clause, along with the privileges and immunities and equal protection clauses of the Fourteenth Amendment, the Ninth Amendment, and the interstate commerce clause, is the source of the right to travel throughout the United States, a right whose "textual source...has proved elusive."[19] Since the right to travel throughout the United States is a fundamental right (see page 356), a law

---

[11] *United Bldg. & Construction Trades Council* v *Mayor of Camden,* 465 US 208 (1984).

[12] *Supreme Court of New Hampshire* v *Piper,* 470 US 274 (1985).

[13] *Supreme Court of New Hampshire* v *Piper,* 470 US 274 (1985); *Supreme Court of Virginia* v *Friedman,* 487 US 59 (1988).

[14] *Barnard* v *Thorstenn,* 488 US 921 (1989).

[15] *Toomer* v *Witsell,* 334 US 385 (1948).

[16] *Hicklin* v *Orbeck,* 437 US 518 (1978).

[17] *White* v *Massachusetts Council of Construction Employers,* 460 US 204 (1983).

[18] *Baldwin* v *Montana Fish and Game Commission,* 436 US 371 (1978).

[19] *Attorney General of NY* v *Soto-Lopez,* 476 US 234 (1986).

limiting that right is subject to careful court scrutiny to ensure that citizens who migrate from one state to another are not disadvantaged simply because of the timing of their migration.

American citizens become citizens of a state the moment they move to a state with the intent to remain. May a state distinguish among its residents by establishing length-of-residency requirements for certain purposes? The Supreme Court has set aside a variety of such *durational residency* requirements. In reviewing such requirements, the Court sometimes uses this clause, sometimes uses the equal protection clause, and sometimes bases its decisions on the right to travel.

A state must show a compelling interest before it will be permitted to deny newly arrived residents the rights accorded all other citizens. To illustrate: a state may not make newly arrived citizens wait a year before becoming eligible for welfare payments, medical care, or voting rights. A day seems to be as long a wait as the Court will tolerate for welfare payments or medical care,[20] fifty days or so for the right to vote.[21] On the other hand, states may impose a one-year durational residency requirement on those seeking divorces because that constraint is not considered such a burden on the right to travel as those declared unconstitutional.[22]

What about a durational requirement to attend public colleges and universities without paying out-of-state fees? A one-year requirement is constitutionally permissible. A state may not, however, create an irrefutable presumption that any person who comes into the state to attend a college is a nonresident of the state, and a state cannot disqualify such a person from acquiring residency while attending school.[23] But those who move into the state just before enrolling in a state-supported university or college may be required to give evidence of their "attachment" to residence in the state by such things as driver's licenses; car registration; voter registration; and continuous, year-round residence. Moreover, if students wish to establish their own residence, they may be required to provide evidence of their financial independence from their parents.

Section 2

2. A Person charged in any State with Treason, Felony, or other Crime, who shall flee from Justice, and be found in another State, shall on Demand of the executive Authority of the State from which he fled, be delivered up, to be removed to the State having jurisdiction of the Crime.

This paragraph provides for what is known as *interstate rendition,* or—more commonly—*extradition.* Although it is a self-executing provision,

---

[20] *Shapiro v Thompson,* 394 US 618 (1969).

[21] *Dunn v Blumstein,* 405 US 331 (1972).

[22] *Sosna v Iowa,* 419 US 393 (1975).

[23] *Vlandis v Kline,* 412 US 441 (1973).

Congress has implemented it by making the governor of the asylum state responsible for returning a fugitive, on the request of the governor or chief magistrate of the state from which the person fled.

Despite the positive language of this clause, in 1861 the Supreme Court held in *Kentucky* v *Dennison* that, although governors are constitutionally obligated to return fugitives on receiving a properly certified request, federal courts lack authority to order them to do so.[24] Until 1987 that decision, based on an obsolete view of the relations between the national government and the states, was left undisturbed. Under that doctrine governors occasionally exercised their discretion and refused to honor extradition requests. For example, in 1976 Governor Jerry Brown of California refused to extradite Dennis Banks, an American Indian activist, to South Dakota, from which he had fled after being convicted of "felony riot." In 1984 Governor Scott M. Matheson of Utah rejected an extradition request from Illinois for a business official wanted for trial for murder because of an industrial accident in one of his company's plants.[25] Then in 1987 the Court reversed *Kentucky* v *Dennison* and made it clear that federal courts do have the power to order governors to fulfill a state's obligation under the extradition clause.[26] Even so, governors occasionally continue to refuse to honor extradition requests: in 1990 Governor Cuomo of New York denied a request from Governor Hunt of Alabama to extradite four executives of a New York company to face charges of transmitting obscene films by satellite. The executives had never been in Alabama and it is highly doubtful if the material in question would have been declared obscene in many jurisdictions, including New York.[27]

Once the governor of the asylum state has issued the warrant of arrest and rendition, the courts of that state have only four issues to consider before delivering up the fugitive: whether the extradition documents are in order, whether the petitioner has been charged with a crime in the demanding state, whether the petitioner is the person named in the request, and whether the petitioner is a fugitive. They have no authority to inquire whether the demanding state had probable cause for an arrest, whether the charges are substantial, or whether the prison conditions of the demanding state violate the Eighth Amendment prohibition against cruel and unusual punishment. Those matters are to be heard in the courts of the demanding state.[28]

Congress has made it a federal crime to engage in interstate or foreign travel with the intent to avoid prosecution or confinement by a state for certain felonies. Those who violate this law are to be brought back to the federal judicial district in which the original crime is alleged to have been committed, making it possible for federal officers to turn the fugitive over to state officials for prosecution or confinement.

---

[24] *Kentucky* v *Dennison*, 24 Howard 66 (1861).

[25] Bill Richards, "Governors' Decisions in Extradition Cases Vary All Over the Map," *The Wall Street Journal* (May 27, 1984): 1.

[26] *Puerto Rico* v *Branstad*, 483 US 219 (1987).

[27] *The New York Times* (June 21, 1990): B4

[28] *Michigan* v *Doran*, 439 US 282 (1978); *Pacileo* v *Walker*, 449 US 86 (1980); *California* v *Superior Court of California*, 482 US 400 (1987).

SECTION 2

3. No Person held to Service or Labour in one State, under the Laws thereof, escaping into another, shall, in Consequence of any Law or Regulation therein, be discharged from such Service or Labour, but shall be delivered up on Claim of the Party to whom such Service or Labour may be due.

The Thirteenth Amendment, abolishing slavery, nullified the fugitive slave clause. Prior to the Civil War it was the source of major contention: some judges in northern states refused to order the return of fugitive slaves. The insistence of southern state officials that northern courts had a legal obligation to do so contributed significantly to the growing tensions that led to the Civil War.

SECTION 3

1. New States may be admitted by the Congress into this Union;

The normal procedure is as follows: (1) the inhabitants of a territory file a petition for admission to the Union, (2) the president approves a congressional resolution authorizing the inhabitants of the territory to draw up a constitution, (3) a majority of both houses of Congress and then the president approve the proposed constitution, (4) the territory is admitted to the Union.

Although Congress and the president may withhold their approval of admission until the territory complies with or agrees to certain conditions, once a state is admitted, it possesses the same political powers as the other states. For example, in 1910 President Taft vetoed legislation admitting Arizona to the Union, because its proposed constitution permitted the voters to recall state judges. After deleting that clause, Arizona was admitted in 1912 and promptly proceeded to restore the objectionable provision. Since the right to determine the method of selection, tenure, and removal of its own judges is a political power enjoyed by each state, Arizona's power in this respect could not be less than that of other states; Taft's condition was unenforceable.

Admission conditions, such as those relating to public lands in the state that do not detract from the state's political power, are, however, enforceable as binding contracts. For example, when Minnesota was admitted to the Union it agreed, in return for certain federal lands, not to tax the remaining land still owned by the national government within the state. The Court enforced this agreement.[29]

After it became apparent that a proposed Constitutional amendment to extend additional representation to the District of Columbia would fail to be ratified, its proponents advocated that the District of Columbia be admitted

---

[29] Compare *Stearns v Minnesota*, 179 US 223 (1900) with *Coyle v Smith*, 221 US 559 (1911).

as a state. Under their plan a small part of the District of Columbia would be retained as the seat of government of the United States, as required by the Constitution, but the rest of it would be admitted as a state. Such action would give the people of the district everything the proposed amendment would have—and more—and could be done with only the vote of a majority of both houses of Congress and the approval of the President.

The District has held a constitutional convention, adopted a proposed constitution, and petitioned Congress for admission of "New Columbia" under the terms of Article IV. Admission of the District as a new state has been endorsed by the Democratic Party and its prospects are more promising with a Democrat in the White House since admission of the district as a state would undoubtedly add two Democratic Senators and one Democratic member of the House.

Puerto Rico, with more than 3 million citizens, presently has commonwealth status: its citizens are American citizens. But while living and working in Puerto Rico they pay no federal taxes and Spanish is the language used in schools and government circles. Puerto Rico has no senators and no voting members in the House of Representatives, although it does have a delegate. In its referendum on November 14, 1993, 48.4 percent of the people of Puerto Rico voted to retain commonwealth status, 46.2 percent for statehood, and 4.4 percent for independence. This vote will probably put to rest the pressure for statehood, at least for the near future.

The Civil War conclusively settled the question of whether or not a state can constitutionally secede from the Union. In the words of the Supreme Court, ours is "an indestructible Union composed of indestructible States."[30]

SECTION 3

1. [continued] but no new State shall be formed or erected within the Jurisdiction of any other State; nor any State be formed by the Junction of two or more States, or Parts of States, without the Consent of the Legislatures of the States concerned as well as of the Congress.

Five states have been formed within the jurisdiction of other states with the consent of the legislatures concerned and of Congress: Vermont from New York in 1791, Kentucky from Virginia in 1792, Tennessee from North Carolina in 1796, Maine from Massachusetts in 1820, and West Virginia from Virginia (by a rump legislature during the Civil War) in 1863. When Texas was admitted to the Union, Congress consented to the division of the state into five states if the Texas legislature should ever so wish and thereby increase the number of senators from Texas to ten!

---

[30] *Texas* v *White*, 7 Wallace 700 (1869).

SECTION 3

2. The Congress shall have Power to dispose of and make all needful Rules and Regulations respecting the Territory or other Property belonging to the United States; and nothing in this Constitution shall be so construed as to Prejudice any Claims of the United States, or of any particular State.

When Puerto Rico, the Philippines, and Hawaii were annexed, the question arose whether or not "the Constitution followed the flag." The Supreme Court met the problem by distinguishing between "fundamental" and "formal" parts of the Constitution. The fundamental provisions are those that provide for fair trials, freedom of speech, and those rights necessary to an ordered scheme of liberty. The formal provisions are those, such as trial by jury, which at that time were considered forms appropriate for Americans but not essential for freedom and not the only way to secure justice.[31] The Court ruled in the *Insular Cases* that unless Congress provides otherwise, in unincorporated territories—those Congress has neither explicitly nor implicitly made an integral part of the Union—only the fundamental provisions apply.

Today Guam, the Northern Marianas, American Samoa, and the Virgin Islands are unincorporated territories. Although the *Insular Cases* have never been specifically overruled, their continuing validity has been questioned and it had been assumed that, as far as the constitutional protections for individuals are concerned, all provisions of the Constitution are applicable to the territories. Then in 1982 the Court gave the *Insular Cases* continuing vitality. It upheld the Commonwealth of Puerto Rico's authority to vest the right to fill vacancies in its legislature in the voters of the party in which the former legislator was a member. Citing the *Insular Cases,* the Court wrote, "It is not disputed that the fundamental protections of the United States Constitution extend to the inhabitants of Puerto Rico."[32] In 1990 the Court in a holding relating to application of the Fourth Amendment to Mexican nationals in Mexico (see page 249), re-endorsed the *Insular Cases'* holding: "Only 'fundamental' constitutional rights are guaranteed to inhabitants of those territories."[33] The significance of these dicta is not clear. Does the Court's use of the words "fundamental protections" and "fundamental constitutional rights" suggest that the nonfundamental parts of the Constitution do not apply? In the modern context, what are the nonfundamental parts? What is the meaning of such a distinction with respect to territories such as Puerto Rico, the Virgin Islands, Guam, and the Northern Marianas, where inhabitants are citizens of the United States?

Outside the context of protection of the rights of American citizens, it is clear that Congress may treat territories differently from states "so long as there is a rational

---

[31] *Hawaii* v *Mankichi,* 190 US 197 (1903); *Balzac* v *Puerto Rico,* 258 US 298 (1922).

[32] *Rodriguez* v *Popular Democratic Party,* 407 US 1 (1982).

[33] *United States* v *Verdugo-Urquidez,* 494 US 259 (1990).

basis for its action."[34] Thus, Congress was allowed to make lower social security payments to dependent children in Puerto Rico than to those in the states. The right to receive financial aid from the federal government is not a constitutionally protected right. Moreover, the distinction between the payments is rational, said the Court, because (1) Puerto Rican citizens, although American citizens, do not pay federal taxes; (2) the cost of treating Puerto Rico as a state would be very high; and (3) the payment of the greater benefits might disrupt the Puerto Rican economy.

SECTION 4
The United States shall guarantee to every State in this Union a Republican Form of Government,

---

The Constitution does not define "a republican form of government." John Adams observed, "The word *republic* as it is used, may signify anything, everything, or nothing."[35] The framers undoubtedly meant a form that, as distinguished from aristocracy, monarchy, or direct democracy, rests on the consent of the people and operates through representative institutions. In the landmark case of *Luther* v *Borden,* the Supreme Court held that what "a republican form of government" means is a political question, a responsibility of the Congress, not of the courts, to answer.[36] Whenever Congress permits the senators and representatives of a particular state to take their seats in Congress, that state must be deemed to have "a republican form of government" within the meaning of the Constitution. In 1902, after Oregon adopted the *initiative,* whereby its citizens are able to legislate directly without the intervention of the legislature,[37] a company that had been taxed under a law passed by the initiative procedure argued that such action transgressed the clause requiring states to have republican forms of government. The Court again refused to intervene, holding that "violation of the...guaranty of a republican form of government...cannot be challenged in the courts."[38]

Because the Court, at least until recently, firmly holds to the view that interpretation of the guarantee clause is a political question and not a justiciable one, the clause is seldom raised in litigation. As the Court said, "We approach the issue with some trepidation, because the Guarantee Clause has been an infrequent basis for litigation throughout our history." Long ago Charles Sumner

---

[34] *Harris* v *Rosario,* 446 US 651 (1980).

[35] C. Gordon Post, review of "The Guarantee Clause of the U.S. Constitution" by William M. Wiececk in *Annals of the American Academy of Political and Social Science* (New York: Cornell University Press, 1972).

[36] *Luther* v *Borden,* 7 Howard 1 (1849).

[37] Simply stated, the initiative procedure calls for two steps: (1) securing signatures of a required number of voters on a petition calling for submission of the proposed law to the electorate and (2) submission of the proposal to the voters in a general election. If approved by a majority of those voting on the proposition, the proposal becomes a law.

[38] *Pacific States Tel. & Tel.* v *Oregon,* 223 US 118 (1912); *Colegrove* v *Green,* 328 US 549 (1946). See also *Baker* v *Carr,* 369 US 186 (1962).

pointed out that the guarantee clause is "a sleeping giant." No other part of the Constitution gives "Congress such supreme power over the states."

Today there are those who argue that the Court should revive the guarantee clause and use it to impose on Congress the responsibility to supervise state activities directly to ensure that they meet the test of a republican form of government.[39] The Supreme Court itself has "suggested that perhaps not all claims under the Guarantee Clause present nonjusticiable political questions,"[40] but the primary restraint on congressional intervention into state matters remains, as it has always been, more political in nature than constitutional. Whenever Congress, responding to national majorities, feels the need to intervene in state matters, this clause is not the only one available to justify its intervention.

SECTION 4

[continued] and shall protect each of them against Invasion; and on Application of the Legislature, or of the Executive (when the Legislature cannot be convened) against domestic Violence.

Invasion of a state by a foreign power would also be an invasion of the United States.

Congress has delegated to the president the authority to send troops into a state to protect it from domestic violence, on the request of the appropriate state authority. In 1842 there were two governments in Rhode Island, each of which claimed to be the legitimate one. When President Tyler indicated that he was prepared to send troops to defend one of these against domestic violence from the other, he was at the same time determining which government was the legitimate one. The Supreme Court, refusing to intervene, called the question political.[41]

When necessary to enforce federal laws or federal judicial decrees or to preserve the property or "the peace of the United States," the president may send federal law enforcement agents or even troops to the scene of resistance. Under such circumstances, the president does not act at the request of state officials and may act even against their wishes: The president is not "ordering troops into a state" but enforcing the laws of the United States, which cover the length and breadth of the land.[42]

---

[39] C. Gordon Post, review of "The Guarantee Clause of the U.S. Constitution" by William M. Wiececk in *Annals of the American Academy of Political and Social Science* (New York: Cornell University Press, 1972). See also L. Tribe, *American Constituitional Law* (2d ed. 1988) p. 398.

[40] *New York* v *United States*, 120 L Ed 2d 130 (1992).

[41] *Luther* v *Borden*, 7 Howard 1 (1849).

[42] *In re Debs*, 158 US 464 (1895).

ARTICLE V: THE AMENDING POWER

The Congress, whenever two thirds of both Houses shall deem it necessary, shall propose Amendments to this Constitution, or, on the Application of the Legislatures of two thirds of the several States, shall call a Convention for proposing Amendments, which, in either Case, shall be valid to all Intents and Purposes, as Part of this Constitution, when ratified by the Legislatures of three fourths of the several States, or by Conventions in three fourths thereof, as the one or the other Mode of Ratification may be proposed by the Congress;

Amendments to the Constitution must be both proposed and ratified. The Constitution provides two ways to propose and two ways to ratify. So far, all amendments have been proposed by Congress, and all but one, the Twenty-first, have been ratified by the state legislatures.

The formal amendatory procedures have been criticized as undemocratic. One-fourth of the states plus one, which could reflect the wishes of much less than one-fourth of the people, could block amendments desired by a large majority. It is also possible for amendments to be adopted without a direct expression of popular opinion. The latter criticism would be largely met were Congress to require ratification by state conventions called for that purpose, rather than by state legislatures chosen to deal with other issues.

Of the many attempts to get Congress to call a constitutional convention to propose an amendment, so far the closest to success came in the spring of 1967, when thirty-three state legislatures, only one short of the number required, petitioned Congress to call a convention to propose an amendment to reverse Supreme Court rulings requiring both chambers of state legislatures to be apportioned on the basis of population. Suddenly, the many unanswered questions about how such a convention might operate ceased to be only of academic interest. But the thirty-fourth state legislature never acted, pressures for a reapportionment amendment abated as many states were reapportioned, and interest in a constitutional convention temporarily died down.

Concerns about a constitutional convention were revived in the 1980s because there are two active campaigns for the calling of such a convention. Some state legislatures have petitioned Congress to call a convention to propose an amendment permitting states to ban abortions. But the most active campaign has been that of the National Taxpayers Union working with the endorsements of Presidents Reagan and Bush, to get the additional two state legislatures it needs (thirty-two have already acted) to pass resolutions calling for a national convention to write and propose an amendment requiring the federal budget to be balanced each year, except during times of war or other emergencies declared by an extraordinary majority of Congress. Opponents of such an amendment, including Common Cause, organized labor, and many constitutional scholars, have been trying to get states that had previously adopted a resolution calling for a convention to repeal their call.

There are many questions relating to a constitutional convention for which there are no clear answers. How would a convention be run? How would delegates be apportioned? How would they be chosen? Could members of Congress become delegates? Are the petitions from the several states sufficiently identical to reflect support for a particular amendment? Have they been presented within a period to indicate there is a "contemporaneous national wish" for such an amendment? Congress, not the courts, would decide such questions.

Of greatest concern is the issue of whether Congress could call for a limited convention, restricting what the convention could consider. Scholars are divided on whether a convention could constitutionally ignore such a congressional limit. Once in session, a convention might, as did the Convention of 1787, "run away" and propose an entirely new constitution. Because of such concerns, many observers believe that, if thirty-four legislatures ever petition Congress to call a convention, they do so in language that makes it clear they all want a particular amendment and that they do it within the proper time. Congress is more likely to propose the amendment itself than to run the risk of calling a national convention.

Proposed amendments must be ratified. Congress decides which of the two methods of ratification will be used—approval by the legislatures of three-fourths of the states or approval by special state conventions in three-fourths of the states. Governors have no role in the ratification process. When Congress proposed the Twenty-first Amendment, repealing the Eighteenth Amendment (prohibition), it left to each state the determination of the manner in which delegates to its ratifying convention would be chosen.

May a state legislature, having rejected an amendment, change its mind and ratify? After it has ratified, may it change its mind and rescind its ratification? If a state constitution requires ratification to be by a two-thirds vote of each chamber of the state legislature, may a majority of that legislature subsequently rescind ratification? When are ratifications untimely? The lack of an absolutely clear and agreed-upon answer to these questions points to a danger spot in our Constitution, for the one thing that we should know for sure is what is and what is not required to amend the Constitution.

The predominant opinion, based on post–Civil War congressional practices, is that after voting against an amendment, a state legislature may reconsider and ratify but that once a legislature has ratified an amendment, its ratification cannot be rescinded and will be counted. On July 20, 1868, Secretary of State William H. Seward certified to Congress that the required twenty-eight states (there were then thirty-seven states) had approved the Fourteenth Amendment; however, Ohio and New Jersey had, prior to that date, "withdrawn their earlier assent." The next day, Congress declared the amendment a part of the Constitution and directed the secretary of state to promulgate it. On July 28 the secretary so certified. In the interim two other states had added their ratification. (Authority to make the initial certification of amendments, subject to ultimate congressional approval, has since been transferred to the archivist of the United States.)

This Fourteenth Amendment precedent was frequently cited during the battles over the ratification of the Equal Rights Amendment (ERA). In the fall of 1978, when Congress extended the period for ratification of the ERA, some members argued that, since the time was being extended, it was only fair that rescissions be counted (four states had already voted to rescind), but Congress refused to authorize rescissions. If the appropriate number of states had ratified, the issue of rescissions would have arisen again when Congress decided whether to certify the amendment.

Ratification of an amendment must take place within a "reasonable time." Congress determines what constitutes a reasonable time, but since it recently endorsed the ratification of the Twenty-seventh Amendment after 202 years it seems that a congressional control over reasonable time for ratification has little meaning. To avoid any danger that the other four long-ago proposed but as yet unratified amendments will become part of the Constitution, the Senate has declared all of them "dead."

What is likely to happen in the future is that Congress will be sure to do what it started to do beginning with the Eighteenth Amendment, submitted in 1917 when it placed a seven-year limit for ratification in the body of the amendment. However, when it submitted the Child Labor Amendment in 1924, it failed to set a time limit. Only twenty-eight state legislatures ratified it, the last in 1937. (Moreover, Supreme Court decisions since 1937 have provided Congress with other means of outlawing child labor, so the amendment is unnecessary.)

Beginning with the Twenty-third Amendment, proposed in 1960, Congress adopted the practice of setting a seven-year limit in the submissions of resolutions rather than making it a formal part of the amendment. Thus, when it appeared that the ERA would not be ratified within the seven-year limit, advocates of extending the time limit successfully argued that since the time limit was not part of the text of the proposed amendment, but was contained only in the resolution submitting it to the states, the time for ratification could be extended by a majority vote of both houses, instead of the two-thirds required to propose an amendment. When, in August of 1978, Congress proposed an amendment to give a greater voice in national affairs to the people of the District of Columbia, it pointedly reverted to previous practice and put the seven-year limit right in the body of the proposed amendment.

More than five thousand amendments have been introduced in Congress, but only thirty-three have been proposed. Twenty-seven of those have been ratified. One of the rejected amendments was proposed along with the ten that were finally ratified as the Bill of Rights. Another that was not ratified (1810) would have withdrawn citizenship from any person who accepted a title of nobility or who received, without the consent of Congress, an office or emolument from a foreign power. On the eve of the Civil War, Congress proposed an amendment that would have prohibited any amendment to the Constitution that interfered with slavery in any of the states.

The rejections of the Child Labor Amendment, the Equal Rights Amendment, and the second District of Columbia Amendment are somewhat unusual. During most of our history, if a coalition of political forces has been strong enough to get two-thirds of both houses of Congress to propose an amendment, it has ordinarily reflected a consensus strong enough to make ratification probable.

One of the stranger ratification stories is that of the Twenty-seventh Amendment. It was first proposed in 1789 as one of the original Bill of Rights. If it had been ratified then it would have become the "Second Amendment." What is now the First Amendment was in fact the third article of amendment proposed in 1789. The first article, which to this day remains unratified, would have limited the number of members of the House of Representatives to a meaningless number (see page 47). The proposed second article was ignored throughout most of our history, but in March 1982 a student at the University of Texas doing a paper on the Equal Rights Amendment came across this bit of history. He learned that only six of the original thirteen states had ratified it, and that during the intervening years only three more states had done so. He decided to start a ratification movement. He got some publicity for his efforts and a few states began to ratify. He and his colleagues had hoped to get the necessary three-fourths by 1989, the two hundredth anniversary of the inauguration of the Constitution.

Most observers felt that the ratification movement for what became the Twenty-seventh Amendment was more in the way of a political exercise to express displeasure about Congress rather than a serious attempt to amend the Constitution. In 1921 the Supreme Court had specifically cited that amendment, along with others then unratified, as examples of long-forgotten proposals which had failed to pass the test of being ratified in a time "sufficiently contemporaneous in that the number of States to reflect the will of the people in all sections at relatively the same period of which of course ratification scattered through a long series of years would not do."[1] However, when Michigan became the thirty-fourth state to ratify the amendment on May 7, 1992, Congress quickly confirmed its ratification (see Twenty-seventh Amendment).

Many questions arising out of Article V, especially those that relate to ratification, are political questions; indeed, it is possible that the Court would, if occasion arose, accept Justice Black's statement, made in 1939, "Congress, possessing exclusive power over the amending process, cannot be bound by and is under no duty to accept the pronouncements upon that exclusive power by this Court."[2]

[continued] Provided that no Amendment which may be made prior to the Year One thousand eight hundred and eight shall in any Manner affect the first and fourth Clauses in the Ninth Section of the first Article;

This provision referred to the importation of slaves and possesses only historical interest today. It is another example of how the framers, although

---

[1] *Dillon v Gloss*, 256 US 368 (1921)
[2] *Coleman v Miller*, 307 US 433 (1939), concurring opinion.

reluctantly willing to make the concessions necessary to secure the assent of the slave-owning states to the Constitution, went out of their way to avoid any overt mention of slaves or slavery.

[continued] and [provided] that no State, without its Consent, shall be deprived of its equal Suffrage in the Senate.

Some consider this provision unamendable, and others contend that there are ways in which even it can be changed. It could be repealed, they say, by amendment, and then another amendment could be adopted that would permit unequal representation in the Senate.

Other Methods of Constitutional Development

The Constitution, written before the industrial and democratic revolutions had made their imprint on the nation, continues to be a living, fundamental law for our powerful industrial democracy. Obviously, the Constitution has had to change as the nation changed. Although the framework is the same, fundamental alterations have been made in the operation of the government within that framework. The formal amending process has been relatively unimportant in this development; less formal, more subtle methods have been employed.

The Unwritten Constitution

Surrounding the formal document are customs and usage, congressional statutes, judicial decisions, and presidential practices that supplement the written Constitution. These rules are sometimes called the "unwritten Constitution."

It has been primarily through the use of informal methods of development and alteration in this unwritten Constitution that our system of government has grown. The Constitution was democratized by the extension of the suffrage within the states and by the extraconstitutional development of national political parties. The national government has been strengthened to meet the emergencies of a national economy and an interdependent world without fundamentally changing the written Constitution. In short, our Constitution provides for a living, organic, and growing governmental system.

Congressional Elaboration

The framers were wise and humble men who doubted that they had either the moral right or the necessary wisdom to prescribe the details of governing the nation for future generations. They knew that a rigid, detailed, and restrictive constitution would have little chance of enduring. They painted in broad strokes, made their grants of power general, and left it to Congress to develop the structure of government by ordinary legislation. Examples of congressional elaboration appear in such legislation as the Judiciary Act of 1789, which laid the foundation of our national judicial system; in the laws establishing the organization and functions of all federal executive officials subordinate to the president; in Congress's application and interpretation of its powers under the impeachment clauses; and in its rules of procedure, internal organization, and practices.

Presidential Practices

The president has great discretion in developing the nature and role of the office. There has been no change in the formal constitutional position of the president, but nowadays the president participates in the making of legislative policy to an extent not anticipated by the Founding Fathers; if they had anticipated it, they would probably have disapproved. With the growth of political parties, the president became a national party leader and an active participant in party battles. In response to crises, the presidency has grown into the pivotal office of our national government, and the president has become a key legislator as well as the nation's chief executive.

Judicial Interpretation

As we have already seen, the courts are the authoritative interpreters of the Constitution. The words of the Constitution are sufficiently broad to accommodate divergent interpretations. As conditions have changed, so have judicial interpretations of the Constitution. In the words of Woodrow Wilson, "The Supreme Court is a constitutional convention in continuous session." At one time, the Supreme Court ruled that the national government could not regulate child labor.[3] Today the national government does so with the approval of the Supreme Court. Earlier the Constitution was interpreted to deny Congress power to regulate discrimination practices of private individuals. Today there are a host of federal regulations designed to protect civil rights against abridgment by other individuals. And so it goes. The Supreme Court's responses to persistent public demand have often made it unnecessary formally to amend the Constitution in order for governmental practices to be brought into balance with public wishes.[4] Perhaps the best illustration of how judicial interpretation has altered our constitutional system is that the power of the courts to interpret the Constitution is itself the result of judicial interpretation.

---

[3] *Hammer v Dagenhart*, 247 US 251 (1918).
[4] *United States v Darby*, 312 US 11 (1941).

It should be noted that, although the Supreme Court has the final judicial say about the meaning of our Constitution, the Constitution is also interpreted daily by the hundreds of federal judges and by thousands of state judges. And judges have no monopoly on constitutional interpretation; the president and members of Congress are also obligated to refrain from violating the Constitution and when exercising their powers they must first interpret the Constitution. In a less formal way every time a prosecutor or a police official or a city council person acts in an official capacity, they too are giving an interpretation to the Constitution.

Customs and Usage

The president's cabinet and the local residence requirement for congressional members are examples of constitutional customs. A more significant example is the custom of presidential electors' pledging themselves to support the candidates of their party, a practice that has transformed the electoral college into an automatic transmitter of the electorate's choice.

ARTICLE VI: THE SUPREMACY ARTICLE

1. All Debts contracted and Engagements entered into, before the Adoption of this Constitution, shall be as valid against the United States under this Constitution, as under the Confederation.

At the time of the Constitutional Convention, the securities and currency issued by the Confederation and the several states had depreciated in value. Later, Alexander Hamilton, Washington's brilliant secretary of the treasury, proposed that the national government assume the debts of the several states and pay in full the debts of the Confederation. Adoption of this proposal did much to strengthen the new Union, at a handsome profit to speculators in Confederation securities.

2. This Constitution, and the Laws of the United States which shall be made in Pursuance thereof; and all Treaties made, or which shall be made, under the Authority of the United States, shall be the supreme Law of the Land;

This clause lays down one of the key principles of the Constitution, a principle that makes federalism work: Within the scope of its powers the national government is *supreme.* Any provision of a state constitution or any state law is null and void if it conflicts with the Constitution, with a federal law passed in pursuance of the Constitution, or with a treaty made under the authority of the United States. State courts, just as much as federal ones, are bound to uphold the supremacy of the Constitution and of national government when acting within the boundaries of the Constitution.

"State law may run afoul of the Supremacy Clause in two distinct ways: the law may regulate the Government directly or discriminate against it ..., or it may conflict with an affirmative command of Congress."[1] State laws may also interfere with a congressional policy. Thus, the Court held unenforceable a Pennsylvania law punishing advocacy of sedition against the United States as unenforceable because it conflicts with a similar federal law.[2] (However, a state law supersedes conflicting regulations of its own subgovernments.)

Preemption

It is not just the Constitution that takes priority over any state's action and renders the enforcement of a state law or action unconstitutional; it is also every law or regulation of the federal government. Federal regulations issued by executive agencies with authority from Congress have no less preemptive effect than federal statutes.[3] Nowadays, a considerable portion of our judges' time is taken trying to determine whether the federal government has preempted a state's action not only through its regulations of commerce, which we have discussed on page 78, but in its exercise of all its other powers.

Preemption may be either expressed or implied. "Absent explicit preemptive language, Congress's intent to supersede a state law may be inferred because the scheme of federal regulation may be so pervasive as to make reasonable the inference that Congress left no room for the States to supplement it, because the Act of Congress may touch a field in which the federal interest is so dominant that the federal system will be assumed to preclude enforcement of state laws on the same subject, or because the object sought to be obtained by federal law and the character of obligations imposed by it may reveal the same purpose."[4] "Even where Congress has not completely displaced state regulation ... state law is nullified to the extent that it conflicts with federal law," as when compliance with both federal and state regulations is impossible.[5]

Discerning the will of Congress with respect to preemption is no easier than discerning the meaning of the Constitution. Take the problems of deciding whether Congress has preempted the regulation of nuclear energy. There is perhaps no field in which the federal government has exercised more pervasive authority than in regulating nuclear plants to ensure their safety. Yet a unanimous Court decided California could impose a moratorium on any new nuclear plants until the state

---

[1] *North Dakota* v *United States*, 109 L Ed 2d 420 (1990).
[2] *Pennsylvania* v *Nelson*, 350 US 497 (1956); *Uphaus* v *Wyman*, 360 US 72 (1959).
[3] *Fidelity Federal S & L Assn.* v *De la Cuesta*, 458 US 141 (1982).
[4] *Pacific Gas & Electric* v *Energy Res. Commission*, 461 US 190 (1983).
[5] *Hillsborough County* v *Automated Med. Labs*, 471 US 707 (1985).

energy commission was satisfied that there was a feasible way to dispose of nuclear waste. California acted, so its legislature declared, not for reasons of safety but to prevent excessive costs to its citizens. "The legal reality remains," concluded the Supreme Court, "that Congress has left sufficient authority in the states to allow the development of nuclear power to be slowed or even stopped for economic reasons. Given this statutory scheme, it is for Congress to rethink the division of regulatory authority in light of its possible exercise by the states to undercut a federal objective. The courts should not assume the role which our system assigns to Congress."[6]

---

2. [continued] and the Judges in every State shall be bound thereby, any Thing in the Constitution or Laws of any State to the Contrary notwithstanding.

Although Congress cannot force a state to create a court, if a state does create a court, state courts have a concurrent duty to enforce federal law according to their regular mode of procedure and cannot fail to do so because the federal law is contrary to the policy of their state. States' neutral rules that apply both to federal or state cases may be applied, but a state may not by denoting something as jurisdictional relieve state courts of their responsibility to enforce federal laws. "The Supremacy Clause requires more than that."[7]

The Existence of the States and the Supremacy Clause

Although the powers of Congress are granted by the Constitution without any reference to the states, Congress is not to exercise its powers in a fashion that impairs the states' integrity or ability to function effectively. This prohibition is made explicit by the Tenth Amendment. Yet it is easier to make this generalization than to cite cases in which the existence of the states has constrained the exercise of congressional powers. The only cases in modern times have been *National League of Cities* v *Usery*, which was overruled nine years later in *Garcia* v *San Antonio Metro Transit Authority*,[8] and *New York* v *United States*,[9] which in practice placed little constraint on Congress.

In *National League of Cities* the Supreme Court, by a sharply divided vote, held that federal wage and hour regulations could not be applied to the employees of state governments. Here Congress, said the Court, had interfered with the states' "freedom to structure integral operations in areas of traditional governmental functions...functions essential to separate and independent existence."[10]

Following *National League of Cities* the Court went out of its way to make it clear that the reach of that decision was exceedingly limited.[11] The Court

---

[6] *Pacific Gas & Electric* v *Energy Res. Commission*, 461 US 190 (1983).
[7] *Howelett* v *Rose*, 496 US 356 (1990).
[8] *Garcia* v *San Antonio Metropolitan Transit Authority*, 469 US 528 (1985).
[9] *New York* v *United States*, 120 L Ed 2d 120 (1992).
[10] *National League of Cities* v *Usery*, 426 US 833 (1976).
[11] *Hodel* v *Virginia Surface Min. & Recl. Assn.*, 452 US 264 (1981).

started to distinguish between traditional state activities that are integral parts of state governments—generally immune from federal regulation—and all other state activities, such as a state-owned railroad, which are not immune from federal regulation.[12] Moreover, the decisions following *National League of Cities* were hard to reconcile with it. Justice Stevens, one of the dissenters, called for its reversal as "inconsistent with the central purpose of the Constitution itself," and as a "modern embodiment of the spirit of the Articles of Confederation."[13]

Then in *Garcia*, Justice Blackmun, who had provided the fifth vote in *National League of Cities*, switched and wrote the opinion for the Court over-ruling it. There is no principled way, he argued, to distinguish between traditional and nontraditional state governmental functions. Although agreeing that "the States occupy a special and specific position in our constitutional system and that the scope of Congress' authority under the Commerce Clause must reflect that position," he clearly rejected the view that the Supreme Court is the primary agency to prevent Congress from extending its powers in such a way as to intrude into the province of the states. Rather, he argued, "the Framers chose to rely on a federal system in which special restraints on federal power over the States inhered principally in the workings of the National Government itself.... State sovereign interests, then, are more properly protected by procedural safeguards inherent in the structure of the federal system than by judicially created limitations on federal power."[14] In *South Carolina v Baker*, the Court not only confirmed Garcia but appeared to close down the possibility that there might be some categories of state activity constitutionally protected from national regulation.[15] There must be some evidence of "extraordinary defects in the national political process" before the Court will entertain a violation of the Tenth Amendment.

Justice Powell, in what for him was an unusually strong opinion, dissented in *Garcia* and accused the majority of rejecting almost 200 years of understanding of the constitutional status of federalism, "of propounding a view of federalism that pays only lip service to the role of the States," of reflecting an "unprecedented view that Congress is free under the Commerce Clause to assume a State's traditional sovereign power, and to do so without judicial review of its action." Justice O'Connor predicted that the principles of *National League of Cities* would "in time again command the support of a majority of the Court" and that "this Court will in time again assume its constitutional responsibility."[16] She came close to being right. Justices subsequently nominated by Presidents Reagan and Bush—Scalia, Kennedy, Souter, and Thomas—are more sympathetic to O'Connor's version of federalism than that of the *Garcia* majority. Yet even the conservative justices acknowledged that if the Court resumes the task of protecting the states, the set of activities protected by state sover-

---

[12] *United Transportation Union* v *Long Island Railroad Co.*, 455 US 678 (1982).

[13] *EEOC* v *Wyoming*, 460 US 226 (1983).

[14] *Garcia* v *San Antonio Metropolitan Transit Authority*, 469 US 528 (1985).

[15] *South Carolina* v *Baker*, 485 US 505 (1988).

[16] Ibid.

eignty from the reach of the national government "may well be negligible."[17] Justice Ruth Bader Ginsberg may be the swing vote on this issue and how she goes may determine whether *Garcia* is reaffirmed or modified.

In fact the Rehnquist Court has already started to modify the *Garcia* doctrine. It refused to apply the Age Discrimination in Employment Act of 1967 to set aside a provision of the Missouri Constitution mandating the retirement of judges at the age of seventy because Congress, although specifically making the law applicable to state employees, had not plainly stated it intended the law to apply to state judges.[18]

Then in *New York v United States* the Court actually held that Congress had violated the Tenth Amendment. Congress had commanded that states must take title to low-level radioactive waste generated in the state if they failed to provide for a site to dispose of internally generated waste by a specific date. (The Court did hold that Congress could allow states that operate disposal sites to charge a surcharge on waste from states that lack such sites.) Whereas *Garcia* involved the application to states of a law generally applicable to private companies, Justice O'Connor for the Court argued, "this is not a case in which Congress has subjected a State to the same legislation applicable to private parties," but rather "it is a command by Congress to a state. Whether one views the take title provision as lying outside of Congress' enumerated powers, or as infringing upon the core of state sovereignty reserved by the Tenth Amendment, the provision is inconsistent with the federal structure of our Government established by the Constitution.... Whatever the outer limits 'of the sovereignty left to the States' may be, one thing is clear: The Federal Government may not compel the States to enact or administer a federal regulatory program." Justice White, with whom Justices Blackmun and Stevens joined, accused the Court of making an illogical distinction from the *Garcia* holding and of engaging in an outdated interpretation of federalism.

Here is another example of how the election of President Clinton is likely to alter the course of constitutional construction. For it is probable that President Clinton's appointees to the federal bench are more likely to strengthen *Garcia* than to use *New York v United States* as the opening to overrule it.

It is not clear whether Congress can be counted upon, as the Court argued in *Garcia*, to protect the states from being overwhelmed by the national government. Members of Congress have their own constituencies and are no longer dependent on state political parties for their funds or for electoral help. State governments do not appear to have great influence in the halls of Congress. Congressional voting on federalism issues suggests moderate levels of support for the concept of federalism,[19] but it is not an overwhelming con-

---

[17] Ibid.

[18] *Gregory v Ashcroft*, 115 L Ed 2d 410 (1991).

[19] Rodney E. Hero, "The U.S. Congress and American Federalism: Are 'Subnational' Governments Protected?" *The Western Political Quarterly* (vol. 42, March 1989), p. 103. See for greater skepticism, Martha Derthick, "Preserving Federalism: Congress, the States, and the Supreme Court," *The Brookings Review* (Winter/Spring 1986), p. 32–37.

cern for most members of Congress. Although a few senators have suggested a constitutional amendment to reverse *Garcia,* the movement to do so has not generated much support. The debate over *National League of Cities* and *Garcia* and the division of opinion among the justices should nonetheless give Congress a mild warning that the existence of the states does set some limits on its exercise of the powers granted to it.

If the principles of federalism are not much of a barrier to congressional exercise of the commerce power, they are even less a barrier when Congress acts to enforce the Fourteenth and Fifteenth Amendments. That congressional actions to enforce those amendments may interfere with essential state functions is of no constitutional consequence.[20]

United States Treaty Power

Treaties are of two types: self-executing and non-self-executing. Self-executing treaties require no implementation by Congress to have internal application as supreme law of the land. If the president, with the consent of two-thirds of the Senate, makes a self-executing treaty giving foreign nationals certain rights in return for reciprocal concessions for American nationals, such a treaty is valid as internal law. It takes precedence over any conflicting state constitutions or laws. Non-self-executing treaties, although establishing a binding international obligation, must be implemented in this country by Congress; the implementing legislation becomes supreme law of the land, enforceable in the courts.

Treaties, like national laws, must conform to the national Constitution. A treaty, or a law implementing a treaty, that abridged First Amendment freedoms would be just as unconstitutional as a law that did the same thing. "This Court has regularly and uniformly recognized the supremacy of the Constitution over a treaty."[21] Nonetheless, the limitations of federalism, such as they are, do not appear to limit the scope of the national government's treaty-making power as they do its law-making powers.

Note that whereas the supremacy clause makes only those "laws of the United States made in pursuance" of the Constitution the supreme law of the land, it makes "all treaties made, or which shall be made, under the authority of the United States" supreme law. Does this difference in constitutional language have any significance? The question came to the Supreme Court in the famous case of *Missouri* v *Holland* (1920). After Congress passed a law in 1913 regulating the hunting of migratory birds, several district judges ruled that the law was unconstitutional because regulation of wild game is not among the powers delegated to the national government. Three years later, the United States became party to a treaty with Canada (through Great Britain) in which the national government promised to protect the birds migrating

---

[20] *Fitzpatrick v Bitzer,* 427 US 445 (1976).
[21] *Reid v Covert,* 354 US 1 (1957).

between Canada and this country in return for a promise by Canada to do the same. To fulfill our obligations under this treaty, Congress passed a law even more stringent than its 1913 enactment. This time the case went to the Supreme Court. Justice Holmes, speaking for a unanimous Court, said,

> Acts of Congress are the supreme law of the land only when made in pursuance of the Constitution, while treaties are declared to be so when made under the authority of the United States.... We do not mean to imply that there are no qualifications to the treaty-making power; but they must be ascertained in a different way.... The only question is whether it is forbidden by some invisible radiation from the general terms of the Tenth Amendment.... We see nothing in the Constitution that compels the Government to sit by while a food supply is cut off and the protectors of our forest and our crops are destroyed.[22]

Discussions today of whether the treaty power is broader than the national lawmaking power have lost much of their significance. With the liberal construction of the national government's legislative powers, there are few subjects of national importance that Congress cannot directly regulate.

3. The Senators and Representatives before mentioned, and the Members of the several State Legislatures, and all executive and judicial Officers, both of the United States and of the several States, shall be bound by Oath or Affirmation, to support this Constitution;

This clause makes it clear that the first allegiance of all Americans, including state officials, is to the national Constitution. If a state governor, for example, is ordered by the state constitution or legislature to perform an act contrary to the national Constitution, the governor's duty is nonetheless to comply with the national Constitution.

3. [continued] but no religious Test shall ever be required as a Qualification to any Office of public Trust under the United States.

This provision applies only to the national government, but as a result of the adoption of the First and Fourteenth Amendments, the same prohibition applies to state and local governments.[23]

Note that Article I, Section 3, paragraph 6, and Article II, Section 1, paragraph 8, on pages 52 and 121, are additional evidence of the framers' concern for religious freedom. Whenever the Constitution calls for an oath to God to tell

---

[22] *Missouri v Holland*, 252 US 416 (1920).
[23] *Torcaso v Watkins*, 367 US 488 (1961).

the truth or to perform responsibilities, an alternative is provided for those who may have convictions against the swearing of such oaths. They, or anyone, may choose merely to affirm that they will tell the truth or carry out their duties.

ARTICLE VII: RATIFICATION OF THE CONSTITUTION

The Ratification of the Conventions of nine States, shall be sufficient for the Establishment of this Constitution between the States so ratifying the Same.

The Constitutional Convention was a revolutionary body. The delegates were representatives of the states acting in response to a call by the Congress of the Confederation. Since the Articles of Confederation could be amended only with the consent of all thirteen state legislatures, and since they created a "perpetual Union," Congress, when it called the convention, had explicitly stated that no recommendations should be effective until approved by Congress and ratified in accordance with the terms of the Articles, that is, by all thirteen state legislatures. Nevertheless, the delegates to the convention boldly assumed power to exceed their mandate and proposed an entirely new government, which was to go into effect upon ratification by specially chosen conventions of only nine of the thirteen states.

Done in Convention by the Unanimous Consent of the States present the Seventeenth Day of September in the Year of our Lord one thousand seven hundred and Eighty seven and of the Independence of the United States of America the Twelfth. *In Witness whereof We have hereunto subscribed our Names.*

For a discussion of the signing of the Constitution, see pages 16–17.

CHAPTER FOUR

AMENDMENTS TO THE CONSTITUTION

THE BILL OF RIGHTS

Much of the opposition to ratification of the Constitution stemmed from its lack of specific guarantees of certain fundamental rights. The Constitutional Convention failed to adopt such guarantees because they were thought to be unnecessary and dangerous—unnecessary because the Constitution itself prohibits bills of attainder, ex post facto laws, and suspension of the writ of habeas corpus except in times of public danger, and requires trial by jury in federal criminal cases; dangerous because prohibitions might furnish an argument for claiming powers not granted the new government. For example, to forbid the national government to abridge freedom of the press might be thought to imply that it had the power to *regulate* the press if it could do so without abridging it. It was also urged that the protection of fundamental rights ultimately rested not on paper guarantees but in the hearts and minds of the nation's citizens.[1]

Despite those arguments, there was a general demand for a bill of rights; the Constitution was adopted with the understanding that the first business of the First Congress would be the consideration of amendments suitable for the purpose. Congress proposed twelve such amendments on September 25, 1789, ten of which were ratified and became part of the Constitution on December 15, 1791. One that was not ratified prescribed the ratio of representation to population in the House of Representatives; the other, which prohibited any increase in compensation to members of Congress until an election for representatives had intervened, was ratified 203 years later to become the Twenty-seventh Amendment (see page 409).

THE BILL OF RIGHTS AND THE STATES

By 1787 most state constitutions contained a bill of rights. In general, people were confident that they had sufficient political power to prevent abuse

---

[1] Alexander Hamilton, *The Federalist*, No. 84.

of authority by state and local officials. But the national government was new, distant, and threatening; the Bill of Rights was added to the Constitution to restrict its powers. In *Barron* v *Baltimore,* John Marshall confirmed the obvious: the Bill of Rights applies only to the national government; it imposes no restraints on state and local authorities.[2]

The national government, however, responsive to a broad-based political community, proved less a threat to civil liberties and civil rights than did state and local governments. Furthermore, the primary responsibility for the administration of justice vests in the states; the failure of the national Constitution to restrain state and local authorities left large segments of governmental activity without federal constitutional limitation. True, state constitutions contain most of the same guarantees as the Bill of Rights; however, state judges, who alone have jurisdiction to construe their respective state constitutions, until very recently seldom applied their state bills of rights so as to restrain state or local officials.

After the adoption of the Fourteenth Amendment, which does apply to state (and local) governments, the Supreme Court was urged to construe the amendment, especially its due process clause, as applying the same limitations to the states that the Bill of Rights applies to the national government. Although in 1895 the Supreme Court brought within the scope of the due process clause a provision of the Bill of Rights forbidding the taking of private property without just compensation,[3] for decades it refused to go further.

Then in 1925, in *Gitlow* v *New York,* the Supreme Court took the momentous step of holding that the word *liberty* in the due process clause of the Fourteenth Amendment includes liberty of speech.[4] By the early 1940s, the Supreme Court had *incorporated* within the due process clause all the provisions of the First Amendment. In short, by construction of the Fourteenth Amendment, the substantive restrictions that the Bill of Rights places on the national government in order to protect freedom of religion, of speech, of the press, of petition, and of assembly are given national constitutional protection against abridgment by state and local authorities.

What of the other parts of the Bill of Rights? If the due process clause of the Fourteenth Amendment imposes on state governments the same limitations that the First Amendment places on the national government, does the rest of the Bill of Rights also come within the scope of the Fourteenth Amendment? For some time, a persistent minority of Supreme Court justices argued that it did; they would have construed the due process clause of the Fourteenth Amendment to mean that the states should follow precisely the same procedures that the Bill of Rights requires of the national government. What national authorities cannot do because of the Bill of Rights, these justices contended, state authorities could not do because of the due process clause of the Fourteenth Amendment. Ultimately, their arguments have almost carried the

---

[2] *Barron* v *Baltimore,* 7 Peters 243 (1833).
[3] *Chicago B & O RR Co.* v *City of Chicago,* 166 US 226 (1895).
[4] *Gitlow* v *New York,* 268 US 652 (1925).

day: the Supreme Court has not gone quite so far as to incorporate into the Fourteenth Amendment all the applicable provisions of the Bill of Rights, but it has come very close to doing so.

The Court applies the *doctrine of selective incorporation,* or, because it was explained by Justice Cardozo in *Palko* v *Connecticut,* the *Palko* test.[5] According to this view, the Fourteenth Amendment's due process clause does not prescribe any specific procedures for the administration of justice or the execution of governmental affairs. Rather, it forbids states to adopt a procedure that "offends some principle of justice so rooted in the traditions and conscience of our people as to be ranked as fundamental," or to deprive people of rights "implicit in the concept of ordered liberty." The application of this general standard of fundamental fairness has resulted in the selective incorporation or absorption, as it is sometimes called, into the due process clause of almost all the provisions of the Bill of Rights. Those few not incorporated, such as the Fifth Amendment requirement of indictment by grand jury, provide certain procedures that will secure justice but they are not the only procedures that will do so: states can and do indict persons, that is, formally charge them with crimes and force them to stand trial, by what is called *information,* that is, charges brought by the prosecutor.

Beginning in the 1930s and accelerating after 1964, the Supreme Court selectively incorporated provision after provision of the Bill of Rights into the requirements of the due process clause of the Fourteenth Amendment. In 1968 a Court majority modified the *Palko* test to permit the easier incorporation of additional provisions: the Supreme Court now asks if a particular procedure is considered fundamental to the *American* system of ordered liberty. Using this standard, the Supreme Court ruled that trial by jury for serious offenses is essential for due process. The Court conceded that in some societies justice is secured without using juries (in England most criminal trials take place before judges without juries), but "in the American states, as in the federal judicial system...a general grant of jury trial for serious offenses is a fundamental right, essential for preventing miscarriages of justice and for assuring that fair trials are provided for all defendants."[6]

By 1970, the Bill of Rights had been, for all practical purposes, incorporated into the Fourteenth Amendment. Today, except for the Second, Third, and Tenth Amendments, which are not applicable, the Fourteenth Amendment imposes on states all the requirements the Bill of Rights imposes on the national government, *except* indictment for serious crimes by a grand jury and trial by jury in all civil cases involving more than $20.

Although the specific provisions of the Bill of Rights provide most of the contours of the limitations on state and local governments, the Court has also held that, since there are no superfluous parts of the Constitution, the due process requirements of the Fifth and Fourteenth Amendments are additional limitations on national and state governments beyond those enumerated in the other provisions of the Bill of Rights. The due process clauses protect other fundamental rights, such as the right of privacy.

---

[5] *Palko* v *Connecticut,* 302 US 319 (1937).
[6] *Duncan* v *Louisiana,* 391 US 145 (1968).

What does it mean to say that the Bill of Rights, or at least most of it, has been absorbed into the Fourteenth Amendment? The absorption has three major consequences: (1) the Supreme Court has jurisdiction to review cases involving the application of these provisions and to establish standards to guide the behavior of state and local, as well as national authorities; (2) the federal district judges, through habeas corpus petitions, have greater jurisdiction to hear complaints by persons alleging that they are being held contrary to the commands of the Constitution; (3) Congress has the power to pass whatever laws are necessary and proper to implement constitutional guarantees in the states.

Harmless Error Analysis

The "nationalization" of the Bill of Rights has not, however, ended constitutional debate, nor is each provision of the Bill of Rights treated in the same fashion. The old battles are being fought in new ways. For example, the Supreme Court now distinguishes between "constitutional rights so basic to a fair trial that their infraction can never be treated as a harmless error" and "constitutional errors which in the setting of a particular case are so unimportant and insignificant that they may, consistent with the Federal Constitution, be deemed harmless, not requiring the automatic reversal of the conviction."[7] Examples of the former are denial of the right to counsel, lack of an impartial judge, conviction by a jury that acted on an indictment by a grand jury from which persons were excluded because of their race, or conviction and death sentence by a jury from which a juror was improperly dismissed because of opposition to the death penalty.[8] Similarly, if a judge fails properly to instruct a jury that it may not convict unless the evidence shows beyond a "reasonable doubt" that the accused is guilty, this is not a harmless error. The defendant has been denied the constitutionally protected Sixth Amendment to trial by a properly instructed and impartial jury.[9]

Examples of possibly harmless errors are comments by a prosecutor about a defendant's failure to take the stand, unconstitutionally overbroad jury instructions at the sentencing stage of a capital case, denial of a defendant's right to be present at a trial, and use of evidence obtained in violation of the Fourth Amendment. A prosecutor's comments violate the right against self-incrimination, but if the state reviewing courts find that in the context of the entire trial and of other evidence presented, these errors were harmless beyond a reasonable doubt," such convictions need not be set aside.[10] Similarly, admitting into evidence a codefendant's confession when the codefendant refused to take the stand, and was therefore not subject to confrontation, violates the confrontation clause of the Sixth Amendment, but in view of the defendant's own minutely detailed and consistent confession, the Court ruled the violation a

---

[7] *Chapman* v *California*, 386 US 18 (1967).

[8] *Vasquez* v *Hillery*, 474 US 254 (1986); *Gray* v *Mississippi*, 481 US 648 (1987).

[9] *Sullivan* v *Louisiana*, June 1, 1993.

[10] *Chapman* v *California*, 386 US 18 (1967).

harmless error.[11] Violation of the right to confront witnesses (see page 516) does not require reversal if the reviewing court "may confidently say, on the whole record, that the constitutional error was harmless beyond a reasonable doubt."[12] Until 1991 the introduction of a coerced confession was thought to render any trial to be a denial of due process, whether or not there was other evidence of guilt, and thus not subject to harmless error analysis. But in that year the Court held that a coerced confession, at least one not obtained by physical violence, can be subjected to harmless error analysis and sustained if after such review this error is thought to be harmless.[13]

There are, apparently, endless refinements to the application of the harmless error doctrine. For example, the standard for its application when a conviction should be set aside because of a federal constitutional error on direct review is that the error "was harmless beyond a reasonable doubt." The standard, however, for determining whether habeas relief must be granted is more difficult: it depends on whether the error "had substantial and injurious effect or influence in determining the jury's verdict."[14]

Provisions Subject to Collateral Habeas Corpus Review

Another variation of the argument about whether some provisions of the Bill of Rights are more fundamental than others concerns the *Teague rule*, which limits federal judges from retroactively applying new rules to petitioners for habeas corpus review of state court decisions to only two exceptions. The first exception is if a new interpretation, that is, a new rule of law, places certain kinds of individual conduct beyond the power of the criminal law-making authority to proscribe. The second exception is for rules which involve those fundamental procedures and provisions of the Constitution that are "implicit in the concept of ordered liberty," and are thereby given greater status, such as the right to counsel at a criminal trial. Judges are not, however, to apply retroactively those new rules that apply to rights that are not so fundamental and that do not diminish the likelihood of obtaining an accurate verdict, for example, a restriction on police-initiated interrogation following a suspect's request for counsel.[15]

State Bills of Rights

After the Supreme Court had incorporated most of the provisions of the Bill of Rights into the Fourteenth Amendment, little attention was paid by state judges or anybody else to the bills of rights in their respective state constitutions.

---

[11] *Schneble* v *Florida*, 405 US 427 (1972).
[12] *Delaware* v *Van Arsdall*, 475 US 673 (1986).
[13] *Arizona* v *Fulminante*, 113 L Ed 2d 202 (1991).
[14] *Brecht* v *Abrahamson*, 123 L Ed 2d 353 (1993); see also *Chapman* v *California*, 386 US 18 (1969).
[15] *Butler* v *McKellar*, 108 L Ed 2d 347 (1990).

"The Supreme Court took such complete control of the field that state judges could sit back in the conviction that their part was simply to await the next landmark decisions."[16] Then, after the United States Supreme Court had begun in the mid-1970s to retreat from an expansive interpretation of some provisions of the Bill of Rights, especially those relating to the rights of persons accused of crimes, some observers, including Justices Brennan and Stevens, began to urge state supreme courts to step into the breach.[17] As former Justice Stanley Mosk of the California Supreme Court pointed out, state supreme courts that were "once thought to be mere bus stops en route to the U.S. Supreme Court," by using their state constitutions, "can have the final word."[18]

In the past the state courts could declare a practice, law, or procedure unconstitutional and by citing both federal and state cases could be ambiguous about whether it was unconstitutional because it violated the federal Constitution and the state judges were merely following the dictates of the U.S. Supreme Court or whether it was unconstitutional because the state judges on their own were so interpreting it under their own state constitutions.[19] Justice Stevens believes that the state courts should strike out on their own more often under their own constitutions, and that, whenever a state supreme court has made use of both federal and state cases, the presumption ought to be that it decided under state constitutional law rather than federal constitutional law. But in *Michigan* v *Long,* the U.S. Supreme Court said that, unless the state courts explicitly stated that they are relying on independent and adequate grounds in their own state constitutions, the Supreme Court will assume that the decision was made on federal grounds and thus the decision could appropriately be reviewed and reversed by the Supreme Court.[20] Henceforth if state judges wish to rely on their own state constitutions they will have to accept the responsibility for making unpopular decisions.

A few state supreme courts have taken up the challenge, providing greater protections for civil liberties through their own constitutions, particularly in the arena of rights of criminal defendants and protection of the press. Rulings of Oregon, California, New Jersey, Wisconsin, Massachusetts, and Washington are noteworthy. Examples include the decision of the Minnesota Supreme Court barring newsroom searches allowed by the U.S. Supreme Court in *Zurcher* v *Stanford* (see page 227); decisions in California, Texas, and other states requiring an equalization of funding among school districts—an equalization not required by the Supreme Court's interpretation of the U.S. Constitution in a case from Texas, *San Antonio School District* v *Rodriguez* (see page 556); and decisions of some state courts requiring exclusion of uncon-

---

[16] *Harvard Civil Rights-Civil Liberties Law Review,* 1973, quoted in Robert Welsh and Ronald K. L. Collins, *The Center Magazine,* 14 (September-October 1981): 6.

[17] William J. Brennan, Jr., "State Constitutions and the Protection of Individual Rights," *Harvard Law Review* 90 (1977), p. 489.

[18] Justice Stanley Mosk of the California Supreme Court as quoted in Fred Barbash, "State Courts Expanding Individual's Rights: Role Reversal in Judicial Systems," *The Washington Post,* sec. A (April 2, 1984): 1.

[19] *Michigan* v *Long,* 463 US 1032 (1983); *Delaware* v *Van Arsdall,* 475 US 673 (1986).

[20] *Michigan* v *Long,* 463 US 1032 (1983).

stitutionally seized evidence, which will keep such evidence out of those state courts despite the Supreme Court's limited good faith exception, announced in *United States* v *Leon* (see page 267).

The trend toward state courts' staking out a different line of interpretation from the U.S. Supreme Court could become more pronounced if the Court moves toward the views of its more conservative justices—less likely as a result of the Clinton Administration's probability of appointing Supreme Court jurists less sympathetic to the constitutional views of the current conservative justices— and as more and more lawyers become familiar with state constitutional law. Yet, despite somewhat more adventurous stands on the part of state courts in relying on their own state constitutions, the United States Supreme Court and the United States Constitution remain the dominant protection for civil liberties and civil rights. Finally, and perhaps most importantly, a majority of state judges who might step into the breach, giving more protection to some rights under their state constitutions than the Supreme Court is giving to the same rights under the national Constitution, lack lifetime tenure. They may make themselves targets for electoral reprisal if they anger significant portions of the electorate.

Amendment I: Religion, Speech, Assembly, and Petition

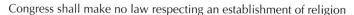

Congress shall make no law respecting an establishment of religion

The First Amendment is directed specifically to Congress. The Fourteenth Amendment, as now interpreted, imposes the same restrictions on the states.

God is not mentioned in the Constitution, and the word religion occurs in only one other place: in the prohibition of any religious test as a qualification for office. The framers of the Constitution were not irreligious. Several of them came from states with established religions, but all probably agreed that religious matters should not fall within the jurisdiction of the national government.

There are two religion clauses—this one, forbidding the establishment of religion, and the next, prohibiting governments from interfering with the free exercise of religion—but they provide no definition of *religion*. The Supreme Court has been reluctant, understandably, to get into this question. "Although, only beliefs rooted in religion are protected by the Free Exercise Clause, ... one can, of course, imagine an asserted claim so bizarre, and so clearly nonreligious in motivation, as not to be entitled to protection under the Constitution."[1] Nonetheless, "religious beliefs need not be acceptable, logical, consistent, or comprehensible to others in order to merit First Amendment

---

[1] *Sherbert* v *Verner*, 374 US 398 (1963); *Thomas* v *Review Board*, 450 US 707 (1981).

protection."[2] "To claim the protection of the Free Exercise clause," one does not have to respond "to the commands of a particular religious organization."[3] It is enough the belief be a sincerely held religious one (see page 195).

As difficult as the cases involving the two religion clauses have been, they promise to become even more complicated as the pervasiveness of governmental actions continue and as the number of less orthodox religious groups expands.

Establishment Clause

Establishment clause cases are not easy. They stir deep feelings, and the justices, reflecting differences in the nation, are often divided among themselves. Jefferson's "wall of separation between church and state" has become "as winding as the famous serpentine wall" he designed for the University of Virginia.[4] "The Establishment Clause ... erects a blurred, indistinct, and variable barrier depending on all the circumstances of a particular relationship."[5]

When a dispute breaks out between factions within a congregation or between a congregation and its own external church authorities, judges have to tread carefully. Obviously, civil judges should not decide in such a dispute which side is orthodox and which heretical. But if the dispute involves questions about who owns church property, the Supreme Court has given judges permission to decide such issues by using rules previously established by the church.[6]

Some have argued that the establishment clause does not forbid governmental support for religion but merely governmental favoritism toward a particular religion. The Supreme Court has rejected this construction,[7] although variations of a *no-preference doctrine* have been espoused by the Chief Justice, Justice Scalia, and Justice Thomas, at least to the extent of reading the Constitution as permitting governments to accommodate the people's religious and spiritual needs, provided there is no state religion and no one is coerced into religious activities. Justices Scalia and Thomas have specifically stated that they find no violation of the establishment clause unless there is an embrace of a *particular* religious sect.[8]

As presently construed, all levels of government must be completely neutral, aiding neither a particular religion nor all religions. "A given law might not *establish* a state religion but nevertheless be one 'respecting' that end in the sense of being a step that could lead to such establishment and hence offend the First Amendment."[9] Indeed, in *Lemon v Kurtzman* the Court established a three-part test a statute must pass to survive an establishment challenge. (1) The statute must have a *secular purpose*. "While the Court is normally defer-

[2] Ibid. See also *United States v Seeger*, 380 US 33 (1965).

[3] *Frazee v Employment Security Dept.*, 488 US 814 (1989), quoting *Thomas v Review Board*, 450 US 707 (1981).

[4] Justice Jackson concurring in *Illinois ex rel McCollum v Board of Education*, 333 US 203 (1948).

[5] *Lynch v Donnelly*, 465 US 668 (1984).

[6] *Jones v Wolf*, 443 US 595 (1979).

[7] *Abington School District v Schempp*, 374 US 203 (1963); *Engel v Vitale*, 370 US 421 (1962).

[8] Concurring in *Lamb's Chapel v Center Moriches Union Free School District*, 124 L Ed 2d 352 (1993).

[9] *Lemon v Kurtzman*, 403 US 602 (1971).

ential to a State's articulation of a secular purpose, it is required that the statement of such purpose be sincere and not a sham."[10] (2) Its primary *effect* must neither advance nor inhibit religion. (3) "*Excessive entanglement*" with religion must be avoided by the government, especially if it sends out a warning signal by engendering political divisiveness along religious lines.

The *Lemon* test survives despite many justices' unhappiness with it and various attempts to modify it. After the Court once again reaffirmed the *Lemon* test Justice Scalia, perhaps its leading critic, quipped that the Court's invocation of the *Lemon* test is "Like some ghoul in a late-night movie that repeatedly sits up in its grave and shuffles abroad, after being repeatedly killed and buried."[11] Sometimes the Court's *accommodationist* wing dominates and gives the *Lemon* test a twist in which, to survive a challenge that a law violates the establishment clause, a statute's "secular legislative purpose" need not be an *exclusively* secular one. The statute must still have a "primary effect that neither advances nor inhibits religion," but a "law is not unconstitutional simply because it 'allows' churches to advance religion."[12] It is okay if the benefit to religion is only slight or incidental or if the law happens to coincide or harmonize with the tenets of some religions. And, although the statute and its administration must still avoid "excessive government entanglement with religion," divisiveness along religious lines is not by itself sufficient to invalidate government conduct.[13] Justice O'Connor has also reformulated the *Lemon* test. She argues that the establishment clause forbids governmental *endorsement of religion,* as she concluded was not the case when a creche was erected on city-owned land at Christmastime.[14] The Court is moving in her direction (see below).

Applying these generalities, we find that the establishment clause forbids states to introduce devotional exercises of any variety into the public school curriculum, including denominationally neutral prayers, devotional reading of the Bible, recitation of the Lord's Prayer, or the posting of the Ten Commandments on the walls of public classrooms.[15] The Court has not, as is often said, made it unconstitutional for students to pray in the public schools. Any student may pray silently anytime he or she wishes to do so. What the Constitution forbids is the sponsorship or encouragement of prayer, directly or indirectly, by public school authorities. The Rehnquist Court, somewhat to the surprise of many observers, reaffirmed its interpretation that public schools may not sponsor or otherwise encourage public school prayer, when it held that the inclusion of an invocation and benediction by a member of the clergy at a public secondary school graduation exercise was a violation of the establishment clause. In an opinion by Justice Kennedy, joined by Blackmun, Stevens, O'Connor, and Souter, the Court held that although the students were

---

[10] *Edwards* v *Aguillard,* 482 US 578 (1987).

[11] Concurring in a *Lamb's Chapel* v *Center Moriches Union Free School District,* 124 L Ed 2d 352 (1993).

[12] *Corporation of Presiding Bishop* v *Amos,* 483 US 327 (1987).

[13] Ibid.

[14] *Lynch* v *Donnelly,* 465 US 668 (1984).

[15] *Abington School District* v *Schempp,* 374 US 203 (1963); *Engel* v *Vitale,* 370 US 421 (1962); *Stone* v *Graham,* 449 US (1980).

not legally coerced, the state in such circumstances was pressuring students to participate in religious exercises. It was the coercive feature of such an environment that was persuasive for Justice Kennedy, whereas Blackmun, Stevens, and O'Connor expressed the view that the establishment clause prohibits governmental endorsement or sponsorship of religion, regardless of whether the students were coerced to conform. Scalia, Rehnquist, White, and Thomas dissented, contending that the only coercion forbidden by the establishment clause is that which is backed by a threat of a legal penalty.[16]

The Court has declared unconstitutional an Alabama statute authorizing public school teachers to hold a one-minute period of silence for "meditation or voluntary prayer," because the state rather clumsily made it clear that the purpose of the statute was to return voluntary prayer to the schools.[17] The Court strongly hinted that if a state law providing for a moment of silence had a more neutrally phrased purpose, it would pass.

The Supreme Court (1981) in *Widmar* v *Vincent* decided that a university that makes its facilities generally available for student activities does not violate the establishment clause if it allows some student groups to use its facilities for religious prayers. On the contrary, if the university were to ban religious activities while allowing other kinds of programs, it would violate the constitutional provision against "prohibiting the free exercise" of religion (see page 194). In this ruling the Court pointedly noted, "University students are, of course, young adults. They are less impressionable than younger students and should be able to appreciate that the University's policy is one of neutrality toward religion."[18] This comment caused some to believe that the Court might treat a similar requirement for the public schools differently.

Congress did not wait, however. In 1984, in what many thought was an attempt to reintroduce school prayer into schools, Congress made it unlawful for any public high school receiving federal funds (almost all of them do) to keep student groups from using school facilities for religious worship if the school opens its facilities for other student meetings. More precisely, Congress made it unlawful for a high school whenever it offers an opportunity for one or more noncurriculum-related student groups to meet on school premises, including such nonideological activities as a stamp or chess club, "to deny equal access to, or discriminate against, any student who wishes to conduct a meeting within that limited open forum on the basis of the religious, political, philosophical, or other content of the speech at such meetings." (Although adopted to provide equal access for worship, this law also provides federal protection for unpopular and unfashionable student groups to hold meetings in high schools during noninstructional times.) The Court sustained this congressional judgment that high school students should not be treated differently from college students in their ability to avoid confusing an equal access policy with state sponsorship of religion. While warning school officials to make it

---

[16] *Lee* v *Weisman*, 120 L Ed 2d 467 (1992).

[17] *Wallace* v *Jaffree*, 472 US 38 (1985).

[18] *Widmar* v *Vincent*, 454 US 263 (1981).

clear that the school does not endorse the views of the religious clubs, the Court held that the law does not conflict with the establishment clause.[19] Then in 1993 the Court ruled, primarily on free speech grounds, that if a school board allows school property to be used after school hours for social, civic, and recreational meetings open to the public, the board may not proscribe the use of school property for religious purposes. The showing of a religious film in question after school hours, not sponsored by the school, and open to the public "created no realistic danger that the community would think that the school district was endorsing religion or any particular creed, and any benefit to religion or to the church would have been more than incidental."[20]

A state may not ban Darwin's theory of evolution from being taught in its public schools because of "its supposed conflict with the biblical account, literally read."[21] Nor may a state forbid the teaching of evolution unless accompanied by instruction in the theory of "creation science."[22] The Constitution does not prevent the study of the Bible or religion in public schools when presented as part of a secular program of education,[23] but school authorities may not permit religious instructors to come into the public school building during the school day to provide religious instruction, even on a voluntary basis.[24] Schools may, however, release students from part of the compulsory school day so that the students can receive religious instruction, provided this instruction does not take place in public school buildings.[25]

An especially troublesome and controversial area is government aid to church-operated schools. The principles are easy to formulate, but application is difficult. A state may provide aid to promote the well-being and education of students; it may not give aid to religion. At the college level, the problems are relatively simple. The students are presumed to be mature, and there is less pervasiveness of religion in the curriculum. Tax funds may be used to build buildings and operate programs at church-operated schools, provided tax funds are not used to support sectarian education. Such grants to colleges require no elaborate intervention by government authority to ensure that they will be used only for secular purposes.[26]

Also at the college level, in a unanimous decision—unanimous decisions are rare in establishment clause cases—the Court held (although it was not unanimous in its reasons) that state rehabilitation aid payments to a blind student for education could be used by that student to study at a Christian college to become a pastor. It is well settled, Justice Marshall said for the Court, that a state may not grant aid to a religion, but it is equally well settled "that

[19] *Westside Community Schools* v *Mergens,* 496 US 226 (1990).

[20] *Lamb's Chapel* v *Center Moriches Union Free School District,* 124 L Ed 2d 352 (1993).

[21] *Epperson* v *Arkansas,* 393 US 97 (1968).

[22] *Edwards* v *Aguillard,* 482 US 578 (1987).

[23] *Abingdon* v *Schempp,* 377 US 203 (1963).

[24] *Illinois ex rel McCollum* v *Board of Education,* 333 US 203 (1948).

[25] *Zorach* v *Clauson,* 343 US 306 (1952).

[26] *Tilton* v *Richardson,* 403 US 672 (1971); *Hunt* v *McNair,* 413 US 734 (1973); *Roemer* v *Board of Public Works of Maryland,* 426 US 736 (1976).

the Establishment Clause is not violated every time money previously in the possession of a State is conveyed to a religious institution."[27] The law was designed to help the visually handicapped and had a secular purpose. That the funds ultimately had the effect of helping a religious school was not a constitutional vice, since the money was paid to the student and it was his independent and private choice as to which kind of education he would seek.

At the elementary and secondary level, "The Court has been particularly vigilant in monitoring compliance with the Establishment Clause...."[28] The secular and religious parts of the institution are more closely interwoven. The students are younger and more susceptible to indoctrination, and the chances are greater that aid given to church-operated schools will seep over to aid religion.[29] Therefore, the Supreme Court, at least the pre-Rehnquist Court, looked at tax assistance to church-operated elementary and secondary schools with much greater skepticism than such aid at the college level.

In drawing the lines between permissible use of tax funds to aid children and impermissible use to support religion, the Court has held that tax funds may be used to provide textbooks,[30] lunches, and transportation to and from school[31] to schoolchildren, including those in church-operated schools (except that textbooks cannot be provided to those that deny admission to pupils because of race or religion).[32] Also approved has been the use of public funds to provide and score standardized tests in church-operated schools, to provide diagnostic services for speech and hearing in church-operated schools, and to provide guidance and remedial services outside church-operated schools.[33] A state may reimburse sectarian schools for the costs of administering state-required and state-prepared tests, and for costs of complying with state attendance and data-collection requirements.[34] In *Mueller* v *Allen*, one of the accommodationist cases, the Court approved a tax deduction for public and private school expenses, including tuition payments, even though the bulk of the deductions are claimed by parents sending children to sectarian schools.[35] These uses of tax dollars are viewed as promoting the health, safety, and secular education of students, not as aiding religion.

In a 1993 case the Court upheld the assignment of a sign-language interpreter, paid for by a federal grant to the state under the Individuals With Disabilities Education Act, to accompany a deaf child to a parochial school. Chief Justice Rehnquist, speaking for a five-person majority, emphasized that no government funds would find their way into "sectarian schools' coffers,"

---

[27] *Witters* v *Wash. Dept. of Serv. for Blind*, 474 US 481 (1986).

[28] *Edwards* v *Aguillard*, 482 US 578 (1987).

[29] Ibid.

[30] *Board of Education* v *Allen*, 392 US 236 (1968); *Wolman* v *Walter*, 433 US 229 (1977).

[31] *Cochran* v *Board of Education*, 281 US 370 (1930); *Everson* v *Board of Education*, 330 US 1 (1947); *Board of Education* v *Allen*, 392 US 236 (1968); *Meek* v *Pittenger*, 421 US 349 (1975).

[32] *Norwood* v *Harrison*, 413 US 455 (1973).

[33] *Wolman* v *Walter*, 433 US 229 (1977); *Meek* v *Pittenger*, 421 US 349 (1975).

[34] *Committee for Public Education* v *Regan*, 444 US 646 (1980).

[35] *Mueller* v *Allen*, 463 US 388 (1983).

and that this action was aid to the student, not to religion, and that in the context of a generally available state program, there was no endorsement of religion. "If the Establishment Clause," wrote the Chief Justice, "did bar religious groups from receiving general government benefits then a church could not be protected by the police and fire departments...." The minority emphasized that since the interpreter would be obliged to follow the deaf student throughout his day, including the Mass, "the interpreter's every gesture would be infused with religious significance," and because of the inextricable intertwinement between the secular and sectarian "governmental assistance to the educational function of the school necessarily entails governmental participation in the schools' inculcation of religion."[36]

On the other side, tax funds may *not* be used directly to maintain facilities; provide instructional equipment such as maps, charts, records, or laboratory equipment;[37] provide auxiliary services such as counseling to students inside church-operated schools; produce teacher-prepared tests; or transport students on field trips.[38] States may not send public school teachers to teach even secular subjects in sectarian schools, even after school hours, even in classrooms leased by the public schools.[39] Similarly, states may not use public funds to provide remedial instruction and guidance services to parochial school students in parochial schools, even if the schools are subject to supervision to ensure that there are no religious influences in these services.[40] A state may not directly reimburse parents for tuition paid to send children to parochial schools.[41] (It may do so indirectly, as we have noted, by providing a tax exemption for expenses of sending children to either public or private schools.)

If taxes can be used for textbooks, why not for teachers? If for standardized tests, why not for teacher-prepared tests? If for transportation to school, why not for transportation on field trips? If for books, why not for maps? If for counseling outside a parochial school, why not inside? If for a sign-language interpreter, why not for a teacher? The answers are: "A textbook is ascertainable," but a teacher's handling of a subject is not.[42] A standardized test is not prepared by church schools, but teacher-prepared tests are an "integral part of the teaching process."[43] Transportation to and from school is a routine round trip every student makes every day and is unrelated to any aspect of the curriculum; field trips are controlled by teachers and are an aid to instructional programs. Counseling outside a school is less likely to involve religious matters than is counseling within the "pervasively sectarian atmosphere of the

[36] *Zobrest v Catalina Foothills School District*, 125 L Ed 2d 1 (1993).
[37] *Committee for Public Education v Nyquist*, 413 US 756 (1973).
[38] *Wolman v Walter*, 433 US 229 (1977).
[39] *Aguilar v Felton*, 473 US 402 (1985).
[40] *Grand Rapids School District v Ball*, 473 US 373 (1985).
[41] *Committee for Public Education v Nyquist*, 413 US 756 (1973); *Sloan v Lemon*, 413 US 825 (1973).
[42] *Levitt v Committee for Public Education*, 413 US 472 (1973).
[43] Ibid.

school."[44] A teacher's comments may readily become sectarian and to provide a teacher is to relieve a parochial school of an expense it may otherwise
incur, whereas a sign-language interpreter does no more than accurately interpret whatever material is presented to the class as a whole. As for its approval
of tax-purchased books but disapproval of tax-purchased records, maps, and
other kinds of instructional materials, the Court has recognized there is a
"tension" between its holdings. Nonetheless, the justices argue, when a standardized textbook is used both in public and church-operated schools, it provides assurance that the books will not be sectarian or used for sectarian
purposes, whereas there is much greater danger that other kinds of teaching
materials may be diverted to religious purposes.[45]

In a decision that marks a more lenient attitude toward governmental
involvement with religious activity, the Court sustained the Adolescent
Family Life Act of 1982. The AFLA provides federal funding for services
relating to counseling adolescents about the problems of sexuality. It
expressly calls for the involvement of "religious and charitable organizations,
voluntary associations, and other groups in the private sector, as well as services provided by publicly sponsored initiatives." The Court distinguished
between what it considered permissible aid to religious institutions to be used
for secular purposes and impermissible aid to "pervasively sectarian" institutions where there is too great a danger that the funds will be used for religious purposes. The Court sustained the law on its face, but instructed the
district court to examine the precise application of the law in the case before
it to ensure that the funds were not being given to institutions that are "pervasively sectarian." For to give funds to "pervasively sectarian" institutions,
said the majority, would be unconstitutional even if they were using the funds
for secular purposes.[46] Dissenting Justices Blackmun, Brennan, Marshall, and
Stevens called the AFLA a "clear and overwhelming governmental endorsement of religion" that called for "a partnership between the clergy and the
fisc in addressing a problem with substantial religious overtones," and
accused the majority of ignoring past precedents and most especially of ignoring the *Lemon* test.

Laws requiring business establishments to close on Sunday—so-called "Blue
laws"—have passed the Supreme Court's tests, even though they cause "free
exercise" problems for those who observe the Sabbath on Saturday. Whatever
their original purpose, they now have a secular purpose and the effect of promoting family living by providing a common day of rest and recreation.[47]

A general tax exemption from property and income taxes for nonprofit
groups including churches has been allowed. Such general tax exemptions neither advance nor inhibit religion; are neither amicable nor hostile; and, unlike
a direct subsidy, do not involve excessive entanglement. In fact such exemp-

---

[44] *Wolman v Walter*, 433 US 229 (1977); *Meek v Pittenger*, 421 US 349 (1975).
[45] Ibid.
[46] *Bowen v Kendrick*, 487 US 589 (1988).
[47] *McGowan v Maryland*, 366 US 420 (1961).

tions may involve less entanglement than if churches were not included within the nonprofit exemption.[48]

In contrast to these general tax exemptions, sales tax exemptions on periodicals published or distributed by a religious faith are not permitted. Such exemptions are unconstitutional for they have a religious purpose, the effect of advancing religion, and produce state entanglement with religion.[49]

The Court has also set aside a Massachusetts law giving churches the right to veto liquor licenses for taverns located within a 500-foot radius of the church. "The mere appearance of a joint exercise of legislative authority by Church and State," said the Court, "provides a significant symbolic benefit to religion."[50]

In *Marsh* v *Chambers* (1983) the Court simply ignored the *Lemon* test to sustain the centuries-old practice of paying chaplains to open sessions of state legislatures and Congress. It merely noted that the nation from its very beginning had opened its legislative sessions in this fashion and that legislators, unlike schoolchildren, are adults "presumably not readily susceptible to... peer pressure."[51] The dissenting justices contended that, "if any group of law students were asked to apply [the three-part test of the *Lemon* decision] to the question of legislative prayer, they would nearly unanimously find the practice to be unconstitutional," suggesting that the dissenters, if professors, would flunk their colleagues in a constitutional law test. The case may also demonstrate that judges believe legislators need the help of prayers more than do students.

Congress exempted religious organizations' nonprofit activities, religious and secular, from the Civil Rights Act's ban on religious discrimination in employment. When the exemption was challenged as favoritism toward religion contrary to the establishment clause, the Court upheld the exemption on accommodationist grounds, with the majority making a distinction between exemptions and regulations. For exemptions, said the Court, there are less rigorous establishment clause standards. Laws discriminating *among religions* are subject to strict scrutiny, whereas laws affording a uniform benefit to all religions are to be analyzed according to the *Lemon* test, and they concluded that exempting religious organizations so that they may hire only members of their own religion for nonreligious but nonprofit activities did not violate that test.[52] (The Court left open the question of the application of this exemption to secular employment by religious organizations in profit-making ventures.)

The Supreme Court has had special difficulty in distinguishing between the permissible and unconstitutional governmental use of religious symbols. It all depends on the context: "The effect of the government's use of religious symbolism depends upon its particular context, upon its particular physical set-

---

[48] *Walz* v *Tax Commission*, 397 US 664 (1970); *Diffenderfer* v *Central Baptist Church*, 404 US 412 (1972).
[49] *Texas Monthly, Inc.* v *Bullock*, 489 US 1 (1989).
[50] *Larkin* v *Grendel's Den*, 459 US 116 (1982).
[51] *Marsh* v *Chambers*, 463 US 783 (1983).
[52] *Corporation of Presiding Bishops* v *Amos*, 483 US 327 (1987).

ting."[53] The Court's holdings have led to this implicit rule: if it appears to endorse religious beliefs it is unconstitutional; if it does not have such an effect it is constitutional. In *Lynch v Donnelly* (1984), the Court held that the city of Pawtucket, Rhode Island, could pay for and display a Nativity scene in the heart of its shopping district, along with Santa's house and sleigh, Christmas trees, lights, and other symbols of the Christmas season. The Court concluded that the city fathers had commercial—not religious—purposes in mind, that the effect provided little or no benefit to religion in general or to the Christian faith in particular, and that there was no excessive entanglement between religion and government. The city, said the Court, "has principally taken note of a significant historical religious event long celebrated in the Western World. . . . The creche in the display depicts the historical origins of this traditional event long recognized as a National Holiday."[54]

Five years later the Court, in two cases, upheld a city display of a creche along with Santa's house and other symbols of the Christmas season in a shopping district, and the Hanukkah menorah on the steps of the Pittsburgh City Hall next to a Christmas tree. These displays, concluded the Court majority, without agreeing precisely why, provided little or no benefit to religion in general or to the Christian or Jewish faiths in particular. The Constitution, said the Court, "[does not] require complete separation of church and state; it affirmatively mandates accommodation, not merely tolerance of all religions, and forbids hostility toward any." In a companion case, the Court ruled the Constitution does *not* permit the *unadorned* display of the Nativity scene in a courthouse because, in this context, the county gave the impression that it was endorsing the display's religious message.[55]

---

or prohibiting the free exercise thereof;

"The Court has struggled to find a neutral course between the two Religion Clauses, both of which are cast in absolute terms, and either of which, if expanded to a logical extreme, would tend to clash with the other."[56] To illustrate: it violates the establishment clause for a state to require employers to give employees an absolute right to be absent from work on their chosen Sabbath,[57] but it violates the free exercise clause for a state to deny unemployment compensation to Sabbatarians who refuse to accept positions requiring them to work on Saturday.[58] Similarly, "The Free Exercise Clause value suggests that a State may not impose a tax on spreading the gospel. . . . The Establishment

[53] *Allegheny County v Greater Pittsburgh ACLU*, 492 US 573 (1989).

[54] *Lynch v Donnelly*, 465 US 668 (1984).

[55] *Allegheny County v Greater Pittsburgh ACLU*, 492 US 573 (1989).

[56] *Walz v Tax Commission*, 397 US 664 (1970).

[57] *Estate of Thornton v Caldor, Inc.*, 472 US 703 (1985).

[58] *Sherbert v Verner*, 374 US 398 (1963); *Thomas v Review Board*, 450 US 707 (1981).

Clause value suggests that a state may not give a tax break to those who spread the gospel that it does not also give to others who actively might advocate disbelief in religion."[59]

What of the congressional practice of exempting from military conscription persons who, by reason of religious belief, are conscientiously opposed to participation in war, but not those who are opposed on "political, sociological, or philosophical grounds"? The Supreme Court, in part to avoid a clash between the two clauses, has construed the word *religious* so broadly that any deeply held humanistic opposition to participation in any and all wars in any form is included within the congressionally granted exemption.[60]

Right to Believe

Because there can be no compulsion by law of any form of worship and because the government recognizes neither orthodoxy nor heresy, everyone has an *absolute right to believe* whatever he or she wishes. A state may not compel a religious belief nor deny any person any right or privilege because of beliefs or lack of them. Abstract beliefs, even of a nonreligious kind, are protected from governmental interference. One can believe whatever one wishes. This does not mean, however, that "the Constitution...erects a per se barrier" to any consideration of beliefs.[61] When belief ripens into conduct, such as when one selects victims for attack because of hatred toward the victims' race, the First Amendment does not prevent a state from making such racially motivated crimes a more serious offense and enhancing the penalty for such crimes.[62]

A religious oath, for example an oath that one believes in the existence of God as a condition of public employment or of eligibility for an elected position, is unconstitutional (see Article VI, Section 3, page 177).[63] So also is disqualification of clergy from serving in public offices. "However widely that view [that clergy would promote the interests of one sect] may have been held in the 18th century by many, including enlightened statesmen of that day, the American experience provides no persuasive support for the fear that clergymen in public office will be less careful of antiestablishment interests or less faithful to their oaths of civil office than their unordained counterparts."[64]

The Right to Practice One's Religion

At a minimum this clause establishes that a law will survive strict scrutiny only in rare cases if it prohibits conduct because it is undertaken for religious reasons. To phrase it differently, the Constitution forbids laws that target religious conduct for distinctive treatment or are aimed at conduct because of its

---

[59] Justice Blackmun concurring in *Texas Monthly, Inc.* v *Bullock,* 489 US 1 (1989).

[60] *Welsh* v *United States,* 398 US 333 (1970); *Gillette* v *United States,* 401 US 437 (1971).

[61] *Wisconsin* v *Mitchell,* 124 L Ed 2d 436 (1993).

[62] Ibid.

[63] *Torcaso* v *Watkins,* 367 US 488 (1961).

[64] *McDaniel* v *Paty,* 435 US 618 (1978).

religious motivation. Thus a unanimous court set aside ordinances of Hialeah, Florida, which made religious animal sacrifice unlawful while at the same time allowing all other forms of animal killing. These ordinances were clearly aimed at the Santeria religion and had as their objective the suppression of its religious rituals.[65]

What of laws that are not aimed at religious practices but have the indirect consequence of forbidding or limiting them? In 1990 the Rehnquist Court in one fell swoop significantly altered the interpretation of the free exercise clause as it relates to such government regulation. Prior to that time the Court had taken the view that the free exercise clause protected religious practices from even indirect governmental prohibition or limitation unless the government could demonstrate that the law in question was in pursuit of "an especially important governmental interest" and that the government was "pursuing this interest by narrowly tailored means."[66] This is known as the "compelling interest" test. In other words, the Constitution was thought to throw a mantle of protection around religious practices and the burden was on the government to justify interfering with them.[67]

In *Employment Division* v *Smith* (1990), the Court, speaking through Justice Scalia, unequivocally discarded the compelling interest test except as applied to laws denying people unemployment compensation. Outside of this narrow field, a government no longer has to show a compelling interest in order to apply its general laws to religious practices. "A law that is neutral and of general applicability need not be justified by a compelling governmental interest even if the law has the incidental effect of burdening a particular religious practice."[68] As long as a law does not single out and ban religious practices because "they are engaged in for religious reasons, or only because of the religious belief they display," a general law may be applied to conduct even if it is religiously inspired. In this particular instance Oregon was allowed to apply its laws against the use of controlled substances to persons who used peyote as part of their religious rituals. Noting that states could if they wish—and many have—exempt sacramental peyote use from their drug prohibition laws, Justice Scalia wrote, "It may fairly be said that leaving accommodation to the political process will place at a relative disadvantage those religious practices that are not widely engaged in." Such a consequence, he concluded, is an unavoidable result of democratic government and to be "preferred to a system in which each conscience is a law unto itself."[69]

Justice O'Connor, although concurring, strenuously objected to this abrupt jettisoning of the strict scrutiny test and to what Justice Blackmun called "a wholesale overturning of settled law." Justice O'Connor wrote, "If the First Amendment is to have any vitality, it ought not be construed to cover only the extreme and hypothetical situation in which a society directly targets a religious practice." And as to leaving disfavored religious practices to the protection of the political process, she quoted Justice Jackson's celebrated words: "The very purpose of a Bill of Rights was to withdraw certain subjects from the vicissi-

[65] *Church of Lukumi Babalu Aye, Inc.* v *City of Hialeah*, 124 L Ed 2d 472 (1993).

[66] *Wisconsin* v *Yoder*, 406 US 205 (1972).

[67] *Bowen* v *Roy*, 476 US 693 (1986).

[68] *Church of Lukumi Babalu Aye, Inc.* v *City of Hialeah*, 124 L Ed 2d 472 (1993)

[69] *Employment Division* v *Smith*, 494 US 872 (1990).

tudes of political controversy, to place them beyond the reach of majorities and officials and to establish them as legal principles to be applied by the courts. One's right to life, liberty, and property, to free speech, a free press, freedom of worship and assembly, and other fundamental rights may not be submitted to vote; they depend on the outcome of no election."[70] Two years later the Court reaffirmed *Employment Division v Smith*. Justices Blackmun and O'Connor made clear their continuing opposition to the *Smith* rule and Justice Souter called for a reexamination of it "in the next case that would turn upon its application."[71] In the Religious Freedom Restoration Act of 1993 Congress attempted to reverse *Employment Division v Smith* by conferring on all persons the right to perform their religious practices unless the government, national or state, can show that the law or regulation in question is narrowly tailored and in pursuit of a "compelling interest." Whether Congress has the authority to so set aside state, in contrast to national, laws or regulations as applied to persons who claim a conflict with their religious practices raises interesting federalism questions.

Even prior to *Employment Division*, in applying the compelling interest test the Court nonetheless found the following religious practices subject to regulation: persons may be required to comply with Sunday closing laws, even if Sunday is not their Sabbath;[72] parents may be compelled to have their children vaccinated as a condition of attending public schools, whether or not vaccination violates their religious beliefs;[73] members of the Society for Krishna Consciousness could be confined to a fixed location for selling and distributing their literature at a state fairgrounds, even though the distribution and selling of religious literature is a ritual for them.[74] An orthodox Jew was not entitled to an exemption from an air force regulation prohibiting the wearing of headgear indoors, even though the wearing of a yarmulke was akin to a silent prayer and prescribed by his religion.[75] (Congress subsequently intervened to permit such practices.) A Native American could be required, as a condition of securing food stamps, to obtain a social security number for his child, even though such an action would violate the parent's religious beliefs.[76] Other unsuccessful attempts to protect activities as part of religious practices include: a church-affiliated school engaging in racially discriminatory practices could be denied the benefit of having its donors receive a tax deduction for their contributions to it.[77] Payments to the Church of Scientology for certain religious services were held to be taxable by the IRS because the taxpayers had received a benefit for their payments.[78] The Forest Service was allowed to construct a road

---

[70] Justice O'Connor in *Employment Division* quoting Justice Jackson in *West Virginia Board of Education v Barnette*, 310 US 586 (1940).

[71] *Church of Lukumi Babalu Aye, Inc. v City of Hialeah*, 124 L Ed 2d 472 (1993).

[72] *Braunfeld v Brown*, 366 US 599 (1961).

[73] *Jacobson v Massachusetts*, 197 US 11 (1905).

[74] *Heffron v International Society for Krishna Consciousness, Inc.*, 452 US 640 (1981).

[75] *Goldman v Weinberger*, 475 US 503 (1986).

[76] *Bowen v Roy*, 476 US 693 (1986).

[77] *Bob Jones University v United States*, 461 US 574 (1983).

[78] *Hernandez v Commissioner*, 489 US 1027 (1989).

through a portion of national forest held sacred by Indians and used by them for religious ceremonies.[79]

As to taxes and religious organizations, generally applicable sales and use taxes may be collected from religious organizations for the sale of religious items such as Bibles and religious pamphlets. (In fact, as noted on page 193, exemption of such literature from taxes while it is collected from other kinds of books may violate the establishment clause.[80]) Flat license taxes that operate as a prior restraint on the distribution of religious materials are a different matter. The Amish can be required to collect and pay social security taxes for their employees, even though both payment and receipt of social security benefits are forbidden by their faith.[81] (Congress exempts from such taxes self-employed persons who have religious scruples, but not employers or employees.)

On the other side, some practices, earlier upheld, have apparently not been invalidated by the Court even though the views sustaining some of them appear to be at odds with the majority opinion in *Employment Division* v *Smith*. Among these are the following: states failed to show a compelling interest in promoting patriotism that would justify forcing Jehovah's Witnesses (or anyone else) to salute the flag, which to witnesses is a symbol of the Evil One, as a condition of attending public schools, nor were states able to justify forcing people to display on license plates a state motto—in this case New Hampshire's motto, "Live free or die."[82] Because of the Amish's long-established tradition concerning education, a state may not compel them to send their children to schools beyond the eighth grade; compelling schooling up to the eighth grade is constitutional.[83] States may not require parents to send children to public schools if parents wish to educate them in religious ones.[84] Nor would the Supreme Court permit states to force persons to choose between "fidelity to religious belief and employment" by denying unemployment compensation to persons who refuse to accept work on their chosen Sabbath.[85] This protection for religious practices was specifically re-endorsed by the Court in *Employment Division* v *Smith*.

or abridging the freedom of speech,

The right of freedom of speech is essential to the preservation and operation of democracy. "Nevertheless, there are categories of communication and

---

[79] *Hernandez* v *Commissioner*, 489 US 1027 (1989); *Lyng* v *Northwest Indian Cemetery Protective Assn.*, 485 US 439 (1988).

[80] *Swaggart* v *California Equalization Bd.*, 493 US 378 (1990).

[81] *United States* v *Lee*, 455 US 252 (1982).

[82] *West Virginia State Board of Education* v *Barnette*, 319 US 624 (1943); *Wooley* v *Maynard*, 430 US 705 (1977).

[83] *Wisconsin* v *Yoder*, 406 US 205 (1972).

[84] *Pierce* v *Society of Sisters*, 268 US 510 (1925).

[85] *Sherbert* v *Verner*, 375 US 398 (1963); *Hobbie* v *Unemployment Appeals Commission*, 480 US 136 (1987); *Frazee* v *Employment*, 488 US 814 (1989).

certain special utterances to which the majestic protection of the First Amendment does not extend because 'they are no essential part of any exposition of ideas, and are of such slight social value as a step to the truth that any benefit that may be derived from them is clearly outweighed by the social interest in order and morality.'"[86] *Libelous speech* is such a category. Anyone (except, under most circumstances, a member of Congress, a judge, or the president) who slanders or libels another may be penalized. *Obscene speech* is another kind not entitled to constitutional protection, nor is *child pornography* protected. *Fighting words* that, by their very utterance, injure and provoke others to imminent attack are outside the pale of protection. So are *seditious incitements* of others to immediate acts of violence.

Constitutional problems have always been involved in the definition and determination of libelous speech, obscene speech, seditious incitement, or fighting words. The Supreme Court has been very suspicious of definitions that cast their nets too wide. Recently the Court has seemed to modify this "categorical" approach. In 1992 Justice Scalia, in an opinion for a five-person majority, wrote that when the Court has written that these categories of expression are "'not within the area of constitutionally protected speech,' or that the 'protection of the First Amendment does not extend' to them," what the Court meant to say "is that these areas of speech can, consistently with the First Amendment, be regulated because of their constitutionally proscribable content (obscenity, defamation, etc.)—not that they are categories of speech entirely invisible to the Constitution." Thus, Justice Scalia illustrated, a government may proscribe libel, but it may not make the further content discrimination of proscribing only libel critical of the government.[87]

Fighting Words

Fighting words must be limited to those that "have a direct tendency to cause acts of violence by the person to whom, individually, the remarks are addressed"—words that are merely abusive, harsh, or insulting are not sufficient.[88] In fact, the Court may have so narrowly applied the category as to virtually eliminate it. Moreover, the fighting-words exception "requires an even narrower application in cases involving words addressed to a police officer, because a properly trained officer may reasonably be expected to exercise a higher degree of restraint 'than the average citizen, and thus be less likely to respond belligerently to fighting words.'"[89] Nonetheless, the Supreme Court has reaffirmed that fighting words—those that "provoke immediate violence"—are not protected by the First Amendment. In fact, the Court has emphasized that "words that create an immediate panic" are not entitled to

---

[86] *Bose Corporation* v *Consumers Union*, 466 US 485 (1984).

[87] *R.A.V.* v *St. Paul*, 120 L Ed 2d 305 (1992).

[88] *Cohen* v *California*, 403 US 15 (1971); *Gooding* v *Wilson*, 405 US 518 (1972).

[89] Justice Powell, concurring in *Lewis* v *City of New Orleans*, 415 US 180 (1974), as quoted approvingly by Justice Brennan in the opinion of the Court in *Houston* v *Hill*, 482 US 451 (1987).

constitutional protection.[90] "Words that create an immediate panic," however, are apparently not a new category of speech outside the scope of the First Amendment, but just another way to talk about fighting words.

The fighting words category has been restored to constitutional interest as many cities, colleges, and universities have tried to deal with so-called "hate speech," speech attacking persons because of their race, religion, gender, or sexual orientation, and most especially racial epithets.[91] The Court dealt with the issue when a St. Paul ordinance provided, "Whoever places on public or private property a symbol, object, appellation, characterization or graffiti, including, but not limited to, a burning cross or Nazi swastika, which one knows or has reasonable grounds to know arouses anger, alarm or resentment in others on the basis of race, color, creed, religion or gender commits disorderly conduct and shall be guilty of a misdemeanor." As written, the ordinance was clearly overbroad, impermissibly content-based and facially invalid (see below), but the Supreme Court of Minnesota narrowly construed the ordinance to reach only expressions that constitute fighting words and not merely those that aroused "anger, alarm, or resentment." Justice Scalia for the majority held that even as so narrowed, the St. Paul ordinance was facially unconstitutional because it applied only to fighting words that "insult, or provoke violence, on the basis of race, color, creed, religion, or gender," and did not apply, for example, to "[t]hose who wish to use 'fighting words' in connection with other ideas—to express hostility, for example, on the basis of political affiliation, union membership, or homosexuality."[92] Justice Blackmun concurred, for he, too, thought the St. Paul ordinance was overbroad and reached beyond fighting words, but he accused Justice Scalia of being distracted from the Court's proper mission "by the temptation to decide the issue over 'politically correct speech' and 'cultural diversity,' neither of which is present here." Along with the other justices in the minority, he found nothing objectionable in the fact that St. Paul had limited its concern to hate speech based on race, color, creed, religion, and gender.

It should be noted that all members of the Court are in agreement that a city—or a public university—cannot punish persons for using hate speech that causes hurt feelings, or because it is offensive, or causes resentment. "The mere fact that expressive activity causes hurt feelings, offense, or resentment does not render the expression unprotected."[93] However, the government may require employers to discipline and even dismiss persons for using words that sexually harass persons in the workplace.[94] And it would seem, although there is no direct Supreme Court ruling on it, that a university would have greater authority to regulate hate speech as used by those who chose to reside in its residence halls than, say, to punish students for what they say in a classroom.

---

[90] *NAACP* v *Clairborne Hardware Co.*, 458 US 886 (1982).

[91] Calvin R. Massey, "Hate Speech, Cultural Diversity, and the Foundational Paradigms of Free Expression," *UCLA Law Review*, vol. 40 October, 1992, pp. 155–197.

[92] *R.A.V.* v *St. Paul*, 120 L Ed 2d 305 (1992).

[93] Justice White concurring in *R.A.V.* v *St Paul*, 120 L Ed 2d 305 (1992).

[94] *Meritor Savings Bank* v *Vinson*, 477 US 57 (1986).

Libel

Libel prosecutions used to be a favorite means of suppressing criticism of government officials and of preventing discussion of public issues. (Libel refers to the written word, slander to the spoken one, although nowadays libel is often used as the generic term to refer to both.) In seventeenth-century England seditious libel was defined to include criticism of the king or his ministers, whether true or false, and the stirring up of public discontent.

Under the Constitution, however, persons cannot be made to pay damages for defaming public officials or public figures merely because they have issued false statements. As established by the Court in the leading case of *New York Times* v *Sullivan,* there must also be clear and convincing evidence—a greater burden than the usual one in a civil case, which is to mean a preponderance of evidence—that the false comment was made with "actual malice," a confusing term which means not that the publisher or reporter had bad motives or dislike for the person who was subject of the article, but made the statements with a reckless disregard for whether they were false or not, which in turn means that "the defendant must have made the false publication with a "high degree of awareness of probable falsity," or must have "entertained serious doubts as to the truth of his publications."[95] Actual malice under the *New York Times* standard, a term which the Court has called an "unfortunate one," should not be confused with the concept of malice as "an evil intent or a motive arising from spite or ill will.... In place of the term actual malice, it is better practice that jury instructions refer to publication of a statement with knowledge of falsity or reckless disregard as to truth or falsity."[96]

"The question whether the evidence in the record in a defamation case is sufficient to support a finding of actual malice is a question of law" for judges, not juries, ultimately to decide. "Judges have a duty to decide independently whether the evidence in the record is sufficient to cross the constitutional threshold that bars the entry of any judgment that is not supported by clear and convincing proof of actual malice."[97] In establishing the fact that a publication was made with knowledge of its falsity or with reckless disregard for its truth, public officials and figures may inquire into the state of mind of editors and publishers: the First Amendment does not protect conversations among news people from judicial scrutiny.[98]

Public officials and public figures cannot collect damages from those who draw, print, or publish outrageous, clearly inaccurate, and false cartoons about them. Everybody is supposed to recognize that a cartoon is a "parody which no one can reasonably believe to be stating actual facts or actual events." Such was the case when *Hustler Magazine* printed an advertisement parodying the Reverend Jerry Falwell and he tried to win damages under a state-law tort for the intentional infliction of emotional distress.[99]

---

[95] *Harte-Hanks, Inc.* v *Connaughton,* 491 US 657 (1989).
[96] Ibid.
[97] Ibid.
[98] *Herbert* v *Lando,* 441 US 153 (1979).
[99] *Hustler Magazine* v *Falwell,* 485 US 46 (1988).

"Imaginative expression" and "rhetorical hyperbole" are protected by the First Amendment. Although the Court refused to provide a categorical exemption from any possible libel action for statements of opinion, that is, to make an "opinion exception," it has established that "a statement on matters of public concern must be provable as false before there can be liability under state defamation law, at least . . . where a media defendant is involved." In other words, a statement of opinion relating to matters of public concern which does not contain "a provable false factual connotation will receive full constitutional protection."[100] In addition, the Court has refused to permit falsity to be established solely by the fact that an author deliberately altered words uttered by a plaintiff but surrounded them by quotation marks. "Although the use of quotations to attribute words not in fact spoken bears in most important way on the inquiry into falsity," "unless the alteration results in a material change in the meaning conveyed by the statement it does not equate with knowledge of falsity for purposes of *New York Times* v *Sullivan*."[101]

Public figures subject to the difficult burden of proof of showing that they have been libeled are of two kinds: famous persons who are public figures for all purposes and in all contexts, and those who are not so famous but who have allowed themselves to be injected into a particular public controversy so that they are public figures for a limited range of issues ("limited purpose public figures"). Yet persons do not lose their status as private individuals merely because their names get into the papers for having been robbed or for having gotten a divorce that received a great deal of publicity or for being a scientist supported by a federal grant whose work a United States senator thinks a waste of public funds.[102]

A different libel rule prevails for comments made about private individuals. A state may permit a private individual to recover damages upon a showing of negligence on the part of those responsible for the defamatory falsehood, for example, by showing that they issued a false statement without taking responsible precautions to check it.[103] In most instances in order to win a defamation action private individuals must show not only negligence or fault but, at least in the case of a media defendant, also falsity—that the statements made were not true. States may constitutionally place on defendants the common law burden of proving truth only when private individuals claim defamation in matters "of exclusively private concern."[104] The reasons for making libel actions by private persons easier than for public figures and officials are that private persons have less effective means of responding to defaming statements, they have not voluntarily exposed themselves to the risk of injury from falsehoods, the public's interest in knowing about them is less compelling, and they are entitled to some protection of their right to privacy.

The amount of damages that may be collected by private individuals is an issue for which there is no coherent and consistent Court majority. No longer

---

[100] *Milkovich* v *Lorain Journal Co.*, 497 US 1 (1990).

[101] *Masson* v *New Yorker Magazine, Inc.*, 115 L Ed 2d 447 (1991).

[102] *Hutchinson* v *Proxmire*, 443 US 111 (1979).

[103] *Gertz* v *Welch*, 418 US 323 (1974); *Dun & Bradstreet* v *Greenmoss Builders*, 472 US 749 (1985).

[104] *Philadelphia Newspapers, Inc.* v *Hepps*, 475 US 767 (1986).

may damages be presumed; plaintiffs must show actual damages. Apparently, to secure punitive damages, in contrast to actual ones, a private defendant in a matter relating to public concern must meet the stringent *New York Times* v *Sullivan* test of proving the defendant published a falsehood knowing that it was false.[105] However, in the case of private individuals bringing suit about private matters, the less stringent requirement of proving that what was published was false and that the publisher of it was negligent is sufficient for punitive damages. An example of a *private* matter would be the publication by a credit firm of a credit rating: such firms are liable for punitive damages if they negligently publish a false statement.[106]

First Amendment and due process concerns do not keep a person who has been libeled from bringing an action in any state in which the magazine or newspaper regularly circulates, even if it causes inconvenience for the defendant to go there to defend.[107] On the other hand, First Amendment considerations do require appellate courts to set aside the normal rule that the findings of trial courts are to be reversed only when they are clearly erroneous. In reviewing libel judgments, appellate courts are to make an independent judgment to "determine whether the record establishes actual malice with convincing clarity."[108]

Obscenity

What of obscenity? Except for child pornography, the possession of obscene materials for private use cannot be made a crime.[109] However, the production, sale, mailing, or transportation of obscene matter is not entitled to constitutional protection. The Supreme Court has had the same difficulty as has everybody else who has tried to define obscenity. As Justice Brennan has written, "No other aspect of the First Amendment has, in recent years, commanded so substantial a commitment of our time, generated such disharmony of views, and remained so resistant to the formulation of stable and manageable standards."[110] Since the Supreme Court entered the field in 1957, almost a hundred separate opinions have been written by the justices.

In *Miller* v *California* (1973) Chief Justice Burger, speaking for five members of the Court, once again tried to clarify the constitutional standards, and that definition of obscenity has lasted for two decades. A work—"a book, a film, a play"—may be considered obscene, provided: (1) the average person, applying contemporary standards of the community in which the court sits, finds that the work, taken as a whole, appeals to a prurient interest in sex; (2) the work depicts in a patently offensive way sexual conduct specifically defined by the law or by decisions of the courts and (3) the work, taken as a whole, lacks

[105] *Gertz* v *Welch*, 418 US 323 (1974).
[106] *Dun & Bradstreet* v *Greenmoss Builders*, 472 US 749 (1985).
[107] *Calder* v *Jones*, 465 US 783 (1984); *Keeton* v *Hustler Magazine, Inc.*, 465 US 770 (1984).
[108] *Bose Corporation* v *Consumers Union*, 466 US 485 (1984).
[109] *Stanley* v *Georgia*, 394 US 557 (1969); *Osborne* v *Ohio*, 495 US 103 (1990).
[110] *Stanley* v *Georgia*, 394 US 557 (1969); *Osborne* v *Ohio*, 495 US 103 (1990).

serious literary, artistic, political, or scientific value.[111] The Chief Justice explicitly rejected part of the previous test, the so-called *Memoirs* v *Massachusetts* formula; namely, that no work should be judged obscene unless it was "utterly without redeeming social value."[112] He argued that such a test made it impossible for a state to outlaw hard-core pornography. He also stipulated, and the Court has since reaffirmed, that the standards of offensiveness are to be those of the community from which the jury comes, rather than what the jury might believe to be the standards of the nation.[113] The jury is to use its common sense and general knowledge about local community standards. Because of the variability of community standards, it is possible for a book, a movie, or record album to be legally obscene in one state or city but not in another. A jury may not, however, take into account the effect of the materials on children in determining community standards; otherwise, it would reduce the adult population to reading or seeing only that which is fit for children.[114]

The Court has never made clear what makes an interest in sex prurient, but it has made clear that a work that appeals to a normal interest in sex or that merely promotes "lust" cannot be declared obscene. "Material that, taken as a whole, does no more than arouse a good, old-fashioned, healthy interest in sex may not be included in the definition."[115]

For the third prong of the Miller test, "whether the work, taken as a whole, lacks serious literary, artistic, political, or scientific value," unlike the first two, community standards are not the measure. Rather, the measure is whether "a reasonable person would find such value in the material, taken as a whole."[116] In other words, a jury is not to find materials obscene merely because most of the people in their community believe the materials to be "trash," but only if a "reasonable person" would find no value in it. What this means, in practical fact, is that defendants may bring forward "experts" to testify on the literary merits of materials alleged to be obscene, and juries are to consider their views.

In determining whether materials are obscene, a jury may consider the motives of sellers to see if they are engaging in commercial exploitation of sexually offensive materials: the circumstances of distribution are relevant in determining whether the materials are being forced on people, and the motives of sellers are relevant in determining whether social importance claimed for materials is a pretense or a reality.[117]

When persons are criminally prosecuted for selling obscene materials, the state must establish its case beyond a reasonable doubt, proving not merely the fact of the sale but also the obscenity of the materials. There is a less burdensome standard of proof in civil actions, for example, an attempt by a gov-

---

[111] *Miller* v *California*, 415 US 15 (1973).
[112] *Memoirs* v *Massachusetts*, 383 US 413 (1966).
[113] *Hamling* v *United States*, 418 US 87 (1974).
[114] *Pinkus* v *United States*, 436 US 293 (1978).
[115] *Brockett* v *Spokane Arcades, Inc.*, 472 US 491 (1985).
[116] *Pope* v *Illinois*, 481 US 497 (1987).
[117] *Splawn* v *California*, 431 US 595 (1977).

ernment to close a theater as a public nuisance by proving it routinely shows only obscene movies. The Supreme Court has not made clear, however, whether the less stringent standard of a preponderance of the evidence will do in judging matter obscene in a civil proceeding or whether states have to use the more demanding "clear and convincing" standard or one of its variants.[118]

Justices Brennan, Marshall, and Stevens, instead of trying to refine the definition of obscenity, wanted to abandon the effort. They came to the conclusion that it is impossible to develop a constitutional definition without endangering protected speech and miring the Court in a "case-by-case determination of obscenity." They would let adults see or read whatever they wish and would permit only narrowly drawn statutes designed to prevent pornography from being forced on persons or made available to minors.[119] Justice Stevens, however, would provide some latitude for civil regulations that treat panderers of obscenity as public nuisances and would find acceptable some time, place, and manner regulations for the sale and distribution of pornography.[120]

Nonobscene but erotic literature and movies, as well as vulgar, offensive, and lewd speech, although constitutionally protected, nonetheless are entitled to less protection than political speech. School authorities may punish students for using "indecent" or "lewd" or "suggestive" speech in schoolrooms and school assemblies. Cities may regulate by zoning ordinance where "adult motion pictures" may be commercially shown. "The state may legitimately use the contents of these materials as a basis for placing them in a different classification from other motion pictures."[121] There are limits, however, to the regulation of offensive, but nonobscene, speech. "When a zoning ordinance infringes upon a protected liberty, it must be narrowly drawn and must further a sufficiently substantial governmental interest." So said the Court when it struck down a zoning ordinance of the Borough of Mount Ephraim in New Jersey that prevented "non-obscene nude dancing" in an adult bookstore by excluding from a small shopping district all live entertainment. (Chief Justice Burger in dissent chided his colleagues for trivializing and demeaning "that great Amendment."[122]) Yet the Court has allowed local officials to justify imposing limits on the location of adult movies because of the negative "secondary effects" (prostitution, for example) said to accompany such facilities. It has also upheld closing of an adult bookstore as a nuisance for the same reason.[123]

When it comes to children, less—considerably less—justification is required in order to restrict materials. Even those members of the Court who would allow adults to read and see anything about adults agree that when it comes to children, the states may step in to make criminal the production or sale of pornographic materials about children or those aimed at them.[124] Sexually

---

[118] *Cooper v Mitchell Brothers*, 454 US 90 (1981).

[119] *Miller v California*, 413 US 15 (1973); *Paris Adult Theatre I v Slaton*, 413 US 49 (1973).

[120] *Young v American Mini Theatres*, 427 US 50 (1976).

[121] Ibid.

[122] *Schad v Mt. Ephraim*, 452 US 61 (1981).

[123] *City of Renton v Playtime Theatres*, 475 US 41 (1986); *Arcara v Cloud Books*, 478 US 697 (1986).

[124] *New York v Ferber*, 458 US 747 (1982); *Ginsberg v New York*, 390 US 629 (1968).

explicit materials either about minors or aimed at minors are not protected by the First Amendment. As a means of protecting children, a state may make the mere possession and viewing of child pornography a crime.[125] State and local governments, provided they act under narrowly drawn statutes, can, for example, ban the knowing sale of "girlie" magazines to minors, even if such materials would not be considered legally obscene if sold to adults. States may make it a crime to depict sexual conduct by children visually, even if the depicted behavior would not be considered obscene if depicted as done by adults.

Pornography

Pornography used to be merely a synonym for *obscenity*. Pressure for regulating pornography came primarily from political conservatives and religious fundamentalists concerned that it undermines moral standards. More recently, many feminists have joined them, arguing that "pornography is central in creating and maintaining sex as a basis for discrimination."[126] They contend pornography promotes sexual abuse of individual women and perpetuates social subordination of women as a class. They define pornographic materials as sexually explicit pictures or words that depict women as sexual objects enjoying pain and humiliation or that present abuse of women as a sexual stimulus for men. These advocates argue that just as sexually explicit materials about minors are not entitled to First Amendment protection, so should there be no such protection for pornographic materials. They propose that civil penalties be imposed on pornographers and that women—and others who have had pornography forced upon them—be given the right to file complaints. Women and men differ significantly in their attitudes about pornography. Men are less likely than women to think pornography damages adults who read it, and women are twice as likely to favor laws banning the sale of pornography, regardless of the age of the buyer, while men tend to favor restricting the sale of pornography to minors.[127]

Not all feminists favor antipornography ordinances, yet those who do have been joined by social conservatives, and thus a new era in the battle over pornography has just begun. For this new antipornography coalition to be successful, a substantial alteration in constitutional doctrine will be required.[128] The Canadian Supreme Court has redefined obscenity to include materials that degrade women, and several U.S. cities have been considering the adoption of

---

[125] *Osborne v Ohio*, 495 US 103(1990).

[126] From "Preamble to Indianapolis City-County Ordinance," cited by Joel B. Grossman, "The First Amendment and the New Anti-Pornography Statutes," *News for Teachers of Political Science* (American Political Science Association), 1985, p. 18.

[127] Barry Sussman, "With Pornography, It All Depends on Who's Doing the Looking," Washington Post-ABC News Poll, *The Washington Post National Weekly Edition*, March 24, 1986, p. 37.

[128] "Anti-Pornography Laws and First Amendment Values," *Harvard Law Review* 98 (1984), p. 460; See also Donald Alexander Downs, *The New Politics of Pornography* (University of Chicago Press, 1990).

antipornography ordinances.[129] Only Indianapolis has passed such a law, which was declared unconstitutional in a decision affirmed by the Supreme Court without opinion.[130]

Seditious Speech

What of seditious speech, that is, speech advocating the use of force as a political tactic or as a means to overthrow the government? Since World War I the Supreme Court has considered issues relating to seditious speech a number of times in a variety of contexts. In 1951, in *Dennis* v *United States,* the Court sustained the application of the Smith Act, a federal statute making it illegal to advocate the violent overthrow of the government, to the leaders of the Communist Party of the United States, even though there was no evidence that they actually urged people to commit specific acts of violence.[131] However, that decision, although never specifically overruled, has been undermined by later rulings. The Supreme Court has made it clear that the Smith Act can be applied only to those who incite imminent lawless action.

The net result is that seditious incitement, if narrowly defined by statute and narrowly applied by the courts, is another exception to the protection of the First Amendment. Stated positively, the First Amendment protects the abstract advocacy of violence and forbids a government to make it a crime or to punish persons for what they advocate, except "where such advocacy is directed to inciting or producing imminent lawless action and is likely to incite or produce such action."[132]

Rules for Protected Speech

Outside the areas of fighting words, libel, obscenity, child pornography, and seditious incitement, the Supreme Court has elaborated a whole series of doctrines to measure the constitutionality of laws that appear to restrict freedom of expression. Even among protected speech, the amount of constitutional protection varies with the kind and character of the speech. "Not all speech is of equal First Amendment concern." Political speech about matters of public concern is "at the heart of the First Amendment's protection."[133] Such speech is so important that "in public debate our own citizens must tolerate insulting, and even outrageous, speech in order to provide adequate breathing space to the freedoms protected by the First Amendment."[134]

Prior Restraint

The Court is especially suspicious of laws that impose restraints prior to publication, including licensing schemes that require permission before a

---

[129] *Butler* v *Her Majesty* S. S.C.R. 452 (1992). See also "Pornography, Equality, and a Discrimination-Free Workplace: A Comparative Perspective," Harvard Law Review, vol. 106 (March 1993), pp. 1075–1092.

[130] *Hudnut* v *American Booksellers,* 475 US 1001 (1986).

[131] *Dennis* v *United States,* 341 US 494 (1951).

[132] *Yates* v *United States,* 354 US 298 (1957); *Brandenburg* v *Ohio,* 395 US 444 (1969).

[133] *Dun & Bradstreet* v *Greenmoss Builders,* 472 US 749 (1985).

[134] *Boos* v *Barry,* 485 US 312 (1988).

speech can be made, a motion picture shown, or a newspaper published or that in any way try to interpose the authority of government between someone trying to communicate something and the audience. Prior restraint is also involved whenever a government seizes or otherwise restrains materials suspected of being obscene or otherwise legally objectionable without a prior judicial determination that they were in fact so.[135] Prior restraints included "injunctive systems which threaten or bar future speech based on some past infraction."[136] The Supreme Court has not gone so far as to declare all forms of prior censorship unconstitutional, but "a prior restraint on expression comes to this Court with a 'heavy presumption' against its constitutionality."[137] The burden against prior restraint is so great that the Court is willing to tolerate such restraints only if (1) any restraint is imposed only for a specified brief period, (2) expeditious judicial review of the decision to restrain must be available, and (3) the censor must bear the burden of going to court to suppress the speech and must bear the burden of proof once in court. (In the case of licensing requirements for First amendment-protected *businesses*— an adult motion picture *theatre* in contrast to a motion picture—only the first two of these safeguards are essential.)[138]

In the celebrated case, *New York Times Company* v *United States* (1971), the Supreme Court held that the government had not met the heavy burden against prior restraint when the attorney general tried to secure a court injunction against publication by *The New York Times, The Washington Post*, and other newspapers, of the so-called Pentagon Papers, a classified study of some of the decisions leading to our involvement in the Vietnam War. Three concurring justices—Black, Douglas, and Brennan—made it clear that, in their view, the First Amendment forbids a court to impose, however briefly and for whatever reasons, any prior restraint on a newspaper. (Justice Brennan might have made an exception for publication of troop movements during time of war.) The dominant view, however, was more limited: in this particular instance, the government had failed to show that the publication of these particular documents would cause immediate and specific damage to the nation's security.[139]

In the Pentagon Papers case, the government attempted to assert its right to act without any specific congressional authorization. But in 1979, when the government learned that *The Progressive* was about to publish an article titled "The H-Bomb Secret: How We Got It, Why We're Telling It," federal prosecutors sought an injunction pursuant to the Atomic Energy Act. The act authorizes the government to enjoin the dissemination of restricted data concerning the design, manufacture, or utilization of atomic weapons. The district judge could "find no plausible reason why the public needs to know the technical details about hydrogen bomb construction" and issued a preliminary restraining order.

---

[135] *Alexander* v *United States*, 125 L Ed 2d 441 (1993).

[136] Justice Kennedy dissenting in *Alexander* v *United States*.

[137] *Organization for a Better Austin* v *Keefe*, 402 US 415 (1971); *Nebraska Press Assn.* v *Stuart*, 427 US 539 (1976).

[138] *FW/PBS, Inc.* v *Dallas*, 493 US 215(1990).

[139] *New York Times Company* v *United States*, 403 US 713 (1971).

The courts refused to expedite the case and it never reached the Supreme Court's docket because the government abandoned the effort to enjoin publication after the information in the article was published in other places.[140]

The Constitution tolerates more regulation of motion pictures than of printed media. A state or city may require motion pictures to be licensed before being shown to the public, whereas such prior censorship is not permitted in the case of printed media.[141] However, even with respect to motion pictures, the Supreme Court is suspicious of prior restraint; it insists on procedures to ensure prompt judicial determination of whether a particular picture is unfit to be shown.[142] And the only permissible grounds on which a license may be withheld is obscenity, as constitutionally defined.[143]

Live performances, such as plays and revues, are, along with motion pictures, entitled to some constitutional protection.[144] Yet live theater is subject to greater regulation than either the printed page or the motion picture. The First Amendment, especially in view of the Twenty-first, does not protect liquor licensees from state regulations forbidding sexually suggestive performances in places where liquor is sold.[145]

Today, other than for motion pictures, and then only for obscenity, one of the few examples of prior censorship to pass Supreme Court muster has been the requirement that reading matter not be distributed on a military base without prior approval of post headquarters. The Supreme Court acknowledged special military interests in keeping military activities free of partisan political entanglements and noted that military bases are not ordinary forums of public discussion.[146] The Court also held that the First Amendment does not preclude the CIA from enforcing employment agreements requiring agents to submit all their writings about the CIA for prepublication review, even those that contain no classified material.[147] The Court has also permitted judges to restrain newspapers from publishing information the newspapers obtained by using pretrial discovery procedures to compel their legal adversaries to produce materials. Said the Court, "An order prohibiting dissemination of discovered information before trial is not the kind of classic prior restraint that requires exacting First Amendment scrutiny."[148] When commercial speech (see pages 219) is involved, such as classified advertisements about jobs, the Court has allowed governments to prohibit announcements for jobs restricted only to men (or women).[149]

---

[140] *United States v The Progressive, Inc.*, 467 F Supp 990 (1979).

[141] *Times Film Corp. v Chicago*, 356 US 43 (1961).

[142] *Teitel Film Corp. v Cusak*, 390 US 139 (1968); *Freedman v Maryland*, 380 US 51 (1965).

[143] *Burstyn v Wilson*, 343 US 495 (1952); *Superior Films v Department of Education*, 346 US 587 (1954); *Kingsley Corp. v Regents*, 360 US 684 (1959).

[144] *Southeastern Promotions, Ltd. v Conrad*, 420 US 546 (1975).

[145] *California v LaRue*, 409 US 109 (1972).

[146] *Greer v Spock*, 424 US 828 (1976); *Brown v Glines*, 444 US 620 (1980); *Secretary of Navy v Huff*, 444 US 453 (1980).

[147] *Snepp v United States*, 444 US 507 (1980).

[148] *Seattle Times Co. v Rhinehart*, 467 US 20 (1984).

[149] *Pittsburgh Press Co. v Human Relations Commission*, 413 US 376 (1973).

The Court's hostility toward prior restraint reinforces Fourth Amendment considerations to provide an exception to the general rule that, with a proper warrant or based on probable cause (see page 254), all contraband, instrumentalities and evidence of crimes may be seized.[150] When the materials involved are presumptively protected by the First Amendment, "While a single copy of a book or film may be seized and retained for evidentiary purposes based on a finding of probable cause, the publication may not be taken out of circulation completely until there has been a determination of obscenity after an adversary hearing."[151] However, the Court did not find prior restraint when the federal government, after a criminal trial convicting a person of selling four obscene magazines and three such videotapes, in addition to imposing a prison term and fine seized and destroyed all the other books and assets in his stores.[152] Chief Justice Rehnquist, speaking for a majority of five, said to lump a forfeiture imposed after a full criminal trial with an injunction enjoining future speech would stretch the term "prior restraint" well beyond the limits established by our cases. Justice Kennedy, writing for the dissenters, contended, "What is at work in this case is not the power to punish an individual for his past transgressions but the authority to suppress a particular class of disfavored speech... by seizing speech presumed to be protected."[153]

The Supreme Court, although agreeing that the First Amendment was involved, nonetheless sustained the right of a high school principal to impose prior censorship upon a school newspaper written and edited by a journalism class. The paper was not a public forum (see page 236) open by policy or practice "for indiscriminate use by the general public" or by student organizations. Rather it was a school-sponsored paper and part of the school's educational program.[154] The First Amendment does not provide the same protection for the student press as it does for nonschool papers, possibly more for a college than for a high school newspaper.

Although not a classic example of prior restraint, the Court has struggled over the question of whether and how the First Amendment restricts a public school board's ability to decide which books may be kept in a public school library. In *Board of Education* v *Pico*, the justices wrote seven different opinions and seventy-four pages, but they were unable to get a majority behind any of the opinions. Apparently, what it comes down to is that the First Amendment does apply— actions of school boards are subject to federal court review; although school boards have wide discretion in deciding which books are suitable for the library, they may not remove books from library shelves simply because they dislike the ideas contained in those books. The dissenting justices felt that the choice of books for a school library should be left completely to the discretion of school boards.[155]

---

[150] *Marcus* v *Search Warrant*, 367 US 717 (1961).

[151] *Fort Wayne Books, Inc.* v *Indiana*, 489 US 46 (1989).

[152] *Alexander* v *United States*, 125 L Ed 2d 441 (1993).

[153] Ibid.

[154] *Hazelwood School Dist.* v *Kuhlmeier*, 484 US 260 (1988).

[155] *Board of Education* v *Pico*, 457 US 853 (1982).

Vagueness and Overbreadth

Laws touching First Amendment freedoms must not be so vague that people are afraid to exercise protected freedoms. Such vague laws have a "chilling effect" on freedom of speech. For example, New York's attempt to ban "sacrilegious movies" and publications of "criminal deeds of bloodshed or lust...so massed as to become vehicles for inciting violent and depraved crimes" was declared unconstitutional because the definitions used were so vague that no one could know what was or was not allowed.[156]

Closely related to vagueness and sometimes shading into it is the overbreadth doctrine. Overbroad statutes, whatever their purpose, that have a "chilling effect upon First Amendment rights" are especially suspect. "Because First Amendment freedoms need breathing space to survive, government may regulate in the area only with narrow specificity."[157] In fact, if an overbroad statute significantly affects freedom of speech, the Court may hold not merely that the law as applied to a particular person is unconstitutional, but that the law on its face is unconstitutional. In such instances, even if the defendant's language might have been punished under a more narrowly drawn statute, the defendant has standing to challenge the law.[158]

To use the overbreadth doctrine to strike down a statute is "strong medicine." Therefore, there must be a "realistic danger that the statute compromises First Amendment protections of parties not before the Court." For example, the Court struck down a regulation forbidding all First Amendment activities within the Los Angeles International Airport. The airport commissioners, by declaring that LAX was not a public forum, were trying to avoid the accusation that they were allowing some but not others to pass out handbills and approach travelers. Their sweeping ban, however, made it possible to find "virtually every individual who enters LAX" to violate the resolution by engaging in some "First Amendment activity."[159] Another example of the use of the overbreadth doctrine is the Court's holding unconstitutional, on its face, a Houston ordinance making it unlawful to assault, strike, or in any manner oppose, molest, abuse, or interrupt any policeman in the execution of his duty. This ordinance was so broad that it prohibited speech that in any manner interrupts an officer. The Constitution does not, wrote Justice Brennan for the Court, "allow such speech to be made a crime."[160] A similar fate befell a Columbus, Ohio, ordinance that made it a crime for a person "to abuse another by using menacing, insulting, slanderous, or profane language."[161] Schaumburg, Illinois, was not allowed to forbid direct solicitation of funds by organizations that did not use at least 75 percent of the money they collected

---

[156] *Burstyn v Wilson*, 343 US 495 (1952); *Winters v New York*, 333 US 507 (1948).

[157] *NAACP v Button*, 371 US 415 (1963).

[158] *Los Angeles City Council v Taxpayers for Vincent*, 466 US 789 (1984); *Secretary of State of Maryland v J. H. Munson Co.*, 467 US 947 (1984).

[159] *Board of Airport Commissioners v Jews for Jesus*, 482 US 569 (1987).

[160] *Houston v Hill*, 482 US 451 (1987).

[161] *Plummer v City of Columbus*, 414 US 2 (1973).

for direct charitable purposes. Such an ordinance was overbroad and unconstitutional on its face. It effectively prevented solicitation by "advocacy organizations," organizations that use funds to advocate such causes as cleaning the
air and banning the bomb.

An overbroad statute cannot be "cured" by a subsequent legislative action
narrowing the statute. It can be cured, however, by a state court giving a narrower construction to it that avoids threatening protected speech. Why the
difference? Justice White has explained, "Legislators who know they can cure
their own mistakes by amendment without significant cost may not be as careful to avoid drafting overbroad statutes as they might otherwise be." But judges
will not be less careful if they are allowed to correct overbreadth, so decided the
Supreme Court in a case involving a state court's narrowing of a law's definition of child pornography in order to avoid the statute's making it a crime
merely to possess nude pictures of children.[162]

Least Restrictive Means

The requirement that governments, in regulating speech, directly or indirectly, do so by the least restrictive means applies to content-based regulation, but
not to time, place, and manner regulations (see page 214). When a legislature is
dealing with a matter that goes to the core of First Amendment freedoms, however important the state's interest, the legislation must be subject to "the most
exacting scrutiny" and the legislature must choose the "least-restrictive means"
of accomplishing its otherwise legitimate goals. To illustrate, a state may protect
the public from unscrupulous lawyers, but it may not do so by forbidding organizations to make legal services available to their members or by forbidding attorneys from advertising. A government may protect foreign diplomats, but it may
not ban displaying abusive signs in front of foreign embassies.[163]

Content Neutrality

Content-neutral laws are much less likely to be struck down than those
that restrict speech based on content. For example, a law forbidding the posting of any signs on telephone poles would be more likely to pass constitutional muster—and has—than one forbidding all posters advocating racism.
As noted (see page 200), the Court invalidated a hate-speech law because
the law made criminal some "fighting words" based on their content. The
Court has also struck down New York's "Son of Sam" law—most states
had a similar law—that required taking from and giving the funds to victims of the crime a criminal's income from books or any other kind of work
such as a television show that described the criminal's conduct. Here were
words and pictures that were not obscene or libelous or others in the category

---

[162] *Osborne* v *Ohio*, 495 US 103 (1990).
[163] *Boos* v *Barry*, 485 US 312 (1988).

that could be forbidden being attacked solely because of their content.[164] (Note: a state could probably accomplish its goal of not allowing criminals to benefit from their crimes by laws confiscating all earnings while in prison or for a period of time regardless of source and then appropriating funds to compensate victims.)

Content neutral is more than viewpoint neutral. "A regulation that 'does not favor either side of a political controversy' is nonetheless impermissible because of the First Amendment's hostility to content-based regulation if it extends...to prohibition of public discussion of an entire topic."[165] However, if a category of speech is involved, such as adult films, and the justification has to do with the *secondary effects* of adult theaters that show such films, that is, the ordinance is not aimed at the suppression of the films but, say, at preventing the degredation of a neighborhood, the Court will require less justification than if the content-based regulation is aimed directly at speech, especially political speech.[166]

Justice Stevens is skeptical about the usefulness of the content-neutral analysis, pointing out that selective regulation of speech based on content underlies much of the Court's First Amendment jurisprudence. "Whether a magazine is obscene, a gesture, a fighting word, or a photograph, child pornography is determined, in part, by its content... it is also beyond question that the Government may choose to limit advertisements for cigarettes and not for cigars."[167]

Time, Place, and Manner Regulations

The Supreme Court has come very close to the view that, except for the narrowly defined categories of libel, obscenity, fighting words, and seditious incitement to violence, pure speech—"that is, speech unconnected with action"—including commercial speech and that of corporations, is constitutionally protected from any except reasonable time, place, and manner regulations. Regulations designed to regulate the time, place, or manner of speech are subject to a three-part test. (The Supreme Court seems partial to three-part tests.)

1. The regulation must be neutral with respect to the content of the expression and it must be applied evenhandedly. (Justice Stevens is also skeptical that this generalization is of help. He quipped, "Any student of history who has been reprimanded for talking about the World Series during a class discussion of the First Amendment knows that it

---

[164] *Simon & Schuster* v *New York Crime Victims Bd.*, 116 L Ed 2d 476 (1991).

[165] Quoted from *Consolidated Edison Co.* v *Public Service Comm'n.*, 447 US 537 (1980) in *Boos* v *Barry*, 485 US 312 (1988).

[166] *City of Renton et al.* v *Playtime Theatres, Inc. et al.*, 475 US 41 (1986); *Boos* v *Barry*, 485 US 312 (1988).

[167] *R.A.V. Paul* v *St. Paul* 120 L Ed 2d 305 (1992).

is incorrect to state that a time, place, or manner restriction may not be based upon either the content or subject matter of the speech.")[168]

2. It must leave open ample alternative channels for communication of the information.

3. Although the least restrictive-means test does not apply, the regulation must be "narrowly tailored" to serve a significant governmental interest. However, "So long as the means chosen are not substantially broader than necessary to achieve the government's interest...the regulation will not be invalid simply because a court concludes that the government's interest could be adequately served by some less speech-restrictive alternative."[169]

An example of congressional time, place, and manner regulations is a federal law, stemming from World War II concerns, requiring foreign agents in the United States to register and to notify the Department of Justice of any materials they intend to distribute in the United States. If the Department of Justice declares that the materials come within the statutory definition, the distributor must see that they are properly labeled as "political propaganda." The Supreme Court sustained the law as an appropriate exercise of congressional authority. The Court concluded that the statute merely gives people additional information about the source of the materials. The dissenting justices contended that even if Congress used the "propaganda" designation with a completely neutral purpose, Congress has burdened political discourse and has given no persuasive justification of the burden. Such a burden, they argued, is contrary to consistent Supreme Court holdings that limitations on First Amendment freedoms can be justified only by a compelling governmental interest.[170] (As a side issue, it is a mark of how far we have gone into modern federalism that we now assume that Congress has authority to act unless a specific constitutional provision forbids it to do so. In this case, there was no discussion by any justice about the precise constitutional authority under which Congress was acting. The statute appears to be based on congressional authority over the mails and over commerce among the states.) Another example comes from a 1992 case in which the Court sustained a Tennessee statute prohibiting solicitation of votes and distribution of campaign literature within 100 feet of the entrance to a polling place. Subjecting the regulation to what the Court claimed to be exacting scrutiny, and indicating that it was one of those rare cases in which a law survives strict scrutiny, the Court concluded that even though it applied to political speech, in a public forum, and was not content-neutral since it did not forbid nonpolitical speech, nonetheless, the state had a compelling interest in protecting the integrity of the vote and the secrecy of the ballot so that a 100-feet limit was narrowly enough drawn to achieve that compelling interest.[171]

---

[168] *Consolidated Edison Company* v *Public Service Commission of New York*, 447 US 530 (1980).

[169] *Ward* v *Rock Against Racism*, 488 US 816 (1989).

[170] *Meese* v *Keene*, 481 US 465 (1987).

[171] *Burson* v *Freeman*, 119 L Ed 2d 5 (1992).

Handbills, Amplification, Sound Trucks, and Billboards

Reasonable content-neutral restraints can be imposed on the time, place, and manner in which handbills may be sold or distributed. A general ban on handbills is unreasonable, as is a ban on handbills that do not carry the name and address of the author.[172] Regulation with any aspect of prior restraint is likely to be struck down.[173] On the other side, the federal government may forbid the use of mailboxes for distribution of leaflets;[174] a city may ban the posting of signs on public property.[175]

Billboards on private property are entitled to constitutional protection, and a San Diego ordinance banning off-site billboards was declared unconstitutional, but the decision was "a virtual Tower of Babel from which no definitive principles can be clearly drawn." A plurality of the justices found that San Diego had erred in allowing on-site commercial billboards but not on-site noncommercial messages. Two other justices felt the vice of San Diego's action was its failure to prove that such action was necessary to promote traffic safety or to improve the beauty of the city.[176]

What of the use of amplification to project music and sound? Provided it proceeds by content-neutral means, a government may ban sound trucks that give out loud and raucous noises, even if the loud and raucous noises are political speeches.[177] As to music, "[It], as a form of expression and communication, is protected under the First Amendment." On the other hand, one does not have the right to play any music any time at any level. A government may regulate reasonable restrictions on sound-amplification equipment in order to avoid undue intrusion into residential areas.[178]

Speech Enmeshed with Conduct

When speech becomes enmeshed with conduct it loses its character as pure speech. Nonetheless, expressive conduct is also subject to First Amendment protection. The Court has repeatedly warned governments that "[they cannot regulate conduct connected with First Amendment freedoms] through the use of sweeping, dragnet statutes that may, because of vagueness, jeopardize these freedoms." "The Constitution does not bar enactment of laws regulating conduct, even though connected with speech, press, assembly, and petition, if such laws specifically bar only the conduct deemed obnoxious and are carefully and narrowly aimed at that forbidden conduct."[179]

---

[172] Talley v California, 362 US 60 (1960).
[173] Organization for a Better Austin v Keefe, 402 US 415 (1971).
[174] United States Postal Service v Greenburgh Civic Assn., 453 US 114 (1981).
[175] Los Angeles City Council v Taxpayers for Vincent, 466 US 789 (1984).
[176] Metromedia v San Diego, 453 US 490 (1981).
[177] Kovacs v Cooper, 336 US 77 (1949).
[178] Ward v Rock Against Racism, 488 US 816 (1989).
[179] Justice Black concurring, Gregory v Chicago, 394 US 111 (1969).

Of course, almost every law may have an effect on speech activities, but the only laws subject to First Amendment scrutiny are those that regulate symbolic speech, conduct with "a significant expressive element," or those that have the "inevitable effect of singling out" expressive activity.[180] Moreover, "We cannot accept the view," wrote Chief Justice Warren, "that an apparently limitless variety of conduct can be labeled speech whenever the person engaged in the conduct intends thereby to express an idea."[181] Or, as Chief Justice Burger has written, "Conduct that the State police power can prohibit on a public street does not become automatically protected by the Constitution merely because the conduct is moved to a bar or a 'live theater' stage, any more than 'live' performance of a man and woman locked in a sexual embrace at high noon in Times Square is protected by the Constitution because they simultaneously engage in a ... political dialogue."[182]

The Court has distinguished between two kinds of governmental regulations of expressive conduct: those where the government's interest is in regulating the expressive conduct directly and those where the government's concern is directed toward some other interest. The relatively lenient "O'Brien test"—first announced in a case relating to federal laws requiring the carrying and preserving of draft cards—applies to laws regulating expressive conduct when the government interest is unrelated to the expressive nature of the conduct. Here the laws are constitutional: (1) if the conduct itself may constitutionally be regulated; (2) if the regulation furthers an important or substantial governmental interest; (3) if the government interest is unrelated to the suppression of free expression; (4) and if the incidental restriction on alleged First Amendment freedoms is no greater than is essential to the furtherance of that interest. On that basis, the Supreme Court unanimously sustained the constitutionality of the 1965 amendment to the Selective Service Act that made it a crime knowingly to destroy or mutilate draft cards.[183] The Court later upheld a National Park Service regulation denying to an organization speaking for the homeless the right to sleep overnight in Lafayette Park across from the White House.[184]

The Supreme Court, applying the O'Brien test, concluded that nude dancing performed in a public place "is expressive conduct within the outer perimeters of the First Amendment, though we view it as only marginally so." (At least the Court did not say "barely so.") Indiana could apply its public indecency law to such dancing and require the dancers to wear at least "pasties" and a "G-string." Such a requirement, said the Court, apparently without recognizing the humor of it, "was narrowly tailored" to achieve the state's purposes. Justice Scalia would have applied no First Amendment test because he found the Indiana statute a general law regulating conduct and not directed at

---

[180] *Arcara* v *Cloud Books,* 478 US 697 (1986).

[181] *United States* v *O'Brien,* 391 US 367 (1968).

[182] *Paris Adult Theatre I* v *Slaton,* 413 US 49 (1973).

[183] *United States* v *O'Brien,* 391 US 367 (1968).

[184] *Clark* v *Community for Creative Non-Violence,* 468 US 288 (1984).

expression that could be enforced against those who chose to use public nudity as a mean of communication. Justices White, Marshall, Blackmun, and Stevens dissenting argued that Indiana was applying its law to nude dancing performances in entertainment establishments for the purpose of preventing customers from receiving the erotic messages the dancers were trying to send.[185]

If, however, the governmental interest is more *directly aimed at the symbolic character of the conduct* then the more demanding standards for regulation of speech come into play. A majority of the justices held that school authorities had violated the Constitution when they suspended two students for quietly and passively wearing black armbands to school to protest the Vietnam War.[186]

The Court sustained the right of Congress to give the US Olympic Committee, a congressionally chartered private corporation, exclusive control of the use of the word "Olympics." The committee had denied to another group the right to promote the "Gay Olympics." The Court treated this federal law as an appropriately aimed trademark regulation of commercial speech, with whatever incidental limit on expressive speech being justified as necessary to further a substantial governmental interest.[187]

Flag Burning

A question arousing considerable heat inside and outside the Court is whether governments may make it a crime to mutilate the American flag. In 1989 a bitterly split Court, by five to four, declared unconstitutional Texas's conviction of a protester at the Republican National Convention for burning the flag as part of a demonstration. *Texas v Johnson* effectively declared unconstitutional a similar federal law and one in all but two states that made it a crime to burn, defile, deface, or trample on the American flag with the *intent to cast contempt on it*. Justice Brennan, speaking for the Court, rejected the application of the *O'Brien* test and declared that Texas's argument cannot depend here on the distinction between speech and conduct for that "distinction...is of no moment where the nonverbal conduct is expressive, as it is here, and where the regulation of that conduct is related to 'expression.'"...Government may not prohibit expression simply because it disagrees with its message." Justice Brennan, knowing that this decision would undoubtedly be greeted with anger, commented "We are tempted to say...that the flag's deservedly cherished place in our community will be strengthened, not weakened, by our holding today. Our decision is a reaffirmation of the principles of freedom and inclusiveness that the flag best reflects...."

Chief Justice Rehnquist, with whom Justices White and O'Connor joined, dissented, accusing the majority of engaging in a "regrettably patronizing civics lecture" and of acting as "Platonic guardians admonishing those responsible to

---

[185] *Barnes v Glen Theatre,*

[186] *Tinker v Des Moines School District,* 391 US 367 (1968).

[187] *San Francisco Arts and Athletics, Inc. v Olympic Committee,* 483 US 522 (1987).

public opinion as if they were truant school children." He contended that "The American flag, throughout more than 200 years of our history, has come to be the visible symbol embodying our Nation... [it] is not simply another 'idea' or 'point of view' competing for recognition in the market place of ideas." It is eminently reasonable and well within the power of legislatures to prohibit "the public burning of the flag on the grounds that it is so inherently inflammatory that it may cause a breach of public order." Justice Stevens, dissenting on the grounds that the case had nothing to do with disagreeable ideas, wrote, "It involves disagreeable conduct that, in my opinion, diminishes the value of an important national asset."[188]

President Bush greeted the decision with a call for a constitutional amendment. Congress responded by passing a content-neutral law, unlike the Texas law, that would make it a crime to burn or deface the flag whatever one's purpose or intent. Congress provided for expedited direct and mandatory review by the Supreme Court of any decision involving this law by a lower court. The president allowed the bill to become law without his signature, insisting that a constitutional amendment was preferable.

The law was promptly tested. Two federal judges, relying on the *Johnson* ruling, declared the law unconstitutional and, in June 1990, nine months after the *Johnson* decision, the Supreme Court again declared it unconstitutional by the same five to four line up as in the *Johnson* case. Justice Brennan, again speaking for the Court in *United States* v *Eichman*, said that, although "Congress cast the Flag Protection Act in somewhat broader terms than the Texas statute at issue in *Johnson*, the Act still suffers from the same fundamental flaw: it suppresses expression out of concern for its likely communicative impact." The government's interest was related to the suppression of free expression and concerned with the content of such expression. Justice Brennan acknowledged the pressures building against flag burning because it is "deeply offensive to many," but even assuming that most Americans are against such expressive activity, "any suggestion that the government's interest in suppressing speech becomes more weighty as popular opposition to that speech grows," wrote Justice Brennan "is foreign to the First Amendment."[189] Justice Stevens, writing for the minority, argued that First Amendment rights are not absolute—"the communicative value of a well-placed bomb in the Capitol does not entitle it to the protection of the First Amendment."

Immediately upon hearing of the decision, President Bush called for a constitutional amendment and one was introduced. It read, "The Congress and the states shall have power to prohibit the physical desecration of the flag of the United States." The House of Representatives failed, however, to muster the necessary two-thirds vote, as did the Senate a few weeks later.

---

[188] *Texas* v *Johnson*, 488 US 884 (1989).
[189] *United States* v *Eichman*, 496 US 310 (1990).

Picketing

The right to picket, when picketing is unaccompanied by threats or violence, is protected by the Constitution; but, since picketing involves "elements of both speech and conduct...picketing can be subjected to controls that would not be constitutionally permissible in cases of pure speech."[190] Even peaceful picketing can be restricted if it is conducted for an illegal purpose, that is, designed to pressure someone to do something that the law forbids them to do.[191]

In recent years the Court has shown somewhat greater concern to protect picketing, especially "public issue picketing."[192] The Constitution forbids statutes aimed at picketing that are not narrowly drawn. At the same time the Constitution, by the equal protection clause of the Fourteenth Amendment as well as the First Amendment, forbids a state to choose by subject matter the kinds of peaceful picketing it will allow. Illinois, for example, found itself in constitutional difficulty when, to draw its ban on picketing of residences as narrowly as possible, it exempted peaceful labor picketing of places of employment.[193] The statute, the Court said, made an impermissible distinction between labor picketing and other peaceful picketing, although dissenting Justice Rehnquist complained that a state's constitutional ability to protect residential privacy was being made almost impossible to enforce.[194] And the Court, with Justices Brennan, Marshall, and Stevens dissenting and with Justice White indicating that he did not believe that the banning of residential picketing in general could be sustained, upheld an ordinance that forbids all picketing "before or about any residence" after construing the ordinance to limit the forbidding of picketing against a single residence.[195] On the other hand, while upholding a congressional prohibition on hostile congregations within 500 feet of a foreign embassy, the Court struck down a prohibition on hostile picketing.[196]

Commercial Speech

Commercial speech is speech that "proposes a commercial transaction."[197] The mere fact that it is uttered for a profit—for example, charitable solicitations by professional fund-raisers, or political advertisements—does not make it commercial speech.[198] Commercial speech is entitled to constitutional protection, but less so than political speech. It is subject to more regulation than are other varieties of speech because of the common-sense differences between it and other kinds of speech. Decisions of the Supreme Court dealing with

---

[190] *Amalgamated Food Employees Local 590 v Logan Valley Plaza, Inc.,* 391 US 308 (1968).
[191] *Building Serv. Employees Union v Gazzam,* 339 US 532 (1950).
[192] *Boos v Barry,* 485 US 312 (1988).
[193] *Carey v Brown,* 447 US 455 (1980).
[194] Ibid.
[195] *Frisby v Schultz,* 487 US 474 (1988).
[196] *Boos v Barry,* 485 US 312 (1988).
[197] *Board of Trustees, SUNY v Fox,* 492 US 469 (1989).
[198] *Riley v National Fed'n. of the Blind,* 487 US 781 (1988).

"more traditional First Amendment problems do not extend automatically to this... area."[199] For example, overbreadth analysis is not applicable, and perhaps neither are the prohibitions against prior restraint.

Commercial speech is subject to a four-part analysis. "(1) For commercial speech to come within [the First Amendment], it at least must concern lawful activity and not be misleading. (2) Next, we ask whether the asserted governmental interest is substantial. If both inquiries yield positive answers, we must determine (3) whether the regulation directly advances the governmental interest asserted, and (4) whether the state has affirmatively established that it is using a narrowly tailored means to achieve the desired objective, a fit that is not necessarily perfect, but reasonable."[200] Although the "least-restrictive-means" test used to measure the constitutionality of political speech is not applicable to commercial speech,[201] the regulating government has a burden to establish a reasonable fit between its legitimate ends and the means used to achieve those ends.[202]

The Court is more likely to sustain disclosure requirements for commercial speech than for noncommerical speech. With political speech, not only may people not be compelled to say things they do not wish to say,[203] but they may not be forced to identify themselves as authors of handbills.[204] In the case of commercial speech, although "unjustified or unduly burdensome disclosure requirements might offend the First Amendment... an advertiser's rights are adequately protected as long as disclosures requirements are reasonably related to the State's interest in preventing deception of consumers."[205]

A law forbidding "false or misleading" political speech would be clearly unconstitutional. Who is to say, in the realm of political matters, what is false or misleading? But, although a state may not forbid professionals such as doctors, lawyers, and pharmacists from advertising the prices they charge or to list their fields of specialization or prohibit them from sending targeted advertisements,[206] it may forbid them from false or misleading advertising. ("Although a state may prohibit misleading advertising entirely, it may not place an absolute prohibition on potentially misleading information if the information may also be presented in a way that is not deceptive.")[207] What is false or misleading advertising is something that can be established. Moreover, advertisers' access to the truth about their products and prices "substantially eliminates any danger that governmental regulation of false or misleading advertising will chill accurate and non-deceptive commercial

[199] Friedman v Rogers, 440 US 1 (1979).

[200] Board of Trustees, SUNY v Fox, 492 US 469 (1989); Central Hudson Gas & Electric Corporation v Public Service Commission of New York, 447 US 557 (1980).

[201] Board of Trustees, SUNY v Fox, 492 US 469 (1989).

[202] Ibid. and Cincinnati v Discovery Network, Inc., 123 L Ed 2d 99 (1993).

[203] Wooley v Maynard, 430 US 705 (1977); West Virginia State Board of Education v Barnette, 319 US 624 (1943).

[204] Talley v California, 362 US 60 (1960).

[205] Zauderer v Office of Disciplinary Counsel, 471 US 626 (1985).

[206] Virginia Pharmacy Board v Virginia Consumer Council, 452 US 746 (1976); Bates v State Bar of Arizona, 433 US 530 (1977); In re RMJ, 455 US 191 (1982); Shapero v Kentucky Bar Assn., 486 US 4665 (1988).

[207] Peel v Disciplinary Com. 496 US 91 (1990).

expression."[208] That which *might* be misleading may be regulated by narrowly drawn restrictions if the state shows that a particular regulation furthers its substantial interest.[209] Professional advertising on radio and television is subject to greater restraint than print advertising.

States may discipline lawyers for direct face to face solicitation of clients,[210] but they may not so discipline accountants. Why the difference? There is a greater danger of overreaching when a lawyer, trained in the art of persuasion, personally solicits an unsophisticated, injured, or distressed lay person than when an accountant does so. Unlike a lawyer, argues the Court, an accountant is not professionally trained in the art of persuasion but rather is trained to emphasize independence and objectivity, not advocacy. Moreover, a typical client of a CPA is far less susceptible to manipulation than are many prospective legal clients.[211]

What a state has made illegal (prostitution, race and gender discrimination, or gambling, for example), it may forbid commercial advertising to promote. Since it is illegal to discriminate in employment on the basis of sex, a city may make it illegal for newspapers to publish want ads under the headings "Male Help Wanted" and "Female Help Wanted," just as it could forbid advertisements for prostitution or illegal drugs. Where the underlying conduct, although legal, is of such a nature that a government could make it illegal, advertising about it may be regulated, even forbidden. Thus, Puerto Rico, although it allowed advertising by legal gambling casinos directed at tourists, could prohibit such advertising aimed directly at island residents.[212] Congress was allowed to prohibit lottery advertising by a broadcaster in a state that does not allow lotteries even though most of its audience lived in a state which sponsored the lottery.[213]

Governments may not, however, forbid newspapers to publish advertisements advocating "sexism or other controversial subjects."[214] Nor may governments forbid political advocacy of controversial or illegal activities, that is, advertisements urging that gambling be made legal, that discrimination be practiced, or that prostitution be legalized. Governments may not ban advertising or contraceptives or abortions that are legal where they are performed. [215] And a city may not ban "For Sale" signs in front of homes, even if the purpose of the ban is to prevent panic selling by whites in neighborhoods becoming racially integrated.[216] Nor may a city ban the distribution of commercial publications through news racks located on public property while allowing other publications to do so.[217] Such a regulation is neither content neutral nor narrowly tailored.

---

[208] Justice Stewart concurring in *Virginia Pharmacy Board* v *Virginia Consumer Council*, 425 US 748 (1976).

[209] *In re RMJ*, 455 US 191 (1982).

[210] *Ohralik* v *Ohio State Bar Assn.*, 436 US 447 (1978).

[211] *Edenfield* v *Fane*, 123 L Ed 2d 543 (1993).

[212] *Posadas de Puerto Rico Assoc.* v *Tourism Co.*, 478 US 328 (1986).

[213] *United States* v *Edge Broadcasting Company*, 125 L Ed 2d 345 (1993).

[214] *Pittsburgh Press Co.* v *Human Relations Commission*, 413 US 376 (1973).

[215] *Carey* v *Population Services International*, 431 US 678 (1977); *Bigelow* v *Virginia*, 421 US 809 (1975).

[216] *Linmark Associates, Inc.* v *Township of Willingboro*, 431 US 85 (1977).

[217] *Cincinnati* v *Discovery Network, Inc.*, 123 L Ed 2d 99 (1993).

In fact, the distinction between political and commercial speech is becoming less and less sharp. There appears to be an emerging Court consensus that "permissible restraints on commercial speech..." should be limited "to measures designed to protect consumers from fraudulent, misleading, or coercive sales techniques."[218] When commercial speech is involved the regulating government has the burden of showing that there is a "reasonable fit" between its legitimate interests and the means it chooses to serve that interest.[219]

Corporate Speech

Corporations, like people, are entitled to freedom of speech. A state may not prohibit corporations from spending money to influence votes on referendum proposals, nor may it prevent public utilities from placing promotional advertisements or statements about public issues in its bills.[220] On the other hand the Supreme Court has upheld substantial restrictions on corporate speech, including speech of a political character, the kind of speech that is entitled to the most protection. The Court has concluded that the state's interest in preventing corruption of the political process justifies some restraints on expressive activity of general purpose business and non-profit corporations.[221] Nonmedia corporations, including not-for-profit ones such as a chamber of commerce but not corporations formed for the express and single purpose of promoting political ideas, may be prohibited from spending money from the corporate general treasury to endorse candidates in elections, although such a law clearly would be unconstitutional as applied to a newspaper, television, radio, magazine, or other kind of media corporation. Nonmedia corporations may, however, promote political ideas by using segregated funds collected expressly for such purposes. Justice Scalia, in dissent, satirically described the law approved by the Court as saying, "Attention all citizens. To assure the fairness of elections by preventing disproportionate expression of the views of any single powerful group, your Government has decided that the following association shall be prohibited from speaking or writing in support of any candidate...." (Similar regulations have been sustained as applied to trade unions that collect dues from members.)

Campaign Finances

Concerned about corruption and about the unfair advantage that people and interests of wealth have in the political process, especially elections,

---

[218]Justice Blackmun concurring in *Cincinnati v Discovery Networks, Inc.* 123 L Ed 2d 99 (1993). Quoting from his concurrence in *Central Hudson Gas & Electric Corp. v Public Service Comm'n of New York,* 447 US 557 (1980).

[219]*Trustees of State Univ. of New York v Fox,* 492 US 469 (1989); *Cincinnati v Discovery Network, Inc.* 123 L Ed 2d 99 (1993).

[220]*First National Bank of Boston v Bellotti,* 435 US 765 (1978); *Central Hudson Gas v Public Service Commission,* 447 US 557 (1980); *Consolidated Edison v Public Service Commission,* 447 US 530 (1980).

[221] *Austin v Mich. Chamber of Commerce,* 494 US 652 (1990).

Congress has regulated campaign financing. Restrictions on what people may *give* to candidates are constitutionally permissible. Restrictions on what people, except for general-purpose corporations, may *spend* in behalf of candidates without consulting candidates are not. Limitations on contributions only marginally restrict a contributor's ability to express political views; limitations on expenditures directly affect what people can say and where, when, and how they can say it.[222] Moreover, only contributions to candidates can be limited, not those to groups that advocate causes or work for or against ballot measures.[223]

Congress may condition the funds it provides to finance presidential campaigns on an agreement by candidates and their political parties to limit the amount that will be spent by the candidate and the party committee that receives them.[224] Congress tried to close an obvious loophole by forbidding any independent political campaign committee from spending more than $1,000 to further the election of a presidential candidate. But the Supreme Court declared the limit unconstitutional. As long as a committee maintains no obvious ties to the presidential candidate, it may spend whatever its members wish to further a candidate's political fortunes.

Congress may subject trade union and commercial corporation political action committees to more regulation than is permissible for other kinds of political action committees. Trade unions and commercial corporations can be forbidden to spend any union or corporate funds to endorse candidates—but they cannot be limited with respect to advocating causes.

Subsidized Speech

Although governments have no obligation to subsidize speech, they may not use their power of the purse in such a way as to control speech. Congress did not infringe the First Amendment when it denied tax-exempt charitable organizations the right to use tax-deductible contributions to support lobbying activities.[225] In a much more controversial ruling, the Court sustained the right of Congress to prohibit federal funds to support family-planning clinics from being used for any kind of advice by doctors or nurses employed in such clinics relating to abortion. (Subsequently Congress and the Clinton Administration removed this limit on the use of federal funds.) The majority did so, however, only after intepreting the implementing regulations to permit abortion referral or counseling in case of a "medical emergency."[226] Justice Blackmun in dissent charged, "The Court, for the first time, upholds viewpoint-based suppression of speech solely because it is imposed on those dependent upon the Government for economic support."

---

[222] *Buckley* v *Valeo*, 424 US 1 (1976).

[223] *Citizens Against Rent Control* v *Berkeley*, 454 US 290 (1981).

[224] *Federal Election Commission* v *National Conservative Political Action Committee*, 470 US 480 (1985).

[225] *Regan* v *Taxation with Representation*, 461 US 540 (1983).

[226] *Rust* v *Sullivan*, 114 L Ed 2d 233 (1991).

---

or of the press;

When "the press" is used, more often than not most people think of print journalism, but these days it covers all the media. The Supreme Court has never defined who is entitled to the protections "of the press," and until recently it has not made much of a difference since the press did not appear to have any freedoms beyond those of other persons. It was assumed that freedom of speech was used as a synonym for freedom of the press. One explanation of the Constitution's speaking of the two freedoms separately is that freedom of speech was thought to protect oral communications, and freedom of the press, written ones. Another explanation is that the framers added the phrase "of the press" because "dissemination" had more often been the object of official restraint than had mere personal expression.

Justice Stewart wrote, "That the First Amendment speaks separately of freedom of speech and freedom of the press is no constitutional accident, but an acknowledgment of the critical role played by the press in American society,"[227] and in fact media defendants are being treated differently. However, the prevailing view remains that expressed by Chief Justice Burger: "The First Amendment does not 'belong' to any definable category of persons or entities; it belongs to all who exercise its freedoms."[228] In 1985 Justice Brennan went out of his way to point out that, at least within the context of defamation law, "at least six Members of this Court...agree today that...the rights of the institutional media are no greater and no less than those enjoyed by other individuals or organizations engaged in the same activities." A year later, Justice O'Connor, in an opinion joined on this point only by Justices Marshall and Powell, carefully established a rule for libel suits by private individuals against *media defendants* (see page 202), reserving for another day the question of whether the same standard would apply against a nonmedia defendant.[229] And as we have noted, the Court has made a distinction between media corporations, which cannot be kept from spending general corporate funds for endorsing political candidates, and nonmedia corporations where such limitations may be imposed. The Court has also acknowledged the press exemption from the Federal Campaign Act's limitation on corporations' expenditures in behalf of political candidates: it is quite clear that such a limitation on a press corporation would be unconstitutional.[230]

The Right of Access

There is no general constitutional right of access that allows news people, or anybody else, to go wherever they wish to interview whomever they desire

---

[227] *Houchins v KQED*, 438 US 1 (1978).
[228] *First National Bank of Boston v Bellotti*, 435 US 765 (1978).
[229] *Philadelphia Newspapers, Inc. v Hepps*, 475 US 767 (1986); *Dun & Bradstreet v Greenmoss Builders*, 472 US 749 (1985).
[230] *FEC v Massachusetts Citizens for Life*, 479 US 238 (1986).

or to see whatever documents they claim are of general public interest. Neither the First nor the Fourteenth Amendment guarantees to the news media a right of access to government information not available to the public generally. However, after the Court had been unwilling under the Sixth Amendment's right to a public trial (see page 311) to order that preliminary trial proceedings be open, in what Justice Stevens called a "watershed case," the Supreme Court did rule in *Richmond Newspapers, Inc.* v *Virginia,* "that the acquisition of newsworthy matter is entitled to some constitutional protection." The Court held that a trial judge could not, even with the consent of the prosecutor and defendant, close a trial to the press and public without a specific finding by the judge that there is some "overriding interest" that would justify such a closure. Said Chief Justice Burger, "It is not crucial whether we describe this right to attend criminal trials to hear, see, and communicate observations as a right to access, or a right to gather information."

Whatever it is called, the Court did find that the right of access to trials is protected by a combination of the First, Ninth, and Fourteenth Amendments. Moreover, even Chief Justice Burger seemed to concede some special role for the press. Although pointedly saying that media representatives enjoy only the same right of access as the public, he did recognize that the media often function as "surrogates for the public" and are "accorded special seating and priority of entry so that they may report what people in attendance have seen and heard."[231] Clearly, if this right of public access is extended to other governmental proceedings beyond trials, the decision will deserve Justice Stevens's accolade.

Since *Richmond,* the Court has talked more enthusiastically about the value of open trials.[232] The Court has extended this First Amendment right of access to preliminary hearings as well as to trials.[233] The Court set aside a Massachusetts statute requiring the exclusion of the press and public during the testimony of a minor victim in a sex offense trial.[234] It also refused to allow a trial judge in a rape and murder case to close the jury selection process to protect the privacy of potential jurors, who were subject to questioning about their past sexual experiences and attitudes. The presumption that trials must be kept open, including questioning of jurors, can be overcome "only by an overriding interest based on findings that closure is essential to preserve higher values and is narrowly tailored to serve that interest."[235] Moreover, the judge must make a finding that there is a "substantial probability"—not merely a "reasonable likelihood"—that a right to a fair trial or hearing will be undermined by the opening of a proceeding.[236] In other words, a trial judge who closes any portion of a trial had better have very persuasive reasons, and must put those reasons in writing.

Note the press does not have a general federal constitutional right to take pictures in courtrooms or to televise the proceedings. States may provide for

---

[231] *Richmond Newspapers, Inc.* v *Virginia,* 448 US 555 (1980).
[232] *Globe Newspaper Co.* v *Superior Court,* 457 US 596 (1982).
[233] Ibid.
[234] Ibid.
[235] *Press Enterprise Co.* v *Superior Court,* 464 US 501 (1984).
[236] Ibid.

televised proceedings, however, if they wish and more and more of them are doing so. However, they have to do so in a fashion that does not create such distractions as to deprive a defendant of a fair trial.

Grand jury proceedings are still not open to the press and the Court has not even hinted that they may become so. It has, however, held that a state may not make it a crime for a witness to make public his own testimony after the grand jury session is over.[237]

Although the Constitution does not require that it do so, Congress has gone far toward opening government files. The Freedom of Information Act of 1965, as amended in 1974, requires federal agencies to make information available on request, with certain exceptions, such as defense secrets, criminal investigation files, and interoffice memorandums relating to pending decisions.

In addition to the problem of getting access to information, there is the problem of getting access to the public. Here the constraints are not as likely to be imposed by the government as by the media. In some places there may be only a single newspaper, and it may also own the local television station. Persons ignored by the media (or attacked by it for that matter) have little recourse. The Court has been hostile to access regulations on the printed media and to laws giving persons a right to reply to media attacks on them. A unanimous Court declared unconstitutional a Florida law giving candidates a right to reply in a newspaper's columns to its critical editorial comments. As the Court declared, "A responsible press is an undoubtedly desirable goal, but press responsibility is not mandated by the Constitution and like many other virtues, it cannot be legislated."[238] The Court has been more tolerant of access requirements for the broadcast media: Congress does have the power to confer upon "legally qualified candidates for Federal office" a right to demand that broadcasters sell them time.[239]

The Press and Immunity

Does the First Amendment confer on news people an immunity from being compelled by a grand jury or another government agency to divulge the sources of their information? Although some states have conferred a qualified privilege on news people so that they may more readily gather the news, the First Amendment provides no such immunity. A reporter has no less an obligation than any other citizen to respond to a grand jury subpoena and answer relevant questions.[240] Nor does the First Amendment protect the files of news people from being searched by the police with a valid search warrant. It does not make any constitutional difference that the news people may themselves be innocent of any

---

[237] *Butterworth v Smith*, 494 US 624 (1990).

[238] *Miami Herald Publishing Co. v Tornillo*, 418 US 241 (1974).

[239] *CBS, Inc. v Federal Communications Commission*, 453 US 775 (1978).

[240] *Branzburg v Hayes*, 408 US 665 (1972).

suspected wrongdoing.[241] Congress has, however, provided news people special protection from such searches. Congress has prohibited courts from issuing warrants to federal, state, and local police officers that would authorize those officers to search "the products of news organizations and others engaged in First Amendment activities," except when the news people are themselves suspected of a crime related to the materials they are holding or when there is reason to believe that the immediate seizure of the materials is necessary to prevent death or serious bodily injury. (Materials in news people's files are still subject to subpoena.) And when suing persons for libel, the First Amendment does not protect news people from being questioned about their thought processes or general inquiries into the procedures and processes used inside the newspaper.[242]

The Court also held that the First Amendment does not protect a newspaper from having to pay damages to an informant to whom it had promised confidentiality and then decided that the public was entitled to know his name. "The application of such general laws against the press is not subject to stricter scrutiny than would be applied to enforcement against other persons or organizations."[243]

Taxes and the Media

Although "generally applicable laws do not offend the First Amendment simply because their enforcement against the press has incidental effects on its ability to gather and report the news,"[244] the Court has been especially solicitous of protecting publications from any kind of taxation that could possibly have an intimidating effect on them. Wrote Justice O'Connor for the Court, "The press plays a unique role, as a check on government abuse, and a tax limited to the press raises concerns about censorship of critical information and opinion."[245] General taxes, along with such economic regulations as fair labor standards acts, antitrust laws, and so on, can be applied to the press. But when Huey Long, as governor of Louisiana, persuaded the legislature to impose a tax on some newspapers that had been critical of him, the Supreme Court, in *Grosjean* v *American Press Co.*, declared the taxation unconstitutional. The Court perceived that the tax had been imposed to punish a select group of newspapers.[246]

So careful is the Court to protect the press from possible government threats that in *Minneapolis* v *Minnesota Comm. of Revenue* it declared a Minnesota tax unconstitutional, even though it had been adopted with no evil intent and in amount less than the sales taxes on other enterprises. Rather than collect a sales tax on every newspaper or magazine sold, Minnesota had

---

[241] *Zurcher* v *Stanford Daily*, 436 US 547 (1978).

[242] *Herbert* v *Lando*, 441 US 153 (1979).

[243] *Cohen* v *Cowles Media Co.*, 115 L Ed 2d 586 (1991).

[244] *Cohen* v *Cowles Media Co.*, 115 L Ed 2d 586 (1991).

[245] *Leathers* v *Medlock*, 113 L Ed 2d 494 (1991).

[246] *Grosjean* v *American Press Co.*, 297 US 233 (1936).

imposed a tax on ink and paper used by publications, exempting the first $100,000 worth of ink and paper consumed in each calendar year so that the tax would fall most heavily on the largest newspaper in the state. "Whatever the motive of the legislature in this case," said Justice O'Connor for the Court, "we think that recognizing a power in the State not only to single out the press but also to tailor the tax so that it singles out a few members of the press presents such a potential for abuse that no interest suggested by Minnesota can justify the scheme."[247] In a similar vein, the Court struck down an Arkansas sales tax applied to general interest magazines but exempted newspapers and magazines published within Arkansas, as well as religious, professional, trade, and sports magazines. Selective taxation of the press is unconstitutional, even where there is no evidence of any improper censorial motive, most especially where, as here, the exemption depends on the content of the magazines. Arkansas could have collected a tax on the sales of all magazines and newspapers, but not on some of them.[248]

Yet the Court sustained an Arkansas general gross receipt sales tax as applied to cable television while exempting newspapers, magazines, and satellite television, in a decision that led Justices Marshall and Blackmun in dissent to charge the Court with retreating from its position of allowing the tax power to discriminate against individual members of the media or the media as a whole. Justice O'Connor, speaking for the Court, stated "differential taxation, of speakers, even members of the press, does not implicate the First Amendment unless the tax is directed at, or presents the danger of suppressing, particular ideas.... We conclude that the State's extension of its generally applicable sales tax to cable television services alone ... while exempting the print media, does not violate the First Amendment."[249]

The Press and the Truth

The Supreme Court has refused to make a blanket declaration that truthful publication may never be punished. It has, however, made it clear that "if a newspaper *lawfully* obtains truthful information about a matter of *public* significance then state officials may not constitutionally punish publication of the information, absent a need to further a state interest of the highest order."[250] The Supreme Court has come pretty close to endorsing the view that truth is an absolute defense where discussion of public affairs is concerned. Yet the Court has left open the possibility of constitutionally constraining even the truthful publication of troop transports in time of war, and, more to the point, "leaving unsettled the constitutional implications of truth-

---

[247] *Minneapolis Star* v *Minnesota Comm. of Rev.*, 460 US 575 (1983).

[248] *Austin* v *Mich. Chamber of Commerce*, 494 US 652 (1990); *Arkansas Writers' Project, Inc.* v *Ragland*, 481 US 221 (1987).

[249] *Leathers* v *Medlock*, 113 L Ed 2d 494 (1991).

[250] *Smith* v *Daily Mail Publishing Co.*, 443 US 97 (1979).

fulness in the discrete areas of purely private libels," and keeping still open the constitutionality of punishing the publication of certain matters if obtained by unlawful methods.[251]

What if the press publishes information of a classified nature? And what if it publishes information in violation of state laws against publication of the names of minors accused of crime, or against publishing the names of victims of sex offenses? The Court refused to permit the imposition of civil damages on a newspaper for publishing against the law the name of a victim of a sexual offense whose name the paper had copied from matters inadvertently put into police records. "We do not hold," the Court went out of its way to make clear, "that truthful publication is automatically constitutionally protected, or that there is no zone of personal privacy within which the State may protect the individual from intrusion by the press, or even that a State may never punish publication of the name of a victim of a sexual offense." Rather it set aside the damages in this case because the newspaper had obtained the information through lawful methods. Justice White, with whom the Chief Justice and Justice O'Connor dissented, would have tipped the balance more in favor of privacy rights. "There is no public interest," wrote Justice White "in publishing the names, addresses, and phone numbers of persons who are the victims of crime— and no public interest in immunizing the press from liability in the rare cases where a State's efforts to protect a victim's privacy have failed."[252] Although the Court has thus not ruled out the possibility that the media, under some circumstances, could be punished for the truthful publication of materials, in recent years the only limitation the Supreme Court has permitted on a newspaper's right to the truthful publication of materials, whether they have obtained such materials lawfully or unlawfully, is on the use of information gained through the discovery process of a court when a newspaper is a party to a suit.[253]

Other Media

The Court has pointed out, "The liberty of the press is not confined to newspapers and periodicals," and its "historical connotation comprehends every sort of publication which affords a vehicle of information and opinion"; [254] in fact it also comprehends all kinds of media beyond publications. The Constitution protects communications by mail, radio, telephones, television, and motion pictures. For each of these media, there are special problems that result in different degrees of protection. "Each method of communicating ideas is 'a law unto itself' and that law must reflect the 'differing natures, values, abuses, and dangers of each method.'"[255]

---

[251] *The Florida Star* v *B. J. F.*, 491 US 524 (1989).

[252] Ibid.

[253] *Seattle Times Co.* v *Rinehart*, 467 US 20 (1984).

[254] *Lovell* v *Griffin*, 303 US 444 (1938)

[255] *Metromedia, Inc.* v *San Diego*, 453 US 490 (1981).

Mail

"The United States may give up the Post Office when it sees fit, but while it carries it on, the use of the mails is almost as much a part of free speech as the right to use our tongues."[256] In striking down the first act of Congress ever to be held in conflict with the First Amendment, an act that required the postmaster general to detain unsealed foreign mailings of "communist political propaganda," Justice Douglas said for the Court, "The Act sets administrative officials astride the flow of mail to inspect it, appraise it, write the addressee about it, and await a response before dispatching the mail.... The regimen of this Act is at war with the 'uninhibited, robust, and wide-open' debate and discussion that are contemplated by the First Amendment."[257] Six years later the Court extended this decision to void laws authorizing postal authorities to make administrative determinations of obscenity, exclude it from the mails, and cut off mail delivery to persons sending it. Although it may not authorize administrative interference with the mails, Congress may make it a crime knowingly to send obscene material through the mails, even if it is sent to adults who have requested it.[258] Any rulings must be reviewable promptly in court and the burden is on the censor (the postal official) to prove obscenity.[259] Customs officials, in contrast to postal authorities, may seize obscene materials. But this administrative action must be reviewed promptly by the courts. Judicial proceedings must be commenced within fourteen days of the seizure and concluded within sixty days.[260] Congress has made it a crime to send obscene matter through the mails, with indictment possible at either the point of mailing or the point of receipt. It is also a crime to transport such materials in interstate commerce, even if it is carried in a briefcase and designed only for private use.[261]

Whereas administrative censorship of the mails is unconstitutional, householder censorship is not. "The mailer's right to communicate must stop at the mailbox of an unreceptive addressee."[262] The Supreme Court upheld a law giving householders and apartment dwellers the absolute right to ask the postmaster to order mailers to delete their names from all mailing lists and to refrain from sending to householders any advertising materials that they, in their sole discretion, believe, to be "erotically arousing or sexually provocative." It makes no constitutional difference if the householder includes in such a category a "dry-goods catalogue." This is not governmental censorship.[263]

---

[256] Justice Holmes dissenting in *Milwaukee Pub. Co.* v *Burleson,* 255 US 407 (1921). His views were adopted by the Supreme Court in *Lamont* v *Postmaster General,* 381 US 301 (1965).

[257] *Lamont* v *Postmaster General,* 381 US 301 (1965).

[258] *Hamling* v *United States,* 418 US 87 (1974); *United States* v *Reidel,* 402 US 351 (1971).

[259] *Blount* v *Rizzi,* 400 US 410 (1971).

[260] *United States* v *Thirty-seven Photographs,* 402 US 363 (1971); *United States* v *Twelve 200-Ft. Reels of Film,* 413 US 123 (1973).

[261] *United States* v *Orito,* 413 US 139 (1973).

[262] *Rowan* v *Post Office Department,* 397 US 728 (1970).

[263] Ibid.

Moreover, Congress may forbid the deposit into any authorized mailbox of any material on which no postage has been paid. Mailboxes are part of the national postal system and do not have public forum status as do streets.[264] (See pages 236-238 for discussion of importance of the nature of the forum.)

Broadcasting

"Of all forms of communications, broadcasting has received the most limited First Amendment protection."[265] "The broadcast media pose unique and special problems not present in traditional free speech cases."[266] "There is no 'unbridgeable' First Amendment right to broadcast comparable to the right of every individual to speak, write, or publish.... This is not to say that the First Amendment is irrelevant... to broadcasting... but it is the right of viewers and listeners, not the right of the broadcasters, which is paramount."[267] Thus the Court has sustained the "fairness doctrine," a requirement that all licensees must provide balanced presentation of all points of view and take positive steps to invite controversial views.

The First Amendment prevents governmental censorship of broadcasters. Although no one has a right to a license, the Federal Communications Commission (FCC), which regulates and licenses broadcasting, may not censor what is broadcast. However, with its authority to forbid the use of indecent language, even language that is not obscene, the FCC can rebuke or fine a station for broadcasting such language and can take into account, in subsequent determinations of license renewals, that a station has broadcast such language. Broadcasting, unlike the printed media, "confronts the citizen, not only in public, but in the privacy of the home" and "is uniquely accessible to children, even those too young to read."[268]

The Supreme Court, in *FCC v League of Women Voters of California*, in a five-to-four watershed decision, declared unconstitutional a federal statute regulating broadcasters. That statute stated, "No noncommercial educational broadcasting station which receives a grant from the Corporation for Public Broadcasting [all public television stations and most public radio stations] may engage in editorializing." Justice Brennan, writing for the majority, distinguished this ban from the previously sustained "fairness doctrine" on the ground that the ban on editorializing "singles out noncommercial broadcasters and denies them the right to address their chosen audience on matters of public importance" was not "narrowly tailored to further a substantial government interest," and strikes at "the heart" of the First Amendment.[269] The dissenting justices felt that those who take government dollars could be subject to

---

[264] *United States Postal Service v Greenburgh Civic Associations*, 453 US 114 (1981).

[265] *Federal Communications Commission v Pacifica Foundation*, 438 US 726 (1978).

[266] *Buckley v Valeo*, 424 US 1 (1976).

[267] *Red Lion Broadcasting Co. v Federal Communications Commission*, 395 US 367 (1969).

[268] *Federal Communications Commission v Pacifica Foundation*, 438 US 726 (1978).

[269] *FCC v League of Women Voters of California*, 468 US 364 (1984).

what the justices considered reasonable limitations designed to protect stations from being unduly influenced by federal authorities, to keep the stations from becoming privileged outlets, and to prevent government subsidies of editorials to which many taxpayers might object.

Perhaps the most important consequences of *FCC v League of Women Voters of California* will be reactions to the footnotes in the majority opinion noting that the "prevailing rationale for broadcast regulation has come under increasing criticism in recent years" because technological changes, such as cable, direct beam broadcast, and videotapes, might be undermining the theory that the scarcity of channels justifies substantial government regulation of television. "We are not prepared, however," said Justice Brennan, "to reconsider our long-standing approach without some signal from Congress or the FCC that technological developments have advanced so far that some revision of the system of broadcast regulation may be required." In another footnote the Court said that if the FCC demonstrated that the fairness doctrine reduces, rather than enhances, free speech, the Court "would then be forced to reconsider the constitutional basis" of its earlier rulings upholding the doctrine. Congress, the president, and the FCC responded to this invitation, but gave the Supreme Court conflicting signals. The Reagan Administration and its FCC appointees repealed the fairness regulation. Congress then tried unsuccessfully to reimpose it. They may have more success with the Clinton Administration.

The Court has yet to determine "whether the characteristics of cable television make it sufficiently analogous to another medium to warrant application of an already existing standard or whether those characteristics require a new analysis."[270] It has decided, however, that cable partakes "of some of the aspects of speech and the communication of ideas as do the traditional enterprises of newspaper and book publishers, public speakers and pamphleteers,"[271] and that when cities regulate cable television they are subject to appropriate First Amendment constraints. What this generalization means will be worked out through case-by-case application. Installation of cable also raises questions under the "taking clause" (see page 304).

Telephones, Fax, and the Electronic Revolution

The Framers did not address the telephone, telegraph, or television, let alone the fax or "E-Mail." Each new medium, the most recent being the fax machine, presents its own problems. As millions of faxes come into use, states are beginning to pass "junk fax laws" making it illegal to fax unsolicited advertisements. Similar problems are being created by "autodialers," which send computer telephone messages into homes. Congress is also considering federal legislation to regulate these intrusions into privacy. And while federal laws protect against eavesdropping on telephone conversations, including those con-

---

[270] Justice Blackmun concurring in *Los Angeles v Preferred Communications*, 476 US 488 (1986).
[271] *Los Angeles v Preferred Communications*, 476 US 488 (1986).

veyed by cellular phones, these laws do not as yet extend to walk-around phones that transmit messages via radio waves. As Congress and the states begin to deal with these problems they, and the judges who will be reviewing these actions as subsequent lawsuits are filed, find the need to apply these traditional constitutional principles to new situations.

For example, what about pornography and obscenity as delivered over telephones? Congress, reflecting constituency concern about "dial-a-porn," especially as directed to persons under eighteen, and unpersuaded that the FCC could by regulation limit access for minors, imposed a total statutory ban on obscene and indecent interstate commercial telephone messages to any person, whatever their age. The Court found no constitutional obstacles to the law as it relates to "obscene" messages, but declared unconstitutional the provision relating to "indecent" messages. "It may well be," wrote Justice White for the Court, "that there is no fail-safe method of guaranteeing that never will a minor be able to access the dial-a-porn system, ... but from all we know ... the FCC's technological approach to restricting dial-a-porn messages to adults who seek them would be extremely effective, and only a few of the most enterprising and disobedient young people will manage to secure access to such messages."[272] The Court also distinguished between the ban on indecent messages over the airwaves that it had sustained[273] and the ban on such messages over telephones. Because of the unique attributes of broadcasting, its messages are readily available to children and they can intrude into the privacy of the home without prior warning. Telephone messages on the other hand are available only to people who want to hear them. It also may be possible, as the Court suggested, more readily to deny minors access to indecent telephone messages than to indecent broadcasting, excepting, of course, "enterprising and disobedient young people."

---

or the right of the people peaceably to assemble,

The Constitution protects the right to assemble peaceably in public places, but those who wish to protest or otherwise express their views have no constitutional right to do so "whenever and however and wherever they please."[274] No one has a right to take over a school, to seize and hold the office of a mayor, or, most especially, to take over a university president's office. State and local governments have the power to make reasonable regulations to preserve order.

Time, place, and manner regulations, designed to preserve the public peace, must be precisely drawn and fairly administered. The courts will look carefully at regulations or police actions that encroach on this right, especially in

---

[272] *Sable Communications* v *FCC*, 492 US 115(1989).
[273] *FCC* v *Pacifica Foundation et al.*, 438 US 726 (1978).
[274] *Adderley* v *Florida*, 385 US 39 (1966).

circumstances that raise suspicion that the law is not being applied evenhand-edly. Not constitutional are regulations permitting authorities to determine which groups will be allowed to hold public meetings or giving police wide dis-cretion to determine whom to arrest and courts latitude to determine whom to convict. For example, the Court struck down a Louisiana law defining "dis-turbing the peace" so broadly that it would permit arrest merely for holding a meeting on a public street or public highway.[275]

Political Protest

Does the Constitution require police officers to protect unpopular groups whose public meetings and demonstrations arouse others to violence? If the answer were no, then the right of unpopular minorities to hold meetings would be seriously curtailed by the "heckler's veto." It is almost always easier for the police to maintain order by curbing the peaceful meetings of the unpopular minority than to restrain those threatening violence. Yet if police were never to have the right to order a group to disperse, public order would be at the mercy of those who might resort to street demonstrations just to create public tensions and provoke street battles.

The Supreme Court has refused to give a categorical answer to the ques-tion; the answer depends on the circumstances. In 1951, in *Feiner* v *New York*, the Court upheld the conviction for unlawful assembly of a sidewalk speaker who continued to talk after being ordered to stop by the only two policemen present. There was no evidence that the police interfered because of objection to what was being said. In view, however, of the hostile response of the audi-ence, the police were fearful a riot might ensue that they could not contain or prevent.[276] The *Feiner* case has never been overruled, but since then the Supreme Court has tended to emphasize the need for governments to move under more precisely drawn statutes.

In *Edwards* v *South Carolina*, the Court reversed the conviction of 187 African-American students for breach of the peace because they had held a protest meeting in front of the South Carolina State House. The police had been afraid that their gathering would provoke a clash with a crowd of onlookers. After trying to keep the groups apart for forty-five minutes, the police told the students to disperse and when they failed to do so, arrested them. "The Fourteenth Amendment," said the Court, "does not permit a State to make criminal the peaceful expression of unpopular views."[277]

The Supreme Court followed the *Edwards* precedent rather than *Feiner* when it dealt with the conviction under a disorderly conduct statute of Dick Gregory and other demonstrators for failing to obey a police command to stop marching in

---

[275] *Cox* v *Louisiana*, 379 US 536 (1965).
[276] *Feiner* v *New York*, 340 US 315 (1951).
[277] *Edwards* v *South Carolina*, 372 US 229 (1963).

front of the house of the mayor of Chicago at a time when a large number of onlookers became unruly toward the demonstrators. The Supreme Court reversed the conviction because Gregory and his followers had been convicted of disorderly conduct when there was no evidence they had been acting disorderly, but the Court made it clear that the situation would have been different if Chicago had acted under ordinances specifically forbidding demonstrations after certain hours in residential areas or making it an offense to disobey a police officer when there is an imminent threat of violence and the police have made all reasonable efforts to protect the demonstrators from hostile bystanders.[278] Similarly, in *Coates* v *Cincinnati,* the Court held as void for its vagueness and overbreadth an ordinance that forbade three or more persons to assemble on sidewalks and there conduct themselves in a manner annoying to persons passing by. "A city is free to prevent people from blocking sidewalks, committing assaults, obstructing traffic, littering streets, but it must do so by ordinances directed with reasonable specificity toward the conduct to be prohibited.... It cannot constitutionally do so through the enactment and enforcement of an ordinance whose violations may entirely depend upon whether or not a policeman is annoyed."[279]

What of public facilities, such as libraries, courthouses, schools, or swimming pools, that are designated to serve purposes other than public assembly? As long as persons use such facilities within the normal bounds of conduct, they may not be constitutionally restrained from doing so. If, however, they attempt, by sit-ins or other kinds of demonstrations, to interfere with programs or to appropriate facilities for their own use, a state has constitutional authority to punish, provided it does so under laws that are not applied in a discriminatory fashion and that properly limit the discretion of those enforcing the laws. "The crucial question is whether the manner of expression is basically incompatible with the normal activity of a particular place at a particular time."[280] To illustrate the application of these general rules: a small group of protesters who quietly remained in a library for ten to fifteen minutes to protest racial discrimination, but did not interfere with the operations of the library, could not constitutionally be charged with violating a general breach of the peace ordinance;[281] a group of protesters could be punished for deliberately making a noise that disturbed the peace and good order of a school under an ordinance directly aimed at preventing demonstrations in and around school buildings;[282] because they were thought to be interfering with the operation of the jail, a group of students could be convicted for trespass when, to protest racial segregation and the arrest of a fellow student, they marched into a jailhouse and refused to leave when so ordered by the sheriff.[283]

---

[278] *Gregory* v *Chicago,* 394 US 111 (1969).

[279] *Coates* v *Cincinnati,* 402 US 611 (1971).

[280] *Grayned* v *Rockford,* 408 US 104 (1972).

[281] *Brown* v *Louisiana,* 383 US 131 (1966).

[282] *Grayned* v *Rockford,* 408 US 104 (1972).

[283] *Adderley* v *Florida,* 385 US 39 (1966).

Public Forums

The extent of government's power to regulate speech and assembly depends on where the speech and assembly take place, that is, the forum. In recent analysis, the Court has focused on the type of forum. The Court has recognized three kinds of public forums: (1) the traditional public forum, such as a street or a park; (2) the public forum created by government designation; and (3) the public-nonpublic forum.[284] A minority of the Court would expand the category and would not confine public forum status to the traditional ones or even to those precisely so designated by the government but would give public forum status to other forms of government property, "if the objective, physical characteristics of the property at issue and the actual public access and uses which have been permitted by the government indicate that expressive activity would be appropriate and compatible with those uses."[285]

Traditional Public Forum—Streets and Parks

Streets and parks, including streets and parks in residential areas,[286] "have immemorially been held in trust for the use of the public and, time out of mind, have been used for purpose of assembly, communicating thoughts between citizens, and discussing public questions."[287] Before a state may limit speech in such areas it must show that regulation "is necessary to serve a compelling state interest and that it is narrowly drawn to achieve that end."[288] In addition, a state may enforce content neutral time, place, and manner regulations that are "narrowly tailored to serve a significant government interest, and leave open ample alternative channels of communication."[289] Thus, the Supreme Court, assuming for purposes of the case but not deciding that "overnight sleeping in connection with a demonstration is expressive conduct protected to some extent by the First Amendment," upheld a National Park Service regulation that allows persons to hold rallies, even to pitch tents and stay in them, but not to sleep in tents on the Mall in downtown Washington, D.C., and in Lafayette Park, across the street from the White House.[290] The Court, while not ruling on a law forbidding a display in the Supreme Court building or on its grounds "of any flag, banner, or device designed or adapted to bring into public notice any party, organization, or movement," held the law unconstitutional as applied to sidewalks surrounding the Supreme Court building. In so doing the justices rejected the solicitor general's contention that since judges, unlike legislators and executives, are supposed to decide cases on the basis only

---

[284] *Cornelius v NAACP Legal Defense & Ed. Fund,* 473 US 788 (1986).

[285] Justice Kennedy concurring in *International Society for Krishna Consciousness v Lee,* 120 L Ed 2d 541 (1992).

[286] *Frisby v Schultz,* 487 US 474 (1988).

[287] *Hague v CIO,* 307 US 496 (1939).

[288] *Perry Education Assn. v Perry Local Educators' Assn.,* 460 US 37 (1983).

[289] Ibid.

[290] *Clark v Community for Creative Non-Violence,* 468 US 288 (1984).

of the record before them, Congress had been justified in outlawing conduct that might create the appearance that judges are subject to outside influences. [291] The Court did uphold an ordinance forbidding picketing "before or about any residence" after construing it to apply only to picketing against a single residence. It left for another day the question of whether a similar ordinance not limited to restraining only a single residence would be sustained.[292]

Public Forums by Government Designation

States may open up public property beyond streets and parks and designate it a public area. Judges, however, are not to rule that a public forum has been created unless the government in question clearly so designated it. However, Justice Kennedy has warned, "if the public forum jurisprudence is to retain its vitality, courts have to reserve the right to review the facts to determine if certain objective characteristics of government property and its customary uses might overrule a regulation designating an area as being unavailable for expressive activities or trying to limit the kind of such activities that can take place there."[293]

Public-Nonpublic Forums

Public property that is "not by tradition or designation a forum for public communication is governed by different standards. . . . In addition to time, place, and manner regulations, the state may reserve the forum for its intended purposes, communicative or otherwise, as long as the regulation on speech is reasonable and not an effort to suppress expression merely because public officials oppose the speaker's view."[294] Moreover, "control over access to a nonpublic forum can be based on subject matter and speaker identity so long as the distinctions drawn are reasonable in the light of the purpose served by the forum and are viewpoint neutral." Thus, as we have noted, a city may ban the posting of handbills on telephone poles and lampposts. School mail facilities are not a public forum and a school board may keep all unions or associations, other than the one that has won collective bargaining rights, from using the interschool mail system and teacher mailboxes.[295] Military commanders may ban persons from military bases.[296]

The post office can forbid solicitation of funds in postal facilities, including on sidewalks from the postal parking lot to the post office itself.[297] The Court, by a five to four vote, also held that a public airport operated by a public authority is not a public forum and face to face solicitation of funds may be

---

[291] *United States v Grace,* 461 US 171 (1983).

[292] *Frisby v Schultz,* 487 US 474 (1988).

[293] Justice Kennedy concurring in *United States v Kokinda,* 497 US 720 (1990).

[294] *Perry Ed. Assn. v Perry Local Ed. Assn.,* 460 US 37 (1983).

[295] Ibid.

[296] *United States v Albertini,* 472 US 675 (1985).

[297] *United States v Kokinda,* 497 US 720 1990).

prohibited there,[298] but by a six to three vote held that even if not a public forum an airport cannot ban peaceful pamphleteering and perhaps not the sale of literature.[299] Justice Kennedy went out of his way to make a distinction between a permissible ban on solicitation and an impermissible ban on the sale of literature, whereas the dissenters would have sustained the banning in airports not merely of solicitation but also leafletting.[300]

A fascinating cluster of issues was raised by a 1980 decision of the California Supreme Court. The United States Supreme Court had previously established that the federal Constitution does not give one a right to go into a privately owned shopping center against the wishes of the owner to distribute handbills or to engage in picketing on matters unrelated to the shopping center's own operations.[301] The Supreme Court of California, however, had ruled that, even though the United States Constitution provides no protection for speech activities in private shopping malls, the California constitution does protect "speech and petitioning, reasonably exercised, even when the centers are privately owned," and thus a group of high school students could set up a card table in the corner of a large shopping center to gather signatures on a petition, even though the owners of the shopping center had ordered them off the property. But what of the rights of the owners of the shopping centers? Can a state compel them to allow their property to be used to express views that they find distasteful? The United States Supreme Court ruled that what California had done in this particular case was acceptable. The justices carefully limited the holding to the facts of the case before them and emphasized that the decision was not "blanket approval for state efforts to transform privately owned commercial property into public forums."[302]

Right to Associate

"While the freedom of association is not explicitly set out in the Amendment, it has long been held to be implicit in the freedoms of speech, assembly, and petition."[303] (There is another aspect of the freedom of association, a "fundamental element of personal liberty" relating to intimate human relationships such as the family and close friends, that is protected by the due process clause; see page 353.)[304] Not every coming together of human beings involves the constitutional rights of association. When Dallas restricted admission to certain dance halls to persons between the ages of 14 and 18, except for parents and guardians, the Court held that this coming together to engage

---

[298] International Society for Krishna Consciousness v Lee, 120 L Ed 2d 541 (1992).

[299] Lee v International Society for Krishna Consciousness, 120 L Ed 2d 669 (1992); International Society for Krishna Consciousness v Lee, 120 L Ed 2d 541 (1992).

[300] Lee v International Society for Krishna Consciousness, 120 L Ed 2d 669 (1992).

[301] Lloyd Corporation v Tanner, 407 US 551 (1972).

[302] Prune Yard Shopping Center v Robins, 407 US 551 (1972).

[303] Healy v James, 408 US 169 (1972).

[304] Roberts v United States Jaycees, 468 US 609 (1984).

in recreational dancing was neither a form of intimate association nor did it involve the sort of expressive association protected by the First Amendment, and thus persons over 18 and under 13 who were excluded from the dances had no valid constitutional complaint.[305]

When the right to associate is asserted for expressive purposes, the Court reviews the regulation of this right with a First Amendment perspective. Thus, although a state college may refuse to grant a student organization the right to use facilities unless the organization agrees to abide by reasonable campus rules, it may not deny such privileges to an organization because of disapproval of its aims or generalized apprehensions that its activities could lead to disruptions.[306]

Before a government may require organizations to make public the names of their members, it must demonstrate some compelling and legitimate need to know.[307] What about the 1974 amendments to the Federal Election Campaign Act of 1971 that compel political parties to maintain records and disclose contributions of more than $10 and disbursements of more than $100? The Supreme Court, conceding that these compelled disclosures could seriously infringe on the rights of association and could have a chilling effect on people exercising the right to associate, somewhat reluctantly upheld these requirements, including their application to minor parties, as necessary and proper ways for the government to enhance voters' knowledge about a candidate's possible allegiances and interests, to deter corruption, and to help enforce contribution limitations.[308] The Court indicated, however, that if a minor party could show that disclosure of its contributors' names might subject such contributors to threats or reprisals or impair the party's ability to receive funds, the disclosure and reporting requirement as applied to that party might well be declared unconstitutional.

True to this promise, in 1982 the Court held that the Ohio campaign law could not be applied to require the Socialist Workers' Party to report the names and addresses of campaign contributors, or even the names and addresses of those with whom it did business. "The First Amendment prohibits a state from compelling disclosures by a minor party that will subject those persons identified to the reasonable probability of threats, harassment, or reprisals. Such disclosures would infringe the First Amendment rights of the party and its members and supporters."[309] Democrats and Republicans, however, can still be required to disclose publicly the contributions to their political parties and hope that the bosses of their contributors are tolerant or are of the same political persuasion.

Recent Supreme Court decisions have applied the right to associate in such a fashion as to strengthen the autonomy of political parties. National party conventions, rather than the state from which delegates come, have the final say on the seating of delegations and the requirements for participation in

---

[305] *Dallas v Stanglin*, 488 US 815 (1989).

[306] *Healy v James*, 408 US 169 (1972).

[307] *Gibson v Legislative Investigation Commission*, 372 US 539 (1963), and cases cited therein.

[308] *Buckley v Valeo*, 424 US 1 (1976).

[309] *Brown v Socialist Workers*, 459 US 87 (1983).

the convention.[310] California's law forbidding the governing bodies of political parties to endorse candidates in primaries was held to violate the party's speech and association rights. Also struck down were provisions of the California law restricting the terms of office for state central committee chairs and requiring a rotation between residents of Northern and Southern California. The state failed, said the Court, to show any compelling interest that would justify this burden on the associational rights of political parties.[311] The right of association protected the Connecticut Republican Party when it ignored a Connecticut closed primary law to the extent of opening some of its primaries to independent voters.[312] Justice Scalia in dissent contended that if the concept of freedom of association is extended to such casual contacts as that of an independent voting in a party primary, "it ceases to be of any analytic use."

The Court has been especially vigilant to protect "the right of citizens to create and develop new political parties," and "to the degree that a State would thwart this interest by limiting the access of new parties to the ballot, we have called for the demonstration of a corresponding interest sufficiently weighty to justify the limitation."[313] It was not persuaded that Illinois could require parties to obtain more signatures to become established and get on a ballot in local districts than was required statewide but it could require a new party to get some signatures from voters in each electoral district in which it wished to field candidates.[314]

Not only is the right to form a political party incorporated within the right to associate, but so is the right to vote for candidates of one's choice at a general election and to register and vote in a party primary. It also includes the right to be able to vote for independent candidates, and to make that right effective, independent candidates have to have a right to get onto ballots. Some states regulate the conditions under which a person can change party registration in order to prevent '"raiding," that is, members of one party entering a primary of their opponents in order to try to nominate the weakest candidate. The Court has upheld regulations that forbid switching party registration when there a "reasonable" waiting period—eight months before a presidential primary and eleven months before other primaries (New York)—and reversed them when the time was "unreasonable"—23 months (Illinois).[315]

State laws regulating how independent candidates can get on a ballot relate not only to the candidate's rights but also to the rights of association of those who would vote for them. Thus, cases relating to ballot access often involve the same questions as voting rights cases since "the rights of voters and the rights of candidates do not lend themselves to neat separation."[316] However, while "it is beyond cavil" that "voting is of the most fundamental significance under

---

[310] Cousins v Wigoda, 419 US 477 (1977); Democratic Party of the United States v La Follette, 450 US 107 (1981).

[311] Eu v San Francisco Democratic Comm., 489 US 214,

[312] Tashjian v Republican Party of Connecticut, 479 US 208 (1986).

[313] Norman v Reed, ll6 L Ed 2d 711 (1992).

[314] Ibid. and Board of Illinois Elections v Socialist Workers Party. 440 US 173 (1983).

[315] Rosario v Rockefeller, 410 US 752 (1973); Kusper v Pontikes, 414 US 51 (1973).

[316] Bullock v Carter, 405 US 134 (1972).

our constitutional system," election laws that impose a burden upon the right to vote are not necessarily an unconstitutional interference with the right to vote. The Court has "repeatedly upheld reasonable, politically neutral regulations that have the effect of channeling expressive activity at the polls."[317]

Contemporary Supreme Court rulings on ballot access began with cases arising from George Wallace's difficulties in getting on ballots when he ran as an independent presidential candidate in 1968. The Court invalidated an Ohio rule that made it difficult for independent parties to get on the ballot because it gave the two major political parties such a decided advantage that it interfered with persons' rights to associate to advance political beliefs and with the rights to cast an effective votes.[318] Then in a series of 1974 holdings, the Court upheld a state requirement preventing persons who had recently been affiliated with a political party from running as an independent.[319] It also upheld a state law requiring parties to achieve a certain proportion of the vote in previous elections in order to have their candidates automatically listed on ballots, but the Court warned that a state may not place an unreasonable burden by requiring too many registered voters' names on a petition to qualify as an independent or new party candidate.[320] The Court has also refused to allow a state to impose unreasonable filing fees. When John Anderson ran for president in 1980 as an independent candidate, he also successfully challenged Ohio's early filing requirements for interfering with his and his followers' rights of association.

More recently, the Court upheld Hawaii's prohibition on counting and reporting of write-in voting in its open primary and general elections, announcing "that when a State's ballot access laws pass constitutional muster as imposing only reasonable burdens on First and Fourteenth Amendment rights..., a prohibition on write-in voting will be presumptively valid."[321] Justices Kennedy, Blackmun and Stevens, in dissent, contended that especially in Hawaii, where the Democratic Party is dominant and Democratic candidates often run unopposed, a ban on the counting of write-in votes was not justified by a legitimate state interest.

Sometimes the constitutional right to associate comes into conflict with persons' rights secured by federal or state law not to be discriminated against because of race, sex, or ethnic origins. The Supreme Court rejected a law partnership's contention that it need not comply with Title VII of the Civil Rights Act of 1965, which forbids sex discrimination in employment, because of its constitutional right of association.[322] The Court also sustained the application of state human rights acts to compel the Jaycees and the Rotary Club to

---

[317] *Burdick v Takushi*, 119 L Ed 2d 245 (1992) with quotation from *Illinois Board of Elections v Socialist Workers Party*, 440 US 173 (1979).

[318] *Williams v Rhodes*, 393 U.S 28 (1968).

[319] *Storer v Brown*, 415 US 724 (1974).

[320] *American Party of Texas v White*, 415 US 767 (1974).

[321] *Burdick v Takushi*, 119 L Ed 2d 245 (1992).

[322] *Hishon v King & Spalding*, 467 US 69 (1984).

admit women. Such acts make it an "unfair discriminatory practice...to deny any person the full and equal enjoyment of goods, services, facilities, privileges, advantages...of a place of public accommodation because of race, color, creed, religion, disability, national origin, or sex." The Jaycees and Rotarians argued, among other things, that the law interfered with their constitutionally protected right to associate with persons of their own choice for the purpose of expressing their views. Justice Brennan, speaking for the majority in the cases relating to the Jaycees, conceded, "There can be no clearer example of an intrusion into the internal structure or affairs of an association than a regulation that forces the group to accept members it does not desire. Such a regulation may impair the ability of the original members to express only those views that brought them together."[323] However, the Court decided that the Jaycees (and in separate cases the law partnership and the Rotarians) were not purely private organizations and that they had failed to demonstrate that allowing women to become members and to vote would change the content or impact of the organization's speech.

The Court's several opinions in these cases limiting the rights of private organizations in selecting their members have been carefully crafted to try to make clear that the right to associate is nonetheless constitutionally protected. And it has declared that for many kinds of human relationships, families and churches, for example, the right to choose and exclude one's associates will take priority over a state public accommodation laws and regulations. The Court has also established that antidiscrimination laws probably cannot constitutionally be applied to associations organized for religious, cultural, or social purposes. Factors to be considered in determining whether an organization may constitutionally be covered by antidiscrimination laws are "size, purpose, policies, selectivity, congeniality."[324] Justice O'Connor, in her concurring opinion in the *Jaycee* case, would have drawn the line between an association that chooses to be expressive, which could not be covered by a public accommodations act and forced to accept memberships, and one that enters the marketplace of commerce in any substantial degree and thus "loses the complete control over its membership that it would otherwise enjoy if it confined its affairs to the marketplace of ideas."

Boycotts

Interesting questions are presented by the application to political boycotts of the Sherman Antitrust Act, which outlaws combinations in restraint of trade. If the boycott brings economic power to bear, the Sherman Act applies, and a "group's efforts to use market power to coerce...through economic means may subject the participants to antitrust liability."[325] But if the boycott brings into play political power, then the First Amendment may protect against antitrust prosecutions. For, as the Court has said, "There are...some activities,

---

[323] *Roberts v United States Jaycees*, 468 US 609 (1984).

[324] *Board of Directors of Rotary International v Rotary Club of Duarte*, 481 US 537 (1987).

[325] From Justice Brennan's dissent in *FTC v Super. Ct. Trial Lawyers Assn.*, 493 US 411 (1990).

legal if engaged in by one, yet illegal if performed in concert with others, but political expression is not one of them."[326]

The First Amendment offers less protection to secondary boycotts by trade unions. Secondary boycotts—"those against someone other than the workers' own employers"—are forbidden by the National Labor Relations Act, but those engaged in such boycotts for political rather than economic purposes have somewhat greater constitutional protection. Nonetheless, when the longshoremen's union refused to unload cargoes shipped from the Soviet Union to protest its invasion of Afghanistan, the Supreme Court held their refusal to be illegal and unprotected. Wrote Justice Powell for the Court, "We have consistently rejected the claim that secondary picketing by labor unions in violation of [the National Labor Relations Act] is protected activity under the First Amendment.... It would seem even clear[er] that conduct designed not to communicate but to coerce merits still less consideration under the First Amendment."[327]

It is not always clear whether a boycott involves the exercise of constitutionally protected political power or the exercise of unprotected economic power. The two elements are often entangled. When black citizens of Claiborne County boycotted white merchants in order to force changes in city policies, their action was protected by the First Amendment since they were struggling to change a social order that had consistently treated them as second-class citizens and the black boycotters were not out to destroy legitimate competition.[328] However, when the trial lawyers of the District of Columbia refused to accept new appointments to defend indigent criminal defendants until the District of Columbia government increased lawyers' compensation, the Sherman Act could be applied to them. True, their purpose was to improve the quality of representation for indigent defendants, but "no matter how altruistic the motives of respondents may have been, ... their immediate objective was to increase the price that they would be paid for their services."[329]

Although violence is not entitled to constitutional protection, even if motivated for political purposes, the mere fact that some violence may flow from a political boycott is not sufficient to permit the imposition of liability on all participants when there is no evidence that they agreed to the use of unlawful means. Thus, the Supreme Court reversed a Mississippi ruling imposing on the NAACP for promoting a Claiborne County boycott. The First Amendment did not, however, bar recovery of damages from those who engaged in violence or threatened it, for losses directly caused by their unlawful conduct.[330]

Right Not to Associate

What of the freedom not to associate? May a state compel lawyers to join bar associations, or may it pass laws allowing employers to make agreements

---

[326] *Citizens Against Rent Control/Coalition for Fair Housing v Berkeley,* 454 US 290 (1981).

[327] *International Longshoremen's Association v Allied International,* 456 US 212 (1982).

[328] *NAACP v Claiborne Hardware,* 458 US 886 (1982).

[329] *FTC v Super. Ct. Trial Lawyers Assn.,* 493 US 411 (1990).

[330] *NAACP v Claiborne Hardware Co.,* 458 US 886 (1982).

with unions that require workers either to join the union or make payments to it as a condition of employment? To oversimplify a complex problem, laws permitting or compelling such arrangements are constitutional provided individuals are not compelled to make contributions for political or ideological purposes. Compelled contributions may be used to support the professional purposes of a bar association, such as disciplining members of the bar or proposing ethical codes for the profession, and the collective-bargaining, contract-administration, and grievance-adjustment purposes of a union, including costs of running conventions, reasonable contributions to the national organization, costs of social activities related to union programs, and general publication expenses. But lawyers compelled by law to join a bar association or employees required to join unions have a constitutional right that fees they pay not be used for political or ideological purposes unrelated to the functions of the bar or union.[331] Employees have a constitutional right to "prevent the Union's spending a part of their required service fees to contribute to political candidates and to express political views unrelated to its duties as an exclusive bargaining representative."[332] Dissenting union members cannot be charged for lobbying or other political activities unrelated to ratification of a collective barginning agreement.[333] A negative check-off of dues for political purposes will not do: it is not sufficient to permit unions to take dues to be used for political purposes from unwilling members or nonmembers in a union or agency shop and then later to rebate to them the funds used for political purposes. Unions must make it possible for such unwilling members to pay the lower dues rates (the ones that do not include funds to be used for political purposes) initially.[334] Moreover, to pass constitutional muster a union's collection of fees from nonmembers must "include an adequate explanation of the basis for the fee, a reasonably prompt opportunity to challenge the amount of the fee before an impartial decision-maker, and an escrow for the amounts reasonably in dispute while such challenges are pending."[335]

Public Employees and the First Amendment

A troublesome question grows out of the conflict between the constitutional right to engage in political activity, to join political organizations and to speak freely, and the right of the government to regulate the conditions of public employment. Justice Holmes, while sitting on the Supreme Judicial Court of Massachusetts, quipped, "A policeman may have a constitutional right to talk politics, but he has no constitutional right to be a policeman."[336] That famous epigram no longer expresses current interpretation of the

---

[331] *Keller v State Bar of California*, 496 US 1 (1990).

[332] *Abood v Detroit Board of Education*, 431 US 209 (1977); *International Association of Machinists v Street*, 367 US 74 (1961).

[333] *Lehnert v Ferris Faculty Assn.*, 114 L Ed 2d 572 (1991).

[334] *Ellis v Railway Clerks*, 466 US 435 (1984).

[335] *Teachers v Hudson*, 475 US 292 (1986).

[336] *McAuliffe v Mayor of New Bedford*, 155 Mass 216 (1892).

Constitution. Today "it is clearly established that a State may not discharge an employee on a basis that infringes an employee's constitutionally protected interest in freedom of speech."[337]

Persons who are actively attempting to overthrow the government by force and who are unwilling to take an oath to support the Constitution may be disqualified from public employment. But neither the national government nor the state governments may make it a condition of employment that employees abandon their constitutional rights of freedom of speech or of association. The Court has struck down all except the most narrowly drawn loyalty oath requirements. Among the requirements invalidated are those that bring within their net persons who are members of organizations that may have unlawful purposes but who themselves do not participate in those unlawful activities or share the unlawful purposes.[338]

Although "a public employee does not relinquish First Amendment rights to comment on matters of public interest by virtue of government employment,"[339] when public employees write or speak about matters of only personal interest that relate to their jobs, they may be fired for insubordination or for disrupting their offices. First Amendment protections extend to public employees only for speech on matters of public concern, and then only to employees who serve no confidential, policymaking, or public contact role.[340] Employees who occupy key policy roles may be dismissed for policy differences and for failure, in pursuing their duties, to support the positions of the department.

A troublesome case involving the speech rights of public employees resulted from the dismissal of a probationary employee from the Harris County, Texas, constable's office. The employee, reacting to a radio announcement that someone had tried to assassinate President Reagan, had said in a brief conversation with a coworker, "If they go for him again, I hope they get him." That remark was overheard by another employee, who related it to the constable. He discharged the employee. The Supreme Court, by five to four, making a distinction between a statement that amounts to a threat to kill the president, which is not protected, and a statement such as this one, which could not properly be criminalized at all, concluded that since this employee did not occupy a confidential, policymaking, or public contact role, and since her comment related to matters of public concern, she could not constitutionally be discharged for having made it.[341]

The First Amendment rights of speech and association do not protect government employees from federal and state regulations forbidding civil servants to take "an active part in the political management of political campaigns." The Hatch Act, as the federal law is known, has been twice sustained, despite the contention that it is overbroad and vague and interferes with

---

[337] *Rankin v McPherson*, 483 US 378 (1987).

[338] *Elfbrandt v Russell*, 384 US 11 (1966); *Connell v Higginbotham*, 403 US 207 (1971).

[339]*Connick v Myers*, 461 US 138 (1983).

[340] Ibid.

[341]*Rankin v McPherson*, 483 US 378 (1987).

the right of association. The Court concluded that it is a reasonable measure to free employees from political pressures and to ensure that they are not coerced into political action in behalf of the party in power.[342] A state may also require certain officeholders to resign if they wish to run for other offices or may make certain officeholders ineligible for certain other posts until after the term for which they were previously elected or appointed has expired.[343]

Minnesota raised the tension between rights to associate and not to associate when it gave unions of state employees, including faculty unions, a special exclusive right (in addition to the regular right to be the collective bargaining agent) "to meet and confer" with administrators and talk with them about matters of common concern beyond issues directly relating to employment. Twenty community college instructors who were not members of the union charged that giving this special privilege to unions deprived faculty members who chose not to join the union of their free speech rights. The Court did not agree. Wrote Justice O'Connor for the Court, instructors "have no constitutional right to force the government to listen to their views. They have no such right as members of the public, as government employees, or as instructors in an institution of higher education." It is of special interest, at least to faculty members, that Justice O'Connor went out of her way to write, "This Court has never recognized a constitutional right of faculty to participate in policy making in academic institutions.... Faculty involvement in academic governance has much to recommend it as a matter of academic policy, but it finds no basis in the Constitution."[344]

Among the more amazing decisions of recent years are those in which the Supreme Court has struck down the political patronage system, a system older than the nation. Senator William L. Marcy is reputed to have said about President Andrew Jackson that Jackson saw nothing wrong in the rule, "To the victor belong the spoils," but a century and a half later Justice Brennan, delivering the opinion of the Court, said, "To the victor belong only those spoils that may be constitutionally obtained."[345] The Court has ruled that those government employees who occupy positions in which party membership is "not relevant" may not be discharged or denied a job or a promotion or a transfer or any other benefit of public employment because of their failure to belong to the winning political party.

Justice Stevens, providing examples of public employees constitutionally protected from discharge or other disadvantage for party reasons, cited a coach of a state university football team. Such a coach, he pointed out, formulates policy, but nonetheless, he argued, "no one could seriously claim that Republicans make better coaches than Democrats, or vice versa." (Justice Stevens apparently does not know very many intense political partisans.) As examples of officials who

---

[342] United Public Workers v Mitchell, 330 US 75 (1947); Civil Service Commission v Letter Carriers, 413 US 548 (1973); Broadrick v Oklahoma, 413 US 601 (1973).

[343] Clements v Flashing, 457 US 957 (1982).

[344] Minnesota Board for Community Colleges v Knight, 465 US 271 (1984).

[345] Rutan v Republican Party of Illinois, 497 US 62 (1990).

could be discharged for political reasons, Justice Stevens mentioned election judges and assistants who help governors write speeches. The immediate cases before the Court have involved deputy sheriffs, assistant public defenders, a rehabilitation counselor, operators of road equipment, a garage worker, and a dietary manager. Although the sheriff and the public defender had been elected in partisan elections, the Court ruled that, once elected, they could not fire their deputy sheriffs and assistant public defenders for belonging to the political party that had lost the election. Justice Powell, in dissent, wondered why the voters, who could also have elected deputy sheriffs and assistant public defenders on party tickets if they had wished, could not delegate to those whom they had elected the authority to hire only those of the winning party faith.[346] Justice Scalia, also in dissent in a more recent case, pointed out the irony that most federal judges, including those on the Supreme Court, owe their appointments to the very patronage system the Court was striking down. So far, no Supreme Court decision has dealt with the power of a president to replace subcabinet policy-making officials of the federal executive branch, but the logic of its decisions and the litigious nature of our times suggest that it may not be long before some discharged or disadvantaged federal official brings the question to the Court.

and to petition the Government for a redress of grievances.

Petitioning for redress of grievances can be writing a letter to your senator or a demonstration at the state capital. The more the petitioning is expressive the more it is protected; the more it involves action, the more it is subject to reasonable regulation. For members of the armed services, even writing a letter can be regulated. They cannot be kept from writing to their own member of Congress, but the military can forbid the joining together of members of the armed services for such petitioning.[347]

Today when we speak of "petitioning the government for the redress of grievances," we generally thinking of lobbying. And lobbying is done primarily through associations. Lobbying, like other protected rights, is not immune from regulation. Congress and most states require associations that spend considerable sums of money to influence legislation to register and make public their records. These laws have been upheld, provided "lobbying" is narrowly defined.

Although lobbying is a constitutional right, "Congress is not required to subsidize lobbying." Nonprofit groups may lose their tax-exempt status and contributions to them may no longer be deductible if "a substantial part of the activities" is "carrying on propaganda, otherwise attempting to influence legislation."[348]

---

[346] *Branti v Finkel*, 445 US 507 (1980); *Elrod v Burns*, 427 US 347 (1976).

[347] *Brown v Glines*, 444 US 348 (1980).

[348] *Regan v Taxation with Representation*, 461 US 540 (1983).

Litigation has become an increasingly important means whereby interest groups pursue their public policy objectives. When states attempted to charge interest groups with barratry, a common law crime of improperly stirring up cases, or "ambulance chasing," for telling people about their rights and helping them sue to achieve certain policy objectives, the Court has upheld the interest group activity as an essential aspect of the right to associate.[349] "The right of access to the courts is an aspect of the First Amendment right to petition the Government for redress of grievances," and although governments may regulate to prevent "baseless litigation," they may not halt the prosecution of lawsuits unless these suits lack any reasonable basis in fact or law.[350]

AMENDMENT II: MILITIA AND THE RIGHT TO BEAR ARMS

A well regulated Militia, being necessary to the security of a free State, the right of the people to keep and bear Arms, shall not be infringed.

State as used in this amendment refers to a generic state rather than a state of the Union.

This amendment was designed to prevent Congress from disarming the state militias, not to prevent it from regulating private ownership of firearms. "The Second Amendment guarantees no right to keep and bear a firearm that does not have 'some reasonable relationship' to the preservation or efficiency of a well-regulated militia."[1] In upholding a federal law making criminal the shipment in interstate commerce of sawed-off shotguns, the Court found no evidence that such weapons had any reasonable relationship "to the preservation or efficiency of a well-regulated militia." The Second Amendment, it held, "must be interpreted and applied" with a view to maintaining a militia. "The Militia which the States were expected to maintain and train is set in contrast with Troops which they were forbidden to keep without the consent of Congress. The sentiment of the time strongly disfavored standing armies; the common view was that adequate defense of country and laws could be secured through the Militia—civilians primarily, soldiers on occasion."[2]

The Second Amendment applies, even to this limited extent, only to the national government. It in no way limits the power of the state and local governments to regulate firearms. As Justice Douglas wrote in an opinion dissenting on another point, "a powerful lobby dins into the ears of our citizenry

---

[349] NAACP v Button, 371 US 415 (1963); In re Primus, 436 US 412 (1978).

[350] Bill Johnson's Restaurants v NLRB, 461 US 731 (1983).

[1] Lewis v United States, 445 US 55 (1980).

[2] United States v Miller, 307 US 174 (1939).

that gun...purchases are constitutional rights protected by the Second Amendment....There is under our decisions no reason why stiff state laws governing the purchase and possession of pistols may not be enacted. There is no reason why pistols may not be barred from anyone with a police record. There is no reason why a State may not require a purchaser of a pistol to pass a psychiatric test. There is no reason why all pistols should not be barred to everyone except the police."[3]

AMENDMENT III: QUARTERING OF SOLDIERS

No Soldier shall, in time of peace be quartered in any house, without the consent of the Owner, nor in time of war, but in a manner to be prescribed by law.

Certain remarks of Justice Miller are appropriate here: "This amendment seems to have been thought necessary. It does not appear to have been the subject of judicial exposition; and it is so thoroughly in accord with all our ideas, that further comment is unnecessary."[1]

AMENDMENT IV: SEARCHES AND SEIZURES

The right of the people to be secure in their persons, houses, papers, and effects, against unreasonable searches and seizures, shall not be violated,

Since the Fourth Amendment has been incorporated into the due process clause, the limitation against unreasonable searches and seizures applies to state and local as well as to federal officers. Private individuals, associations, and corporations are not constrained by the Fourth Amendment unless they are operating as instruments or agents of the government, as for example when the railroads, as a result of regulations of the Federal Railroad Administration, administer blood, urine, and breath tests to certain of their employees.

The "people" whose right to be secure against unreasonable searches and seizures is not to be violated include American citizens wherever they may be

---

[3] *Adams v Williams,* 407 US 143 (1972).
[1] Samuel F. Miller, "The Constitution," as quoted in *The Constitution Annotated* (1964), 923.

and all aliens "when they have come within the territory of the United States and developed substantial connections with this country." Although the Court has never unequivocally declared that the Amendment protects illegal aliens voluntarily in the United States, it has assumed that it does. The Court has declared that the Fourth Amendment does *not* protect aliens outside of the United States from unreasonable searches and seizures by federal agents.[1]

The Amendment protects against both searches and seizures. "A search compromises the individual interest in privacy; a seizure deprives the individual of dominion over his or her person or property."[2]

The Constitution does not forbid *all* searches and seizures but forbids only "unreasonable ones by agents of the government." What distinguishes a reasonable search and seizure from an unreasonable one is "an opaque area of the law."[3] It is also an area in which the justices are divided. The Warren Court took the view that, with few limited exceptions, any search or seizure without a warrant is unreasonable.[4] The Burger and Rehnquist Courts tend more to the view that "it is not whether it was reasonable to procure a search [or arrest] warrant, but whether the search itself was reasonable."[5]

In the application of the Fourth Amendment, each decision often depends on refinements in the facts; the justices are not often of one mind, and the Court has had difficulty in developing generalizable doctrines. We shall try, however, to make some sense of the hundreds of decisions relating to the Fourth Amendment.

Police Detentions and Arrests

People have somewhat less Fourth Amendment protection from searches of their person and their own seizure, that is detention or arrest, than does their property. Although police have no general right to stop people, not all police stops are limited by the Fourth Amendment; in other words, the Fourth Amendment does not require police to have a justification to approach persons just to ask them questions.

It is difficult to draw the line between police questioning of someone who consents to respond, which is not restricted by the Fourth Amendment, and police constraint, which brings Fourth Amendment limits into play. If all that happens is police asking questions in a noncoercive atmosphere, there is no detention. The Supreme Court, in an opinion with Fourth Amendment over-

---

[1] *United States v Verdugo-Urquidez*, 494 US 259 (1990).

[2] *Horton v California*, 496 US 128 (1990).

[3] *Schneckloth v Bustamonte*, 412 US 218 (1973); and quoting Justice Harlan in *Ker v California*, 374 US 23 (1963).

[4] *Chimel v California*, 395 US 752 (1969); *United States v Harris*, 403 US 573 (1971).

[5] *United States v Edwards*, 415 US 800 (1974); and for the Burger Court, *Michigan State Police Department v Sitz*, 496 US 444 (1990).

tones, declared unconstitutional for vagueness an ordinance giving police authority to ask persons who loiter or wander the streets to give "credible and reliable" identification and to account for their presence.[6] But if the person refuses to answer and the police take additional steps to obtain an answer, then the Fourth Amendment applies. (So does the Fifth Amendment's protection against self-incrimination, and so may the Sixth Amendment's right to counsel; see pages 275 and 319.) Or if, by *intentionally applied* physical force or a show of authority, police restrain the movement of people, even though there is no arrest, the Fourth Amendment comes into play.[7]

The test of whether a person has been seized within the meaning of the Fourth Amendment, the so-called "*Mendenhall* test" first formulated by Justice Stewart in *United States* v *Mendenhall,* is "If, in view of all the circumstances surrounding the incident a reasonable person would have believed that he was not free to leave,"[8] and, as explained by Justice Scalia for the Court, the test for "a show of authority is an objective one: not whether the citizen perceived that he was being ordered to restrict his movement, but whether the officer's words and actions would have conveyed that to a reasonable person."[9] As Justice Scalia went on to explain, this test is merely a necessary but not a sufficient condition. Even if there has been a show of authority but there was no compliance and the person flees, there is no constitutional seizure and evidence abandoned by fleeing persons may be used to prosecute them (see exclusionary rule, page 266).

Police may make *arrests* only when they have "probable cause" (see discussion of the second part of this amendment) or an arrest warrant. Sometimes the police lack probable cause to make an arrest but have the objective justification to detain a person for questioning and, as a result of the interrogation (see page 256 for ground rules that apply to such interrogations), get the evidence they need to justify a probable-cause arrest.

Persons found in *public places* may be detained without probable cause, however, for an investigatory stop, called a *Terry* stop, after the case *Terry* v *Ohio,* for which this exception was first elaborated, (see page 252).[10] Police may make such investigatory stops if they have "some objective manifestation that the person stopped is or is about to be engaged in criminal activity, or that there is reasonable grounds to believe the person is wanted for past criminal conduct."[11] To illustrate, the Court upheld a *Terry* stop of a suspect based on an anonymous telephone tip some of whose details were corroborated by the police's own observations which, given the totality of the circumstances, furnished reasonable suspicion that the suspect was engaged in criminal activity.[12] Police may make a *Terry* stop (and search) of a suspect if they have

---

[6] *Kolender* v *Larson,* 461 US 352 (1983).

[7] *Brower* v *County of Inyo,* 489 US 593 (1989).

[8] *United States* v *Mendenhall,* 446 US 544 (1980).

[9] *California* v *Hodari D.,* 113 L Ed 2d 690 (1991).

[10] *Terry* v *Ohio,* 392 US 1 (1968).

[11] *United States* v *Cortez,* 449 US 411 (1981).

[12] *Alabama* v *White,* 496 US 325 (1990).

a "wanted" flier that makes it clear that the police department issuing it possessed a reasonable suspicion that the person in question had committed a felony.[13] Such investigatory stops cannot continue indefinitely, but the Court has refused to set a time limit. Rather, the test is "whether the police diligently pursued a means of investigation that was likely to confirm or dispel their suspicions quickly." During an investigatory stop, the police may also fingerprint persons "if there is a reasonable suspicion that the suspect has committed a criminal act, if there is a reasonable basis for believing that fingerprinting will establish or eliminate the suspect's connection with the crime, and if the procedure is carried out with dispatch."[14] *Terry* v *Ohio* was extended again when the Court approved a "protective sweep" of a home by officers who were making an arrest of a suspect in his home pursuant to an arrest warrant to be sure that it did not harbor any person posing a danger to the officers or others. Such a sweep is permissible if the officers "possess a reasonable belief based on 'specific and articulable facts' which, taken together with the rational inferences from those facts, reasonably warrant the officer to believe that the area might harbor an individual posing a danger to the officer or others."[15]

Here are a few other examples of the application of these generalizations: there was no constitutional violation when officers approached a person in an airport and requested identification and the person responded. The situation was not considered a detention. But when the police asked another person if he would consent to a search of his suitcases, and took him to a small room for the search, their actions created an in-custody detention, which requires police to have some objective justification beyond a mere suspicion.[16] Police approaching people on buses and seeking their consent to search them or their luggage does not necessarily constitute a "seizure" within the meaning of the Fourth Amendment, a holding which the dissenters said "trivializes the values that underlie the Fourth Amendment."[17] The Court gave a green light to the Immigration and Naturalization Service's use of "factory sweeps" to catch illegal aliens. The INS, either with the employer's consent or with a broadly worded search warrant, sends its agents into factories where it thinks illegal aliens may be working and has the agents question all the workers about their citizenship. Having INS agents posted at the exits, said Justice Rehnquist for the majority, did not turn the encounter into a detention. It was merely a classic case of a consensual encounter between individuals and officials.[18] Justice Brennan, in his dissent, wrote, "It is simply fantastic to conclude that a reasonable person could ignore all that was occurring throughout the factory and have the temerity to believe that he was at liberty to refuse to answer the questions and walk away."[19]

[13] *United States* v *Hensley*, 469 US 221 (1985).
[14] *Hayes* v *Florida*, 470 US 811 (1985).
[15] *Maryland* v *Buie*, 494 US 325 (1990).
[16] *Florida* v *Royer*, 460 US 491 (1983).
[17] *Florida* v *Bostick*, 115 L Ed 2d 389 (1991).
[18] *INS* v *Delgado*, 466 US 210 (1984).
[19] *INS* v *Delgado*, 466 US 210 (1984).

The Fourth Amendment provides more protection against stops, arrests, and detentions for persons in *private homes* than for persons in public places. Without some exigent circumstance—as when somebody's life is in danger, when evidence is about to be destroyed, or when the police are in hot pursuit of a person seen committing a *serious* crime—police may not break into a private home to make an arrest unless they have a warrant.[20] "Police bear a heavy burden when attempting to demonstrate an urgent need that might justify warrantless searches or arrests in a private home. [Moreover] . . . application of the exigent-circumstances exception in the context of a home entry should rarely be sanctioned when there is probable cause to believe that only a minor offense . . . has been committed."[21]

An arrest may sometimes be justified on the basis of a *search* warrant: a warrant to search for contraband carries with it the authority to detain the occupants of the premises while the search is conducted, and, if the search uncovers evidence that establishes probable cause, to arrest the persons found on the premises.[22] A search warrant for particular items in a particular place permits this detention of the persons found there; it does not permit their personal search, except to ensure they do not have dangerous weapons. However, if the search uncovers evidence justifying their arrest on probable cause, then they can be searched to the same extent as if they had been arrested with a warrant.

Although warrantless arrests are permitted for probable cause, persons arrested without a warrant must promptly be brought before a neutral magistrate for a judicial determination of probable cause.[23] How promptly? The Constitution does not "impose on the States a rigid procedural framework, but the Court has defined 48 hours as the time when the burden shifts to the government to demonstrate the existence of a bona fide emergency or other extraordinary circumstance." Prior to that time the arrested individual has the burden to show that the state failed to provide a prompt hearing.[24]

The Fourth Amendment not only limits when police may seize people: It also limits *how* they may do so. Under the common law, police could use whatever force was necessary to effect the arrest of a fleeing felon, though not of a misdemeanant. Not so under the Fourth Amendment. A police officer may not seize an unarmed, nondangerous suspect "by shooting him dead," as Justice White rather bluntly put it for the Court.[25] Deadly force may be used only when the officer has probable cause to believe that the suspect poses a threat of serious physical harm, either to the officer or to others. Thus, if a suspect threatens the officer with a weapon or there is probable cause to believe that the suspect has committed a crime involving the infliction or threatened

---

[20] *Payton* v *New York*, 445 US 573 (1980).

[21] *Welsh* v *Wisconsin*, 466 US 740 (1984).

[22] *Michigan* v *Summers*, 452 US 693 (1981).

[23] *Gerstein* v *Pugh*, 420 US 103 (1975).

[24] *County of Riverside* v *McLaughlin*, 114 L Ed 2d 49 (1991).

[25] *Tennessee* v *Garner*, 471 US 1 (1985).

infliction of serious physical harm, and after, where feasible, some warning has been given, then, and only then, may the officer use a weapon that could kill to prevent the escape of the fleeing and dangerous felon.

"All claims that law enforcement officers have used excessive force—deadly or not—in the course of an arrest or investigatory stop, or other 'seizure' of a free citizen" are to be measured against the standard whether or not the officers' actions are "objectionable or reasonable" in light of the facts and circumstances confronting them, without regard to their intentions and with awareness that police officers are often forced to make split-second judgments about the amount of force necessary. "Not every push or shove, even if it may later seem unnecessary in the peace of a judge's chambers violates the Fourth Amendment," but police are not to use more force than is necessary.[26]

Unreasonable Searches

The distinction between reasonable and unreasonable searches in general, but these days with more and more exceptions, is that reasonable searches are based on a search warrant or probable cause and unreasonable ones are not. "With proper warrant or probable cause or with one of the exceptions, (see p. 255) police may seize all contraband and all instrumentalities and evidence of crime except for materials protected by the First Amendment. Single copies of expressive materials may be seized but none may be taken where the result is to impose prior restraint upon the sale or distribution or viewing of books or films or other such materials just because police believe they may be obscene or otherwise evidence of a crime. Incriminating letters and documents, however, are not generally considered expressive materials.

"It is a cardinal principle that searches conducted outside the judicial process, without prior approval by a judge or a magistrate, are per se unreasonable under the Fourth Amendment—subject only to a few specifically established and well-delineated exceptions."[27] However, "neither a warrant nor probable cause, nor indeed, any measure of individualized suspicion, is an indispensable component in every circumstance."[28] In fact the number of exceptions keeps growing, and they are not so well delineated.

For the most part the issues are those of procedure, but there are some searches that are unreasonable and thus unconstitutional, even if surrounded by the appropriate procedural safeguards. For example, absent a showing of a compelling need, a state could not force a person to undergo surgery to produce a bullet that might be useful evidence to prove his or her guilt, no matter how careful the procedures it used or how many warrants it obtained.[29]

---

[26] *Graham* v *Connor*, 488 US 816 (1989).

[27] *Mincey* v *Arizona*, 437 US 385 (1970); *Thompson* v *Louisiana*, 469 US 17 (1985).

[28] *National Treasury Employees* v *Von Raab*, 489 US 656 (1989).

[29] *Winston* v *Lee*, 470 US 753 (1985).

Exceptions for Police Searches without Warrants

To begin with, there are a variety of searches by government agents not designed to uncover crimes. Such searches are discussed later. Here we concentrate on exceptions for searches without warrant by law enforcement officers. Furthermore, not all inspections are searches. "A truly cursory inspection—one that involves merely looking at what is already exposed to view, without disturbing it—is not a 'search' for Fourth Amendment purposes."[30] Thus, police committed no violation when, without warrant or probable cause, they merely recorded the serial numbers of some stereo equipment. They did commit a violation, however, when they picked up the equipment, for that action was a search.[31]

Where the Amendment applies, the exceptions to the general rule against warrantless searches and seizures of what is found by police and customs officials are as follows:

1. *The automobile exception:* "The law of search and seizure with respect to automobiles is intolerably confusing. The Court apparently cannot agree even on what it has held previously, let alone on how these cases should be decided."[32] The exception is justified in part because of the mobility of automobiles and in part because persons are not entitled to the same expectations of privacy in their automobiles as in their homes or other places. Police have no general right to stop automobiles or to search the occupants of an automobile. But if officers have probable cause to believe that an automobile is being used to commit a crime, even a traffic offense, or that it contains persons who have committed crimes or that it contains evidence of crimes or contraband, they may stop the automobile, detain the persons found therein, and search them and any containers or packages found inside the car.[33] The scope of a warrantless search of an automobile "is defined . . . by the object of the search and the places in which there is probable cause to believe that it may be found."[34] Officers may conduct a warrantless search of the vehicle even after it has been impounded and is in police custody. The automobile exception applies fully to mobile motor homes in public places,[35] but probably not to trailers on private land.

2. *The* Terry *exception:* As noted, officers may make *Terry* searches. These brief investigatory stops and searches were first justified only when officers had reason to believe they were dealing with armed and dangerous persons but have subsequently been expanded to cover stops when the police have reason to believe that a person has committed or

---

[30] *Arizona v Hicks,* 480 US 321 (1987).

[31] Ibid.

[32] Justice Powell concurring in *Robbins v California,* 453 US 420 (1981).

[33] *United States v Ross,* 456 US 798 (1982).

[34] *United States v Ross,* 456 US 798 (1982).

[35] *California v Carney,* 471 US 386 (1985).

is about to commit a criminal offense, and when the intrusion is limited to a quick pat-down to check for weapons that might be used to assault the arresting officer, to check for contraband, to determine identity, or to maintain briefly the status quo while obtaining more information.[36] If an officer stops and frisks a suspect to look for weapons but instead finds criminal evidence that might justify an arrest, then the officer can make a full search. To illustrate: an officer, acting on an informer's tip, approached a man sitting in a car. The officer ordered the suspect to get out of the car, but the suspect merely rolled down the window. The officer saw a bulge on the suspect's waistband. He reached over and into the car and removed a gun from the suspect's waistband. The officer arrested the suspect, although the mere possession of a weapon was not a crime, made a search, and found heroin. Justice Rehnquist, speaking for the Court, said, "The Fourth Amendment does not require a policeman who lacks the precise level of information necessary for probable cause to arrest to simply shrug his shoulders and allow a crime to occur or a criminal to escape." The dissenting justices argued that the majority had ignored the fact that the stop-and-frisk exception to the warrant requirement had been begrudgingly granted only to protect the safety of officers of the law.[37] The Court has now held that an "officer may seize nonthreatening contraband," for example, cocaine, "detected during a protective patdown search of the sort permitted by *Terry*."[38] This is what is known as a "plain patdown," that is, the officer must only pat down a suspect's outer clothing, and make no additional invasion of the suspect's privacy beyond that authorized by a search for weapons. This kind of plain patdown is analogous to the "plain view exception" (see below).

3. *Searches Subsequent to Valid Arrest:* When making a lawful arrest, either with an arrest warrant or because of probable cause, police may make a warrantless full search of the persons involved, the areas under their immediate control, and all the possessions they take with them to the place of detention, and, as we have noted, they may make a protective sweep of the immediate area to be sure it does not harbor other dangerous persons.[39]

4. *Evidence:* When there is probable cause to make an arrest, even if one is not made, limited searches are permitted if necessary to preserve easily disposed-of evidence, such as scrapings under fingernails.[40]

5. *Inventory searches:* Searches that are part of the routine procedures incident to incarceration of an arrested person are acceptable. These

[36] *Terry v Ohio,* 392 US 1 (1968); *United States v Sharpe,* 470 US 675 (1985); *Hayes v Florida,* 470 US 811 (1985).

[37] *Adams v Williams,* 407 US 143 (1972).

[38] *Minnesota v Dickerson,* 124 L Ed 2s 334 (1993).

[9] *Chimel v California,* 395 US 752 (1969); *United States v Edward,* 415 US 800 (1974); *Illinois v Lafayette,* 462 US 640 (1983).

[40] *Cupp v Murphy,* 412 US 291 (1973).

include searches of articles in the possession of the person being arrested, including his or her car and items in the car,[41] provided there are established rules for inventory searches so that such a search does not become "a ruse for a general rummaging in order to discover incriminating evidence."[42]

6. *Consent:* Searches based on voluntary consent are allowed even if the persons who give the consent are not told they have a right to refuse to grant permission.[43]

7. *Border Searches:* Searches of persons and the goods they bring with them are permissible, under customs and immigration laws, at border crossings,[44] but the Court has imposed limits on roving border patrols greater than those applicable to fixed check points, and has limited situations in which extensive interviews beyond initial inquiries can take place. The border search exception also permits officials to open mail entering the country if they have "reasonable cause" to suspect it contains merchandise imported contrary to the law.[45] (The border search exception does not extend to searches by Puerto Rican authorities of persons coming from the continental United States; such persons are not making an international crossing.)[46]

8. *Plain view:* The plain-view exception permits officers to search and seize evidence without a warrant if (1) they are lawfully in a position from which the evidence can be viewed, (2) it is immediately apparent to them that the items they observe are evidence of a crime or are contraband, and (3) they have probable cause—a reasonable suspicion will not do— that the evidence uncovered is contraband or evidence of a crime.[47] (In 1990 the Court removed the requirement that the evidence seen under the plain view exception had to be discovered inadvertently.)[48]

9. *Exigent circumstances:* Searches and seizures are permissible under "exigent circumstances," that is, when officers do not have time to secure a warrant before evidence is destroyed or a criminal escapes capture or when there is need "to protect or preserve life or avoid serious injury." Here are some examples of exigent circumstances: fire fighters and police may enter a burning building without a warrant and may remain there for a reasonable time to investigate the cause of the blaze after the fire has been extinguished. However, after the fire has been put out, the emergency is not to be used as an excuse to make an exhaustive,

---

[41] *Colorado v Bertine*, 479 US 367 (1987).

[42] *Florida v Wells*, 495 US 1(1990).

[43] *Schneckloth v Bustamonte*, 412 US 218 (1973); *United States v Matlock*, 415 US 164 (1974).

[44] *Almeida-Sanchez v United States*, 413 US 266 (1973); *United States v Ortiz*, 422 US 891 (1975).

[45] *United States v Ramsey*, 431 US 606 (1977).

[46] *Torres v Puerto Rico*, 442 US 465 (1979).

[47] *Coolidge v New Hampshire*, 403 US 443 (1971); *Texas v Brown*, 460 US 730 (1983); *Arizona v Hicks*, 480 US 321 (1987).

[48] *Horton v California*, 496 US 128 1990).

warrantless search for evidence not in plain sight.[49] Police may enter a building in hot pursuit of a fleeing felon or in search of immediate aid needed to save life or to avoid injury and may seize any evidence that is in plain view during the course of their legitimate emergency activities. They may make a prompt warrantless search of an area where, they have reason to believe, a person has been injured or murdered, to see if there are other victims or if a killer is still on the premises.[50] Films, books, and other materials that might be protected by the First Amendment may be seized under the exigent-circumstances exception only if copies of the seized materials are left undisturbed.

Premises and Persons Protected

The premises and things protected against warrantless police searches include all places where a person has a legitimate expectation of privacy, including hotel rooms, rented homes, first class mail, and even telephone booths.[51] The Amendment does not, however, cover all places where one has a legitimate right to be; it covers only those where one has *legitimate expectations of privacy,* "those expectations that society is prepared to recognize as reasonable."[52]

In other words, first, a person has to make clear that he or she has an expectation of privacy, and second, the Supreme Court has to decide that society is willing to recognize that expectation as reasonable.[53] Strangely enough, the Court has not established clearly whether the burden of proving that an expectation of privacy is reasonable is upon the person claiming a violation of the Fourth Amendment or upon the prosecution attempting to use evidence.[54]

Since no one has a legitimate expectation of privacy in the glove compartment of a car in which one is merely a passenger, or in the numbers one dials into a telephone system, evidence taken from such places can be used even if taken without a warrant.[55] Nor is there any reasonable expectation of privacy with respect to what is contained in garbage bags left on the curb in front of houses. Police need no warrant to search such garbage.[56] Nor may a shopkeeper successfully raise constitutional objections if he offers to sell books and magazines and they are purchased by police officers and used as evidence in a prosecution for the distribution of obscene literature.[57]

In addition, only those whose rights are directly violated have standing to challenge an improper search. One Jack Payner discovered this fact, to his

---

[49] *Michigan* v *Tyler,* 436 US 499 (1978); *Mincey* v *Arizona,* 437 US 385 (1978).
[50] *Thompson* v *Louisiana,* 469 US 17 (1984).
[51] *Minnesota* v *Olson,* 109 US 2d 85 (1990).
[52] *Oliver* v *United States,* 466 US 170 (1984).
[53] *California* v *Ciraolo,* 476 US 207 (1986).
[54] See Justice Blackmun's dissenting opinion on this issue in *Florida* v *Riley,* 488 US 445 (1989).
[55] *United States* v *Salvucci,* 448 US 83 (1980).
[56] *California* v *Greenwood,* 486 US 35 (1988).
[57] *Maryland* v *Macon,* 472 US 463 (1985).

unhappiness. Payner was brought to trial because internal revenue agents had found incriminating evidence against him in his banker's briefcase. The agents had used a female private investigator to lure Payner's banker out to dinner. During the dinner the agents had swiped the briefcase from his apartment, copied documents found in it, and then returned it to the apartment. Federal courts found the agents had knowingly and willfully violated the Fourth Amendment rights of the banker but that Payner had no expectations of privacy in his banker's briefcase. Since Payner's rights had not been violated, evidence taken in the briefcase caper could be used against him.[58]

The Fourth Amendment does not protect open fields. Such fields may be searched by police officers without warrants or probable cause.[59] The Amendment does apply, however, to the *curtilage,* the common-law term for the land immediately surrounding and associated with a home. In determining the dividing line between curtilage and open fields, the centrally relevant consideration is "whether the area in question is so intimately tied to the home itself that it should be placed under the home's 'umbrella' of Fourth Amendment protection."[60] This question is to be resolved with reference to four factors: the proximity to the home of the area claimed to be curtilage, inclusion of the area within an enclosure surrounding the home, the nature of the uses to which the area is put, and the steps taken by the resident to protect the area from observation by people passing by. Applying these factors the Court apparently has concluded that most barns on most farms most of the time are not part of the curtilage.[61]

As aerial surveillance and satellite technology become more sophisticated, judges are once again being asked to apply the principles of the Fourth Amendment to the electronic age. The Court has ruled that there was no violation of the Amendment when police officers rented an airplane to fly within 1,000 feet above the backyard of a person suspected of growing marijuana nor was there a violation when a helicopter was used for this same purpose from a height of 400 feet. Said the Court, "The Fourth Amendment simply does not require the police traveling in the public airways at this altitude to obtain a warrant in order to observe what is visible to the naked eye."[62]

People do not have an expectation of privacy from aerial surveillance that society is prepared to recognize as reasonable, although in the case of the low-flying helicopter only four justices based their views upon the legal right of the police to be there, with Justice O'Connor indicating that she might be persuaded to go along with the dissenting four if evidence was presented that helicopters circling over the curtilage of a home at that height are sufficiently rare that it would violate reasonable expectations of privacy, despite compliance with

---

[58] *United States v Payner,* 447 US 727 (1980).
[59] *Oliver v United States,* 466 US 170 (1984).
[60] *United States v Dunn,* 480 US 294 (1987).
[61] Ibid.
[62] *California v Ciraolo,* 476 US 207 (1986).

FAA safety regulations.[63] A closely divided Court also held that the Fourth Amendment did not prevent the Environmental Protection Agency from using aerial photography to observe Dow Chemical Company's compliance with the antipollution laws. However, the Court made quite clear that if government agents, going beyond mere eyeballing or the use of conventional cameras commonly used in map making, use "highly sophisticated surveillance equipment not generally available to the public, such as satellite technology," the use of such equipment might well be constitutionally proscribed, without a warrant.[64] In other words, flying over and taking pictures with a regular camera of people's backyards or of industrial plants presents a different constitutional issue from using more highly sophisticated aerial observation and modern technology to disclose to the police "those intimate associations, objects or activities otherwise imperceptible to police or fellow citizens."[65]

Searches by Authorities Other than the Police

The Fourth Amendment protects commercial buildings as well as homes, covers civil as well as criminal investigations, and includes searches by government officers other than the police, such as internal revenue agents, probation officers, health inspectors, occupational and safety inspectors, and public school teachers and administrators. The standards for searches by other than police for purposes other than law enforcement are much less stringent.[66] Searches by such officials may take place without warrant or probable cause. "Where a Fourth Amendment intrusion serves special governmental needs, beyond the normal need for law enforcement, it is necessary to balance the individual's privacy expectations against the Government's interests to determine whether it is impractical to require a warrant or some level of individual suspicion in the particular context."[67]

Take public elementary and secondary school officials. They need not obtain a warrant before searching a student, nor must they have probable cause to believe that the student has violated or is violating a law. Rather, a search by school officials is justified if there are reasonable grounds for suspecting that it will turn up evidence that the student has violated or is violating either the law or a rule of the school and if the search is reasonably related to its objectives and "is not excessively intrusive in light of the age and sex of the student and the nature of the infraction."[68]

The federal government requires the searching of all passengers and their baggage seeking to enter a commercial airliner without any basis in suspecting any particular passenger. "Where...the possible harm against which the Government seeks

---

[63] *Florida v Riley*, 488 US 455 (1989).

[64] *Dow Chemical Co. v United States*, 476 US 227 (1986).

[65] From footnote to *California v Ciraolo*, 476 US 207 (1986) reserving this question.

[66] *Griffin v Wisconsin*, 483 US 868 (1987).

[67] *National Treasury Employees v Von Raab*, 489 US 656 (1989).

[68] *New Jersey v TLO*, 469 US 325 (1985).

to guard is substantial, the need to prevent its occurrence furnishes an ample justification for reasonable searches calculated to advance the Government's goal."[69]

The Fourth Amendment applies to supervisors of government employees, but a search of offices for noninvestigatory work-related purposes or an investigatory search for evidence of suspected work-related employee misconduct does not require a warrant or probable cause.[70] It is judged merely by the standard of reasonableness. Justice Blackmun, dissenting from this view, was so incensed that he accused the plurality, whose opinion had been penned by Justice O'Connor, of being motivated by a dislike for public employees.[71]

Health, building, and safety inspectors must secure a warrant before they may enter a home or most businesses if the occupants refuse to give them entry.[72] However, in such instances an *administrative search warrant*, rather than a criminal search warrant is all that is required. Inspectors do not have to prove to a magistrate that they have probable cause to believe that violations are taking place; they must prove merely that an inspection is authorized by law, that it is based on a general administrative plan for the enforcement of the law, and that they are acting reasonably to enforce it.

No warrants at all, administrative or otherwise, are required to search a few kinds of businesses. First, such searches are permitted for industries "that have such a history of governmental oversight that no reasonable expectation of privacy . . . could exist for a proprietor over the stock of such an enterprise." Liquor and firearms are industries of this type. When entrepreneurs embark on such businesses, they have voluntarily chosen to subject themselves to a full arsenal of governmental regulation.[73]

Second, although governments cannot authorize warrantless inspections of all businesses, they may do so for specific businesses when they "reasonably" determine that warrantless searches are necessary to further a regulatory scheme and when the regulatory presence is so comprehensive and so well defined that the owner of the commercial property cannot help being aware that the property will be subject to periodic inspections undertaken for specific purposes. Mines and car junkyards are examples of such pervasively regulated industries. Thus, Congress may constitutionally authorize warrantless inspections of the nation's underground and surface mines, and a state may regulate car junkyards even to the extent of allowing police to make warrantless inspections that lead to arrests for criminal violations.[74]

Warrantless inspections, however, even in the context of pervasively regulated businesses, will be deemed to be reasonable only so long as (1) there is a substantial government interest, (2) the warrantless inspections are necessary to further the regulatory scheme, and (3) the regulatory statute performs the

---

[69]*National Treasury Employees* v *Von Raab*, 489 US 656 (1989).

[70]*O'Connor* v *Ortega*, 480 US 709 (1987).

[71]Ibid.

[72]*Marshall* v *Barlow's*, 436 US 307 (1978); *See* v *City of Seattle*, 387 US 541 (1967); *Camara* v *Municipal Court*, 387 US 523 (1967).

[73]*Colonnade Catering Corp.* v *United States*, 397 US 72 (1970); *United States* v *Biswell*, 406 US 311 (1972).

[74]*Donovan* v *Dewey*, 452 US 594 (1981); *New York* v *Burger*, 482 US 691 (1987).

functions of a warrant by advising the owner that the search is being made pursuant to the law and by carefully limiting the search in time, place, and scope.

Drug Testing

Blood sampling by health care professionals at the instruction of police in the case of persons suspected of drunken driving or of being under the influence of drugs, as well as police-administered breath tests of persons thought to be under such influences, have been sustained without too much judicial questioning.[75]

But the Fourth Amendment restricts the way governments can impose drug tests on their own employees or require certain industries to drug test their employees. A drug testing requirement for all government employees merely as a condition of employment would in all probability be declared unconstitutional. Yet the Supreme Court has upheld some drug testing when it has been persuaded that such testing is closely related to some special need. The Court upheld a requirement of the U.S. Customs service that employees engaged in drug enforcement duties or who carry firearms must submit to urinalysis. Those who test positive for drug use and who can offer no satisfactory explanation are to be dismissed from the service. The Court, speaking through Justice Kennedy, concluded that these suspicionless searches, while doubtlessly infringing on "some privacy expectations, do not outweigh the Government's compelling interests in safety and the integrity of our borders."[76] Justice Scalia, joining the dissenters, "searched in vain for real evidence of a real problem that will be solved by urine testing of Customs Service employees." The Court also upheld federal regulations requiring breath, blood, and urine testing of railroad employees who had been involved in an accident: the long history of the problems of alcohol use in railroads "and the demonstrated connection between such use and the needs of public safety rendered such searches a reasonable means of protecting society."[77] Justices Stevens, Brennan and Marshall dissented, with the latter writing, "The majority's acceptance of dragnet blood and urine testing ensures that the first and worst, casualty of the war on drugs will be the precious liberties of our citizens."

[continued] and no Warrants shall issue, but upon probable cause, supported by Oath or affirmation, and particularly describing the place to be searched, and the persons or things to be seized.

[75] *Schmerber* v *California*, 384 US 757 (1966).
[76] *O'Connor* v *Ortega*, 480 US 709 (1987).
[77] *Skinner* v *Railway Labor Exec. Assn.*, 489 US 602 (1989).

"Our constitutional fathers were not concerned about warrantless searches, but about overreaching warrants. It is perhaps too much to say that they feared the warrant more than the search, but it is plain enough that the warrant was the prime object of their concern."[78] "Since the general warrant, not the warrantless search, was the immediate evil at which the Fourth Amendment was directed, it is not surprising that the Framers placed precise limits on its issuance. The requirement that a warrant only issue on showing of a particular probable cause was the means adopted to circumscribe the warrant power."[79]

When a search warrant is required, it must be granted by a magistrate—a judicial officer—or a clerk of a court who may serve as a neutral judicial officer for that purpose. The police must appear before such a magistrate and, under oath, indicate they have "probable cause" to believe the search will produce criminal evidence. If it subsequently appears that the police knowingly or recklessly made a false statement to the magistrate, the evidence obtained by the search cannot be used (see the material, later in this section, on the exclusionary rule).[80] The magistrate who issues warrants need not be a legally trained judge, but a prosecutor or a state's attorney will not do, nor will justices of the peace who receive a fee if they issue a warrant but no fee if they refuse to do so.[81] The magistrate must "perform his 'neutral and detached' function and not serve merely as a rubber stamp for the police."[82] Thus, it was impermissible for a town justice to issue an open-ended search warrant and then go along with the police on a raid of an adult bookstore in which the justice made an on-the-spot decision about which items should be included in the warrant and which excluded. The fact that the judge visited the scene was not the problem: he acted not as a judicial officer, but as an adjunct law enforcement officer. "He did not manifest that neutrality and detachment demanded of a judicial officer."[83]

The "probable cause" that justifies the issuance of a warrant is hard to define; it is a "fluid concept." It requires, however, that a magistrate be able reasonably to conclude, based on the totality of the circumstances, that there is a substantial basis for believing that a search will uncover evidence of wrongdoing.[84] "The task of the issuing magistrate is simply to make a practical, common-sense decision whether, given all the circumstances set forth in the affidavit before him, ... there is a fair probability that contraband or evidence of a crime will be found in a particular place. And the duty of a reviewing court

---

[78]T. Taylor, *Two Studies on Constitutional Interpretation* (Columbus: Ohio State University Press, 1969), as quoted by Justice Stevens, dissenting in *Marshall v Barlow's*, 436 US 307 (1978).

[79]*Marshall v Barlow's*, 436 US 307 (1978).

[80]*Franks v Delaware*, 438 US 154 (1978).

[81]*Shadwick v Tampa*, 407 US 345 (1972); *Coolidge v New Hampshire*, 403 US 433 (1971); *Connally v Georgia*, 429 US 245 (1977).

[82]*Aguilar v Texas*, 378 US 108 (1964).

[83]*Lo-Ji Sales, Inc. v New York*, 442 US 319 (1979).

[84]*Illinois v Gates*, 462 US 213 (1983).

is simply to ensure that the magistrate had a 'substantial basis for . . . conclud[ing]' that probable cause existed."[85]

The warrant the magistrate issues must specify the places to be searched and the things to be seized. A blanket authorization to search indiscriminately is a *general search warrant* and violates the Constitution. A magistrate may issue a warrant to enter any public place if the police demonstrate to the magistrate's satisfaction that there is evidence of a crime in that place. That the place is owned by an innocent party or that the person in possession of the things to be searched is not suspected of any law violations makes no constitutional difference.[86] A warrant to search a public place, however, such as a tavern, does not authorize a warrantless search of customers in the place.[87]

Once a valid search warrant has been obtained, the Fourth Amendment does not prohibit police from using force or stealth to execute the search warrant if that is the only way the warrant can be effectively executed. When there is a warrant to engage in electronic surveillance, a separate warrant to enter the premises to install the device is not needed and the installation may be done by stealth.

Electronic Searches

The inventions of science have confronted judges with novel problems in applying the prohibitions against unreasonable searches and seizures. Obviously, the framers of the Fourth Amendment had in mind physical objects such as books, papers, letters, other kinds of written documents, weapons, and other physical evidence. But what of tapping phone wires or using electronic devices to eavesdrop? In *Olmstead* v *United States,* decided in 1928, a bare majority of the Supreme Court held that there was no unconstitutional search unless there was seizure of physical objects or an actual physical entry into a place. Justices Holmes and Brandeis, in dissent, argued that the Constitution should be kept up with the times; the "dirty business" of wiretapping produced the same evil invasions of privacy that the framers had in mind when they wrote the Fourth Amendment.[88]

Forty years later, in *Katz* v *United States,* the Supreme Court adopted the Holmes-Brandeis position: "The Fourth Amendment protects people—and not simply 'areas'—against unreasonable searches and seizures." The use by police officers of electronic devices to overhear a conversation in a public telephone booth is a search and seizure within the meaning of the Constitution. "Wherever a man may be [since modified to wherever a person has a legitimate

---

[85] *Illinois* v *Gates,* 462 US 213 (1983); *New York* v *P. J. Video, Inc.,* 475 US 868 (1986).

[86] *Zurcher* v *Stanford Daily,* 436 US 547 (1978).

[87] *Ybarra* v *Illinois,* 444 US 85 (1979).

[88] *Olmstead* v *United States,* 277 US 438 (1928).

expectation of privacy], he is entitled to know that he will remain free from unreasonable searches and seizures."[89]

After conversations became constitutionally protected, legislatures and judges had to develop rules for the conditions under which conversations would be allowed to be intercepted. The basic federal legislation is contained in the Crime Control and Safe Streets Act of 1968, which makes it a crime for any unauthorized person to tap telephone wires or use or sell electronic bugging devices in interstate commerce. Yet the act authorizes the attorney general to secure permission for federal agents to engage in bugging by applying for a warrant from a federal judge. The attorney general must authorize the wiretapping personally or through an assistant specifically designated for that purpose.[90] At the state level, the act authorizes the principal prosecuting attorney of any state or its political subdivision to apply to a state judge for a warrant approving wiretapping or mechanical devices for felonies.

Judges are to issue warrants only if they decide that probable cause exists that a crime is being, has been, or is about to be committed and that information relating to that crime may be obtained only by the intercept. In addition to intercepts under warrant, the act permits police officers to act without a warrant for forty-eight hours in "an emergency situation relating to conspiratorial activities threatening the national security" or involving organized crime.

The Crime Control Act of 1968 specifically left undisturbed whatever constitutional authority the president might have to authorize, without securing a warrant, bugging and tapping to protect our national security. But the Supreme Court has held that the president's authority to act to protect the nation against foreign attack and violent overthrow does not include the right, without judicial warrant, to authorize electronic surveillance of persons suspected of *domestic* subversion. Justice Powell, speaking for the Court, said, "The danger to political dissent is acute where the government attempts to act under so vague a concept as the power to protect domestic security."[91] The Court pointedly did not rule on the scope of the president's authority to authorize surveillance of foreign agents inside or outside of the country.

In 1978, by the Foreign Intelligence Surveillance Act, Congress forbade all officials except those of the National Security Agency—the agency in charge of making and breaking codes—to bug foreign agents, except with a warrant from the United States Foreign Intelligence Surveillance Court. This court, consisting of seven designated federal district judges, grants secret warrants permitting the bugging of foreign agents.

It needs to be noted that, as long as the police make no illegal entries and do not violate the laws by using illegal electronic devices, neither the Constitution nor any federal law requires police officers to secure warrants before they resort to undercover tactics, including the use of secret cameras or recording devices on their persons or on undercover agents. Police may use the devices of science to extend the range of their "eavesdropping" by expanding what they can hear, see,

---

[89] *Katz v United States*, 389 US 347 (1967).
[90] *United States v Giordano*, 416 US 505 (1974).
[91] *United States v United States District Court*, 407 US 297 (1972).

film, record, or smell. These "modern devices" include dogs trained to sniff luggage and to detect the presence of drugs.[92] The Court upheld the warrantless installation of an electronic tracking device, a beeper, inside a container of chemicals being transported in an automobile when it revealed no information that could not have been obtained through visual surveillance.[93] However, the Court has shown some concern about the warrantless use of these electronic devices when they are smuggled inside a person's home, where there is the greatest expectation of privacy.[94]

One must choose one's friends with care, for there is no violation of the Constitution if one tells a friend a secret and the friend in turn informs the police. Except inside your own home, and not always even then, if your "friend" is wired for sound so that what you say is transmitted back to police officers, there is no constitutional violation. Similarly, police may listen in on a telephone conversation over an extension phone with the consent of one of the parties to the conversation but without the knowledge of the other.[95]

The Exclusionary Rule

How to enforce the Fourth Amendment? Officers who engage in unreasonable searches and seizures are, under most circumstances, guilty of violating the criminal laws. They can also be sued for civil damages by those whose rights have been violated,[96] and under some circumstances the governments that employ them can also be sued. However, victims of unreasonable searches are often not in a position to sue the police. Nor are police and prosecutors likely to move against fellow officers for engaging in unlawful searches.

To enforce the Fourth Amendment, we rely on the exclusionary rule.[97] (It also is used to enforce the Fifth and Sixth Amendments.) Under this rule, evidence obtained in an improper fashion, that is, in violation of the Constitution or of statute, cannot be introduced against those whose Fourth Amendment rights have been violated. By excluding such evidence, judges hope to deter officers from violating the Fourth (or Fifth or Sixth) Amendments.

The exclusionary rule does not apply to a grand jury. Such a jury may not instruct its agents to violate the Fourth Amendment and may not issue subpoenas that do; but if illegally procured evidence becomes available to a grand jury, the jury may consider it, even though the evidence may not be used in a subsequent criminal trial.[98] Nor does the exclusionary rule apply to civil proceedings, not even to deportation proceedings to determine eligibility to remain in this country.[99]

---

[92] *United States v Place,* 462 US 696 (1983).

[93] *United States v Knotts,* 460 US 276 (1983).

[94] Ibid.

[95] *Lee v United States,* 343 US 747 (1952); *Hoffa v United States,* 385 US 293 (1966); *United States v White,* 401 US 745 (1971).

[96] *Bivens v Six Unknown Named Agents of the Bureau of Narcotics,* 403 US 388 (1971).

[97] *Weeks v United States,* 232 US 383 (1914); *Mapp v Ohio,* 367 US 643 (1961).

[98] *United States v Calandra,* 414 US 338 (1974).

[99] *INS v Lopez-Mendoza,* 468 US 1032 (1984).

There have always been critics of the exclusionary rule. "Why," they quote Justice Cardozo, should the criminal "go free because the constable has blundered?"[100] They argue that the rule is ineffective, that there are more desirable ways to prevent police misconduct, that it keeps relevant and reliable evidence from the trier of the facts, and that it deflects the search for the truth. Defenders of the rule respond that not only does the exclusionary rule have a deterrent effect on police misconduct, but judges, who also are agents of the government, should have no part in violating the Fourth Amendment.[101]

In 1971 the Court began to back away from the full sweep of the exclusionary rule. In *New York* v *Harris* it allowed unconstitutionally obtained evidence to be used to contradict a defendant's testimony and to challenge the defendant's credibility.[102] (The Court has refused, however, to extend this exception to the exclusionary rule to allow the use of evidence obtained illegally from a defendant to be used to impeach the testimony of defense witnesses.)[103]

The major exception to the exclusionary rule is the "objective good faith" exception. For years some members of the Court, as well as many outside, have urged the Court to make a good faith exception that would "not require the exclusion of evidence obtained by the police in a reasonable belief that they have obtained it in a constitutional manner."[104] The Court has not gone that far—yet. It has ruled, however, that if a police officer has obtained a search warrant from a magistrate who acted in the proper neutral and detached way, evidence so obtained should not be excluded, even if it subsequently is established that the magistrate lacked probable cause to issue the warrant [105] or if it turns out that the warrant was defective.[106] This does not mean that evidence may be used if the police obtained the warrant by knowingly or recklessly submitting false information or if they acted on a warrant that they knew to be improperly issued. The police officers' belief in the validity of the warrant must be "objectively reasonable. An officer's subjective belief, based on ignorance of constitutional requirements, will not protect an invalid warrant." The Court left for another day the question of whether the good faith exception would apply to good faith warrantless searches.

The Court has also refused to apply the exclusionary rule to bar the use of a statement made by a suspect at the police station after police had entered his *home* without warrant—the place that is most protected by the Fourth Amendment from unreasonable search and seizure—but for whom they had probable cause to arrest for murder.[107]

---

[100] *People* v *Defore*, 242 NY 13 (1926).
[101] Justice Brennan dissenting in *United States* v *Leon*, 468 US 897 (1984).
[102] *Harris* v *New York*, 401 US 222 (1971); *United States* v *Havens*, 446 US 620 (1976).
[103] *James* v *Illinois*, 493 US 307 (1990).
[104] *Illinois* v *Gates*, 462 US 213 (1983).
[105] *United States* v *Leon*, 468 US 897 (1984).
[106] *Massachusetts* v *Sheppard*, 468 US 981 (1984).
[107] *New York* v *Harris*, 495 US 14 (1990).

By five to four, the Court has extended the exception to cases in which officers have acted in objectively reasonable reliance on a statute authorizing warrantless administrative searches but where the statute is ultimately found to violate the Fourth Amendment. This exception to the exclusionary rule is not likely to be very significant, since it will apply only to searches occurring before the declaration by a court of the unconstitutionality of the particular law authorizing administrative searches. Justice Blackmun for the Court wrote, "A statute cannot support objectively reasonable reliance if, in passing the statute, the legislature wholly abandoned its responsibility to enact constitutional laws. Nor can a law enforcement officer be said to have acted in good-faith reliance upon a statute if its provisions are such that a reasonable officer should have known that the statute was unconstitutional."[108] It is not likely that there will be many examples of legislative bodies wholly abandoning responsibilities. One also wonders if we really want law enforcement officers to decide for themselves which laws are unconstitutional and thus not to be relied on for the purposes of making administrative searches.

AMENDMENT V: GRAND JURIES, DOUBLE JEOPARDY, SELF-INCRIMINATION, DUE PROCESS, AND EMINENT DOMAIN

No person shall be held to answer for a capital, or otherwise infamous crime, unless on a presentment or indictment of a Grand Jury,

---

The Fifth Amendment introduces us to the oldest institution known to the Constitution: the grand jury. It hails from the days of William the Conqueror; the trial, or petit (also spelled petty) jury, is an offshoot of it (see the Sixth Amendment). Like its English forerunner, the federal grand jury is composed of not more than twenty-three members, of whom any twelve are sufficient to make a presentment or to return an indictment—that is, to accuse some person or persons of an offense against the laws of the United States, on the basis either of evidence gathered by the grand jury itself or of evidence laid before it by a prosecuting officer.

The grand jury operates in a courthouse and "under judicial auspices," but "its institutional relationship with the judicial branch has traditionally been ...at arm's length," and the courts exercise no general supervisory authority over it. "It belongs to no branch of the institutional government, serving as a kind of buffer or referee between the Government and the people."[1]

---

[108] *Illinois v Krull*, 480 US 340 (1987).
[1] *United States v Williams*, 118 L Ed 2d 352 (1992).

"The function of the grand jury is to inquire into all information that might possibly bear on its investigation until it has identified an offense or has satisfied itself that none has occurred."[2] Since the "accused" is not being tried, a grand jury's proceedings may be one sided (ex parte), with only the government being represented, and kept secret. (A state, however, may not make it a crime for witnesses before a grand jury to disclose their own testimony after the term of the grand jury has expired.)[3] Strict observance of trial rules is not followed and persons brought before grand juries have no right to have attorneys with them in the grand jury room, although the federal government permits such persons to consult with their lawyers anytime they wish in adjacent quarters. The Fourth Amendment's exclusionary rule also does not apply, and, although the investigatory powers of the grand jury are not unlimited, the grand jury can investigate "merely on suspicion that the law is being violated, or even just because it wants assurance that it is not."[4]

Grand juries, like all other juries, must be selected without respect to race, sex, or ethnic origin. To discriminate violates the constitutional rights of those who are indicted, as well as the rights of any person who might be denied the opportunity to serve on a grand jury. Systematic discrimination in selection of grand jurors requires reversal of a conviction based on an indictment brought by such a jury. The Supreme Court concluded, however, that reversing the conviction and dismissing the indictment was inappropriate in a case in which the grand jury otherwise properly selected had been presided over by a foreman alleged to have been selected in a discriminatory fashion. The office of grand jury foreman, unlike the grand jury itself, is not established by the Constitution and "the ministerial role is not such a vital one that discrimination in the appointment of an individual to that post significantly invades the distinctive interests of the defendant protected by the due process clause."[5]

After an indictment has been returned, it may not be broadened except by the grand jury itself. Any conviction of a defendant for an offense different from those included in the indictment, unless they are for lesser included offenses to the ones charged, violates the Fifth Amendment. However, "As long as the crime and the elements of the offense that sustain the conviction are fully and clearly set out in the indictment, the right to a grand jury is not normally violated by the fact that the indictment alleges more crimes or other means of committing the same crime."[6]

Indictment by grand jury is the one provision of the Bill of Rights relating to criminal prosecutions not incorporated into the due process clause of the Fourteenth Amendment. States are, therefore, free to proceed against an accused by other means, and they have been using the grand jury less and less. In many states and for most crimes, the prosecuting attorney simply files an

---

[2] *United States v R. Enterprises, Inc.*, 498 US 292 (1991).
[3] *Butterworth v Smith*, 494 US 624 (1990).
[4] *United States v Morton Salt Co.*, 357 US (1950).
[5] *Hobby v United States*, 468 US 339 (1984).
[6] *United States v Miller*, 471 US 130 (1985).

affidavit, called information, that there is evidence available to justify a trial.[7] (To hold a person in custody, however, the prosecutor's information must be followed by a hearing before a magistrate for presentation of evidence showing probable cause.)[8]

except in cases arising in the land or naval forces, or in the Militia, when in actual service in time of War or public danger;

The significance of this exception goes far beyond merely dispensing with grand jury indictments for persons in the armed forces. This clause, along with Article I, Section 8, giving Congress the power to make "rules for the Government and Regulation of the land and naval Forces," means that persons subject to trial before military courts are not entitled to the same procedural rights as are civilians.

Which persons are subject to trial before military courts? Since 1960 only members of the armed forces have been subject to military trials, and from 1969 to 1987, only for service-connected crimes. In 1987 the Court reversed a 1969 precedent and held that jurisdiction of military tribunals extends to members of the armed services for crimes committed during their military service, whether or not the crimes are service connected.[9] Military jurisdiction does not extend, however, to civilian employees of the armed forces, here or overseas, nor to civilian dependents of military personnel, including those who accompany a member of the armed forces overseas.[10] Nor may persons be tried by the military after they have been discharged, even for crimes committed while they were in the service.[11]

Congress has created a Uniform Code of Military Justice and established a Court of Military Appeals, the so-called GI Supreme Court. That court has construed the Uniform Code to extend to armed forces personnel's rights to speedy trial, to confront witnesses, to protection against unreasonable searches and seizures, to public trial, to compulsory service of process, to Miranda-like warnings and the privilege against self-incrimination.[12]

nor shall any person be subject for the same offence to be twice put in jeopardy of life or limb;

---

[7] Marvin E. Frankel and G. P. Naftalis, *The Grand Jury: An Institution on Trial* (New York: Shill & Way, 1977), 18–19.

[8] *Gerstein v Pugh*, 420 US 103 (1975).

[9] *Solorio v United States*, 483 US 435 (1987), reversing *O'Callahan v Parker*, 359 US 258 (1969).

[10] *Kinsella v Singleton*, 361 US 234 (1960), and companion cases.

[11] *Toth v Quarles*, 350 US 11 (1955).

[12] *McLucas v De Champlain*, 421 US 21 (1975).

This provision is now extended to the states by means of the Fourteenth Amendment.[13] Although the constitutional language "jeopardy of life or limb" suggests proceedings in which only the most serious penalties can be imposed, "the clause has long been construed to mean something far broader than its literal language."[14] It now applies to all crimes, including prosecutions for criminal contempt of court.[15] It protects against both multiple punishment and multiple prosecutions. It does not apply to civil suits between private persons.

The guarantee consists of three separate constitutional protections. "It protects against a second prosecution for the same offense after acquittal. It protects against a second prosecution for the same offense after conviction. And it protects against multiple punishments for the same offense."[16] The problem with this often-quoted statement, as Justice Rehnquist has pointed out, is that "same offense" is "a phrase deceptively simple in appearance but virtually kaleidoscopic in application."[17]

"Historians have traced the origins of our constitutional guarantee against double jeopardy back to the days of Demosthenes.... Despite its roots in antiquity, however, this guarantee seems both one of the least understood and, in recent years, one of the most frequently litigated provisions of the Bill of Rights."[18] Since 1971, when Congress authorized government appeals in all criminal prosecutions except when banned by the double jeopardy clause, the Supreme Court, in a series of confusing decisions, has tried, without much success, to "create order and understanding" about the meaning of double jeopardy. Here is what the Court seems to be saying:

Jeopardy attaches in both national and state jury trials as soon as the jury has been sworn in and, in nonjury trials, as soon as the judge begins to hear the evidence.[19] (In contrast, common law and current English interpretation restrict the limitations against double jeopardy to cases in which there has been a complete trial, ending in acquittal or conviction.)

If a trial ends in acquittal, the double jeopardy clause unequivocally bars reprosecution for that offense.[20]

If a trial ends with a guilty verdict, "the general rule is that the Clause does not bar reprosecution of a defendant whose conviction is overturned on appeal," or set aside by the judge.[21] But, if the verdict is set aside because it is based on insufficient evidence, it has the same effect as a judgment of acquittal, "because it means that no rational factfinder could have voted to convict the defendant."[22] However, if the verdict of guilty is set aside because of "the

---

[13] *Benton v Maryland*, 359 US 784 (1969).

[14] *Breed v Jones*, 421 US 519 (1975).

[15] *United States v. Dixon*, 125 L Ed 2d 556 (1993).

[16] *North Carolina v Pearce*, 395 US 711 (1969).

[17] *Whalen v United States*, 445 US 684 (1980).

[18] Ibid.

[19] *Crist v Bretz*, 437 US 28 (1979).

[20] *Albernaz v United States*, 450 US 333 (1981).

[21] *Justices of Boston Municipal Court v Lydon*, 466 US 294 (1984).

[22] *Tibbs v Florida*, 457 US 31 (1982).

weight of the evidence," the state may reprosecute. Such a reversal does not mean that acquittal was the only proper verdict, but merely that the reviewing court sits as a "thirteenth juror" and disagrees with the jury's resolution of conflicting testimony. "This difference of opinion no more signifies acquittal than does a disagreement among the jurors themselves."[23]

If a trial terminates before a final verdict, the double jeopardy clause may or may not prevent retrial. It prevents retrial if an indictment is dismissed or the case is terminated because the evidence is insufficient to justify conviction. Such action is tantamount to an acquittal.[24] But most midtrial terminations are not likely to prevent reprosecution, despite the Court's generalization that once jeopardy attaches and a trial starts, a defendant is ordinarily entitled to have it run its course and not again to be placed in the agony of having to be retried. For the Court has a counter generalization: "The double jeopardy clause... does not offer a guaranty to the defendant that the State will vindicate its societal interest in the enforcement of the criminal laws in one proceeding."[25] Persons may be retried if the jury is unable to agree on a verdict (that is, if there is a hung jury); if, at the defendant's request, the judge terminates the proceedings because of the failure of the government to frame the indictment properly; or even if a prosecutor's action causes the judge to declare a mistrial, unless the "prosecutor's actions... were done in order to goad the defendant into requesting a mistrial."[26]

The Supreme Court sustained an act of Congress (an act of Congress has never been held to violate the double jeopardy clause) permitting the federal government to ask the court of appeals to review a sentence imposed by a district judge. Under such circumstances, the defendant is not placed in jeopardy again, but merely has to defend against an increase in the severity of the sentence imposed.[27]

A single act may violate several statutory provisions. The Court has refused to adopt the single-transaction view of double jeopardy, for example that one robbery of several people should be treated as one crime. Instead, in order to determine whether two prosecutions or punishments for two offenses violates this clause, the Court uses the so-called "same-elements" or *Blockburger test*.[28] The double jeopardy clause prevents reprosecution or additional punishment for the same offense as defined separately under several laws or separate provisions of a single law unless "each provision requires proof of a fact that the other does not."[29]

The double jeopardy clause prevented the reprosecution of a man named Ashe after he had been acquitted of participating with others in the armed robbery of one of six men who were playing poker. The acquittal was based chiefly

[23] Ibid.

[24] *Hudson v Louisiana*, 450 US 40 (1981); *Burks v United States*, 437 US 1 (1978).

[25] *Oregon v Kennedy*, 456 US 667 (1982).

[26] *Oregon v Kennedy*, 456 US 667 (1982); *United States v Scott*, 437 US 82 (1978); *Arizona v Washington*, 434 US 497 (1978); *United States v Martin Linen*, 430 US 564 (1977).

[27] *United States v DiFrancesco*, 449 US 117 (1980).

[28] *Blockburger v United States*, 284 US 299 (1932).

[29] Ibid.

on the matter of identification. Six weeks later Ashe was convicted of robbing another of the poker players. The Supreme Court set his conviction aside because he had already been tried for the offense of being one of the robbers of the poker players. Chief Justice Burger argued in dissent, "What the Court is holding, is, in effect, that the second and third and fourth criminal acts are 'free' unless the accused is tried for the multiple crimes in a single trial."[30]

Conviction of a lesser offense probably precludes prosecution for the greater offense, but the same is not true of a guilty plea to the lesser offense. To illustrate, Kenneth Johnson was indicted for murder, involuntary manslaughter, aggravated robbery, and grand theft. His guilty pleas to the charges of manslaughter and grand theft were accepted by the court over the state's objection. Johnson then argued that it would be double jeopardy if the state were to prosecute him for murder. The Supreme Court rejected his contention: "The acceptance of a guilty plea to a lesser included offense while charges on the greater offense remain pending...has none of the implications of an 'implied acquittal' which results from a verdict convicting a defendant on lesser included offenses rendered by a jury charged to consider both greater and lesser included offenses."[31]

There is no double jeopardy in trying persons both for a substantive offense and for conspiring to commit that same offense.[32] And the double jeopardy clause does not prevent a civil suit by a government against a person who has been acquitted of a crime, provided the purpose of a civil action is remedial and not punitive and the civil penalty sought bears some relation to the loss sustained and appears to be compensation and not additional punishment.[33] Here are three examples of the application of these generalizations: after a person was acquitted of smuggling, the government was allowed to seek forfeiture of the goods alleged to have been illegally brought into the country;[34] after a person was acquitted of knowingly engaging in selling firearms without a license, the government was allowed to institute civil proceedings to force him to give up the weapons;[35] on the other side, after a person had been convicted and fined for submitting $585 worth of false Medicare claims, he could not be subjected to a civil suit by the government for the recovery of a civil penalty of $130,000 since this penalty bore no rational relation to the sum of the government's actual loss and costs and was in effect really a second punishment for the same act.[36]

The double jeopardy clause does prevent a government from trying delinquents for the same offense in the regular courts after trying them in juvenile courts.[37] (If, after a mere preliminary hearing on whether or not to try a person as a juvenile, a decision was made to transfer the case to adult court, there would not be double jeopardy.)

---

[30] *Ashe* v *Swenson*, 397 US 436 (1970).

[31] *Ohio* v *Johnson*, 467 US 493 (1984).

[32] *Ianelli* v *United States*, 420 US 770 (1975). See also *United States* v *Felix*, 118 L Ed 2d 25 (1992).

[33] *United States* v *One Assortment of 89 Firearms*, 465 US 354 (1984).

[34] *One Lot Emerald Cut Stones and One Ring* v *United States*, 409 US 232 (1972).

[35] *United States* v *One Assortment of Firearms*, 465 US 354 (1984).

[36] *United States* v *Halper*, 489 US 1004 (1989).

[37] *Breed* v *Jones*, 421 US 519 (1975).

The double jeopardy clause prevents only trial by the *same government* for the same offense. It does not keep both national and state governments from trying a person for the same act if it violates the law of each government, even if the defendant is acquitted of the charge in the courts of the first government.[38] It should be noted that, although prosecution for the same act by the national and state governments is not forbidden by the Constitution, in most instances federal policy precludes federal prosecution if there has been a previous state prosecution for the same act.[39] (Whenever federal civil rights violations are involved, the Department of Justice is more likely to reverse the presumption against federal prosecution as it did in the 1993 trial and conviction of Los Angeles police officers after they had been acquitted in a California case on charges stemming from the beating of Rodney King.)

The double jeopardy clause does not bar prosecution of Indians both in tribal courts and in federal courts, since tribal courts, even though their jurisdiction is subject to supervision by Congress, receive their jurisdiction from the tribes—independent sovereigns, at least for this purpose—and they are not arms of the federal government.[40] Nor does the clause prevent two or more states from trying a person for the same act.[41] In contrast, trial by both a state and one of its municipalities for the same act is double jeopardy:[42] municipal corporations are creatures of the state, and, constitutionally speaking, a city and its state are the same government. The same is true of the national government and a territorial government, and probably of the national government and the District of Columbia.

The double jeopardy clause does not apply to sentencing decisions with the same force that it applies to redeterminations of guilt or innocence. On the other hand, due process considerations are often brought to bear with respect to sentencing. On retrial, if the responsibility for setting a sentence is vested in a jury, a defendant may receive a more severe sentence than was received at the first trial. However, because of the due process clause, if a judge is responsible for the sentence, as is true in most jurisdictions, the judge may not ordinarily impose a harsher punishment than was given in the first trial. If the judge does so, he or she must justify such action in writing, or the reasons for doing so must be otherwise clear.[43] However, this presumption of vindictiveness does not apply when the first sentence was based on a guilty plea, which is then set aside, followed by a second trial with a second sentence.[44]

A state cannot impose the death penalty on retrial if at the first trial the jury declined to do so, nor may a judge impose the death penalty on a person after the life sentence he or she had initially received has been set aside on appeal.[45]

---

[38] *Bartkus v Illinois*, 359 US 121 (1972).

[39] *Rinaldi v United States*, 434 US 22 (1977); *Petite v United States*, 361 US 529 (1960).

[40] *United States v Wheeler*, 435 US 313 (1978).

[41] *Heath v Alabama*, 474 US 82 (1986).

[42] *Waller v Florida*, 397 US 387 (1970).

[43] *Texas v McCullough*, 475 US 134 (1986); *Bullington v Missouri*, 451 US 430 (1981); *North Carolina v Pearce*, 395 US 711 (1969).

[44] *Alabama v Smith*, 488 US 1003 (1989).

[45] *Bullington v Missouri*, 451 US 430 (1981); *Arizona v Rumsey*, 467 US 203 (1984).

The double jeopardy clause does not prohibit multiple punishments after a single trial for an act that is contrary to several statutes: "It does no more than prevent the sentencing court from prescribing greater punishment [under each statute] than the legislature intended."[46]

---

nor shall be compelled in any criminal case to be a witness against himself,

---

Originally construed to mean only that persons might not be forced to testify against themselves in criminal prosecutions, this provision has been broadened in a variety of highly significant ways. It is now included within the Fourteenth Amendment as a limitation on the states,[47] thereby permitting a person to refuse to testify before the authorities of either the national or state governments in order to avoid the risk of criminal prosecution by either government.[48]

The privilege against self-incrimination is designed, not "to enhance the reliability of the fact-finding," but to prevent the use of evidence obtained in a manner "that offends an underlying principle in the enforcement of our criminal law: that ours is an accusatorial and not an inquisitorial system."[49] The individual has no responsibility whatsoever to prove innocence; the government has the full burden to demonstrate guilt.

Persons are not entitled to refuse to answer questions merely because the answers might be embarrassing, lead to public ridicule, or incriminate others, but they are entitled to refuse to answer questions that may furnish the police with links to evidence that could result in their being prosecuted, even if the ultimate outcome would be acquittal.

It is in the area of protection for persons accused of a crime that the self-incrimination clause has had its most important and controversial extensions. The clause gives defendants the right to refuse to take the stand at their trials; they may thus refrain from answering any question, incriminating or not. The burden is on the government to prove guilt; the defendant has no responsibility to help. If defendants choose not to take the stand, nothing can prevent jurors from speculating about why they stand mute in the face of a criminal accusation. Yet a prosecutor may not comment about a defendant's refusal to testify.[50] A judge may, and must if requested to do so, use the unique power of the jury instruction to reduce speculation to a minimum by instructing the jurors that a defendant has a constitutional right not to testify and that the defendant's failure to testify should not be used to infer guilt and should not prejudice the jury against the defendant in any way.[51] If

---

[46] *Missouri* v *Hunter*, 459 US 359 (1983).

[47] *Malloy* v *Hogan*, 378 US 1 (1964).

[48] *Murphy* v *Waterfront Commission*, 378 US 52 (1964).

[49] *Allen* v *Illinois*, 478 US 364 (1986).

[50] *Griffin* v *Illinois*, 351 US 12 (1956).

[51] *Griffin* v *California*, 380 US 609 (1965); *Bruno* v *United States*, 308 US 287 (1939); *Carter* v *Kentucky*, 450 US 288 (1981); *James* v *Kentucky*, 466 US 341 (1984).

defendants do take the stand, the prosecution may cross-examine them on all of their testimony, even including their failure to respond to police accusations and questions before their arrest.

Right to Testify

The privilege against self-incrimination, although protecting persons only from criminal prosecution, may be invoked to keep persons from being compelled to answer incriminating questions put by any government agency, for example, the Federal Trade Commission, if such answers could lead to criminal proceedings against that person. Furthermore, it provides some protection from complying with certain laws—specifically aimed tax laws, for example—when compliance would expose a person to a "real and appreciable risk" of self-incrimination by furnishing evidence of illegal activities. For instance, professional gamblers cannot be made to pay a special excise tax on receipts from professional gambling if doing so would provide evidence of their illegal activity.[52] On the other hand, the self-incrimination clause does not prevent a state from requiring drivers involved in accidents to stop and notify the owner or person in charge of the property damaged of their name and address, since such a statute is more general and is not directly aimed at uncovering illegal action.[53]

The clause does not protect against future transgressions of the law; hence, Congress may require persons who sell or give certain kinds of firearms to file with federal authorities the names, addresses, and fingerprints of the transferees. The information provided cannot be used as evidence in a criminal proceeding for a prior or concurrent violation, but failure to file the information may be made a crime, such as the possession of an unregistered weapon.[54]

Nor does this clause preclude Congress from requiring persons in charge of offshore facilities to report any discharge of oil into navigable waters and to pay a penalty for the discharge. Such action may also be a criminal offense, but since the penalty imposed is civil, it does not trigger the protections afforded by the Constitution to a criminal defendant.[55] (The statute provides some limited immunity in that the fact of notification of oil discharge cannot be used against the reporting person as evidence of other crimes.)

The privilege does not prevent the use of admissions made to examining psychiatrists in proceedings designed to determine whether persons are "sexually dangerous" and should be committed to institutions for treatment. This is true even though the commitment proceedings—in this particular instance, in Illinois—are triggered only after the state has brought criminal charges and even though confinement is in a maximum security institution run by the Illinois Department of

---

[52] *Marchetti* v *United States*, 390 US 39 (1968); *Haynes* v *United States*, 390 US 85 (1968); *Leary* v *United States*, 395 US 6 (1969).

[53] *California* v *Byers*, 402 US 424 (1971).

[54] *United States* v *Freed*, 401 US 601 (1971).

[55] *United States* v *Ward*, 448 US 242 (1980).

Corrections. That the purpose is to treat rather than to punish did not persuade a skeptical minority of four justices that this was a civil and not a criminal proceeding.[56] However, a defendant's statements to a psychiatrist may not be used in sentencing proceedings unless the defendant has been properly warned.[57]

The self-incrimination clause provides some protection for public employees. They may not be fired merely for invoking the clause when questioned by their superiors. However, they may be dismissed if they refuse to answer questions directly relating to the performance of their official duties, provided they are not required to relinquish their constitutional immunity; nor may such compelled evidence be used against them in subsequent criminal prosecutions. Similarly, unless they are given immunity, contractors may not be denied the right to do future business with a state merely because they have refused to testify before a grand jury about past contracts.[58]

The Supreme Court quickly disposed of the claim that the Solomon Amendment compels persons to testify against themselves. This provision requires men applying for federal student financial assistance to furnish proof that they had registered with the selective service system. It was argued that men who had not registered would be compelled to testify if they applied for such aid. Chief Justice Burger wrote for the Court, "a person who has not registered clearly is under no compulsion to seek financial aid."[59] Justices Marshall and Brennan, who dissented, felt that the problem was not that simple. Wrote Justice Marshall, "If appellees assert their Fifth Amendment privilege by their silence, they are penalized for exercising a constitutional right by the withholding of education aid. If they succumb to the economic coercion either by registering, or by registering but claiming the privilege as to particular disclosures, they have incriminated themselves."[60]

The protection against self-incrimination extends only to incriminating testimonial evidence, not to protect a suspect from being compelled by the state to produce "real or physical evidence."[61] "In order to be testimonial, an accused's communication must itself, explicitly or implicitly, relate a factual assertion or disclose information."[62] One cannot claim the right in order to refuse to submit handwriting samples, to give voice samples, to be fingerprinted, to appear in a police lineup, to submit to a breath test, or even to give a blood sample. Moreover, the mere fact that one refused to give fingerprints or submit to a breath test or give blood samples may be used as incriminating evidence in court.[63] Nor may the right of refusal to self-incrimination be used by a parent under the court's supervision to avoid production of an abused child in response to a court order to do so.[64]

---

[56] *Allen v Illinois*, 478 US 364 (1986).

[57] *Estelle v Smith*, 451 US 454 (1981).

[58] *Garrity v New Jersey*, 385 US 493 (1967); *Spevack v Klein*, 385 US 511 (1967); *Gardner v Broderick*, 392 US 273 (1968); *Sanitation Men v Sanitation Comm.*, 392 US 281 (1968); *Lefkowitz v Turley*, 414 US 70 (1973).

[59] *Selective Service System v Minnesota Public Service Research Group*, 468 US 841 (1984).

[60] Ibid.

[61] *Pennsylvania v Munitz*, 496 US 582 (1990).

[62] Ibid., quoting *Doe v United States*, 487 US 201 (1988).

[63] *Schmerber v California*, 384 US 757 (1966); *South Dakota v Neville*, 459 US 553 (1983).

[64] *Baltimore Soc. Serv. v Bouknight*, 493 US 549 (1990).

The self-incrimination clause, at least for the moment, also protects against subpoenas of one's personal books and papers in one's own possession. The important conditions are that the material be personal and in one's possession. Tax records in the hands of one's accountant are not protected, for example, nor are books or papers that one might have as a union officer or that belong to a corporation of which one is an officer or that belong to a partnership, nor are the papers of a one-person business firm.[65] However, in the last example the act of producing incriminating documents may be protected, since the mere act of producing them may amount to testifying against oneself. But even this minimal protection for business records should not be read too generously. The Supreme Court, although not there yet, appears to be moving toward Justice O'Connor's position "that the Fifth Amendment provides absolutely no protection for the contents of private papers of any kind."[66]

"When a person assumes control over items that are the legitimate object of the government's non-criminal regulatory powers, the ability to invoke the privilege is reduced."[67] "The Fifth Amendment privilege may not be invoked to resist compliance with a regulatory regime construed to effect the State's public purpose unrelated to the enforcement of its criminal laws."[68] Thus, to take possession of papers that the government requires be kept, or a child that the state has appropriately decided is subject to the state's regulatory interests, one assumes the obligation to produce the records or the child over whom one has custody.

What about the right to testify? The Constitution does not explictly provide for such a right and it was not one known to the common law. However, "The right to testify on one's own behalf in a criminal proceeding is made explicit by federal statute, and, we [the Supreme Court] have said, it is also a right implicit in the Constitution."[69]

A defendant's right to testify does not, however, include a right to commit perjury.[70] Thus the right is not compromised by a United States Sentencing Guideline that a court may "enhance" the punishment of a person who the court finds committed perjury at trial so long as the court makes a specific finding that the accused did commit perjury.

Plea Bargaining

Although governments cannot compel persons to incriminate themselves, most cases are disposed of by guilty pleas. Increasingly, such pleas result from bargaining in which prosecutors agree to drop more serious charges in return for defendants' guilty pleas to lesser ones. It was not until 1971 that the

---

[65] *Couch v United States,* 409 US 322 (1973).

[66] Concurring *in United States v Doe,* 465 US 605 (1984).

[67] *Baltimore Soc. Serv. v Bouknight,* 493 US 549 (1990).

[68] Ibid.

[69] *Rock v Arkansas,* 483 US 44 (1987); *Nix v Whiteside,* 475 US 157 (1986).

[70] *United States v Dunnigan,* 122 L Ed 2d 445 (1993).

Supreme Court, in *Santobello v New York,* dispelled any "lingering doubts about the legitimacy of the practice...and...plea bargaining was no longer shrouded in secrecy and deliberately concealed."[71] A year earlier, in *Brady v United States,* the Court had listed the arguments for plea bargaining: "For a defendant who sees slight possibility of acquittal, the advantages of pleading guilty and limiting the probable penalty are obvious.... For the State there are also advantages—the more promptly imposed punishment after an admission of guilt may more effectively attain the objectives of punishment; and with the avoidance of trial, scarce judicial and prosecutorial resources are conserved for those cases in which there is a substantial issue of the defendant's guilt or in which there is substantial doubt that the State can sustain its burden of proof. It is this mutuality of advantage that perhaps explains the fact that at present well over three-fourths of the criminal convictions in this country rest on pleas of guilty."[72] The Court has upheld prosecutors' actions carrying out a threat, made during plea negotiations, to reindict on more serious charges, and reindicting a defendant for these charges when the defendant refused to plead guilty to lesser ones.[73]

Since *Santobello,* the Court has established ground rules for plea bargaining that ensure that the guilty plea is knowingly made and the prosecutor's promise is upheld. (A prosecutor may withdraw an offer and then the defendant has a right to withdraw a guilty plea.) Counsel must be present during plea negotiations, and a record must be made to show that the plea was knowingly and voluntarily made with a full understanding of its consequences.[74]

Granting Immunity

If a government grants immunity from prosecution as broad as the protection provided by the self-incrimination clause, then a witness may be compelled to respond under pain of fine or imprisonment. Often the government would rather have the evidence than prosecute, and for many decades Congress authorized the granting of "transactional immunity," meaning that a person who was denied the right to claim self-incrimination and was compelled to testify could not be prosecuted for any transactions mentioned in the compelled testimony.

In 1970 Congress restricted the immunity. No longer does it grant immunity for any crimes mentioned. The immunity conferred only denies the government the right to use any information derived directly or indirectly from the compelled testimony. The Court has said this "use and derivative use immunity" is coextensive with the Fifth Amendment requirement and that, therefore, persons given "use and derivative use immunity" may not claim the privilege to refuse to answer incriminating questions. However, if they are subsequently prosecuted, the government has to prove that the evidence it proposes to use was derived from legitimate sources wholly independent of the compelled testimony.

[71] Quoted in *Blackledge v Allison,* 431 US 63 (1977); *Bordenkircher v Hayes,* 434 US 357 (1978).
[72] *Brady v United States,* 397 US 742 (1970).
[73] *Bordenkircher v Hayes,* 434 US 357 (1978); *United States v Goodwin,* 457 US 368 (1982).
[74] *Mabry v Johnson,* 467 US 504 (1984).

Any testimony given under immunity, however, may be used in a prosecution for perjury. It may also be used in most civil suits.[75] Persons previously granted immunity from criminal prosecution may claim the Fifth Amendment right not to respond to incriminating questions in a civil deposition lest that testimony be used against them in a criminal prosecution.[76]

The *Miranda* Warning and Custodial Interrogations

Traditionally, the right to refuse to incriminate oneself applied only at the time of formal trial. But what good was this right, or the right to assistance of counsel, or the presumption of innocence, if long before the accused was brought before a judge he or she was detained and, without the help of an attorney, forced to prove innocence or confess to the police? Do not such procedures reduce the courtroom proceedings to a mere formality?

In the 1930s the Supreme Court began to move against these "third degree" tactics. At first it used the more general due process standards to reverse convictions obtained by using evidence secured by torture, by prolonged psychological coercion, or by involuntary confession. It acted not so much because these practices amount to self-incrimination as because such brutal procedures and the use of coerced confessions, whether true or false, offend constitutional principles.[77] "The use against a defendant of his involuntary statement is a denial of due process of law, 'even though there is ample evidence aside from the confession to support the conviction.'"[78]

In 1966, in *Miranda* v *Arizona*, the Supreme Court abandoned case-by-case determination of whether police interrogation had gone too far. It brought the self-incrimination clause into play.[79] The Court announced that, henceforth, no conviction could stand if evidence introduced at the trial, even though voluntarily given, had been obtained by the police as a result of "custodial interrogation" unless suspects had been (1) notified that they are free to remain silent; (2) warned that what they say may be used against them in court; (3) told they have a right to have their attorneys present during the questioning; (4) informed that if they cannot afford to hire their own lawyers, attorneys will be provided for them; and (5) permitted at any stage of the police interrogation to terminate it. The Miranda warning does not have to be given literally word by word. The requirement is that the warnings reasonably convey to suspects their *Miranda* rights.[80] Failure to comply with the *Miranda* requirements will lead to reversal of a conviction, even if other independent evidence would have been sufficient to establish guilt.

Custodial interrogation includes any questioning by police, including Internal Revenue Service agents, when the investigators have fixed on the per-

---

[75] *United States* v *Apfelbaum,* 445 US 115 (1980).

[76] *Pillsbury* v *Conboy,* 459 US 248 (1983).

[77] *Haynes* v *Washington,* 373 US 503 (1963); *Lego* v *Twomey,* 404 US 477 (1972).

[78] *Mincey* v *Arizona,* 437 US 385 (1978).

[79] *Miranda* v *Arizona,* 384 US 436 (1966).

[80] *Duckworth* v *Eagan,* 492 US 195 (1989).

son questioned for possible criminal prosecution.[81] Custodial interrogations do not depend on whether persons are in custody in a police station or have been placed under formal arrest. They cover all investigations in which persons are deprived of freedom of action "to a degree associated with a formal arrest."[82]

Miranda warnings are not required, however, for undercover agents, including questioning by such agents of persons who are in jail on charges *unrelated* to those for which the agent is trying to get information.[83] Nor are such warnings required for police to talk with suspects, even in police stations, if suspects have voluntarily gone to the station, are free to go whenever they wish, and are under no legal restraint.[84] Even if suspects are under restraint, a *Miranda* warning is not necessary to ask "routine booking questions" in order to get the biographical material such as name, address, height, weight, eye color, date of birth, and current age to complete booking or pretrial services.[85] Nor are *Miranda* warnings required at routine traffic stops.[86] Nor are such warnings required when a probation officer questions a probationer about an earlier crime or when a person has been called to appear before a grand jury.[87]

The Supreme Court has also created a "public safety" exception to the *Miranda* requirement. In *New York* v *Quarles* the Court was faced with the following facts: Officers were patrolling in Queens, New York, when a young woman approached the car and told them that she had just been raped by a man who had then gone into an A & P market and that he was carrying a gun. The officers drove the woman to the store, saw the suspect, frisked him, and discovered he was wearing an empty shoulder holster. After handcuffing him, one officer asked him where the gun was and the suspect said, "The gun is over there," and pointed to some empty cartons. The officer retrieved a loaded .38-caliber revolver, formally placed the defendant under arrest, and then read him his *Miranda* rights. The lower courts held that neither the gun nor the defendant's statement "The gun is over there" could be introduced at his trial, since that evidence had been obtained before the *Miranda* warning had been given. The Supreme Court agreed that prior decisions would have required such a result, but speaking through Justice Rehnquist, concluded, "There is a 'public safety exception' to the requirement. . . .We do not believe that the doctrinal underpinnings of *Miranda* require that it be applied in all its rigor to a situation in which police officers ask questions reasonably prompted by a concern for the public safety."[88] The Court did acknowledge that the exception lessened the clarity of the *Miranda* rule.

---

[81] *Berkemer* v *McCarty*, 468 US 420 (1984); *Mathis* v *United States*, 391 US 1 (1968); *Orozco* v *Texas*, 394 US 324 (1969).

[82] *California* v *Beheler*, 463 US 1121 (1983).

[83] *Illinois* v *Perkins*, 110 L Ed 2d 243 (1990).

[84] *Oregon* v *Mathiason*, 429 US 492 (1977); *California* v *Beheler*, 463 US 1121 (1983).

[85] *Pennsylvania* v *Muniz*, 496 US582 (1990).

[86] *Berkemer* v *McCarty*, 468 US 420 (1984); *Pennsylvania* v *Bruder*, 488 US 9 (1988).

[87] *Minnesota* v *Murphy*, 465 US 420 (1984).

[88] *New York* v *Quarles*, 467 US 649 (1984).

After a *Miranda* warning has been given and a suspect has requested that an attorney be present, police are in danger of violating the suspect's rights "even if what they say to a suspect is not punctuated by a question mark." If suspects answer questions in the absence of attorneys, the prosecution must be prepared to demonstrate that the suspects knowingly and intelligently waived their rights to remain silent and to have their own lawyer present. In *Edwards v Arizona,* the Court established a rule that once a suspect asks to have an attorney present, no waiver of that right, however voluntary, can be valid if made in response to further police questioning.[89] "Once a suspect has invoked the right to counsel, any subsequent conversation must be initiated by him."[90] "When counsel is requested, interrogation must cease, and officials may not reinitiate interrogation without counsel present, whether or not the accused has consulted with his attorney."[91] Of course, not all conversation between the police and the accused must cease. Yet, if in such conversations the suspect makes incriminating statements away from counsel, the statements may not be introduced in court against the suspect unless they clearly were not provoked by the police, directly or indirectly. There continues, however, to be some confusion among the courts as to determining how precise must be the request for the assistance of counsel.[92]

The *Edwards* rule, although dogmatically stated, has not been rigorously applied. Even when a suspect has asked for an attorney, the Court has regularly found conditions that make the *Edwards* rule inapplicable, and the questioning has been allowed. In a particularly important case reducing police obligations under *Miranda,* the Court concluded that there had been no violation of *Miranda* in the use of a confession obtained by police after they failed to inform a suspect that his counsel had tried to communicate with him and and he had been assured that there would be no further questioning until the next day.[93] More recently, the Court said that a defendant's appearance with a lawyer at a court hearing for one offense is not to be considered a *Miranda* request for a lawyer on other offenses about which the defendant was questioned, so that his confession about the latter offense could be used.[94]

The *Miranda* doctrine applies in a modified form to state-initiated psychiatric examinations to determine if an accused is mentally competent to stand trial. The accused is not entitled to have an attorney present during the examination. However, the state may not use evidence derived from such an examination to determine guilt or severity of the sentence unless it gave the suspect a *Miranda* warning.[95]

---

[89] *Edwards v Arizona,* 451 US 477 (1981); *Rhode Island v Innis,* 446 US 291 (1980); *Michigan v Jackson,* 475 US 625 (1986).

[90] *Solem v Stumes,* 465 US 638 (1984).

[91] *Minnick v Mississippi,* 112 L Ed 2d 489 (1990).

[92] *Muller v Virginia,* April 19, 1993.

[93] *Moran v Burbine,* 475 US 412 (1986).

[94] *McNeil v Wisconsin,* 115 L Ed 2d 158 (1991).

[95] *Estelle v Smith,* 451 US 454 (1981).

Miranda prohibitions apply primarily to evidence relating to issues of guilt or innocence. Thus, a prosecutor, to challenge a defendant's credibility, may introduce evidence obtained in violation of the *Miranda* ruling to contradict statements a defendant volunteers from the witness stand. Otherwise, a defendant might give perjured testimony free from the risk of confrontation by prior inconsistent utterances. The exception may put pressure on defendants to refrain from taking the stand in their own defense, since their testimony may open the way for the prosecution to use evidence that could not otherwise be introduced.[96]

nor be deprived of life, liberty, or property, without due process of law;

Due Process Clauses

A parallel clause is found in the Fourteenth Amendment as a limitation on the states. The due process clauses of the Fifth and Fourteenth Amendments, along with their companion, the equal protection clause of the Fourteenth, have resulted in more cases and controversies than any others in the Constitution. The Fifth Amendment contains no equal protection clause to parallel the Fourteenth Amendment, but the Supreme Court in *Bolling* v *Sharpe* has interpreted the due process clause of the Fifth Amendment to limit the national government in precisely the same way that the equal protection clause of the Fourteenth Amendment limits the state governments.[97] Since then the Court has referred to this as "the implied equal protection guarantee of the Due Process Clause."[98]

Due process has many components, which the Supreme Court has developed primarily through cases testing actions taken by state or by local governments and which are challenged under the Fourteenth Amendment's language, "nor shall any State deprive any person of life, liberty, or property, without due process of law." But due process as applied to the national government because of the Fifth Amendment is the same as the due process applied to state and local governments by the Fourteenth Amendment, so we will discuss both clauses here.

Despite the number of cases applying and interpreting the two due process clauses, it is impossible to give due process any exact, final, and completely satisfactory explanation. Indeed, the Supreme Court itself has refused to give due process a precise definition, stating that it prefers to rely on "the gradual process of judicial inclusion and exclusion."[99]

---

[96] *Harris* v *New York*, 401 US 222 (1971).

[97] *Bolling* v *Sharpe*, 347 US 497 (1954).

[98] *Federal Communications Commission* v *Beach Communication, Inc.*, 124 L Ed 2d 211 (1993).

[99] *Davidson* v *New Orleans*, 96 US 97 (1878).

How to determine what due process means continues to be one of the major points of contention among sitting justices, as it has divided their predecessors. Justice Scalia, for example, takes every opportunity to press his contention that due process means, and is limited to meaning, those processes known to the English Common Law at the time of our Independence as modified by the consensus of American experience as reflected in the practices of our legislatures and courts during the last two hundred years. He is joined in these views by Chief Justice Rehnquist and Justice Kennedy. On the other side, former Justice Brennan led those justices who believe that due process is more than historical tradition: they argue that judges have a responsibility to make an independent enquiry to determine what is fair and just. Justices O'Connor and Souter have also refused to go along with the Scalia-Kennedy-White and apparently Thomas point of view: Justice O'Connor, joined by Justice Souter, "against the historical status quo," would "allow some weight to be given countervailing considerations of fairness in operation."[100]

This battle over how to interpret the meaning of due process breaks out in many forms and over many issues. Recently, the question was a rather simple one: whether a California court had jurisdiction over a New Jersey man when he came to California on business and to visit his children and was served a summons from a California court obtained by his former wife. All the justices agreed that California had jurisdiction, but they could not agree why.[101] The Chief Justice and Justices Kennedy and Scalia argued that the California court had jurisdiction because, under the continuing traditions of our legal system, physical presence in a state has always been thought to confer jurisdiction: everybody who goes into a state should know that he or she will be subject to the jurisdiction of the courts of that state. Justices Brennan, Marshall, Blackmun, and O'Connor agreed that California had jurisdiction. They argued, however, that this is so not just because of historical tradition but because "all rules, even ancient ones must satisfy contemporary notions of due process," and their enquiry persuaded them that for California to claim such jurisdiction is fair. Justice White went along with the argument of Justice Scalia that in this case the due process had been served because of the traditional rule that physical presence in a state confers jurisdiction, but he said that he could be persuaded otherwise if in a particular case the application of this traditional rule to a defendant would be "so arbitrary and lacking in common sense as not to be due process." Justice Stevens concurred with no other justice about how to determine due process, concluding that under all approaches in this case there had been no denial of due process: "For me," he wrote, "it is sufficient to note that the historical evidence and consensus identified by Justice Scalia, the consideration of fairness identified by Justice Brennan, and the common sense displayed by Justice White, all combine to demonstrate that this is an easy case."

---

[100] *Medina* v *California*, 120 L Ed 2d 353 (1992).
[101] *Burnham* v *Superior Court*, 495 US 604 (1990).

It should be noted that this debate among the justices on how to decide what is and what is not due process is not just an academic one. It really is a debate about the proper role of judges with very real consequences. The Scalia school contends that judges should be historians with limited discretion: judges should try to find out what the words of the Constitution mean and what are the prevailing practices of Americans and that what judges think is fair and just is beside the point. The Brennan school contends that judges should be philosophers and try to find out what is just and that what judges think is fair and just is the point.

To Whom Do the Due Process Clauses Apply? What Is State Action?

The due process clause restricts the actions of governments, not of private individuals. "[N]othing in the language of the Due Process clause ... requires the State to protect the life, liberty, and property of its citizens against invasion by private actors," wrote Chief Justice Rehnquist for the Court when it held that county officials had not deprived a child of his liberty without due process when they failed to stop his father from beating him. "Its purpose," as the Chief Justice has more recently reminded us, "was to protect the people from the State, not to ensure that the State protected them from each other. The Framers were content to leave the extent of governmental obligation in the latter area to the democratic political process."[102]

A question that for decades was significant only for the application of the equal protection clause (see page 350) has become an issue in the application of the due process clauses; namely, when is an action an action of the state and when is it merely private action? (When we get to the Fourteenth Amendment equal protection clause we will discuss at greater length the factors that caused the Court to decide that state action is involved.) In part, the issue of what is and what is not state action comes about because of the more expansive application of the protections of the due process clauses to more and more arenas. In part, the question has become more important because of the Supreme Court's liberal construction of 42 USC 1983 permitting citizens to bring suits for damages against those who act "under color of any statute, ordinance, regulation, custom, or usage of any State to deprive them of any rights, privileges, or immunities secured by the Constitution and laws."

An example of the debate over what is state action arising out of the due process clause flowed from a decision by a private nursing home, after a utilization review, required by federal regulations, to transfer some Medicaid patients, whose expenses were paid by federal and state funds, to a facility providing lower levels of care. The patients argued they had been denied due process because they had not been given a hearing. The Supreme Court decided the due process clause did not apply. True, the nursing home was extensively

---

[102] *De Shaney v Winnegago County Department of Social Services,* 489 US 189 (1989); *Burnham v Superior Court,* 495 US 604 (1990).

regulated by the state—the state paid the expenses—but the decision about the appropriate level of care turned on medical judgments made by private parties, and the nursing home was not performing a function that has traditionally been the exclusive prerogative of the state.[103] When Jerry Tarkanian, alias Tark the Shark, then the basketball coach of the University of Nevada, Las Vegas, sued the NCAA for violating his rights by ordering the university to dismiss him as coach, the Supreme Court ruled that the action of the NCAA was not state action but that of a private organization of universities.[104]

What Life, Liberty, and Property Interests Are Protected

Before deciding whether a state has deprived somebody of due process, the Court must first decide if there is a life, liberty, or property interest involved. The Court has expanded the scope of the life, liberty, and property interests, especially liberty, protected by the due process clauses.

What is meant by life, when it begins and when it ends, was not subject to much discussion until modern times. Even these days, the Court prefers not to get into these matters directly but rather to do so as part of its interpretation of the liberty interest of individuals. For example, the Court has established what is sometimes referred to as "the right to die," as part of the liberty interest. A person does have a constitutional right, at least when he or she is terminally ill and in a vegetative state, to refuse medical treatment and to refuse to take food and water. (The right can be realistically exercised only if clearly stipulated in advance.) In Justice O'Connor's words: "[T]he liberty guaranteed by the Due Process Clause must protect, if it protects anything, an individual's deeply personal decision to reject medical treatment, including the artificial delivery of food and water."[105]

As to the liberty interests, originally, the liberty protected was only freedom from physical restraint. "Freedom from bodily restraint has always been at the core of the liberty protected by the Due Process Clause from arbitrary governmental action."[106] Nowadays liberty denotes "not merely freedom from bodily restraint but also right of the individual to contract, to engage in any of the common occupations of life, to acquire useful knowledge, to marry, to establish a home and to bring up children, to worship God according to the dictates of his own conscience, and generally to enjoy those common law privileges long recognized as essential to the orderly pursuit of happiness by free men."[107]

Until 1937 the most important part of this "new liberty" protected was "liberty of contract,"[108] that is, business liberty. Since 1937 the Supreme Court has abandoned the doctrine of "liberty" of contract, but its action did not fore-

---

[103] Blum v Yaretsky, 457 US 991 (1982).

[104] NCAA v Tarkanian, 488 US 179 (1989).

[105] Concurring in Cruzan v Director, Missouri Dept. of Health, 497 US 266 (1990).

[106] Foucha v Louisiana, 118 L Ed 2d 437 (1992).

[107] Meyer v Nebraska, 262 US 390 (1923).

[108] Lochner v New York, 198 US 45 (1905); Muller v Oregon, 208 US 424 (1908); West Coast Hotel v Parrish, 300 US 379 (1937).

shadow a return to the old narrow conception of liberty. On the contrary, the liberty of the Fifth and Fourteenth Amendments has been expanded to include the basic civil liberties. Also now included in the liberty protected by due process is the right of privacy, a largely undefined right, within which "marital privacy" has received the most protection.

Outside of constitutionally created liberty, that is, those liberty interests secured by the Constitution itself, there are some liberty interests the government—national or state—creates that are also entitled to due process protection. The fact that certain state-created liberty interests have been found to be entitled to due process protection, while others have not, is not the result "of the court's judgement as to which interests are more significant than others," but, "stated simply a State creates a protected liberty interest by placing substantive limitations on official discretion" and "makes those limits mandatory."[109]

For example, the specific liberty and property interests to which prisoners are entitled depended in large part on what liberty and property expectations a state provides by its laws. When a state takes a person into custody, as in a mental institution or a jail, a state then acquires a due process obligation to assume some responsibility for safety and general well being. There are, however, some liberty interests protected by the Constitution itself.[110] Prisoners, for example, must be provided reasonable opportunities to exercise their religious freedoms; to get married; to petition the government; and they must not be subject to cruel and unusual punishments.[111]

How one determines if a particular liberty interest is constitutionally protected is an ongoing debate. For example, Justice Scalia insists that, when deciding whether there is a liberty interest at stake, judges are bound by our specific historical tradition. The point in contention was whether a man who claimed to be the father of a child had a constitutionally protected liberty interest—a parental right—against a state law that presumes that the father of a child is the husband of the mother at the time of the child's birth. Argued Justice Scalia, for a plurality of the Court, "we are not aware of a single case, old or new," or a single state law that in fact has recognized substantive parental rights of "the natural father of a child conceived within and born into an extant marital union that wishes to embrace the child." "This is not," wrote Justice Scalia, "the stuff of which fundamental rights qualifying as liberty interests are made."[112] Justice Brennan retorted, "In construing the Fourteenth Amendment to offer shelter only to those interests specifically protected by historical practice . . . the plurality ignores the kind of society in which our Constitution exists. . . . The document that the plurality construes today is unfamiliar to me. It is not the living charter that I have taken to be our Constitution; it is instead a stagnant, archaic, hidebound document steeped in the prejudices and superstitions of a time long past."[113]

---

[109] *Kentucky v Thompson,* 490 US 454 (1989).
[110] *Turner v Safley,* 482 US 78 (1987); *Washington v Harper,* 494 US 210 (1990).
[111] *Washington v Harper,* 494 US 210 (1990).
[112] *Michael H. v Gerald D.,* 491 US 110 (1989).
[113] Ibid.

Property rights protected by due process have also been expanded. At one time the property protected by the Constitution was primarily physical things. Today, property includes a whole bundle of rights. Welfare, housing, education, employment, professional licenses, and so on are now more and more matters of entitlement, and to deprive someone of them calls into play some form of due process protection. However, unlike the liberty protected by the due process clause, which primarily comes from the Constitution itself, property interests are not created by the due process clause itself. Rather, the clause extends various *procedural* safeguards to property interests created by other parts of the Constitution or, more commonly, by state law.[114]

These expansive definitions of liberty and property have blurred the distinction between a privilege—something given by the government as a matter of grace—and a right—something to which one is entitled.[115] Yet despite these expansive interpretations "not every grievous . . . loss invokes [the] protections of the Due Process Clause."[116] "The due process clause does not transform every tort"—that is, a legal wrong—"committed by a state actor into a constitutional violation."[117] For example, a child has no Constitutional right to governmental protection against an abusive father. Nontenured faculty members at state colleges or universities have no property or liberty right in their jobs flowing from the Constitution. (The state, by its own laws and procedures, can confer property rights in teaching jobs, and if it does so, then it cannot take such rights away without due process.) True, teachers are entitled to freedom of speech, along with everybody else, and they cannot be denied that freedom without due process, but "the interest in holding a job at a state university, simpliciter, is not itself a free speech interest . . . nor one that cannot be denied without procedural due process."[118]

One has no constitutional liberty right to a government job, but one may have a legally conferred property right and if a law confers some kind of security of employment, employees may not be dismissed without appropriate due process.[119] (As noted, the First Amendment does limit the reasons for which most government employees may be dismissed.)[120] If the reasons for a dismissal are publicized, the publicity might amount to governmental imposition of a stigma on a person, which would infringe on that person's liberty and thus require some kind of due process.[121]

In a unanimous opinion, a rather rare occasion these days, the Supreme Court had no difficulty in concluding that the due process clause does not provide municipal employees with a constitutional right to be properly trained

---

[114] *Board of Regents of State Colleges v Roth*, 408 US 564 (1972) reaffirmed in *Delaware v New York*, 123 L Ed 2d 211 (1993).

[115] *Goldberg v Kelly*, 397 US 254 (1970).

[116] *Meachum v Fano*, 427 US 215 (1976); *Jago v Van Curen*, 445 US 14 (1981).

[117] *DeShaney v Winnebago Soc. Ser.*, 489 US 189 (1989).

[118] *Board of Regents v Roth*, 408 US 564 (1972).

[119] *Cleveland Board of Education v Loudermill*, 470 US 532 (1985).

[120] *Givhan v Western Line Consolidated School District*, 439 US 410 (1979); *Rankin v McPherson*, 483 US 378, 1056 (1987).

[121] *Bishop v Wood*, 426 US 341 (1976).

so that they will not be harmed during the course of their work.[122] The Court has also held that alien children have no fundamental liberty interest to be placed in the custody of private custodians rather than to be institutionalized if there is no available parent, close relative, or legal guardian.[123]

Procedural Due Process

There are two forms of due process: *procedural* and *substantive.* Procedural due process refers to how a law is applied and to whether it is being applied fairly. Substantive due process refers to whether the law itself is fair. First, we are going to talk about procedural due process, which is the older form.

Procedural due process, to paraphrase Daniel Webster's famous definition, requires a procedure that hears before it condemns, proceeds upon inquiry, and renders judgment only after [a] trial or hearing of some sort in which the essentials of justice have been preserved. Or as the Court has said more recently, "the fundamental requirement of due process is the opportunity to be heard at a meaningful time and in a meaningful manner."[124]

Procedural due process is the special preserve of lawyers and it is the area where judges are supposed to have a particular competence, unlike substantive due process, which is more clearly the domain of legislators. The issues presented by what procedural due process means, however, are so complex that judges, even those on the Supreme Court, or perhaps we should say, especially those on the Supreme Court, are not of one mind about what is required. For example, when Congress authorized the secretary of labor to order employers to reinstate immediately employees who claimed they had been discharged for refusing to operate unsafe trucks, with a hearing for the employers to follow later, the justices reached a variety of conclusions about whether such procedures provided employers with due process. Justices Marshall, Blackmun, Powell, and O'Connor said "no" because due process requires the secretary of labor, before ordering an employer to reinstate an employee, to give the employer notice of the employee's allegations, notice of the substance of the relevant supporting evidence, an opportunity to submit a written response, a chance to meet with the investigating official, and an opportunity to present statements from rebuttal witnesses. But to these justices, due process does not require that the employer be allowed to confront and cross-examine witnesses, provided a prompt postreinstatement hearing is made available. Justices Brennan and Stevens, although agreeing that Congress had not provided due process, contended that due process also requires that, in addition to the rights listed by the plurality, the employer be given a chance before being forced to reinstate employees to cross-examine witnesses and test the evidence in an

---

[122] *Collins v Harker Heights,* 117 L Ed 2d 261 (1992).
[123] *Reno v Flores,* 123 L Ed 2d 1 (1993).
[124] *Mathews v Eldridge,* 424 US 371 (1971).

adversary proceeding. On the other side, Chief Justice Rehnquist and Justices White and Scalia thought that, by providing for a postreinstatement hearing, Congress had provided employers all the due process the Constitution requires.[125]

Vagueness

Although procedural due process is primarily concerned with how executive and judicial officials apply a law, there are several ways in which a law itself may violate procedural due process. First, there is a violation if a law is too vague, for "a statute which either forbids or requires the doing of an act in terms so vague that men of common intelligence must necessarily guess at its meaning and differ as to its application" violates the first essential of due process of law.[126] Not only does a vague statute run the risk of entrapping the innocent, but it also "impermissibly delegates basic policy matters to policemen, judges, and juries...on an *ad hoc* and subjective basis, with the attendant dangers of arbitrary and discriminatory application."[127] A vague statute "furnishes a convenient tool for 'harsh and discriminatory enforcement by local prosecuting officials,'"[128] ... "confers on police a virtually unrestrained power to arrest and charge persons with a violation,"[129] and "entrust[s] lawmaking to the moment-to-moment judgment of the policeman on the beat."[130]

Examples of statutes struck down for vagueness are "a suspicious person ordinance," providing that any persons found on a street at late or unusual hours of the night without any visible or lawful business and who did not give satisfactory accounts of themselves, might be fined or imprisoned,[131] and a statute requiring persons who loitered or wandered on the streets, under circumstances that made police suspicious, to provide "credible and reliable" identification to account for their presence when asked by a police officer to do so.[132] A similar fate befell a vagrancy ordinance declaring vagrants to be a wide variety of ill-defined classes such as "rogues and vagabonds," "dissolute persons who go about begging," "common night walkers," and so on.[133] Yet another example: a Pennsylvania statute that was held void for vagueness made doctors criminally liable who, after determining that a fetus "is viable or... may be viable," failed to exercise "that degree of professional skill, care, and diligence necessary to preserve the life and health of the fetus" and to adopt the particular abortion technique "which would provide the best opportunity for the fetus to be aborted alive so long as a different technique would not be necessary in order to preserve the life or health of the mother."[134]

---

[125] *Brock v Roadway Express Co.*, 481 US 252 (1987).
[126] *Connally v General Construction Co.*, 269 US 385 (1926).
[127] *Grayned v Rockford*, 408 US 104 (1972).
[128] *Papachristou v City of Jacksonville*, 405 US 156 (1972), quoting *Thornhill v Alabama*, 310 US 88 (1940).
[129] *Lewis v City of New Orleans*, 415 US 130 (1974).
[130] *Smith v Goguen*, 415 US 566 (1974).
[131] *Palmer v City of Euclid, Ohio*, 402 US 544 (1972).
[132] *Kolender v Lawson*, 461 US 352 (1983).
[133] *Papachristou v City of Jacksonville*, 405 US 156 (1972).
[134] *Colautti v Franklin*, 439 US 379 (1979).

On the other side, the Court ruled that an ordinance requiring a business to obtain a license if it sells any items "designed or marketed for use with illegal cannabis or drugs," that is, if it is a "head-shop," was not unconstitutionally vague on its face.[135] The Court also upheld an ordinance directing the chief of police, prior to making a recommendation to the city council, to consider whether an applicant for a license to run a coin-operated amusement center has any "connection with criminal elements." The Court pointed out that, although the ordinance would be too vague to convict a person of the offense of having such a connection, and might even be too vague to support the denial of a license, the Constitution does not preclude a city from giving vague directions to officials authorized to make investigations and recommendations to the city council.[136]

When the Court upheld a punitive damage award of an Alabama jury despite a claim that the damages were excessive, Justice O'Connor in dissent objected on vagueness grounds. Under the common law, juries had full discretion to impose punitive or exemplary damages. Most states still leave juries wide discretion to set whatever damages they wish, the only check being the power of the court to set aside damages where there is evidence that the jury has been unduly influenced by "passion, prejudice, partiality, or corruption, or where it clearly evinces a mistake of the law or the facts of the case." The Supreme Court, although not as yet setting aside any such award, has warned the states that due process requires a "general concern" for reasonableness and adequate court guidance for a jury.

A second way in which a law itself may violate procedural due process is by creating an improper burden of proof. For most civil proceedings, the preponderance-of-evidence standard—the side with the most evidence wins—meets due process requirements; but, in some proceedings due process may impose a "clear and convincing" evidence standard.[137] For example, a state may not commit an individual to a mental institution unless the state can present clear and convincing evidence that the person is mentally ill and that the person requires hospitalization for his or her own welfare and protection of others. Proof beyond a reasonable doubt is not required, but proof by a preponderance of the evidence falls short of satisfying due process.[138]

For criminal trials where there must be a presumption of innocence, due process places the burden on the government to prove guilt beyond a reasonable doubt. The state must present proof of every fact necessary to constitute the crime with which a defendant is charged.[139] Instructions to a jury defining "reasonable doubt" in terms of "grave" or "substantial" uncertainty when combined with the need for "moral certainty" rather than "evidentiary certainty" allow a finding of guilt based on a degree of proof below that required by the due process clause.[140] The level of

---

[135] *Hoffman Estates v Flipside Hoffman Estates*, 455 US 489 (1982).
[136] *City of Mesquite v Aladdin's Castle*, 455 US 283 (1983).
[137] *Rivera v Minnich*, 483 US 574 (1987).
[138] *Addington v Texas*, 323 US 418 (1979); *Foucha v Louisiana*, 118 L Ed 2d 437 (1992).
[139] *In re Winship*, 397 US 358 (1970); *Estelle v Williams*, 425 US 501 (1976); *Taylor v Kentucky*, 436 US 478 (1978); *Kentucky v Whorton*, 441 US 786 (1979); *Francis v Franklin*, 471 US 307 (1985).
[140] *Cage v Louisiana*, 498 US 39 (1990).

proof to demonstrate delinquency must be the same as that required in a criminal trial—namely, proof beyond any reasonable doubt—but, the juvenile is not entitled to have the decision made by a jury.[141]

The burden of proof cannot be be shifted by a law that creates a presumption of criminal guilt, unless the fact the law infers "is more likely than not... to flow from the fact proved."[142] For example, the Court has declared unconstitutional laws creating the presumption that possessors of marijuana or cocaine obtained the drugs through illegal importation.[143] The constitutionality of such a presumption in the case of heroin has been sustained, since little, if any, heroin is made in this country, and virtually all heroin is illegally imported and anyone convicted of its possession has more likely than not obtained it illegally.[144]

Although the due process clause prevents the criminal prosecution of a person who is not competent to stand trial, it does not forbid a state to require a defendant who alleges incompetence to stand trial to bear the burden of proving incompetence by a preponderance of the evidence.[145]

Denial of a Hearing

A third way a law can violate procedural due process is if it takes away a liberty or property interest without a hearing. Here are just a few examples of laws declared unconstitutional on such grounds: a law providing for automatic revocation of a driver's license after an accident;[146] a law permitting the listing in liquor stores of the names of persons who have engaged in "excessive drinking" and forbidding sales of liquor to such persons, with no provisions for those whose names were listed to be first notified and given a hearing;[147] and a law disqualifying unwed fathers as fit parents without giving such fathers a hearing to determine their fitness.[148]

There are a few exceptions to the requirement for a pre-deprivation hearing. In emergency situations, when protection of public health and safety is paramount, summary administrative actions may be taken, provided there is provision for a post-deprivation hearing or a law suit tort remedy available. For example, an unsafe mine may be closed or a passport revoked with only a statement of reasons and an opportunity for a prompt post-revocation hearing.[149] The national government may seize property being brought illegally into the country and follow with a hearing within a reasonable time. The Court recently held that an eighteen-month delay in filing civil proceedings for forfeiture of currency, which had been seized by customs officials because it had been improperly listed on a form, was not a denial of due process.[150]

---

[141] *In re Winship*, 397 US 358 (1970).

[142] *Ulster County Court v Allen*, 442 US 140 (1979).

[143] *Leary v United States*, 395 US 6 (1969).

[144] *Turner v United States*, 396 US 398 (1970).

[145] *Medina v California*, 120 L Ed 2d 353 (1992).

[146] *Bell v Burson*, 402 US 535 (1971).

[147] *Wisconsin v Constantineau*, 400 US 433 (1971).

[148] *Stanley v Illinois*, 405 US 645 (1972).

[149] *Hodel v Virginia Surface Min. & Recl. Assn.*, 452 US 264 (1981); *Haig v Agee*, 453 US 280 (1981).

[150] *United States v Eight Thousand Eight Hundred and Fifty Dollars*, 461 US 555 (1983).

What Process Is Due?

In a *courtroom*, due process requires the full panoply of rights outlined in the Constitution. Moreover, courtroom due process goes beyond the specific provisions of the Bill of Rights. A court could follow each particular provision of the Bill of Rights and still deny due process if, for example, the judge, in manner or mood, showed bias against the defendant or if the judge had a financial interest in the outcome of the trial. In other words, due process requires fundamental fairness—a fair and impartial trial.[151] Thus, it is impossible to provide a fair trial for a person not mentally competent to understand the nature of the proceedings or not able to consult with counsel or to assist in the preparation of a defense.[152] Similarly, a state may not compel a defendant to take medication in order to make the defendant competent to stand trial without some showing of the necessity for such medication. The Court is not clear whether a state must first find that the medication is medically appropriate and, considering less intrusive alternatives, essential for the sake of the defendant's own safety or the safety of others or whether a state may be able to justify medically appropriate involuntary treatment with the drug if it could establish it could not obtain an adjudication of guilt or innocence by using less intrusive means.[153]

In juvenile court procedures, not considered criminal trials, a juvenile cannot be declared delinquent without a hearing in which the juvenile is given the right to confront hostile witnesses and to cross-examine them, to present oral evidence, and to be represented by counsel.

Noncriminal Proceedings

Due process does not necessarily require that criminal procedures be used in *noncriminal proceedings*. The question in each instance is what must be done to ensure fundamental fairness. It is hard to generalize because of the wide variety of governmental proceedings involved. Among the many situations in which procedural due process is required are disbarment proceedings; determinations of eligibility for welfare payments; parole and probation revocation hearings; legislative contempt proceedings; hearings before congressional committees and administrative tribunals; disciplinary proceedings in state universities, colleges, and public schools; and proceedings for confinement in mental institutions.[154]

In deciding what due process requires in noncourtroom proceedings, the Court asks three questions, outlined in its decision in *Mathews* v *Eldridge*. (1) What are the private interests at stake? (2) What is the government's interest? (3) What are the risks the procedures used will lead to an erroneous decision?[155]

---

[151] *Ward* v *Village of Monroeville*, 409 US 57 (1972).

[152] *Drope* v *Missouri*, 420 US 162 (1975).

[153] *Riggins* v *Nevada*, 118 L Ed 2d 479 (1992).

[154] *Groppi* v *Leslie*, 404 US 496 (1972); *Goldberg* v *Kelly*, 397 US 254 (1970); In re *Gault*, 387 US 1 (1967); *Thorpe* v *Housing Authority*, 393 US 268 (1969).

[155] *Mathews* v *Eldridge*, 424 US 319 (1976).

Due process requires, at a minimum, adequate notice and an opportunity to be heard. Hearings do not have to be formal or adversary in nature. To illustrate: unless the student's presence poses a continuing danger to persons or property, a student is entitled to a notice and to an informal hearing before being suspended from a public school for disciplinary reasons, but the informal hearing perhaps could be only a brief talk with the principal.[156] For long-term disciplinary expulsion the procedures must be a little more formal. (Dismissal from a state college or university for academic reasons does not require any kind of hearing.)[157] A municipally owned utility, before terminating service for failure to pay bills, must notify customers of procedures that permit them to protest the proposed termination.[158] Apparently the federal government must provide some kind of hearing for persons whose claims under the Medicare program have been turned down, but the hearing does not have to be before a legally trained officer.[159] A state does not have to provide a judicial hearing before treating a prisoner with antipsychotic drugs: a hearing before a committee consisting of a psychiatrist, a psychologist, and another prison official will do.[160]

Here are additional examples of how much due process is due: before children may be taken by the government from the custody of natural parents, those parents must be given an opportunity to be heard in a rather formal proceeding, and the state is required to support by "clear and convincing proof" its allegations that the children's welfare requires such an action.[161] Parents do not, however, have an automatic right to court-appointed counsel in such a proceeding: the trial judge must make a decision in each instance of whether or not due process requires the assistance of counsel. In fact, the Court has suggested that due process probably requires the automatic appointment of counsel for indigents in noncriminal proceedings only in situations in which they "may be deprived of physical liberty."[162]

Procedures for admissions to mental institutions have caused considerable litigation. Commitment to a mental hospital "entails a massive curtailment of liberty" and requires due process protection. The nature and duration of the commitment must bear some reasonable relation to the purposes of the commitment, and it requires either valid consent or commitment by a carefully prescribed involuntary placement hearing.[163] Children are entitled to due process before they can be placed by their parents in mental institutions, but due process does not require a formal adversarial hearing, merely a neutral medical determination by a doctor or other professional.[164] Nor is there a

---

[156] *Goss v Lopez,* 419 US 565 (1975).

[157] *Board of Curators, University of Missouri v Horowitz,* 435 US 78 (1978).

[158] *Memphis Light, Gas & Water Division v Craft,* 436 US 1 (1978).

[159] *Schweiker v McClure,* 465 US 188 (1982).

[160] *Washington v Harper,* 494 US 210 (1990).

[161] *Santosky v Kramer,* 455 US 745 (1982).

[162] *Lassiter v Department of Social Services,* 452 US 18 (1981).

[163] *Vitek v Jones,* 445 US 480 (1980); *Addington v Texas,* 441 US 418 (1979); *Zinermon v Burch,* 1494 US 113 (1990).

[164] *Parham v JR,* 442 584 (1979).

denial of due process if a state allows parents and other close relatives of a mentally retarded person to participate in commitment hearings.[165]

Prisoners, even though not entitled to due process before being transferred from one prison to another, are entitled to such protection before being taken from prison and placed in a mental hospital, even if the placement is for a period within the period of their sentence. Moreover, before being transferred to a mental hospital, a prisoner must be given written notice, a hearing before an independent decision maker, an opportunity to present evidence and cross-examine witnesses, and a written statement of the decision.[166] And persons held in a mental institution as a result of being acquitted based on an insanity plea may not be kept in such an institution after it is determined that they are no longer mentally ill even if state authorities believe that such a person might be dangerous.[167]

An issue that has caused considerable division within the Court has to do with the due process requirements for state proceedings affording relief for creditors against delinquent debtors. Before the garnishment of wages there must be a hearing.[168] (Garnishment is a process by which an employer is ordered by a court to pay directly to an employee's creditors amounts deducted from the wages due the employee.) A hearing is necessary before goods sold on the installment plan can be repossessed.[169] A prerepossession hearing is not necessary if a judge orders a sheriff to take possession of property in which title is still vested in the seller.[170] A hearing is necessary before a creditor can place a hold on and garnish a bank account.[171] Along these same lines, state courts cannot place an attachment on real estate without a hearing or the posting of bond in order to protect a possible judgment for the owner.[172] Whether such an attachment without a hearing is valid to protect a working person's interest in payment for work on real estate—a so-called mechanic's lien—has not been clearly established.[173] When a creditor using procedures established by Virginia law went into a Virginia court to attach property of one of his debtors, the debtor was allowed to sue the creditor under Section 1983 on the grounds that the creditor, acting under color of state law, had violated the debtor's due process rights.[174]

Substantive Due Process

Whereas procedural due process places limits on the manner in which governmental power may be exercised, *substantive due process* withdraws certain subjects from the full reach of governmental power regardless of the

---

[165] *Heller v Doe,* 125 L Ed 2d 257 (1993).
[166] *Vitek v Jones,* 445 US 480 (1980).
[167] *Foucha v Louisiana,* 118 L Ed 2d 437 (1992).
[168] *Sniadach v Family Finance Corp.,* 395 US 337 (1969).
[169] *Fuentes v Shevin,* 407 US 67 (1972).
[170] *Mitchell v W. T. Grant,* 416 US 600 (1975).
[171] *North Georgia Finish, Inc. v Di-Chem Inc.,* 419 US 601 (1975).
[172] *Connecticut v Doehr,* 115 L Ed 2d 1 (1991).
[173] *Spielman-Fond, Inc. v Hanson's Inc,* 417 US 901 (1974), as modified by *Connecticut v Doehr.*
[174] *Lugar v Edmonson Oil Co.,* 457 US 922 (1983).

procedures used. Substantive due process requires that the Court be convinced that a law—not merely the procedures by which the law is to be enforced, but its very purpose—is fair, reasonable, and just.

Before 1937 the Supreme Court used substantive due process to strike down many laws the justices thought to be unreasonable regulations of business liberty. Indeed, the Supreme Court for a time became the final arbiter of our economic and industrial life. During that period the Court struck down laws regulating hours of labor, establishing minimum wages, regulating prices, forbidding employers to discharge workers for union membership, on the grounds that they were unreasonable interferences with the liberty of employers and employees to contract with one another.[175]

Since 1937 the Supreme Court has refused to apply substantive due process to laws regulating the economy.[176] This rejection does not mean that the Court has abandoned the doctrine of substantive due process. Quite the contrary, the doctrine has been given new life as a judicially imposed limitation on both state and federal governments' power to regulate civil liberties and civil rights.

For a while, the Court applied substantive due process but was reluctant to admit that it was doing so. However, in recent decades, it has openly begun to inspect laws for "reasonableness." For example, the Court declared unconstitutional an ordinance limiting occupancy in homes to single families and defining single families in a way that excluded a grandmother living with two grandchildren who were cousins rather than brothers. Justice Powell, speaking for a plurality of four, conceded that "substantive due process has at times been a treacherous field for this Court. There are risks when the judicial branch gives enhanced protection to certain substantive liberties without the guidance of the more specific provisions of the Bill of Rights. As the history [of the earlier use of due process to strike down many welfare laws] demonstrates there is reason for concern lest the only limits to such judicial intervention become the predilections of those who happen at the time to be members of this Court. That history counsels caution and restraint. But it does not counsel abandonment." Justice White, in dissent, reminded his colleagues "that the Court has no license to invalidate legislation which it thinks merely arbitrary or unreasonable.... The Court should be extremely reluctant to breathe still further substantive content into the Due Process Clause so as to strike down legislation adopted by a state or a city to promote its welfare. Whenever the Judiciary does so, it unavoidably preempts for itself another part of the governance of the country without express constitutional authority."[177]

The Court's return to the use of substantive due process, openly inspecting laws for "reasonableness," is primarily but not exclusively related to state laws and local ordinances. The Court is more deferential to Congress, as it also is with respect to First Amendment concerns, than to state and local govern-

---

[175] West Coast Hotel v Parrish, 300 US 379 (1937).

[176] Hodel v Virginia Surface Min. Recl. Assn., 452 US 264 (1981); Exxon v Maryland, 437 US 117 (1978); National Road Passenger Corporation v AT & SFR, 470 US 451 (1985).

[177] Moore v East Cleveland, 431 US 494 (1977).

ments. Nonetheless the Court has never repudiated the notion that substantive due process is any less a limitation on the actions of the national than of the state and local governments.

Closely related to the revival of the doctrine of substantive due process, and often merging with it, has been the Supreme Court's development of new tests to determine whether or not a state or federal law deprives a person of the equal protection of the law. The equal protection clause, as presently interpreted, has many similarities to substantive due process (see page 350). Indeed, it is sometimes difficult to determine whether the Supreme Court is striking down a law because it violates the due process clause or because it is a denial of equal protection. Take several examples: the Supreme Court declared unconstitutional a federal law aimed at preventing non-needy college students from getting food stamps. The law made ineligible for food stamps any household that contained any person over the age of eighteen who had been claimed as a tax dependent the prior year by somebody not living in that house. The Supreme Court ruled that the law created an unreasonable irrebuttable presumption because there is often no relation between the need of a household and the fact that it contains a person claimed the year before as a tax dependent by someone not living in the house.[178] Along the same lines, when Congress, to deny food stamps to "hippie communes," declared ineligible for such stamps any household containing an individual not related to any other member of the household, the Supreme Court declared the "classification to be wholly without any rational basis."[179] And then there was the regulation of the Cleveland Board of Education that no pregnant teacher should be allowed to teach beyond the fifth month of her pregnancy or to return to work until her child was three months old. Justice Stewart announced in *Cleveland Board of Education* v *LaFleur* that the "maternity leave rules directly affect 'one of the basic civil rights of man [sic],'" that they were "wholly arbitrary and irrational," and that they hence violated the due process clause of the Fourteenth Amendment.[180]

In a case of some interest to students, teachers, and university administrators, the Supreme Court, assuming that federal judges may review academic decisions of public universities and colleges under substantive due process standards, has concluded, "When judges are asked to review the substance of a genuinely academic decision, such as the dismissal of a student, they should show great respect for the faculty's professional judgment. Plainly, they may not override it unless it is such a substantial departure from accepted academic norms as to demonstrate that the person or committee responsible did not actually exercise professional judgment."[181]

Another example of contemporary use of substantive due process is the Court's declaring unconstitutional Louisiana's statute that allows a criminal defendant found not guilty by reason of insanity to be committed to a psychiatric

---

[178] *US Dept. of Agriculture* v *Murray*, 413 US 508 (1973).
[179] Ibid.
[180] *Cleveland Board of Education* v *LaFleur*, 414 US 632 (1974).
[181] *Regents of University of Michigan* v *Ewing*, 474 US 214 (1986).

hospital and kept there until he could prove to a trial court that he was no longer mentally ill or dangerous. In addition to the procedural inadequacies of Louisiana's statute in placing an improper burden of proof on the committed person, the Court concluded that the substantive component of the due process clause bars a state from keeping a mentally well person in a mental hospital without clear and convincing evidence produced by the state that he is both mentally ill and dangerous.[182]

At times the justices cannot even agree among themselves as to whether they are faced with a substantive or a procedural due process question, for what they are really struggling with are questions of right and wrong for which the written words of the Constitution provide little guidance. Take the case of *Michael H. v Gerald D.* which, as we noted on page 287, involved a California law providing that a child of a married woman cohabiting with her husband is presumed to be a child of that marriage when the husband is not impotent or sterile. This law was applied to a putative father—not the husband—with the results that the California courts refused to entertain the motions of the putative father—or the daughter—to establish paternity. Justice Scalia, speaking for a plurality, held that there was no procedural due process question here such as, Was the putative father denied his constitutional rights because he could not have a hearing on his claim? Rather, Justice Scalia argued, the Court was presented with a substantive question: Does a putative father who is not the husband have a liberty interest in establishing his paternity when there are a husband and wife living together at the time of the birth? On this basis, the plurality concluded there is no constitutional protected liberty interest of such a putative father. Our traditions provide no such right to what Justice Scalia kept calling an "adulterous natural father." Justice Brennan, on the other hand, in a scathingly bitter dissent accused Justice Scalia of "make-believe" and argued that the natural father had been denied his procedural due process rights. "The question before us," Justice Brennan insisted, "is whether California has an interest so powerful that it justifies granting Michael, the putative father, *no* hearing before terminating his paternal rights."[183]

The Court applied substantive due process standards when it dealt with the question of whether Missouri violated the Constitution by requiring that persons not be allowed to exercise the so-called right to die unless their wishes be established by "clear and convincing evidence." Such a requirement makes it very difficult, if not impossible, for persons to claim this right if they have failed to make known their wishes before they lapse into a comatose state.[184] Justices Brennan, Marshall, and Blackmun dissented on the grounds that Missouri had acted unfairly since the right to be free of unwanted forced feeding is a fundamental right and the procedures required by Missouri impermissibly burden that right. Justice Scalia concurred with the majority that Missouri had acted constitutionally but used the occasion to attack once again the doctrine

---

[182] *Foucha v Louisiana*, 118 L Ed 2d 437 (1992).

[183] Ibid.

[184] *Cruzan v Director, Missouri Dept. of Health*, 497 US 260 (1990).

of substantive due process. "The constantly increasing power of science to keep the human body alive for longer than any reasonable person would want to inhabit it," raises "difficult, indeed agonizing, questions and issues, the answers to which are neither set forth in the Constitution nor known to the nine Justices of this Court any better than they are to nine people picked at random from the Kansas City telephone directory." The standards of proof that should be required before a person is allowed to terminate such treatment, he argued, "should be decided by the state legislatures not by the federal courts.... Our salvation is the equal protection clause, which requires the democratic majority to accept for themselves and their loved ones what they impose on you and me. This Court need not, and has no authority to, inject itself into every field of human activity where irrationality and oppression may theoretically occur, and if it tries to do so it will destroy itself."[185]

Substantive Due Process and Abortion

The Court has written somewhat apologetically about its substantive due process jurisprudence, "while our decisions... do not form checkerboard bright lines between black squares and red squares," substantive due process today is likely to be bound by "the individual's freedom of choice with respect to certain basic matters of procreation, marriage, and family life."[186] Perhaps the most celebrated, certainly the most controversial, illustration of the modern Supreme Court's use of substantive due process are its rulings relating to abortion. In the first of these, *Roe* v *Wade* (1973), the Court announced that women do have a liberty interest protected by the Constitution to decide whether or not to have an abortion. The Court elaborated a trimester rationale to evaluate state regulation of abortions.[187] During the first trimester (about the first three months), it would be unreasonable and unconstitutional for a state to interfere with a woman's right to choose an abortion or to interfere with her doctor's medical judgments about how to carry it out. During the second trimester, when the point of viability—the ability of the fetus to live outside the womb—is reached, the state's interest in protecting not merely that fetus but also the health of women who undergo abortions becomes compelling, and a state may make reasonable regulations about how, where, and when abortions may be performed. During the third trimester, the state's interest in protecting the unborn fetus is so important that the state can proscribe abortions altogether, except when necessary to preserve the life or health of the mother.

Four years later, in *Maher* v *Roe,* the Court concluded that, although a woman has the constitutional right to an abortion during the early months of pregnancy, she has no right to have the state pay for it. A state may refuse to

---

[185] Ibid.
[186] *Kelley* v *Johnson*, 425 US 238 (1976); *Harrah Independent School District* v *Martin*, 440 US 194 (1979).
[187] *Roe* v *Wade*, 410 US 113 (1973).

pay the medical expenses for poor women for nontherapeutic abortions, even if the state covers medical expenses related to childbirth.[188]

Debates over abortion quickly became "the most politically divisive domestic legal issue of our time."[189] As each abortion case came before the Court, the justices could "look forward to . . . carts full of mail from the public, and streets full of demonstrators."[190] But during the 1970s and early 1980s the Court majority held fast to *Roe* v *Wade,* turning down almost every attempt by states to regulate women's choices about abortions.

As new members of the Court were appointed by President Reagan, speculation grew as to how they might vote about abortion issues. With the appointment of Justice Scalia—whose opposition to *Roe* v *Wade* was known—and Justice Kennedy—whose opposition could be assumed—it appeared that Justice O'Connor would have the "swing vote." She had made known her skepticism about the underlying rationale of the *Roe* v *Wade* trimester framework and had voted to sustain a variety of state regulations as to where, when, and how abortions might be obtained.

As the 1989 term came to an end, national attention was focused on the Court because it had before it a Missouri law that declared in its preamble that the life of each human being begins at conception, mandated that unborn children be given all the rights of other persons, forbade the use of public dollars or facilities for abortions, and required doctors prior to performing an abortion on any woman who the physician had reason to believe was carrying a fetus of 20 or more weeks gestational age to perform certain tests to ascertain whether the unborn child was viable. (The woman would still have the choice to proceed with the abortion.)

In *Webster* v *Reproductive Health Services,*[191] in a series of opinions notable for the strong language reflecting their strong feelings, Chief Justice Rehnquist, speaking for himself and three other justices, acknowledged that women have a constitutional liberty interest to have an abortion, but abandoned the trimester framework of *Roe* v *Wade,* and Justice O'Connor, although she did not join this part of the plurality's opinion, repeated her skepticism about the trimester framework. Although refusing to reverse *Roe* v *Wade,* the plurality nonetheless upheld Missouri's right to forbid the use of tax funds or facilities to perform abortions and sustained Missouri's right to require these tests about viability. Justice Scalia chided the plurality and Justice O'Connor for the refusal to overrule *Roe* v *Wade* and to return the regulation of abortion to the discretion of the state legislatures. "Our retaining control, through *Roe,* of what I believe to be, and many of our citizens recognize to be, a political issue, continuously distorts the public perception of this Court."

Justice Blackmun, the author of *Roe* v *Wade,* bitterly dissented. He wrote "Today, *Roe* v *Wade* and the fundamental constitutional right of women to decide whether to terminate a pregnancy, survive but are not secure." The

---

[188] *Maher* v *Roe,* 412 US 464 (1977).

[189] From Justice Blackmun's concurrence and dissent in *Webster* v *Reproductive Health Serv.,* 492 US 490 (1989).

[190] From Justice Scalia's concurrence in *Webster* v *Reproductive Health Serv.,* 492 US 490 (1989).

[191] *Webster* v *Reproductive Health Serv.,* 492 US 490 (1989).

Court, he charged, "implicitly invites every state legislature to enact more and more restrictive abortion regulations." "The plurality opinion is filed with winks, and nods, and knowing glances to those who would do away with Roe explicitly.... I fear for the liberty and equality of the millions of women who have lived and come of age in the 16 years since *Roe* was decided. I fear for the integrity of, and public esteem for, this Court."

Following *Webster,* the Court splintered over whether a state can constitutionally require minors to notify, or have doctors notify, parents before young women obtained abortions. In fact Justice Stevens, who wrote the opinion for the Court, also dissented from that opinion. Differing majorities formed and reformed to decide the two cases before them. The result: a state may require that a pregnant young woman inform *both* her parents before having an abortion, *provided* the state establishes an alternative "judicial bypass" permitting a judge to authorize an abortion without such notification if the young woman can show she is mature or that the abortion is in her best interest and it would be adverse to her interests to secure and wait for both parents' notification. A *one-parent notification* statute is constitutionally permissible. The Court left open whether a "judicial bypass" is necessary to sustain the constitutionality of such a state law, although it has previously decided that a judicial bypass is necessary to sustain a law that requires the *consent* of at least one parent.[192]

The key abortion case of the 1991-1992 Term was *Planned Parenthood* v *Casey,* involving Pennsylvania's abortion regulations which provided that a husband must be notified before a married woman could have an abortion and that the doctor must wait for twenty-four hours after providing the woman with information about the risks, and the likely gestational age of her fetus. Many anticipated that *Roe,* if not reversed, would be so limited that the Court would open abortion to almost unlimited state legislative regulation. But to the surprise of most, Justices O'Connor, Kennedy, and Souter—three Reagan and Bush appointees—along with Blackmun and Stevens provided a majority necessary to confirm the essential holding of *Roe* v *Wade.* Justices O'Connor, Kennedy, and Souter, although setting aside the trimester framework of Roe, held (1) a woman has a constitutional right to choose to have an abortion before viability and to obtain it without undue interference from the state, (2) a state has the power to restrict abortions after fetal viability, if the law contains exceptions for pregnancies which endanger a woman's life or health, and (3) the state has a legitimate interest from the outset of the pregnancy in protecting the health of the woman and the life of the fetus that may become a child. The joint opinion's authors defended their holding on a variety of grounds, not the least of which was to preserve the legitimacy of the Court by not backing down from an established precedent in the face of political pressures from the White House and elsewhere. Chief Justice Rehnquist, joined by Justices White, Scalia, and Thomas in dissent, would have reversed *Roe* and allowed states to regulate an abortion subject only to the standard that the regulations must be reasonable.[193]

---

[192] *Ohio* v *Akron Center for Reproductive Health,* 497 US 502 (1990); *Hodgson* v *Minnesota,* 497 US 417 (1990).

[193] *Planned Parenthood* v *Casey,* 120 L Ed 2d 674 (1992).

As a consequence of the plurality's position in *Casey*, states may not, prior to a fetus's viability, impose an undue burden on a woman's choice to have an abortion. "An undue burden exists, and therefore a provision of a law is invalid, if its purpose or effect is to place a substantial obstacle in the path of a woman seeking an abortion before the fetus attains viability." Applying this standard, the Court upheld, except for a medical emergency, a 24-hour waiting period before an abortion could be performed starting from the time a physician informed the woman of the nature of the procedure, the health risks, and the probable gestational age of the unborn child. It did, however, strike down the provision requiring women to notify their husbands prior to obtaining an abortion.

The pro-choice–pro-life debate divides the nation, and feelings run deep. This same division is felt strongly among the justices. Justice Blackmun, the author of the Roe opinion, charged the anti-*Roe* v *Wade* justices with using "hyperbole that can have but one result: to further incite an American press, public, and pulpit."[194] He argued in *Casey* that now that the Court has reaffirmed that women have a constitutional liberty to terminate pregnancy but that this liberty is not beyond reasonable state regulations, " the contending sides" should "end their national division by accepting a common mandate rooted in the Constitution."[195] On the other side, the anti-Roe jurists, speaking through Justice Scalia, charged that the opinions of the Court contain "outrageous arguments," and that the Court's decision merely prolongs and intensifies the anguish and that the Court "should get out of this area, where we have no right to be, and where we do neither ourselves nor the country any good by remaining."[196]

Justice Blackmun, concurring in *Casey*, wrote, "Three years ago, in *Webster* v *Reproductive Health Services* four Members of this Court appeared poised to 'cast into darkness the hopes and visions of every woman in this country' who had come to believe that the Constitution guaranteed her the right to reproductive choice.... All that remained between the promise of Roe and the darkness of the plurality was a single, flickering flame.... But now, just when so many expected the darkness to fall, the flame has grown bright." He said, "I am 83 years old. I cannot remain on this Court forever, and when I do step down, the confirmation process for my successor well may focus on the issue before us today. That, I regret, may be exactly where the choice between the two worlds will be made."[197] Justice Scalia, responding, "If, indeed, the 'liberties' protected by the Constitution are, as the Court says, undefined and unbounded, then... confirmation hearings for new Justices *should* deteriorate into question-and-answer sessions in which Senators go through a list of their constituents' most favored and most disfavored alleged constitutional rights and seek the nominee's commitment to support or oppose them.... Justice Blackmun not only regards this prospect with equanimity, he solicits it."[198]

---

[194] Justice Blackmun dissenting in *Ohio* v *Akron Center for Reproductive Health*, 497 US 502 (1990).
[195] Ibid.
[196] Ibid.
[197] Ibid.
[198] Ibid.

This colloquy made even more pointed Bill Clinton's pledge as a presidential candidate not to appoint to the Court anybody who might vote against *Roe* v *Wade*. Although President Bush refused to make such a categorical statement and in fact attacked Clinton for imposing an improper litmus test for judicial candidates, nonetheless he made it clear that if he were reelected he would implement his pledge to appoint jurists who are "constitutional conservatives" and unwilling to write modern concepts about privacy into the Constitution. Perhaps seldom in American history did the electorate have such a direct voice in determining how subsequent lines of constitutional decisions would be resolved. When they voted for Clinton over Bush that made it highly unlikely that *Roe* v *Wade* will be reversed, at least for the immediate future.

President Clinton came through on his promise when he nominated Ruth Bader Ginsburg, a known supporter of the conclusions of *Roe* v *Wade*, although a critic of its rationale.

Gays and Lesbians, Substantive Due Process, and the Right of Privacy

The abortion decisions, and those relating to the sale and use of contraceptives, are grounded in substantive due process but are also tied to a more generalized right of privacy that has been construed to flow from due process as well as the Ninth Amendment. The Court has refused, however, to extend this constitutional right of family privacy to gays and lesbians. The Court, by five to four, held that homosexual activity is not protected by what the Court described as this "fundamental individual right to decide whether or not to beget or bear a child." The dissenters angrily responded that the Court's unwillingness to strike down the Georgia antisodomy law is a betrayal of a value deeply rooted in our nation's history, namely, that governments have no right to deprive individuals of the choice of how to conduct their most intimate relationships. Sex practices in private bedrooms between consenting adults, said the dissenters, are protected by the Constitution against governmental regulation.[199]

These cases relating to abortion and to the rights of gays and lesbians are but one more round of the never-ending debate about the proper role of the courts in a democracy and about the use and alleged abuse of the doctrine of substantive due process.

Limits on Jury Awards in Civil Cases

In the face of some large punitive damage awards that seem to have no relationship to the civil wrong for which they are imposed, the Court, or at least a plurality of the justices, has announced that the Fourteenth Amendment "imposes a substantive limit on the amount of a punitive damages award." (Compensatory awards are to make whole the person damaged, punitive damage awards are to punish the party who committed the wrong.) Despite being

---

[199] *Bowers* v *Hardwick*, 478 US 186 (1986).

asked to do so in five recent cases, the Court has never set aside an award for being excessive. In 1991 when it sustained an award four times that of the compensatory damages, it said that this "may be close to the line" of constitutionality.[200] Nonetheless, in 1993 the Court refused to set aside a punitive damage award 526 times the compensatory award. Moreover, the Court refused to formulate a test to be used by the lower courts. Rather, said the plurality, it had to be decided on a case-by-case basis that the awards are "grossly excessive." In this case the Court refused to declare the award excessive because it was rational for the jury to place great weight on the deliberate, wrongful conduct in determining that such large award was required "to serve the goals of punishment and deterrence," and thus there was no "unfair, arbitrary, or irrational seizure of... property." "In the end," said Justice Stevens for the plurality, "in determining whether a particular award is so 'grossly excessive' as to violate the Due Process Clause...[w]e need not, and indeed we cannot, draw a mathematical bright line between the constitutionally acceptable and the constitutionally unacceptable that would fit every case. We can say, however, that [a] general concern of reasonableness...properly enters into the constitutional calculus."[201]

---

nor shall private property be taken for public use, [without just compensation, *discussed later*]

This clause was the first provision of the Bill of Rights to be incorporated in the Fourteenth Amendment and thus to be made applicable to the states.[202] (A regulation that "goes too far" may also violate the due process clause.)[203] This clause places a restriction on the government's power of *eminent domain*—that is, the power to take property for public use.

Although the clause refers to private property, the national government may take property belonging to a local government, as may a state, but an interesting question not definitively decided is whether the national government may take property owned and used by a state for a direct governmental purpose.

Property may be taken under eminent domain, even if the owner is fairly compensated, *only for public use*. The Court found no difficulty in finding a public purpose when the U.S. Government via the Interstate Commerce Commission took 48.8 miles of railroad track from the Boston and Maine Railway and gave it to Amtrak in order to faciliate its passenger railroad service.[204] In *Hawaii Housing Authority et al.* v *Midkiff*, the Supreme Court put to rest the notion that the words "public use" should be read literally to mean

---

[200] *Pacific Mutual Life Ins. Co.* v *Haslip*, 499 US 1 (1991).

[201] *TXO Production Corp.* v *Alliance Resources Corp.* 125 L Ed 2d 366 (1993).

[202] *Chicago, Milwaukee & St. Paul Ry.* v *Minnesota*, 134 US 418 (1890).

[203] *Williamson Planning Comm.* v *Hamilton Bank*, 473 US 172 (1985), quoting from Justice Holmes's opinion for the Court in *Pennsylvania Coal* v *Mahon*, 260 US 393 (1922).

[204] *National Railroad Passenger Corp.* v *Boston & Maine Corp.*, 118 L Ed 2d 52 (1992).

that the taken property must be owned and operated by a government and open to use by the public. The Hawaii legislature in 1967 had adopted a land reform act empowering authorities to condemn the land of large landowners, to transfer ownership of the condemned land to tenants, and to lend funds to arrange for the financing of the land so purchased. The landowners who lost their property argued that the act violated the Constitution in that it took property from one person and made it available to others for their own private use. The Court of Appeals for the Ninth Circuit agreed. In its judgment, the act was simply "a naked attempt on the part of the state of Hawaii to take the private property of A and transfer it to B solely for B's private use and benefit." But the Supreme Court said that although "one person's property may not be taken for the benefit of another private person without a justifying public purpose, even though compensation be paid,"[205] it can be taken if it serves a public purpose. It is the legislature which determines what constitutes a public use. "The Court... will not substitute its judgment for a legislature's judgment as to what constitutes a public use unless the use be palpably without reasonable foundation.... The Hawaii Legislature's judgment to break up land oligopolies and correct the evils associated with such concentrated landownership was a classic exercise of a State's police powers and clearly serves a public use."[206]

The question of what constitutes a taking for purposes of the Fifth Amendment has occupied a considerable portion of the Court's time, most especially in recent years. In fact, the taking jurisdiction of the modern-day Supreme Court has become a new battleground, replacing pre-1937 substantive due process, in the war between those who favor governmental regulation, especially of land development, and those who are suspicious of such government actions.

Ordinarily, but not always, a taking must be direct, some kind of permanent physical occupation authorized by the government. Taxes are not takings, even if a tax is so stiff as to drive a person out of business.[207] "A reasonable user fee is not a taking if it is imposed for the reimbursement of the cost of government services."[208] The government does not have to pay damages when it temporarily occupies a building in the course of restoring order in a riot situation.[209]

When there is a physical occupation, even if minor, the taking clause requires compensation. "Thus, whether the government floods a landowner's property or does no more than require the landowner to suffer the installation of a cable, the Takings Clause requires compensation if the goverment authorizes a compelled physical invasion of property."[210]

Government regulations are not ordinarily considered takings and do not ordinarily require compensation (but see below), even if the government action results in a property loss. Government regulation of utility rates and general

---

[205] *Thompson v Consolidated Gas Corp.*, 300 US 55 (1937).

[206] *Hawaii Housing Authority et al. v Midkiff*, 467 US 229 (1984).

[207] *Pittsburgh v Alco Parking Corp.*, 417 US 369 (1974).

[208] *United States v Sperry Corp.*, 489 US 1009 (1989).

[209] *Hawaii Housing Authority et al. v Midkiff*, 467 US 229 (1984).

[210] *Yee v Escondido*, 118 L Ed 2d 153 (1992).

price control regulations are not takings unless the rates set are considered by the courts to be confiscatory.[211] For many decades the Supreme Court struggled with the formulas by which states could set rates charged by utilities. Nowadays, "the guiding principle" is that all that the taking clause protects is that the rates be set higher than at a confiscatory level, that is, that rates not be set so low as to "destroy the property for all the purposes for which it was acquired."[212] Thus, Pennsylvania could disallow utilities' recovery of a return on the funds invested in nuclear power projects that were never brought into service, because the total rates the utilities earned were not confiscatory.

Governments closely regulate land uses, requiring permits and, these days, environmental impact reports (EIRs) before land is entitled and its owners allowed to use it for any number of purposes. There are elaborate regulations of what can be built on land and how the buildings can be used. There is not a taking of this property through such land use regulation if it "substantially advances legitimate state interests" and does not deny an owner "economically viable use of his land."[213] For example, a government may designate a building a "historic landmark" and may impose on the owner of such a building requirements for its maintenance and restrictions on its development without having to pay "just compensation," as the owners of Grand Central Terminal in New York discovered. They were denied the right to make changes in the structure, changes that would have increased their rental returns.[214]

On the other side, even when title is left in the hands of the owners, sometimes the courts will find that the government has "taken" property and owes compensation to its owners. Such a so-called regulatory taking occurs when "the purpose of the regulation or the extent to which it deprives the owner of the economic use of the property suggest that the regulation has unfairly singled out the property owner to bear a burden that should be borne by the public as a whole."[215] To illustrate: if airplanes take off and land over property adjacent to airports at such levels that the land is no longer suitable for its prior use, say, raising chickens, this is a compensable taking.[216] Similarly, the Supreme Court indicated that, if a congressional program to keep the bankrupt northeastern railroads operating resulted in such significant losses to them that it amounted to an "erosion taking," the government would be liable for just compensation for having taken railroad property by forcing them to continue to operate at huge losses.[217] Along these same lines, the government must provide compensation if it wants to provide public access to a private lagoon that the owners have dredged out at their own expense.[218] More recently, the Court established a categorical rule that if a state regulation denies *all* benefi-

---

[211] *FCC* v *Florida Power Corp*, 480 US 245 (1987).

[212] *Duquesne Light Co.* v *Barasch*, 488 US 299 (1989).

[213] *Agins* v *City of Tiburon*, 447 US 255 (1980).

[214] *Penn. Central Transportation Co.* v *City of New York*, 438 US 104 (1978).

[215] *Yee* v *Escondido*, 118 L Ed 2d 153 (1992).

[216] *United States* v *Causby*, 328 US 256 (1946).

[217] *Regional Rail Reorganization Act Cases*, 419 US 102 (1974).

[218] *Kaiser Aetna* v *United States*, 444 US 164 (1979).

cial or productive use of land, it is a taking even if justified by perfectly proper and compelling governmental interests. Such total regulatory takings must be compensated, although if the state can show that the proscribed use interests were not part of the title of the owner of the land to begin with, it does not have to compensate the owner for such a taking.[219]

It is difficult to draw the lines between what is a reasonable regulation and what goes "too far" and thus becomes a taking. Where and how the constitutional lines are drawn rests ultimately on ideas of fairness and justice rather than on precise constitutional language. In 1922 Justice Holmes, the leading light of judicial deference, speaking for the Court in *Pennsylvania Coal Co.* v *Mahon,* held that Pennsylvania had gone too far when it restricted the mining of coal on land owned by mining companies if it might cause damage to buildings on adjacent land.[220] This restriction, said Justice Holmes, took the mine owners' property from them for the benefit of the few people whose buildings might be damaged. For sixty-five years the case was cited as an example of regulation that went "too far." Then in 1987, by a five-to-four vote, the Supreme Court, distinguishing but not overruling *Mahon,* upheld another Pennsylvania law requiring miners to leave a certain amount of coal— 27 million tons—in the ground for support of buildings and to pay for damage to structures, even if the surface owners had waived any claim to such damages when they sold the rights to mine under their land. The coal that had to be left underground, a limitation on the miners' purchased interest in mining the coal, was not a taking, said the majority, but a regulation in the public interest.[221]

In the same term, following this less rigorous application of the taking clause, the Court signaled, in a pair of cases, a more restrictive application of the clause to governmental land regulations. The first, *First Lutheran Church* v *Los Angeles County,* warned governments that they have to pay compensation for regulations that are subsequently judged to be takings (see page 308). The second, *Nollan* v *California Coastal Commission,* established that governments may not impose mitigating conditions on land use without paying just compensation, unless there is a substantial relation between the governmental purpose and the condition imposed. The particular case before it was an attempt by the California Coastal Commission to deny a permit to remodel a beach home unless the owners agreed to extend public access to the beach. The Court held there was no relation between the remodeling and public access and that this was a taking entitled to just compensation.[222] Justice Scalia, for the Court, stated that the commission's action is the "same as if California law forbade shouting fire in a crowded theater, but granted dispensations to those willing to contribute $100 to the state treasury.... In short, unless the permit condition serves the same governmental

---

[219] *Lucas v So. Carolina Coastal Council,* 120 L Ed 2d 798 (1992).

[220] *Pennsylvania Coal Co. v Mahon,* 260 US 393 (1922).

[221] *Keystone Coal Association* v *DeBenedictis,* 480 US 470 (1987).

[222] *First Lutheran Church* v *Los Angeles County,* 482 US 304 (1987); *Nollan* v *California Coastal Commission.,* 483 US 825 (1987).

purpose as the development ban, the building restriction is not a valid regulation of land use but an 'out-and-out plan of extortion.'"

without just compensation.

In cases of disagreement between the government and the individual about what price is just, decision is referred to a disinterested body; ultimately, a court of law makes the final decision. What is just compensation is not always an easy question to answer. By and large, "the owner is entitled to receive what a willing buyer would pay in cash to a willing seller at the time of the taking."[223] An owner is not entitled to compensation for the special value of the property to the owner: an old, broken-down house that is loved dearly will still bring only compensation for an old, broken-down house. When the property is owned by a public entity, that entity is entitled to no more than the fair market value of the condemned property, even if it will cost more to acquire a substitute facility that the entity has a duty to acquire.[224]

What happens if, after a long, drawn-out legal battle, there is a final judicial determination that a regulation was in fact a taking? The government involved may amend the invalid regulation, withdraw it, or exercise eminent domain and pay compensation. But what about the losses while the proceedings are taking place? Does the Constitution confer a right to compensation for these "temporary takings"? In an important decision on *inverse condemnation*—the right to sue for compensation—that will spawn considerable additional litigation and may, as the Court conceded, significantly slow down land use regulations, the Court, considering an ordinance that denied a church all use of its property for a considerable period of time, decided that the church was entitled to just compensation for that temporary taking. The Court limited its holding to the facts of the case and did not "deal with the quite different questions that would arise in the case of normal delays in obtaining building permits, changes in zoning ordinances, variances, and the like which are not before us."[225]

Another interesting taking and compensation case involved Indian lands. In 1980 the Supreme Court ruled that the national government had exceeded its powers to abrogate Indian treaties and to manage tribal lands and, in 1877, had acted in bad faith by taking the Black Hills from the Sioux Indians. The Indians, ruled the Court, were entitled to the $17 million that the Black Hills had been worth in 1877, plus 5 percent annual interest compounded since then, for a total of almost $100 million.[226]

[223] *United States v 564.54 Acres of Land*, 441 US 506 (1979).
[224] *United States v 50 Acres of Land*, 469 US 24 (1984).
[225] *First Lutheran Church v LA County*, 482 US 304 (1987).
[226] *United States v Sioux Nation of Indians*, 448 US 371 (1980).

AMENDMENT VI: CRIMINAL COURT PROCEDURES

In all criminal prosecutions, the accused shall enjoy the right to a speedy [trial]

"This guarantee is an important safeguard to prevent undue and oppressive incarceration prior to trial, to minimize anxiety and concern accompanying public accusation, and to limit the possibilities that long delay will impair the ability of an accused to defend himself."[1] "This right differs from other constitutional rights in that there is a societal interest in providing a speedy trial which exists separate from, and at times in opposition to, the interests of the accused," who often finds advantage in delay. It also differs in that if it is determined that a defendant has been denied a speedy trial, the only remedy is the drastic one of dismissal of the charges without the possibility of their reinstatement, for the fault is not correctable by retrial, as are other violations of the Sixth Amendment.[2]

The constitutional right to a speedy trial protects against the states as a result of the Fourteenth Amendment. What might not violate the Sixth Amendment might violate one of the due process clauses: undue and prejudicial delay by the prosecution before indictment, or between dropping charges and reinstating them, could create a due process claim.[3]

A trial clearly may be "speedy" in a legal sense even though it admits of considerable delay, especially delays caused by the counsel for the accused. "The many procedural safeguards provided an accused mean that the ordinary procedures for criminal prosecution are designed to move at a deliberate pace."[4] The constitutional right to a speedy trial starts from the time a person has been formally charged, not from the time of arrest.[5] (Federal law for federal prosecutions starts the clock from time of arrest or from the time the police discover evidence of a crime.) The speedy trial guarantee does not apply when the government, acting in good faith, has formally dropped charges and then later reinstates them.

The Supreme Court has refused to give the words "speedy trial" any precise time limit.[6] Rather, the Court has listed four factors that must be taken into account in determining whether the right to a speedy trial has been violated. First, there is the length of the delay. The longer the time, the greater the burden on the government to justify it.

---

[1] *United States v Ewell*, 383 US 116 (1966).
[2] *Strunk v United States*, 412 US 434 (1973).
[3] *United States v Marion*, 404 US 307 (1971).
[4] *United States v Ewell*, 383 US 116 (1966).
[5] *Doggett v United States* 120 L Ed 2d 520 (1992).
[6] *United States v Lovasco*, 431 US 783 (1977).

Second are the reasons for the delay. If the delay is intentional, it will weigh heavily against the government; if it is the result of "diligent prosecution" the defendant must show prejudice from the delay. Delay as the result of "official negligence" "occupies the middle ground" between "diligent prosecution and bad-faith delay." "While not compelling relief in every case where bad-faith delay would make relief virtually automatic, neither is negligence automatically tolerable simply because the accused cannot demonstrate exactly how it has prejudiced him . . ." "toleration of such negligence varies inversely with its protractedness."[7]

Third, a defendant's demand for waiver of the right to an immediate trial would work against him or her. Finally, the fourth factor is any disadvantage to a defendant because of the delay.[8]

Adding up these factors when the federal government took 8½ years between the time it indicted a person for importing and distributing cocaine until they arrested him, the Court set aside his conviction because he had been denied the right to a speedy trial even though during these years he had never been put in jail and in fact did not even know that he had been indicted.[9]

Congress adopted the 1974 Speedy Trial Act to expedite criminal trials in federal courts. It provides time limits for various stages of a case, from arrest through indictment to trial, with some exclusions of time for various purposes. If any of the specified deadlines is not met, the judge is to decide whether to dismiss the charges with prejudice, which will bar reprosecution, or to dismiss them without prejudice, which will allow for reproduction. Although it is not clear that defendants' causes are advanced when charges against them are dropped without prejudice, such action expresses a congressionally defined goal that justice should move more swiftly in the future than it has in the past.

and public trial,

A public trial is essential for due process and therefore is secured to defendants in state as well as federal courts.[10] The right to a public trial belongs to defendants and not to television camera operators, photographers, or newspaper reporters. The requirement of a public trial is satisfied if the members of the public and press have an opportunity to attend the trial and to report what they observe. The press does not have a right to be allowed to broadcast or tape the trial. Nor does the First Amendment grant the press any right to information about the trial superior to that of the general public.[11]

---

[7] *Doggett v United States,* 120 L Ed 2d 520 (1992).
[8] *Barker v Wingo,* 407 US 514 (1972).
[9] *Doggett v United States,* 120 L Ed 2d 520 (1992).
[10] *In re Oliver,* 333 US 257 (1948).
[11] *Nixon v Warner Communications,* 435 US 589 (1978).

After some initial floundering about the matter, the Court established that an accused has a Sixth Amendment right to insist on a public trial, including pretrial suppression hearings, and judges' authority to close trials or preliminary hearings is limited to those few instances when they can show an overriding need to do so.[12]

There is no constitutional right to a private trial. Federal rules of criminal procedure forbid radio or photographic coverage of criminal cases in federal courts, but most states now permit electronic, including television, coverage of courtroom proceedings.[13] A state may permit the televising of trials notwithstanding the objections of the defendants.[14] Defendants, however, always have the right to present evidence that television interfered with their particular trials, prevented fair hearings, and deprived them of due process. For example, the televising of the trial may occur in such a way as to create such distractions that it denies the defendant due process.

---

by an impartial jury

Despite the fact that Article III requires trial by jury for all federal crimes, the right was considered so important that it was further guaranteed by the Sixth Amendment. The Fourteenth Amendment "guarantees a right of jury trial in all [state] criminal cases which, were they tried in a federal court, would come within the Sixth Amendment's guarantee of trial by jury."[15] Defendants may waive the right to a jury trial, but a judge may insist on a jury trial even against the wishes of the defendant, for there is no constitutional right *not* to be tried by a jury.[16] However, defendants can, by a plea of guilty, waive the right to any kind of trial.

Trial by jury is a constitutional requirement for serious but not petty crimes. Serious crimes are those punishable by more than six months in prison and a $500 fine.[17] Although offenses carrying a maximum prison term of six months or less do not automatically qualify as petty offenses, defendants are entitled to jury trials in such circumstances if they can demonstrate that any additional statutory penalties are so severe that they clearly reflect a legislative determination that the offense in question is a "serious one." This means in effect that no jury trial is required for crimes carrying less than six months incarceration except "in the rare situation"—so far the Supreme Court has

---

[12] *Press-Enterprise Co.* v *Superior Court of California,* 464 US 501 (1984); *Waller* v *Georgia,* 467 US 39 (1984).

[13] Susanna Barber, *News Cameras in the Courtroom: A Free Press-Fair Trial Debate* (Ablex Publishing Corporation, 1987), p. 9.

[14] *Chandler* v *Florida,* 449 US 560 (1981).

[15] *Duncan* v *Louisiana,* 391 US 145 (1968).

[16] *Singer* v *United States,* 380 US 24 (1965).

[17] *Dyke* v *Taylor Implement Manufacturing Co.,* 391 US 216 (1968).

found none—"where a Legislature packs an offense it deems 'serious' with onerous penalties that nonetheless 'do not puncture the 6-month incarceration line.'"[18]

The jury trial requirement applies to convictions for criminal contempt if
the penalty imposed exceeds imprisonment for six months.[19] It does not apply
to civil contempt or to other noncriminal proceedings, such as deportation or
loyalty and security hearings.

Trial by jury was once thought to include all the elements recognized by common law at the time the Constitution was adopted, the most important being a jury
of exactly twelve members and the requirement of a unanimous verdict for conviction. In 1970, however, the Supreme Court decided that a twelve-person jury is not
an "indispensable component of the Sixth Amendment,"[20] at least as applied to
the states, and a jury composed of at least six people will do. Fewer than six, the
Court has decided, promotes inaccurate and biased verdicts, causes lack of consistency in verdicts, and prevents juries from adequately representing a cross-section
of the community. Moreover, reduction below six provides no particular saving in
court time or costs.[21] Although the Sixth Amendment no longer requires a twelve-
member criminal jury, most states and the federal government continue to use such
juries, but six-person juries may be used in federal *civil* cases.

Unanimity is constitutionally required for conviction in federal courts,
but not in state courts. This result came about because Justice Powell, who
had the swing vote on the issue, took the view that the Sixth Amendment,
which applies to the federal government, calls for unanimous verdicts but that
the Fourteenth Amendment, which applies to the states, while requiring states
to use juries for serious crimes, does not require that state juries be unanimous for conviction. How much less than unanimous is not clear. The Court
has approved convictions by the votes of nine jurors out of twelve.[22] The Court
has said, however, that if a state uses the minimum number of jurors permitted under the Constitution—that is, six—the decisions must be unanimous.[23]

A person is entitled to trial by an *impartial* jury, which means a jury drawn from
a panel that represents a "fair cross section" of the community and a jury from
which no person has been excluded because of race, sex, national origin, or religion. The fair cross-section requirement applies to the panels—venires, they are
called—from which juries are drawn, not to the actual composition of the jury
itself.[24] There is no Sixth Amendment violation if the jury is not a representative
one of the ethnic, sex, or race composition of the community, provided it has been
drawn from a fair cross-section of the community. The Sixth Amendment does not
guarantee a representative jury, only an impartial one.[25]

---

[18] *Blanton v North Las Vegas*, 489 US 538 (1989); reaffirmed in *United States v Nachtigal*, 122 L Ed 2d 374
(1993).

[19] *Bloom v Illinois*, 391 US 194 (1968); *Frank v United States*, 395 US 147 (1969).

[20] *Williams v Florida*, 399 US 78 (1970).

[21] *Ballew v Georgia*, 435 US 223 (1978).

[22] *Apodaca v Oregon*, 406 US 404 (1972); *Johnson v Louisiana*, 406 US 356 (1972).

[23] *Burch v Louisiana*, 419 US 522 (1975).

[24] *Lockhart v McCree*, 476 US 162 (1986); *Buchanan v Kentucky*, 483 US 402 (1987).

[25] *Holland v Illinois*, 493 US 474 (1990).

A defendant does not have to be a member of an excluded class to object to a trial by a jury from which persons have been excluded because of race, sex, national origin, or religion; that is, a white person may object to the absence of black people and a man to the absence of women.[26]

Practices or statutes that bias the selection of particular categories of persons may run afoul of the fair cross-section requirement. Thus, a Missouri statute was declared unconstitutional that allowed women, but not men, to be excused from jury duty merely by so requesting.[27] There is no violation of the Constitution, however, if a judge exempts women from service who request it because of the need to stay home with small children, even if the granting of such requests results in an all-male jury.

To ensure that the jury is impartial, both the prosecution and the defense have a right to question prospective jurors, a so-called voir dire examination, about their possible biases, and based on that examination, the judge may exclude them from the jury "for cause." A defendant accused of a violent interracial crime is entitled, on request, to have prospective jurors informed of the race of the victim and questioned on the issue of racial or ethnic bias;[28] except for such cases, there is no automatic constitutional rule that permits a defendant to question jurors about racial prejudice. If the trial court determines, however, that "there are substantial indications of the likelihood of racial or ethnic prejudice affecting the jurors in a particular case," it may permit such questions. The Supreme Court has also left to the discretion of the trial judge whether to conduct a voir dire examination with respect to the ability of a prospective juror to remain impartial in the face of extensive pretrial publicity[29] and whether defendants with beards may interrogate potential jurors about their possible prejudice against bearded persons.[30]

Of a more serious nature, at least to persons without beards, the Court has ruled that a jury from which persons have been excluded because of their general objections to the death penalty cannot be impartial in choosing between a sentence of life and a sentence of death and that such a jury does not represent a fair cross-section of the community.[31] Jurors may be excluded, however, if they make it 'unmistakably clear' that they would 'automatically' vote against capital punishment without regard to the evidence or that their attitude toward penalty would prevent them from making an impartial decision as to the defendant's guilt."[32] Or, as the Court more recently explained about the constitutionality of "death-qualified" juries, a juror may be excluded for views that would "prevent or substantially impair the performance of his duties as a juror in accordance with his instructions and his oath."[33] However, the Court has been unwilling to rule that

[26] *Peters v Kiff,* 407 US 493 (1972); *Taylor v Louisiana,* 419 US 522 (1975).
[27] *Duren v Missouri,* 439 US 357 (1979).
[28] *Turner v Murray,* 476 US 28 (1986); *Aldrige v United States,* 283 US 308 (1931).
[29] *Mu'Min v Virginia,* 114 L Ed 2d 493 (1991).
[30] *Ham v South Carolina,* 409 US 524 (1973).
[31] *Witherspoon v Illinois,* 391 US 510 (1968); *Adams v Texas,* 448 US 38 (1980).
[32] *Wainwright v Witt,* 469 US 412 (1985).
[33] *Wainwright v Witt,* 469 US 412 (1985); *Lockhart v McCree,* 476 US 162 (1986).

excluding those who object to the death sentence from the portion of the trial in which guilt is determined produces an unfairly drawn jury.

Interesting equal protection clause as well as Sixth Amendment questions related to the impartial jury requirement are raised by the long-established practice of giving both the prosecution and defense the right peremptorily to exclude a certain number of people from the jury. Potential jurors removed by peremptory challenges are in addition to the unlimited number that the judge may remove for cause on the recommendation of the prosecutor or the defense attorney. No reason has to be given for a peremptory challenge: one can excuse fat people or tall people or people with college degrees or people without them or rich people or poor people—any person or group of persons one wishes.

Until recently a state prosecutor could, through peremptory challenges, exclude all white people or all black people from a jury. However, in *Batson* v *Kentucky,* the Supreme Court held, not for Sixth Amendment reasons of ensuring an impartial jury, but for equal protection reasons, "that a race-based exclusion is no more permissible at the individual petit jury stage than at the venire stage,"[34] and that a prosecutor's use of peremptory challenges to exclude all blacks from a jury trying black defendants establishes a prima facie case of purposeful racial discrimination.[35] The burden then shifts to the prosecution to provide a neutral explanation that relates to the particular case. It will not do merely to assert that black jurors as a group will be unable to consider impartially the case against a black defendant.[36] It also violates the equal protection clause for a prosecutor to use the state's peremptory challenges to exclude otherwise qualified and unbiased persons from a jury solely by reason of their race regardless of the race of the defendant. The equal protection clause also prohibits *defendants* from using peremptory challenges to exclude jurors based on their race.[37] Peremptory challenges based on race have also been held impermissible in civil trials.[38]

There is no precise holding with respect to whether black defendants can use such challenges to exclude white jurors, but the Court's language suggests that such a practice would also be unconstitutional. The Court has not ruled precisely with respect to peremptory challenges based on gender, but it would appear that they too violate the equal protection clause.

Free speech often clashes with claims for an impartial jury. When newspapers and television report in vivid details the facts of a crime, interview prosecutors and police, question witnesses, and hold press conferences for defendants and their attorneys, they may so inflame the public that conducting a fair trial is difficult. In England, strict rules determine what the media may report, and judges do not hesitate to punish newspapers that comment on

---

[34] *Holland* v *Illinois,* 493 US 474 (1990); interpretation of the *Batson* decision: See also *Hernandez* v *New York,* 114 L Ed 2d 395 (1991).

[35] *Batson* v *Kentucky,* 476 US 79 (1986).

[36] Ibid.

[37] *Georgia* v *McCollum,* 120 L Ed 2d 33 (1992).

[38] *Edmonson* v *Leeseville Concrete Co.,* 114 L Ed 2d 660 (1991).

pending criminal proceedings. In the United States, in contrast, free comment is emphasized. The Supreme Court has even set aside contempt citations against editors who threatened judges with political reprisals unless the judges imposed severe punishments on certain named defendants. Yet the Supreme Court has not been indifferent to protecting persons on trial from inflammatory publicity. Its remedies have been to order new trials or to instruct judges to impose sanctions on prosecutors and police, not on reporters. "Lawyers representing clients in pending cases may be regulated under a less demanding standard than that established for regulation of the press."[39] They may be disciplined for their comments prior to or during a trial even if the comments do not present a clear and present danger but merely if their comments are "substantially likely to have a materially prejudicial effect."[40] And if a judge allows news people to hound witnesses or permits the prosecutor to make damaging statements to the press that deprive the defendant of a right to trial by an impartial jury free from outside influences, such actions create due process problems. As the Supreme Court said, "Trial courts must take strong measures to ensure that the balance is never weighted against the accused."[41]

of the State and district wherein the crime shall have been committed, which district shall have been previously ascertained by law,

Early English juries were always from the neighborhood of the accused, which was sometimes an advantage for the accused, sometimes not. One of the grievances against George III was that his government had forced American colonists to stand trial in England for offenses alleged to have been committed in America.

To prevent the national government from using such procedures, both Article III and the Sixth Amendment require trials to be held in the state in which the crime was committed (the Sixth Amendment adds district). Defendants may, however, petition for removal of the trial from the district on the grounds that the community has been so inflamed and prejudiced against them that it would be impossible to select a fair and impartial jury in the district in which the crime was committed.

and to be informed of the nature and cause of the accusation;

[39] *Gentile v State Bar of Nevada*, 115 L Ed 2d 888 (1991).
[40] Ibid.
[41] *Sheppard v Maxwell*, 384 US 333 (1966).

The charges against the accused—whether in the grand jury's indictment or in an information filed by a prosecutor—must be specified, and a defendant can seek a "bill of particulars" to obtain greater specificity. This is related to the requirement, which is part of due process, that a statute must state precisely the acts that are forbidden and must include all the ingredients essential to a proper judgment of guilt of the crime. A law violates this requirement if it is so vague as to provide no clear notice that an action has been made criminal and no clear standard to guide judge and jury in determining guilt.

to be confronted with the witnesses against him;

This clause provides two types of protection for criminal defendants: the right physically to face those who testify against them—this is the so-called face-to-face guarantee—and the right to conduct cross-examination of one's accusers. The cases involving the clause fall into two general categories: (1) cases that relate to the admission of testimony by a person not available for cross-examination and (2) cases in which the opportunity to cross-examine has been restricted by law or by a court ruling.[42]

The right to confront witnesses should not be equated with the general rule prohibiting the admission of hearsay statements. There are those who argue that all the constitutional clause protects is the right of a defendant to confront and cross-examine only those witnesses who appear and testify at a trial. The Supreme Court has not construed the clause so narrowly, but it has not so broadly construed it as to rule out all hearsay evidence, although under most circumstances a witness's evidence cannot be introduced at a trial unless the witness is available for cross-examination.[43] There are some traditional "hearsay" exceptions, such as deathbed statements.[44] There is also the rule of necessity for so-called "residual hearsay exceptions," for evidence given at a prior judicial proceeding by a witness who has since moved to a foreign country, and evidence given at a preliminary hearing by a witness no longer available to testify,[45] particularly if the witness was cross-examined at the earlier time. "The prosecutor must either produce the accusatory witnesses or demonstrate their unavailability." If witnesses are shown to be unavailable, their written statements can be used only when there are ample "indicia of reliability."[46] There must be specific findings, based on the totality of the circumstances, that the evidence is "so trustworthy that cross-examination of the declarant would be of marginal utility."[47]

---

[42] *Pennsylvania v Ritchie*, 480 US 39 (1987); *Kentucky v Stincer*, 482 US 730 (1987).

[43] *Dutton v Evans*, 400 US 74 (1970).

[44] *White v Illinois*, 116 L Ed 2d 848 (1992).

[45] *Mancusi v Stubbs*, 408 US 204 (1972).

[46] *Ohio v Roberts*, 448 US 56 (1980).

[47] *Idaho v Wright*, 111 L Ed 2d 638 (1990).

Defendants may lose their right to confront adverse witnesses if they engage in such disruptive behavior that their trials cannot proceed while they remain in the courtroom, or if they voluntarily absent themselves from the proceedings.[48]

A difficult problem is how to handle the confessions of nontestifying codefendants. Although it is ordinarily assumed that juries will follow instructions, defendants are deprived of their rights under the confrontation clause when the confessions of nontestifying codefendants naming them as participants in a crime are introduced at a joint trial, even if the jury is instructed to consider a confession only against the defendant who made it.[49] The codefendant's confession is admissible, however, if it is edited to omit any reference to the other defendants.[50]

The right to confront witnesses does not require the government to make pretrial disclosure of any and all information that might be useful to defendants. However, the failure of the state to produce material evidence in its possession could raise serious due process considerations.

"Notice and hearing requirements" that call upon defendants to notify judges, prosecutors, and witnesses in advance of their intention to call certain witnesses and about the nature and scope of the interrogation of them may violate the Sixth Amendment right of defendants to confront witnesses, but they are not per se unconstitutional. Many states have such requirements as part of rape-shield statutes precluding questions about a rape victim's prior sexual relationship with a criminal defendant unless he follows certain procedures.[51]

Although the right to confront is stated in categorical terms, in recent years the Court, under the pressure of legislation designed to protect victims of sexual abuse, especially children, has upheld some limitations on face-to-face confrontation. In response to a number of child-abuse programs many states have tried to protect victims from having to confront in a face-to-face manner those accused of abusing them. This is a frightening experience for adults; for children it can be a trauma almost equal to their abuse. A defendant was excluded from a hearing held to determine the competency of two child witnesses to testify against him at a subsequent trial for child sexual molestation. The Court held that this did not violate this clause because the purpose of the hearing was to establish whether the children were able to remember basic facts and to distinguish between telling the truth and telling a lie, because the defendant's attorney was allowed to remain to cross-examine, and because the defendant would have an opportunity for full and effective cross-examination of the two witnesses during the trial. The dissenters argued that the clause plainly envisions that witnesses against the accused shall testify in the defendant's physical presence at all stages of the formal hearings; its purpose is not merely to secure the right of cross-examination. "Not until today," wrote Justice Marshall for the three dissenters, "has this Court gone so far as

---

[48] *Illinois v Allen,* 397 US 337 (1970); *Taylor v United States,* 414 US 17 (1973).

[49] *Bruton v United States,* 391 US 123 (1968); *Richardson v Marsh,* 481 US 200 (1987).

[50] *United States v Inadi,* 475 US 387 (1986).

[51] *Michigan v Lucas,* 114 L Ed 2d 205 (1991).

to substitute a defendant's subsequent opportunity for cross-examination for his right to confront adverse witnesses in a prior testimonial proceeding."[52]

With respect to the actual trial itself, an Iowa statute authorized the judge to place a one-way screen between the witness stand and the defense table. But the Court held that the Iowa law was unconstitutional since the right to confront witnesses is the core of this clause and it means the right to confront all witnesses who appear and give evidence at the trial face to face. Exceptions may be made, said the Court, only on a case-by-case basis with specific findings of fact by the judge why it was necessary in this individual case. A generalized legislative imposed presumption of trauma will not do.[53]

The next term, the Court was presented with a procedure for such a specific finding of fact. Maryland, along with many other states, provided that if a judge made a finding that the child witness will suffer "serious emotional distress such that the child cannot reasonably communicate," the child could be allowed to testify via closed circuit television. Once the procedure was invoked "the child witness, prosecutor, and defense counsel withdraw to a separate room; the judge, jury, and defendant remain in the courtroom. The child witness is examined and cross-examined in the separate room, while a video monitor records and displays the witness's testimony to those in the courtroom. Although the witness cannot see the defendant, the defendant remains in electronic communication with defense counsel, and objections may be made and ruled on as if the witness were testifying in the courtroom."

A five-justice majority sustained this procedure holding that, although the confrontation clause guarantees defendants the right to confront their accusers, "we have never insisted on an actual face-to-face encounter at trial in *every* instance in which testimony is admitted against a defendant."[54] So long as a trial court makes such a case-specific finding of necessity, the confrontation clause does not prohibit a state from using a one-way closed circuit television procedure for the receipt of testimony. Justice O'Connor, for the Court, noted the procedure preserves the other elements of confrontation—oath, cross-examination, and observation of the witness's demeanor. Justice Scalia, for the dissenters, contended, "Seldom has this Court failed so conspicuously to sustain a categorical guarantee of the Constitution against the tide of prevailing current opinion."

As to limiting the scope of cross-examination of witnesses, a "court may ... impose reasonable limits on defense counsel's inquiry into the potential bias of a prosecution witness ... to take account of such factors as harassment, prejudice, confusion of the issues, the witness' safety, or interrogation that [would] be repetitive or only marginally relevant,"[55] but the limitation cannot restrict a defendant's right to testimony that may relate to the witness's background and bias, a conflict that is becoming increasingly troublesome in balancing equities between victims and defendants in rape cases.

---

[52] *Kentucky* v *Stincer*, 482 US 730 (1987).
[53] *Coy* v *Iowa*, 487 US 1012 (1988).
[54] *Maryland* v *Craig*, 111 L Ed 2d 666 (1990).
[55] *Olden* v *Kentucky*, 488 US 227 (1988).

to have compulsory process for obtaining witnesses in his favor,

This clause has been incorporated into the Fourteenth Amendment as a limitation on the states.[56]

Under eighteenth-century English common law, persons accused of felonies or treason were not allowed to introduce any witnesses in their own defense. England abolished this general disqualification in 1787 but retained a number of restrictions on the kind of witnesses who could be called. For a while we followed English practices, but in 1918 the Supreme Court declared that all persons of competence who may have knowledge of the facts involved in a case should be allowed to be called, with a few exceptions. Among these exceptions is the husband-wife privilege, but it has been limited. A husband may no longer deny his wife, and vice versa, the right to testify if she (or he) wishes to do so.[57] However, common-law testimonial privileges protecting communications between lawyer and client, priest and penitent, and doctor and patient are today provided by federal rules or state rules of evidence. The disqualification of witnesses because of mental infirmity or infancy remains undisturbed.

The Supreme Court "has had little occasion to discuss the contours of the Compulsory Process Clause.... At a minimum... criminal defendants have the right to the Government's assistance in compelling the attendance of favorable witnesses at a trial and the right to put before a jury evidence that might influence the determination of guilt."[58] A state has no authority to compel the attendance in its court proceedings of witnesses outside its jurisdiction. Nonetheless, it must make a good faith effort to secure witnesses for the defense, wherever they are.[59]

This clause does not by its terms grant criminal defendants the right to secure the attendance and testimony of any and all witnesses; it guarantees them only compulsory process for obtaining "witnesses in their favor." Thus, defendants cannot establish a violation of their constitutional right to compulsory process merely by showing that the government has not helped to produce a witness; they must make some "plausible showing of how" the witness's testimony would have been both material and favorable to their defense.[60]

and to have the Assistance of Counsel for his defence.

---

[56] *Washington* v *Texas*, 388 US 14 (1967).

[57] *Burber* v *Page*, 390 US 719 (1968).

[58] *Pennsylvania* v *Ritchie*, 480 US 39 (1987).

[59] *Burber* v *Page*, 390 US 719 (1968).

[60] *United States* v *Valenzuela-Bernal*, 458 US 866 (1982).

What was once a right of defendants to be represented by an attorney during trial, provided they could afford to obtain such assistance, has now become a positive obligation—for federal authorities since *Johnson v Zerbst* (1938) and for state authorities since *Gideon v Wainwright* (1963)—to secure lawyers for those who are unable to pay for their own. Attorneys are furnished to those unable to afford to hire their own; in some jurisdictions, judges assign lawyers from the community. However, the growing practice in the larger states and cities in both federal and state courts is to create an office of the public defender using tax funds.

"Where assistance of counsel is a constitutional requirement, the right to be furnished counsel does not depend on request."[61] Unless the record clearly shows that defendants, with full awareness of what they were doing, waived their right to counsel, the absence of such counsel will render criminal proceedings unconstitutional. "The right to counsel of one's own choice is not unlimited: one cannot, for example, choose a nonlawyer, a lawyer one cannot afford, or a lawyer who in the judgment of the judge has a conflict of interest."[62] A defendant unable to afford counsel is not entitled to the attorney of his or her choice, and thus is not entitled "to insist on representation by an attorney he cannot afford."[63] In fact, defendants are not guaranteed a "meaningful attorney-client relationship," only that counsel will be competent.[64] How competent? The Sixth Amendment right to counsel is the right to the *effective* assistance of counsel. However, the burden is on the defendant to prove that counsel provided was ineffective, and the "defendant must show, first, that counsel's performance was deficient because of serious errors and, second, that this deficient performance did in fact prejudice the defense to such an extent that the defendant was deprived of a fair trial."[65]

Does the right to the assistance of counsel—or its more significant corollary, the right to have the government furnish and pay for counsel if one cannot afford it—extend only to trials for serious offenses or to all trials? "No accused may be deprived of his liberty as the result of any criminal prosecution, . . . whether or not a jury trial is required . . . in which he was denied the assistance of counsel."[66] The only trials exempt from the assistance-of-counsel requirement are those in which fines are the sole penalty *actually* imposed; in other words, there is to be no incarceration without counsel.[67] To this extent this requirement for legal assistance differs from that for jury trials. A jury trial must be offered for any crime for which imprisonment for more than six months may be imposed, even if in fact only a fine is levied. Likewise, a juvenile is entitled to counsel in proceedings in which institutionalization may result.[68]

---

[61] *Johnson v Zerbst*, 304 US 458 (1938); *Miranda v Arizona*, 384 US 436 (1966).

[62] *Wheat v United States*, 486 US 153 (1988).

[63] *Wheat v United States*, 486 US 153 (1988).

[64] *Morris v Slappy*, 461 US 1 (1983).

[65] *United States v Cronic*, 466 US 648 (1984); *Strickland v Washington*, 466 US 668 (1984); *Hill v Lockhart*, 474 US 52 (1985), *Lockhart v Fretwell*, 122 L Ed 2d 180 (1993).

[66] *Argersinger v Hamlin*, 407 US 25 (1972).

[67] *Scott v Illinois*, 440 US 367 (1979).

[68] *US ex rel. Hughes v Gault*, 271 US 1142 (1926).

The Sixth Amendment protects the right to the help of a trained lawyer, but the Supreme Court, proceeding more from due process than Sixth Amendment considerations, has established a variety of conditions under which psychiatric or clinical psychological help is also constitutionally necessary. For example, when defendants in a criminal prosecution make a preliminary showing that their sanity at the time of the offense is likely to be a significant factor at their trial, they are entitled access to a psychiatrist even if they cannot otherwise afford such professional help. They are also entitled to such help at the time of sentencing if a question of their future dangerousness is involved.[69]

In order to avoid a case-by-case inquiry to determine whether the defendant's waiver of the right to be represented by counsel was "voluntary, knowing, and intelligent," and in order to protect the Sixth Amendment rights of an accused to communicate with the state only through his or her attorney, the Supreme Court has adopted a "bright-line rule" for deciding whether an accused who has asserted the Sixth Amendment right to counsel has subsequently waived that right. In *Michigan* v *Jackson* the Court held that, once formal criminal proceedings have begun and after a defendant has requested assistance of counsel, any waiver of Sixth Amendment rights given in a discussion initiated by police is presumed invalid, and evidence obtained pursuant to such a waiver is inadmissible in the prosecution's case in chief, that is, in the prosecution's case against the defendant.[70] Yet like the *Miranda* exception, evidence obtained in the absence of the defendant's attorney as the result of a voluntary statement made in response to a police-initiated inquiry still may be used if the defendant takes the stand in order to impeach a defendant's inconsistent trial testimony.[71] Moreover, invocation of right to counsel under the Sixth Amendment is offense-specific and prevents any police-initiated questioning about that particular offense, but that waiver does not preclude such questioning about other offenses.[72]

To complicate the issue, the right to assistance of counsel includes the right *not* to be assisted by counsel, provided the record clearly shows that defendants—again with full awareness of what they were doing—asked the judge for the right to defend themselves[73] Although a judge must grant such a request, the appointment of standby counsel by the judge does not violate defendants' rights to conduct their own defense, provided the standby counsel's participation does not interfere with the defendants' actual control over the presentation of their defense and cannot reasonably be thought to have undermined the defendants' appearance before the jury in the status of representing themselves.[74]

"The Sixth Amendment right to counsel does not attach until after the initiation of formal charges."[75] (Under the Fifth Amendment, however, persons

---

[69] *Ake* v *Oklahoma*, 470 US 68 (1985).

[70] *Michigan* v *Jackson*, 476 US 625 (1986).

[71] *Michigan* v *Harvey*, 494 US 344 (1990).

[72] *McNeil* v *Wisconsin*, 115 L Ed 2d 158 (1991).

[73] *Gideon* v *Wainwright*, 372 US 335 (1963); *Faretta* v *California*, 422 US 806 (1975).

[74] *McKaskle* v *Wiggins*, 465 US 168 (1984).

[75] *Moran* v *Burbine*, 475 US 412 (1986); *United States* v *Gouveia*, 467 US 180 (1984).

not formally accused of a crime but subject to custodial interrogation have the right to refuse to answer questions until provided an attorney.) After criminal charges have been initiated, whether by indictment or information or at a preliminary hearing, or arraignment, defendants are entitled to have a lawyer at their side whenever and wherever they appear and substantial rights may be affected. Included are occasions when defendants are subject to identification by victims, as in lineups (but not when arrays of photographs are used); arraignments, if a plea may be taken; preliminary hearings; the trial itself, of course; the time when the judge instructs the jury; and the sentencing.[76]

Confessions and other evidence secured in violation of the right to the assistance of counsel are subject to essentially the same exclusionary rules as are applied to enforce the Fourth Amendment. And what police and prosecutors may not do directly—namely, cross-examine defendants without counsel when counsel has been requested—they may not do indirectly. For example, although there is no constitutional prohibition against the use of undercover agents, prosecutors violated the Sixth Amendment when they instructed a paid informer in the same jail with the accused to listen for and report any damaging statements made by the accused. The government had intentionally created a situation likely to induce the accused to make incriminating statements without the assistance of counsel.[77] (This situation is to be distinguished from the use of undercover agents to get information from persons who are in jail after conviction for crimes *unrelated* to those for which the agent is trying to get information.)[78] In short, after being formally charged with a crime, the accused has a right to communicate with the state only through his or her lawyer.

Perhaps the decision that went to the limit of the application of this principle was the five-to-four decision in *Brewer* v *Williams* reversing a conviction for murdering a child because it was based on a confession made to the police while they were transporting the accused to jail after his attorney had requested that he not be questioned that evening. The police had induced the confession by telling Williams that because it was snowing so hard, the child might not be able to have "a Christian burial" unless he told them where the body could be found.[79] (On retrial, Williams was convicted again and that conviction was affirmed, on the basis that there would have been "inevitable discovery of the body.")[80]

A defendant has a right to the assistance of counsel not only at the trial, but at the sentencing stage. If placed on probation, a person is entitled to legal help whenever there is a hearing to revoke probation.

The Constitution does not require that there be an appeal to a higher court, but when a right of appeal has been established (all jurisdictions now provide

---

[76] *Herring v New York*, 422 US 853 (1975); *Kirby v Illinois*, 406 US 682 (1972); *United States v Wade*, 388 US 218 (1967); *Moore v Illinois*, 434 US 220 (1977).

[77] *Massiah v United States*, 377 US 201 (1964); *United States v Henry*, 447 US 264 (1980); *Maine v Moulton*, 474 US 159 (1986).

[78] *Illinois v Perkins*, 110 L Ed 2d 243 (1990).

[79] *Brewer v Williams*, 430 US 387 (1977).

[80] *Nix v Williams*, 467 US 431 (1984).

at least one appeal for all criminal convictions), a defendant is constitutionally entitled to the help of an attorney in making the *first* appeal.[81] (This right to an effective attorney for an appeal was held to be guaranteed by due process and equal protection requirements rather than Sixth Amendment considerations, but it seems that the Court, although saying "due process," was thinking Sixth Amendment.) For further appeals, including taking cases to the United States Supreme Court, a state has no federal constitutional obligation to furnish attorneys at public expense.[82] Nor is the right to an attorney constitutionally guaranteed for what are known as postconviction "collateral proceedings."[83]

Although states may not deprive prisoners of opportunities to consult with lawyers and to have access to lawbooks and other legal materials, they do not have to provide attorneys for prisoners, including those on death row, seeking postconviction relief, filing for habeas corpus or other subsequent attacks on the constitutional validity of the trial.[84] "Postconviction proceeding is not part of the criminal process itself, but is instead a civil action designed to overturn a preemptively valid criminal judgment. Nothing in the Constitution requires the States to provide such proceedings or to follow a federal model."[85]

AMENDMENT VII: TRIAL BY JURY IN COMMON-LAW CASES

In Suits at common law, where the value in controversy shall exceed twenty dollars, the right of trial by jury shall be preserved, and no fact tried by a jury, shall be otherwise re-examined in any Court of the United States, than according to the rules of the common law.

This provision refers to litigation in *federal* courts and has not been incorporated into the due process requirement of the Fourteenth Amendment. It concerns suits at common law. It does not apply to equity proceedings, which are seldom before a jury, or to those disputes which Congress has entrusted to administrative agencies.

The amendment was not the source of much litigation until 1974 and it was generally thought that the constitutional right to jury trial extended only to actions arising under the common law, not to those arising out of statutes enacted by Congress. In 1974 the Supreme Court declared the contrary: "The

---

[81] *Evitts v Lucey,* 469 US 387 (1985).

[82] *Ross v Moffit,* 417 US 600 (1974); *Pennsylvania v Finley,* 481 US 551 (1987).

[83] *Pennsylvania v Finley,* 481 US 551 (1987).

[84] *Murray v Giarratano,* 492 US 1 (1989).

[85] Justice O'Connor concurring in *Murray v Giarratano,* 492 US 1 (1989).

Seventh Amendment does apply to actions enforcing statutory rights, and requires a jury trial upon demand, if the statutes create legal rights and remedies, enforceable in an action for damages in the ordinary courts of law."[1]

To determine what makes an action one "at common law"—which provides individuals a constitutional right to a jury trial—requires the examination of a variety of technical niceties, including the nature of the issues involved and the remedy sought.[2] The amendment applies only "if a cause of action is legal in nature and it involves a matter of 'private right.'" (If it is a legal remedy, money damages most often are sought.) But this is not all. The Seventh Amendment only protects those particular legal actions involving private rights which are of the nature that must be heard by Article III courts, not those legal actions that Congress may entrust to administrative agencies. But, as we have noted, which particular legal actions involving private rights that Congress may not entrust to administrative agencies is itself a question for which there are no precise answers.

Although a legal dispute between two individuals ordinarily is a private right action and only hearable before an Article III court, it does not follow that just because the government is not a party to a case that Congress must entrust its resolution to an Article III court. The crucial question, in cases not involving the Federal Government, is whether "Congress... has created a seemingly 'private' right that is so closely integrated into a public regulatory scheme as to be a matter appropriate for agency resolution with limited involvement by the Article III judiciary."[3] In short, a private right that must be protected by the jury trial requirements of the Seventh Amendment ceases to become one if Congress thinks it could be better adjudicated elsewhere and a majority of the Supreme Court agrees with it.

The Seventh Amendment is, however, more than a paper tiger. Although "Congress may devise novel causes of action involving public rights free from the strictures of the Seventh Amendment," nonetheless, the Court will occasionally hold that "[Congress] lacks the power to strip parties contesting matters of private right of their constitutional right to a trial by jury." Such was a 1989 decision of the Supreme Court in which the Court declared unconstitutional a provision of the bankruptcy laws. Congress had entrusted to the bankruptcy courts a certain action that a majority of the Court concluded was protected by the Seventh Amendment since it was legal in nature and involved a private right and could not be assigned to an equity court.[4]

The Seventh Amendment does not guarantee that a jury will establish the amount of the damages and penalties to be awarded. Congress, if it wishes, can give that responsibility to a judge.[5]

---

[1] *Lorillard v Pons*, 434 US 575 (1978); *Curtis v Loether*, 415 US 189 (1974).
[2] *Chauffeurs, Teamsters & Helpers v Terry*, 108 L Ed 2d 519 (1990).
[3] *Thomas v Union Carbide*, 473 US 568 (1985).
[4] *Granfinanciera v Nordberg*, 492 US 33 (1989).
[5] *Tull v United States*, 481 US 412 (1987).

The Seventh Amendment does not require that the jury be of the size and character known in common law. Thus, in civil cases in federal courts, as long as a jury has not less than six members it is satisfactory.[6] Most federal district courts are presently employing some form of jury with fewer than twelve members for civil cases, although some judges insist on twelve. Alternates are now regularly used so that the final number voting may be between twelve and six with the precise number depending on how many jurors drop out during the trial because of illness, disqualifications, or personal excusable emergencies.[7]

There is no holding whether less than unanimous verdicts would be constitutionally permissible in federal civil trials should Congress ever choose to implement such a process.

AMENDMENT VIII: BAIL AND CRUEL AND UNUSUAL PUNISHMENTS

Excessive bail shall not be required,

Until the Court's decision in *United States* v *Salerno* (1987), it was thought that everybody is entitled to bail except those accused of a capital crime, and that bail higher than reasonably calculated to ensure the presence of a defendant at trial would be "excessive."[1] Since persons are innocent until their guilt has been determined by trial, the sole constitutional justification for bail was thought to be to prevent flight. Thus, persons accused of capital crimes—because under some circumstances no amount of bail might be sufficient to ensure their presence at trial—might be denied bail, but this phrase was thought to guarantee that no other accused person could be detained without bail until *after* conviction.

In *United States* v *Salerno* the Court upheld the preventive detention provisions of the Bail Reform Act of 1984 against the charge these provisions violated both the due process clause and the Eighth Amendment. That act, similar to laws in thirty or so states, authorizes federal judges to deny bail to "dangerous persons" charged with certain felonies, including serious drug offenses, crimes of violence, and crimes in which firearms were used or possessed for whom no conditions will reasonably assure the appearance of such persons at their trial and the safety of any other persons in the community. Suspects are

---

[6] *Colegrove* v *Battin,* 413 US 149 (1973).

[7] Junda Woo, "Role of Alternative Juror Expands, Allowing an Equal Voice and Vote," *The Wall Street Journal,* December 26, 1991, p. 10. Charles Roberts, "Alternate Jurors Now Will Vote in Federal Court," *Los Angeles Daily Journal,* January 3, 1992, p. 1.

[1] *Stack* v *Boyle,* 342 US 1 (1951); *Schlib* v *Kuebel,* 404 US 357 (1971).

entitled to a hearing on the matter within five days, although failure to provide a hearing within the time limit does not require the release of a defendant later found to be dangerous or likely to flee.[2] Judges (in fact most hearings are before magistrates) must explain in writing why they believe there is clear and convincing evidence that no conditions of pretrial release can reasonably ensure the safety of other persons and of the community. Detention orders may be appealed.

In sustaining the law, Chief Justice Rehnquist stated for the Court, "This Clause . . . says nothing about whether bail shall be available at all . . ." but only that when required it not be excessive. "We believe," he continued, "that when Congress has mandated detention on the basis of a compelling interest other than prevention of flight, as it has here, the Eighth Amendment does not require release on bail."[3]

nor excessive fines imposed,

It was not until 1989 that the Court gave any attention to this clause when it held that it did not limit the award of punitive damages to a party in a civil suit when the government neither had prosecuted the action nor had any right to receive a share of the damages, but did apply to limit the power of governments to impose fines.[4] Then in 1993, the Court concluded that this clause does limit "the Government's power to extract payments, whether in cash or in kind," as punishment, "including civil procedures for the forfeiture of property, what is called an *in rem* civil forfeiture proceeding."[5] The key is not whether the proceedings are criminal or civil but whether the action taken by the government is *punishment*. The specifics in the 1993 case relate to South Dakota's seeking forfeiture of a mobile home and auto body shop which were owned by and had been used by a person as the locale for the sale of two grams of cocaine. Although the Court held that the excessive fines clause did apply to these civil proceedings, it returned to the lower courts the initial responsibility to develop a test to decide when a forfeiture is in fact constitutionally "excessive."

nor cruel and unusual punishments inflicted

---

[2] *United States v Montalvo-Murillo*, 109 L Ed 2d 720 (1990).

[3] *United States v Salerno*, 481 US 739 (1987).

[4] *Browning-Ferris v Kelco Disposal*, 492 US 257 (1989).

[5] *Austin v United States*, 125 L Ed 2d 488 (1993).

This ban limits government in three ways. First, it limits barbaric punishments, such as burning at the stake, crucifixion, breaking on the wheel, use of the rack and the thumbscrew, and service in chains at hard labor. "Moreover, the Eighth Amendment's proscriptions are not limited to those practices condemned by the common law in 1789. . . . [T]he Amendment also recognizes the evolving standards of decency that mark the progress of a maturing society."[6] Second, the clause prohibits punishments that are "grossly out of proportion to the severity of the crime or that make no measurable contribution to acceptable goals of punishment and hence are nothing more than the purposeless and needless imposition of pain and suffering." Third, the clause limits what can be considered a criminal offense.

As to the latter, merely being addicted to drugs or being a chronic alcoholic, for example, cannot be made a crime, for making it a crime would inflict punishment simply for being ill.[7] However, being drunk in public or buying drugs or possessing them can be made criminal, for such statutes punish persons for their behavior, not for being ill.[8]

The Eighth Amendment prohibition against cruel and unusual punishments applies only to criminal sanctions; it does not protect public school children from corporal punishment by their teachers.[9]

Barbaric Punishments

In discerning what are the evolving standards of decency, the Court has looked at "objective" evidence of how our society views a particular punishment, such as legislation enacted by the state legislatures, sentences imposed by juries, and recently it has even considered public sentiment as viewed by public opinion polls as well as the sentiments expressed by organizations concerned with such matters.[10] Justice Scalia, joined by three other justices, has gone out of his way to point out that it is "*American* conceptions of decency that are dispositive," rejecting the contention that the sentencing practices of other countries are relevant. He has also emphasized that in discerning evolving standards of decency the standard should be the practice of American society as a whole "and should not be, or appear to be, merely the subjective views of individual Justices."[11] Justice Brennan, in dissent, with the concurrence of Justices Marshall, Blackmun, and Stevens, rejoined, "Justice Scalia's approach would largely return the task of defining the contours of Eighth Amendment protection to political majorities," and he insisted that the justices must exercise their own judgment as to what punishments are cruel and unusual.[12]

---

[6]*Ford* v *Wainwright*, 477 US 399 (1986).

[7]*Robinson* v *California*, 370 US 660 (1962).

[8]*Powell* v *Texas*, 392 US 514 (1968).

[9]*Ingraham* v *Wright*, 430 US 651 (1977).

[10]*Penry* v *Lynaugh*, 492 US 302 (1989).

[11]*Stanford* v *Kentucky*, 492 US 361 (1989).

[12]Ibid.

Although it is unlikely that the Court would consider execution by cyanide gas to be a cruel and unusual way to inflict the death penalty, the Supreme Court recently sidestepped the issue. Only California, Maryland, and Arizona currently mandate execution by gas.[13]

Prisoners and Prisons

Justice White, speaking for the Court, announced, "It is undisputed that the treatment a prisoner receives in prison and the conditions under which he is confined are subject to scrutiny under the Eighth Amendment."[14] Justice White may have meant "It should not be disputed," since in the very decision in which he made his statement, Justices Scalia and Thomas dissented. Their view is that the word 'punishment' in the Eighth Amendment refers to the penalty imposed for the commission of a crime and does not cover at all conditions of confinement or restrict the behavior of prison officials.[15] Until 1976 this was also the view of the Court—that the clause applied only to punishments specified by statutes and handed out by judges but not to the conduct of prison officials and guards. But since 1976 the Court has applied the clause to review complaints about conditions of confinement in prisons.[16]

The Constitution does not mandate comfortable prisons, and conditions that are "restrictive and even harsh...are part of the penalty criminals pay for their offenses."[17] To prove cruel and unusual punishments in the operation of prisons, the standard now apparently being applied includes an objective standard of the "unnecessary and wanton" infliction of pain and the subjective one that this action was taken by prison officials intentionally or as the result of "deliberate indifference" to the improper conditions of confinement.[18]

In the case of the use of force to put down a riot, there is no violation of the cruel and unusual punishment clause unless the force used to restore order was so wanton and unjustified that it was "tantamount to a knowing willingness that it occur."[19] Outside of a riot situation when force is being applied the standard is whether prison officials "maliciously and sadistically" use force to cause harm. "Not every malevolent touch by a prison guard gives rise to a federal cause of action," and there must be something beyond a minimal use of force but there is no requirement that the prisoner be subject to significant injury.[20] The Court has not yet definitely decided whether the cruel and unusual clause comes into play for "isolated and unauthorized"

---

[13]*Gomez v US District Court*, 118 L Ed 2d 293 (1992).
[14]*Helling v McKinney*, 125 L Ed 2d 22 (1993).
[15]*Helling v McKinney*, 125 L Ed 2d 22 (1993).
[16]*Estelle v Gamble*, 429 US 97 (1976).
[17]*Rhodes v Chapman*, 452 US 337 (1981).
[18]*Wilson v Seiter*, 115 L Ed 2d 271 (1991).
[19]*Whitley v Albers*, 475 US 312 (1986).
[20]*Hudson v McMillian*, 117 L Ed 2d 156 (1992).

misconduct on the part of a prison official, and the lower courts are divided on the issue.[21]

"Double-celling" is not a violation. But when governments confine persons without proper diet in excessively crowded and unsanitary conditions or knowingly deny prisoners needed medical care, they violate the Constitution.[22] In the case of exposure to health risks, such as when a prisoner was assigned a cell with another inmate who smoked five packs of cigarettes a day, the tests are the subjective one of "deliberate indifference" to imposing unnecessary and wanton infliction of pain contrary to contemporary standards of decency and an objective one of showing that the prisoner was in fact being exposed to an unreasonable risk of serious damage to health.[23]

Federal judges have declared unconstitutional the manner in which almost half the states have operated their prisons, in some cases their entire prison systems. In 1980, Congress in the Civil Rights for Institutionalized Persons Act authorized the Department of Justice to act whenever conditions in state prisons were thought to violate constitutional rights. The department obtained court orders involving prisons in five states for lack of medical care and overcrowding.

Disproportionate Punishments

An example of a punishment grossly out of proportion to the severity of the crime would be life imprisonment for overtime parking. To use an example from real life, the Court set aside the sentence of death for the crime of rape of an adult woman in the absence of additional physical attack or abuse.[24] Outside the context of capital punishment, successful challenges to the proportionality of particular sentences have been exceedingly rare. The Court held that the Eighth Amendment does not prevent Texas from applying its recidivist statute for mandatory life imprisonment of any person convicted of a felony for the third time to William James Rummel. Rummel's convictions were for relatively minor offenses: fraudulent use of a credit card to obtain $80 worth of merchandise, passing a forged check in the amount of $28.36, and accepting $120.75 to repair an air conditioner that he never intended to repair.[25] Two years after its Rummel decision, the Court reaffirmed its unwillingness to get involved in the review of the proportionality of sentences and refused to set aside a forty-year sentence and a $20,000 fine for the crime of intending to distribute nine ounces of marijuana. The Court reaffirmed that, for crimes classifiable as felonies, the length of the sentence imposed is purely a matter of legislative prerogative.[26]

The only successful challenge to disproportionate sentencing not involving capital punishment came when the Court in *Solem v Helm* put aside South

---

[21]*Helling* v *McKinney*, 125 L Ed 2d 22 (1993).
[22]*Estelle* v *Gamble*, 429 US 97 (1972).
[23]*Helling* v *McKinney*, 125 L Ed 2d 22 (1993).
[24]*Coker* v *Georgia*, 433 US 588 (1977); *Hutto* v *Finney*, 437 US 678 (1978).
[25]*Rummel* v *Estelle*, 445 US 263 (1980).
[26]*Hutto* v *Davis*, 454 US 370 (1982).

Dakota's sentencing of Jerry Helm to life in prison without possibility of parole after his conviction for his seventh nonviolent felony. For determining whether punishments are disproportionate, the Court majority set forth three guidelines: (1) the gravity of the offense and the harshness of the penalty, (2) the sentences imposed on other criminals in the same jurisdiction, and (3) the sentences imposed for the commission of the same crime in other jurisdictions.[27] Chief Justice Burger, with whom Justices White, Rehnquist, and O'Connor joined in dissent, accused the majority of ignoring the *Rummel* decision and of adopting a view that amounts to nothing more than a determination "that a sentence is unconstitutional if it is more severe than five justices think appropriate."

In a 1991 decision that left *Solem v Helm* still standing but very shaky, the Rehnquist Court edged away from proportionality review outside of the context of the death penalty. Before the Court was the constitutionality of a Michigan statute imposing a life sentence without the possibility of parole for possession of 650 grams or more of certain controlled substances as applied to a person for possessing 672 grams of cocaine.[28] Although writing for the Court, Justice Scalia, in a part of an opinion joined only by Chief Justice Rehnquist, argued that the framers chose not to include within the Eighth Amendment guarantee any limitation against disproportionate sentences and that outside of the death penalty context the decision as to severity of punishment should be left to the discretion of the legislature. However, he hedged: "This is not to say that there are no absolutes; one can imagine extreme examples that no rational person, in no time or place, could accept." Justices Kennedy, O'Connor, and Souter would retain the constraint against "grossly disproportionate" sentences, but would have reinterpreted the *Solem* three-part test to call for a consideration of punishments passed out for other crimes both inside the jurisdiction and in other states only in "the rare case in which a threshold comparison of the crime committed and the sentence imposed leads to an inference of gross disproportionality." Thus, *Solem* is alive but not kicking.

Capital Punishment

What of capital punishment? After much soul-searching and many decisions, the Supreme Court ruled that the death penalty is not per se cruel and unusual punishment for the crime of murder. But it must be properly imposed. Death is different from any other punishment, both in severity and finality. The sentencing process as well as the trial itself must satisfy both due process and Eighth Amendment requirements.[29]

"The death penalty may be properly imposed only as to crimes resulting in the death of the victim."[30] For a while the Court's standard was that the death penalty could not be imposed on anyone who was not actually the "trig-

---

[27]*Solem v Helm*, 463 US 277 (1983).

[28]*Harmelin v Michigan*, 115 L Ed 2d 836 (1991).

[29]*Gardner v Florida*, 430 US 349 (1977); *Woodson v North Carolina*, 428 US 280 (1976).

[30]Chief Justice Burger in *Coker v Georgia*, 433 US 584 (1977).

german" convicted of having killed, attempting to kill, or intending to kill someone. Merely having participated in a felony in which persons were killed by others would not do. In fact, there was some language that seemed to suggest that the death penalty could properly be imposed only on those who had committed an "outrageously wanton and vile murder."[31] However, the Rehnquist Court has modified that standard and announced that persons participating in felonies may be given the death penalty even if they did not kill or intend to kill anybody, provided their participation in the felony was "major" and showed a reckless indifference to human life.[32]

The Court in 1972 set aside state laws imposing a death penalty because they were being applied in a capricious manner[33] in which blacks were much more likely than whites to be sentenced to death. Many states responded with mandatory death sentence statutes, that is, requiring the imposition of the death penalty on all persons convicted of certain crimes. This, too, said the Court, is unconstitutional.[34] Moreover, the mandatory imposition of the death sentence for every person convicted of a specified capital offense—for example, murder of a police officer or murder while serving a life sentence—will not do.[35]

As a result states have to harmonize two competing commandments of the Eighth Amendment. "On the one hand . . . States must limit and channel the discretion of judges and juries to ensure that death sentences are not meted out wantonly or freakishly." On the other hand, states "must confer on the sentencer sufficient discretion to take account of the character and record of the individual offender and the circumstances of the particular offense to ensure that death is the appropriate punishment in a specific case."[36]

The Court has also held that the Eighth Amendment forbids the execution of certain categories of persons because of their status. No person may be executed who is insane at the time of the execution and the amendment requires that a state provide an opportunity for some kind of hearing on this issue to dispose of claims of insanity.[37] The amendment does not categorically prohibit a death sentence for a mentally retarded person, but the accused is entitled to jury instructions as to the mitigating effect of mental retardation and childhood abuse.[38] A state may not execute any person for crimes committed before the accused was sixteen years old,[39] but the Court has endorsed the constitutionality of capital punishment for persons sixteen and seventeen years old at the time they committed the crimes.[40] And of course, "a truly persuasive demonstration of 'actual innocence' made after trial would render the execution of a defendant unconstitutional."[41]

---

[31]*Godfrey v Georgia*, 446 US 420 (1980); *Enmund v Florida*, 458 US 782 (1982).
[32]*Tison v Arizona*, 481 US 137 (1987).
[33]*Furman v Georgia*, 408 US 238 (1972).
[34]*Roberts v Louisiana*, 431 US 663 (1977), but see *Gregg v Georgia*, 428 US 153 (1976).
[35]*Roberts v Louisiana*, 431 US 663 (1977); *Sumner v Shuman*, 483 US 66 (1987).
[36]*Graham v Collins*, 122 L Ed 2d 260 (1993).
[37]*Ford v Wainwright*, 477 US 399 (1986).
[38]*Penry v Lynaugh*, 492 US 302 (1989).
[39]*Thompson v Oklahoma*, 487 US 815 (1988).
[40]*Stanford v Kentucky*, 488 US 887 (1989).
[41]*Herrera v Collins*, 122 L Ed 2d 203 (1993).

In 1987 a substantial attack was made on the death penalty, based on persuasive statistical evidence that in Georgia those convicted of murdering a white person were much more likely than those convicted of murdering a black person to be given a death sentence. The evidence, it was argued, showed that the death penalty in Georgia was being imposed under a sentencing procedure that created a substantial risk that punishment would be inflicted in an arbitrary and capricious manner. A majority of the Court rejected this argument on the grounds that the sentence of death for the crime charged was not disproportionate merely because other defendants did not receive the death penalty. The dissenters responded that the evidence conclusively proved that in Georgia a jury would more likely than not have spared the defendant's life if his victim had been black, and they said that this fact alone demonstrated that the sentencing procedures of Georgia, in addition to violating the equal protection clause, by their arbitrariness amounted to cruel and unusual punishment.[42]

After guilt has been established, most states leave to the jury the responsibility of deciding whether the sentence should be life or death. A few states—Arizona, Florida, Alabama, and Indiana—allow a judge to override a jury's recommendation of life imprisonment, and the Court has concluded that "placing the responsibility on a trial judge to impose the sentence in a capital case is [not] so fundamentally at odds with contemporary standards of fairness and decency" that the practice violates either the Eighth Amendment or the due process clause of the Fourteenth.[43]

How much discretion do sentencers have in capital punishment cases? On the one hand, the death sentence may not be mandatory. On the other, a state may not leave the decision of whether to impose capital punishment on a particular defendant solely to "the untrammeled discretion of a jury."[44] Nor may a state adopt a vague standard to guide judges and juries in distinguishing between those persons convicted of murder who will be subject to the death penalty and those who will not.[45] The state must ensure that judge or jury imposes the penalty only after careful consideration of all mitigating circumstances including the character and record of the person convicted and the circumstances of a particular crime.[46] It is essential that the capital sentencing decision allows for any mitigating circumstances that may be relevant to either the particular offender or the particular offense. Whoever sets the sentence, judge or jury, "may not refuse to consider or be precluded from considering any relevant mitigating evidence" that the defendant wishes to present.[47] And

---

[42]*McCleskey* v *Kemp*, 481 US 279 (1987).

[43]*Spaziano* v *Florida*, 468 US 447 (1984); *Hildwin* v *Florida*, 490 US 638 (1989); *Walton* v *Arizona*, 111 L Ed 2d 511 (1990).

[44]Justice Brennan concurring in *Adams* v *Texas*, 448 US 38 (1980).

[45]*Godfrey* v *Georgia*, 446 US 420 (1980).

[46]*Mills* v *Maryland*, 486 US 367 (1988); *McKoy* v *North Carolina*, 494 US 433 (1990).

[47]*McKoy* v *North Carolina*, 494 US 433 (1990); *Skipper* v *South Carolina*, 476 US 1 (1986); *Hitchcock* v *Dugger*, 481 US 393 (1987).

the fundamental principle is that "to satisfy the Eighth and Fourteenth Amendments, a capital sentencing scheme must 'suitably direct and limit' the sentencer's discretion so as to minimize the risk of wholly arbitrary and capricious action. . . . The State must 'channel the sentencer's discretion by clear and objective standards that provide specific and detailed guidance, and that make rationally reviewable the process for imposing a sentence of death.'"[48]

In a matter of great importance for what a jury may consider, in 1987 and confirmed in 1989, the Supreme Court in essence held that information about the victim or about the effect of the crime on the victim's family or statements by the victim's family cannot be considered at the time of sentencing. Such evidence, said the Court, "creates a constitutionally unacceptable risk that the jury may impose the death penalty in an arbitrary and capricious manner."[49] "The defendant's punishment must be tailored to his guilt and comments by the prosecutor or the victim's family about the victim's personal characteristics could result in imposing the death sentence irrelevant to the defendant's decision to kill."[50] In 1991 the Court concluded that its earlier decisions on victim impact statements were wrongly decided and ruled that a state could, if it wished, permit evidence and argument relating to the victim and the impact of the victim's death on the victim's family at a capital sentencing hearing,[51] but left undisturbed its holding with respect to the admission of a victim's family members' characterizations and opinions about the crime, the defendant, and the appropriate sentence. In a bitter dissent Justice Marshall argued, "Power, not reason, is the new currency of this Court's decisionmaking. . . . Neither the law nor the facts supporting . . . [the earlier rulings] underwent any change in the last four years. Only the personnel of this Court did."

Justices Brennan and Marshall were so opposed to capital punishment that they refused to be bound by the precedents of the Court upholding it and on every occasion recorded their opposition and their conviction that it violates the Constitution. On the other side, Chief Justice Rehnquist and Justice Scalia believe that the Supreme Court's unwillingness to accept the plain words of the Constitution endorsing capital punishment has created such uncertainty and unpredictability that persons sentenced to a death have an opportunity to postpone their punishment for years and years and have effectively blocked the operations of "swift or even timely justice."[52]

---

[48]*Lewis v Jeffers*, 497 US 764 (1990); quoted in *Arave v Creech*, 123 L Ed 2d 188 (1993).

[49]*Booth v Maryland*, 482 US 496 (1987); confirmed and extended in *South Carolina v Gathers*, 489 US 1006 (1989).

[50]Ibid.

[51]*Payne v Tennessee*, 115 L Ed 2d 720 (1991).

[52]Justice Scalia, concurring in *Walton v Arizona*, 111 L Ed 2d 511 (1990).

AMENDMENT IX: RIGHTS RETAINED BY THE PEOPLE

The enumeration in the Constitution, of certain rights, shall not be construed to deny or disparage others retained by the people.

This amendment embodies the dominant political thought of eighteenth-century America, which taught that before the establishment of government, people existed in a state of nature and lived under the natural law, which endowed them with certain natural rights. When, by mutual consent, people created government, they granted to it their natural right of judging and executing the natural law but retained the rest of their natural rights. In accordance with this theory, the Bill of Rights did not "confer" rights but merely "protected" those already granted by the natural law. The Ninth Amendment made it clear that the enumeration of rights to be protected did not imply that the other natural rights not mentioned were abandoned.

Although the Ninth Amendment had been mentioned in passing,[1] until 1965 no law had been declared unconstitutional because of disparagement of any of these unenumerated rights, nor had there been any suggestion that this amendment limited the powers of the states. Then in *Griswold* v *Connecticut* (1965), a decision that has turned out to be one of the more important of recent decades, the Court ruled that a Connecticut law forbidding the use of contraceptives violated the right of marital privacy and stated that this right is "within the penumbra of specific guarantees of the Bill of Rights" and is one of the fundamental rights reserved by the Ninth Amendment to the people against disparagement by a state or the national government.[2] More recent decisions tend to peg the right of privacy on the protections of the due process clauses of the Fifth and Fourteenth Amendments.

Among the other rights found in the Ninth Amendment, but always in connection with other constitutional provisions, are the right to be presumed innocent, the right to be judged by a standard of proof beyond a reasonable doubt of guilt in a criminal trial, the right to travel among states, and the right to attend a criminal trial.

After the incorporation of most of the specific provisions of the Bill of Rights into the Fourteenth Amendment, some anticipated that the "glittering generalities" of the Ninth Amendment would become a new constitutional battleground. But the justices who want to protect from governmental intrusion what they consider basic rights not otherwise specifically secured in the Constitution have found the language of the due process and equal protection clauses sufficiently commodious to suit their needs.

---

[1] *United Public Workers* v *Mitchell*, 330 US 75 (1947).
[2] *Griswold* v *Connecticut*, 381 US 479 (1965).

AMENDMENT X: RESERVED POWERS OF THE STATES

The powers not delegated to the United States by the Constitution, nor prohibited by it to the States, are reserved to the States respectively, or to the
people.

This amendment was adopted to assuage fears. It does not alter the distribution of powers between the national and state governments. It adds nothing
to the Constitution; in the words of Justice Stone, "It is merely a truism."[1]
Nonetheless, for decades after John Marshall's death, the Supreme Court from
time to time held that some of the reserved powers of the states were sovereign powers and hence set a limit to the delegated powers of the national government. When the national government used its specifically granted taxing and
spending powers to regulate agriculture, its action was held by the Supreme
Court, in *United States v Butler* (1936), to be repugnant to this amendment,
since the regulation of agriculture is a power reserved to the states.[2] Earlier
the Supreme Court had ruled that, since the power to regulate conditions of
employment is reserved to the states, Congress could not use its powers to
regulate interstate commerce, *Hammer v Dagenhart,* or to tax, *Child Labor
Tax Cases,* for the purpose of driving employers of children out of the interstate
market.[3] In short, under what is called the doctrine of *Dual Federalism,* the
Supreme Court used the Tenth Amendment to limit some of the enumerated
powers of the national government.

Subsequently, however, the Court reversed *Butler, Dagenhart,* and the
Child Labor Tax Cases and returned to Marshall's view that the Tenth
Amendment and the reserved powers of the states do not limit the national government in exercising the powers given it by the Constitution.[4] Today it makes
no constitutional difference whether or not an act of Congress touches or governs matters otherwise subject to state regulation. Congressional regulation
supersedes any conflicting state regulation.

When it comes to the application of national laws directly to the states,
that is, to the way that states and local governments exercise their powers, "the
Tenth Amendment... is not without significance." It declares "the constitutional
policy that Congress may not exercise power in a fashion that impairs the States'
integrity or their ability to function effectively in a federal system."[5]

Yet, as already noted, after a temporary flirtation with the doctrine of Dual
Federalism in *National League of Cities,* the Court by a five-to-four vote in

---

[1] *United States v Butler,* 297 US 1 (1936).
[2] Ibid.
[3] *Hammer v Dagenhart,* 247 US 251 (1918); *Child Labor Tax Cases,* 259 US 20 (1922).
[4] *United States v Darby Lumber Co.,* 312 US 100 (1941); *Wickard v Filburn,* 317 US 111 (1942).
[5] *Fry v United States,* 421 US 542 (1975).

Garcia v San Antonio Metropolitan Transit Authority returned to the more traditional view that the Tenth Amendment is not to be construed as setting any substantial judicially enforceable limits on the national government's full exercise of the powers granted to it. In essence the Court told the states to look to the structure of federalism—that states are represented in the Senate, that members of the House of Representatives champion their districts, that electoral votes for president are cast by states—and not to the federal courts to protect them from overreaching federal power. Justice Powell, writing for the dissenters, accused the majority of failing "to recognize the broad, yet specific areas of sovereignty that the Framers intended the States to retain." "Indeed," he continued, "the Court barely acknowledges that the Tenth Amendment exists.... The Court recasts the language [of the Tenth Amendment] to say that the States retain their sovereign powers 'only to the extent that the Constitution has not divested them of their original powers and transferred those powers to the Federal Government.'"[6]

The Court has not, however, abandoned its role in applying the Tenth Amendment. For example, it upheld the right of a state to mandatorily retire its judges: it did so by interpreting the coverage of a federal anti-discrimination statute, but the constitutional overtones of the ruling were clear (see page 175).[7]

In 1992 the Supreme Court, in an almost unprecedented ruling, actually declared part of an act of Congress to be in violation of the Tenth Amendment (see page 175) because Congress had ordered states to take title to low-level radioactive waste if by a certain date they had not made proper arrangements for the disposal of such waste generated within their boundaries. As the dissenters pointed out, the actual impact of that holding is limited. Congress could accomplish all it sought to accomplish by avoiding a direct order to a state. Using its commerce clause powers Congress could forbid the shipment of any such waste out of the state if the state failed by a deadline to provide for its appropriate disposal. Yet, the Court's use of the Tenth Amendment to limit congressional action is another warning, however mild, to Congress that the Tenth Amendment is part of the Constitution and that, as Justice O'Connor wrote for the Court and quoting from *The Federalist No. 39*, "States are not mere political subdivisions of the United States. The Constitution instead 'leaves to the several states a residuary and inviolable sovereignty,' reserved explicitly to the States by the Tenth Amendment."[8]

The relationships between the national government and the state governments are not symmetrical. The national government represents all the people, each state only some of them. Although national regulations may be applied to the states, no state may tax or otherwise regulate a federal agency, except with the consent of Congress. To give one of many examples: no state may levy any tax on liquor sold for use in military installations.[9] But Congress

---

[6]*Garcia v San Antonio Metropolitan Transit Authority*, 469 US 528 (1985)
[7]*Gregory v Ashcroft*, 115 L Ed 2d 410 (1991).
[8]*New York v United States*, 120 L Ed 2d 120 (1992).
[9]*United States v Tax Commission of Mississippi*, 421 US 599 (1975).

can collect from the states aircraft registration fees for helicopters, including state-owned helicopters used for police work.[10]

Note that the Tenth Amendment does not say that powers not *expressly* delegated to the United States are reserved to the states. The framers of the Tenth Amendment specifically rejected such a statement, for its adoption would have seriously curtailed the scope of national powers. Moreover, it should be emphasized that the states must exercise their reserved powers subject to the national government's supremacy and to national constitutional limitations. For example, states have the reserved power to establish public schools, but they may not exercise this power contrary to the Fourteenth Amendment or to any other constitutional limit. Nor may they exercise it in such a way as to conflict with national regulations—for example, by compelling an eighteen-year-old drafted to serve in the United States armed forces to attend school. The national power to raise and support armies and navies takes precedence over a state's power to educate.

PRE–CIVIL WAR AMENDMENTS

AMENDMENT XI: SUITS AGAINST STATES

The Judicial power of the United States shall not be construed to extend to any suit in law or equity, commenced or prosecuted against one of the United States by Citizens of another State, or by Citizens or Subjects of any Foreign State.

This amendment was proposed March 4, 1794, and proclaimed January 8, 1798.

Article III, Section 2, paragraph 1, among other things, extends the judicial power of the United States to "cases and controversies between a state and citizens of another state." During the struggle over ratification of the Constitution, many persons objected to this clause on the ground it would permit a private individual to hail a state before a federal court; they were assured by Hamilton and others that, because of the doctrine of "sovereign immunity," no state could ever be sued without its own consent. In 1792, however, the Supreme Court applied the literal terms of the Constitution and upheld the right of the federal courts to take jurisdiction in a case commenced by a citizen of South Carolina against Georgia.[1] Since many states were in

---

[10] *Massachusetts v United States,* 435 US 444 (1978); *New York Gaslight Club v Carey,* 447 US 54 (1980).

[1] *Chisholm v Georgia,* 2 Dallas 419 (1793).

default on their debts, there was a great alarm lest a series of similar suits result. Immediately after the Supreme Court's decision, the Eleventh Amendment was proposed, and its ratification in effect "recalled" the decision.

The amendment covers states.[2] It does not cover counties, cities, school boards, or regional authorities created by states.[3] It does not protect states from being sued in federal courts by other states or by the United States government. It does not protect a state against suit in the courts of another state. It does protect states from being sued in federal courts by other nations and by Indian tribes.[4] However, the immunity does not depend on the state's being named as a party; it includes suits in which private individuals seek to impose a liability that must be paid from public funds.[5] In short, the Court reads the amendment to find a surrender of immunity by the states in "only two contexts: suits by sister States... and suits by the United States."[6]

If a state commences a prosecution in a state court, the Eleventh Amendment does not prevent the person prosecuted from appealing the decision of a state court to the Supreme Court. The taking of the case from state courts to the Supreme Court is not considered the initiation of a new case by the individual against the state; it is merely the continuation of the one originally commenced or prosecuted by the state.

Debates over the meaning of the Eleventh Amendment continue to stir deep passions and illustrate that what appear to be relatively technical and nonsubstantive issues can generate considerable heat and have major policy consequences. Former Justice Brennan led a minority who would have narrowly construed the Eleventh Amendment to preserve maximum freedom for those who believe that their constitutional rights have been violated to seek vindication in federal courts. He would have applied the amendment in its literal terms only to immunize a nonconsenting state against federal court suits in law and equity brought by citizens of another state or by citizens of a foreign state. He would have reversed an 1890 precedent, *Hans* v *Louisiana*,[7] that incorporated the doctrine of sovereign immunity into the Eleventh Amendment to prevent federal suits by a state's own citizens. Justices Blackmun and Stevens are the only justices left who take this position. Justice Stevens has chided the Court majority for what he terms "the Court's love affair with the doctrine of sovereign immunity," a doctrine that, he points out, "despite its ancient lineage,... is nothing but a judge-made rule."[8] The amendment, however, continues to be construed to extend to states' immunity from federal suits of all kinds,

---

[2] *Lake Country Estates* v *Tahoe Regional Planning Agency*, 440 US 391 (1979); *Mt. Healthy City Board of Education* v *Doyle*, 429 US 274 (1977).

[3] *Nevada* v *Hall*, 440 US 410 (1979).

[4] *Blatchford* v *Native Village of Noatak*, 115 L Ed 2d 686 (1991).

[5] *Edelman* v *Jordan*, 415 US 651 (1974); *Florida Department of Health* v *Florida Nursing Home Association*, 450 US 147 (1980).

[6] *Blatchford* v *Native Village of Noatak*, 115 L Ed 2d 686 (1991).

[7] *Green* v *Mansour*, 474 US 64 (1985); *Welch* v *Department of Highways*, 483 US 468 (1987).

[8] Dissenting on another but related issue in *United States* v *Nordic Village*, 117 L Ed 2d 181 (1992).

including those in admiralty brought by foreign nations and, more importantly, those by a state's own citizens.[9]

In the landmark case *Ex parte Young*, the Supreme Court declared that the Eleventh Amendment does not prevent federal courts, on the application of private individuals, from issuing injunctions restraining state officers who are acting unconstitutionally.[10] By the principle of the *rule of law*, a state officer who acts beyond the law ceases to be an officer and thus ceases to be a representative of the state. However, when state officers act beyond the law, their action is nevertheless state action for the purposes of the Fourteenth Amendment. This result is inconsistent but fortunate for the protection of constitutional rights.

Ex parte Young clearly opens federal courts to private individuals seeking injunctions to protect them from alleged violations by state officials of federal laws and the federal Constitution. Should the federal courts provide similar protection against allegations of violations by state authorities of their own state constitutions and state laws? Justice Powell, speaking for the Court majority, refused in *Pennhurst II*, as the case came to be called, to extend the *Young* doctrine to such suits. As he said in a reaffirming decision, such action "would emasculate the Eleventh Amendment."[11]

Although the Eleventh Amendment does not bar injunctive relief to prevent state officials from acting or continuing to act in an unconstitutional fashion, it does, absent consent or clear and unmistakable language by Congress setting aside the immunity, prevent suits for money damages to recover from "state" funds (in contrast to personal funds of the state officials) for past misconduct by state or local officials. The distinction between injunctions and suits for damages is a distinction between actions that are designed to bring an end to ongoing and present violation of federal law and suits designed to compensate for past violations of federal law.[12]

The Eleventh Amendment must be read in connection with other constitutional provisions, most especially the Fourteenth Amendment, that to some extent have modified the Eleventh. When Congress exercises authority granted to it by Section 5 of the Fourteenth Amendment, it can open federal courts to suits against state officials "which are constitutionally impermissible in other contexts."[13] By a somewhat shakier majority (the Brennan Group—Brennan, Marshall, Blackmun, and Stevens, joined by White), the Court decided that the authority of Congress to subject unconsenting states to suit in federal court is not confined to the Fourteenth Amendment, and upheld the right of Congress under the commerce clause to subject states to suits for money damages in federal courts to help clean up hazardous waste sites.[14]

---

[9] *Hans v Louisiana*, 134 US 1 (1890).

[10] *Ex parte Young*, 209 US 123 (1908).

[11] *Papasan v Allain*, 478 US 265 (1986); *Pennhurst State School & Hospital v Halderman*, 465 US 89 (1984).

[12] *Green v Mansour*, 474 US 64 (1985).

[13] *Employees v Missouri Health Department*, 411 US 279 (1973); *Atascadero State Hospital v Scanlon*, 473 US 234 (1985).

[14] *Pennsylvania v Union Gas Co.*, 488 US 810 (1989).

The extent of state immunity continues to be whittled down. Congress may make a state's participation in a federal program conditional on the state's willingness to waive its immunity, but the state must waive its immunity in express language or by such "overwhelming implications from the text as [will] leave no room for any other reasonable construction." (The Court in 1987 overruled a holding that permitted tacit state consent.)[15] However, when Congress wishes to strip states of Eleventh Amendment immunity, whether acting under the Fourteenth Amendment, the commerce clause, the bankruptcy clause, or any other clause, it must do so in unmistakably clear language. "In this area of the law," wrote Justice Kennedy for the Court, "evidence of congressional intent must be both unequivocal and textual."[16] The Court appears to be saying that, if Congress wants to deprive states of their immunity, it must make explicit reference to the Eleventh Amendment or to state sovereign immunity. Legislative history, legislative committee reports, and floor debates are considered irrelevant. Congress must say it.[17] Justices Scalia and O'Connor have spoken out that they would not read the Constitution to give Congress the authority to take away state immunity from suit in federal courts whether it says so clearly or not.[18]

Congress has authorized civil suits against officials who have willfully deprived persons of their constitutional rights, even if they acted under color of law, that is, on behalf of the government. (Any action in an official role is under color of law, whether or not specific action is authorized.) To collect damages from officials, one must prove they acted knowingly or with malicious intent to deprive persons of their constitutional rights.[19] Damages may be collected only from the state officials, not from the state.[20] Municipalities, in contrast to states, may be required to pay compensatory damages for wrongs by their officials, even if done in good faith, if they were done according to policy or custom.[21]

AMENDMENT XII: ELECTION OF THE PRESIDENT

The Electors shall meet in their respective states and vote by ballot for President and Vice-President, one of whom, at least, shall not be an inhabitant of the same state with themselves; they shall name in their ballots the person voted for as President, and in distinct ballots the person voted for as Vice-President, and they shall make distinct lists of all persons voted for as

---

[15] *Welch v Department of Highways*, 483 US 468 (1987).

[16] Ibid.

[17] *Hoffman v Connecticut Income Dept.*, 492 US 96 (1989).

[18] Ibid.

[19] *Ex parte Young*, 209 US 123 (1908).

[20] *Kentucky v Graham*, 473 US 159 (1985).

[21] *Scheuer v Rhodes*, 416 US 213 (1974); *Wood v Strickland*, 420 US 308 (1975); *Monroe v Pape*, 365 US 167 (1961); *Kentucky v Graham*, 473 US 159 (1985).

President, and of all persons voted for as Vice-President, and of the number of votes for each, which lists they shall sign and certify, and transmit sealed to the seat of the government of the United States, directed to the President of the Senate;—The President of the Senate shall, in the presence of the Senate and House of Representatives, open all the certificates and the votes shall then be counted;—The person having the greatest number of votes for President, shall be the President, if such number be a majority of the whole number of Electors appointed; and if no person have such majority, then from the persons having the highest numbers not exceeding three on the list of those voted for as President, the House of Representatives shall choose immediately, by ballot, the President. But in choosing the President, the votes shall be taken by states, the representation from each state having one vote; a quorum for this purpose shall consist of a member or members from two-thirds of the states, and a majority of all the states shall be necessary to a choice. *And if the House of Representatives shall not choose a President whenever the right of choice shall devolve upon them, before the fourth day of March next following, then the Vice-President shall act as President, as in the case of the death or other constitutional disability of the President [emphasis added].*— The person having the greatest number of votes as Vice-President, shall be the Vice-President, if such number be a majority of the whole number of Electors appointed, and if no person have a majority, then from the two highest numbers on the list, the Senate shall choose the Vice-President; a quorum for the purpose shall consist of two-thirds of the whole number of Senators, and a majority of the whole number shall be necessary to a choice. But no person constitutionally ineligible to the office of President shall be eligible to that of Vice-President of the United States.

This amendment was proposed December 8, 1803, and declared in force by the secretary of state September 25, 1804. The emphasized portion of this amendment has been superseded by the Twentieth Amendment and modified by the Twenty-fifth.

The presidential electoral system is the classic example of how custom and usage have amended and democratized the Constitution. As previously mentioned, the authors of the Constitution expected electors to be distinguished citizens who would in fact, as well as in form, choose the president and the vice president. Their expectations were not fulfilled because of the rise of national political parties. By the election of 1800, electors had come to be party puppets, pledged in advance to vote for the candidates nominated by their respective parties. In that election the Republican-Democratic electors were in a majority. Since under the original provisions for selecting the president and the vice president each elector voted for two individuals without indicating which was his choice for president and which for vice president, Aaron Burr, the Republican-Democratic candidate for vice president, received the same number of electoral votes as Thomas Jefferson, the Republican-Democratic candidate for president. This circumstance transferred the election to the House of Representatives, where the Federalists were in control. Although many Federalists favored Burr as the lesser of two evils, Alexander Hamilton threw his great influence on the side of Jefferson, who was finally elected on the thirty-sixth ballot. The Twelfth Amendment was designed to prevent such a situation from occurring again.

The two major differences between the Twelfth Amendment and the original provisions of the Constitution, which were repealed by it, are as follows. First, electors today are required to cast separate votes clearly designating their choice for president and their choice for vice president. Second, in the event no person receives a majority of the electoral votes for president, the House of Representatives chooses from the three persons with the most electoral votes (rather than five, as in the original provision). Each state has one vote in the House. If no person receives a majority of the electoral votes for vice president, the Senate chooses between the two persons with the most electoral votes, each senator having one vote.

Presidential and vice-presidential candidates today are chosen by political parties in national nominating conventions. On the first Tuesday after the first Monday in November, the voters select the electors, who are morally pledged to cast their electoral votes for the candidates chosen by their particular national convention. The electors' names do not even appear on the ballot; only the names of the candidates to whom they are pledged appear. Thus, the electors have been reduced to automatons and the electoral college, as the electors are known collectively, to an automatic registering device.

The development of the two-party system had another consequence for the electoral college that the framers did not anticipate. It greatly lessened the probability that the House of Representatives would be called on to make the final selection. Only once since 1801 has the House exercised this duty. In the election of 1824, before the full development of our party system, Andrew Jackson, John Quincy Adams, and William Crawford received the most electoral votes, but not one of them had a majority. The House, voting by states, chose John Quincy Adams. The only time the Senate has been called upon to make the final selection for the vice presidency was in 1837, when it favored Richard M. Johnson over Francis Granger. With only two major political parties there is no dispersion of the vote, and one party is assured of a majority of the electoral votes. Whenever a strong third party develops, such as George Wallace's American Independent Party in the 1968 election, John Anderson's independent candidacy in 1980, and in 1992 Ross Perot's major run at the White House, the probability of final selection by the House and Senate is greatly increased.

All the states except Maine now provide for the selection of electors on a general statewide, straight-ticket basis. Each voter casts one vote for all the electors of one party or independent candidate. This statewide, straight-ticket voting means that the party that receives the most popular votes in a state receives all that state's electoral votes. For example, in 1992 Bill Clinton (that is, the Democratic electors) received 46 percent of the popular vote in California; George Bush received 32 percent and Ross Perot received 21 percent. Clinton nevertheless received all 54 of California's electoral votes.

It is even possible for a person to obtain a majority of the total popular vote without receiving a majority of the electoral votes. Let us take a hypothetical case involving two states to illustrate this point:

State X (20 electoral votes):   1,800,000 Republican popular votes
                                 1,700,000 Democratic popular votes
State Y (5 electoral votes):   200,000 Republican popular votes
                                   400,000 Democratic popular votes

Results:
Republican popular votes: 2,000,000 Republican electoral votes: 15
Democratic popular votes: 2,100,000 Democratic electoral votes: 5

Such a thing happened in 1876, when Samuel Tilden received more popular votes but lost the electoral vote to Rutherford B. Hayes after a commission awarded contested votes to Hayes, and again in 1888, when Grover Cleveland, despite his larger popular vote, was defeated by Benjamin Harrison.

Despite the widely supported view that the electoral college needs to be reformed, it has been difficult to secure agreement about what reforms should be made. The 1980 and 1992 elections temporarily revived and intensified the concerns about the risks inherent in our present arrangements: if John Anderson in 1980 or Ross Perot in 1992 had secured enough electoral votes to keep either major party candidate from obtaining a majority, electors might have been tempted to exercise some discretion, or, more probably, the election would have been thrown into the House of Representatives, where the Anderson supporters in 1980 or the Perot followers in 1992 might have had the balance of power votes necessary to determine the presidential choice between the two major-party candidates. The discomfort that could result from the installation of a president selected through such procedures is hard to exaggerate.

Representatives of the less populous states have opposed proposals to provide for direct popular election. Since states have as many electoral votes as they have senators and representatives, the smaller states carry greater weight in the electoral college than they would in a nationwide direct election. Some people have proposed that we do away with the individual electors but retain the system of electoral votes and distribute a state's electoral vote in the same ratio as its popular vote. Such a change would eliminate any danger of an elector's disregarding the wishes of the voters (as happened in 1956, 1960, 1968, and 1972), lessen the influence of strategically located minorities, weaken the one-party system where it now exists, and ensure the election of the candidate with the largest popular vote. This change has been opposed by those who fear it would weaken the influence of people living in large cities, who often have the balance of power in presidential elections. These same objections hold even more strongly against proposals to have electors chosen by congressional districts rather than on statewide tickets.

CIVIL WAR AMENDMENTS

The Thirteenth, Fourteenth, and Fifteenth Amendments were adopted after and as a result of the Civil War. They were, so to speak, the terms of surrender dictated by the North to the South. Congress, for example, insisted that the southern states ratify the Fourteenth Amendment before federal troops were withdrawn and the states restored to full participation in Congress.

The purpose of these three amendments was to free the slaves, grant them citizenship, and protect their rights, especially the right to vote, against infringement by the states. As Justice Miller wrote, "No one can fail to be impressed with the one pervading purpose of them all, ... the freedom of the slave race, the security and firm establishment of that freedom, and the protection of the newly-made free man and citizen from the oppression of those who formerly exercised unlimited dominion over him."[1] Clearly the purpose of these amendments was to deprive the states of the "right" to impose disabilities on African Americans because of their race, color, or previous condition of servitude. It was to take almost three-quarters of a century, however, before the Civil War amendments were to be used for this purpose.

AMENDMENT XIII: SLAVERY

SECTION 1
Neither slavery nor involuntary servitude, except as a punishment for crime whereof the party shall have been duly convicted, shall exist within the United States, or any place subject to their jurisdiction.

This amendment was proposed on January 31, 1865, and declared in force by the secretary of state on December 18, 1865.

Before the adoption of this amendment, each state could determine for itself whether or not slavery should be permitted within its borders. The Thirteenth Amendment deprived both the states and the national government of that power. The amendment was aimed at black slavery. Without violating the amendment, a government may still compel persons to help build public roads (under the common law, men could be drafted for a certain number of days every year for this purpose, although in some cases, payment of taxes exempted them from such duties), to pay alimony, or to serve on a jury, in the militia, or in the armed forces.

Several state laws which made failure to work after receiving money to do so *prima facie* evidence of intent to defraud have been held contrary to the

---

[1] *Slaughter House Cases*, 16 Wallace 36 (1873).

Thirteenth Amendment; in effect, such laws made it a crime punishable by imprisonment to fail to work after securing money on the promise to work.[2] They established a condition of *peonage,* involuntary servitude forced on a person to work off a debt.

Section 1 of the Thirteenth Amendment is one of the two provisions of the Constitution (the other is the Twenty-first) that an individual can violate directly, that is, without the government's involvement. It is also self-executing. By its "own unaided force and effect" the Thirteenth Amendment abolished slavery and established universal freedom.

After all these years, the Supreme Court has not decided "whether the Thirteenth Amendment itself reaches practices with a disproportionate effect as well as those motivated by discriminatory purpose, or indeed whether it accomplished anything more than the abolition of slavery."[3]

SECTION 2
Congress shall have power to enforce this article by appropriate legislation.

"Whether or not Section 1 by its own force did anything more than abolish slavery is still an open question. But it is no longer open that under Section 2 Congress has the power to determine what are the badges and incidents of slavery, and the authority to translate that determination into effective legislation."[4] This more expansive interpretation of congressional power is of recent origin. Before 1968 the prevailing view was that all Section 2 did was to give Congress power to prevent the imposition of slavery and peonage, narrowly defined. Hence, it was ruled that Congress had no power under Section 2 to legislate against racial discrimination.[5]

Then, in *Jones* v *Mayer,* the Supreme Court construed Section 2 in a significantly new way, or some would say the Court finally got around to interpreting the section as its framers intended. The case grew out of a suit filed by Mr. and Mrs. Joseph Lee Jones against a developer in St. Louis County, Missouri, who refused to sell them a home because Mr. Jones was an African-American. The Joneses cited an almost unused section of the Civil Rights Act of 1866, enacted pursuant to the Thirteenth Amendment, that reads, "All citizens of the United States shall have the same right, in every State and Territory, as is enjoyed by white citizens thereof to inherit, purchase, lease, sell, hold, and convey real and personal property." Few thought that the Joneses had a good case; almost 90 years earlier, the Court had ruled that Congress lacked power under the Fourteenth Amendment (see page 350) to legislate against discrimination unless

---

[2] *Pollock* v *Williams,* 322 US 4 (1944).
[3] *General Building Contractors* v *Pennsylvania,* 458 US 375 (1982).
[4] *Jones* v *Alfred H. Mayer Co.,* 392 US 409 (1968); *Memphis* v *Greene,* 451 US 100 (1981).
[5] *Civil Rights Cases,* 109 US 3 (1883).

it was imposed or supported by governmental action. The Thirteenth Amendment was thought to cover only slavery; the Civil Rights Act of 1866 had always been construed to cover only state-imposed discrimination. Besides, in 1968 Congress had just passed a civil rights act covering discrimination in housing, which many thought superseded any impact the 1866 law might have had.

As anticipated, the district court dismissed the complaint and the court of appeals affirmed the decision, both courts concluding that the Civil Rights Act of 1866 applied only to state action and did not reach private refusals to sell. But the Supreme Court reversed the decision. Significant beyond the immediate facts of this case was the Supreme Court's interpretation of Section 2 of the Thirteenth Amendment. Justice Stewart, speaking for the Court, proclaimed,

> The Thirteenth Amendment authorized Congress to do more than merely dissolve the legal bond by which the Negro slave was held to his master; it gave Congress the power rationally to determine what are the badges and the incidents of slavery and the authority to translate that determination into effective legislation....
>
> When racial discrimination herds men into ghettos and makes their ability to buy property turn on the color of their skin, then it too is a relic of slavery....
>
> At the very least, the freedom that Congress is empowered to secure under the Thirteenth Amendment includes the freedom to buy whatever a white man can buy, the right to live wherever a white man can live. If Congress cannot say that being a free man means at least this much, then the Thirteenth Amendment made a promise the Nation cannot keep.[6]

Since the Jones decision the Supreme Court has several times reaffirmed its validity.[7] Furthermore, it has ruled that Congress intended the civil rights act passed during Reconstruction to protect not merely blacks but "identifiable classes of persons who are subject to intentional discrimination solely because of their ancestry or ethnic characteristics, such as Jews and Arabs."[8]

In short, Section 2, as now construed, gives Congress the authority to enact whatever legislation is necessary and proper to overcome all incidents and badges of slavery, no matter their source.

---

[6] *Jones v Alfred H. Mayer Co.*, 392 US 409 (1968).

[7] *McDonald v Santa Fe Trail Transportation Co.*, 427 US 273 (1976); *Runyon v McCrary*, 427 US 160 (1976); *Tillman v Wheaton-Haven Recreation Association*, 410 US 431 (1973); *Sullivan v Little Hunt Park*, 376 US 226 (1969).

[8] *Saint Francis College v Al-Khazraji*, 481 US 604 (1987); *Shaare Tefila Congregation v Cobb*, 481 US 615 (1987).

Amendment XIV: Citizenship, Privileges, and Immunities of United States Citizenship, Due Process, and Equal Protection of the Laws

Section 1

All persons born or naturalized in the United States, and subject to the jurisdiction thereof, are citizens of the United States and of the State wherein they reside.

This amendment was proposed June 13, 1866, and declared in force by the secretary of state July 28, 1868.

In the *Dred Scott* case (1857), Chief Justice Taney declared that the framers did not include African Americans as part of the sovereign "people of the United States"; he wrote: "[Negroes] were not intended to be included, under the word 'citizen' in the Constitution, and can therefore claim none of the rights and privileges which that instrument provides for and secures to citizens of the United States. On the contrary, they were at that time considered as a subordinate and inferior class of beings, who had been subjugated by the dominant race, and, whether *emancipated or not* [italics added], yet remained subject to their authority, and had no rights or privileges but such as those who held the power and the government might choose to grant them."[1] The opening sentence of the Fourteenth Amendment reversed this decision.

Persons born in the United States but not subject to the jurisdiction thereof are children of foreign diplomats and children born of alien enemies in the event of a hostile occupation of the United States. Although the Native American tribes are subject to the jurisdiction of the United States, they have been considered a special category, and the Fourteenth Amendment did not directly confer citizenship on them. However, all Native Americans are now citizens of the United States by act of Congress. All other children born in the United States become citizens even if their parents are aliens.

The clause confers citizenship by the principle of *jus soli*—that is, by reason of place of birth; it does not prevent Congress from conferring citizenship by *jus sanguinis*—by reason of blood. Citizenship may also be acquired by naturalization.

The Constitution confers citizenship on all persons born or naturalized in the United States. Although naturalization secured by fraud may be canceled through proper judicial action and persons may under certain conditions voluntarily renounce their citizenship, what the Constitution confers, Congress cannot constitutionally take away. At various times Congress has tried. It has

---

[1] *Scott* v *Sandford*, 19 Howard 393 (1857).

declared that persons who did certain things—for example, voting in elections in other nations, joining the military forces of another nation, and leaving the United States during time of war to avoid the draft—would be construed as having expatriated themselves and would be subject to having their citizenship taken from them by judicial action. The Supreme Court, however, has held those provisions unconstitutional. Expatriation depends on the will of the citizen rather than on the will of Congress.[2]

Congress has the power, nonetheless, to declare that persons who perform certain acts, for example, swearing allegiance to another country, create a presumption that they intend to relinquish citizenship. In such an instance a court may take citizenship away if the government proves by a preponderance of the evidence that the person both voluntarily performed the expatriating act and did so with the "intent to abandon citizenship."[3]

The Fourteenth Amendment confers citizenship on persons born or naturalized in the United States. Congress can confer citizenship on others. It has done so for children born to American citizens outside the United States. Since it is Congress (not the Constitution) that confers this citizenship, Congress may set reasonable conditions on the obtaining and retaining of such citizenship. Thus, the Court sustained a provision expatriating persons born outside the United States to a citizen parent and an alien if such persons do not return to the United States and live here for five continuous years between the ages of fourteen and twenty-eight (since changed to two years).[4]

SECTION 1
[continued] No State shall make or enforce any law which shall abridge the privileges or immunities of citizens of the United States;

After the adoption of the Thirteenth Amendment, several southern states that had been restored to full rights of statehood by President Johnson promptly adopted legislation that, in the words of Justice Miller, "imposed upon the colored race onerous disabilities and burdens, and curtailed their rights in the pursuit of life, liberty, and property to such an extent that their freedom was of little value." Those laws convinced Congress, again to quote Miller, "that something more was necessary in the way of constitutional protection to the unfortunate race who had suffered so much."[5] Accordingly, Congress insisted on the ratification of the Fourteenth Amendment as a condition of its agreeing to restoring the rest of the southern state governments to full

---

[2] *Vance v Terrazas,* 444 US 252 (1980); *Trop v Dulles,* 356 US 86 (1958); *Kennedy v Mendoza-Martinez,* 372 US 144 (1963); *Schneider v Rusk,* 377 US 163 (1964); *Afroyim v Rusk,* 387 US 253 (1967).

[3] *Vance v Terrazas,* 444 US 252 (1980).

[4] *Rogers v Bellei,* 401 US 815 (1971).

[5] *Slaughter House Cases,* 16 Wallace 36 (1873).

participation in the government of the Union. Despite the obvious purpose of the Fourteenth Amendment, to protect blacks from the "oppressions of those who had formerly exercised unlimited dominion" over them, it was not until the 1940s that the amendment was used primarily for this purpose. And it has not been the privileges and immunities clause that has been used, but rather the due process and equal protection clauses.

The Supreme Court in the *Slaughter House Cases* so narrowly construed the privileges and immunities clause in the very first case in which the Fourteenth Amendment came before it that it has never had much significance. The Court held that there are two distinct citizenships, state and federal, and that the "fundamental" civil and political rights that we enjoy are privileges or immunities stemming from *state,* not *United States,* citizenship. In other words, this clause conferred no new rights on United States citizens but merely made explicit a federal guarantee against abridgment of already established rights. The privileges and immunities of United States citizens (which this clause forbids states to abridge) are those that owe their existence to the Constitution and the laws and treaties of the United States, such as the right to travel in the United States, the right to engage in interstate and foreign commerce, the right to the protection of the national government on the high seas and in foreign countries, and the right to vote in primaries and general elections in which members of Congress and presidential electors are chosen and to have that vote properly counted. And although the Supreme Court in past decisions has held that some important rights are not privileges or immunities of United States citizens—such as the right to be secure in one's home, the right to refuse to give self-incriminatory evidence in state courts, the right to engage in a legal occupation, the right to attend public schools, the right to vote in state elections[6]— the significance of those decisions has been undermined by more recent rulings. Those rights may not be privileges of United States citizens, but today they are protected by the due process and equal protection clauses of the Fourteenth Amendment. Furthermore, with the expansion of federal civil rights laws, there are a large number of such rights that owe their existence to federal laws and are thus protected from state (or private, for that matter) abridgment.

SECTION 1
[continued] nor shall any State deprive any person of life, liberty, or property, without due process of law;

As has been noted, after the Supreme Court's interpretation of the privileges and immunities clause rendered it ineffective as a protector of "fundamental rights," an attempt was made to make the due process clause serve

---

[6] *Twining v New Jersey,* 211 US 78 (1908).

this purpose, an attempt that was not completely successful until the 1960s. The Supreme Court still has not gone so far as to make the due process clause of the Fourteenth Amendment a mirror image of the Bill of Rights, although, as noted, most provisions of the Bill of Rights have been incorporated into the due process clause.

What we had to say about the due process clause of the Fifth Amendment (see pages 283–304) is equally applicable to the due process clause of the Fourteenth Amendment. With minimal exceptions, the Fourteenth Amendment due process clause imposes on the states the same limits that the Fifth Amendment due process clause imposes on the national government—which is not true for the equal protection clause (see page 381).

SECTION 1

[continued] nor deny to any person within its jurisdiction the equal protection of the laws.

The equal protection clause, often merging into substantive due process, is the Court's major instrument for scrutinizing state regulations. As noted, there is no equal protection clause limiting the national government; however, just as the due process clause of the Fourteenth Amendment has been used to apply provisions of the Bill of Rights to the states, so has the due process clause of the Fifth Amendment been used to prevent national discriminatory legislation.[7] In *Bolling* v *Sharpe*, the companion case to *Brown* v *Board of Education*, the Court held that equal protection principles are embedded in the Fifth Amendment's due process clause. Just as the states could no longer do so, neither could the national government operate segregated schools in the District of Columbia. "It would be unthinkable that the same Constitution would impose a lesser duty on the Federal Government."[8] In fact, however, Congress has considerably greater leeway in considering race as a relevant category in national legislation than do the states or municipal governments.

State Action

As also noted when discussing the due process clause (see page 285) the equal protection clause, as well as the privileges and immunities clause, is directed to the actions of governments and governmental officials. Private wrongs—wrongful acts of private individuals—if not sanctioned in some way by a state, do not violate the Fourteenth Amendment. Discrimination by pri-

---

[7] *Bolling* v *Sharpe*, 347 US 497 (1954); *Washington* v *Legrant*, 394 US 618 (1969); *Richardson* v *Belcher*, 404 US 78 (1971).

[8] *Bolling* v *Sharpe*, 347 US 497 (1954).

vate individuals may violate a law, but such action does not violate the equal protection clause or, as we have seen, the due process clause, unless it is state supported or positively encouraged by the state. Thus, one of the more important issues growing out of the equal protection and due process clauses is what is and what is not state action.

The first inquiry is "whether the claimed...deprivation has resulted from the exercise of a right or privilege having its source in state authority" or involves a right for which there is no state governmental source, for example a right to have access to a big league baseball team. The second inquiry is "whether the private party charged with the deprivation can be described as a state actor" and in deciding that the Court applies three principles: (1) "the extent to which the 'private actor' relies on governmental assistance"; (2) whether the private actor is performing a traditional governmental function; and (3) "whether the injury caused is aggravated in a unique way by the incidents of governmental authority," that is, whether the harmful action takes place in such a circumstance that it appears to be supported and sanctioned by the government.[9]

The Supreme Court inspects closely whenever there is a suspicion of state involvement in discriminatory conduct. For certain traditional sovereign functions exclusively reserved to governments, the equal protection clause applies regardless of who actually does the discriminating. Thus, if a state delegates responsibility for running governmental elections, including primaries, to private associations such as political parties, the actions of party officers are state actions subject to constitutional restraint.[10] Similarly, if a state allows a private corporation to perform the municipal functions of running a company town, the actions of company officials are state actions.[11]

On the other side, the management of a private shopping center is not state action, nor is the action of a private warehouse operator, or a private utility, even though its franchise is given to it by a state.[12] Although Congress has by law subjected private schools to some equal-protection-like restraints and conditioned nonprofit status for educational institutions on their not discriminating because of race, private schools are ordinarily not subject to constitutional limitations. Providing an education, unlike holding elections, is not a function that has traditionally been "the exclusive prerogative of the State."[13]

Covenants placed in deeds to restrict the use of property to persons of particular races or religions are not by themselves state action (although they may violate federal and state laws), but no court or public official may help to enforce such covenants.[14] A liquor license granted by the state does not make the discriminatory action of a private club state action,[15] yet when a state

---

[9] *Georgia v McCollum*, 120 L Ed 33 (1992), summarizing holdings in *Lugar v Edmondson Oil Co.*, 457 US 922 (1982).

[10] *Terry v Adams*, 345 US 461 (1953).

[11] *Marsh v Alabama*, 326 US 501 (1946).

[12] *Flagg Brothers, Inc. v Brooks*, 436 US 14 (1978), and cases cited therein.

[13] *Rendell-Baker v Kohn*, 457 US 830 (1982).

[14] *Shelley v Kraemer*, 344 US 1 (1948); *Barrows v Jackson*, 346 US 249 (1953).

[15] *Moose Lodge No. 107 v Irvis*, 407 US 163 (1972).

leased space to a restaurant in a building designed to provide public parking, the action of the restaurant was no longer considered "purely private" and became subject to equal protection limitations.[16]

As noted, the Court has extended the prohibition against using peremptory challenges to keep persons from serving on juries because of their race to attorneys in civil cases and to lawyers for criminal defendants. In order to make such decisions, it had to hold that these practices involve state action. It did so by concluding that peremptory challenges are established by state law, that the jury system could not exist without the participation by the state, that those who exercise peremptory challenges perform a traditional function of government in providing for a fair jury, and that in the context of a courtroom setting discrimination implicates the state and undermines confidence in the fairness of its legal proceedings.[17]

Sometimes when a state does nothing, or tries to do nothing, it may still be supporting, encouraging, or abetting discriminatory conduct. The mere repeal of race-related legislation or policies not required in the first place by the Constitution is not necessarily unconstitutional, but it may be. Take, for example, California's action when it adopted a constitutional amendment that repealed previously existing legislation forbidding racial discrimination in the private sale of houses and, in addition, explicitly made nondiscriminatory housing legislation unenforceable. It was argued that no state action was involved when individuals refused to sell property to African Americans. But the Court concluded that when California amended its Constitution, it was not being neutral. Rather it was encouraging discrimination by making it more difficult for black people than for white people to buy homes. This was state action forbidden by the Constitution.[18] On the other hand, California's action was ruled constitutionally neutral when it repealed legislation encouraging judges to order busing and forbade them to do so unless required to by the U.S. Constitution (see page 368).[19]

The conflict over whether a particular act is strictly that of a private individual or is that of the state shades at times into tension between the constitutionally protected rights of association and privacy on one side and the rights to equal protection of the law on the other. A state may not, for example, directly discriminate in operating a public park, nor may it grant exclusive use to a group that excludes persons because of race. However, if a city were merely to make its parks available to all comers without condition or reservation, it would not violate the Constitution to let segregated groups use the facilities. In fact, "the exclusion of any person or group—all Negro, all oriental, or all white—from public facilities infringes upon the freedom of the individual to associate as he chooses."[20]

---

[16] *Burton v Wilmington Parking Authority,* 365 US 715 (1961).

[17] *Georgia v McCollum,* 120 L Ed 2d 33 (1992).

[18] *Reitman v Mulkey et al.,* 387 US 369 (1967).

[19] *Crawford v Los Angeles Board of Education,* 458 US 527 (1982).

[20] *Gilmore v City of Montgomery,* 417 US 556 (1974).

The Constitution precludes "government from interfering with private clubs or groups. The associational rights which our system honors permit all white, all black, all brown, and all yellow clubs to be established. Government may not tell a man or a woman who his or her associates must be. The individual may be selective as he desires."[21] Yet, "although the Constitution does not proscribe private bias, it places no value on discrimination.... Invidious private discrimination may be characterized as a form of exercising freedom protected by the First Amendment, but it has never been accorded affirmative constitutional protections."[22]

In contrast to private matters, there is no constitutionally protected right to discriminate in public dealings with other persons. Thus, an important question becomes, where is the line to be drawn between private associative behavior, which, however discriminatory, is constitutionally protected and beyond government regulation, and public associative behavior, which can be regulated by the state? As we have noted, the Supreme Court has upheld the application of state public accommodations laws to the Jaycees and Rotarians, because their actions with respect to admitting members fell on the public rather than private side of the line.[23] The same is true of a law partnership with respect to admission of partners.[24] When groups, associations, or businesses open their doors and invite in the public, they may be compelled by the state to stop discriminating.

On the other side are such associations as families, social clubs, and churches. "The freedom to enter into and carry on certain intimate or private relationships is a fundamental element of liberty protected by the Bill of Rights."[25] Public accommodations or other civil rights laws cannot be applied to these intimate relationships. Moreover, as we have noted, the right to engage in activities protected by the First Amendment implies a "corresponding right to associate with others in pursuit of a wide variety of political, social, economic, educational, religious and cultural ends."[26] Thus, as noted on page 239, for certain purposes even political associations have some constitutionally protected right to discriminate for certain expressive purposes.

The national government has not left the protection of civil rights against private discrimination to the states. Today there are federal laws protecting the rights of minorities and women with respect to housing, employment, schools, commerce, and many other activities. Owners of places of public accommodation and businesses affecting interstate commerce—and most businesses do—may not discriminate against persons because of race, religion, or handicap; employers in businesses affecting interstate commerce may not discriminate against persons because of race, sex, national origin, religion, or handicap.

---

[21] *Moose Lodge No. 107* v *Irvis*, 407 US 163 (1972).

[22] *Norwood* v *Harrison*, 413 US 455 (1973); *Hison* v *King & Spaulding*, 467 US 69 (1984).

[23] *Roberts* v *Jaycees*, 468 US 609 (1984); *Bd. of Dirs. of Rotary Int'l.* v *Rotary Club of Duarte*, 481 US 537 (1987).

[24] *Hison* v *King & Spaulding*, 467 US 69 (1984).

[25] *Bd. of Dirs. of Rotary Int'l.* v *Rotary Club of Duarte*, 481 US 537 (1987).

[26] *Hunter* v *Underwood*, 471 US 222 (1985).

In summary, "while the principle that private action is immune from the restrictions of the equal protection clause is well established and easily stated, the question whether particular conduct is 'private,' on the one hand, or 'state action' on the other, frequently admits of no easy answer."[27]

Three Tiers

When a *state* law is challenged as a violation of the equal protection clause, the Court chooses among three different tiers or tests. The lowest, or least stringent, is the traditional rational basis test. Under this test, "it's enough that the State's action be rationally based and free from invidious discrimination."[28] "It does not offend the Constitution merely because the classification is not made with mathematical nicety or because in practice it results in some inequality."[29] When using this test, the justices emphasize that the Constitution does not forbid governments from making distinctions among people, for it could not legislate without doing so. What it forbids is *unreasonable* classification when there is no relation between the classes the law creates and permissible governmental goals. When the act relates to social and economic legislation and neither employs suspect classifications (see page 357) nor impinges on fundamental rights (see page 356), such legislation carries with it a presumption of rationality that can only be overcome by a clear showing of arbitrariness and irrationality. It is likely to be upheld against equal protection attack if the legislative means are rationally related to a legitimate governmental purpose.[30] As the Court recently said, "We many times have said . . . rational-basis review in equal protection analysis 'is not a license for courts to judge the wisdom, fairness, or logic of legislative choices.'"[31] In areas of social and economic policy, a statutory classification that neither proceeds along suspect lines nor infringes fundamental constitutional rights must be upheld against equal protection challenge if there is any reasonably conceivable state of facts that could provide a rational basis for the classification."[32]

The *rational basis test* has been applied primarily but not exclusively to legislation impinging on business activities or the distribution of public benefits under general legislation such as social security. It essentially means that any law is constitutional so long as it serves some legitimate governmental purpose, even if not the purpose stated by the legislature.[33] There is no need for purposes of rational-basis review for a legislature or administrative agency to articulate at any time the rationale supporting its classification and a legislative purpose may be ascertained even when the legislative or administrative history is silent.

[27] *Jackson* v *Metropolitan Edison Co.*, 419 US 345 (1974).
[28] *Dandridge* v *Williams*, 397 US 471 (1970); *Jefferson* v *Hackney*, 406 US 535 (1972).
[29] Ibid.
[30] *Hodel* v *Virginia Surface Min. & Recl. Assn.*, 452 US 264 (1981).
[31] *Heller* v *Doe*, 125 L Ed 2d 257 (1993).
[32] *Federal Communications Commission* v *Beach Communications, Inc.*, 124 L Ed 2d 211 (1993).
[33] *Califano* v *Jobst*, 434 US 47 (1977).

Nevertheless, there must be a reasonably conceivable purpose and policy and the classificatory scheme under review must advance a reasonable and identifiable governmental interest.[34] "It is entirely irrelevant for constitutional purposes whether the conceived reason for the challenged distinction actually motivated the legislature."[35]

When the legislature has made clear the purpose it intends a statute to serve, thus assuring the courts that the legislature has made a conscious policy choice, such action should receive "the most respectful deference." But when no clear legislative purpose appears from a reading of the statute and the only purpose before the Court is one stated by a government lawyer litigating the constitutionality of the statute, various justices—Powell, Brennan, Marshall, and Stevens—have at times argued that the rational basis test should be firmed up slightly. They would apply what is sometimes called "a meaningful rational basis test," a rational basis test with a bite. They argue that, under these circumstances, the Court should require that the classification bear a "fair and substantial relation" to the asserted purpose. "While the absence of a clear statement of purposes need not doom a statute under rationality review, our task must always be to determine whether a particular rational purpose actually motivated the Legislature."[36] The rational basis test, argues Justice Stevens, requires that legislators "logically believe that the classification would serve a legitimate public purpose that transcends the harm to the members of the disadvantaged class."[37] "This more demanding scrutiny indirectly would test the plausibility of the tendered purpose."[38] The Court, however, has rejected this twist on the rational basis test and it is probably accurate to say, as Justice Stevens has charged, that once the Court decides that the rational basis test should be applied, "any 'conceivable basis' for a discriminatory classification will repel a constitutional attack . . . [and] judicial review . . . constitute[s] a mere tautological recognition of the fact that Congress [or a state legislature] did what it intended to do."[39] Or as Justice Kennedy reemphasized for the Court, "A statutory classification fails rational-basis review only when it 'rests on grounds wholly irrelevant to the achievement of the State's objective."[40]

The top tier, under the equal protection clause, the most stringent standard, is called *strict scrutiny*. When this test is applied there is a reversal of the normal presumption of constitutionality: the burden is on the state to demonstrate that its actions serve a "compelling governmental interest" and that it has "adopted those means to accomplish the intended ends that put the least possible restraint on the fundamental right in question."[41] This test is used

---

[34] *Nordlinger* v *Hahn*, 120 L Ed 2d 1 (1992).

[35] *Federal Communications Commission* v *Beach Communications, Inc.*, 124 L Ed 2d 211 (1993).

[36] Justice Marshall dissenting in *Bowen* v *Owens*, 476 US 340 (1986).

[37] Justice Stevens dissenting in *Kadrmas* v *Dickinson Pub. Schools*, 487 US 450 (1988), quoting his concurrence in *Cleburne* v *Cleburne Living Center*, Inc., 473 US 432 (1985).

[38] Justice Powell concurring in *Schweiker* v *Wilson*, 450 US 221 (1981).

[39] *United States Railroad Retirement Board* v *Fritz*, 449 US 166 (1980).

[40] *Heller* v *Doe*, 125 L Ed 2d 257 (1993), quoting *Holt Civic Club* v *Tuscaloosa*, 439 US 60 (1978), which in turn quoted a long line of precedents.

[41] *Dunn* v *Blumstein*, 405 US 330 (1972).

whenever suspect classes—race, ethnic origin, alienage under certain conditions—or fundamental rights are involved.

There is also a middle tier test. This test is not as rigid as the strict scrutiny-compelling state-interest test or as relaxed as the rational basis test. This intermediate tier, often called *heightened scrutiny,* requires that the law be more than a rational means to a legitimate governmental end but not that it be the least restrictive means to accomplish a compelling government interest. Rather the law must serve "important governmental objectives and must be substantially related to the achievement of these objectives."[42]

This intermediate tier applies when the law affects neither a suspect class nor a fundamental right but involves an almost suspect, or "disfavored," classification. At the moment gender or illegitimacy are the only classifications so evaluated by the Court, having rejected requests that different effects of governmental action on the wealthy, the poor, and the mentally retarded be subject to the heightened scrutiny of the middle tier test.[43]

Obviously, it makes a substantial difference as to which kind of equal protection test is applied. If the Court uses the least stringent rational basis test it seldom declares a law unconstitutional. If it decides that the more stringent strict scrutiny test should be used, it almost never declares the law constitutional. If it decides that the middle tier test applies, the outcome is more difficult to predict.

What, then, determines which test is to be applied? Although various critics, including some of the justices, contend that justices make up their minds about the results and then choose the level of scrutiny to fit, the established doctrine is that the upper tier test applies only if the law impinges on *fundamental rights* or deals with *suspect classifications.* The intermediate tier test applies to laws that deal with "almost suspect classifications."

Fundamental Rights

Which rights are fundamental and which are not? The justices have not been very clear on this point. Beyond those rights "readily identifiable in the Constitution's text," the Court, "[s]triving to assure itself and the public" that much more is involved than "the imposition of the Justices' own choice of values," has given various formulations over the years. One is that fundamental liberties are those "'implicit in the concept of ordered liberty,' such that 'neither liberty nor justice would exist if [they] were sacrificed.'" Another formulation characterizes these rights as "those liberties that are 'deeply rooted in this Nation's history and tradition.'"[44]

---

[42] *Craig v Boren,* 429 US 190 (1976).

[43] *Heller v Doe,* 125 L Ed 2d 257 (1993). *Kadrmas v Dickinson Pub. Schools,* 487 US 450 (1988).

[44] Justice White for the Court quoting from Justice Cardozo in *Palko v Connecticut,* 302 US 319 (1937), and from Justice Powell in *Moore v East Cleveland,* 431 US 494 (1977); *Bowers v Hardwick,* 478 US 186 (1986).

Clearly, it is not a right's importance that makes it fundamental in a constitutional sense. For example, the rights to food, shelter, and education are basic, but they are not in a constitutional sense fundamental rights. They are not rights the Constitution "explicitly or implicitly" guarantees. The following rights, among others, have been declared fundamental in a constitutional sense: free speech, freedom of religion, freedom to associate, personal privacy, freedom to travel in the United States (but not abroad) if one is under no legal restraint and is not fleeing from officials, access to the courts, the right to marry, freedom from government interference with marital privacy, and the right to obtain an abortion during the early stages of pregnancy (a right deriving from the right to privacy—the right of women to make "intimate decisions" affecting their bodies).[45]

The Court, although refusing to extend the protection of fundamental rights to education, has reserved the question "whether a minimally adequate education is a fundamental right and whether a statute alleged to infringe that right should be accorded heightened equal protection review."[46] Thus, although there is no fundamental right to an adequate or good education, there may be one to at least enough education to be able to read and write.

The Supreme Court has refused to extend the fundamental right of marital privacy to the right of homosexuals to engage in consensual sodomy, because that right of privacy does not relate to procreation, marriage, or the right to decide whether or not to beget or bear a child.[47]

Suspect Classifications

The suspect classification criterion grew out of what may be the most famous Supreme Court footnote of all time, footnote 4 in Justice Stone's opinion in *United States* v *Carolene Products Co.* In that footnote Justice Stone indicated that judges should subject certain kinds of legislation to greater constitutional scrutiny, including statutes directed at discrete and insular religious, national, or racial minorities.[48] Taking off from this language Justice Powell explained that the traditional criteria for determining which groups fall into a suspect, and therefore especially protected, class are "an immutable characteristic determined solely by the accident of birth, or a class saddled with such disabilities, or subjected to such a history of purposeful unequal treatment, or regulated to such a political powerlessness as to command extraordinary protection from the majoritarian political process."[49]

---

[45] *San Antonio School District* v *Rodriguez*, 411 US 1 (1973); *Roe* v *Wade*, 410 US 113 (1973); *Beal* v *Doe*, 432 US 464 (1965); *Jones* v *Helms*, 452 US 412 (1981); *Haig* v *Agee*, 453 US 280 (1981); *Califano* v *Aznarorian*, 439 US 179 (1978); *Illinois Elections Board* v *Socialist Workers Party*, 440 US 173 (1979); *Attorney General of New York* v *Edwardo Soto-Lopez*, 476 US 898 899 (1986).

[46] *Papasan* v *Allain*, 478 US 265 (1986).

[47] *Bowers* v *Hardwick*, 478 US 186 (1986).

[48] *United States* v *Carolene Products Co.*, 304 US 144 (1938).

[49] *San Antonio School District* v *Rodriguez*, 411 US 1 (1973).

Classifications based on race or national origin (or, as it is now called, ethnicity) are clearly suspect as far as state and local governments are concerned. And as far as states are concerned, so is alienage (the condition of being an alien). Since Congress has the power to regulate immigration and to implement the Fourteenth Amendment (see page 387), national legislation affecting aliens and race is not subject to the same rigid scrutiny as are state laws.[50] Religion is probably a suspect classification, although there is no specific Supreme Court decision to this effect other than those stemming from the First Amendment.

Almost Suspect Classifications

Disfavored classifications, at the moment, include illegitimacy and sex. "Illegitimacy is analogous in many respects to the personal characteristics that have been held to be suspect," wrote Justice Powell for the Court. "We nevertheless conclude that the analogy is not sufficient to require our most exacting scrutiny."[51] Yet, in reviewing laws imposing disabilities on illegitimate children, the Court has made it clear that the intermediate test to scrutinize such laws is "not a toothless one."[52]

As to gender-based classifications, the Supreme Court has waffled. At one time it came close to declaring sex classifications suspect. More recently it has treated such classifications as merely disfavored.

Race was thought to be the paradigmatically "suspect class." "Classifications of citizens solely on the basis of race are by their very nature odious to a free people whose institutions are founded upon the doctrine of equality."[53] Yet the Supreme Court has thrown doubt on the matter so far as national legislation is concerned when it adopted the heightened rather than strict scrutiny standard for dealing with *national* legislation as it relates to race, the same standard that is applied to classifications based on gender (see page 381). But as far as *state and local* legislation is concerned, race remains a suspect classification whether the classifications are "benign" or "remedial" or motivated by "illegitimate notions of racial inferiority."[54]

Judicial construction of the equal protection clause is instructive in showing how judges move from the simple to the complex. As judges are presented with new applications of old rules, they proceed to make distinctions that are more and more refined until the picture becomes so confused and complicated that the judges try to rationalize past decisions and again provide more simple guidelines. We started with an interpretation of the equal protection clause that used one test—the rational basis test. Then the judges added a more stringent requirement—an overriding public purpose. Then they came up with a test to be

---

[50] *Nyquist v Mauclet*, 432 US 1 (1977); *Graham v Richardson*, 403 US 365 (1971); *Fiallo v Bell*, 430 US 787 (1977).

[51] *Trimble v Gordon*, 430 US 762 (1977); *Matthews v Lucas*, 427 US 495 (1976).

[52] Ibid.

[53] *Shaw v Reno*, 125 L Ed 2d 511 (1993), quoting *Hirabayashi v United States*, 320 US 81 (1943),

[54] *Shaw v Reno*, 125 L Ed 2d 511 (1993).

applied in some instances that is less rigid than the overriding public-purpose test, but more demanding than the rational basis test; that test is whether a law is "substantially related to important governmental objectives." And now there is a tendency to break the rational basis test into two tests—one when the legislature has clearly stated the purposes it wants to achieve, and another when it has not. Perhaps the next step will be a completely new restructuring and new guidelines.

To summarize, the Supreme Court has been using the equal protection clause and a multi-tiered analysis to differentiate among various kinds of laws and to subject these laws to varying degrees of scrutiny. Critics of the newer, more rigid equal protection tests contend that the judges are substituting their own policy judgments for those of the legislatures. Justice Rehnquist, for example, has written in dissent, "This Court seems to regard the Equal Protection Clause as a cat-o'-nine-tails to be kept in the judicial closet as a threat to legislatures which may, in view of the judiciary, get out of hand and pass 'arbitrary,' 'illogical,' or 'unreasonable' laws. In enforcing the generalities of the Equal Protection Clause, judges are in the position of Adam in the Garden of Eden and the Court's decisions can fairly be described as an endless tinkering with legislative judgments, a series of conclusions unsupported by any central guiding principle."[55]

From the opposite side of the Court, Justice Marshall was no fan of the "intellectually disingenuous 'two-tier' equal protection analysis."[56] He believed it does not describe the more subtle analysis that the Court should undertake. And from what might be called the middle of the Court, Justice Blackmun has expressed his "unrelieved discomfort with what seems to be a continuing tendency in this Court to use as tests such easy phrases as 'compelling state interest' and 'least drastic means.'...I have never been able fully to appreciate just what a compelling state interest is. If it means 'convincingly controlling,' or 'incapable of being overcome upon any balancing process,' then of course, the test merely announces an inevitable result, and the test is no test at all. And, for me, 'least drastic means' is a slippery slope and also the signal of the result the Court has chosen to reach. A judge would be unimaginative indeed if he could not come up with something a little less 'drastic' or less 'restrictive' in almost any situation, and thereby enable himself to vote to strike legislation down."

Rational-basis Test

Let us see how the tests have been applied. Applying the rational basis test, the Court sustained an Illinois law that exempted individuals from personal property taxes but imposed such taxes on corporations. "Where taxation is concerned and no specific federal right, apart from equal protection, is imperiled, the States have large leeway in making classifications and drawing lines which in their judgment produce reasonable systems of taxation."[57] Despite this leeway, the Supreme Court, by a unanimous decision no less, held that a West Virginia assessor violated the Constitution when on her own initiative she

---

[55] *Trimble* v *Gordon*, 430 US 762 (1977).
[56] *Beal* v *Doe*, 432 US 438 (1977).
[57] *Lenhausen* v *Lake Shore Auto Parts Co.*, 410 US 356 (1973).

decided to assess property on its original purchase price and not on its current value with the result that some people's property was assessed at 8 to 35 times more than comparable neighboring property.[58] Three years later, however, the Court upheld California's celebrated Proposition 13 that established a system for assessing property for tax purposes based on its value at time of acquisition, not on its current market value. As a result property taxes in California vary tremendously between those who purchased their homes or business years ago as against those who more recently acquired them. The Court, applying the rational basis text, upheld Proposition 13 since the state had given a plausible reason for treating newer and older owners differently—namely to create an acquisition-based system in order to preserve local neighborhoods and to protect property owners' legitimate expectations about the amount of property taxes that would be assessed against their property. The Court distinguished West Virginia's program because Webster County, West Virginia, had failed to give any rational reason for its unequal assessment practice but on the contrary had tried to defend its practices on the ground that its scheme was rationally related to the purpose of assessing properties at true current value. (They had the wrong arguments.)[59] It should be noted that the Court left open what it might decide if Proposition 13 is challenged by one moving to California on the ground that it infringed on the right to travel, a fundamental right.

Other examples of the rational basis test: there was no constitutional violation in the Texas practice of providing educational revenues for local schools largely from local property taxes, even though the practice produced fewer dollars to educate children in poor districts than to educate children in districts where more valuable property was located.[60] The village of Belle Terre, New York, was sustained when it adopted zoning regulations that effectively excluded anyone except single families and groups of no more than two individuals from occupying houses in the village. Six students at the State University of New York at Stony Brook challenged the ordinance as violating their rights, but the Court said, "The police power is not confined to elimination of filth, stench, and unhealthy places. It is ample to lay out zones where family values, youth values, and the blessings of quiet seclusion and clean air make the area a sanctuary for people."[61]

Still more examples of the application of the rational basis test: a state may deny unemployment benefits to those who attend day schools while making them available to those who attend night school, it being reasonable to assume that those who go to school during the day are less likely to be available for employment than are those who go to school after the workday.[62] New York could subject harness-racing trainers to more drastic restrictions than thoroughbred-racing trainers because of a legislative determination that the former

---

[58] *Allegheny Pitt.* v *Webster County*, 488 US 336 (1989).
[59] *Nordlinger* v *Hahn*, 120 L Ed 2d 1 (1992).
[60] *San Antonio School District* v *Rodriguez*, 411 US 1 (1973).
[61] *Village of Belle Terre* v *Boraas*, 416 US 1 (1974).
[62] *Idaho Employment* v *Smith*, 434 US 100 (1977).

kind of activity justifies more stringent regulation.[63] Minnesota could ban the sale of milk in plastic nonreturnable bottles while allowing its sale in paperboard nonreturnable cartons.[64] Congress could provide death benefits to widows, widowers, and divorced spouses responsible for the care of minor children but deny such aid to unwed mothers.[65] Congress could authorize survivor's benefits to widows who remarried after age 60 and not to surviving divorced and remarried spouses. "Governmental decisions to spend money... in one way and not another are 'not confined to the courts. The discretion belongs to Congress, unless the choice is clearly wrong, a display of arbitrary power, not an exercise of judgment.'"[66] Congress could permit veterans' organizations, but not others, to engage in lobbying activities without jeopardizing their tax-exempt status. "Our country has a long-standing policy of compensating veterans for their past contributions by providing them with numerous advantages."[67]

Until recently, in almost every instance, when the Court concluded that the rational basis test should be applied, it was in effect concluding that the law was constitutional. After all, if a majority of a state legislature has voted for a particular law, it is rather presumptuous for judges to declare that the legislators have acted without any rational basis. Moreover, until recently the rational basis test was used almost exclusively to judge legislation regulating businesses reflecting the perspective of some justices that courts should let legislatures regulate the economy almost as they wished. However, the Supreme Court ruled that Alaska had failed to pass even the minimal test when it proposed to distribute income derived from its oil revenues to its citizens in varying amounts based on the length of each citizen's residency in Alaska. In language reminiscent of Justice Holmes, who at the beginning of the century often reminded the then conservative majority that it had no mandate to impose its views on states, Justice Rehnquist wrote in dissent, "In striking down the Alaskan scheme, the Court seems momentarily to have forgotten 'the principle that the Fourteenth Amendment gives the federal courts no power to impose upon the States their view of what constitutes wise economic or social policy.'"[68] The Court told Vermont that it was "wholly arbitrary" for it to charge new Vermont residents a use tax to register cars purchased out of state while exempting long-time Vermont residents from the same tax for cars they purchased out of state.[69] After specifically refusing to hold that the mentally retarded are a quasi-suspect classification calling for a more exacting standard of judicial review than is normally accorded economic and social legislation, the Court held that a city had violated the rational basis test by requiring a special zoning use permit for homes for a group of mentally retarded persons when it did not require such permits for other multiple-dwelling units. The requirement, said the majority,

---

[63] Barry v Barchi, 443 US 55 (1979).
[64] Minnesota v Clover Leaf Creamery Co., 449 US 456 (1981).
[65] California v Boles, 443 US 282 (1980).
[66] Bowen v Owens, 476 US 340 (1986).
[67] Regan v Taxation with Representation, 461 US 540 (1983).
[68] Zobel v Williams, 457 US 55 (1982).
[69] Williams v Vermont, 472 US 14 (1985).

appeared to have been based on an irrational prejudice, not a rational basis.[70] On the other hand, the Court, using the rational basis test, held that Kentucky had proffered more than adequate justifications for the differences in treatment between the mentally retarded and the mentally ill because of the difference in the two conditions, and it could apply a less rigorous standard—clear and convincing evidence—to involuntarily commit the mentally retarded than the one it applied— beyond a reasonable doubt— to commitments for the mentally ill.[71]

The rational basis test has also been applied to evaluate the constitutionality of distinctions between state regulations of corporations chartered in the state with regulations for corporations chartered elsewhere. A couple of months after the equal protection clause was used to tell Alabama it could not favor Alabama-chartered insurance companies,[72] the Court held that the clause does permit states to favor in-state and regional banks. The difference appears to be that the Court interprets the equal protection requirement to permit laws motivated by legislative desires to protect consumers, but not those designed merely to favor local businesses.[73]

The Court would not allow Arkansas (in 1927) to restrict suits against domestic corporations to counties where such corporations maintained a place of business but to expose foreign corporations authorized to do business in Arkansas to file suit in any county. Such a distinction, said the Court, lacks a rational basis and deprived foreign corporations of equal protection.[74] But a half century later it allowed Montana to permit suits against domestic corporations only in the county of the *principal place* of business, but to permit suits in any county against a corporation incorporated elsewhere. The difference, said the Court, is that the Arkansas any-county rule applied to almost all foreign corporations while Montana's any-county rule probably does not apply to most foreign corporations since not many of them have their principal place of business in Montana.[75]

Strict Scrutiny and Fundamental Rights

An example of how the Court has applied strict scrutiny to judge laws that affect fundamental rights is a ruling on one of the most judicially favored fundamental rights—the constitutional right to travel. This right, having various constitutional sources, ensures new residents who move into a state the same rights to vital governmental benefits and privileges in the state to which they migrate as are enjoyed by long-term residents. As already noted (page 156), Article IV, Section 2, protects citizens who move from one state to another,

---

[70] *Cleburne* v *Cleburne Living Center*, 473 US 432 (1985).

[71] *Heller* v *Doe*, 125 L Ed 2d 257 (1993).

[72] *Metropolitan Life Insurance Co.* v *Ward*, 470 US 869 (1985).

[73] *Northeast Bancorp* v *Board of Governors FRS*, 472 US 159 (1985).

[74] *Power Manufacturing Co.* v *Saunders*, 274 US 490 (1927).

[75] *Burlington Northern R. Co.* v *Ford*, 119 L Ed 2d 432 (1992).

and those protections often merge with equal protection considerations (the latter also extending to aliens as well as to citizens). Durational residency requirements for eligibility for certain benefits are suspect because of their impact on the right to travel (see page 157). However, the right to travel does not include the right to take with one benefits of the place from which one came; therefore, Congress may limit social security benefits to the residents of the states and the District of Columbia and may exclude persons who move to Puerto Rico.[76] Nor does it impermissibly infringe on the right to travel for a state to set a harsher criminal penalty for parents who abandon their children and leave the state than for parents who abandon their children but remain in the state.[77]

Here are other examples of state actions that impinged on fundamental rights, were subject to rigorous scrutiny and declared unconstitutional: laws making property ownership a requirement for serving on a school board;[78] requirements that allowed only persons who had paid some kind of property tax to vote in city bond elections;[79] requirements that permitted only parents or taxpayers to vote in school board elections;[80] laws making it a crime for a doctor to prescribe a contraceptive device to an unmarried person, but not to a married one;[81] laws denying unwed fathers, but not unwed mothers, an opportunity to take custody of children on the death of the other parent;[82] the provision of religious services for Christians and Jews in prisons, but not for Buddhists;[83] and laws imposing such high fees on candidates in primaries that it is difficult for those without funds or without backers to run.[84]

The Court has also, in the words of the dissenting justices, patched "together bits and pieces of what might be termed quasi-suspect-class and quasi-fundamental-rights analysis"[85] to declare unconstitutional a Texas statute denying illegal alien children the right to a free public education. Although illegal aliens are not a suspect class and the right to an education is not a fundamental right, the Court nonetheless held that Texas had to "offer something more than a rational basis for its classification."[86] Texas failed to prove to the justices' satisfaction that its action was justified by a substantial state interest in saving money or discouraging illegal aliens from moving to Texas, particularly since the regulation of immigration is a congressional, not a state, responsibility. Six years after this Texas decision, *Plyler v Doe,* the more conservative Rehnquist Court seemingly ignored it when

---

[76] *Califano v Torres,* 435 US 1 (1978).
[77] *Jones v Helms,* 452 US 412 (1981).
[78] *Turner v Fouche,* 396 US 346 (1970).
[79] *Hill v Stone,* 421 US 289 (1975).
[80] *Kramer v Union Free School District,* 395 US 621 (1969).
[81] *Eisenstadt v Baird,* 405 US 438 (1972).
[82] *Stanley v Illinois,* 405 US 645 (1972).
[83] *Cruz v Beto,* 405 US 319 (1972).
[84] *Bullock v Carter,* 405 US 134 (1972).
[85] Chief Justice Burger dissenting in *Plyler v Doe,* 457 US 202 (1982).
[86] *Plyler v Doe,* 457 US 202 (1982).

it sustained a North Dakota statute authorizing certain school districts, but not others, to charge school bus fees.[87]

Race

The most suspect of suspect classifications is race. The Fourteenth Amendment, and most especially its equal protection clause, was adopted precisely for the purpose of protecting African Americans against discrimination by state and local governments, so we have had more constitutional experience with classifications based on race than we have had with other suspect classifications. The "core purpose of the Fourteenth Amendment was to do away with all governmentally imposed discrimination based on race. Classifying persons according to their race is more likely to reflect racial prejudice than legitimate public concerns; race, not the person, dictates the category. Such classifications are subject to the most exacting scrutiny; to pass constitutional muster, they must be justified by a compelling governmental interest and must be 'necessary ...to the accomplishment' of its legitimate purpose."[88]

More recently, the Court has made a distinction between the use by Congress of racial categories and their use by state governments (see page 382). Although "this Court never has held that race-conscious state decision making is impermissible in all circumstances," it approaches such with suspicion and has "held that the Fourteenth Amendment requires state legislation that expressly distinguishes among citizens because of their race to be narrowly tailored to further a compelling governmental interest." Such stringent test is applied not only "to legislation that contains explicit racial distinctions, but also to those 'rare' statutes that, although race-neutral, are on their face 'unexplainable on grounds other than race.' In the case of national legislation, however, the test is the less stringent heightened scrutiny, that is, racial classifications created by Congress are constitutionally permissible to the extent that they serve important governmental objectives and are substantially related to achievement of those objectives."[89]

Although the Fourteenth Amendment was adopted for the protection of the recently freed slaves, at first it was not applied in that regard. In fact, in *Plessy v Ferguson* (1896) the Supreme Court held that a state could compel racial segregation in the use of public facilities, provided equal facilities were available for all races. Only Justice Harlan dissented, saying, "In view of the Constitution, in the eye of the law, there is in this country no superior, dominant ruling class of citizens. There is no caste here. Our Constitution is colorblind, and neither knows nor tolerates classes among citizens. In respect of civil rights, all citizens are equal before the law."[90]

---

[87] *Kadrmas v Dickinson Pub. Schools*, 487 US 450 (1988).

[88] *Palmore v Sidoti*, 466 US 429 (1984).

[89] *Metro Broadcasting v Federal Communications Commission*, 497 US 547 (1990).

[90] *Plessy v Ferguson*, 163 US 537 (1896).

Under the guise of the "separate but equal" formula, Jim Crow laws, as segregation laws came to be known, were passed in southern states to cover all phases of life from birth to death, from hospitals to burial grounds. For decades, the facilities provided for blacks were separate but not equal. In the 1940s the Supreme Court began to insist that states must either stop requiring segregation in the use of public facilities or start providing blacks with exactly equal facilities.

School Desegregation

Finally, in the spring of 1954, in *Brown* v *Board of Education*, the Supreme Court reversed its 1896 holding as applied to public schools and ruled that "separate but equal" is a contradiction in terms and that segregation is itself discrimination.[91] In the years that immediately followed, all forms of segregation in public facilities were declared unconstitutional. Furthermore, the Constitution requires authorities not merely to *cease* discriminating, but also to take action to remedy the consequences of their past segregative conduct.

However, the amount of action required to overcome past discrimination varies with the area: the most is required in the case of public schools, the least in the case of such things as 4-H clubs, which southern states used to operate on a segregated basis. In the case of schools, states must take positive steps to overcome the effects of prior segregative practices. In the case of the 4-H clubs, all the Constitution requires is the disestablishment of segregated clubs and nondiscrimination against any person who seeks to join them.[92]

A year after its decision in *Brown* v *Board of Education,* the Court, in the second Brown decision, ordered school boards to proceed with all deliberate speed to desegregate public schools at the earliest practical date.[93] In 1969, fifteen years after its first ruling that school segregation was unconstitutional, and in the face of massive resistance to compliance in many parts of the South, the Supreme Court withdrew its earlier grant of time to school authorities to work out the problems in desegregating schools. The Court stated: "The time for mere 'deliberate speed' has run out.... Delays in desegregating school systems are no longer tolerable.... The burden of a school board today is to come forward with a plan that promises realistically to work and promises realistically to work now."[94]

In 1964 Congress authorized the Department of Justice to enter the fray by filing school desegregation suits. It also stipulated in Title VI of the Civil Rights Act that "No person ... shall on the ground of race, color, or national origin, be excluded from participating in, be denied the benefits of, or be subjected to discrimination under any program or activity receiving federal financial assistance," which meant that federal funds could be cut off from any district that

---

[91] *Brown* v *Board of Education,* 347 US 483 (1954).
[92] *Bazemore* v *Friday,* 478 US 385 (1986).
[93] *Brown* v *Board of Education,* 349 US 294 (1955).
[94] *Alexander* v *Board of Education,* 396 US 19 (1969).

refused to desegregate. By the time schools opened in the fall of 1970, de jure segregated school systems had been abolished. No longer was any school legally defined to be only for blacks or only for whites.

If schools were previously legally segregated, authorities have a duty to take positive action to overcome the past segregation. School authorities and judges formulating desegregation decrees may require, as a means of dismantling a previously legally segregated school system, the assignment of pupils and teachers to schools on a racial basis. "Just as the race of students must be considered in determining whether a constitutional violation has occurred so must race be considered in formulating a remedy. To forbid, at this stage, all assignments made on the basis of race, would deprive school authorities of the one tool absolutely essential to the fulfillment of their constitutional obligation to eliminate existing dual school systems."[95]

For schools in which segregation is not the result of prior intentional governmental action, there is no constitutional requirement that authorities act to integrate the schools. In determining appropriate remedies, the Court has continued to maintain this distinction between school districts where racial imbalance is the continuing consequence of a prior segregated school system or the result of purposeful intent to segregate and districts where racial imbalance is not the result of governmental segregative purposes.[96] In school districts that were previously intentionally segregated, judges may impose system wide remedies, force authorities to take a positive action to disestablish any vestiges of a dual school system, even to order school districts to raise taxes and issue bonds.[97] Where racial imbalance is *not* the result of purposeful governmental action, judges lack any such authority. Therefore, a crucial finding is whether or not any racial imbalance that exists is a consequence of prior violations of the equal protection clause.

When it is found that racial imbalance is the result of prior segregative governmental action, judges formulating desegregation decrees may require remedial programs, including the busing of pupils from one school within the district to another.[98] In a unanimous but cautiously worded decision, the Supreme Court held in *Swann v Charlotte-Mecklenburg Board of Education* (1971) that a federal judge has authority to order, among other things, that students be bused a reasonable distance beyond their own neighborhoods as a means of eliminating all vestiges of state-imposed segregation. No students should be bused so far that the time or distance of travel presents risk to their health or impinges on the educational process. The Court rejected the notion that the constitutional command to desegregate means that every school in every community must always reflect the racial composition of the school system as a whole. Exact racial balance is not required. And "all things being equal with

---

[95] *Swann v Charlotte-Mecklenburg Board of Education*, 402 US 1 (1971). See also Chief Justice Burger's further elaboration in *Winston-Salem/Forsythe Board of Education v Scott*, 404 US 122 (1971).

[96] *Columbus Board of Education v Penick*, 443 US 449 (1979).

[97] *Missouri v Jenkins*, 488 US 888 (1990).

[98] *Milliken v Bradley*, 433 US 267 (1977).

no history of discrimination, it might well be desirable to assign pupils to schools nearest their homes." But in districts that previously operated segregated systems, "desegregation plans cannot be limited to walk-in schools."[99]

What about interdistrict busing? In many cities blacks are crowded into the central city and there has been "white flight" to the suburbs. In such situations it is difficult to achieve integration if the central city and suburban schools are considered separately. But unless it is demonstrated that school district lines have been drawn for the purpose of maintaining segregation and that the suburban districts are being operated in a racially discriminatory fashion, a judge may not require cross-district busing.[100] A judge may, however, require the central city district to raise its taxes and improve its schools in order to make these schools magnets to attract back to them nonminority students who may have gone elsewhere.[101]

Despite the best efforts of some school boards to eliminate the vestiges of segregation and to move from a dual segregated system to a unitary one in which there are no longer "white" or "black" schools, many schools have become resegregated as a result of all kinds of factors, including "white flight." "Where resegregation is a product not of state action but of private choices, it does not have constitutional implications. It is beyond the authority and beyond the practical ability of the federal courts to try to counteract these kinds of continuous and massive demographic shifts."[102] And where there has been "good faith compliance of the district with the court ordered" integration over a reasonable period of time, the mere fact of current racial imbalance enables a district court to accept a board's representation that it has accepted the principle of racial equality and will not "impose intentional discrimination in the administration of the schools."[103]

Although the Constitution does not require states to take corrective action to overcome *de facto* segregation, or in Justice Scalia's words, "the constitutional right is equal racial access to schools, not access to racially equal schools,"[104] states, if they wish, may act to create racial balance in their public schools. In March of 1978 the Seattle School Board decided that mandatory reassignment of students was necessary to eliminate the racial isolation in its schools caused by segregated housing patterns. This action generated so much opposition that a statewide initiative measure forbidding any board to order mandatory reassignment of students for the purpose of achieving racial balance was overwhelmingly approved. The Supreme Court, however, struck down this action, not because the state of Washington had an obligation to provide such busing, but because the initiative petition had a racially discriminatory purpose and Washington had unconstitutionally distorted its political process to place special burdens on the ability of blacks to achieve legislation they felt would benefit them.[105]

---

[99] *Swann v Charlotte-Mecklenburg Board of Education,* 402 US 1 (1971); *Milliken v Bradley,* 433 US 267 (1977).

[100] *Milliken v Bradley,* 418 US 717 (1974).

[101] *Missouri v Jenkins,* 488 US 888 (1990).

[102] *Freeman v Pitts,* 118 L Ed 2d 108 (1992).

[103] Ibid.

[104] Concurring in *Freeman v Pitts,* 118 L Ed 2d 108 (1992).

[105] *Washington v Seattle School District No. 1,* 458 US 457 (1982).

On the very same day, however, the Supreme Court refused to overturn a California action, also adopted as the result of an initiative, that stripped California courts of the power to order mandatory busing unless it was necessary to remedy a violation of the United States Constitution. The consequence of the action was to set aside a busing plan that the California courts had imposed on Los Angeles on the grounds that the California Constitution required school boards to overcome racial segregation regardless of whether it was de facto or de jure. The United States Supreme Court held that the mere repeal of legislation not required by the federal Constitution in the first place is not unconstitutional. California, having by the action of its courts gone beyond the requirements of the federal Constitution, was free to return by the action of its voters to "the standard prevailing throughout the United States." Those who had initiated the action were not motivated, said the Supreme Court, by discriminatory purposes. Moreover, even though California courts could no longer order school boards to adopt busing to overcome de facto segregation, the boards themselves, unlike those in Washington, retained the power to adopt such busing.[106] In short, it is unconstitutional for a state to take from a school board the power to order mandatory busing to overcome racial imbalance not caused by the state, but it is all right for the state to take from its courts the power to order such busing without a finding of a violation of the United States Constitution.

Although there has never been any question that racial segregation at the college level is as unconstitutional as it is at the primary and secondary level, not until 1992 did the Supreme Court establish the standards for desegregation of public higher education. Does a state that previously operated a segregated higher education system—some colleges and universities only for whites and others for African Americans—have the same responsibilities it has for desegregation of primary and secondary schools, of actively working to integrate its colleges and universities, or is it enough simply to open the doors to all students and let students make their choices? The fact that historically black institutions remain predominantly black and historically white universities and colleges remain predominantly white does not by itself constitute a constitutional violation. However, the Supreme Court rejected the argument that the Constitution requires no more of states than to open admissions to all institutions of higher education to persons regardless of race. Rather states must, consistent with sound educational practices, eliminate all policies that continue to foster segregation. A state does not have to achieve any particular level of racial balance, but states with a history of de jure segregation must review admissions policies and continued duplication of "non-essential" programs between historically black and historically white institutions, and must even consider whether the retention of the number of schools that it operates affects student choices and perpetuates segregated higher education.[107] The Court made clear that there is no constitutional right to maintain historically black institutions.

---

[106] *Crawford v Los Angeles Board of Education*, 458 US 527 (1982).
[107] *United States v Fordice*, 120 L Ed 2d 575 (1992).

Brown v *Board of Education* applied only to public schools. But discrimination in private schools may be a violation of federal civil rights laws based on the Thirteenth Amendment, which gives Congress the right to get rid of racial discrimination, a "badge of slavery."[108] Nor may such schools retain their federal tax exemption.[109]

Since *Brown* the Supreme Court has declared unconstitutional laws requiring segregation in any public facility or place. Any use of governmental power to keep people of different races apart is clearly unconstitutional.[110] Today any law or government practice that invidiously discriminates against any person because of race is unconstitutional.

Nowadays governmentally sanctioned discriminatory action is not likely to be overt, although there are still examples. Only two and a half decades ago the Court had to set aside state laws making marriage between persons of different races illegal.[111] And as late as 1984, the Court had to reverse a state court's decision to take from a mother custody of her child because of her remarriage to a person of a different race.[112] The Court did so unanimously and in one of its briefest opinions in recent years.

Gender

What of classifications based on sex? It was 1971 before any classification based on sex was declared to violate the equal protection clause. Before that, state laws excluding or restricting women's participation on juries had been sustained, as well as many laws purporting to provide special protection for women, such as one in Ohio forbidding any woman other than a wife or daughter of a tavern owner to serve as a barmaid.[113]

Then in 1971 a unanimous Court stated in *Reed* v *Reed* that the arbitrary preference Idaho gave fathers over mothers in the administration of their children's estates "cannot stand in the face of the Fourteenth Amendment's command."[114] Soon after, in *Frontiero* v *Richardson,* the Court invalidated a federal law that permitted a serviceman to claim his wife as his dependent but allowed a servicewoman to claim her husband as a dependent only if he was in fact dependent on her for more than half of his support. Justice Brennan wrote for a plurality that "there can be no doubt that our Nation has had a long and unfortunate history of sex discrimination. Traditionally, such discrimination was rationalized by an attitude of 'romantic paternalism' which, in practical effect, put women not on a pedestal, but in a cage."[115] Although Justice Brennan would have made gender

---

[108] *Runyon* v *McCrary,* 427 US 160 1976).

[109] *Bob Jones University* v *U.S.,* 461 US 574 (1983).

[110] *Mayor* v *Dawson,* 350 US 877 (1956); *Gayle* v *Browder,* 352 US 903 (1956).

[111] *Loving* v *Virginia,* 388 US 1 (1967).

[112] *Palmore* v *Sidoti,* 466 US 429 (1984).

[113] *Goesaert* v *Cleary,* 335 US 464 (1948).

[114] *Reed* v *Reed,* 404 US 71 (1971).

[115] *Frontiero* v *Richardson,* 411 US 677 (1973).

a suspect category, with laws classifying on the basis of sex subject to strict scrutiny, he did not win a majority for this position.

Among the sex-based distinctions declared unconstitutional since then are the following: a law specifying that males are entitled to child support from their fathers until they are twenty-one but females only until they are eighteen;[116] a state law prohibiting the sale of beer to males under twenty-one but to females under eighteen;[117] laws making women but not men eligible for alimony;[118] laws giving unwed mothers, but not unwed fathers, the right to consent to the adoption of their children;[119] social security provisions providing aid to children with unemployed fathers but not to those with unemployed mothers;[120] and the policy of the Mississippi University for Women of limiting enrollment to women in its school of nursing (as well as all its other schools).[121] (Note that a good many of the laws were struck down because they discriminated against men.) Nor may governments—and because of the equal protection interpretation of the due process clause of the Fifth Amendment (see page 283), members of Congress are included—discriminate because of sex in the selection of public employees.[122]

On the other side, the Court has sustained some sex-based distinctions: Upholding a Florida law granting a $500 exemption from the state property tax to widows but not to widowers, the majority said, "There can be no dispute that the financial difficulties confronting the lone woman in Florida or in any other State exceed those facing the man." The dissenters pointed out that there are such things as rich widows and poor widowers and argued that the need for the exemption would not appear to be related to one's sex.[123] A naval regulation was upheld that permitted male naval officers only nine years in which to be either promoted or discharged, while providing thirteen years for women, because women have less opportunity within the naval service for promotion.[124] A social security regulation was sustained giving women but not men the right to eliminate some low-earning years from the calculation of their retirement benefits in order to compensate them for past economic discrimination.[125] Congress may give preference in admission to the country to alien mothers of illegitimate children over alien fathers of such children.[126] A state may treat fathers of illegitimate children differently from mothers of such children, for example, by requiring that mothers must always be notified prior to the adoption proceedings of their children but that only those fathers who have shouldered some responsibility or acknowledged their responsibility for their children must be notified.[127]

---

[116] *Stanton v Stanton*, 421 US 7 (1976).

[117] *Craig v Borden*, 429 US 190 (1976).

[118] *Orr v Orr*, 440 US 268 (1979).

[119] *Caban v Mohammed*, 441 US 380 (1979).

[120] *Califano v Westcott*, 443 US 76 (1979).

[121] *Mississippi University for Women v Hogan*, 458 US 718 (1982).

[122] *Davis v Passman*, 442 US 228 (1979).

[123] *Kahan v Shevin*, 416 US 351 (1974).

[124] *Schlesinger v Ballard*, 419 US 498 (1975).

[125] *Califano v Webster*, 430 US 313 (1977).

[126] *Fiallo v Bell*, 430 US 787 (1977).

[127] *Lehr v Robertson*, 463 US 248 (1983).

A narrowly divided Court sustained the conviction by California of a seventeen-year-old male for the statutory rape of a sixteen-year-old female under a law that makes it a crime for a male to have intercourse with a female under eighteen, but not for a female to have intercourse with an underage male. The Court majority argued that such a law was based, not on archaic assumptions about the proper role of the sexes, but on a legitimate state interest in avoiding teenage pregnancies, and that since only women can become pregnant, men and women are not similarly situated with respect to the risks associated with pregnancy. The minority argued that the law discriminated against men and the state could have accomplished its objectives just as well with a gender-neutral law making it a crime for both teenage men and women to engage in sex.[128]

Veterans' preference laws have also been sustained, even though such laws adversely affect women. The Supreme Court upheld a Massachusetts law giving veterans a lifetime preference in public employment, because the law reflects no purpose to discriminate against women, but is designed to favor those who have served in the armed forces, male and female.[129] And as already noted, the Court upheld the power of Congress to order the registration of males and not of females for potential military conscription, largely on the grounds that only men could be assigned to combat duty. "This is not a case," wrote Justice Rehnquist for the majority, "of Congress arbitrarily choosing to burden one of two similarly situated groups, such as would be the case with an all-black or all-white, or an all-Catholic or all-Lutheran, or an all-Republican or all-Democratic registration. Men and women, because of the combat restrictions on women, are simply not similarly situated for purposes of a draft or registration for a draft." The dissenters did not challenge the exclusion of women from combat posts, but charged the Court with placing its "imprimatur on one of the most potent remaining public expressions of 'ancient canards about the proper role of women' by categorically excluding women from a fundamental civic obligation." The armed forces, they argued, need many people beyond those given combat assignments. Women are presently serving with great glory and honor in the armed forces and should not be excluded from the obligation to register, which can be divorced from conscription, since the purpose of the registration requirement is "to provide an inventory of what the available strength is within the military qualified pool in this country."[130]

To summarize, state classifications based on sex are not subject to scrutiny as severe as are state classifications based on race, but to sustain a classification based on sex the burden is on the state and local government to show that it serves "important governmental objectives" and is substantially related to the achievement of these objectives. Treatment of women differently from men is forbidden when supported by no more substantial justification than "archaic and overboard generalizations," "old notions," and "the role-typing society has long imposed upon women."[131]

---

[128] *Michael M. v Superior Court of Sonoma County*, 450 US 464 (1981).

[129] *Personnel Administrator of Massachusetts v Feeny*, 442 US 256 (1979).

[130] *Rostker v Goldberg*, 453 US 57 (1981).

[131] *Califano v Webster*, 430 US 313 (1977), and cases cited therein.

What is allowed by the Constitution, however, may still be illegal. Congress has used its powers to make sex-based distinctions illegal in many areas of employment and education. For example, as the Court has interpreted the Civil Rights Act of 1964, Title VII, a state may not require that prison guards be over 5 feet 2 inches tall and weigh more than 120 pounds, because the impact of such a law discriminates against women. (On the other hand, the practice of denying women the right to be prison guards in all-male, maximum-security institutions is not illegal.[132]) Similarly, the Civil Rights Act of 1964 made illegal the practice of the Los Angeles Department of Water and Power of charging women more than men for pension benefits.[133] Although women live longer than men, the statute makes it unlawful to discriminate against any individual because of such individual's race, color, religion, sex, or national origin and precludes treatment of an individual woman differently from a man, even though, "unless women as a class are assessed an extra charge, they will be subsidized, to some extent, by the class of male employees."[134]

In his opinion in *Regents of the University of California* v *Bakke*, Justice Powell suggested that preferential programs designed to assist women offer fewer constitutional obstacles than those "premised on racial or ethnic criteria." With respect to gender he wrote, "There are only two possible classifications. The incidence of the burdens imposed by preferential classification is clear. There are no rival groups who can claim that they, too, are entitled to preferential treatment. Classwide questions as to the group suffering previous injury and groups which fairly can be burdened are relatively manageable for reviewing courts."[135] On the other side, the Fourteenth Amendment was intended to protect blacks, not women, and its extension to sex discrimination is of recent origin. Of almost a dozen cases relating to affirmative action, only one has related directly to sex discrimination, but in that one the Court held that neither the Constitution nor the Civil Rights Act, Title VII, forbids public employers from giving preference to women in promotions "to positions within a traditionally segregated job classification in which women have been significantly under represented."[136]

Other Classifications

Decisions regarding state laws relating to aliens "have not formed an unswerving line."[137] So far as the states are concerned, "restrictions on lawfully resident aliens primarily affecting economic interests are subject to heightened judicial scrutiny," but such "strict scrutiny is out of place when the

---

[132] *Dothard* v *Rawlinson*, 433 US 321 (1977).

[133] *Los Angeles Department of Water and Power* v *Manhart*, 435 US 702 (1978); *General Electric Co.* v *Gilbert*, 429 US 125 (1976).

[134] Ibid.

[135] *Regents of the University of California* v *Bakke*, 438 US 265 (1978).

[136] *Johnson* v *Transportation Agency*, 480 US 616 (1987).

[137] *Ambach* v *Norwich*, 441 US 68 (1979).

restriction primarily serves a political function. . . . Some state functions are so bound up with the operation of the State as a governmental entity as to permit the exclusion from those functions of all persons who have not become part of the process of self-government."[138] In other words, some state laws regulating aliens are subject to strict scrutiny, some are not.

The Court has declared unconstitutional laws imposing a blanket prohibition against all public employment of aliens, forbidding them to practice law or civil engineering, denying them financial assistance for higher education, and depriving them of the right to serve as notaries public.[139] Yet, although the Court has said that the political exception is to be narrowly construed, that exception has been used to uphold state regulations that exclude aliens from serving as state police officers, probation officers, and public school teachers and that keep aliens from voting, serving on juries, and fulfilling "important nonelective executive, legislative, and judicial positions."[140]

In 1982 Justice Brennan, speaking for the Court, ignored the whole question whether lawfully admitted aliens should be treated as a suspect classification and, resorting to federal supremacy principles, set aside a practice of the University of Maryland of charging nonimmigrant aliens (children of diplomats and persons who work for international associations) out-of-state tuition. Said the Court, "State regulation not congressionally sanctioned that discriminates against aliens lawfully admitted to the country is impermissible if it imposes additional burdens not contemplated by Congress."[141] In his dissenting opinion, in which Chief Justice Burger joined, Justice Rehnquist argued that there is reason to doubt whether political powerlessness is any longer a legitimate reason for treating aliens as a "suspect classification" deserving of "heightened judicial solicitude."[142]

Then, in 1984, after appearing to have been wavering on the issue, the Court, in an opinion in which every justice except Rehnquist joined, reaffirmed in rather strong language that so far as state regulation is concerned, aliens are to remain a suspect classification other than for the political exception, and that exception is to be narrowly construed; "otherwise the exception will swallow the rule and depreciate the significance that should attach to the designation of a group as a 'discrete and insular' minority for whom heightened judicial solicitude is appropriate."[143]

Classifications based on *illegitimacy* are not considered suspect and thus are not subject to the Court's most exacting scrutiny. However, "in view of the history of treating illegitimate children less favorably than legitimate ones," the Court has "subjected statutory classifications based on illegitimacy to its heightened intermediate test." The scrutiny applied to them is not a "tooth-

---

[138] *Cabel v Chavez-Salido*, 454 US 432 (1982).

[139] *Bernal v Fainter*, 467 US 216 (1984); *Graham v Richardson*, 403 US 365 (1971); *Nyquist v Mauclet*, 432 US 1 (1977).

[140] *Foley v Connelie*, 435 US 291 (1978); *Ambach v Norwich*, 441 US 68 (1979).

[141] *Toll v Moreno*, 441 US 458 (1979), quoting *DeCana v Bica*, 424 US 351 (1976).

[142] *Toll v Moreno*, 441 US 458 (1979).

[143] *Bernal v Fainter*, 467 US 216 (1984).

less one." A classification based on illegitimacy is unconstitutional unless it "bears an evident and substantial relation to the particular...interests [the] statute is designed to serve."[144]

Poverty is not ordinarily a suspect classification. A state has no federal constitutional duty to see to it that school districts where most people are poor have the same funds for their schools as do districts where many of the people are well-to-do.[145] Poverty, however, is not always without significance in equal protection analysis. Laws that prevent the absolutely destitute, rather than those who are merely poor, from being able to enjoy some legal benefits because of their poverty have received close judicial scrutiny; while laws barring access to the divorce courts if one could not pay a fee have been declared unconstitutional, the filing fee for federal bankruptcy court has been upheld even when some are "too poor to go bankrupt."[146] And although the right to run for office is not a fundamental right, the Court has been especially suspicious of filing fee provisions that may make it difficult for those without funds to run for office, since "economic status is not a measure of a prospective candidate's qualifications to hold elective office, and a filing fee alone is an inadequate test of whether a candidacy is serious or spurious."[147]

The equal protection clause, often combined with due process considerations, also provides some protection for the poor in courtroom situations. In addition to forbidding discrimination in the administration of justice, the clause imposes on states a limited positive obligation to see to it that the poor have treatment equal to that of persons who can afford proper legal counsel, investigators, appeals, and so on. If a state makes a transcript a requirement for an appeal, it must furnish transcripts to those unable to afford them.[148] As mentioned earlier, for all appeals that each state provides as a matter of right, it must provide indigents with attorneys to help them carry their appeals to the next higher court; the state does not, however, have to provide an attorney at public expense for discretionary appeals, including those to the United States Supreme Court.[149]

Although defendants' poverty in no way immunizes them from punishment, "a state cannot force into jail those who cannot pay fines or it cannot revoke probation because of failure to pay a fine or restitution upon which probation had been conditioned." A state may imprison someone for willfully refusing to pay court costs or a fine or for failing to make a genuine effort to get a job or borrow the money to pay the fine; it cannot imprison a person solely because he or she lacks the resources to pay.[150]

---

[144] *Pickett v Brown*, 462 US 1 (1983); *Mills v Habluetzel*, 456 US 96 (1982), and cases cited therein.

[145] *San Antonio School District v Rodriguez*, 411 US 1 (1973).

[146] *United States v Kras*, 409 US 434 (1973); *Boddie v Connecticut*, 401 US 371 (1971).

[147] Justice Rehnquist for a plurality in *Clements v Flashing*, 457 US 957 (1982).

[148] *Griffin v Illinois*, 351 US 12 (1956); *Douglas v California*, 372 US 353 (1963); *Meyer v City of Chicago*, 404 US 189 (1971).

[149] *Ross v Moffit*, 417 US 600 (1974).

[150] *Bearden v Georgia*, 461 US 660 (1983).

In contrast to criminal prosecutions, where the state "hails a defendant into court," states have less of an equal protection and due process obligation to provide the poor with equal access to the civil courts. Yet even here there are some constitutional requirements. As noted above, a state may not, for example, deny access to its courts to those unable to pay filing fees for a divorce. The right to marry and to get a divorce are basic rights, and the state has a monopoly in regulating the marital relationship: to deny the poor access to the courts is, in effect, to deny them a divorce.[151] In contrast, the United States may deny access to its courts to persons unable to pay a small fee for filing a bankruptcy petition. There is no constitutional right to be absolved of one's debts, and there are ways of handling debts other than by becoming legally bankrupt. As Justice Stewart said in dissent, "Some of the poor are too poor even to go bankrupt."[152] A state may also collect a general filing fee from those wishing to appeal decisions of welfare agencies.[153] And although the precise grounds were denial of due process, the equal protection aspect was prominent when the Supreme Court ruled that a state must pay for the blood-typing of a person involved in a paternity suit who lacks the funds to pay for the test.[154]

The equal protection clause also prohibits states from imposing poll taxes as a condition of eligibility to vote; this prohibition is apart from that contained in the Twenty-fourth Amendment. Even if there is no evidence that a poll tax might discriminate against blacks or the poor, it establishes an unreasonable classification based on wealth. "Wealth, like race, creed, or color, is not germane to one's ability to participate intelligently in the electoral process."[155]

Congress has made some *age* classifications illegal, but age is not a constitutionally suspect classification. The Court has never struck down a law as unconstitutional because of an age classification. On the contrary, it has sustained a Massachusetts law disqualifying persons from being state police officers after age fifty, and an act of Congress making retirement from the foreign service compulsory at age sixty.[156]

Mentally ill persons, according to some of the lower federal courts, should be considered a suspect classification. The mentally ill, they argue, "historically have been subjected to purposeful and unequal treatment; they have been relegated to a position of political powerlessness; and prejudice against them curtails their participation in the pluralist system and strips them of political protection against discriminatory legislation."[157] But so far the Supreme Court has sidestepped the issue, although it specially refused to treat the mentally retarded as a suspect classification.[158]

---

[151] *Boddie v Connecticut*, 401 US 371 (1971).

[152] *United States v Kras*, 409 US 434 (1973).

[153] *Ortwein v Schwab*, 410 US 656 (1973).

[154] *Little v Streater*, 452 US 1 (1981).

[155] *Harper v Board of Elections*, 338 US 663 (1966).

[156] *Massachusetts Board of Retirement v Murgia*, 427 US 307 (1976); *Vance v Bradley*, 440 US 93 (1979).

[157] *Schweiker v Wilson*, 450 US 221 (1981).

[158] *Heller v Doe*, 125 L Ed 2d 257 (1993).

Intent and Effect—Proving Discrimination

How is discrimination proved? If a law should classify persons based on a suspect classification, such as race, or a semi-suspect classification, such as sex, the mere fact that the law has a discriminatory *effect* raises serious equal protection claims. However, for laws or practices that are not based "on an overtly discriminatory classification,"[159] the mere fact that a law or governmental practice has a differential *impact* on persons of different races (or sexes) does not by itself establish the law as *unconstitutional*. "The invidious quality of a law claimed to be racially discriminatory must ultimately be traced to a racially discriminatory purpose. Disproportionate impact is not irrelevant, but it is not the sole touchstone of an invidious racial discrimination forbidden by the Constitution. Standing alone, it does not trigger the rule that racial classifications are to be subjected to the strictest scrutiny and are justified only by the weightiest of considerations."[160]

Examples of discriminatory intent being shown are rather rare these days since legislators who intend to discriminate are not likely to admit it. Such was not the case with respect to a provision of the Alabama Constitution adopted in 1901, which added misdemeanors to the crimes covered by provisions disenfranchising persons convicted of crimes involving moral turpitude. The whole purpose of the provision, said those who worked for its adoption, was to disenfranchise blacks. Although the state argued that regardless of the original purpose, events occurring since then had made the provision legitimate, the Supreme Court, "without deciding whether [that provision] would be valid if enacted today without any impermissible motivation," concluded that it had been adopted with the desire to discriminate, continued to have that effect, and was thus unconstitutional.[161]

"Once racial discrimination is shown to have been a 'substantial' . . . factor behind enactment of the law, the burden shifts to the law's defenders to demonstrate that the law would have been enacted without this factor."[162] The fact of disproportionate effect, although by itself not proof of discrimination, is not unimportant. If a practice of a state or local government adversely affects members of one race, the burden of proof often shifts to the government to demonstrate that it has not engaged in discriminatory conduct.[163] For example, if a test has a racially discriminatory impact, or if in some districts none or only a few members of a race or ethnic group are called for jury service, the burden shifts to the government to show that the results are not the consequence of an intent to discriminate.

Discriminatory impact, however, does not always shift the burden. A defendant in a Georgia murder case presented powerful statistical evidence that

---

[159] Justice Powell for the Court in a footnote in *Wayte v United States,* 470 US 598 (1985).
[160] *Washington v Davis,* 426 US 229 (1976); *Mobile v Bolden,* 446 US 55 (1980); *Arlington Heights v Metro Housing Corp.,* 429 US 252 (1977).
[161] *Hunter v Underwood,* 471 US 222 (1985).
[162] Ibid.
[163] *Dothard v Rawlingson,* 433 US 321 (1977).

in that state there was a great disparity in the imposition of the death sentence based on the race of the murder victim and to a lesser extent the race of the defendant. According to an analysis of 2,000 Georgia murder cases tried during the 1970s, taking into account 230 variables that could have explained the disparity on nonracial grounds, defendants charged with killing a white person were 4.3 times as likely to receive a death sentence as defendants charged with killing a black person. Black defendants who killed white victims had the greatest likelihood of receiving the death penalty.

The Court majority, speaking through Justice Powell, rejected this analysis as evidence of discriminatory intent and distinguished this rejection from the Court's willingness to accept statistics as proof of intent to discriminate with respect to employment and in the selection of juries in particular districts. In jury sentencing, the statistics relate to many juries, with many other variables to be explained, and the various juries have no opportunity to explain the statistical disparity. Moreover, discretion is essential to the criminal justice process and is the very essence of judicial verdicts and sentencing. Nor could the evidence be considered persuasive in proving that the state of Georgia as a whole had violated the equal protection clause by adopting its capital punishment statute and allowing it to remain in force despite its alleged discriminatory application. For such an argument to prevail, argued Justice Powell, it would have to be established "that the Georgia legislature enacted or maintained the death penalty statute 'because of' an anticipated racially discriminatory effect."[164] Justice Blackmun, speaking for himself and Justices Marshall, Brennan, and Stevens, argued that the defendant had established a prima facie case of discriminatory intent and that the burden had then shifted to Georgia to demonstrate that the challenged effect was due to permissible racially neutral selection criteria, which it had failed to do. Although there was no evidence of racial discrimination in the case before them, the dissenters would have reversed, and some would have narrowed the class of defendants eligible for the death penalty to those that had committed such heinous murders under such bizarre circumstances that, according to the study, prosecutors would consistently seek and juries would consistently impose the death penalty, without regard to the race of the victim or the race of the offender.

In a series of cases that overlap Fifteenth Amendment considerations, the Court has moved back and forth over the question of the evidence necessary to prove discrimination in at-large election systems—those in which city council members or county representatives are elected citywide or countywide rather than by election districts. The effect of such systems in most cities, even if there is a substantial African American or Hispanic population, is to keep the city council all Anglo. The constitutional standard under the Fourteenth Amendment is the same as under the Fifteenth: there must be evidence of an *intent* to discriminate.[165] But even if no or few African Americans get elected,

---

[164] *McCleskey v Kemp*, 481 US 279 (1987).

[165] *Mobile v Bolden*, 446 US 55 (1980); *Rogers v Lodge*, 458 US 613 (1982).

it is hard to prove that it was the intent of those who established the system, and it is even harder to prove that it is the intent of those who maintain it.

Civil Rights Laws and Burden of Proof

What is not unconstitutional, however, may be illegal. The Civil Rights Act of 1866 (now 42 USC 1981), although covering private as well as governmental discrimination, reaches only purposeful discrimination and in the case of a suit against a state or municipal official there must be a showing that the official in action had final policy making authority or was acting in accord with policy or long-standing practice or custom.[166] It provides that "all persons within the jurisdiction of the United States shall have the same right in every State and Territory to make and enforce contracts, to sue, be parties, give evidence, and to enjoy the full and equal benefit of all laws and proceedings for the security of persons and property as is enjoyed by white citizens." The Court construed Section 1981 only to cover *intentional* racial discrimination in initial hiring decisions, not to cover on the job discrimination.[167] In 1991 Congress amended the law to reverse this decision, to provide broader coverage and to allow damage suits by women and those who suffer discrimination based on religion or national origin.

In 1982 Congress amended the Voting Rights Act of 1965 to cover discriminatory *impact* after the Court had interpreted the Act to require proof of intent to discriminate. As amended, the act stipulates that, although blacks and ethnic minorities have no legal right to have members elected in numbers equal to their proportion in the population, where they make up a substantial proportion of the population, the fact that few or none of them get elected because of some practice or procedure, such as at-large elections, is part of the "totality of circumstances" judges may take into account to determine if there has been a violation of the act.[168]

Congress, in Title VI of the Civil Rights Act of 1964, has also stipulated that federal grants are not to be used in any way to discriminate against blacks, women, the aged, or the disabled. Congress has made it illegal to use federal funds for practices that have a discriminatory effect even if those practices fall short of being unconstitutional because there is no proof of discriminatory purpose. In addition, Title VII of the Civil Rights Act of 1964 provides that, even though a job standard, test, or practice to determine eligibility for employment or promotion may be neutral on its face, if it has a *differential impact* on persons by race or sex, even if there is no intent to discriminate, there is nonetheless a violation of the law unless the employer can come forward with evidence that the practice in question has a legitimate business justification.[169]

---

[166] *General Building Contractors v Pennsylvania,* 458 US 375 (1983); *St. Louis v Praprotnik,* 485 US 112 (1988); *Jett v Dallas Ind. School Dist.,* 488 US 940 (1989).

[167] *Patterson v McLean Credit Union,* 491 US 64 (1989).

[168] *Thornburg v Gingles,* 478 US 30 (1986).

[169] *Board of Education of New York v Harris,* 444 US 130 (1979); *Texas Department of Community Affairs v Burdine,* 450 US 248 (1981); *Griggs v Duke Power Co.,* 401 US 424 (1971); *Wards Cove Packing Co. v Antonio,* 104 L Ed 2d 733 (1989).

There has been considerable controversy in these disparate impact cases about who has the burden of proof. The Rehnquist Court narrowed Title VII disparate impact analysis to place the burden of proof on plaintiffs even if the statistical evidence shows disparate impact. Congress, in the Civil Rights Act of 1991, overturned the Court's narrow reading and restored the earlier interpretation of the law, which eased the burden of proof for those charging racial discrimination.

The Civil Rights Act of 1991 counters the effects of nine Supreme Court decisions. It places a greater burden on employers to justify practices that negatively affect women and minorities by requiring employers to justify such practices as being job related for the position in question, being a business necessity, or showing that there are no alternative practices which would have a less negative impact on the protected group. It authorizes limited compensatory damages for intentional discrimination and punitive damages if the defendant acted with malice or reckless indifference to the rights of the individual based on sex, religion, or disability. (Unlimited damages are allowed for racial or ethnic bias under a Reconstruction civil rights law.) It amends the 1866 civil rights law, now 42 USC 1981, to prohibit not merely racial discrimination in initial hiring but other forms of race bias in the workplace, for example, in promotions. It prohibits "race norming" of tests used for employment or promotion, that is, setting different cutoff scores on the bases of race or ethnic origin. The act also establishes a commission, appointed by the president and Congress, to examine the "glass ceiling" that seems to keep women from becoming executives and to make recommendations on how to increase promotion of women and minorities to management positions.

Affirmative Action

What if governments adopt programs to remedy disadvantages that minorities and women suffer because of the lingering effects of past discrimination against them? What if governments adopt programs, or require private employers to adopt race-conscious remedies, popularly known as *affirmative action* by those who support them and as *reverse discrimination* by those who oppose, that provide special protections for minorities? What of benign race-conscious measures that are not directly remedial of specific findings of discrimination against particular individuals but are designed to serve governmental objectives such as bringing about an integrated police force, or diversity in a school student body, or diversity of ownership of radio and television stations? Do such programs create suspect classifications? Are they unconstitutional?

This is one of the more hotly debated constitutional issues of our time. In recent years the Supreme Court has dealt with the issue of affirmative action a dozen or so times. The justices, like the rest of the nation, are not of one mind on these issues and have never been able to muster clear majorities behind a definitive set of doctrines.

The first major statement of the Court on these perplexing issues came in a celebrated case relating to university admissions. Allan Bakke, a white male who was a top student at Minnesota and Stanford universities, as well as a Vietnam Veteran, applied in both 1973 and 1974 to the medical school of the University of California, Davis. In each of those years the school admitted new students, 84 in a general admissions program and 16 in a special admissions program created for African Americans, Chicanos, Asian Americans, and Native Americans—groups who had been underrepresented there until the special admissions program was established. Bakke's application was rejected each year, but students with lower grade-point averages, test scores, and interview ratings were admitted under the special admissions program. After his second rejection Bakke brought a suit in federal court claiming he had been excluded because of his race, contrary to both the Constitution and Title VI of the Civil Rights Act of 1964.

In *Regents of the University of California v Bakke* (1978), the Supreme Court ruled the Davis Plan was unconstitutional.[170] But in an opinion by Justice Powell, which no other member of the Court completely shared, the Court also declared that affirmative action programs are not necessarily unconstitutional. In order to get a diversified student body, a state university may properly take race and ethnic background into account as *one of several* factors in choosing students. (However, the university's goal may not be to redress past misconduct by society or to ensure that more minority members become doctors.) The problem with the California plan was it created a category of admissions from which whites were excluded solely because of their race.

Following *Bakke* the Court dealt with a variety of affirmative action programs, sustaining most, but not all of them. Yet as Justice White said, "Agreement upon a means for applying the Equal Protection Clause to an affirmative-action program has eluded the Court every time the issue has come before us."[171] Among the affirmative action programs approved was one in which Congress had required that ten percent of the funds for certain federal public works projects be set aside for minority-owned businesses.[172] Then in *Richmond v Croson* (1989), the Court struck down a plan of the city of Richmond requiring nonminority city contractors to subcontract at least 30 percent of the dollar amount of their contracts to one or more minority business firms. Said Justice O'Connor for the Court in language that seemed to call into question the validity of most affirmative action plans, when a state or local legislative body "chooses to employ a suspect classification, it cannot rest upon a generalized assertion as to the classification's relevance to its goals." "Race-sensitive remedial measures are to be justified only after a strong basis in evidence has established that remedial action is necessary to overcome the consequences of past discriminatory action."[173] Justice Marshall, in dissent,

---

[170] *University of California Regents v Bakke*, 438 US 265 (1978).
[171] Concurring in *Wygant v Jackson Board of Education*, 476 US 267 (1986).
[172] *Fullilove v Klutznick*, 448 US 448 (1980).
[173] *Richmond v Croson*, 488 US 469 (1989).

contended that there is a "profound difference separating governmental actions that themselves are racist, and governmental actions seeking to remedy the effects of prior racism." The proper test for governmental racial classifications seeking to remedy the effects of prior racism, he argued, is not the most stringent one, "strict scrutiny," but merely the intermediate one, "heightened scrutiny," that is, race-conscious classifications designed to further remedial goals merely have to be justified as serving important governmental objectives and be substantially related to the achievement of those objectives. He accused the Court of sounding "a full-scale retreat from the effort to deliver on the century-old promise of equality and scuttled the efforts of a city to surmount its discriminatory past."

Four years after *Richmond* v *Croson* the Court held that groups disadvantaged by these affirmative action programs had standing to sue without having to show that they would in fact have gotten the contract but for the challenged ordinance. "When the government erects a barrier that makes it more difficult for members of one group to obtain a benefit than it is for members of another group, a member of the former group seeking to challenge the barrier need not allege that he would have obtained the benefit but for the barrier in order to establish standing." The possible denial of equal treatment flows "from the imposition of the barrier, not the ultimate inability to obtain the benefit."[174]

Although *Richmond* v *Croson* was interpreted by most observers to signal a hardened attitude by the Court toward affirmative action, reflecting the growing strength of the Reagan appointments to the Court, at the end of the 1989–1990 term, to the surprise of most, Justice Brennan, speaking for a five-person majority—including Justice White, who had voted with the *Croson* majority—adopted the middle tier test for the scope of governmental power with respect to race classifications *so far as the national government is concerned.*[175] Furthermore, the national government is not, said the Court in *Metro Broadcasting* v *Federal Communications Commission* (1990), limited to using race-sensitive measures in order to overcome past discrimination but may use them for other legitimate governmental objectives. The Court upheld the right of the Federal Communications Commission, in response to congressional mandates, to take race into account as one of the factors in the granting of licenses for radio and television stations and under certain conditions to limit the transfer of certain existing radio and television broadcast stations *only* to minority-controlled firms. Justice Brennan's language was sweeping: "Benign race-conscious measures mandated by Congress—even if those measures are not remedial in the sense of being designed to compensate victims of past governmental or societal discrimination—are constitutionally permissible to the extent that they serve important governmental objectives within the power of Congress and are substantially related to achievement of those objectives."[176]

---

[174] *Northeastern Florida Chapter of the Associated General Contractors of America* v *City of Jacksonville*, 124 L Ed 2d 586 (1993).

[175] *Metro Broadcasting* v *FCC*, 497 US 547 (1990).

[176] Ibid.

He repeated these rather startling words again, "We...find that a congression-ally mandated benign race-conscious program that is substantially related to the achievement of an important governmental interest is consistent with equal pro-tection principles so long as it does not impose *undue* burdens on non-minorities." Justice O'Connor, author of the *Croson* opinion, wrote in dissent, "'Benign-racial classification' is a contradiction in terms. Governmental distinctions among citizens based on race or ethnicity, even in the rare circumstances permitted by our cases, exact costs and carry with them substantial dangers. To the person denied an opportunity or right based on race, the classifica-tion is hardly benign. The right to equal protection of the laws is a per-sonal right."[177]

Where does all this Supreme Court decision making leave us with respect to race? The Court still firmly adheres "to the traditional view that racial clas-sifications that stigmatize—because they are drawn on the presumption that one race is inferior to another or because they put the weight of government behind racial hatred and separatism—are not only suspect, but outlawed."[178] But because of shifting majorities, there are major differences between the power of Congress and those of the state and local governments with respect to questions about race. Congress's action is to be judged by the tests outlined by Justice Brennan in the *Metro* case: benign classifications closely related to legitimate governmental objectives are permissible if they do not unduly burden the nonminority groups.[179] State and local governments, on the other hand, are to be judged by the stringent standards outlined by Justice O'Connor in the *Richmond* case: all racial classifications, including those justified for benign or remedial purposes are suspect, and are subject to the strict scrutiny test to ensure that they are neither motivated by illegitimate notions of racial inferi-ority or simple racial politics.

The law of affirmative action is still evolving. There are more decisions to come as the Court—and the nation—engage in the never-ending business of clarifying constitutional guidelines.

Voting

The equal protection clause also protects access to the ballot and voting power. Except where the Constitution provides otherwise, as with respect to apportionment of presidential electors and senators among the states, the equal protection clause prohibits most electoral schemes that give one person's vote more weight than another. Thus, Georgia's county unit system for counting votes for governor had to go because it gave rural voters a much greater voice in the selection of statewide executive officers than voters living in cities.[180]

---

[177] Ibid.
[178] Justice Marshall in *Fullilove v Klutznick*, 448 US 448 (1980).
[179] *Fullilove v Klutznick*, 448 US 448 (1980).
[180] *Gray v Sanders*, 372 US 368 (1963).

An Illinois law suffered the same fate because it gave more weight to rural than to urban signatories on petitions to secure a place on statewide ballots, by requiring that of the 25,000 signatures needed, at least 200 must come from each of 50 of the state's 102 counties.[181] But certain special purpose units of government, such as water control or irrigation districts, that perform limited functions affecting definable groups have been permitted to distribute votes according to the value of the land owned,[182] and the one-person–one-vote principle does not apply to the selection of judges.[183] And as noted (see page 241) a state law prohibiting the counting and reporting of write-in votes does not violate the equal protection clause, at least in a state such as Hawaii which makes it easy for parties to get on the ballot and for candidates to get their names on ballots.[184]

As previously noted, the Supreme Court has applied equal protection considerations to insist that state legislatures be apportioned on the basis of population.[185] In the forty-nine two-chambered state legislatures (Nebraska has only one chamber), the membership of both chambers must be based on population.[186] The requirement of equal population districts also covers all local government units that exercise legislative functions, such as county commissions[187] and junior college districts.[188] Local units do not, however, have to meet such precisely mathematically equal standards as those required for congressional districts, nor do state legislatures have to meet the same rigid standards for their own districts as they are required to meet when laying out congressional districts.[189] However, the Supreme Court did not hesitate to declare unconstitutional the Board of Estimates of New York City, which gave each borough president an equal vote although the boroughs they represented vary widely in population. The fact that three officials elected citywide— the mayor, comptroller, and council president—were also on the Board and whose two votes each reduced the amount of underrepresentation of the more populous boroughs did not save this system of representation.[190]

If a legislature fails to reapportion when required to do so, the task may fall to a federal judge. The Supreme Court has instructed the judges to avoid multimember districts and has told them that they are obliged to achieve more population equality among districts than might be required if the legislature had proposed the reapportionment plan.[191]

---

[181] Moore v Ogilvie, 394 US 814 (1969).

[182] Sayler Land Co. v Tulare Lake Basin Water Storage District, 410 US 719 (1973); Associated Enterprises, Inc. v Toltec District, 410 US 743 (1973); Ball v James, 455 US 355 (1981).

[183] Wells v Edwards, 409 US 1095 (1973).

[184] Burdick v Takushi, 119 L Ed 2d 245 (1992).

[185] Reynolds v Sims, 377 US 533 (1964), and companion cases.

[186] Wells v Rockefeller, 394 US 542 (1969); Kirkpatrick v Preisler, 394 US 526 (1969).

[187] Avery v Midland County, 390 US 474 (1968).

[188] Hadley v Junior College District of Kansas City, 397 US 50 (1972).

[189] Abate v Mundt, 403 US 182 (1971); Connor v Williams, 404 US 549 (1970); Mahan v Howell, 410 US 315 (1973).

[190] Board of Estimates of New York City v Morris, 488 US 938 (1989).

[191] Chapman v Meier, 420 US 1 (1975); Connor v Finch, 431 US 407 (1977).

Racial Gerrymandering

Racial gerrymandering, that is, to draw election district lines in such a way as to minimize or dilute the votes of people because of their race, violates not only the equal protection clause but also the Voting Rights Act of 1965. But what if, in order to comply with the Voting Rights Act of 1965, a legislature draws electoral district lines in such a way as to maximize the votes of a protected minority? In *United Jewish Organizations* v *Carey,* the Court ruled that a state acting under provisions of the Voting Rights Act may draw district lines for the state legislature in a way that ensures that African Americans will be in a majority in certain voting districts. "Where a plan presents no racial slur or stigma with respect to whites or any other race and does not deprive whites, as a group, of 'fair representation,'" it is constitutional, even though as a consequence of the plan in the case decided, a Hasidic Jewish community was split into two voting districts and thereby had its voting strength diluted.[192]

However, the equal protection clause does prevent a reapportionment scheme that is "so irrational on its face that it can be understood only as an effort to segregate voters into separate voting districts because of their race."[193] So the Court declared when it reviewed the action of North Carolina, which after the 1990 census enacted a reapportionment plan that included only one majority-black congressional district. Then, because of the objection of the attorney general of the United States under Section 5 of the Voting Rights Act of 1965 (see page 392), it created a second majority-black district which cut in places no wider than a super-highway through towns, districts, and counties, winding snake-like for 160 miles. As a state legislator described this congressional district, "If you drove down the interstate with both car doors open, you'd kill most of the people in the district."[194] The Court, speaking through Justice O'Connor, declared: "A reapportionment plan that includes in one district individuals who belong to the same race, but who are otherwise widely separated by geographical and political boundaries, and who may have little in common with one another but the color of their skin, bears an uncomfortable resemblance to political apartheid."[195] States may take race into account in drawing of district lines, "but racial classifications with respect to voting carry particular dangers and such plans must be narrowly tailored to further a compelling governmental interest." Here North Carolina's plan violates the equal protection clause because "the redistricting legislation can be viewed only as an effort to segregate the races for purposes of voting, without regarding for traditional districting principles and without sufficiently compelling justification." The dissenting justices emphasized that the white voters were not injured and were not in any way impaired in their opportunity to participate in the political process. "The conscious use of race in redistricting does not violate the Equal Protection Clause unless the effect of the redistricting plan is to deny a

---

[192] *United Jewish Organizations* v *Carey,* 430 US 144 (1977).
[193] *Shaw* v *Reno,* 125 L Ed 2d 511 (1993).
[194] Ibid.
[195] Ibid.

particular group equal access to the political process or to minimize its voting strength unduly."[196] Justice Souter in dissent would distinguish between equal protection claims involving conscious use of race for affirmative action in employment and contracting from the use of race in drawing the electoral district lines. The latter does not diminish the effectiveness of the individual as a voter, whereas use of race for employment or contracting places some persons at a disadvantage because of their race.

Old-Fashioned Political Gerrymandering

The most recent group to secure constitutional protection against discrimination in the drawing of electoral district lines are the major political parties. In the past they had to depend on their own political strengths. Gerrymandering, which is about as old as the Republic, is the practice of the party controlling a legislative body drawing legislative district lines in such a fashion as to make any given number of votes for their party produce the largest number of winning legislators. It can be done by a variety of techniques, one of which is to draw the lines in such a fashion that all the opposition voters are concentrated in as few districts as possible, known as "stacking," or by splitting the opposition voters into as many districts as possible so that they will never carry an election, known as "cracking." With the use of computers it is now possible to draw election district lines so that there are equal numbers of people in each district depending on how the lines are drawn, ensuring that one party gets more seats than if the lines were drawn another way.

The Supreme Court has held that political gerrymandering raises justiciable questions but the standard to measure it is not the strict scrutiny used for racial gerrymandering. In the case of partisan gerrymandering the Court has been unable to come up with a standard to guide federal judges in deciding which gerrymandering is unconstitutional and which is not. A plurality has announced a complicated test that requires proof not only that there has been an intent to discriminate—which gerrymandering is by definition—but also that the effect has been to "consistently degrade a voter's or a group of voters' influence on the political process as a whole." The plurality emphasized that a single election cannot be relied on to prove unconstitutional partisan discrimination; there must be proof that a party has been consigned to minority status for a decade, with no hope of doing any better after the next reapportionment. Clearly this is not the last word on the subject.[197]

SECTION 2
Representatives shall be apportioned among the several States according to

---

[196] Ibid.
[197] *Davis v Bandemer*, 478 US 109 (1986).

their respective numbers, counting the whole number of persons in each State, excluding Indians not taxed.

This section supersedes Article I, Section 2, paragraph 3. Originally, three-fifths of the number of slaves was added to the number of free persons to determine representation.

***

SECTION 2

[continued] But when the right to vote at any election for the choice of electors for President and Vice President of the United States, Representatives in Congress, the Executive and Judicial officers of a State, or the members of the Legislature thereof, is denied to any of the male inhabitants of such State, being twenty-one years of age, and citizens of the United States, or in any way abridged, except for participation in rebellion, or other crime, the basis of representation therein shall be reduced in the proportion which the number of such male citizens shall bear to the whole number of male citizens twenty-one years of age in such State.

This provision has never been enforced by Congress, and may today be regarded as obsolete through disuse and also, possibly, through obvious disharmony with the Nineteenth and Twenty-sixth Amendments. This provision has been mentioned only twice by the Supreme Court. Once it was cited in support of a decision upholding a state suffrage regulation that denied the vote to felons who had completed their sentences.[198] The other time, a unanimous Court ruled that this section did not exempt a state from complying with the equal protection clause. Thus, Alabama had violated the Constitution, notwithstanding Section 2, in applying a law denying the right to vote to persons convicted of a crime involving moral turpitude. It was clear that this provision had been adopted in 1901 for the express intent of keeping blacks from voting.[199]

***

SECTION 3

No person shall be a Senator or Representative in Congress, or elector of President and Vice President, or hold any office, civil or military, under the United States, or under any State, who, having previously taken an oath, as a member of Congress, or as an officer of the United States, or as a member of any State legislature, or as an executive or judicial officer of any State, to support the Constitution of the United States, shall have engaged in insurrection or rebellion against the same, or given aid or comfort to the enemies thereof. But Congress may by a vote of two-thirds of each House, remove such disability.

---

[198] *Richardson v Ramirez*, 418 US 24 (1974).
[199] *Hunter v Underwood*, 471 US 222 (1985).

This section politically disabled those who had led the Southern states into the Confederacy. It was placed in the Fourteenth Amendment by the radical Republicans and was a factor in their struggle with President Johnson. It limited the president's power to pardon the leaders of the Confederacy and thus restore their political and civil rights. Congress removed this disability on June 6, 1898.

SECTION 4

The validity of the public debt of the United States, authorized by law, including debts incurred for payment of pensions and bounties for services in suppressing insurrection or rebellion, shall not be questioned. But neither the United States nor any State shall assume or pay any debt or obligation incurred in aid of insurrection or rebellion against the United States, or any claim for the loss or emancipation of any slave; but all such debts, obligations and claims shall be held illegal and void.

This section invalidated all the securities and other evidences of debt of the Confederacy and reaffirmed those of the Union.

SECTION 5

The Congress shall have power to enforce, by appropriate legislation, the provisions of this article.

Until recent decades this clause was narrowly construed. In 1883, in the *Civil Rights Cases*, the Supreme Court restricted the power of Congress under this section to the prevention or correction of state (including local) government action that abridged the privileges or immunities of a United States citizen; deprived any persons of life, liberty, or property without due process; or denied them the equal protection of the laws. The Supreme Court held that since the Fourteenth Amendment forbids only state action, Section 5 did not authorize Congress to make it a federal crime for innkeepers and other proprietors of public places to deny accommodations to persons because of race. Congress could adopt legislation under Section 5 only to prevent state discrimination, not abridgment of civil rights by private groups or persons.[200]

In view of the Supreme Court's holdings in the *Civil Rights Cases*, Congress relied on the commerce clause when it adopted the Civil Rights Act of 1964, which forbids discrimination by employers and by operators of places of public accommodation. In view of Supreme Court doctrine since 1964, if Congress had chosen to base the 1964 act more directly on Section 5, the Supreme Court would very likely have sustained it.

---

[200] *Civil Rights Cases*, 109 US 3 (1883).

Beginning in 1966 the Supreme Court started to give new life to Section 5. In that year it held that Section 5 authorizes Congress to do whatever it thinks is necessary and proper to enforce the rights guaranteed by the Fourteenth Amendment, even to the extent of superseding state regulations that are not themselves an unconstitutional denial of Fourteenth Amendment rights! This ruling came about in a challenge to a section of the Voting Rights Act of 1965 that stipulates that no person who has had a sixth grade education under the American flag shall be denied the right to vote for not being literate in English. This section was adopted to set aside a literacy requirement of New York that was keeping many citizens who had come to New York from Puerto Rico from voting. Even though the New York law was constitutional, the Court majority held, Congress is empowered by Section 5 to use its own judgment in determining what legislation is needed to keep states from denying persons equal protection of the laws. Justices Harlan and Stewart dissented on the grounds that Congress was exercising judicial power. So long as a state is not denying any person the equal protection of the laws and is operating within its constitutional sphere, according to the dissenting justices, Congress has no power to act under Section 5.[201]

Then in his *Bakke* opinion, Justice Powell noted significantly that the Congress had greater authority to act against racial discrimination than perhaps did the states because of congressional powers pursuant to Paragraph 2 of the Thirteenth Amendment and Paragraph 5 of the Fourteenth Amendment to remedy the effects of prior discrimination. "We have previously recognized the special competence of Congress to make findings with respect to the effects of identified past discrimination and its discretionary authority to take appropriate remedial measures."[202] When Congress authorizes racial classifications to provide remedial programs for blacks and other ethnic minorities, such programs are on stronger constitutional foundations than are similar programs adopted by trustees of universities or other agencies not empowered by Section 5 of the Fourteenth Amendment "to enforce, by appropriate legislation, the provisions of this article."

In *Fullilove* v *Klutznick,* the Court sustained a federal law calling for set-asides in public construction projects for blacks, minorities, and women and referred to the great latitude of Congress under Section 5 in deciding what actions might be needed to overcome past discrimination.[203] "We are bound to approach our task," wrote Chief Justice Burger for himself and two other Justices, "with appropriate deference to the Congress, 'a co-equal branch charged by the Constitution with the power...to enforce, by appropriate legislation,' the equal protection guarantees of the Fourteenth Amendment."

But the most significant expansion of Congressional powers under Section 5 came in *Metro Broadcasting* v *Federal Communications Commission* where, speaking for the Court, Justice Brennan held that Congress under Section 5 is

[201] *Katzenbach* v *Morgan,* 384 US 641 (1966).
[202] *Regents of the University of California* v *Bakke,* 438 US 256 (1978).
[203] *Fullilove* v *Klutznick,* 448 US 448 (1980).

not limited to overcoming past discrimination but may take action to further other governmental goals, as for example in securing diversity of opinion in the media, and in so doing Congress is not limited by the same standards as the states in fashioning race-sensitive programs.[204] Justice Brennan supplemented his argument for expansive congressional authority under Section 5 by pointing to congressional power that flows from the commerce clause, the spending clause, and the other Civil War Amendments. Justice O'Connor and her three colleagues, dissenting in *Metro*, would limit congressional power under this section to enforce requirements of the equal protection clause and would hold Congress to the same standards as the states.

Congressional legislation enacted pursuant to Section 5 has a "special status."[205] When acting under Section 5, Congress, unlike when it acts under its powers under the commerce and spending clauses, is not "constrained by the principles of federalism that might otherwise be an obstacle to congressional authority." The Civil War Amendments "were specifically designed as an expansion of federal power and an intrusion on state authority."[206] "When Congress acts pursuant to Section 5, not only is it exercising legislative authority that is plenary within the terms of the constitutional grant, it is exercising that authority under one section of a constitutional Amendment whose other sections by their own terms embody limitations on state authority."[207] However, the Court has adopted a "plain-statement rule" as the appropriate test for determining when Congress intends to enforce the guarantees of the Fourteenth Amendment and to determine that Congress is not just acting under the spending clause or commerce clause. For example, "Because Congress nowhere stated its intent to impose mandatory obligations on the States under its Section 5 powers," the Court concluded that Congress had not done so and refused to apply a provision of the Age Discrimination Employment Act forbidding mandatory retirement provisions to set aside Missouri's requirement that its judges retire at age 70.[208]

In the post–Civil War period the Court not only narrowly construed Section 5, it narrowly construed the civil rights acts that Congress did adopt. As a result Section 5 and the statutes enacted under it for decades were of little use in protecting the civil rights of blacks or anyone else. The Civil Rights Act of 1871, now known as 42 USC 1983, has taken on new life. That Act makes personally liable for damages any person acting under color of law or custom of any state who subjects any other person to the deprivation of any rights, privileges, or immunities secured by the Constitution. This statute is being broadly construed by the Court to permit persons to bring actions against public officials, including judges, for any violation of any right protected by the Constitution or federal laws, including the interstate commerce and other clauses of the Constitution and not just those that stem from the Fourteenth Amendment.[209] Such suits are now an

---

[204] *Metro Broadcasting* v *FCC*, 487 US 547 (1990).

[205] So designated by Justice White concurring and dissenting in *Gregory* v *Ashcroft*, 115 L Ed 2d 410 (1991).

[206] *City of Rome* v *United States*, 446 US 156 (1980).

[207] *Fitzpatrick* v *Bitzer*, 427 US 445 (1976).

[208] *Gregory* v *Ashcroft*, 115 Ed 2d 410 (1991).

[209] *Dennis* v *Higgins*, 498 US 439 (1991).

important part of the business of federal courts. Although municipalities are subject to such suits for violations of civil rights, state governments and state officials acting in their official capacity are not considered "persons" covered by Section 1983. And as we noted (see page 339), damages against state officials represent Eleventh Amendment problems of a different order of magnitude than do injunctive actions to prevent alleged violations of civil rights.

AMENDMENT XV: THE RIGHT TO VOTE

SECTION 1

The right of citizens of the United States to vote shall not be denied or abridged by the United States or by any State on account of race, color, or previous condition of servitude.

This amendment was proposed February 26, 1869, and declared in force by the secretary of state on March 30, 1870.

"The Fifteenth Amendment nullifies sophisticated as well as simple-minded modes of discrimination."[1] Yet, for many decades white southerners in charge of registration and voting readily circumvented the Fifteenth Amendment. They had an arsenal of discriminatory schemes. But at the end of World War II, the Supreme Court declared unconstitutional the devices used to keep blacks from registering and voting. The first to go was the white primary. Under the pretense that there was no state action involved, in most southern states blacks were kept from voting in the Democratic party primaries, in many areas the only elections that really mattered. In *Smith* v *Allwright* (1944) the Supreme Court said, "When primaries become a part of the machinery for choosing officials . . . the same tests to determine the character of discrimination...would be applied to the primary as are applied to the general election."[2] The discriminatory use of understanding and good character tests was also enjoined.[3] The Constitution was amended to forbid the requirement of a poll tax payment as a condition for voting for presidential electors or for members of Congress, and the Supreme Court construed the Constitution to forbid the requirement of a poll tax payment as a condition for voting in any public election. In lawsuit after lawsuit, the federal courts struck down one discriminatory scheme after another.

The Court in 1982 reinvigorated an 1875 precedent, *Minor* v *Happersett*,[4] to the effect that "the Constitution 'does not confer the right of suffrage upon any one'" and "the right to vote, per se, is not a constitutionally protected

---

[1] *Lane* v *Wilson*, 307 US 368 (1939).

[2] *Smith* v *Allwright*, 321 US 649 (1944); *Terry* v *Adams*, 345 US 461 (1953).

[3] *United States* v *Mississippi*, 380 US 128 (1965); *Louisiana* v *United States*, 380 US 145 (1965).

[4] *Minor* v *Happersett*, 21 Wallace 162 (1875).

right."[5] This holding has little significance for the Fifteenth Amendment, but removes the right to vote from the fundamental rights especially protected by the equal protection clause of the Fourteenth Amendment.

SECTION 2

The Congress shall have power to enforce this article by appropriate legislation.

Until the Voting Rights Act of 1965, Congress used its powers under Section 2 very little, and when it did use them, it was only to open federal courts for action against discriminatory state practices. This case-by-case litigation was inadequate to combat widespread and persistent discrimination because of the inordinate amount of time and energy required to overcome the obstructionist tactics encountered in those lawsuits. Even after a lawsuit had been won, there was no assurance that African Americans would be permitted to vote. So in 1965 Congress, using its authority under this section to do whatever is necessary and proper to ensure that no state shall deprive any person of the right to vote because of race, adopted a new approach.

By the Voting Rights Act of 1965—three times extended and strengthened by Congress, once in 1970, again in 1975, and most recently in 1982—Congress set about implementing the Fifteenth Amendment in two ways: first, by securing for blacks the right to vote and second by ensuring that their votes would not be diluted. As a result of the Voting Rights Act of 1965 and its amendments, for the first time in a hundred years, the Fifteenth Amendment became an operating reality throughout the nation.

To accomplish these purposes, the act does several things. It prohibits literacy tests everywhere. The act requires that any otherwise qualified persons be allowed to vote for presidential electors even if they fail to meet a state's residency requirements, orders states to keep registration for presidential elections open until thirty days before the election, and lowers from twenty-one to eighteen the voting age in all elections.

In Section 2, it forbids governments—any governments anyplace in the United States—from adopting voting or electoral procedures, regardless of intent, that have the purpose or effect of limiting minorities from full political participation, that is, that result in the *dilution* of voting power.

In those states and counties, mostly but not exclusively in the South, that had a persistent history of violating the Fifteenth Amendment, the act authorizes the attorney general to send federal officials to observe elections and, if necessary, to enroll voters. If local election officials turn away any voter who federal examiners find entitled to vote, the examiners may secure an order from a federal district court impounding all ballots until all persons entitled to vote have been allowed to do so. The attorney general may also appoint poll watchers to ensure that the votes of all qualified persons are properly counted.

---

[5] *Rodriguez v Popular Democratic Party*, 457 US 1 (1982).

Section 5 prescribes that in the areas specifically covered by the law, that is, those areas that have had a persistent history of low registration or voting rates, or with 10 percent of voting-age citizens who belong to language minorities—persons of Spanish heritage, Asian Americans, American Indians, and Alaskan natives—no new voting law or practice that affects the electoral process is effective unless approved by the attorney general or by the United States District Court for the District of Columbia. Bilingual election materials must be provided for language minorities. The attorney general or the District Court for the District of Columbia do not have to show that the purpose of the change is to discriminate against minorities in order to set it aside. It is sufficient that the attorney general find that the proposed change would result in the dilution of the voting influence of a protected class. This rather drastic intrusion into local matters has been justified by the Court on the grounds that the Fifteenth Amendment was specifically designed as an expansion of federal powers: it gives Congress authority to adopt legislation to enforce its provisions, even if such legislation overrides principles of federalism that might otherwise be an obstacle to congressional authority.[6]

A state may "bail out" from the prior-clearance requirements for electoral changes only if it proves to the District Court for the District of Columbia that it has had a clean voting rights record for the preceding ten years.[7]

The Supreme Court, making it clear that "Congress may use any rational means to effectuate the constitutional prohibition of racial discrimination in voting,"[8] has upheld all provisions of the act except the one lowering the voting age to eighteen in elections for state and local officials (the Twenty-sixth Amendment now governs the age requirement for voting in all elections for all officials).[9]

The act goes considerably beyond protecting the right to vote provided by the Fifteenth Amendment. For one thing, it makes it easier for states to do certain things in response to the prompting of that act than it would be to do those things without such prompting. Yet, as we noted in discussing the Fourteenth Amendment, complying with an order of the attorney general under Section 5 does not immunize the states from having to respond to claims that they have violated the Constitution. We did note that in *United Jewish Organizations* v *Carey*, the Court ruled that a state acting under provisions of the Voting Rights Act may draw district lines for the state legislature in a way that ensures that African Americans will be in a majority in certain voting districts.[10] But we also noted that it could not do so by only taking race into account and had to act by the means most narrowly tailored to protect the rights of minorities.[11]

The Voting Rights Act, especially as amended in 1982, goes beyond the Fifteenth Amendment in another very important way. Electoral arrangements that

---

[6] *South Carolina* v *Katzenbach*, 383 US 301 (1966); *City of Rome* v *United States*, 446 US 156 (1980).

[7] *Rome* v *United States*, 446 US 156 (1980).

[8] *South Carolina* v *Katzenbach*, 383 US 301 (1966).

[9] *Oregon* v *Mitchel*, 400 US 112 (1970).

[10] *United Jewish Organizations* v *Carey*, 430 US 144 (1977).

[11] *Shaw* v *Reno*, 125 L Ed 2d 511 (1993).

do not relate directly to voting and are neutral on their face are not violations of the Fifteenth Amendment, even if they *dilute* the voting power of minorities, unless they are motivated by a discriminatory "purpose." In fact, the Court "has not decided whether the Fifteenth Amendment applies to vote-dilution claims...."[12] What does not violate the Fifteenth Amendment, however, may violate the Voting Rights Act. A Supreme Court plurality opinion in *Mobile* v *Borden* had declared that, to establish a violation of either the Voting Rights Act or the Fourteenth or Fifteenth Amendment, minority voters had to prove that a contested electoral mechanism was intentionally adopted or maintained by state officials for a discriminatory purpose.[13] The 1982 amendments set aside this limitation.

As a result, today most of the litigation involving the Voting Rights Act is not about the right to vote, but about the right not to have the votes of minorities *diluted*. What precisely constitutes dilution and how it is to be measured is the subject of much litigation. Although the 1982 amendments do not guarantee "members of a protected class a right to have members...elected in numbers equal to their proportion in the population," they do make it illegal for governments to adopt or maintain procedures, regardless of intent, if such procedures result in the dilution of African-American (or Chicano, or Native American, or Asian-American) voting power. Where African Americans make up a substantial proportion of the population, the fact that few or none of them get elected is part of the "totality of circumstances" judges must take into account in determining whether there has been a violation of the act.[14]

What about multimember electoral districts? Does their mere existence violate Section 2 of the Voting Rights Act? Although the existence of multidistrict plans, as well as at-large plans, generally pose greater threats to minority-voter participation in the political process than do single-member districts, and federal courts strongly prefer single-member districts, their mere existence does not necessarily violate Section 2.[15] However, if (1) a minority group is sufficiently large and geographically compact to constitute a majority in a single-member district, (2) the minority group is politically cohesive, and (3) the white majority usually votes as enough of a bloc to defeat the minority-preferred candidate, then the multimember district system is a violation of Section 2. To prove this set of facts exists, plaintiffs have to show that a significant number of minority group members usually vote for the same candidate, whatever the candidate's race, and that, in general, a white bloc vote normally has defeated the combined strength of minority support plus white "crossover." It is not necessary to prove that the white voters intend to discriminate against blacks or that blacks vote for blacks only because of race. The mere fact of bloc voting is enough.[16]

In the context of single-member districts there can also be violations of Section 2, for example, intentionally dividing a minority group among various districts so that there is a majority in none—that is, fragmenting the vote. Or at the other

---

[12] *Voinovich* v *Quilter*, 122 L Ed 2d 500 (1993).

[13] *Mobile* v *Bolden*, 446 US 64 (1980).

[14] *Thornburg* v *Gingles*, 478 US 30 (1986).

[15] *Growe* v *Emison*, 122 L Ed 2d 388 (1993).

[16] Ibid.

extreme, minority voters can be concentrated into a few districts so that they cannot influence districts in which they might constitute an influential minority. The court has not yet decided whether influence-dilution claims of this kind violate Section 2 but has assumed so for the purpose of deciding some cases.[17]

TWENTIETH-CENTURY AMENDMENTS

AMENDMENT XVI: INCOME TAXES

The Congress shall have power to lay and collect taxes on incomes, from whatever source derived, without apportionment among the several States, and without regard to any census or enumeration.

This amendment was proposed July 12, 1909, and declared in force by the secretary of state February 25, 1913.

During the Civil War an income tax was levied as part of the war-financing program. As was generally expected, the Supreme Court upheld the national government's right to levy such a tax. In 1894 the Wilson-Gorham Tariff levied a 2 percent tax on incomes over $4,000. The year following, after hearing the tax assailed as the opening wedge of populism, communism, and the like, the Supreme Court ruled that a tax on income from property was tantamount to a tax on the property itself and hence a direct tax, which had to be apportioned among the several states according to population (see Article I, Section 2, paragraph 3).[1] The levying of income tax was thus rendered impractical until the adoption of the Sixteenth Amendment in 1913.

AMENDMENT XVII: DIRECT ELECTION OF SENATORS

1. The Senate of the United States shall be composed of two Senators from each State, elected by the people thereof for six years; and each Senator shall have one vote. The electors in each State shall have the qualifications requisite for electors of the most numerous branch of the State legislatures.

This amendment was proposed May 13, 1912, and declared in force by the secretary of state May 31, 1913.

---

[17] *Voinovich* v *Quilter*, L Ed 2d 500, (1993).
[1] *Pollock* v *Farmers Loan & Trust Co.*, 158 US 601 (1895).

The adoption of universal suffrage and the growing strength of the democratic spirit made it inevitable that United States senators should be chosen directly by the people. During the last half of the nineteenth century, dissident labor and farmer parties had called for direct election. The revelation of certain senators' great wealth and of their obligations to various large economic interests reinforced those demands. By the turn of the century, all the major parties supported proposals for direct election; the House of Representatives several times passed resolutions proposing an amendment to make the change. Finally, in 1912 the Senate capitulated. As a matter of fact, by that date the voters in half of the states had obtained the right to indicate their preference for senator in the party primaries; the state legislatures normally followed the wishes of the voters. The adoption of the Seventeenth Amendment merely rounded out a reform that had long been under way.

---

2. When vacancies happen in the representation of any State in the Senate, the executive authority of such State shall issue writs of election to fill such vacancies: Provided, That the legislature of any State may empower the executive thereof to make temporary appointments until the people fill the vacancies by election as the legislature may direct. Most vacancies are filled by temporary appointments. 3. This amendment shall not be so construed as to affect the election or term of any Senator chosen before it becomes valid as part of the Constitution.

Most vacancies are filled by temporary appointments.

AMENDMENT XVIII: PROHIBITION

SECTION 1
After one year from the ratification of this article the manufacture, sale, or transportation of intoxicating liquors within, the importation thereof into, or the exportation thereof from the United States and all territory subject to the jurisdiction thereof for beverage purposes is hereby prohibited.

This amendment was proposed December 18, 1917, and declared in force by the acting secretary of state January 29, 1919.

It was repealed by the Twenty-first Amendment. There have always been those who have waged war on demon rum. As long ago as 1842 the state of Maine went dry, and the Prohibition Party has had a candidate on the ballot in at least a few states in every presidential election since 1872. But it was the Anti-Saloon Leagues—a pressure group deluxe, formed in 1895—that gave the prohibition movement its greatest impetus. During World War I, the necessity of saving grain lent prohibition a guise of patriotism. Although the Eighteenth Amendment was ultimately ratified by all the states except Rhode Island and Connecticut, it always lacked the support of large groups of citizens, especially in the large cities.

SECTION 2

The Congress and the several States shall have concurrent power to enforce this article by appropriate legislation.

The Volstead Act went into effect January 17, 1920. By 1929 three states had repealed their enforcement acts; most states left it to the national government to implement this amendment.

SECTION 3

This article shall be inoperative unless it shall have been ratified as an amendment to the Constitution by the legislatures of the several States as provided in the Constitution, within seven years from the date of the submission hereof to the States by the Congress.

AMENDMENT XIX: WOMAN SUFFRAGE

1. The right of citizens of the United States to vote shall not be denied or abridged by the United States or by any State on account of sex.

The Nineteenth Amendment was proposed June 4, 1919, and declared in force by the secretary of state August 26, 1920.

This amendment was the culmination of a struggle that began in the 1840s. In 1890 women were admitted to full suffrage rights in Wyoming; by the time the amendment was adopted, fifteen states and Alaska had given women full suffrage, fourteen states had given women "presidential suffrage," and two states had given women the right to vote in primaries. Many of the arguments advanced against woman suffrage were ludicrous. Much of the opposition came from certain business groups (especially the liquor industry), who feared that women would vote for regulation.

The Nineteenth Amendment did not affect laws dealing with ownership of property, jury service, marriage and divorce, labor regulations, and so forth. Three years after the amendment had been ratified, the first equal rights amendment was introduced in Congress. Forty-nine years later, Congress finally proposed an Equal Rights Amendment and submitted it to the states. Although it had overwhelming support in both houses of Congress and at first appeared likely to be ratified quickly, it failed to secure the necessary number of votes, even though the time limit for ratification was extended by almost four years.

The Supreme Court, as well as the courts in many states, has started to provide more protection for equal rights for women under existing constitutional language. Although these cases do not arise under the Nineteenth Amendment, that women vote is not unrelated to greater judicial sensitivity to equal rights.

2. Congress shall have power to enforce this article by appropriate legislation.

Congress has had little need to use this power. Despite the intensity of the opposition to the proposal of this amendment and the time it took to bring about this constitutional change, once the Nineteenth Amendment was ratified, in contrast to the Fifteenth, there was no attempt to delay or obstruct its implementation.

AMENDMENT XX: THE LAME-DUCK AMENDMENT

SECTION 1
The terms of the President and Vice President shall end at noon on the 20th day of January, and the terms of Senators and Representatives at noon on the 3d day of January, of the years in which such terms would have ended if this article had not been ratified; and the terms of their successors shall then begin.

This amendment was proposed March 3, 1932, and declared in force by the secretary of state February 6, 1933.

This amendment was eventually ratified by all the states. Senator George W. Norris of Nebraska was the moving force behind the amendment, which is sometimes given his name. Its adoption brought to a close the Progressive Movement's contribution to constitutional reform, a movement that led to the Sixteenth through Twentieth Amendments.

Before the adoption of the Twentieth Amendment, the president and members of Congress elected in November did not take office until the following March, and newly elected members of Congress did not (unless called into special session) actually begin their work until the following December, thirteen months after their election. Meanwhile, members defeated in the November election, "lame ducks," continued to serve until the following March 4 and, although repudiated at the polls, continued to represent their constituencies in the December-to-March session.

SECTION 2
The Congress shall assemble at least once in every year, and such meeting shall begin at noon on the 3d day of January, unless they shall by law appoint a different day.

This section supersedes Article I, Section 4, paragraph 2, which called for Congress to meet on the first Monday in December and so necessitated every other year a short, ineffective "lame-duck" session. The Twentieth Amendment does away with this session, which was frequently marked in the Senate by filibusters.

Normally Congress meets on the constitutionally designated January 3, but occasionally Congress exercises its option and convenes on the day before or after, especially if January 3 is a Sunday.

SECTION 3

If, at the time fixed for the beginning of the term of the President, the President elect shall have died, the Vice President elect shall become President. If a President shall not have been chosen before the time fixed for the beginning of his term, or if the President elect shall have failed to qualify, then the Vice President elect shall act as President until a President shall have qualified; and the Congress may by law provide for the case wherein neither a President elect nor a Vice President elect shall have qualified, declaring who shall then act as President, or the manner in which one who is to act shall be selected, and such person shall act accordingly until a President or Vice President shall have qualified.

It should be noted that, within the meaning of the Constitution, there is no president-elect or vice-president-elect until the electoral votes have been counted by Congress or, in the event that no person has a majority of the electoral votes, until the House of Representatives and the Senate have made their choices.

Congress has now made the same provision for succession in the event of the disability or disqualification of the president-elect and the vice president-elect as in the case of the president and the vice president (see page 405).

SECTION 4

The Congress may by law provide for the case of the death of any of the persons from whom the House of Representatives may choose a President whenever the right of choice shall have devolved upon them, and for the case of the death of any of the persons from whom the Senate may choose a Vice President whenever the right of choice shall have devolved upon them.

Congress has failed to act under this section.

SECTION 5

Sections 1 and 2 shall take effect on the 15th day of October following the ratification of this article.

SECTION 6

This article shall be inoperative unless it shall have been ratified as an amendment to the Constitution by the legislatures of three-fourths of the several States within seven years from the date of its submission.

AMENDMENT XXI: REPEAL OF PROHIBITION

SECTION 1

The eighteenth article of amendment to the Constitution of the United States is hereby repealed.

This amendment was proposed February 20, 1933, and declared in force by the secretary of state December 5, 1933.

It soon became apparent that the Eighteenth Amendment had failed to diminish the amount of liquor consumed; instead, it diverted taxes and profits from legitimate interests into the hands of bootleggers and criminals and was endangering respect for the Constitution and the laws of the land. The demand for repeal became insistent. In 1928 Alfred Smith, the Democratic candidate for president, advocated repeal; by 1932 the platforms of both major parties were, in the phrase of the day, "dripping wet."

SECTION 2

The transportation or importation into any State, Territory, or possession of the United States for delivery or use therein of intoxicating liquors, in violation of the laws thereof, is hereby prohibited.

This section turned back to each state the responsibility for deciding whether intoxicating liquors would be allowed to be transported, used, or sold within its boundaries. States may, if they wish, ban completely the transportation or importation of intoxicating liquors.

Although the Twenty-first Amendment gives states greater authority to regulate intoxicating beverages than to regulate other items of interstate commerce, its current construction does not deny the federal government the right to use the commerce clause to interfere with the exercise by the states of their powers under the Twenty-first Amendment. The test is "whether the interests implicated by a state regulation are so closely related to the powers reserved by the Twenty-first Amendment that the regulation may prevail, notwithstanding that its requirements directly conflict with express federal policies." In other words, the states must persuade a majority of the Supreme Court that what they want to do is more important than what conflicting federal law requires.

Even absent the action by Congress, the commerce clause continues to restrain state power to regulate alcoholic beverages. In 1987 the Supreme Court ruled that a price-maintenance arrangement of New York, an arrangement regulating the prices at which alcoholic beverages could be sold, violated the Sherman Antitrust Act and was not withing the authority reserved to the states by this section. Similarly the Court has struck down so-called "affirmation laws" in which states tried to require brewers and importers to post prices and affirm that they were not be sold at a lesser price in any other state. It makes not difference whether the affirmation is prospective or retrospective since they "have the inherent practical extraterritorial effect of regulating liquor prices in other States."[1]

In 1964 the Court set aside a Kentucky tax on each gallon of whiskey imported from Scotland as a violation of the export-import clause. Justice Black, in dissent, quipped, "Although I was brought up to believe that Scotch whiskey would need a tax preference to survive in competition with Kentucky bourbon, I never understood the Constitution to require a State to give such preference."[2] Similarly, in 1984 the Court set aside a Hawaii 20-percent tax on wholesale liquor sales, from which tax certain locally produced alcoholic beverages were exempt.[3]

That drinking and driving do not mix and that the national government may impose conditions on a state's receipt of federal highway funds—conditions relating both to speed limits and to the minimum age of drivers—despite state regulations to the contrary was established in *South Dakota* v *Dole*.[4]

Despite an occasional state victory, there is some merit to the charge of Justices O'Connor and Stevens: "The Court has, over the years, so completely distorted the Twenty-first Amendment 'that [it] now has a barely discernible effect in Commerce Clause cases.'"[5] And made it "toothless except when freedom of speech is involved."[6]

States' powers under the Twenty-first amendment to regulate the conditions of sale and possession of intoxicating liquors have fared somewhat better in First Amendment contexts. Examples of its application when freedom of speech is involved include the Court's approval of California's prohibition of certain kinds of live and filmed sexual entertainment in places that serve alcohol. The Court recognized that some of the entertainment forbidden could not be deemed obscene but said that just as a state may forbid the sale of liquor where food is not served, where dancing is permitted, where gasoline is sold, and within so many feet of a

---

[1] *Healy* v *The Beer Institute, Inc.*, 488 US 954 (1989).
[2] *Dept. of Revenue* v *James Beam Co.*, 377 US 341 (1964).
[3] *Bacchus Imports, Ltd.* v *Dias*, 468 US 263 (1984).
[4] *South Dakota* v *Dole*, 483 US 203 (1987).
[5] Justice O'Connor dissenting in *324 Liquor Corp.* v *Duffy*, 479 US 335 (1987), quoting from Justice Stevens's dissent in *City of Newport* v *Iacobucci*, 479 US 92 (1986).
[6] *City of Newport* v *Iacobucci*, 479 US 92 (1986).

church or a school, so, because of the Twenty-first Amendment, may it ban enter-tainment.[7] "The Amendment does not license the States, [however,] to ignore their obligations under other provisions of the Constitution."[8] Thus, as we have noted, a city cannot delegate to a church authority to decide whether a liquor license should be granted to a tavern in the church's neighborhood: that action would violate the establishment-of-religion provisions of the First Amendment.

The power of the states under this amendment to regulate the transportation or importation of intoxicating liquors is also subject to limitation by the supremacy clause. When an Oklahoma law, purportedly authorized by the amendment, that forbade advertisements of wine on cable television came into conflict with an FCC regulation permitting such advertising, the Supreme Court concluded that since Oklahoma permitted circulation of out-of-state newspaper and magazine advertisements of wine, its interest in discouraging consumption by forbidding cable television to advertise wine was not of the same stature as the FCC's interest in ensuring the widespread availability of cable television throughout the United States.[9] (It is doubtful that if Oklahoma had tried to ban all advertising of alcoholic beverages, it would have made any difference.)

There have been several cases dealing with the power of states to regulate the importation of intoxicating liquors as applied to liquors on their way to be used in federal enclaves, national parks, military bases, or airports. In most instances the state laws have been struck down, but the Court did uphold a North Dakota requirement that persons sending or bringing liquor into the state, even that destined for federal bases, must report their sale and if they sold directly to a federal enclave they had to affix labels, indicating that the liquor is for domestic consumption only within the federal enclave.[10]

SECTION 3

This article shall be inoperative unless it shall have been ratified as an amendment to the Constitution by conventions in the several States, as provided in the Constitution, within seven years from the date of submission hereof to the States by the Congress.

This is the only amendment Congress submitted to conventions in the several states for ratification rather than to the state legislatures. Congress chose this method because it believed that the "drys" had more influence within some of the rural legislatures than they would have in special ratifying conventions.

Congress left to the judgment of each state legislature how to organize

---

[7] *California v LaRue*, 409 US 109 (1972); *New York State Liquor Authority v Bellanca*, 452 US 714 (1981), *City of Newport v Iacobucci*, 479 US 92 (1986).

[8] *Capital Cities Cable, Inc. v Crisp*, 467 US 691 (1984).

[9] Ibid.

[10] *North Dakota v United States*, 495 US 423 (1990).

and hold the ratifying conventions. Delegates ran on "dry" and "wet" slates so, in effect, the voters in each state made the decision, and the conventions merely ratified the decisions of the voters.

AMENDMENT XXII: THE NUMBER OF PRESIDENTIAL TERMS

SECTION 1

No person shall be elected to the office of the President more than twice, and no person who has held the office of President, or acted as President, for more than two years of a term to which some other person was elected President shall be elected to the office of the President more than once.

This amendment was proposed March 24, 1947, and certified as adopted by the administrator of general services March 1, 1951.

It is one of the few amendments, perhaps the only amendment, adopted since 1787 that, instead of expanding the power of the electorate, places direct curbs on it. It was adopted in reaction to Franklin D. Roosevelt's election to four terms in office. Decades later, during the early years of President Reagan's second term, many Republicans suggested that this amendment might be repealed. When it became apparent that Reagan would not be a viable candidate for a third term, their interest in its repeal began to wane. They subsequently have turned their attention toward a way to limit congressional terms.

The maximum period that a person can serve is ten years—two years by elevation to the office through the death or disability of the elected president and two elected terms of four years. In some cases, a person might be limited to six years, since elevation for two years and a day, through death, disability, or resignation of the elected president, would make a person eligible for only one elected term of four years.

SECTION 1

[continued] But this article shall not apply to any person holding the office of President when this Article was proposed by the Congress, and shall not prevent any person who may be holding the office of President, or acting as President, during the term within which this Article becomes operative from holding the office of President or acting as President during the remainder of such term.

The person in office was Harry Truman, and if he had chosen to run again, which he did not, and had been reelected, his term would have extended beyond ten years.

SECTION 2

This article shall be inoperative unless it shall have been ratified as an amendment to the Constitution by the legislatures of three-fourths of the several States within seven years from the date of its submission to the States by the Congress.

Within four years after submission, forty-one state legislatures ratified this amendment. There was very little discussion of its significance; in some instances, the legislators voted for ratification without debate.

What has been the effect of the Twenty-second Amendment on the influence of the president? When it was possible, even if unlikely, that a president might seek a third term, that president had considerably more influence than presidents who made known their decisions not to run again. Congressional members, governors, and politicians were much less inclined to oppose the person who might be the head of their ticket than the person who was about to retire to the role of elder statesman. The adoption of this amendment has eliminated even the outside possibility of a second-term president's running again.

AMENDMENT XXIII: PRESIDENTIAL ELECTORS FOR THE DISTRICT OF COLUMBIA

SECTION 1

The District constituting the seat of Government of the United States shall appoint in such manner as the Congress may direct:

A number of electors of President and Vice President equal to the whole number of Senators and Representatives in Congress to which the District would be entitled if it were a State, but in no event more than the least populous State; they shall be in addition to those appointed by the States, but they shall be considered, for the purposes of the election of President and Vice President, to be electors appointed by a State; and they shall meet in the District and perform such duties as provided by the twelfth article of amendment.

This amendment, proposed on June 16, 1960, was ratified March 29, 1961.

Congress set the usual seven-year time limit for ratification when it submitted the Twenty-third Amendment to the state legislatures, but it took only nine months to secure approval of the legislatures in three-fourths of the states. (Tennessee was the only southern state to ratify.)

Since the least populous state, Wyoming, has only three electoral votes, that is the number this amendment assigns to the District of Columbia.

On August 22, 1978, Congress proposed an amendment that, if ratified, would have repealed this one. That amendment would have given the District of

Columbia the same number of members of Congress that it would have if it were a state, as well as giving the District the same number of electoral votes for president and vice president and the right to participate in the ratification process for constitutional amendments. It did not even come close, however, to being ratified.

As noted, the District of Columbia is now seeking admission as a state, to be called New Columbia.

SECTION 2

The Congress shall have power to enforce this article by appropriate legislation.

AMENDMENT XXIV: THE ANTI–POLL-TAX AMENDMENT

SECTION 1

The right of citizens of the United States to vote in any primary or other election for President or Vice President, for electors for President or Vice President, or for Senator or Representative in Congress, shall not be denied or abridged by the United States or any State by reason of failure to pay any poll tax or other tax.

SECTION 2

The Congress shall have power to enforce this article by appropriate legislation.

This amendment, proposed August 27, 1962, was readily ratified within the seven years stipulated by Congress and became part of the Constitution on January 23, 1964. At the time it was submitted, only five states imposed a poll tax as a requirement for voting.

The anti-poll-tax amendment by its own terms forbids payment of a poll tax as a condition for voting for presidential electors and members of Congress. In 1966, the Supreme Court, in *Harper* v *Virginia Board of Electors*, decided that the equal protection clause precludes a state from imposing a poll tax as a requirement to vote in any election.[1] Thus, the equal protection clause as presently interpreted forbids for all governmental elections what this amendment forbids for elections of members of Congress and presidential electors.

---

[1] *Harper* v *Virginia Board of Elections*, 383 US 663 (1966).

AMENDMENT XXV: PRESIDENTIAL DISABILITY; VICE PRESIDENTIAL VACANCIES

In the case of the removal of the President from office or of his death or resignation, the Vice President shall become President.

At the time Congress submitted this proposal, on July 6, 1965, it stipulated that ratification would have to take place within seven years to be effective. The amendment was ratified February 10, 1967.[1]

This section merely confirms what has been the consistent practice (see page 120) of the eight vice presidents who have acceded to the presidency on the death of the president. It also deals with an additional situation, the resignation of a president. By making the vice president the president, not merely acting president, after the incumbent resigns, the amendment precludes a person from resigning and then attempting to return to office.

The only incumbent ever to resign was Richard Nixon. The amendment does not deal with the way presidents submit their resignation. Nixon did so by sending a two-line letter to the secretary of state. Thus, the precedent has been established.

SECTION 2
Whenever there is a vacancy in the office of the Vice President, the President shall nominate a Vice President who shall take office upon confirmation by a majority vote of both Houses of Congress.

The vice presidency has been vacant eighteen times. Fortunately, during those periods there has been no need to continue down the line of presidential succession that Congress has provided by law: speaker of the House, president pro tempore of the Senate, and then members of the cabinet in order of the creation of their departments.

The procedure provided by Section 2 has some resemblance to that normally followed in the original selection and election of a vice president. Once a party selects its presidential candidate by a vote of the delegates to its national convention, that candidate normally chooses a vice presidential running mate, who, after confirmation by the national convention and election along with the president, becomes vice president. Section 2 calls on Congress to serve in lieu of the electorate to confirm the presidential choice.

Section 2 received little attention at the time of the adoption of the amendment. Because of President Eisenhower's illness and Kennedy's assassination,

---

[1] See John D. Feerick, *The 25th Amendment* (Fordham Press, 2nd Edition, 1992).

congressional and public attention was focused on the problems of presidential disability dealt with in Section 3. It was generally assumed that Section 2 would be used after the death of a president had elevated into the White House the elected vice president, thereby creating a vacancy in the vice presidency. But the first time Section 2 was used was in the unanticipated set of circumstances created by the resignation of Vice President Spiro T. Agnew after pleading no contest to federal criminal charges at the same time that President Nixon himself was under the cloud of suspicion created by the Watergate affair. President Nixon nominated Gerald Ford, a Republican, then minority leader in the House. The Democratic Party controlled both chambers of Congress, but Congress, in keeping with the spirit of the Constitution, limited its investigation to questions of Ford's fitness and integrity, rather than probing such issues as his policy attitudes, in order that the vice president might be a person reflecting, through the elected president, the wishes of the majority of the voters in the immediately preceding election.

During the interim between Ford's nomination by Nixon and his confirmation by Congress, some wondered what would happen if President Nixon resigned or was removed from office. The speaker of the House would become acting president. Would the Ford nomination for vice president still stand if the speaker were to send another name to Congress? Would Congress have the right to choose between the two nominees? The fact that there are any open questions about presidential succession is, of course, dangerous, for there is nothing more threatening to a constitutional democracy than doubts about who has the legitimate right to govern. But the constitutional crisis passed, and the amendment appeared to work.

Very soon thereafter, President Nixon resigned to escape being impeached, and Ford became president, once again creating a vacancy in the vice presidency. President Ford nominated Nelson Rockefeller, a former four-term governor of New York and a well-known public figure. After a long examination of Rockefeller's record, Congress finally confirmed the nomination.

Although for the first time in our history we had both a president and a vice president who had not been elected by the voters, there was never any question about the rights of President Ford and Vice President Rockefeller to exercise to the full the powers vested in their offices by the Constitution. Nonetheless, some outside and some inside Congress called for a reconsideration of Section 2. President Ford suggested that some time limit should be placed on congressional confirmation. Some in Congress argued that, in the event of a vacancy in the presidency with more than two years of a term still to expire, another election should be held. But the consensus seemed to be that, if Section 2 worked under the circumstances in which it was first used, it was likely to work under constitutionally less trying conditions.

SECTION 3

Whenever the President transmits to the President pro tempore of the Senate and the Speaker of the House of Representatives his written declaration that

he is unable to discharge the powers and duties of his office, and until he
transmits to them a written declaration to the contrary, such powers and
duties shall be discharged by the Vice President as Acting President.

Until this amendment, Congress had never established procedures to determine how it should be judged whether or not the president was unable to discharge the duties of office. Six times in our history this question has caused
difficulty: when President Garfield suffered a lingering death from an assassin's
bullet; when President Wilson had a physical breakdown during the closing
years of his second term; when there was concern about President Roosevelt's
health just before his fatal stroke; when President Eisenhower was temporarily disabled, first by a heart attack and later by a serious operation; and when
President Reagan was briefly disabled by a gunshot wound. The only time since
the adoption of this provision that it might have been brought into play was
in this last case, when President Reagan was disabled as the result of an
attempted assassination in 1982 and was out of commission in the emergency
room of George Washington University Hospital for about twenty-four hours.
His aides did not invoke the Twenty-fifth Amendment, and the cabinet was not
asked to consider the matter.

In July of 1985, when President Reagan underwent a several-hour operation, he made a deliberate decision not to invoke Section 3. "I am mindful,"
he wrote to Vice President George Bush, "of the uncertainties of its application to such brief and temporary periods of incapacity. I do not believe that
the drafters of this amendment intended its application to situations such as the
instant one." Nevertheless, the president sent a letter to the speaker and to the
president pro tempore of the Senate saying, "consistent with my long-standing arrangement with Vice President George Bush, and not intending to set a
precedent binding anyone privileged to hold this Office in the future, I have
determined and it is my intention...that Vice President George Bush shall discharge those powers and duties in my stead commencing with the administration of anesthesia to me in this instance." After he was once again alert, he
sent off a second letter affirming his intention to resume his duties.[2] This following of Section 3 procedures without formally invoking it was the first formal temporary transfer of presidential power in our history.

SECTION 4
Whenever the Vice President and a majority of either the principal officers of
the executive departments or of such other body as Congress may by law provide, transmit to the President pro tempore of the Senate and the Speaker of the

---

[2] *Time* (July 22, 1985): 24.

> House of Representatives their written declaration that the President is unable
> to discharge the powers and duties of his office, the Vice President shall imme-
> diately assume the powers and duties of the office as Acting President.

Section 4 deals with situations in which a president may be unable to declare the inability to discharge the duties of the office. The responsibility then vests in the vice president *and* the cabinet to declare it. The declaration of presidential disability by a majority of the cabinet is subject to a vice presidential veto. However, whenever the cabinet and the vice president believe the president is unable to discharge the powers and duties of the office, the vice president *immediately* assumes the powers and duties of the presidency; but is only the acting president. The disabled president remains president; however, until determined able again (see the remainder of Section 4, which follows the next paragraph), the president is without authority to act.[3]

It is interesting to note that, although the Constitution in Article II, Section 2, mentions "the principal officers of the executive departments," in other words the cabinet, this section is the first to assign the cabinet a collective responsibility. Although Congress by statute designates which positions have "cabinet rank," the precise composition of the cabinet has varied from president to president, and there has not been a very precise definition of its membership. Vesting this constitutional responsibility in the cabinet as an entity suggests the need for a more formal definition of its composition.

Section 4

[continued] Thereafter, when the President transmits to the President pro tempore of the Senate and the Speaker of the House of Representatives his written declaration that no inability exists, he shall resume the powers and duties of his office unless the Vice President and a majority of either the principal officers of the executive department or of such other body as Congress may by law provide, transmit within four days to the President pro tempore of the Senate and the Speaker of the House of Representatives their written declaration that the President is unable to discharge the powers and duties of his office. Thereupon Congress shall decide the issue, assembling within forty-eight hours for that purpose if not in session. If the Congress, within twenty-one days after receipt of the latter written declaration, or, if Congress is not in session, within twenty-one days after Congress is required to assemble, determines by two-thirds vote of both Houses that the President is unable to discharge the powers and duties of his office, the Vice President shall continue to discharge the same as Acting President; otherwise, the President shall resume the powers and duties of his office.

---

[3] See William Safire, *Full Disclosure* (Garden City, N.Y.: Doubleday & Company, 1977), for a political novel dealing with the ramifications of the Twenty-fifth Amendment.

In case of a conflict between the president, on one side, and the vice president and a majority of the cabinet on the other, over the issue of the president's fitness to assume presidential duties, Congress decides. However, the advantage is in favor of the president; a two-thirds vote of both houses is required to retain the vice president as acting president in the face of a declaration by the president of the ability to resume the duties of office.

A contingency still not covered is a method for filling postelection vacancies caused by the death of a winner of an election before there is in a constitutional sense a president-elect or a vice president-elect.

AMENDMENT XXVI: EIGHTEEN-YEAR-OLD VOTE

The right of citizens of the United States, who are eighteen years of age or older, to vote shall not be denied or abridged by the United States or by any State on account of age.

This amendment, proposed on March 23, 1971, was ratified on June 30, 1971, after only five weeks—the fastest ratification of any amendment.

After the Supreme Court ruled that Congress lacked authority to set the voting age for state and local elections but could do so for national elections, Congress proposed this amendment. Ratification was swift, in large part because without the amendment many states would have been faced with the costly and administratively difficult task of operating separate registration books, ballots, and voting apparatuses for election of federal officers and for election of state and local officers.

SECTION 2

The Congress shall have the power to enforce this article by appropriate legislation.

AMENDMENT XXVII: THE MADISON AMENDMENT

No Law, varying the compensation for the services of the Senators and Representatives, shall take effect, until, an election of representatives shall be intervened.

---

[1] William Van Alstyne, "What Do You Think About the Twenty-seventh Amendment," *Constitutional Commentary* (The University of Minnesota Law School), vol. 10, No 1, p. 15

This amendment was proposed in September 1787 and ratified on May 7, 1992.

As noted, Congress proposed twelve amendments to the states as part of the original Bill of Rights, of which this was the second, but the states ratified at the time only ten. If this had been ratified then it would have become the First Amendment.

Only six of the original thirteen states ratified the amendment and during the next almost two hundred years only three more states did so. It was reasonably assumed that the time for ratification of a proposal submitted so long ago had expired. As the two-hundredth anniversary of the ratification of the Constitution approached, a graduate student at the University of Texas, while writing a paper on the Equal Rights Amendment, came across the fact that this amendment had never been ratified.

He started a movement for ratification and hoped to get the necessary three-fourths by 1989, the two-hundredth anniversary of ratification. Because of a contemporary concern about congressional salaries, the movement took hold. State legislatures began to ratify. On May 7, 1992, Michigan became the thirty-fourth state legislature to do so. The first reaction of some congressional leaders was to doubt the effectiveness of this action in view of the fact that the Supreme Court (see page 167) had made it clear that amendments must be ratified within a reasonable time, but when the archivist promulgated the amendment as part of the Constitution the political pressures on Congress were such that on May 21, 1992, by a concurrent resolution Congress declared the Twenty-second Amendment to be "valid as part of the Constitution of the United States." The vote was not even close: 99–0 in the Senate, 414–3 in the House.

It is conceivable, but not likely, that the Supreme Court could someday rule that the amendment had not been properly ratified. One scholar has noted that "In the supplement to my casebook," [the Twenty-seventh Amendment] will go in with an asterisk."[1]

The amendment, it should be noted, prevents the implementation of any change, whether up or down, in the compensation for members of the House and Senate without the intervention of an election for members of the House.

---

[1] William Van Alsstyne, "What Do You Think About the Twenty-seventh Amendment," *Constitutional Commentary* (The University of Minnesota Law School), vol. 10, No. 1, p. 15

CHAPTER FIVE

EPILOGUE

THE CONSTITUTION AND THE POLITICAL PROCESS

The Supreme Court has always played an active role in our political life. This was especially so during the fifteen eventful years before the 1968 election, when the Supreme Court under the leadership of Chief Justice Earl Warren declared racial segregation in all its forms unconstitutional, enlarged the authority of Congress to legislate against racial discrimination, expanded the protection of the Bill of Rights to apply to actions by state and local officials, expanded protection for speech, limited the authority of states to regulate obscenity, raised higher the wall of separation between church and state, and insisted that legislative bodies be apportioned to reflect equal voting power among voters regardless of where they live.

The Warren Court's involvement in our political life was not unique. And since interpretation of the Constitution is in the highest sense a political matter—that is, a choice among conflicting political values—the justices have frequently been attacked by those who differ with their decisions. Until the Warren Court, however, the more usual pattern was for the Supreme Court to reflect conservative views and for the criticism to come from those of liberal persuasion. The Warren Court reflected the attitudes of the less conservative members of our society. Its critics tended to be those who believe that justices should show more restraint about imposing their own values on society. Those critics charged that the Court had moved too quickly, had opened too wide the opportunities for persons to distribute "offensive" materials, had imposed too many restraints on police and prosecutors, and had forced on the nation the justices' own ideas of how best to establish representative legislative bodies.

Ever since the Warren Court, conservatives have been trying to bring the federal courts, especially the Supreme Court, "under control." In the 1968 presidential campaign, Nixon promised that if elected, he would fill judicial vacancies with persons who shared his own "strict-constructionist" constitutional views. Once in office, a somewhat unusual combination of circumstances made it possible for him to select four Supreme Court justices during his first term. To replace the retiring Earl Warren, he selected Warren Burger, a judge from the Court of Appeals for the District of Columbia. The Senate rejected his first two choices to replace the resigning Justice Abe Fortas, but finally confirmed his third choice, Harry A. Blackmun, another Federal Appeals Court judge and a close friend of the recently appointed chief justice. In the fall of 1971 Justice Hugo Black and Justice John Harlan retired. To replace them, President Nixon nominated Lewis Franklin Powell, Jr., a veteran of private practice and bar leadership from Virginia, and William Hubbs Rehnquist, an Arizonan who had served the Nixon administration in the Department of Justice. In December of 1971, the Senate finally confirmed both appointees, although Justice Rehnquist faced considerable opposition because of his conservative views, especially with respect to civil liberties and civil rights issues.

President Ford was in office too short a time to have much impact on the federal judiciary. However, in November 1975, illness finally forced Justice William O. Douglas—who many thought was trying to hold on until 1977, when a Democrat might be in the White House—to retire after 35 years of service, the longest of any member of the Supreme Court. President Ford nominated John Paul Stevens, from the Court of Appeals for the Seventh Circuit. Justice Stevens has turned out to be an independent jurist, more likely to vote with the liberal justices than with the Nixon and Reagan appointees.

THE BURGER COURT

The differences between the Warren Court and the Burger Court, although subject to exaggeration, were significant. The Burger Court was slightly more reluctant than was the Warren Court to use judicial power to set aside legislative decisions or to interfere with administrative arrangements, and was more apprehensive about judges participating actively and openly in the political process. It moved to a more "accommodationist" stance on separation between church and state, was more favorable toward interpretations of the Constitution that strengthen the hands of the police, and was less protective of the rights of the accused. It gave state governments more leeway in determining how justice should be administered and which movies should be considered obscene.

However, from the perspective of many conservatives, the Burger Court was a revolution that did not happen. It did not reverse outright any of the major initiatives of the Warren Court. Moreover, the Burger Court was the Court that issued the decision declaring most state laws against abortion unconstitutional, perhaps the greatest example in recent years of judicial intervention in the political process. In *INS* v *Chadha* (see page 66), it called into constitutional question more acts of Congress than all of its predecessors combined.[1] It approved affirmative action programs in hiring and education, especially those established by Congress.

---

[1] *INS* v *Chadha,* 462 US 919 (1983).

JIMMY CARTER AND THE FEDERAL COURTS

President Carter was the first full-term president who did not select at least one Supreme Court justice. (Franklin D. Roosevelt appointed no member of the Court during his first term, but picked eight of them in his subsequent terms). However, soon after Carter took office, Congress created 117 new district judgeships and 35 new court of appeals positions, which, along with normal vacancies created by deaths, retirements, and resignations, gave President Carter the unprecedented opportunity to appoint more than 250 federal judges. He selected substantially more blacks and women than had ever been appointed before. These Carter-selected judges reflected in general the perspective of the administration that appointed them, substantially slowing down the drift toward judicial conservatism of the Nixon-Reagan appointees. Until the Reagan appointees began to take over, the presence of Carter appointees made the lower federal courts more liberal and activist than the Supreme Court.

RONALD REAGAN, THE REHNQUIST COURT, AND "THE CONSERVATIVE JUDICIAL REVOLUTION"

Ronald Reagan made it no secret that one of his highest priorities was to pack the federal courts with those of ideology similar to his. He pledged that if elected he would appoint judges who would interpret the Constitution according to the original intent of the framers; that is, he would appoint judges who would be less inclined to set aside criminal convictions, more inclined to allow states to regulate abortions, more likely to permit states greater leeway in introducing religious exercises in the public schools, and more likely to oppose affirmative action programs that include race-sensitive remedies and programs.

During his two terms, President Reagan appointed 385 federal judges, almost half of all federal judges—168 full-time appeals judges and 575 district judges—and almost all of whom are white males who share his constitutional views.[2] Although he acted no differently from other presidents in the appointment of judges from his own party, his administration more zealously investigated to assure itself that the men and women he did recommend would, once appointed, make the kind of decisions that would meet with the approval of the president and the approval of those who had elected him.

During Reagan's first term, his only opportunity to select a member of the Supreme Court came with Justice Potter Stewart's retirement. Reagan chose Justice Sandra Day O'Connor. (The year before, perhaps anticipating her appointment, the members of the Court had decided to stop referring to each other as Mr. Justice, but had decided to refer to each other simply as Justice.)

---

[2] Joan Biskupic, "Bush Lags in Appointments to the Federal Judiciary," *Congressional Quarterly* (January 6, 1990): 38–40, and Stuart Taylor, Jr., "The One-Pronged Test for Federal Judges: Reagan Puts Ideology First," *The New York Times*, Sec. E (April 22, 1984): 5.

Justice O'Connor, at the time of her appointment, was a member of the Arizona Court of Appeals. Although she was a lifelong Republican, the views and values she had expressed were considerably less conservative than those of many other judges nominated by President Reagan.

As President Reagan finished his first term, the Burger Court was split five to four on many important decisions. Chief Justice Burger and Justice Rehnquist held down the conservative end of the Court, with Justice Rehnquist the most articulate and conservative justice. Justice O'Connor frequently voted with them. Justices Byron White, Lewis Powell, Harry Blackmun, and John Paul Stevens served as the swing votes with Justice White tending more toward the conservative side, and Justice Blackmun having moved toward the liberal side. Justices William Brennan and Thurgood Marshall, who were often joined by Justice Stevens, represented the diminished liberal wing. Brennan and Marshall became the Court's most frequent dissenters.

The conservatives still did not control the Supreme Court, but they were getting closer. With five of the nine justices seventy-six or older, it appeared unlikely that all of them would be able to remain active for another four years. If the liberal justices were following the precedent of some previous justices, they were doing their best to hold off retiring or dying until there was a president in the White House congenial to their constitutional views. In the past, many justices have successfully outlived their political opponents. Oliver Wendell Holmes served until he was ninety, Roger Taney and Hugo Black until eighty-five, and another five, including Louis Brandeis, served beyond their eightieth birthdays.

In the summer of 1986, at the end of the 1985 term, Chief Justice Burger retired. President Reagan quickly nominated Justice Rehnquist to become the chief justice, and to replace Rehnquist he picked a member of the Court of Appeals for the District of Columbia, Antonin Scalia, a man known both for his wit and for his conservatism. The Senate Judiciary Committee rather easily recommended the confirmation of Justice Scalia. Democratic minority members lodged allegations of improper partisanship by Rehnquist prior to his service on the Court and recommended the confirmation of Rehnquist as chief justice only after an exhaustive hearing in which it was widely recognized that what was at stake was the question of constitutional views. The Senate then finally confirmed Rehnquist's elevation to the center chair.

In the 1986 elections, somewhat unexpectedly, the Democrats regained control of the Senate and of the Judiciary Committee, the committee that processes Senate confirmation of presidential judicial selections. Although the rules of the game call for considerable deference to presidential discretion, the Democrats made clear that they would subject all judicial appointments to careful senatorial scrutiny. The likelihood of senatorial opposition, if any weaknesses in qualification or competence or integrity could be found, somewhat constrained the Reagan administration. It could put on the federal bench only those conservative lawyers with a relatively uncontroversial political record and of the highest legal qualification.

The promotion of Rehnquist to the center chair and the appointment of Scalia to replace Burger did not immediately alter the Court's balance. What had happened was that one younger conservative had taken over a post previously occupied by an older conservative, and an even younger conservative had taken over his post.

With the Democrats in control of the Senate, Ronald Reagan coming to the end of his tenure, and the liberal justices continuing to hold on—although Reagan had put many conservative judges into place in the lower federal courts—it was not at all clear that President Reagan would be successful in securing a constitutionally conservative Supreme Court. Then, suddenly he was given that opportunity. In July 1987, as the term ended, Justice Powell, who held the swing vote in many five-to-four cases, announced his retirement. President Reagan promptly nominated Judge Robert Bork, a former Yale law professor and a public law scholar known for his outspoken criticism of judicial activism who was, like Justice Scalia, from the Court of Appeals for the District of Columbia. Through books, articles, lectures, and judicial opinions Bork was on record with the view that judges should declare unconstitutional only those laws and regulations that are clearly in violation of the language of the Constitution or contrary to the original intent of its framers.

Bork's nomination generated strong opposition from many quarters, most especially from black and women's groups, and led to one of the most exhaustive and divisive confirmation battles in our history. During the Senate Judiciary Committee's hearings, Judge Bork himself was subject to intense questioning about the constitutional views he had espoused in his many articles and speeches over the years. The Bork confirmation battles also produced extensive discussions both before the Senate Judiciary Committee and on the floor of the Senate about constitutional doctrines and the proper role of courts in our democracy. After almost four months of national debate, twelve days of extensive questioning by the members of the Senate Judiciary Committee, and twenty-three hours of debate on the Senate floor, the Senate voted 58 to 42 against Bork's confirmation.

An angry President Reagan quickly nominated Douglas H. Ginsburg, another judge from the Court of Appeals for the District of Columbia. He was a purported judicial conservative but he had written little outside of his relatively few judicial opinions and his votes on major constitutional issues were unknown. His name was never sent to the Senate, however: he asked that it be withdrawn as the result of the publicity arising from his admission that as a younger man and while a law professor he had in the past occasionally smoked marijuana.

On the third try President Reagan nominated Judge Anthony Kennedy from the Court of Appeals for the Ninth Circuit, a judge of conservative constitutional views but who had stated them primarily from the bench in his judicial opinions and in a much less challenging manner than had Judge Bork. Although there was rather extended discussion between the nominee and members of the Senate Judiciary Committee about his judicial orientations, a consensus quickly developed about his suitability for the Supreme Court, and he was confirmed without difficulty. Justice Kennedy quickly joined the conservative wing of the Court, making it the controlling one on most issues. Finally, Reagan had done what he promised those who elected him he would do, produce a conservative Supreme Court.

GEORGE BUSH AND THE FEDERAL COURTS

During his presidential campaign George Bush made clear his admiration for Judge Bork and promised, if elected, to continue the conservative constitutional revolution. He got off to a slow start. During his first year there were no Supreme Court vacancies and Bush became embroiled in a battle with the Senate over the selection of district court judges. President Bush insisted that it was his constitutional authority to nominate federal judges and that home state senators should give him a list of at least three persons from which he could nominate one. But the Senate, even though controlled by the Democrats, supported the practice of senatorial courtesy, was slow to confirm presidential nominations that did not have the support of the Republican senators from the state where the judges are to sit, and in some cases even refused to act. Said Senator Joseph Biden, Jr., a Democrat and Chair of the Judiciary Committee, "Home-state senators know better the quality of the people in their states.... Unless the administration has consulted with, discussed with, and had the input of senators from the states from which these judges originate, they will have a great deal of difficulty moving through the committee."[3]

President Bush had a major impact on the federal courts. In addition to appointing 185 district and appeals court judges who, in general, are from the more conservative side of the law, he was able to select two Supreme Court justices. In July of 1990, at the end of the 1989 term, Justice Brennan resigned, after suffering two minor strokes. Justice Brennan, a veteran of thirty-four years and increasingly the most influential member of the liberal block, had authored some of the more controversial five-to-four opinions of recent years. His leaving the Court clearly would make a difference in many areas, but most of the media attention was focused on how his successor might vote on *Roe* v *Wade*, the 1973 abortion ruling.

President Bush quickly nominated Judge David Souter, who had served for seven years on the New Hampshire Supreme Court and had been on the Court of Appeals for the First Circuit for two months, during which time he did not decide any cases. Although announcing that Judge Souter was a believer in strict constitutional construction and opposed to "judicial legislation," President Bush insisted that he had not inquired into how Judge Souter would vote on specific issues such as abortion and did not believe that such a litmus test would be appropriate. Members of the Judiciary Committee engaged Judge Souter in discussions about his views on constitutional doctrine in general and about the appropriate role of the courts in the political process. He steadfastly refused to respond to questions relating to cases that might come before him. Souter was easily confirmed and has turned out in the first several years of his service to be a more moderate and balanced jurist than might have been anticipated by either his backers or opponents.

Following the contention over the Bork battle and the success of the Souter Solution, many observers assumed that President Bush would be cautious in making future Supreme Court nominees and select persons, like Souter, whose

---

[3] Joan Biskupic, "Senators Demonstrate They Prefer to Judge Nominees for Themselves," *Congressional Quarterly* (January 6, 1990): 40–41.

record, judicial or otherwise, could not be as readily attacked as a person who had been so involved in the debates of recent years as Bork. Yet when Justice Thurgood Marshall retired in 1991, President Bush, to the surprise of many observers, sent to the Senate the name of a controversial jurist, Judge Clarence Thomas, then sitting on the Court of Appeals for the District of Columbia. Thomas was an outspoken conservative African American. Prior to his brief service on the Court of Appeals, Judge Thomas had served in the Reagan administration as chair of the Equal Employment Opportunity Commission (EEOC) and in the Office of Civil Rights in the Department of Education. He had participated in debates about affirmative action, and his nomination aroused the suspicion and eventually the opposition of women's groups and civil rights groups, who were fearful of how he would vote not only on questions relating to affirmative action but also those about abortion.

During five days of grueling questions about his constitutional views, Judge Thomas, as had his predecessors, refused to respond as his answers might reveal how he might vote on specific cases. He told his Senate interrogators that he had not made up his mind about the constitutionality of state regulation of abortion and had not focused his attention on the merits or demerits of Roe v Wade. The Senate Judiciary Committee narrowly recommended his confirmation.

Two days before the Senate was due to vote on his confirmation, documents were leaked to the press that revealed that a former associate of Judge Thomas, Anita Hill, had accused him of sexually harassing her when she worked for him. There was an explosion of outrage on the part of women's and liberal groups and an insistence that the Judiciary Committee take these allegations seriously. There followed three days of dramatic and emotion-charged hearings telecast to the nation in which Judge Thomas categorically denied charges presented persuasively by his accuser. The reports of the hearings were presented to the entire Senate, Judge Thomas was confirmed by the Senate 52-48, the closest Supreme Court vote to confirm in modern times, and he was sworn in as Justice of the United States Supreme Court on October 18, 1991.

During the remaining days of the Bush Administration, the Senate, in the hands of the Democrats, slowed down the nomination process, in anticipation that Democrats would be in charge of the White House after the 1992 elections. Even so, 584 of the 828 federal judgeships were filled by Ronald Reagan and George Bush and they, especially Bush, picked relatively young persons, so the influence of the Bush-Reagan years will linger on well into the next century.

BILL CLINTON AND THE FEDERAL COURTS

When Bill Clinton took over there were 115 federal vacancies, a record number.[4] Clinton had campaigned on the promise of selecting federal judges

---

[4] Richard B. Schmitt, "Advocates for More Judges Feel Favorable Political Wind," *The Wall Street Journal*, February 24, 1993, p. B2. See also Stephen Labaton, "Clinton Expected to Change Makeup of Federal Courts," *The New York Times*, March 8, 1993, p. A1.

who would be sensitive to the concerns of minorities and who would protect the right of privacy, most especially the right of a women to have an abortion. Moreover, with the Democrats in control of both chambers of the Congress it is highly probable that Congress will respond to the pressures to add to the 846 federal judgeships. The Judicial Conference, the policy arm of the federal judiciary, called for the addition of 35 judges, including the addition of 10 more to the Ninth Circuit, the court in San Francisco with jurisdiction over nine states and two territories and which is frequently at odds with the Supreme Court. Congress will no doubt add judges not only because they are needed to take care of the legal business but also because they will make it possible for Clinton to help shape the direction of constitutional law, to dilute the influence of the Reagan-Bush judges, and provide more opportunities to award loyal campaign supporters. Such an addition to the number of federal judges has been the normal practice after a political party takes over the White House if it also controls the Congress.

President Clinton Makes His First Appointment

Almost immediately after President Clinton was sworn in, Justice Byron White, appointed by President Kennedy but in recent years a justice who had been part of the Court's conservative wing, announced that he would retire at the end of the Court's 1992–1993 term. His departure from the Court gave Clinton his first opportunity to stop the "turn to the right." After several months of deliberation, in June, just before the end of the term, he nominated Judge Ruth Bader Ginsberg, another veteran of the Court of Appeals for the District of Columbia, to which she had been appointed by President Carter. Prior to her appointment to that court she had been a professor of law at Columbia and active in behalf of women's equity, having represented women (and men) in cases challenging such practices as denying women military dependents the same benefits as men and laws preferring fathers over mothers as executors of estates. She was readily confirmed by the Senate and took her seat for the 1993–1994 term.

By the end of his term Clinton could very well have a chance to fill at least half of the federal judgeships. He had pledged to appoint federal judges who will be more "representative" of the ethnic makeup of the United States. As Senator Joseph Biden, Jr., chair of the Senate Judiciary Committee, has said, "There will not be an ideological blood test, like there was during the Reagan and Bush years, to see if the candidate is a moderate or liberal, but there will be an insistence upon diversity."[5] But there is also no doubt that he will work to make good his campaign pledge to checkmate the decades-long drive by conservatives to appoint federal judges who will be less active, more deferential to the political process, and more conservative in their interpretation of the Constitution.

---

[5] Stephen Labaton, "Clinton Expected to Change Makeup of Federal Courts," *The New York Times*, March 8, 1993, p. A1.

Once more, as in the past, what the Constitution means and will mean is decided as much by the outcome of elections as by what happens inside the Marble Palace. Although not too many voters cast their ballots for presidential or senatorial candidates explicitly because of convictions about judicial appointments, the ballot provides the vital link between the electorate and the appointing authorities that helps to ensure that what the Supreme Court decides does not vary too often, for too long, or by too much from what most of the people want it to decide.

It may be shocking to some to discover that how judges decide what the Constitution means is linked to which politicians win elections. But this is the vital link that means that our Constitution reflects what the people who elect those politicians want it to mean. For it is "We the people" who created the Constitution. And it is we the people who are responsible for making it a living document. The process of Constitution-making is a continuing one in which we all play a part.

CHAPTER SIX

THE CONSTITUTION OF THE UNITED STATES OF AMERICA[1]

We the People of the United States, in Order to form a more perfect Union, establish Justice, insure domestic Tranquility, provide for the common defence, promote the general Welfare, and secure the Blessings of Liberty to ourselves and our Posterity, do ordain and establish this Constitution for the United States of America.

ARTICLE. I.

Section. 1. All legislative Powers herein granted shall be vested in Congress of the United States, which shall consist of a Senate and House of Representatives.

Section. 2. The House of Representatives shall be composed of Members chosen every second Year by the People of the several States, and the Electors in each State shall have the Qualifications requisite for Electors of the most numerous Branch of the State Legislature.

No Person shall be a Representative who shall not have attained to the Age of twenty five Years, and been seven Years a Citizen of the United States, and who shall not, when elected, be an Inhabitant of that State in which he shall be chosen.

Representatives and direct Taxes[2] shall be apportioned among the several States which may be included within this Union, according to their respective Numbers, which shall be determined by adding to the whole Number of free Persons, including those bound to Service for a Term of Years, and excluding Indians not taxed, three fifths of all other Persons.[3] The actual Enumeration

---

[1] From the engrossed copy in the National Archives. Original spelling, capitalization, and punctuation have been retained.

[2] Modified by the Sixteenth Amendment.

[3] Replaced by the Fourteenth Amendment.

shall be made within three Years after the first Meeting of the Congress of the United States, and within every subsequent Term of ten Years, in such Manner as they shall by Law direct. The Number of Representatives shall not exceed one for every thirty thousand, but each state shall have at Least one Representative; and until such enumeration shall be made, the State of New Hampshire shall be entitled to chuse three; Massachusetts eight; Rhode Island and Providence Plantations one; Connecticut five; New York six; New Jersey four; Pennsylvania eight; Delaware one; Maryland six; Virginia ten; North Carolina five; South Carolina five; and Georgia three.

When vacancies happen in the Representation from any State, the Executive Authority thereof shall issue Writs of Election to fill such Vacancies.

The House of Representatives shall chuse their Speaker and other Officers; and shall have the sole Power of Impeachment.

Section. 3. The Senate of the United States shall be composed of two Senators from each State, chosen by the Legislature thereof, for six Years; and each Senator shall have one vote.[4]

Immediately after they shall be assembled in Consequence of the first Election, they shall be divided as equally as may be into three Classes. The Seats of the Senators of the first Class shall be vacated at the Expiration of the second Year, of the second Class at the Expiration of the fourth Year, and of the third Class at the Expiration of the sixth Year, so that one third may be chosen every second Year; and if Vacancies happen by Resignation, or otherwise, during the Recess of the Legislature of any State, the Executive thereof may make temporary Appointments until the next meeting of the Legislature, which shall then fill such Vacancies.[5]

No Person shall be a Senator who shall not have attained to the Age of thirty Years, and been nine Years a Citizen of the United States, and who shall not, when elected, be an Inhabitant of that State for which he shall be chosen.

The Vice President of the United States shall be President of the Senate, but shall have no Vote, unless they be equally divided.

The Senate shall chuse their other officers, and also a President pro tempore, in the Absence of the Vice President, or when he shall exercise the Office of President of the United States.

The Senate shall have the sole Power to try all Impeachments. When sitting for that Purpose, they shall be on Oath or Affirmation. When the President of the United States is tried, the Chief Justice shall preside: And no Person shall be convicted without the Concurrence of two thirds of the Members present.

Judgment in Cases of Impeachment shall not extend further than to removal from Office, and disqualification to hold and enjoy any Office of honor, Trust or Profit under the United States: but the Party convicted shall nevertheless be liable and subject to Indictment, Trial, Judgment and Punishment, according to Law.

Section. 4. The Times, Places and Manner of holding Elections for Senators and Representatives, shall be prescribed in each State by the Legislature thereof,

[4] Superseded by the Seventeenth Amendment.
[5] Modified by the Seventeenth Amendment.

but the Congress may at any time by Law make or alter such Regulation, except as to the Places of chusing Senators.

The Congress shall assemble at least once in every Year, and such Meeting shall be on the first Monday in December, unless they shall by Law appoint a different Day.[6]

Section. 5. Each House shall be the Judge of the Elections, Returns and Qualifications of its own Members, and a Majority of each shall constitute a Quorum to do Business; but a smaller Number may adjourn from day to day, and may be authorized to compel the Attendance of absent Members, in such Manner, and under such Penalties as each House may provide.

Each House may determine the Rules of its Proceedings, punish its Members for disorderly Behaviour, and, with the Concurrence of two thirds, expel a Member.

Each House shall keep a Journal of its Proceedings, and from time to time publish the same, excepting such Parts as may in their Judgment require Secrecy; and the Yeas and Nays of the Members of either House on any question shall, at the Desire of one fifth of those Present, be entered on the Journal.

Neither House, during the Session of Congress, shall, without the Consent of the other, adjourn for more than three days, nor to any other Place than that in which the two Houses shall be sitting.

Section. 6. The Senators and Representatives shall receive a Compensation for their Services, to be ascertained by Law, and paid out of the Treasury of the United States. They shall in all Cases, except Treason, Felony and Breach of the Peace, be privileged from Arrest during their Attendance at the Session of their respective Houses, and in going to and returning from the same; and for any Speech or Debate in either House, they shall not be questioned in any other Place.

No Senator or Representative shall, during the Time for which he was elected, be appointed to any civil Office under the Authority of the United States, which shall have been created, or the Emoluments whereof shall have been encreased during such time; and no Person holding any Office under the United States, shall be a Member of either House during his Continuance in Office.

Section. 7. All Bills for raising Revenue shall originate in the House of Representatives; but the Senate may propose or concur with Amendments as on other Bills.

Every Bill which shall have passed the House of Representatives and the Senate shall, before it become a Law, be presented to the President of the United States; If he approve he shall sign it, but if not he shall return it, with his Objections to that House in which it shall have originated, who shall enter the Objections at large on their Journal, and proceed to reconsider it. If after such Reconsideration two thirds of that House shall agree to pass the Bill, it shall be sent, together with the Objections, to the other House, by which it shall likewise be reconsidered, and if approved by two thirds of that House, it shall become a Law. But in all such Cases the Votes of both Houses shall be determined by yeas and Nays, and the Names of the Persons voting for and against

---

[6] Superseded by the Twentieth Amendment.

the Bill shall be entered on the Journal of each House respectively. If any Bill shall not be returned by the President within ten Days (Sundays excepted) after it shall have been presented to him, the Same shall be a Law, in like Manner as if he had signed it, unless the Congress by their Adjournment prevent its Return, in which Case it shall not be a Law.

Every Order, Resolution, or Vote to which the Concurrence of the Senate and House of Representatives may be necessary (except on a question of Adjournment) shall be presented to the President of the United States; and before the Same shall take Effect, shall be approved by him, or being disapproved by him shall be repassed by two thirds of the Senate and House of Representatives, according to the Rules and Limitations prescribed in the Case of a Bill.

Section. 8. The Congress shall have the Power To lay and collect Taxes, Duties, Imposts and Excises, to pay the Debts and provide for the common Defence and general Welfare of the United States; but all Duties, Imposts and Excises shall be uniform throughout the United States;

To borrow Money on the credit of the United States;

To regulate Commerce with foreign Nations, and among the several States, and with the Indian Tribes;

To establish an uniform Rule of Naturalization, and uniform Laws on the subject of Bankruptcies throughout the United States;

To coin Money, regulate the Value thereof, and of foreign Coin, and fix the Standard of Weights and Measures;

To provide for the Punishment of counterfeiting the Securities and current Coin of the United States;

To establish Post Offices and post Roads;

To promote the Progress of Science and useful Arts, by securing for limited Times to Authors and Inventors the exclusive Right to their respective Writings and Discoveries;

To constitute Tribunals inferior to the supreme Court;

To define and punish Piracies and Felonies committed on the high Seas, and Offences against the Law of Nations;

To declare War, grant Letters of Marque and Reprisal, and make Rules concerning Captures on Land and Water;

To raise and support Armies, but no Appropriation of Money to that Use shall be for a longer Term than two Years;

To provide and maintain a Navy;

To make Rules for the Government and Regulation of the land and naval Forces;

To provide for calling forth the Militia to execute the Laws of the Union, suppress Insurrections and repel Invasions;

To provide for organizing, arming, and disciplining, the Militia, and for governing such Part of them as may be employed in the Service of the United States, reserving to the States respectively, the Appointment of the Officers, and the Authority of training the Militia according to the discipline prescribed by Congress;

To exercise exclusive Legislation in all Cases whatsoever, over such District (not exceeding ten Miles square) as may, by Cession of particular States, and the Acceptance of Congress, become the Seat of the Government of the United States, and to exercise like Authority over all Places purchased by the Consent of the Legislature of the State in which the Same shall be, for the Erection of Forts, Magazines, Arsenals, dock-Yards, and other needful Buildings;—And

To make all Laws which shall be necessary and proper for carrying into Execution the foregoing Powers, and all other Powers vested by this Constitution in the Government of the United States, or in any Department or Officer thereof.

Section. 9. The Migration or Importation of such Persons as any of the States now existing shall think proper to admit, shall not be prohibited by the Congress prior to the Year one thousand eight hundred and eight, but a Tax or duty may be imposed on such Importation, not exceeding ten dollars for each Person.

The Privilege of the Writ of Habeas Corpus shall not be suspended, unless when in Cases of Rebellion or Invasion the public Safety may require it.

No Bill of Attainer or ex post facto Law shall be passed.

No Capitation, or other direct, Tax shall be laid, unless in Proportion to the Census or Enumeration herein before directed to be taken.

No Tax or Duty shall be laid on Articles exported from any State.

No Preference shall be given by any Regulation of Commerce or Revenue to the Ports of one State over those of another: nor shall Vessels bound to, or from, one State, be obliged to enter, clear, or pay Duties in another.

No Money shall be drawn from the Treasury, but in Consequence of Appropriations made by Law, and a regular Statement and Account of the Receipts and Expenditures of all public Money shall be published from time to time.

No Title of Nobility shall be granted by the United States: And no Person holding any Office of Profit or Trust under them, shall, without the Consent of the Congress, accept of any present, Emolument, Office, or Title, of any kind whatever, from any King, Prince, or foreign State.

Section. 10. No State shall enter into any Treaty, Alliance, or Confederation; grant Letters of Marque and Reprisal; coin Money; emit Bills of Credit; make any Thing but gold and silver Coin a Tender in Payment of Debts; pass any Bill of Attainder, ex post facto Law, or Law impairing the Obligation of Contracts, or grant any Title of Nobility.

No State shall, without the Consent of the Congress, lay any Imposts or Duties on Imports or Exports, except what may be absolutely necessary for executing its inspection Laws: and the net Produce of all Duties and Imposts, laid by any State on Imports or Exports, shall be for the Use of the Treasury of the United States; and all such Laws shall be subject to the Revision and Controul of the Congress.

No State shall, without the Consent of Congress, lay any Duty of Tonnage, keep Troops, or Ships of War in time of Peace, enter into any Agreement or Compact with another State, or with a foreign Power, or engage in War, unless actually invaded, or in such imminent Danger as will not admit of delay.

ARTICLE. II.

Section. 1. The executive Power shall be vested in a President of the United States of America. He shall hold his Office during the Term of four Years, and, together with the Vice President, chosen for the same Term, be elected, as follows:

Each State shall appoint, in such Manner as the Legislature thereof may direct, a Number of Electors, equal to the whole Number of Senators and Representatives to which the State may be entitled in the Congress: but no Senator or Representative, or Person holding an Office of Trust or Profit under the United States, shall be appointed an Elector.

The Electors shall meet in their respective States, and vote by Ballot for two Persons, of whom one at least shall not be an Inhabitant of the same State with themselves. And they shall make a List of all the Persons voted for, and of the Number of Votes for each; which List they shall sign and certify, and transmit sealed to the Seat of the Government of the United States, directed to the President of the Senate. The President of the Senate shall, in the Presence of the Senate and House of Representatives, open all the Certificates, and the Votes shall then be counted. The Person having the greatest Number of Votes shall be the President, if such Number be a Majority of the whole Number of Electors appointed; and if there be more than one who have such Majority, and have an equal Number of Votes, then the House of Representatives shall immediately chuse by Ballot one of them for President; and if no Person have a Majority, then from the five highest on the List the said House shall in like Manner chuse the President. But in chusing the President, the Votes shall be taken by States, the Representation from each State having one Vote; A quorum for this Purpose shall consist of a Member or Members from two thirds of the States, and a Majority of all the States shall be necessary to a Choice. In every Case, after the Choice of the President, the Person having the greatest Number of Votes of the Electors shall be the Vice President. But if there should remain two or more who have equal Votes, the Senate shall chuse from them by Ballot the Vice President.[7]

The Congress may determine the Time of chusing the Electors, and the Day on which they shall give their Votes; which Day shall be the same throughout the United States.

No Person except a natural born Citizen, or a Citizen of the United States, at the time of the Adoption of this Constitution, shall be eligible to the Office of President, neither shall any Person be eligible to that Office who shall not have attained to the Age of thirty five Years, and been fourteen Years a Resident within the United States.

In Case of the Removal of the President from Office, or of his Death, Resignation, or Inability to discharge the Powers and Duties of the said Office, the Same shall devolve on the Vice President, and the Congress may by Law provide for the Case of Removal, Death, Resignation, or Inability, both of the President and Vice President, declaring what Officer shall then act as President,

---

[7] Superseded by the Twelfth Amendment.

and such Officer shall act accordingly, until the Disability be removed, or a President shall be elected.[8]

The President shall, at stated Times, receive for his Services, a Compensation, which shall neither be encreased nor diminished during the Period for which he shall have been elected, and he shall not receive within that Period any other Emolument from the United States, or any of them.

Before he enter on the Execution of his Office, he shall take the following Oath or Affirmation:—"I do solemnly swear (or affirm) that I will faithfully execute the Office of President of the United States, and will to the best of my Ability, preserve, protect and defend the Constitution of the United States."

Section. 2. The President shall be Commander in Chief of the Army and Navy of the United States, and of the Militia of the several States, when called into the actual Service of the United States; he may require the Opinion, in writing, of the principle Officer in each of the executive Departments, upon any Subject relating to the Duties of their respective Offices, and he shall have Power to grant Reprieves and Pardons for Offences against the United States, except in Cases of Impeachment.

He shall have Power, by and with the Advice and Consent of the Senate, to make Treaties, provided two thirds of the Senators present concur; and he shall nominate, and by and with the Advice and Consent of the Senate, shall appoint Ambassadors, other public Ministers and Consuls, Judges of the supreme Court, and all other Officers of the United States, whose Appointments are not herein otherwise provided for, and which shall be established by Law; but the Congress may by Law vest the Appointment of such inferior Officers, as they think proper, in the President alone, in the Courts of Law, or in the Heads of Departments.

The President shall have Power to fill up all Vacancies that may happen during the Recess of the Senate, by granting Commissions which shall expire at the End of their next Session.

Section. 3. He shall from time to time give to the Congress Information of the State of the Union, and recommend to their Consideration such Measures as he shall judge necessary and expedient; he may, on extraordinary Occasions, convene both Houses, or either of them, and in Case of Disagreement between them, with Respect to the Time of Adjournment, he may adjourn them to such Time as he shall think proper; he shall receive Ambassadors and other public Ministers; he shall take Care that the Laws be faithfully executed, and shall Commission all the Officers of the United States.

Section. 4. The President, Vice President and all civil Officers of the United States, shall be removed from Office on Impeachment for, and Conviction of, Treason, Bribery, or other high Crimes and Misdemeanors.

ARTICLE. III.

Section. 1. The judicial Power of the United States, shall be vested in one supreme Court, and in such inferior Courts as the Congress may from time to

---

[8] Modified by the Twenty-fifth Amendment.

time ordain and establish. The Judges, both of the supreme and inferior Courts, shall hold their Offices during good Behaviour, and shall, at stated Times, receive for their Services, a Compensation, which shall not be diminished during their Continuance in Office.

Section. 2. The judicial Power shall extend to all Cases, in Law and Equity, arising under this Constitution, the Laws of the United States, and Treaties made, or which shall be made, under their Authority;—to all Cases affecting Ambassadors, other public Ministers and Consuls;—to all Cases of admiralty and maritime Jurisdiction;—to Controversies to which the United States shall be a Party;—to Controversies between two or more States;—between a State and Citizens of another State;[9]—between Citizens of different States,—between Citizens of the same State claiming Lands under Grants of different States, and between a State, or the Citizens thereof, and foreign States, Citizens or Subjects.

In all Cases affecting Ambassadors, other public Ministers and Consuls, and those in which a State shall be Party, the supreme Court shall have original Jurisdiction. In all the other Cases before mentioned, the supreme Court shall have appellate Jurisdiction, both as to Law and Fact, with such Exceptions, and under such Regulations as the Congress shall make.

The Trial of all Crimes, except in Cases of Impeachment, shall be by Jury; and such Trial shall be held in the State where the said Crimes shall have been committed; but when not committed within any State, the trial shall be at such Place or Places as the Congress may by Law have directed.

Section. 3. Treason against the United States, shall consist only in levying War against them, or in adhering to their Enemies, giving them Aid and Comfort. No Person shall be convicted of Treason unless on the Testimony of two Witnesses to the same overt Act, or on Confession in open Court.

The Congress shall have Power to declare the Punishment of Treason, but no Attainder of Treason shall work Corruption of Blood, or Forfeiture except during the Life of the Person attainted.

ARTICLE. IV.

Section. 1. Full Faith and Credit shall be given in each State to the public Acts, Records, and judicial Proceedings of every other State. And the Congress may by general Laws prescribe the Manner in which such Acts, Records and Proceedings shall be proved, and the Effect thereof.

Section. 2. The Citizens of each State shall be entitled to all Privileges and Immunities of Citizens in the several States.

A Person charged in any State with Treason, Felony, or other Crime, who shall flee from Justice, and be found in another State, shall on Demand of the executive Authority of the State from which he fled, be delivered up, to be removed to the State having Jurisdiction of the Crime.

---

[9] Modified by the *Eleventh Amendment.*

No Person held to Service or Labour in one State, under the Laws thereof, escaping into another, shall, in Consequence of any Law or Regulation therein, be discharged from such Service or Labour, but shall be delivered up on Claim of the Party to whom such Service or Labour may be due.

Section. 3. New States may be admitted by the Congress into this Union; but no new State shall be formed or erected within the Jurisdiction of any other State, nor any State be formed by the Junction of two or more States, or Parts of States, without the Consent of the Legislatures of the States concerned as well as of the Congress.

The Congress shall have Power to dispose of and make all needful Rules and Regulations respecting the Territory or other Property belonging to the United States; and nothing in this Constitution shall be so construed as to Prejudice any Claims of the United States, or of any Particular State.

Section. 4. The United States shall guarantee to every State in this Union a Republican Form of Government, and shall protect each of them against Invasion; and on Application of the Legislature, or of the Executive (when the Legislature cannot be convened) against domestic Violence.

ARTICLE. V.

The Congress, whenever two thirds of both Houses shall deem it necessary, shall propose Amendments to this Constitution, or, on the Application of the Legislatures of two thirds of the several States, shall call a Convention for proposing Amendments, which, in either Case, shall be valid to all Intents and Purposes, as Part of this Constitution, when ratified by the Legislatures of three fourths of the several States, or by Conventions in three fourths thereof, as the one or the other Mode of Ratification may be proposed by the Congress; Provided that no Amendment which may be made prior to the Year One thousand eight hundred and eight shall in any Manner affect the first and fourth Clauses in the Ninth Section of the first Article; and that no State, without its Consent, shall be deprived of its equal Suffrage in the Senate.

ARTICLE. VI.

All Debts contracted and Engagements entered into, before the Adoption of this Constitution, shall be as valid against the United States under this Constitution, as under the Confederation.

This Constitution, and the Laws of the United States which shall be made in Pursuance thereof; and all Treaties made, or which shall be made, under the Authority of the United States, shall be the supreme Law of the Land; and the Judges in every State shall be bound thereby, any Thing in the Constitution or Laws of any State to the Contrary notwithstanding.

The Senators and Representatives before mentioned, and the Members of the several State Legislatures, and all executive and judicial Officers both of the

United States and of the several States, shall be bound by Oath or Affirmation, to support this Constitution; but no religious Test shall ever be required as a Qualification to any Office or public Trust under the United States.

ARTICLE. VII.

The Ratification of the Conventions of nine States, shall be sufficient for the Establishment of this Constitution between the States so ratifying the Same.

done in Convention by the Unanimous Consent of the States present the Seventeenth Day of September in the Year of our Lord one thousand seven hundred and Eighty seven and of the Independence of the United States of America the Twelfth. **In witness** whereof We have hereunto subscribed our Names,

Articles in Addition to, and Amendment of, the Constitution of the United States of America, Proposed by Congress, and Ratified by the Legislatures of the Several States, Pursuant to the Fifth Article of the Original Constitution.

AMENDMENT I[10]

Congress shall make no law respecting an establishment of religion, or prohibiting the free exercise thereof; or abridging the freedom of speech, or of the press; or the right of people peaceably to assemble, and to petition the Government for a redress of grievances.

AMENDMENT II

A well regulated Militia, being necessary to the security of a free State, the right of the people to keep and bear Arms shall not be infringed.

AMENDMENT III

No Soldier shall, in time of peace, be quartered in any house, without the consent of the Owner, nor in time of war, but in a manner to be prescribed by law.

AMENDMENT IV

The right of the people to be secure in their persons, houses, papers, and effects, against unreasonable searches and seizures, shall not be violated, and

---

[10] The first ten amendments were passed by Congress September 25, 1789. They were ratified by three-fourths of the states December 15, 1791.

no Warrants shall issue, but upon probable cause, supported by Oath or affirmation, and particularly describing the place to be searched, and the persons or things to be seized.

AMENDMENT V

No person shall be held to answer for a capital or otherwise infamous crime, unless on a presentment or indictment of a Grand Jury, except in cases arising in the land or naval forces, or in the Militia, when in actual service in time of War or public danger; nor shall any person be subject for the same offence to be twice put in jeopardy of life or limb; nor shall be compelled in any criminal case to be a witness against himself, nor be deprived of life, liberty, or property, without due process of law; nor shall private property be taken for public use, without just compensation.

AMENDMENT VI

In all criminal prosecutions, the accused shall enjoy the right to a speedy and public trial, by an impartial jury of the State and district wherein the crime shall have been committed, which district shall have been previously ascertained by law, and to be informed of the nature and cause of the accusation; to be confronted with the witnesses against him; to have compulsory process for obtaining witnesses in his favor, and to have the Assistance of Counsel for his defence.

AMENDMENT VII

In suits at common law, where the value in controversy shall exceed twenty dollars, the right of trial by jury shall be preserved, and no fact tried by a jury, shall be otherwise reexamined in any Court of the United States, than according to the rules of common law.

AMENDMENT VIII

Excessive bail shall not be required, nor excessive fines imposed, nor cruel and unusual punishments inflicted.

AMENDMENT IX

The enumeration in the Constitution, of certain rights, shall not be construed to deny or disparage others retained by the people.

AMENDMENT X

The powers not delegated to the United States by the Constitution; nor prohibited by it to the States, are reserved to the States respectively, or to the people.

AMENDMENT XI[11]

The Judicial power of the United States shall not be construed to extend to any suit in law or equity, commenced or prosecuted against one of the United States by Citizens of another State, or by Citizens or Subjects of any Foreign State.

AMENDMENT XII[12]

The Electors shall meet in their respective States and vote by ballot for President and Vice-President, one of whom, at least, shall not be an inhabitant of the same State with themselves; they shall name in their ballots the person voted for as President, and in distinct ballots the person voted for as Vice-President, and they shall make distinct lists of all persons voted for as President, and of all persons voted for as Vice-President, and of the number of votes for each, which lists they shall sign and certify, and transmit sealed to the seat of the government of the United States, directed to the President of the Senate;—The President of the Senate shall, in the presence of the Senate and House of Representatives, open all the certificates and the votes shall then be counted;—The person having the greatest number of votes for President, shall be the President, if such number be a majority of the whole number of Electors appointed; and if no person have such majority, then from the persons having the highest numbers not exceeding three on the list of those voted for as President, the House of Representatives shall choose immediately, by ballot, the President. But in choosing the President, the votes shall be taken by states, the representation from each state having one vote; a quorum for this purpose shall consist of a member or members from two-thirds of the states, and a majority of all the states shall be necessary to a choice. And if the House of Representatives shall not choose a President whenever the right of choice shall devolve upon them, before the fourth day of March next following, then the Vice-President shall act as President, as in the case of the death or other constitutional disability of the President.—The person having the greatest number of votes as Vice-President, shall be the Vice-President, if such number be a majority of the whole number of Electors appointed, and if no person have a majority, then from the two highest numbers on the list, the Senate shall choose the Vice-President; a quorum for the purpose shall consist of two-thirds of the

---

[11] Passed March 4, 1794. Ratified January 23, 1795.
[12] Passed December 9, 1803. Ratified June 15, 1804.

whole number of Senators, and a majority of the whole number shall be necessary to a choice. But no person constitutionally ineligible to the office of President shall be eligible to that of Vice-President of the United States.

Amendment XIII[13]

Section 1. Neither slavery nor involuntary servitude, except as a punishment for crime whereof the party shall have been duly convicted, shall exist within the United States, or any place subject to their jurisdiction.

Section 2. Congress shall have the power to enforce this article by appropriate legislation.

Amendment XIV[14]

Section 1. All persons born or naturalized in the United States, and subject to the jurisdiction thereof, are citizens of the United States and of the State wherein they reside. No state shall make or enforce any law which shall abridge the privileges or immunities of citizens of the United States; nor shall any State deprive any person of life, liberty, or property, without due process of law; nor deny to any person within its jurisdiction the equal protection of the laws.

Section 2. Representatives shall be apportioned among the several States according to their respective numbers, counting the whole number of persons in each State, excluding Indians not taxed. But when the right to vote at any election for the choice of electors for President and Vice-President of the United States, Representatives in Congress, the Executive and Judicial officers of a State, or the members of the Legislature thereof, is denied to any of the male inhabitants of such State, being twenty-one years of age, and citizens of the United States, or in any way abridged, except for participation in rebellion, or other crime, the basis of representation therein shall be reduced in the proportion which the number of such male citizens shall bear to the whole number of male citizens twenty-one years of age in such State.

Section 3. No person shall be a Senator or Representative in Congress, or elector of President and Vice-President, or hold any office, civil or military, under the United States, or under any State, who, having previously taken oath, as a member of Congress, or as an officer of the United States, or as a member of any State legislature, or as an executive or judicial officer of any State, to support the Constitution of the United States, shall have engaged in insurrection or rebellion against the same, or given aid or comfort to the enemies thereof. But Congress may by a vote of two-thirds of each House, remove such disability.

Section 4. The validity of the public debt of the United States, authorized by law, including debts incurred for payment of pensions and bounties for services in suppressing insurrection or rebellion, shall not be questioned. But

---

[13] Passed January 31, 1865. Ratified December 6, 1865.
[14] Passed June 13, 1866. Ratified July 9, 1868.

neither the United States nor any State shall assume or pay any debt or obligation incurred in aid of insurrection or rebellion against the United States, or any claim for the loss or emancipation of any slave; but all such debts, obligations, and claims shall be held illegal and void.

Section 5. The Congress shall have the power to enforce, by appropriate legislation, the provisions of this article.

AMENDMENT XV[15]

Section 1. The right of citizens of the United States to vote shall not be denied or abridged by the United States or by any State on account of race, color, or previous condition of servitude.

Section 2. The Congress shall have power to enforce this article by appropriate legislation.

AMENDMENT XVI[16]

The Congress shall have power to lay and collect taxes on incomes, from whatever source derived, without apportionment among the several States, and without regard to any census or enumeration.

AMENDMENT XVII[17]

The Senate of the United States shall be composed of two Senators from each State, elected by the people thereof, for six years; and each Senator shall have one vote. The electors in each State shall have the qualifications requisite for electors of the most numerous branch of the State legislatures.

When vacancies happen in the representation of any State in the Senate, the executive authority of such State shall issue writs of election to fill such vacancies: *Provided,* That the legislature of any State may empower the executive thereof to make temporary appointments until the people fill the vacancies by election as the legislature may direct.

This amendment shall not be so construed as to affect the election or term of any Senator chosen before it becomes valid as part of the Constitution.

AMENDMENT XVIII[18]

Section 1. After one year from the ratification of this article the manufacture, sale, or transportation of intoxicating liquors within, the importation

---

[15] Passed February 26, 1869. Ratified February 2, 1870.
[16] Passed July 12, 1909. Ratified February 3, 1913.
[17] Passed May 13, 1912. Ratified April 8, 1913.
[18] Passed December 18, 1917. Ratified January 16, 1919.

thereof into, or the exportation thereof from the United States and all territory subject to the jurisdiction thereof for beverage purposes is hereby prohibited.

Section 2. The Congress and the several States shall have concurrent power to enforce this article by appropriate legislation.

Section 3. This article shall be inoperative unless it shall have been ratified as an amendment to the Constitution by the legislatures of the several States, as provided in the Constitution, within seven years from the date of the submission hereof to the States by the Congress.

AMENDMENT XIX[19]

The right of citizens of the United States to vote shall not be denied or abridged by the United States or by any State on account of sex.

Congress shall have power to enforce this article by appropriate legislation.

AMENDMENT XX[20]

Section 1. The terms of the President and Vice-President shall end at noon on the 20th day of January, and the terms of Senators and Representatives at noon on the 3d day of January, of the years in which such terms would have ended if this article had not been ratified; and the terms of their successors shall then begin.

Section 2. The Congress shall assemble at least once in every year, and such meeting shall begin at noon on the 3d day of January, unless they shall by law appoint a different day.

Section 3. If, at the time fixed for the beginning of the term of the President, the President elect shall have died, the Vice-President elect shall become President. If a President shall not have been chosen before the time fixed for the beginning of his term, or if the President elect shall have failed to qualify, then the Vice-President elect shall act as President until a President shall have qualified; and the Congress may by law provide for the case wherein neither a President elect nor a Vice-President elect shall have qualified, declaring who shall then act as President, or the manner in which one who is to act shall be selected, and such person shall act accordingly until a President or Vice-President shall have qualified.

Section 4. The Congress may by law provide for the case of the death of any of the persons from whom the House of Representatives may choose a President whenever the right of choice shall have devolved upon them, and for the case of the death of any of the persons from whom the Senate may choose a Vice-President whenever the right of choice shall have devolved upon them.

Section 5. Sections 1 and 2 shall take effect on the 15th day of October following the ratification of this article.

---

[19] Passed June 4, 1919. Ratified August 18, 1920.
[20] Passed March 2, 1932. Ratified January 23, 1933.

Section 6. This article shall be inoperative unless it shall have been ratified as an amendment to the Constitution by the legislatures of three-fourths of the several States within seven years from the date of its submission.

AMENDMENT XXI[21]

Section 1. The eighteenth article of amendment to the Constitution of the United States is hereby repealed.

Section 2. The transportation or importation into any State, Territory, or possession of the United States for delivery or use therein of intoxicating liquors, in violation of the laws thereof, is hereby prohibited.

Section 3. This article shall be inoperative unless it shall have been ratified as an amendment to the Constitution by conventions in the several States, as provided in the Constitution, within seven years from the date of the submission hereof to the States by the Congress.

AMENDMENT XXII[22]

No person shall be elected to the office of the President more than twice, and no person who has held the office of President, or acted as President, for more than two years of a term to which some other person was elected President shall be elected to the office of the President more than once.

But this Article shall not apply to any person holding the office of President when this Article was proposed by the Congress, and shall not prevent any person who may be holding the office of President, or acting as President, during the term within which this Article becomes operative from holding the office of President or acting as President during the remainder of such term.

AMENDMENT XXIII[23]

Section 1. The District constituting the seat of Government of the United States shall appoint in such manner as the Congress may direct:

A number of electors of President and Vice President equal to the whole number of Senators and Representatives in Congress to which the District would be entitled if it were a State, but in no event more than the least populous State; they shall be in addition to those appointed by the States, but they shall be considered, for the purposes of the election of President and Vice President, to be electors appointed by the State; and they shall meet in the District and perform such duties as provided by the twelfth article of amendment.

---

[21] Passed February 20, 1933. Ratified December 5, 1933.

[22] Passed March 12, 1947. Ratified March 1, 1951.

[23] Passed June 16, 1960. Ratified April 3, 1961.

Section 2. The Congress shall have power to enforce this article by appropriate legislation.

AMENDMENT XXIV[24]

Section 1. The right of citizens of the United States to vote in any primary or other election for President or Vice President, or for Senator or Representative in Congress, shall not be denied or abridged by the United States or any State by reason of failure to pay any poll tax or other tax.

Section 2. The Congress shall have power to enforce this article by appropriate legislation.

AMENDMENT XXV[25]

Section 1. In case of the removal of the President from office or of his death or resignation, the Vice President shall become President.

Section 2. Whenever there is a vacancy in the office of the Vice President, the President shall nominate a Vice President who shall take office upon confirmation by a majority vote of both Houses of Congress.

Section 3. Whenever the President transmits to the President pro tempore of the Senate and the Speaker of the House of Representatives his written declaration that he is unable to discharge the powers and duties of his office, and until he transmits to them a written declaration to the contrary, such powers and duties shall be discharged by the Vice President as Acting President.

Section 4. Whenever the Vice President and a majority of either the principle officers of the executive department or of such other body as Congress may by law provide, transmit to the President pro tempore of the Senate and the Speaker of the House of Representatives their written declaration that the President is unable to discharge the powers and duties of his office, the Vice President shall immediately assume the powers and duties of the office of Acting President.

Thereafter, when the President transmits to the President pro tempore of the Senate and the Speaker of the House of Representatives his written declaration that no inability exists, he shall resume the powers and duties of his office unless the Vice President and a majority of either the principle officers of the executive department or of such other body as Congress may by law provide, transmit within four days to the President pro tempore of the Senate and the Speaker of the House of Representatives their written declaration that the President is unable to discharge the powers and duties of his office. Thereupon Congress shall decide the issue, assembling within forty-eight hours for that purpose if not in session. If the Congress, within twenty-one days after receipt of the latter written declaration, or, if Congress is not in session, within twenty-one days after

---

[24] Passed August 27, 1962. Ratified January 23, 1964.
[25] Passed July 6, 1965. Ratified February 11, 1967.

Congress is required to assemble, determines by two-thirds vote of both houses that the President is unable to discharge the powers and duties of his office, the Vice President shall continue to discharge the same as Acting President; otherwise, the President shall resume the powers and duties of his office.

Amendment XXVI[26]

Section 1. The right of citizens of the United States, who are eighteen years of age or older, to vote shall not be denied or abridged by the United States or by any State on account of age.

Section 2. The Congress shall have power to enforce this article by appropriate legislation.

Amendment XXVII[27]

No law, varying the compensation for the services of the Senators and Representatives, shall take effect, until, an election of representatives shall be intervened.

---

[26] Passed March 23, 1971. Ratified July 5, 1971.
[27] Passed September 25, 1789. Ratified May 7, 1992.

CREDITS

INDEX

Abortion, 290, 299–303, 412, 416
Access, right of, 224–226
Adams, John, 2, 4, 13, 28, 132
Adams, John Quincy, 342
Adams, Samuel, 13
Adjournment *sine die,* 65
Adjournments of Congress, 64–65, 131–132, 133
Administrative agencies, delegation of congressional power to, 25–26. *See also names of specific agencies*
Administrative search warrants, 261
Administrative searches, 261, 268
Adolescent Family Life Act of 1982 (AFLA), 192
Adoption, 370
Advertising, 219–222, 400
Affirmative action, 33, 372, 379–381, 388–389
AFLA. *See* Adolescent Family Life Act of 1982
African Americans. *See also* Racial discrimination: Slavery boycotts by, 243; death penalty and, 331; discrimination in election systems, 377–378; *Dred Scott* case and, 347; housing discrimination against, 345–346; protection by Fourteenth Amendment, 349; protest activities of, 234–235; and race as suspect classification under equal protection clause, 358, 364–369; racial gerrymandering and, 384; standing to sue and, 33, 34; voting rights for, 390–393
Age Discrimination in Employment Act of 1967, 77, 175, 389
Age requirements: for alcohol use, 71; for driving, 400; Fourteenth Amendment and, 375; for members of Congress, 43, 51; for president, 119–120; for voting, 56, 391, 408–409
Agnew, Spiro T., 55, 138, 405
Air Force, 94
Alcohol: advertising of, 400; age requirements for use, 71; driving under the influence, 400; prohibition in Eighteenth Amendment, 166, 395, 433–434; regulation of, 76, 193, 209, 399–401; repeal of prohibition, 166, 395, 398–401, 432; taxes on, 139, 336
Aliens. *See* Illegal aliens
Alimony, 370
Allen v. *Wright,* 34
Almost suspect classifications, and equal protection clause, 358–359
Ambassadors, 128, 133, 143, 147, 150

Amendments. *See specific amendments*
American Bar Association, 129
American Indians. *See* Native Americans
Amish, 198
Amplification, 215
Anderson, John, 241, 342, 343
Appellate courts, 140
Appointments clause, 128–131
Apportionment, 35–36, 41–42, 44–48, 383–386
Appropriations clause, 105–106
Archbald, Robert W., 137
Aristotle, 5
Armies. *See* Military forces; State militia
Arrests, 250–254, 256, 309–310
Article I (legislative) courts, 131, 141–142
Articles of Confederation: accomplishments of government under, 11–12; amendment of, 178; approval of, 10; attempts to amend, 12; Constitutional Convention and, 12, 14–16; currency system under, 108, 171; structure of government under, 10–11
Articles of the Constitution. *See* Constitution
Assembly, right of, 233–238
Association: right not to associate, 243–244; right to, 238–243, 353
Atlantic Charter, 127
Atomic Energy Act, 208
Attainders of treason, 154
Attorney general, 26, 391
Attorneys. *See* Lawyers
Automobile exception, 255

Bacchus Imports, Inc. v *Dias,* 139–140
Bail, 325–326
Bail Reform Act of 1984, 325
Baker v *Carr,* 36
Bakke, Allan, 372, 380
Bakke decision, 372, 380, 388
Bandemer decision, 45
Bankruptcy, 88, 141, 142, 143, 374
Bankruptcy courts and judges, 141, 142, 374
Bankruptcy Reform Act of 1978, 142
Banks, Dennis, 159
Barbaric punishments, 327–328
Barratry, 248
Barron v *Baltimore,* 180
Batson v *Kentucky,* 314
Beirut, 123
BIA. *See* Bureau of Indian Affairs (BIA)
Bicameral legislature, 39–40
Biden, Joseph, Jr., 416, 418
Bilingual election materials, 392
Bill of attainder, 102–104, 108